Modern Government

2nd edition

Modern Government

*democracy
and
authoritarianism*

ROBERT WESSON
*University of California, Santa Barbara
Hoover Institution, Stanford University*

Prentice-Hall, Inc.   Englewood Cliffs, New Jersey 07632

Library of Congress Cataloging in Publication Data

WESSON, ROBERT G.
  Modern government.

  Includes index.
  1. Comparative government. I. Title.
JF51.W44 1985   320.3   84-8288
ISBN 0-13-594953-X

*Editorial/production supervision and
  interior design: Linda Benson*
Cover design: George Cornell
Manufacturing buyer: Ron Chapman/Barbara Kelly Kittle

Printed in the United States of America

10 9 8 7 6 5 4 3 2 1

ISBN 0-13-594953-X   01

Prentice-Hall International, Inc., *London*
Prentice-Hall of Australia Pty. Limited, *Sydney*
Editora Prentice-Hall do Brasil, Ltda., *Rio de Janeiro*
Prentice-Hall Canada Inc., *Toronto*
Prentice-Hall of India Private Limited, *New Delhi*
Prentice-Hall of Japan, Inc., *Tokyo*
Prentice-Hall of Southeast Asia Pte. Ltd., *Singapore*
Whitehall Books Limited, *Wellington, New Zealand*

Contents

The Democratic World

6
JAPAN   150

II
The Third World

7
THIRD WORLD POLITICS   181

8
INDIA   211

9
NIGERIA   242

III
The Communist World

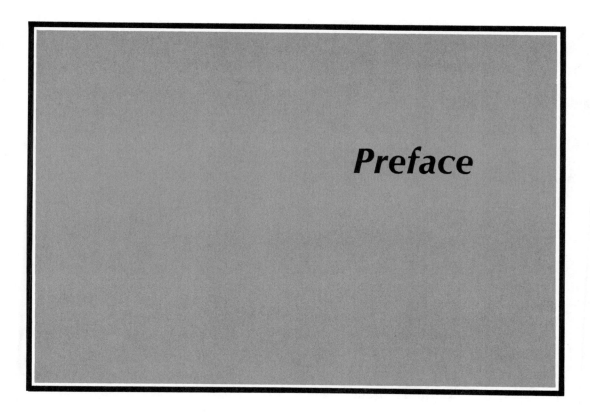

Preface

In no domain of human endeavors has there been less progress over the past two thousand years than in the art or science of government. The elaborately structured participatory democracy of Athens and the constitutional authoritarianism of the Roman republic were far more orderly in the allocation of power than the great majority of modern governments and probably more satisfactory in terms of filling the needs of their peoples. Modern states are, to an unhappy degree, unresponsive to their citizens, abusive of power, wasteful, exploitative, and ineffective in promoting the general welfare. Yet governmental guidance and support seem increasingly necessary in the entanglements of modern civilization.

This human failure was depressingly apparent in the 1930s when the industrial nations were writhing in a depression brought about by misguided policies, and two ideologies of intellectual negativism, fascism (or nazism) and communism, were battling for the world of the future. The same failure is evident today as the most productive states are hard pressed to cope with economic disorders, the world cowers under the threat of calamitous war, and much of humanity exists in virtually subhuman poverty despite a wealth of knowledge capable of providing abundance. Government is the big unsolved problem of modernity, and our inability to govern ourselves is the chief reason why the twenty-first century may well be much poorer than the twentieth.

The problem is perhaps unsolvable, but it should be the highest intellectual challenge. It conceivably gives a purer satisfaction to probe the origins and destiny of the universe, but such probings can hardly advance much further unless we learn better how to organize the guidance of society.

Hence it has been profoundly satisfying to prepare this inquiry into how the world is governed, with the hope that it might furnish students material for thinking about their own and other governments. Perhaps, too, it may stimulate some people to dig much deeper into the political reality that mostly lies neglected or hidden from unwelcome viewers, which is—beyond the simple need for an up-to-date, factual, nonideological, broad survey of the political universe—the basic justification for this book.

The primary organizational question for a discussion of political institutions in several countries is whether to treat them serially, each in its peculiar complexities, or to abstract important institutions or functions of the political system as they appear in various countries. This book adopts a compromise approach, leaning to the country-by-country method because of a feeling that each political system is a coherent whole, the interlocking parts of which are strongly interdependent. That is, when one is dealing with quite diverse countries, it probably makes more sense to consider the administrative system, the selection of leadership, the courts, the process of socialization, the representation of interests, and so forth, in the nexus of a political system and in isolation from more or less close counterparts in other systems than in relation to their counterparts and in isolation from other components of the political system. There is much to be said for dealing with a polity as a whole before trying to deepen understanding by generalizing about elements of the system. To take an extreme example, the rubberstamp legislative bodies in the Soviet state are much more understandable as components of that way of government than in terms of parliamentary institutions. The Soviet (or Chinese or Romanian) Communist party likewise is the key institution in the Communist state with functions very different from those of Western political parties; the similarity of name conveys more disinformation than information.

It would be wrong, however, to look only at individual countries singly. Much can be usefully said about the state in general, amorphous as this concept is, and here a chapter is given to it. The state everywhere has to perform certain functions; and all states do somewhat the same things, only in different proportions. There are no absolutes in political science. Moreover, the states of the world may be divided into three reasonably well-defined categories: the modern democratic; the Communist-ruled; and the more heterogeneous residual group of the non-Western, mostly feebly industrialized non-Communist states of Latin America, Africa, and Asia, usually called collectively the "Third World," for want of a better name. (The Third World is "Third" because it took shape and was baptized after the "Free World" had taken a stance against the Sino-Soviet bloc in the 1950s.) Within each of these three groups, institutions have much the same meaning over a wide range of countries. Thus the British Parliament has a basic resemblance to the German Bundestag and to parliamentary bodies in Scandinavia, Portugal, or Japan. An Australian uses the word *party* in very much the same way as an Austrian, a Canadian, or a Dane. This is even more true of the Communist states, in which the governing party has virtually the same role and quite similar structures in all countries. It is even true to a large extent in the diverse Third World, where in a large majority of countries a political party is primarily a personal following based on patronage. Consequently it seems logical to devote a chapter to a generalized discussion of the political ways of each category.

Most space, however, is given to the nine countries discussed in some detail. This raises problems of selection and the omission of many of the most interesting states. The most important of all, the United States, is regrettably left out except for incidental comparisons because it is conventionally studied by itself. Unfortunately, space did not permit inclusion of many other important and instructive countries, such as Canada, Scandinavian democracies, Italy, Israel, and Yugoslavia. The United Kingdom is necessarily included because of its pioneer role in representative government and the enormous influence it once exercised. France seems essential for similar reasons. West Germany and Japan merit inclusion both because of their intrinsic importance—Germany is among the world's leading exporters, and Japan is the world's second economic power, at least in terms of civilian production—and because they have exceptionally well-functioning democratic systems. In the Third World, choice is more difficult. But it seems imperative to look at India, the world's second largest human mass, although it is typical of the Third World only in its problems. Nigeria is likewise atypical of Africa, but it is by far the most populous and wealthy country of black Africa and had (for some years, at least) the most orderly political system. Mexico similarly is hardly typical of Latin America, but it is economically important and has been relatively successful, at least in terms of stability, with its unique political system. Among the Communist states, it is obviously necessary to deal with the Soviet Union as the military superpower and China as home of nearly a quarter of all humanity.

The treatment of these countries is somewhat more historical than has been customary in books comparable to this. Emphasis on history seems justifiable in part because the past has given us the present; political institutions are made more by historical developments than by human design. An historical approach also goes with the country-by-country treatment, and it implies a more descriptive than comparative-analytical-theoretical handling of contemporary institutions.

This book does not lack theory in the broader sense, however. Behind it lies a political philosophy in terms of which institutions are assessed. Its chief axiom is simple: governments differ fundamentally in the extent to which the rulership acts arbitrarily or legally, coercively or consensually, on its own behalf or for the benefit of the community. Specific institutions and states as a whole may be graded in such terms. The approach is normative so far as it is accepted that the purpose of government is to serve the community, but controversy usually arises over the factual question of whether a given institution or government really serves the general welfare or only pretends to do so. The related fundamental question, the extent to which the state is materially capable of carrying out whatever policies may be selected, is probably secondary.

In this view, the most important question for the future of humankind is the extent to which political institutions can be improved to better serve the interests of those over whom they stand—or how or whether community-serving institutions will be developed where, as in most of the world, the state seriously falls short of its fundamental tasks. The outlook generally is not good; pessimism sometimes seems proportional to the depth of digging beneath sometimes optimistic surfaces. However, the picture is not all dark. There are many effective and well-designed political institutions. And the better we understand conditions and the more broadly we study negative and positive aspects, the greater the likelihood that improvements can be made.

I would like to acknowledge the contributions of the reviewers of this edition: Frank C. Darling, Principia College; and Henry J. Steck, SUNY—Cortland.

Modern Government

Introduction: The Problem of Political Inquiry

The map of the world is partitioned into 150-odd compartments, called sovereign states. The word "sovereign" means that each has its own governing body responsible to no one else; each is free to make its own rules and deals with others as it sees fit, buying and selling, permitting or controlling movement across its borders, even possibly using mayhem and murder against others—that is, making war. The states of the world are extremely diverse in area, from the size of a modest farm to that of a continent; in population, from a handful of people to a billion; in wealth, from primitive poverty to modern affluence; and in the relation of the rulers and the ruled, from cordial near-equality to the harshest tyranny.[1]

[1] There are many handbooks, such as the *Political Handbook of the World, 19__* (New York: McGraw-Hill, 1975 etc.). For a compendium of sketches indicating the quality of governments, see Department of State, *Country Practices on Human Rights* for 1982 (etc.) (Washington, D.C.: Government Printing Office, 1982 etc.).

The state or government is indispensable in civilized society; it is the sovereign human institution. It is as universal as the family, and indeed much like it. To rebel against it is somewhat like rebelling against parental authority. The quality of the state has much to do with the character of our lives and our well-being; it forms the framework within which we work and live. It makes possible creative life, and it can destroy us.

An enormous amount of attention has been given to the state; it has been analyzed more or less systematically from the time of Plato and Aristotle. In recent decades, especially since World War II, the volume of writing has been overwhelming. Yet there is no real theory of the state, and there are few laws of political behavior. Not only the results but also the nature, basic concepts, and goals of comparative politics are confused and nebulous. The study of government has bravely called itself "political science" instead of "politology," but there is little agreement concerning how it should be scientific. There is even uncertainty about the questions we want to answer.

One reason is the complexity of the subject. The behavior of individuals defies the predictive powers of psychology, and the interaction of large numbers of persons through complex channels and within frameworks called institutions is the most complicated affair in our universe. The frustrations of studying it are multiplied by the poor quality and shortage of information. Politics is ultimately a matter of decisions made by persons exercising authority, but those who make decisions do not often analyze and explain why they did what they did. They probably do not know, or know only superficially. And although responsible persons in a few countries may be fairly candid (at least in retrospect), this is far from universal.

In Communist states, very little information about politics is divulged, and it may be swamped by disinformation. Things political are secret in principle. A major difficulty in the study of the politics of the Third World is lack of data. Most of its governments publish little or nothing of their inner workings, the controlled press is uninformative, and snooping political scientists are not welcome.

A third barrier to understanding is that government deeply affects the lives and fortunes of us all, and no one can be indifferent to it or wholly objective about it. Political theory is always more or less mixed with political advocacy, because the state is part of the lives of all of us. Everyone wants something from government, from social services to national security; we sacrifice to it in the form of taxes, and we feel its restraints. We identify with the nation in relation to other nations and to parties within the nation. Hence, when politics comes in, reason takes flight; and in political matters, sane and intelligent people ignore facts perhaps more freely than in any other arena of human affairs.

Indeed, in many ways objectivity in political affairs is not rewarding. A chemist achieves success by mastery of facts; a political personage, by persuasiveness that may be quite unrelated to facts. Neither Hitler nor Lenin won power by moderation and rationality but rather by their defiance of accepted canons. Political theorists, too, become great by appeal to emotions as well as logic. It matters little for Marxism that Marx was often self-contradictory and inconsistent, because the cause he advocated was powerfully appealing. From the Marxist viewpoint, on the other hand, ideology in general represents class interest.

Although political studies, including this one, are inevitably value-laden, and conclusions are inevitably influenced by attitudes, choice of materials, and methods, it is the duty of the student to endeavor to respect reality, sort out facts scrupulously, remain open to contrary interpretations, and judge carefully. Objectivity is a worthy ideal, even though it is buried under involvement, complexity, and scarcity of facts. One may hope, with a good will, to discern at least the rough outlines of truth in political questions.

This does not mean that we pretend to eschew values entirely but that we hope our values are broad and humane. To direct political inquiry to human needs does not in principle have to be more unscientific than medical research, which seeks remedies for ailments. One may even contend that "value-free" studies are usually deceptive and probably blind to the needs of the human situation.

POLITICAL THOUGHT: THE HISTORICAL TRADITION

Traditional political thought has been strongly normative or purposeful. Plato in his *Republic* endeavored to sketch an ideal state (governed by thinkers like himself) with little reference to specific reality. His pupil Aristotle's goal was a community of politically involved citizens rationally conducting their own affairs, in which state and society were equivalent. Much more empirically minded than Plato, he allegedly studied the institutions of 158 Greek city-states, although only one description, that of Athens, has survived. Aristotle classified governments as being in the hands of the many (democracy), the few (oligarchy), or a single ruler (monarchy); he then judged each class qualitatively as sound and legal or abusive and illegal.

In the Roman Empire, political theory was replaced by moral philosophy and then by religious controversy. When political discussion began to revive in the Middle Ages, much of it centered on the conflicting claims of the papacy and the Holy Roman Empire to universal authority. Descriptive and normative writing grew with the emergence of the nation-states of Europe in the fifteenth century. The Italian Machiavelli, for example, found virtue in republics yet urged amoral tactics for princes for the sake of power that would lead to the unification and liberation of Italy. Jean Bodin exalted in theory the supremacy that the French king was achieving in practice.

The seminal idea of early modern analysis of the state was the idea of contract. Out of the medieval notion of society as resembling the human body, with the lower classes equivalent to the legs and trunk and the higher classes to the head, there grew the concept of a compact whereby the masses agreed, for the sake of order, that certain persons should rule. Thomas Hobbes expressed this theory most clearly and elegantly in his *Leviathan:* without government, life was "solitary, poor, nasty, brutish, and short," because of the mutually destructive tendencies of humans. For a civilized society,

it was necessary for all to submit themselves to a monarch, whose power had to be total for the sake of good order.

Hobbes's doctrine was intended to support the absolutist claims of the Stuart kings of England, but it was actually destructive of the theory of the divine right of kings. It was easy to turn it around, as John Locke did a little later, and assert that the people, from whom sovereignty ultimately derived, could withdraw power if it was abused or entrust only limited authority to their rulers. In Locke's view, the people are naturally peaceable (contrary to Hobbes's assumption), so political power was a revocable trust. Something of this philosophy was incorporated in the Glorious Revolution of 1688, which overthrew the Stuarts and hedged the power of British kings with the rights of Parliament.

Institutions and theory interact: if the development of the British form of limited government after 1688 owed much to Locke and others with similar ideas, it in turn became the starting point for a new generation of thinkers. Montesquieu, finding in the British system of king, cabinet, and Parliament considerably more than was there, developed a scheme of rational government through separation of powers. The fledgling United States incorporated this in its Constitution of 1789, the rationale for which was given by James Madison and others in the *Federalist Papers*. Madison, like Montesquieu, Locke, and Rousseau, assumed that the goal of politics was liberty and a just order for the benefit of the people and that institutions were to be devised by observation and reason.

The study of political institutions grew steadily through the nineteenth century. British and American thinkers took for granted the general kind of society in which they lived: the rule of law, popular representation, a complex of public and private organizations expressing demands and interests, and executive and legislative powers operating more or less openly and within the guidelines of a constitution. It was assumed that this general kind of society was normal and that progress consisted simply in securing more perfect justice and more rational modes of operation. Comparative politics a century ago was consequently a rather simple discipline. It was especially concerned with describing the British system, the world's political model as well as its greatest power, in its complicated but understandable and essentially rational interactions. Other countries were measured by comparison with the model.

The traditional approach of comparative politics has remained until recently fairly close to its nineteenth-century outlook. It has dealt primarily with institutions and has been historical and descriptive, taking its examples from the past. Much writing, especially on the British system, still emphasizes precedents in the assumption of continuity: the way things work is to be judged from the way they have worked. Comparative politics was close to the study of law. It was parochial, focused on the European experience. Basic courses in comparative government in the United States dealt with Britain, France, Germany, and the Soviet Union. Other countries were considered unimportant or were simply unknown. The study was not so much comparative as sequentially descriptive; it was easier to try to grasp the political system of a country as a whole than to look at parliaments in several countries, and then at parties, cabinets, and so forth.

This legalistic-descriptive approach gradually became less satisfactory for several reasons. Increasing sophistication and the prestige of science made it seem superficial and stimulated a search for realities beneath and behind the institutions. Scientific inquiry had to seek the causes, general relationships, and motives of which the political process was

the result. At the same time, attitudes toward the state evolved. Popular demands arose for more protection and assistance from the government, which evolved from the keeper of order and defender of the nation to a major redistributor of resources. The study of politics came to concern itself with "who gets what, when, and how," an idea that would have been heretical to the Victorians. Moreover, as a result of World War II, the dominance of Britain and Europe ended. A set of ideas mainly British in inspiration and development seemed increasingly inadequate.

CHANGING APPROACHES

One of the earliest critics of the traditional system was Karl Marx, although his ideas did not become influential until the 1890s, long after his death. He rejected the Industrial Revolution and the "bourgeois" political order he associated with it. In his view, the reality of politics was not institutional or legal structures but class struggle; government was simply the instrument of the class that dominated by virtue of its economic position, that is, in the modern West, the capitalists. Long after Marxism had become powerful as political ideology, its radicalism kept it from serious consideration by most scholars. But with World War I, the victory in Russia of a party professing Marxism, the economic depression of the 1930s, the rise of fascism, the victory of the Soviet Union in World War II, and the subsequent difficulties of the more traditional economic and political systems, its prestige grew. It surged in the United States, especially during and shortly after the Vietnam war (1965–1973). Marxism is stronger in economics and sociology than in political science, however, because it downgrades the significance of constitutions and political structures.

Other critics have been less passionate or less violently destructive of the Western tradition than Marx. Two Italians, Gaetano Mosca (whose *Elementi di Scienza Politica* was first published in 1896) and Vilfredo Pareto (whose *Trattato di sociologia generale* was published in 1916), went part of the way with Marx by emphasizing that the essence of politics was the rule of a dominant elite. From this point of view, the important facts were not the formal processes of government but the way the elite was recruited and how it exercised its power. Following them, a German-Italian, Robert Michels, in his *Political Parties* (1914), emphasized that oligarchy prevailed in all large organizations; even in those most dedicated to the rights of the many—for example, the Social Democratic (Marxist) parties of Europe—power went by an "iron law" to the few. A German sociologist, Max Weber, whose major works were published in the 1920s, held somewhat similar ideas. His chief contribution was an analysis of the bureaucratic apparatus as a prime factor in the political system. In the British context, it was easy to ignore the civil servants who carried out the orders of the ministers. But in Weber's Prussia, not to speak of systems such as imperial China, the bureaucracy obviously played a vital part in its own right. Weber also studied with a fresh eye the sources of political authority and classified them—and the corresponding rulerships—as traditional (obeyed because of long custom), rational (obeyed because it fulfilled needs), or charismatic (obeyed because of the fascination of a personality, such as Napoleon or Hitler).

A further change in the approach to political inquiry was induced in the 1950s and 1960s by the behaviorist revolution in psychology. The central idea was that psychologists should concentrate on observable, measurable behavior and not on undefinable concepts of ideas and feelings. Only thus could psychology be scientific and produce useful and verifiable theories. Many political scientists of the postwar period turned in somewhat the same direction. Weary of vague, value-laden writing, they envied the solid success of the natural sciences, especially physics, and sought to emulate the movement of economics, anthropology, and sociology toward the production of quantitative and supposedly reliable and exact results. They felt that socioeconomic data, survey data, and the like should be used to confirm or reject hypotheses about political behavior.

Results, however, have yet to come up to expectations. It has been too easy, in some cases, for elaborate methodology to take the place of inquiry into real issues and for scholasticism to swamp analytical reasoning. Political affairs seldom lend themselves to quantification, and behaviorists looking for computer fodder may be led away from critical questions. The results of quantitative studies are seldom cited (except elementary data such as electoral results or public opinion polls) in practical or policy-oriented studies, just as sophisticated theories of international relations are ignored by those who deal with foreign affairs. The imprint of behaviorism remains strong, however, and it has brought about great efforts to develop data so that different types of states can be more accurately compared—that is, so that comparative politics can be truly comparative.

Comparative politics was also broadened by including the whole world, not just Western states, and by focusing on the gap between the rich and poor nations. A major problem of American political science became political modernization, the improvement of the institutions of the less favored nations.

The retreat of Europe from world leadership inclined observers to look elsewhere, and the creation of a multitude of new states as colonial empires disintegrated after the war opened a large new field of investigation. It also gave the political scientist a new mission. As long as the political order was stable, they had no other goal than to describe and understand. Now the world was obviously in flux, dangerously so, and analysis could perhaps bring improvement, through reform or revolution. There was new interest in the question of the stability of liberal democracy, the form generally accepted as desirable. There was not so much new and exciting to be said about the old nations; but with the new nations, or the Third World, political scientists could take on a grand and inspiring task: to discern the factors holding back the poorer nations and to prescribe remedies.

This mission took on real significance in the cold war, which seemed at times to be a dubious contest for influence in the Third World between the Soviet Union and the United States, each promoting its political system. It was assumed that economic modernization, if not a guarantee of democratic development, was at least prerequisite for it; failure would surely mean tyranny and very likely a Communist regime. Political modernization was also widely regarded as prerequisite to economic advance; and it was usually, though by no means universally, equated with progress toward something like the American or West European model. The student of Third World politics had a genuine calling: first, to assist the development of states that would be congenial to the United States and its values for the sake of a livable world order, and concurrently to help to overcome the morally repugnant gap between the overfed and the hungry.

Like behavioralism, however, the idea of political modernization has lost momentum. The research difficulties were and are forbidding. The descriptive, institutional approach was obviously unsuitable for the non-Western world, in which formal institutions were frequently insignificant and practice was often contrary to the rules, while little information was made public about the internal processes of politics. Students seeking exact results were driven to skimpy and unreliable statistics, and they could seldom develop their own data in the countries of their interest. More important, the whole concept of political development or modernization came to seem a fantasy. There were numerous and inconsistent definitions, most of which implied comparison with the country of the large majority of investigators, the United States.[2] Ironically, the political scientists who sought above all to be objective and nonethnocentric were led to ethnocentrism by the value orientation that inspired them. For Western students, ethnocentrism was almost unavoidable because of the difficulty of conceiving of progress in other than Western terms, which were also the terms of those who desired to share in the Western economic achievement.

The study of political development also suffered from the near invisibility of its object. Into the mid-1960s, it was generally assumed that economic and social modernization, rising material wealth, urbanization, the spread of literacy and education, and so on would be accompanied by political awareness; better-organized, more stable, effective, and reliable government; growing popular participation; and liberalization or democratization of the state. For some years this assumption appeared to be confirmed, or at least not refuted, by the efforts of the new nations to establish democratic or ostensibly democratic regimes. But Samuel Huntington perceived that modernization might lead to instability and a reversal of the

[2]James A. Bill and Robert L. Hardgrave, Jr., *Comparative Politics: The Quest for Theory* (Columbus: Charles Merrill, 1973), p. 66.

movement toward Western democracy, or "political development." His views were vindicated in the late 1960s and early 1970s as political freedom receded in most parts of the Third World. Fragile or sham democracies were replaced by military governments in Africa, Latin America, and Southern Asia. Only a handful of functioning democracies were left in the Third World. Political scientists were frustrated and confused.

CURRENT THEORIES

The confusion and uncertainty remain. No generally accepted theory yet exists; at best there are a number of semitheories or approaches, all of which point to certain elements or variables and none of which is without serious shortcomings.[3] For example, the class approach, predominantly but not entirely Marxist, is more useful for anti-Western or anti-Establishment agitation and organization than for the analysis of political problems. Marx himself broke off when he once attempted to define the classes about which he had written so much. And he did well, because no useful and plausible definition is possible. When Marx discussed concrete political happenings in England or France, he wrote much less in terms of classes than in terms of interests and personalities, like other journalists of his day. Since Marx's time the difficulty of analysis in terms of class in the Marxist sense (as understood in relation to the means of production) has steadily increased with the vastly increased complexity of economic relations, the growth of nonproletarian and noncapitalist sectors, and the "bourgeoisification" of a large part of the employed classes.

Emphasis on the elite, as opposed to an economically defined governing class, is realistic in that a relatively small number of persons hold positions of power in all societies. But to a large extent *elite theory* (as propounded, for example, by Sorel, Mosca, and C. Wright Mills) is, like Marxism, as much protest against injustice as penetrating analysis. There is no real definition of the elite except the tautology that the elite are those who have influence and govern society. How and why they are able to govern remain unanswered questions, and if a new group acquires influence or power, one can only say that the old elite has been overturned by a new one. Elite theory is basically static in orientation and uninformative regarding revolutionary change; in fact, it implies the impossibility of change. To search for causes of the fall of old and the rise of new elites is to go outside elite theory.

Group theory is broader. Contrary to the elite approach, which stresses the preeminence of a single sector, group theory sees the interaction of an indefinite number of groups of varying influence, coherence, and size. It is also more realistic than a class approach. A person is born into a class and is usually considered to have little or no choice in the matter; but the same person may belong by choice to various overlapping groups. Humans form groups everywhere, and these necessarily affect the political process in all societies, even totalitarian ones. Stressing their role is entirely appropriate, as David Truman made clear,[4] and the focus has added to our understanding of politics.

The principal achievement of group theory, however, is to look behind the scenes of democratic politics by breaking down the po-

---

[3]A number are given by Donald M. Freeman, ed., *Foundations of Political Science: Research, Methods, and Scope* (New York: Free Press, 1977). See also David E. Apter, *Introduction to Political Analysis* (Cambridge, Mass.: Winthrop, 1977).

[4]See David Truman, *The Governmental Process* (New York: Knopf, 1951).

litical body into smaller units understandable in terms of interests. It is less applicable to Communist politics, in which the increasing autonomy of subsectors is equivalent to evolution away from the totally centralized and integrated state. In the Third World also, progress toward political liberalism—modernization—may be measured by the growth and differentiation of interest groups, which are the hallmark of the developed pluralist society. But Third World countries generally have few and weak interest groups in the ordinary sense. The dominant groups are usually the bureaucracy, the military, or a political machine—groups whose thrust is quite different from that proposed by group theory. They do not so much exert pressure as exercise authority. Group theory, moreover, leads to few generalizations, and it deals with only one aspect of the state. The approach sees groups interacting, bargaining, exerting pressures, compromising, or contending within a framework out of which there emerge decisions. Study of the groups tells us little about the process of integration or the accepted framework within which they operate, how they secure results, or their effect on the system.

The group approach deals with organized pressures on the political apparatus; the political culture approach stresses psychological determinants. *Political culture,* a term invented by Gabriel Almond and applied by him (with Sidney Verba),[5] is the whole set of attitudes toward political institutions and processes—people's ideals, norms, and expectations. It calls attention to the fact that the psychological environment for politics differs in countries of different historical experience; and it rather reasonably assumes, for example, that if there is general accep-

tance and expectation of tyranny, there will probably be tyranny. On the other hand, democracy seems to require a people prepared to participate in political life with expectations of influencing official actions.

The idea of political culture is useful, but it raises difficulties. Obviously, the attitudes of lords and peasants toward authority may be very different, and there are no indications of how different attitudes should be weighed. Attitudes are also difficult to determine; people are often prone to give the answers they think the questioner wants. Mind-sets are complex: the French have traditionally been regarded as highly individualistic, yet they accept paternalistic government. And apparently deep-rooted attitudes may change sharply. Much has been made of the deferential attitude of the British toward social superiors, and this has been treated as a major factor in the evolution of the British political system. Yet there is nothing deferential in the attitude of British workers toward their bosses. Maoist China seemed to be the most conformist of societies, with total acceptance of superior wisdom; but two years after Mao's death, Chinese seemed to be much concerned with civil liberties.

It is unwarranted, moreover, to assume a direct causal relation in which political culture is the independent variable and institutions are the dependent variable. This may have been the dominant experience of Western democratic countries, in which government has evolved more or less in response to popular sentiments; but many governments have clearly been imposed by a minority. Causation is two-way. Education contributes to political culture over the course of generations perhaps more than any other factor, and education is ordinarily controlled by the state. The more authoritarian the state, generally, the more determined an effort it makes to generate a political culture

---

[5]See Gabriel A. Almond and Sidney Verba, *The Civic Culture: Political Attitudes and Democracy in Five Nations* (Boston: Little, Brown, 1965).

suitable for itself—for example, the attempt to cultivate the "New Soviet Man." Results, however, may be quite different from those desired by the rulership, perhaps apathy in lieu of dedication.

One may guess that the political culture of South Korea is quite different from that of North Korea after thirty years of different indoctrination, and that the difference between the two Koreas is greater than that between North Korea and Mainland China or between South Korea and Taiwan. It is commonly said that the political cultures of Russia and China are basically authoritarian. But this amounts to little more than rephrasing the historical fact that these countries have had authoritarian or despotic regimes over a long period of time. If the Russian or Chinese people are indeed prone to accept strong government, the causes lie not in genetic makeup but in the national experience. In sum, the idea of political culture is suggestive but lacks explanatory power. Like most other approaches, it implies fixity and tells us little about change.[6]

Structural-functionalism is a broader approach. It postulates that institutions must fulfill a useful function and are inevitably shaped by their purpose. Hence they can be understood in terms of their utility. It is typically asserted that the political system must serve the needs of the community.[7] Unfortunately, however, this basic concept does not add much to our understanding, since it is obvious that the state usually serves some people much better than others. It is a truism that the state must perform its duties well enough to continue to exist, but it may perform them well or poorly in various ways. Institutions can, by almost any standard, be either functional or dysfunctional. It also ap-

pears that the results of political action may be unintended or unforeseeable. Supposedly most states serve much the same functions, yet the organization of power is certainly diverse. If states serve different purposes, structural-functionalism fails to explain the differences.

Gabriel Almond tried to sharpen the structural-functional approach by specifying the functions a political system should fulfill.[8] He named the following seven: political socialization and recruitment, interest articulation, interest aggregation, political communication, rule-making, rule application, and adjudication. The first three are input functions, the fourth (communication) is two-way, and the last three are output functions. This list is suggestive, but it is hardly complete. States have fulfilled many other functions, such as defense, maintenance or imposition of a common culture, performance of religious duties, and fostering economic growth; and a major output of the modern state is the redistribution of wealth. A further weakness is that the relation between functions and the structures serving them is obscure. There are many ways of performing broadly defined functions, aside from the fact that the state may encourage or discourage certain inputs. Another weakness is that the state apparatus is given a mechanical role, like the computer that returns a certain output for a certain input. But the people who carry out the functions of the state have their own purposes and interests.

This failure to take full account of the fact that the state is a dynamic entity in its own right and with its own purposes is a weakness shared by structural-functionalism, a class or elite approach, group theory, and the political culture emphasis. The state not only receives influences but applies force. It not only

---

[6]As observed by Bill and Hardgrave, *Comparative Politics*, p. 114.

[7]See Stanley Rothman, *European Society and Politics* (Indianapolis: Bobbs-Merrill, 1970), p. 7.

[8]See Gabriel Almond and James Coleman, eds., *The Politics of Developing Areas* (Princeton, N.J.: Princeton University Press, 1960).

responds to and serves the community but also initiates policies and serves itself, always to some extent, sometimes virtually to the neglect of nonofficial interests.

Various other attempts have been made to find logical order in political affairs and institutions, but they too have chiefly been able to indicate things to look for or to suggest ways to start thinking about matters that defy fully rational analysis. Many handy terms have been introduced; but the chief virtue of the newer terminology over the older, including such terms as civil liberties, legality, and tyranny, is that the former is less normative or value-laden. No theory or approach has sufficient power to be of much use to historians.

To make such criticisms is a little unfair. The atoms composing the political organism are complex, varied, and plastic humans, whose behavior often defies understanding in the simplest circumstances. The interactions of large numbers of these individually unpredictable atoms are infinitely complex. The political system at the same time resists dissection. It is a web of interactions, formal and informal, with its own mental environment. To isolate parts or specific factors does not reflect the real situation. A sound approach should be based on as much information as possible, but it must necessarily be somewhat intuitive. It may be that humans are simply not intelligent enough fully to comprehend the institutions by which they govern themselves; and if they become more intelligent, their government must grow even more complex.

We do not have a deep understanding of our own government, much less of alien governments concerning which we have much less information and whose actors are further from our ways and culture. It should be useful, however, to survey political problems and institutions around the world. One learns something of the human condition and the fundamental problems of organization of civilized society. Not least, we should gain a better understanding of our own institutions and possibly garner some ideas as to how they might be improved.

The State

Everyone knows what the *state* is: the maker of laws, collector of taxes, defender of the national territory and independence, punisher of crime, provider of social services, promoter of material well-being, decider of quarrels, regulator of activities, educator of youth, issuer of money, and recourse in case of emergency or destitution. It is represented by the police, the military, the social worker, the legislator, the park warden, the bureaucrat who processes papers. Yet the state is more than all these functions put together. It is an entity with its own purposes and direction, and it has varied enormously among cultures and over time. As a result, defining it is difficult.

CHARACTERISTICS OF THE STATE

It is commonly stated that the state is the only organization entitled to apply coercive force. But this definition is too limited; the mail carrier can no more apply force than the grocer, and in all countries, even those most dedicated to private enterprise, many agencies serving the community are nationalized or state owned and operated. In some countries with centrally directed economies, almost everything outside the family is more or less official and touched by politics. The boundary is blurred. In the United States, public universities are an emanation of the political power and private universities are not, but the latter may be almost as much regulated as the former. It is true, however, that the right to use force is the most striking and distinctive characteristic of the state. The state stands over all, and people submit not only because it is useful and the alternative is anarchy but also because there may be unpleasant consequences if they do not. Force is the backbone of the state in democracies as well as in military dictatorships.

Another way of defining the state is to say that it is an entity recognized as such by the international community of states. This is not a circular definition, because the state takes form and meaning to a large extent in interaction with others. Historically its primary function has been the representation of the community and defense of its interests and integrity against rival communities. This role continues to be basic, although other responsibilities, such as regulation of the economy and social services, have come to take most of its attention and revenues. The strongest claim of any government on the loyalty of citizens is patriotism, the sense of the in-group against the outside world. The state represents the strength and position of the society in the international community, so for a person to fail to support it is disloyal and injurious to one's fellows. There are, of course, other actors on the world scene, such as multinational corporations and international private and governmental organizations, and many of them may be more powerful than smaller states. But they lack the essential ingredients of statehood, territory and police powers; and they have no comparable claim on the loyalty of their members.

The state represents power in international relations. This is why we speak of "superpowers," "small powers," and "minipowers." The state incorporates sovereignty or supremacy over a geographic territory—the national soil—delimited by the territories of other states or international waters.

The state is also more or less associated with nationality, the common heritage of a people sharing language, customs, and historical traditions, such as the Swedes or the French. But this principle is really true only in Europe, the homeland of the modern nation-state. And even in Europe, there are many deviations from the correspondence of nationality with statehood: Britain includes Scots and Welsh; Belgium, Flemings and Walloons; Switzerland, speakers of German, French, Italian, and Romansch; and so forth. Outside Europe, only a minority of states closely coincide with clear-cut ethnic divisions. Many Third World states, such as India or Indonesia, contain dozens of linguistic or cultural groups.

Yet political unity imposed over a long period of time may wear down cultural diversity, impose common patterns, and give a sense of nationhood. One example is Russia, which expanded from a small territory through several centuries. Parts of the land, such as Central Asia, remain culturally alien, but much of the huge expanse of territory contains peoples who have been effectively assimilated. A more recent example is Nigeria, a synthetic collection of many diverse ethnic groups that seems to be finding its way to "One Nigeria." The United States, of course, has absorbed much cultural, racial, and ethnic diversity into a single nationality.

The state is primarily an organization of direction, and hence it must have existed ever since human society became sufficiently complicated to require and tolerate a set of persons somehow elevated to command their fellows. Statelike organization must thus be older than the historical record of it. Elaborately structured states have existed in preliterate peoples. Cro-Magnon hunters in all probability had a command structure, and it is probable that some groups of Paleolithic stone ax-wielders subdued others in the manner of humans throughout history. Megalithic monuments dating from the fifth millennium B.C. required millions or tens of millions of manhours of labor.

Ape societies, and those of many other animals, have a hierarchy whereby some, generally the strongest or most aggressive males, are recognized as superior and enjoy corresponding privileges. They are also likely to exercise the responsibilities of watching over or protecting the troop or pack. Similarly, in the state, political control is forcibly imposed and/or represents an answer to a need. One theory of the origin especially of larger states is conquest. The war organization of a victorious tribe would be kept in being in order to maintain the ability to loot and enslave the weaker tribe. On the other hand, all governments perform at least some useful services by keeping order; some states may have arisen primarily through general consent and the need for leadership.

A political system reflects inequality of strength. And political organization accentuates differences by increasing the capacity of the stronger to work their will for their advantage. The state is a means of transfer of resources, sometimes to the needy, more often to the unneedy. Thus rulers can exact tribute or taxes, which enrich them and improve their ability to impose their will; the reward of power becomes the means of increasing it. Thanks to the control of the state, weak successors of strong empire builders can sustain themselves. Rulers or ruling groups are never overthrown from within unless or until they lose the will or ability to employ force or the military forces become alienated. Even in the best democracy, there is some element of fear in the relations of ordinary citizens to the political authority. For these reasons, it is sometimes said that there is no really good government, only some that are less bad.

Many idealists would have no state at all, and the conventional utopia depicts happy people cooperating rationally with no compulsion marring human relations. The thesis of anarchism (from Greek, "no-statism") has always been attractive, although it is unworkable because anarchists can neither agree nor organize.[1] Government is nonetheless a

necessity of human life. The individual alone is nothing; society implies specialization and coordination, not all of which can always be done by simple consent. The more highly developed and complex the society becomes, the more dependent people are on order and the greater the need for structure and organization. We all want security, a framework within which to act, and a group identity. Organization is almost a synonym for government, although the latter term is usually reserved for the sovereign organization that can coerce those under its jurisdiction. To reach broadly binding decisions, it is necessary to have a frame of authority, a state. Even a scholarly university has its government and its politics. Organization, like political power, implies inequality and accentuates and perpetuates it, as some are thrust or thrust themselves into positions of command while others, perhaps no less worthy, must obey.

There are likewise overlapping and intermingling motivations for seeking leadership roles, that is, for going into politics. One is to gain power, which means the ability to shape the actions of others and which is convertible into status and perhaps wealth. Political power in traditional societies, as in Europe during the Middle Ages, is almost equivalent to hierarchical rank and to landholding; only in rather sophisticated societies is there a real but never total separation between political and economic status. Material rewards are probably secondary, however, to the enjoyment of power; politics, from the viewpoint of the politician, is less concerned with "who gets what" than with "who gets ahead of whom." It implies dealing with, helping, and using people; being in command at the center of events; sitting in judgment over proposals and people; and being among the leaders of society. No game is more fascinating, and people give themselves to it with an enthusiasm hardly to be

[1]See J. Roland Pennock and John W. Chapman, *Anarchism* (New York: New York University Press, 1978).

found elsewhere, except perhaps in high business positions, where the rewards are similar.

There is also an unselfish motivation. One not only gets the better of rivals and rises to a position of leadership but also serves the community and promotes the welfare of all or of the social group with which one identifies. Altruism can hardly be so dominant as many politicians pretend, but their dedication is real and strong.

There is idealism in political affairs because the state, even a despotism, always represents something of an ideal. Purely material interests are an inadequate basis for solidarity, and government is always wrapped up in doctrines of some kind. Not only does something of the feeling of kinship loyalty go into the state; this incorporates a share of the ideal values of the society. Myths are the foundation of the political order, from the ancestral spirit world to the ideologies and political philosophies of our day.

LEGITIMACY AND LAW

Although coercive power is characteristic of the state, it is a last resort. No state could operate effectively if coercion were needed in the conduct of daily affairs. All governments rely instead on *legitimacy*—a sense that they, like parents, should be respected and heeded because of what they are and represent.

Legitimacy may be supported by evidence of power and the possession of force, because most people are ready to assume that uncontested force has right. One does not quibble with a gunman, and hostages often admire their captors. Stable government, however, requires a better foundation. Among the bases on which government can rest are rationality (the conviction that the leaders act reasonably), tradition (people are

accustomed to the present system), and charisma (people are drawn to a particular personality).[2] To this list may be added philosophic or ideological legitimation (the belief that the state somehow corresponds to the higher order of the universe), legitimation by revolution (the winners are presumed to have right on their side), and legitimation by success (a system that works is to be supported).

A number of these bases may exist in varying proportions at different times. There is always some idea that the government favors goals necessary or beneficial to the community, so it can properly take private wealth for public ends. At the same time, all governments use myth, tradition, and ritual to surround ordinary mortals with an extraordinary aura. Even very commonplace persons at the summit of power are invested with a certain charm elevating them above the ordinary. Formerly, rulers were magical beings—as in the tradition of healing by the king's touch—or became father figures for the people. The early Sumerian city-states were temple-centered, and the ancient pharaohs were more high priests and gods than civil rulers. Modern states present themselves as the incarnation of a philosophic good, or at least an approach to higher values.

For ideological legitimation, the state must correspond to the outlook of the age. Primitive kings could rest their authority on ancestral myths and tabus; similarly, the right of the Chinese emperors was sustained by Confucianism, which saw hierarchic order as the basis of the universe. European monarchs of the seventeenth and early eighteenth centuries asserted divine appointment to office. As education progressed and philosophers of rationality (the "Enlighten-

---

[2]Max Weber, *The Theory of Economic and Social Organization* (New York: Free Press, 1947), pp. 324–429.

ment") became popular in the latter part of the eighteenth century, it became necessary to claim to govern for the benefit of the people ("benevolent despotism").

In our day, the will of the people has become generally accepted as the source of political authority, so even the most authoritarian rulers try to convince the world that they rest on popular consent and demand. In the 1930s Hitler claimed to represent the German people far better than any legislature and held plebiscites to prove it. Stalin and his successors and imitators in the Soviet Union and elsewhere insisted and insist that the people stand fervently and unanimously behind them, all of which is held so self-evident that no plebiscite is necessary. They claim a popular right through Marxism and the theory that the governing party represents the workers, the most numerous class of the future, if not the present, and the one historically anointed to rule in the socialist order. Democratic states base their legitimation on the expression of popular sentiments through freely contested elections.

The essence of traditional legitimation is that if one's forebears have always bowed, and one has bowed many times, it is easy to bow again. Ritual and ceremony add dignity and mystery, as people watch and share in solemn actions of symbolic meaning, gestures that are to be performed because they have always been performed. Governments that rely heavily on traditional or mystical sanctification make great use of ceremony. The French monarchy, for example, prescribed the motions surrounding the king's dinner in enormous detail, and thousands of servants were required to perform all the rituals correctly. A revolutionary regime, like that of Russia in the first years after the Communist seizure of power, throws formality to the wind because its legitimacy rests on something very different, the promise of a new social order. But as the revolution has

receded and ideological fervor has cooled, the Soviet state has become more and more fond of symbols and protocol.

A democracy has less need for ceremony, because it has the legitimation of popular votes, and it is rightly felt that trappings and paraphernalia of the American presidency are undemocratic in spirit. No one objects, however, to the sacredness commonly attributed to the Constitution. The British system relies more on ritual, as in the colorful opening of Parliament by the monarch, than other democratic countries, perhaps because it lacks a written constitution and is guided to a large extent by tradition and convention. Prewar Japan treated the emperor as divine; the new and more democratic Japan pays little attention to a figurehead who has formally renounced divinity. Education, modern sophistication, and awareness of other customs and cultures tend to reduce the effectiveness of the mystical or ceremonial aspects of the state; people are held together instead by ideological solidarity and a sense of themselves as a cultural-economic unit with shared problems and hopes.

Traditional merges into rational legitimacy as the nation contests with others for power, prestige, security, and material advantages. The state demands loyalty because it is the incorporation of the people in rivalry or struggle with external powers. Hence all states glorify their history at least a little.

The need to stand together against the foreign enemy is perhaps the most forceful claim of the state to obedience. To oppose the government in this situation is to aid a real or alleged enemy. Patriotism or loyalty to the state is virtue, and even when people find their government oppressive they probably feel they must bear with it in the face of an external danger. The consequence is that shaky governments have often undertaken foreign adventures in order to recover the loyalty of their people. This purpose led the French government into war with Prussia in 1870, for example. In this case, defeat discredited the regime.

Governments also earn legitimacy by material services to their people. For example, the American system has been credited with giving its people the world's highest standard of living; for most Americans, this is good reason to support the government, or at least the general political system. Few are likely to think seriously of overthrowing a system such as the Swedish, which not only presides over a very productive economy but also furnishes a multitude of social services. The Soviet Union frequently reminds its citizens of the free education and medical services they receive.

Admiration, gratitude, loyalty, and love may be for a system or for a particular person who stands at the head of it. The charismatic leader usually comes to the fore when the state itself is weak or new, as in a revolutionary or postrevolutionary situation. Thus Napoleon and Lenin presided over new and unsettled regimes, and the new nations of the post-World War II period were led by a galaxy of striking figures, such as Mohandas Gandhi and Jawaharlal Nehru of India, Kwame Nkrumah of Ghana, Julius Nyerere of Tanzania, Jomo Kenyatta of Kenya, Sékou Touré of Guinea, and Sukarno of Indonesia. Successors have usually been less notable or at least less celebrated. Authoritarian states build up the image of leading personalities regardless of their personal qualities. For example, whereas Lenin stood out in his own right, the less attractive personality of Stalin was far more glorified, and the secondary figures of Khrushchev and Brezhnev were inflated disproportionately to their contributions.

In the authoritarian state, to oppose the exalted leader is to oppose the state and practically the entire system. In the constitutional and democratic system, however, the two are separated; it is accepted that a person may be fully loyal to the country and the government while hostile to the current president or prime minister. The leader may then be charismatic for some and hateful to others, as was true of Franklin Roosevelt in the 1930s in America.

Legitimacy of the state or the political regime implies loyalty to it—the willingness of citizens to pay taxes, take mandated actions, and refrain from breaking rules (or committing crimes). Government implies regulations or laws, and legitimacy determines the spirit in which laws are accepted and executed. A simple criterion of the effectiveness of government is the degree to which its mandates are heeded by the people. Another is the extent to which the state and its leaders themselves conform to laws. Insofar as they do, they can boast of a rule of law, which is the basis for freedom. This is also in the long run the basis for prosperity, because production cannot thrive unless people can count on the consequences of their actions. Legality is a prerequisite for rationality in the social order and a major factor of legitimacy.

LEADERSHIP

No one can command beyond the willingness of followers to obey; even a Stalin or Hitler rules not simply by command but also by political juggling, by keeping various powers in the state at odds and preventing subordinates from combining or getting too strong. The dictator is dictator, however, through the power of choosing or removing lieutenants, fixing status, and rewarding loyalty or punishing its failure.

Whether or not a single person is strongly dominant, the tendency toward *oligarchy,* or rule by a small group, is universal. This elite group may be broad or narrow; it may be responsive to popular needs, capable, hard-working, and unselfish, or the opposite. It may be a closed caste, or it may be open to all those of talent. The character of government depends to a large extent on the means by which people are brought into positions of authority.

How Leaders Are Chosen

One of the commonest means is by heredity. The children of the rich or powerful have a headstart in the most egalitarian of societies because of superior education, self-confidence, perhaps inherited talents, easy access to high circles, and the ability of parents to pass wealth and frequently position to their offspring. When the advantages of aristocrats are fixed by custom and strongly held, there is a hereditary nobility. Since supreme rulers desire the highest office for their children, hereditary *monarchy* has been the most common type of government in the past. Even where monarchy was not a recognized institution, as in the Italian republics of the later Middle Ages or modern Latin America, dictators have often sought to found dynasties. The inheritance of rulership is not very rational, however, because the child often does not inherit a parent's strength of character and because being born to the throne is poor preparation for kingship. It would probably be fair to say that most hereditary monarchs have been more or less incompetent.

The institution has advantages, however. When a long-time leader dies, his son is the likeliest candidate for the succession because he supposedly has virtues inherited from his father, because of respect for the dead leader, and because it is easier to agree on the son of the old chief than anyone else. Inheritance gives a clear decision regarding the succession without opening a Pandora's box of contentions. It works rather well when monarchs are strictly circumscribed in their powers, as they usually were by tradition in the Middle Ages, so that the possibilities of abuse are limited. It works best if the monarch reigns without ruling, leaving the government to ministers and exercising only symbolic power. Then permanent kingship provides continuity for the state while facilitating changes of leadership.

Another means of succession is by choice of the dying or retiring ruler. The Roman empire had many good rulers because childless emperors adopted an outstanding general as son and heir, thus applying the hereditary principle with rational choice. When the emperor had a natural son, however, the result was usually unfortunate. The philosopher-emperor Marcus Aurelius was the last of a series of excellent adoptees; his son Commodus was among the worst of the Caesars. Recently presidents have been chosen by outgoing presidents in Brazil and Mexico (with formal election). This procedure does not confer as much legitimacy as genuine election, but it has proved satisfactory. It is the advantage of the Mexican and Brazilian systems that the president has a fixed term, the last duty of which is to turn the administration over to his political heir.

When the ruler's tenure is indefinite or for life, the procedure is less satisfactory. The ruler may be reluctant to plan for his own demise, as though preparing for it brought it closer. Moreover, to tap an individual or heir-apparent is to encourage him to think of hastening his accession, perhaps in fear that the chief may change his mind. It also exposes the designated individual to the intrigues of rivals, who now have a common interest in displacing him. Unhappily also, choice by the outgoing ruler frequently implies inferior capacities. The ruler's favorite is probably his most intimate collaborator; and the ruler seldom brings to his side those who might threaten his position or overshadow him but may prefer the subordinate who is most blindly loyal. At the same time, if the boss has been too long on top, resentments have probably accumulated below. Hence the designated successor may find it difficult to step into the shoes of the departed patron.

For this reason, strong rulers have seldom been able to project their power by designating heirs. Hardly ever have Latin American dictators done so; their departures have usually been accompanied by minirevolutions. Communist leaders likewise have never transferred power to a favored successor. In looser political systems, a leader can only give his choice a strategic advantage in the tussle. The decision is usually with peers and near-peers in the political group, party, or military coterie. By consent or self-imposition, someone emerges or makes oneself the acknowledged head of the group, the chief others support because they see that person as effective and share his or her political fortunes. For example, leaders in the British Conservative party are formally elected by fellow members of Parliament. We may assume that they are chosen for a variety of reasons: their colleagues like them or are indebted to them, they show the ability to head a government, or they seem capable of leading their party to electoral victory and control of the administration. Lenin became recognized head of his Bolshevik faction or party long before he led it to victory in the revolution because he formed the party around himself and was its focus. Stalin rose to supremacy first by making himself useful to his superior, Lenin, and then to his peers, and finally by replacing them with men attached only to himself.

If the appeal of the leader is personal magnetism independent of organizational strength, he or she may be called charismatic. This implies some capacity to elicit awe and is usually associated with a myth, such as Hitler's proclamation of German superiority or Lenin's claim to be the genuine representative of the workers. The charismatic leader also offers the people redress of grievances and the fulfillment of deep hopes. A charismatic leader appears in times of uncertainty and disorder, when customary ways and people seem inadequate, and authority is fortified by success. Hitler and Lenin, to use outstanding examples, affirmed their authority by victories, the former by foreign policy successes followed by spectacular military triumphs, the latter by presiding over revolution and victory in the civil war. When charismatic authority has once been sanctified by amazing success, it is remarkably resistant to erosion. Hitler retained the aura of a very special personality even when all the conquered territories had been lost, and Lenin remained unchallenged as a leader after the civil war despite the utter misery into which Russia had been plunged. The charismatic leader gets credit for the glorious deeds, and the failures are blamed on others.

How genuine and overwhelmingly popular the charismatic or supposedly charismatic leadership may be one cannot tell. The Hitlers and Lenins, or the Sukarnos or Castros, do not care to test the totality of popular affection by free elections. Mao appeared to have been genuinely admired by most Chinese, but not long after his death Chinese leaders were pointing to his faults. Stalin, a man of unattractive personality, whipped the people (or many of them) into loving him.

Changing Leadership

The disorder of a revolutionary situation usually brings to the top capable or at least dynamic leaders. The purpose of revolutions may be, in the view of the masses, to change the social order and abolish the ruling classes: the humble and long-suffering people, goaded to the end of their patience, take things in hand, kick out the oppressors, and make a new start on principles of justice. Revolution is especially appealing in authoritarian societies that have no other means of removing the holders of privilege, and it answers the sense of right for the oppressed, for the weak against the strong and the cruel. But the effect of revolution is not to do away with elites but to replace one elite with a new, uninhibited, probably more capable and inspired elite.

Revolution is consequently an effective way of changing leadership. However, it is messy and usually bloody and requires a painful reestablishment of the legal order. It never places power in the hands of the surging multitude but usually concentrates it still more than the previous regime. Revolutions, moreover, are never made to order simply by the will of the revolutionaries; they require appropriate conditions, usually the turmoil of war and the misery and disorganization of defeat. In normal times, revolution has little chance of success because most people, especially those in positions of influence, prefer to keep things more or less as they are.

It is broadly true that political systems represent vested interests and fixed relations and status. Any system, once established, settles down and becomes routine. The difference between revolutionary and conservative regimes is only temporary, because the aim of the successors of the revolutionary elite soon becomes the preservation of status. A fixed elite becomes not only conservative but decadent. The aging system spends more energy on maintenance and less on performance.[3] Even if the leader does not want personal privilege for himself, followers will not be so self-denying. An elite ac-

customed to superiority appropriates more than its share of goods and comes to regard this as a right. This has been the story of many an imperial regime in the past and, it would appear, of all states that do not have a mechanism for renewal of leadership.

Changing leadership in a regular, rational, and orderly way is thus one of the greatest problems of politics. It is necessary both to check corruption and to renew energies and admit new ideas, but it runs counter to the fact that the most powerful persons in the state do not want to be replaced. Legitimation by election at fixed intervals is one answer. So far as this is accepted, leaders do not try to overstay their terms because they and everyone else know that they would have no title to rule. In most countries, however, the custom of contested elections is not firmly fixed and tenure of office is indefinite. The satisfactions of an unlimited term of office are reduced by its dangers; there is much less incentive to oust or murder the temporary leader. But it is not human nature to like to step down from the summit, so the problem remains a real one.

THE BUREAUCRACY

The people at the top can decide what they want to do and give orders, but they can no more carry out their policies without an army of officials than generals can fight battles without soldiers. The government functions through a staff, like a school or a business; and the staff carries out the decisions handed down to it while generating information and sometimes policies from below. It consists of persons of prescribed powers and duties, all under the orders of superiors in a chain of command like that of the military, all supposed to be applying general rules and specific instructions, but all with some capability for influencing the reality of government.

[3] Thomas Koebernick and Matthew Melko, "Normal Times, Relational Ideologies," *Quarterly Journal of Ideology* 1 (Spring 1977), p. 40.

Although it never presents itself as such, the bureaucracy may well be the most important part of any political system because it endures while leaders come and go.

The only line of demarcation between bureaucracy and the political leadership is that the civil service is ordinarily permanent, whereas the politicians are temporary. At the top, the civil service is more or less politicized in most democratic countries, as high officials are designated by political leaders to be their aides. In more authoritarian systems, the administration is inseparable from the leadership. Officials are promoted from the administrative or party apparatus to decision-making positions. Careers are made by climbing ladders. Bureaucracy implies professionalism because it generally means tenure, and hence time to acquire skills and knowledge.

The staff is the muscle of the system, but its obedience to the leadership is not complete and automatic. On the one hand, bureaucrats have a large say in the formulation of policies, even though probably not present at high councils, because they provide most or sometimes all the information on the basis of which the leaders decide. On the other hand, if policies to which the bureaucracy is opposed are adopted, it finds a thousand ways to bring up difficulties, to delay, sabotage, or neglect fulfillment. American presidents, French premiers, and Soviet general secretaries have found that they could give orders, but nothing would happen. Moreover, a bureaucracy may effectively make policy by the way it implements directives. For example, in the United States affirmative action programs have been made and shaped largely by the officials of the Department of Health, Education and Welfare, applying their interpretation of the law.

It is commonly assumed that in the totalitarian state, bureaucratic obedience must be total, but the reality is different. Control by the top may be more difficult than in the democratic state because information flows less freely and lines of authority are more complicated. As the system ages and the leadership becomes feebler, the bureaucracy is likely to fill the vacuum and become virtually the rulership. The party and state bureaucracy has become the ruling class of the Soviet Union, as it was of prerevolutionary Russia; and the Soviet apparatus has far more in common with its tsarist predecessor than with Lenin's revolutionaries. On the other hand, the permanent, highly qualified, and generally incorruptible higher staff of such governments as the British, French, German, and Japanese provides stability and competence even when the political apparatus seems to flounder.

Like any other organization that provides its members with a livelihood and status, the bureaucracy is self-protective. It is to a considerable extent governed from within, and it uses its resources to strengthen itself. The ponderous, immobile bureaucracy is a prime obstacle to change. It gladly undertakes new programs that enhance its role, but it fiercely resists liquidation of old functions. When the Social Democrats in Sweden were replaced by a conservative coalition in 1976, the programs of the Social Democratic government continued as though nothing had happened. Civil servants want security of tenure for themselves above all, and they have generally obtained it in the advanced countries. In principle, entry is by objective competitive examination, and the idea of dismissal for political reasons is virtually unknown in the democratic countries. Even in the Soviet Union, officials have tenure despite the theoretical power of superiors to dismiss them, because everyone wants security.

Officials remain in place indefinitely whether or not they have real work to do; idleness is no problem because more papers can always be circulated. Unless it can be shaken up from above, the bureaucracy may bog down in waste motion and futile, probably outdated, procedures. It is most efficient when new; it soon becomes inefficient because it lacks an adequate criterion, such as profitability, of the quality of performance. A business retreats from areas of unprofitability; a bureaucracy expands to cover failures. Bureaucratic politics implies bargaining for advantages among agencies. The fiercest battles in the bureaucracy are not over policies but over jurisdiction and boundaries; resistance is much less to new programs than to threats to the structure. The bureaucracy normally favors socialist measures because they involve governmental controls and greater bureaucratic power; the drive for socialism (a rather vague idea, the chief ingredients of which are nationalization or collectivization of the economy, the welfare state, and egalitarianism) amounts to an idealization of the bureaucratic order. Bureaucracies dislike private interest groups because they interfere with solutions or policies dictated by bureaucratic expertise. There is pressure for more responsibilities, bigger budgets, and larger staffs. In a choice between two programs, one of which requires much administration, whereas the other is largely self-administered, officials will sponsor and promote the one that involves more bureaucratic management.

The problem is much broader than the self-protection of the organization; it is an unsolved and perhaps unsolvable problem of government. The bigger and more complex social systems become, the poorer their performance. Demands on government outrace its capacity; the need for problem-solving soars, although the ability to solve problems may even shrink. More and more areas are turned over to experts or specialists, while the ordinary person feels impotent if not abandoned. One of the greatest problems of government, then, is how the bureaucracy is to be organized, by what criteria officials should be selected and promoted, how they can be controlled and yet permitted independence and security from political meddling, and how to ensure that they serve the public interest rather than personal or corporate interests.

KINDS OF GOVERNMENT

Political structures differ in various ways— size, differentiation, complexity, degree of centralization, openness, legality, responsiveness, and degree and kind of political participation by groups or persons outside the center of authority. There are correspondingly various ways in which states may be classified by structure and character, from authoritarian to democratic, closed to open, traditional to modern, conservative to revolutionary, and so forth. One of the commonest modes of description, however, is as "rightist" or "leftist."

Right to Left

The Right-Left distinction originated in the French Assembly after the 1789 revolution. In the old Estates-General, the nobles took their places to the right of the presiding officer, as was their privilege. In the new republican assembly, the deputies who were more sympathetic to the old order took the places vacated by the nobility and clergy, and those who saw more virtues in the new way sat on the opposite side. Since then, *leftist* has come broadly to mean populist, antiprivilege (at least, antieconomic privilege), antiaristocratic, and antitraditional; *rightist*, tradition-bound and favorable to the "better classes." To some extent, leftists have been prodemocratic in demanding more participation in government by ordinary people, while rightists have looked more kindly on kings, dictators, and military juntas. Leftist has also come to mean favorable to expanding the role of the state, which implies more power for a political leadership, whereas rightists have often but not always proposed cutting governmental costs and functions, thereby restricting the scope of the state.

This classification was fairly applicable to European politics through the nineteenth century and in the first decade of the twentieth. Now, however, the labels have become confused. The Communist movement, guided and supported after 1919 by the Soviet Union, claimed to be left of the Left, yet it was (and is) essentially elitist, giving power to a small inner circle or to a single leader. Leftist ideology goes with rightist policies. It has been assumed that military organizations were inevitably rightist by inclination, but in many cases military coups in the Third World have proclaimed leftist, or at least antiaristocratic, goals. Left versus Right has generally been less applicable to the non-European world, and it has often degenerated into a synonym for pro-Communist versus anti-Communist. In the United States, *liberal* has taken on much of the meaning formerly given to *leftist,* and libertarian has acquired some of the meaning formerly attached to liberal, repugnance for state interference. In much Third World politics, as in India, Left versus Right is largely irrelevant, although leftist may mean anti-Western or pro-Soviet.

The distinction of Right and Left is also closely related to whether political power is held by persons related to traditional holders of authority, primarily persons of wealth, or by new claimants, whose trade is more likely in words and who probably seek support by appealing to popular feelings. For this reason, intellectuals are instinctively more inclined to leftist than rightist philosophies. Revolutionary movements that look to broad social change are almost by definition leftist, but equally by definition they cease to be leftist when a new set of owners is installed. Radical leftists and radical rightists in fact have much in common: German fascism may be considered rightist because it violently opposed the leftists, although it was to a considerable extent socially leveling and raised up new elites while cooperating with old ones.

The Political Spectrum

There are no clear-cut and satisfactory classifications into which states can be pigeonholed, but numerous categorizations have been proposed. Writers concerned with political modernization, especially in the 1960s, have often stressed ineffective traditional versus effective modern systems, or preindustrial agrarian versus industrial. Others have discussed states as consensual, fragmented, totalitarian, or traditional, or have divided political systems into dictatorial, oligarchic, and representational.

The last-mentioned classification is close to that of eighteenth-century writers such as Montesquieu, who in his *Spirit of the Laws* described despotic empires, conventional kingdoms, and republics. This is in the tradition of Aristotle's government by the one, the few, and the many; and an acceptable general classificatory spectrum is from the strongest rule of the smallest number (totalitarian dictatorship) to the lightest rule of the largest number (libertarian democracy). Toward one end of the spectrum, the democratic, pluralistic, or open society has a free press, contested and reasonably honest elections, competing political parties, civil rights, market economy, independent courts, rule of law, constitutional regulation of power, authoritative legislative body, limited terms of office, and some local self-government. It has little in the way of ideology, only some general, unobligatory beliefs in its virtues. In it the agencies of force, police and military, play no consequential overt political role.

The thoroughgoing authoritarian state is in all these respects the opposite. It controls the press and other media of expression; it has elections, if at all, only for show; it allows no open political competition; it denies civil rights; it has a centralized economy, although some small-scale private production and trade may be tolerated; its courts are subject to political direction; law is secondary to politics; and power is unshackled by constitutional limitations. If there is something like a legislative body, its function is only to ratify decisions of the rulership. Terms of office are not fixed, and in practice leaders remain in power indefinitely. Local government amounts only to administrative decentralization. There is more or less of an officially prescribed creed, probably including a cult of the leader. Agencies of force, the army or a militarized police force, play a major part in the state.

In contemporary practice, the pluralistic group is almost equivalent to the states of the West European tradition, and the totalitarian-monistic states generally take their inspiration from the Russian Revolution and Marxism-Leninism. This division, however, is the result of historical events, including the destruction of fascist regimes in World War II. The dichotomy represents a fundamental and general cleavage in political affairs and the nature of society, extending much beyond any particular ideologies. It embraces many antitheses, such as

pluralism	monism
individualistic	collectivist
self-will	submission
rationalistic	doctrinaire
heretical	conformist
local autonomy	centralized administration

innovative	conservative
freedom	order
socially open	exclusive
libertarian	authoritarian
responsible	insulated
market economy	controlled economy
noncoercive	coercive
legalistic	arbitrary
achievement status	ascriptive status
open	secretive
competitive	organized

Between the two extremes, there are, of course, many qualified, limited, or ineffective authoritarianisms and limited or qualified democracies. In fact, a majority of the world's states are less than total dictatorships, many of them military, which permit much more latitude of private action than the Marxist-Leninist states. There are also various outwardly more or less democractic states in which real power is in the hands of a monopolistic political party (as Mexico) or the military (as Honduras). Even thoroughly democratic states bear the marks of and retain some institutions of an earlier, less democratic condition. For example, British society, despite prolonged political democratization and decades of rule by Labour governments, is socially still rather deferential; there is considerable fondness for the monarchy, along with snobbery based on family, education, and accent; and education is somewhat elitist. This is understandable in terms of the continuity of British institutions since the Middle Ages and the emphasis on tradition. France has relatively little local self-government because of habits of centralization under a strong monarchy. On the other hand, authoritarian states coming out of a social revolution, such as Leninist Russia, Maoist China, or to some degree even Hitlerian Germany, may be innovative, outwardly egalitarian, and socially mobile, opening careers to all (politically acceptable) for a good many years. The revolution is a sort of democratic event, leveling and loosening, until the political structure cements society in place again and hardens differences. Moreover, dictatorial states often borrow terms and forms from the democratic.

With these qualifications, the broad dichotomy, rule by few or many, has been evident throughout history. There have been almost unstructured primitive villages and preliterate despotic empires, such as the Inca of Peru; there have been free, libertarian city-states, such as those of ancient Greece, and stern imperial states, such as the Assyrian, Persian (Achaemenid), or Roman. In the nineteenth century, European near-democracies or constitutional monarchies contrasted with Oriental despotisms. The twentieth century has seen free democracies and modernized despotisms, now called totalitarian states, such as Nazi Germany and Soviet Russia. During most of history, any considerable amount of political freedom has been exceptional, the product of locally favorable conditions. It is a modern phenomenon that authoritarianism now is possibly on the defensive. No other political ideology on the world stage has prestige comparable to the democratic.

The Authoritarian Cluster

Extreme modern authoritarianism is commonly called *totalitarianism*. The term has been attacked as overly value-laden and insufficiently expressive of visible change within Communist societies. It is true that the word has been used in a propagandistic fashion. It is also true that any implication that totalitarian states were frozen and incapable of change was erroneous; the Hitlerian state could certainly not have endured unaltered under a senile Hitler, and the pressures of older Communist states today are far less than in the heyday of Stalinism, although some of the newer, such as North Korea, leave little to be desired in repressiveness.

Totalitarianism was associated with claims to the total reordering of society and corresponding demands on the citizens and terror against all who fell short of complete obedience.[4] After a few decades, however, the rulership loses interest in social change of any kind, without ceasing to claim total command of society. In fact, despite the boasts of leaders, Italian and German totalitarianism never approached total control of the life of the nation, and Stalinism was a good deal less effective than it pretended. The term remains, however, fairly handy to describe societies wherein, in principle, whatever is not officially approved is forbidden and the state would guide all the thoughts and actions of its citizens. It distinguishes between them and more traditional authoritarian societies that do not bother ordinary citizens very much as long as they pay taxes and stay clear of politics. This is especially relevant to the control of information. The conventional authoritarian state censors what it considers subversive views. The totalitarian state tries not only to prohibit all publications it finds harmful but also to direct literary and other creativity into politically suitable lines.

The label "totalitarian" was invented and worn proudly by fascist Italy, which adopted a Hegelian idealization of the state. But the totalitarianism of Mussolini was mostly bombast; and the fascist society was, from the dictator's point of view, distressingly loose and ineffective, as demonstrated by its poor performance in World War II. There is obviously no clear demarcation between totalitarian and merely dictatorial-authoritarian

[4]Carl Friedrich and Zbigniew Brzezinski, *Totalitarian Dictatorship and Autocracy* (Cambridge, Mass.: Harvard University Press, 1965).

regimes. The postrevolutionary Communist states slide down the scale, with the erosion not of desires to control but of capacities. Lesser fascistic or fascistoid states, such as Franco's Spain, Salazar's Portugal, or Perón's Argentina, had more or less aspiration to totalitarianism, but they never managed to atomize their societies or place the people fully at their mercy.

It is often assumed that totalitarianism is a modern by-product of electronic communications and sophisticated organizational and behavioral control methods. Yet ancient despotisms sometimes exercised sternly pervasive control. The Incas, for example, replaced the religion and myth of the peoples they conquered as effectively as any modern dictatorship; and Chinese dynasties at times had sophisticated thought-control methods. The favorite propaganda method of the Leninists was face-to-face agitation, the oldest of all methods of influence. Neither is ideology a new weapon; Confucianism has probably been more effective as an instrument of social control than any modern theory. Perhaps the simplest criterion is the degree to which the state apparatus stands above the people, able to treat them as it pleases; in this regard modern despotisms (to use an unfashionable word) have been comparable to innumerable predecessors.

Authoritarian rule is based fundamentally on force, supplemented by more or less persuasion and some effort to earn the support of people by looking to their material and psychological needs. In the worst cases, the main instrument of rule is simply terrorism, arbitrary except that the victims are real or supposed opponents of the powers. This is scotomocracy, or government by murder; an example was the Idi Amin regime in Uganda. All governments must, of course, please some people, but the beneficiaries may be principally a small number of armed followers, whose biggest reward is license to bully their fellow citizens.

Many authoritarian states have been established by some sort of military victory. Successful generals have convincing title to command, and foreign conquests strengthen the state. Territorial expansion is highly favorable for autocracy for several reasons: the greatness of the state is proved by its endless dominion, the individual is dwarfed by the resources of the state, and it is more difficult to organize effective opposition over a wide expanse. Control of the center is easier to maintain when it can call upon many provinces, and despotism is justified as the only means of maintaining the empire. The size of the territory also makes the empire more of a world to itself. Foreign travel is usually restricted if not prohibited except for a few emissaries, as under Stalin and in traditional Oriental despotisms. Sealing off the state reduces contamination by alien ideas and ensures a more docile people.

Well-managed dictatorships have the ability to sustain themselves even in the face of real trouble, when a large majority of the people would seem to have good reason to seek a change of regime. This is done by placing control of force in the hands of persons bound to it. For example, a political police stands by an unpopular regime because its fall would cost them status and prosperity. A tyrant has only to reward enough strategically placed persons to offset the discontent of the unfavored multitude.

Traditional autocracies have been agrarian, and a relatively simple and stable agricultural economy suits them much better than industry or commerce. Scattered peasants are defenseless, and it is difficult for them to move, hide, or disguise capital to elude the tax collector. Manufacturing and trade present more problems. It is difficult for the state to manage them effectively because the political criteria are contrary to economic progress. On the other hand, when commerce is allowed freedom of operation, the result is private wealth, or private power. The commercial spirit is antipathetic to the political; private property gives independence of the apparatus, but the officials would usually prefer to have wealth under their own custody.

It is consequently in the historical pattern when modern autocracies deny rights of private ownership and production and complete political power by joining economic power to it. As long as there is a large independent sector, governmental control is not absolute; but if economic power is joined to political, there is not much protection from either.[5] Thus Mussolini tried to organize the Italian economy into estates under his aegis. The Nazis, although they came to power with the help of big business (especially because of promises to help heavy industry by rearmament), proceeded to statization by Aryanization, state-owned combines, and manifold controls reducing the owner effectively to manager for the state. It has been a strength of the Marxist-Leninists to use economic egalitarianism as justification for taking all productive property into their own hands. In the corporate state, people have status corresponding to their functions, and all activities are tied together through an officially sanctioned and directed organization.

Inequality is the fact of the authoritarian system. The more power is concentrated, the higher some rise over others, until the emperor or dictator is something like a god. Petty officeholders stand over ordinary people, whose powerlessness may become equivalent to worthlessness. Characteristic of the system is a net of patron-client relations, in which career advancement is through attachment to powerful persons. The ruling class is, of course, more or less equivalent to the state (or party) bureaucracy. Relationships become more personal than legal; law is an equivocal concept because the ruling powers can make, unmake, or disregard it. The way to wealth is through politics, or at least political connections; no enterprise can prosper without protection. The government may desire to satisfy popular needs for goods, if only for its own security, but it can do this only poorly because of its inefficiency and lack of feedback.

A corollary is the shackling of intelligence. Governments interpret criticism as disloyalty and act to repress it. The absolutist state, moreover, undertakes general philosophic guidance and indoctrination, which is seen as a duty to its unenlightened citizenry as well as a convenience to itself. There is little room for original thinking. From the point of view of the government, the truth is known and inquiry is likely to be heresy. Faith and resignation become prime virtues.

A great weakness of the authoritarian society is resistance to change. Perhaps after a phase of reordering society, the authoritarian government tends toward immobility because the powerholders are fearful that change might dislodge them or at least reduce their status. The apparatus of control deprives forces outside the system of the means of pressing for change and reduces the awareness of needs and demands. Then, if political life remains compressed, insecurity and disinterest in the broader world drive people to the shelter of smaller groups such as the family or clan, within which personal relations are useful and more reliable. Under the impact of power, the authoritarian personality shows itself: cynical, lacking in self-assurance, custom-bound, outwardly conformist, servile to superiors and harsh

[5]As observed by the French president, Valery Giscard d'Estaing, *La démocratie* (Paris: Fayard, 1976), p. 102.

toward inferiors.[6] Europeans exploring the globe met societies more or less of this sort wherever they went, and the ordinary portrait of the traditional society is very much like that of the imperial or authoritarian society.[7]

If more or less authoritarian states have been so common through history and are still prevalent despite the widespread awareness of democratic institutions and the erosion of the authority of monarchy and other traditional rulership, one must suppose that authoritarianism has genuine attractions, at least for influential people. It may indeed appeal to psychological needs; the uncertainties of freedom are often burdensome. The unequivocal ruler may assure order and assert effectively a community will. Dictatorship frequently functions efficiently when it is new, and it may promote economic growth by giving security and opportunity for investment. The authoritarian regimes of Taiwan, South Korea, and Singapore have done so with remarkable success—using political unfreedom to support economic freedom. By economic growth they have, of course, secured the acceptance if not enthusiastic support of many people of all classes.

It must be suspected, however, that the chief reason for the commonness of nondemocratic governments is that, whereas a few armed men can overthrow a democratic state, to establish a viable democracy it is necessary not only to push aside rulers with guns in one hand and the levers of the government in the other but also to erect a sophisticated institutional structure. And if the democracy gets into trouble because of economic problems or inability to keep order in a deeply divided society, it may fall to the next dictator with armed forces behind him.

The Pluralistic Cluster

Why it has been possible, at a few times in certain areas, for mobile, innovative, and progressive states to arise is not wholly clear.[8] Such societies are generally open, less rigidly governed, and pluralistic. One condition for their growth has been an international system of independent and competitive yet culturally related states. There have been only a few such state systems of importance, perhaps a dozen in all history; that of the nation-states of the West has been the largest and most creative.

In some cases geography has certainly played a major part, as in the case of the Greek city-states, which arose on a multitude of islands and rugged peninsulas, and the nation-states of the West, partially protected by seas and mountains. Europe, especially the more open western part, is a peninsula of many peninsulas and islands, with mountain ranges helping to set off Spain, France, Italy, and so on. Without such geographical divisions, nation-states could hardly have grown and maintained their independence. In other cases, the primary condition may have been political. For example, in China prior to the Qin unification (221 B.C.), the weak suzerainty of a powerless emperor seems to have permitted vassal states to become independent while hindering their destroying one another. In medieval Italy, the powers of the papacy and the Holy Roman Empire offset one another effectively enough to permit many cities to become free states for a few centuries; the result was the magnificence of the Italian Renaissance.

[6]Everett E. Hagen, *On the Theory of Social Change* (Homewood, Ill.: Dorsey Press, 1962), chap. 5.

[7]See Robert Wesson, *The Imperial Order* (Berkeley: University of California Press, 1967), chaps. 6–8.

[8]See Robert Wesson, *State Systems* (New York: Free Press, 1978), passim.

However it may have arisen, the coexistence of numerous smallish polities in close communication seems to have been the necessary precondition not only for outstanding cultural creativity but also for limited government and some approach to republican or democratic institutions. Many small entities mean more or less open boundaries, and easy travel abroad undercuts mind control and facilitates criticism by comparison. When commerce between states is important, rulers cannot squeeze the mercantile class so severely. On the contrary, it takes on an importance impossible under authoritarian empires, perhaps becoming the major power in the regime. Pluralism per se implies restraint of authority, and territorial division of power leads to its allocation among the people. Finally, states living in close association are inevitably competitive, if not combative (if they are excessively combative they will destroy independence and the state system), and competition is liberating. It evokes rationality and a critical approach to questions, including those of power. It makes ordinary people valuable, because the state needs its human resources; and it gives community of purpose to elite and nonelite, a shared cause that provides a basis for the constitutional consensus essential to political freedom.

The results of the restriction of power in the ideal open society, like those of the magnification of power in the closed society, are many. Limitation of power at the top makes possible local self-government and freedom of organization, which is almost synonymous with political freedom. The economy is predominantly private and market-regulated. There is no single truth, but a variety of competing opinions. In the open, competitive order, people feel able to improve themselves or called upon to improve the world—the essence of the Protestant ethic, which Weber credited with the rise of modern industry.[9] The bureaucratic apparatus is relatively less weighty, and careers are made mostly outside it. The political process is more or less public, in contrast to the secrecy of the authoritarian state. Politics, like other aspects of life, is frankly competitive, with some of the character of a sport. Law, seen as an expression of the will of the community, is usually respected.

In the open society, there is more interaction among equals or near equals, and relations are less stiffly hierarchic. Mercantile contract replaces political status as the dominant mode of action. Innovation and change are easier. All systems suffer inertia because they provide status for persons of influence; but the open, pluralistic society also permits influence to those who may expect to benefit from change. The society favorable to easy interaction and receptive to innovation, which at the same time encourages and rewards productive effort, has a better chance for general prosperity. The association of pluralism with affluence has been noted. Wealth makes it easier for a society to be legalistic and open, perhaps democratic; but causation seems to work mostly in the opposite direction, as the open social-political order favors productivity. Historically rich countries or areas, such as Renaissance Italy, Sweden, Switzerland, the Netherlands, Britain, and the United States, have all been relatively free before they became exceptionally prosperous.

Productivity and prosperity, as well as military capacity, have made it possible for democratic systems to maintain themselves against larger authoritarian powers and have led others to borrow their institutions. The Greeks of pre-Roman times fended off the mighty Persian Empire, and the form of the Greek *polis* was copied all around the Med-

[9]Max Weber, *The Protestant Ethic and the Spirit of Capitalism* (New York: Scribners, 1958).

iterranean world, even where geographic conditions were quite different from the Greek homeland of islets and fingerlike peninsulas. This imitation must have been at least partly the result of the successes of the polis. Similarly, in the nineteenth century the fact that Britain led the world in trade and industry was persuasive evidence of the virtues of liberal parliamentary government and must have been a major cause—perhaps the greatest cause—for the spread of that form. Nowadays the most persuasive argument for political freedom is the relative prosperity of the United States, Western Europe, and Japan.[10]

ORDER AND FREEDOM

The ideal democracy is a small trading community in which people do as they please as long as they follow the rules established to protect the rights of others. The people gather to decide together the questions that affect the community. There is much voluntary mutual assistance, but government is minimal and interferes little in the lives of individuals. All beliefs are tolerated, including those destructive of tolerance. The chief demand of the community on its members is to join in contests against some neighbor and rival, but this they do willingly because it is the cause of their community.

This is an idealized pattern, to which Greek city-states, Swiss cantons, Netherlands towns in the war for liberation from Spain, and various others have come reasonably near. It is at the opposite end of the spectrum from the totalitarian empire. Most existing

[10]If the closed economic system had proved able to produce rapid economic growth, most countries would rush to adopt it. The nonrepresentative system has the advantage that it can be imposed by pressures or force, whatever the interests and ideas of a large majority of the people.

states stand somewhere between the extremes: all governments serve in part public interests, in part the interests of the governors. People need to get together for safety and for joint enterprises and set up institutions accordingly; at the same time, some assert dominion over others and organize themselves accordingly. Organization is in any case necessary, and it necessitates unequal distribution of power.

Government always represents a "they" against the "we" of the people; the crucial question is how autonomous "they" are, to what extent they are disposed and able to work their will over the will or interests of those they are supposed to serve. In other words, the kind of government depends on the extent to which the elite responds to inputs from outside that are against its own interests or impulses. Individuals are influential partly because they serve a function, partly because they hold levers of power. For example, generals are powerful in war because they are needed; they may be powerful in peace because they command physical force.

The monism-pluralism dichotomy of government is related to the opposite needs of society for order and freedom. Order and discipline are necessary for a workable society, yet order limits freedom. The balancing of freedom and order is a crucial problem of government, around which a thousand controversies revolve: How far should freedom of the press protect writing offensive to some people? Should people be required to serve in the armed forces? Are landlords free to dispose of their property or raise rents as they see fit? There are also the broader questions of whether the governors are masters or servants, how far and through what means they are responsible to and controlled by those over whom they stand.

Yet the order-freedom antithesis is by no means equivalent to the dichotomy of authoritarianism-monism versus democracy-pluralism. There is no liberty without order, and it may well be argued that there is maximum real liberty in the best-ordered state. Perhaps the authoritarian state is incapable of maintaining good order over an extended period. Ruthlessness may assist discipline and make the streets safe, but the state run by a self-chosen and self-perpetuating elite has no real defense against corruption. As the state ages, its mandates lose force; for example, the black and gray markets swell in countries of planned economy. Some freedom reasserts itself as disorder, perhaps insurrectionist impulses or protests as in Poland (1956, 1980), Hungary (1956), Chile (1983), and Czechoslovakia (1968).

THE QUALITY OF GOVERNMENT

To speak of Swiss farmers meeting to thrash out their problems with their neighbors on the one hand, and on the other of the imperial despot secluded in his palace with his harem, suggests a value judgment. It is more pragmatic to ask what purposes political structures are to fulfill and how well designed they are for these ends.

One quality of government that is occasionally overlooked by those of better-governed countries is negative, simply that the political authorities not be exploitative and abusive of their power. Unhappily, a common use of the powers of government is to keep an elite in power—an elite that may be more or less economic but is commonly political. That is, the state may be used by oligarchic landholders to sustain a semifeudal order, or by a variety of economic interests to support monopolistic practices. It is also used to provide jobs and status, and political position is converted into economic standing at least as often as the reverse.

It is to be desired that those who wield authority should not misuse it. Humans unfortunately gain satisfaction from demonstrating and exercising their power over their fellows. Even in democratic societies such as France or the United States, police are sometimes inclined to kick suspects or disturbers of the peace harder than necessary to subdue them, and in authoritarian states, from Argentina to the Soviet Union, they have seemed to take pleasure in brutality beyond political utility. What is true of security forces in physical confrontations is true more broadly and more subtly of any leadership not responsible to its people: those on top are almost certain to enjoy the exercise of power in ways that affirm their superiority, from displays of might to repression of unthreatening dissent.

More positively, many things are sought from governments, a number of which are suggested by the names of ministries or departments. A government should represent the nation in dealings with other states, provide for the general security, protect the people and their property, settle differences legally, promote conditions under which people can beneficially produce, assist the needy and promote economic justice, protect health and provide other social services, educate, and construct roads and other facilities beyond the reach of private enterprise. Most people would also consider it desirable that the state observe and protect human rights and freedoms, such as those of press, speech, religion, and artistic creativity, and that it foster social mobility, the freedom to better oneself. All these should be accomplished with maximum efficiency and minimal costs. These consist primarily of taxation but include conscription and regulation.

It would be appropriate to judge the quality of states by their ability to fulfill these requirements, just as the efficiency of an economic enterprise is judged in terms of its ability to put together the factors of production to produce the desired outputs. That is, political institutions can be judged in terms of securing decisions leading to desired outcomes. In practice, it is difficult to make assessments, because hardly any two persons will agree on how to weigh the various values sought (such as social services against low taxation) or how the performance of any particular government should be rated in a given category. From scanning the world panorama, one would probably conclude that the democratic states generally deserve better marks than the more absolutist. But some democratic states obviously function much better than others, just as some authoritarian states are more progressive, more efficient, and less oppressive than others—a difficult subject to which very little attention has been given.

Another quality, however, demands special consideration in our age—the ability to adapt to rapidly evolving technological needs, to facilitate desired innovation and to bring about appropriate responses. A well-structured political system should be capable of making good use of new inventions. Like an organism, a political entity must at the same time have self-stabilization and the capacity to change. This is difficult: A complex society needs more guidance, more organization, and more fixing of goals by a central authority—yet it is not clear that the political authority is necessarily capable of rational direction.

This may be perhaps the greatest problem of our times; and future generations, like past, will have to find their own answers. But some things seem clear. Change and adaptation require intellectual openness and adequate freedom of exploration and expression. It is indispensable that communication flow easily between rulers and ruled. It would seem essential that those in power be responsible to someone outside the power structure, preferably the citizenry in general. The fundamental problem of regulating the regulators has been sometimes fairly well solved by republican or democratic institutions; unless it is resolved somehow, degeneration is inevitable.

It is nearly the same thing to say that leaders should be selected for merit and not birth or ability at intrigue, that they should be given adequate but not excessive authority, and that terms of office, especially of the highest office, should be limited. There should be nonarbitrary means of allocating power and of removing dysfunctional individuals and organizations. Competitiveness within the state apparatus is indispensable for its effectiveness, as is competition of ideas and policies outside it. Decisions must be made at proper levels, as many persons as possible should be drawn into the making of policy that affects them, and different levels of decision making should be properly linked.[11] The citizens should be as equal as permitted by differences of natural endowment.

The most rational political structure should maximize order and freedom. This is achievable when a common purpose permits and encourages individual initiative. Basic agreement permits laws to be enforced with minimal cost and coercion, and toleration is natural when the community is confident in its basic unity. In the past, common purpose has been given largely by the competition among states. But international conflict no longer serves as an inspiration for nations, and we cannot yet tell whether awareness of common needs may be enough to replace it.

[11]As proposed by Edgar Owens and Robert Shaw in *Development Reconsidered* (Lexington, Mass.: Lexington Books, 1972).

Democracy

2

If a democractic nation is defined as one in which opposition parties have a fair chance of winning office, only about a quarter of the 156 members of the United Nations (ministates excluded) can be counted as democratic;[1] and the fraction has declined over the last decade. This is remarkable in view of the fact that the popular will is, practically speaking, the only respectable claim to power. The authority of monarchy is discredited, fascism has no intellectual standing, simple ad hoc dictatorship has to apologize for its existence, military government is based pretty frankly on guns, and racial philosophies are generally abhorrent. Theocracy is not broadly acceptable, while egalitarianism is almost universally considered a value.

[1]For a survey, see Freedom House, *Freedom in the World: Political Rights and Liberties, 1984* (Boston: S. K. Hall, 1984).

Democracy, however, is the system of the prosperous modern industrial world and of all the states with very high gross national product (GNP) per capita (except some oil-producing states of small population, such as Kuwait). It corresponds to the modern mentality, and intellectuals everywhere aspire to it, even though they may want a different form of it and believe that it is necessary to undergo a violent revolution in order to achieve it. It is probably fair to say that the better informed people are, the more prone they are to favor democracy—and the better able to make it work. Moreover, democracy comes easily in human affairs. If people get together to form a social club, a trade union, a robber band, a security force, an administration of irrigation works, or a political party, they probably pick leaders by consent of the members. There is a good deal of folk democracy among African or

Indian villagers and Latin American shanty town dwellers. If a group is complex enough to require definite rules, the straightforward procedure is that they are adopted by general approval and derive validity from this fact: they are to be obeyed because they represent the will of the whole body, or at least, a majority.

Various alternatives are less attractive. One is to place authority in the hands of someone born to lead, who probably is the son (or sometimes daughter) of someone who led or ruled by virtue of descent from someone else, and so on. The corollary is that laws are right because they have always been known to be the law or are duly sanctioned by persons born to authority. But this manner of selection of rulers suffers familiar drawbacks, and monarchy is a satisfying form of government only if the character of the monarch is not important—that is, if he or she does not really govern. Monarchy may compromise with oligarchy by having some kind of council elect kings. But this does not fully solve the problem, only pushes it backward to the question of determining who has the privilege of acting as electors. And elective monarchy has not been widespread. Government by religiously sanctioned authority also lacks practicality. In not many countries is any church or theocratic organization fully enough accepted to be able to assert itself as sovereign power. Moreover, religious organizations are inherently ill prepared to govern modern communities, with their host of nonreligious problems.

Monarchy and theocracy in any event are discordant with modernity, and nowadays the common alternative to leadership by general consent is leadership by imposition, usually by force or threat of force. The boss of a neighborhood gang may be boss because the others are afraid of him (and respect is close to fear). For a variety of reasons, the military establishment may make itself or one of its leaders the governing power; this is the commonest kind of "constitution" in the world today. All manner of dictatorships or illegitimate rulerships based on force and assisted by persuasion may last for many years and are usually succeeded by another dictatorship. Yet such governments are also impractical or inefficient in that they can hardly be accepted by their subjects in the same way as governments to which the people have given their consent. Basically coercive governments are also intrinsically subject to ills of rigidity and lack of information.

Yet democracy is an exceptional form of government. Indeed, in the pure sense, it is impractical except perhaps in a very small country. There is always an elite with far more than its share of power, and principles of authority and order are essential everywhere. If the members of a legislative assembly faithfully mirrored the views of the various regions and sectors of a large country, coherent policy would probably be impossible. Democracy as we understand and practice it is not rule by the people as a whole (through their representatives) but a system which ensures that ordinary people have rights and can make themselves heard, and it provides a means of checking and renewing the holders of high office.

Even though everyone may in theory favor equality, many yearn to assert their superiority; and in the best of democracies some lord it over their fellows by virtue of special knowledge, status, birth, or power. For this reason, democratic and authoritarian political strains are inextricably mixed. For example, in democratic countries much power remains in the hands of party leaders who decide, with more or less consultation, who is to be presented to the people at elections. Party leadership is weakest in the United States because direct primaries transfer the choice of candidates from the organization to the voters; for this reason primary elections are not used in Britain, France, Germany, and so forth. Parties in power usually have a marked advantage, so replacement of the governing party is apt to be infrequent. In Italy, for example, the Christian Democrats have been at the helm since World War II, and practically the same party has governed Japan since 1949. Of course, where one party is so strong that elections are largely a formality, as in Mexico, we cease to call it democratic.

In contrast, there are almost always democratic elements in the most authoritarian regimes. Roman Caesars were often elected or deposed by the "vote" of the legions. For a considerable part of its history, the Soviet Union has had collective leadership, that is, the "democracy" of the Politburo; and the Central Committee has sometimes made major decisions by vote. There is some effort to observe democratic procedures in the Soviet and other Communist parties, if only because the higher authorities want to check the middle echelons. Latin American dictators have almost always held regular elections. The European minority in Rhodesia (Zimbabwe) governed itself democratically enough for many years while excluding 19/20 of the population from the political process. Moreover, the responsibility of the rulers to the people is theoretically accepted almost everywhere. Even the nearly deified emperors of premodern China considered themselves responsible for the welfare of their subjects.

This general notion of responsibility is perhaps the most widespread of political ideas. It is simple and easily understood, although never totally effective in practice. Democracy means literally, as in the understanding of the Greeks who invented the word and the concept, rule by the "demos," the people as a whole, rather than by kings, tyrants, or aristocrats. We may properly use the word for a system in which the people, although not ruling themselves in any real sense, can in fact hold the rulers responsible.

THE DEVELOPMENT OF DEMOCRACY

In this sense, democracy is probably older than history, perhaps as old as humankind. There are hints of democratic or semidemocratic practices in the records of the Sumerians of Mesopotamia some 4,000 years ago, including a sort of charter of liberties with promises of relief from offensive official acts, from curbing tax collectors to reducing fees for shearing sheep. But the beginnings of government by consent in the Near East were crushed by wars and conquests. The famed libertarians of ancient times were the Greeks, whose political forms have been the more esteemed because of association with their intellectual achievements.

The Greek City-State

The Greek city-states arose on the islands and peninsulas in and around the Aegean Sea between Greece and Asia Minor. Villages grew up on the trade between Europe and Asia, when island hopping was the best means of navigation; as they grew prosperous, they expelled or demoted their kings, leaving government to a council and an assembly of citizens. The statelets were sometimes more oligarchic, giving power to a council of aristocrats; sometimes they were more democratic, opening the council to commoners and making it subordinate to the assembly of citizens. Politics then became a major engagement of the people.

The only Greek democracy whose constitution is known in detail (thanks mostly to

Aristotle's description of it) is Athens. Its central principles included the equal access of all upstanding citizens to governmental positions; short terms of office, usually without reeligibility; and administration by amateur boards. Juries of some hundreds of citizens, with no professional judges, applied the public's ideas of law and justice. There were almost no police, and generals were elected. There were personal followings in the assembly, but no political parties and no politicking in the modern sense because there were no material rewards of office.

The Greeks realized that election favored the experienced and well-connected few, so in the democratic city-states most offices were filled by lottery. Thus the average man (women shared in the game of politics only through their men) had an equal chance to become a member of one of the many administrative boards for a year, a member of the governing council for a month, or president of the assembly for a day. Ordinary citizens, educated by democratic participation, competently fulfilled these duties; the collectivity in any case reduced the risks of foolish actions. The sensitive post of general was subject to election (and reelection), but no general ever seems to have tried to use his position to coerce his fellow citizens.

This system was far more democratic than would be considered possible in our time; we consider it enough that the people elect representatives and governors without themselves governing. But the rule of the citizens worked well for Athens and many other democratic city-states. They not only endowed the world with art, literature, and philosophy but also prospered in commerce and for several centuries defended themselves against much larger powers by virtue of morale, organization, and good weaponry. They were overcome only when Macedon and later Rome, borrowing technol-

ogy from the Greeks, built up professional armies the small city-states could not match.

Medieval City-States

After the collapse of the Roman Empire and the anarchic times of the barbarian invasions, democratic or republican forms reemerged in the towns of medieval Europe. Communities grew up as order returned and commerce expanded after the tenth century. To protect their interests and themselves from bandits and nobles, the townsfolk would form a sort of club, a "commune," with rules of self-government. As a commune they would seek recognition from ecclesiastical and princely powers. Communes grew strong in southern France, Spain (especially Catalonia), Flanders, the Baltic ports, and central and northern Italy. For the most part, feudal authorities, gaining power over larger jurisidictions, managed fairly soon to crush or subject them. Only in Italy, where the power of the papacy counterbalanced and largely canceled that of the Holy Roman emperor, could the increasingly independent towns maintain themselves for several centuries, growing into small states by the absorption of the weaker by the stronger, until they were overcome by the rising nation-states of France and Spain after the French invasion of 1494.

The government of the medieval commune was a little like that of the Greek city-state. There was an assembly of citizens, summoned by the great bell that symbolized the liberties of the commune (and was the prototype of America's Liberty Bell). There was a council or councils, places on which were frequently determined by lottery. However, perhaps because commercial interests predominated, guilds, unions of merchants or producers, played a major role in the town government. And the democratic principle, although strong at first, lost ground as the towns grew in size and wealth. Moreover, while the Greeks were their own masters, the burghers of medieval towns, even though they might count themselves free, almost everywhere acknowledged the suzerainty of undemocratic authorities: counts, dukes, kings, or the Holy Roman emperor, who claimed to inherit the powers of the Roman Caesars. Hence, even in Italy, where the communes were freest, there was never popular participation comparable to that of the Greeks. One city after another fell under tyrannies that became permanent and hereditary. By the time of foreign domination of Italy, republicanism was moribund.

Yet the towns at least gave legal government and freedom with respect for rights, the rational and orderly regime that merchants want. The towns were the fountains of creativity in medieval Europe, not only in art and literature but also in the humbler skills of production. Italy produced the unsurpassed works of its Renaissance—Florence being the Athens of Italy—and at the same time manufactured so efficiently and organized its business, especially banking, so skillfully that it became wealthier than all the rest of Europe together.

Medieval Parliaments

Free towns and villages grew into republican states in Switzerland and the Netherlands, but modern democratic government traces its ancestry more directly to the representative institutions of the Middle Ages. In the feudal order, kings could demand only traditional and accepted taxes, and they were supposed not to make new law but to govern by the law that had existed from time immemorial. In order to change the rules, particularly in order to levy new taxes, they had to secure the consent of their subjects. They did this by summoning representatives of the orders composing medieval society—nobles, clergy, and commoners, who were for practical purposes the townsfolk. It was especially desirable to secure the agreement of the townsfolk, because it was difficult for the king to collect money without the concurrence of those who had most of it, the merchants.

Across medieval Europe, especially around the thirteenth century, parliaments, estates, or diets checked the power of kings, mostly by control of taxation. But the period of consolidation of nation-states and monarchies in France, Spain, Portugal, England, and Sweden, through the latter part of the seventeenth century, was a time of declining freedom in general and of parliaments in particular. The Spanish Cortes lost power after the unification of Spain in 1474 and especially as the new empire in the Americas poured wealth into the king's coffers. The French Estates-General was reduced to insignificance; after 1614 kings did not summon it at all until 1789. Even the English Parliament was reduced to impotence under Henry VIII (1509–1547), and Charles I got along for many years without a Parliament until foreign troubles forced him to seek its help, which led to his decapitation in 1649.

Monarchs were strengthened legally by the revival of Roman law and materially by centralization, better communication, more effective weapons (especially cannons), and better-organized bureaucracies. Kingship thus grew from the status of primacy among the nobles, subject to the general law, to theoretically absolute monarchy; the exalted sovereign was deemed ruler by divine sanction. The tightening and hardening of structures was general in the sixteenth and seventeenth centuries. The distance between commoners and nobles grew along with the distance between nobles and royal lord. Even such relatively libertarian countries as Switzerland and the Netherlands became more hierarchical and aristocratic.

Monarchy climaxed in the reign of Louis XIV (1643–1715), presiding over his brilliant and fawning court, the Sun King of the dominant nation of Europe. All over Europe, lesser potentates imitated the glory and styles of Versailles. Absolutism was the mode from Sweden to Spain and from Britain to Prussia. But Louis XIV failed in his several wars, and the amalgamation of territories proceeded no further. Change, arising from the growing stream of improvements, partly based on the great scientific strides of the age, mostly generated by countless little technical innovations, began to undermine authority. Charles I of England was overthrown by the forces represented in Parliament, primarily the commercial classes of the ports. The Stuarts came back, and Charles II seemed able to act the autocrat fairly well, but his successor James II could not. The Glorious Revolution of 1688 established the permanent superiority of Parliament; after that, kings might try to manage Parliament but never to oppose it.

The Age of Revolution

On the Continent, the changing temper of the age was expressed in the concept of "benevolent despotism." Rulers, although claiming full powers, admitted a certain responsibility for the welfare of their subjects, with the implication that their authority rested on service to the people. The eighteenth-century Enlightenment, with its rationalism and skepticism, undermined authoritarian claims. The philosophers of the Enlightenment, from Montesquieu to Rousseau, sought not revolution but change by education, but their message was unmistakable: the king had no rights superior to the needs of the people.

The Catholic Church declined in authority and ceased to be a powerful support of the social order. The nobility was decadent. New classes outside the old social framework, especially the so-called bourgeoisie—much more mercantile than manufacturing interests—clamored for a larger share in the state.

The ideas of the Enlightenment, the demand of the unrepresented classes for a share of power, and the traditional rights of Englishmen inspired the rebellion of Britain's American colonies against the effort of Parliament to impose some rather insignificant taxes. The 1776 Declaration of Independence was a bold statement of the new ideas, and the success of the Americans against their king was a potent example for the civilized world. Democracy and freedom became stylish, especially in England and France. The United States also pioneered in the writing of a constitution to fix the fundamentals of the state—an idea derived from the grand documents of British constitutional history (Magna Carta, the Petition of Right, and the Declaration of Rights of 1689), the covenants of the Calvinist churches (exemplified in the Mayflower Compact), colonial charters, social contract theory, and writings of Locke and Rousseau. The written constitution, although in recent times borrowed by autocratic states, is basically democratic: to spell out political relations almost inescapably means to set forth responsibilities and rights.

The old regime collapsed in France under the weight of debts and incompetence in 1789, and the revolution that followed opened modern times. The revolutionaries, attempting to fulfill the ideals of the philosophers and political writers of previous generations, proclaimed equality of all citizens and the Rights of Man, and drew up a succession of constitutions deriving the powers of government from the assent of the governed.

Thereby began the era of modern nationalism, which combined with democracy: the state, making itself the vehicle of the equal rights of its citizens, called upon them for loyalty and sacrifices. Partly for this reason, partly because of the egalitarianism of French philosophy, the French Revolution shifted the direction of liberal political thought from the Anglo-Saxon emphasis on limitation of state power to the rights of all and the value of equality. This opened the era of populist versus conservative ideologies, because the traditional aristocratic forces, seeing themselves as true custodians of national greatness, refused to fade away for many generations. The term *democracy,* revived by the French Revolution after many centuries of disuse, for much of the nineteenth century was dyslogistic, implying disorder or tyranny of the masses.[2] Well into this century, some rightist Frenchmen were trying to give their nation a king, while many leftists dreamed of renewing the great revolution.

Revolutionary France engaged in wars with ideological enemies representing most of the rest of Europe, fell under the sway of a gifted general, Napoleon Bonaparte, briefly acquired a vast empire, and was defeated on the battlefield by the conservatives. But the new ideals corresponded to the trend of the times, and they gathered strength as the century progressed. Autocratic institutions held on in many places, especially to the east of France; but the ideals of the French Revolution inflamed antiregime movements in Germany, Austria, Italy, and the Balkans. The implementation of a democratic order lagged in much of Europe because of the existence of a conservative peasantry and an aristocracy for which traditional privileges were beyond price. It was more difficult on

[2]Jens A. Christophersen, *The Meaning of "Democracy"* (Oslo: Universitetsforlaget, 1967), passim.

the Continent than in England, in Central and Eastern than in Western Europe.

The Spread of Parliamentary Government

Britain—commercial, progressive, and prosperous far beyond most other European powers, libertarian although aristocratic in traditions—led the way toward popular government, not as a march toward an ideal but as a series of sensible responses to needs and problems. Change was retarded by the wars with revolutionary France, but a decisive step was taken in the reform of 1832. Parliament (the House of Commons) had become increasingly unrepresentative because electoral districts (boroughs) had not been redrawn for over a century. By the reform, the gross inequalities were evened out and the franchise was somewhat expanded; it was thus accepted that Parliament should be representative of the nation. Further expansion of the electorate came slowly, but it could not be turned back; the middle classes demanded equality with the privileged, which led logically to equality for all. Moreover, in an open, pluralistic system those without the vote could organize and agitate for it, and there was no way in the philosophy of the liberal state to deny it to them. In 1867 the Conservative party took Britain a long way toward universal manhood suffrage.

With modernization and the spread of rationalism, the ideas of constitutionalism, representation of the people, and limitation of the powers of the state advanced across Europe, even into Russia around the turn of the century. Railroads and the telegraph made democratic participation over a large area possible. Parliamentary government came to be the accepted mode; liberalism, thriving on the economic strength of liberal England, was the advanced political philosophy; and democratic theory found powerful expression in the writings of such men as John Stuart Mill and Jeremy Bentham. Autocracy was obsolete: science, rationalism, liberalism, and nationalism joined to promise the indefinite advancement of civilization.

But these trends were not uncontested. The French Revolution inspired not only democracy but also socialism. This current, in the first part of the nineteenth century strongest in France, was anti–middle class, anticommercial, and in part anti-industrial. Socialism thus coincided with the conservative reaction to the Industrial Revolution and the dissolution of feudal society. Socialists, like conservatives, attacked the selfishness and crudity of capitalism. Like conservatism, socialism sought to regulate the market economy, somewhat in the mercantilist spirit of the eighteenth century. But the socialist reaction was more intellectual and based on a nonconservative faith in progress and science, a progress that was to be guided for the preservation of the idealized values of the simpler society. Until the latter part of the century, socialism was the hobby of a few intellectuals and a fringe movement; in the 1880s and 1890s, however, it allied itself with the effort of industrial labor to better its condition by organization and political action and became a powerful current in several countries, primarily Germany and France.

A major issue of the late nineteenth and early twentieth centuries in the industrial democratic countries thus became the role of industrial workers and the urban masses in general. When the masses got the vote the nature of the state changed, and liberal democracy—emphasizing individual freedom and the minimization of the role of the state—gave way to populist democracy, which emphasized the role of the state in the promotion of welfare, the protection of the weak, and the amelioration of economic inequality. This became the principal theme of democratic evolution in the first half of the twentieth century.

The United States meanwhile had become a pioneer of progressive democratic institutions. From about 1890, it became the world's premier industrial power; but it held itself apart from world politics and European diplomacy until it was drawn into World War I. In 1917, with the entry of the United States and the overthrow of the tsarist regime in Russia, the war became a contest between the democratic Allies and the militaristic-authoritarian (although not dictatorial) Central Powers. The defeat of the Central Powers was consequently seen as the triumph of democracy, and in its wake democratic parliamentary governments were set up all across Europe up to the Russian border, especially in numerous new states carved from the Austro-Hungarian Empire and lands that seceded from the Russian Empire. The United States had believed that it was fighting to "make the world safe for democracy," and it seemed in 1919 that it had succeeded.

Between the Wars: Fascism, Communism, and Democracy

But the wave of victory carried democracy much further than it could be sustained in troubled times, and the democratic regimes of eastern Europe began to topple in the early 1920s. One reason, it may be assumed, was lack of custom and understanding. Democratic structures had been erected in the euphoria of Allied success and the high prestige of the United States, but after victory came practical problems. And the United States, rejecting the Treaty of Versailles and the League of Nations, withdrew from leadership in European politics.

Moreover, the war had brought to power in Russia a powerful challenge to the outlook and philosophy prevailing in the West. Lenin and his followers turned values around; they proclaimed the social order of the West to be wholly evil and its political achievement, representative government through elections, to be a hoax and a cover for exploitation. The Communist movement complicated politics, caused ideological confusion, and turned radicalism and socialism into authoritarian channels. Soviet communism, a messianism materially as well as morally backed by a large state, challenged not only the middle classes but also the basis of Western life; and it injected violence of language and extremist thinking. Partly in imitation of it, partly as a reaction to it, there arose Italian fascism and German National Socialism, or nazism, hypernationalist, anti-intellectual movements that mixed premodern barbarism with modern propaganda and organization and lashed out against liberalism and communism alike.

In the tumult of the ideological contest between fascism and communism in the 1930s, democracy often seemed a weary bystander. The Communists took the lead (until Stalin's cynical pact with Hitler) in the opposition to nazism. It was easy for many people to conclude that liberalism was obsolete and that the future belonged to dictatorship, charismatic leadership, mobilizing ideology, and the new organizational forms of the mass party. Democracy seemed dull and unpromising beside the hypnotizing rallies of a Hitler or the power of a Stalin to whip backwardness into modernity. The first part of World War II also showed the feebleness of the democratic states, as German armies swept easily over Poland, Norway, the Low Countries, and France. But they halted at the English Channel, and the British defense of their island restored democratic morale. The war subsequently became an apocalyptic contest of the freer nations, led by the United States, allied with Stalinist Russia, against the aggressive militaristic-dictatorial powers—Germany, Japan, and Italy.

The outcome was a grand victory for the democratic cause, more total than in World War I but shared with Soviet communism. On the one hand, Japan, Italy, and three-quarters of what remained of Germany were reshaped into the mold of free, pluralistic states with popular-based governments. On the other hand, the prestige of communism was elevated, and that form of government was extended, partly by native revolutions (Yugoslavia and Albania), partly by Soviet forces (Bulgaria, Romania, Hungary, Poland, East Germany, North Korea), partly by a mixed process (Czechoslovakia). In East Asia, a native party brought communism to China.

The Postwar World

The result of this split victory was the cold war, which began in earnest in 1947, lasted until about 1970, was more or less replaced by détente for about a decade, and was revived from 1980 by new antagonisms. It amounted to a contest over the division of spheres between the two victorious sides. It was a standoff; neither side, through many crises and innumerable diplomatic moves, was able decisively to change the situation as it existed at the close of hostilities. Some probes of the Communist side, particularly in Korea, were repulsed, but the Communist sphere scored victories in Southeast Asia, Africa, and the Caribbean. On the other hand, first Yugoslavia and then China defected from the Soviet bloc. Whatever modest efforts the United States made to loosen the Soviet grip on Eastern Europe were fruitless.

Democracy was solidified in the non-Communist parts of Europe with the recovery from wartime destruction and the un-expectedly rapid advance in most countries to new levels of productivity. Colonial territories given their freedom after the war also regularly started out with representative institutions patronized by the former governing power. India, Burma, other countries of South Asia, and a host of new African countries were added to the list of free states. It was reasoned that modernization meant movement to a market economy, literacy, occupational specialization and mobility, industrialization, individualism, and rationalism, all of which, in the optimistic view, would support free and democratic political institutions. Nearly all the new democracies, however, soon became more or less dictatorships under one-party rule or military regimes. The years of the Vietnam war, especially 1965–1971, were especially negative for the image of democracy in the world, as the leading power of the West was engaged in a cruel and futile struggle with a small, nonindustrialized nation. It was a conflict which appeared to many as that of capitalism against popular forces, or American technological power against poverty-stricken Asians. By the early 1970s, democracy seemed clearly on the retreat and virtually a lost cause in the Third World.

After the American disengagement from Vietnam, the Soviet Union and other Communist states could again be seen as tyrannies, and the prestige of political freedom somewhat revived. Democracy was restored to Greece, came to Spain after the demise of the long Franco dictatorship, and managed to defeat a Communist bid for power in Portugal after the overthrow of the Salazar dictatorship. In Latin America a prolonged trend toward military dictatorship was halted in the latter 1970s. Human rights, a longtime motif of American foreign policy, became a worldwide theme; and human rights are essentially the values of democracy.

The outlook for democratic government is better at present than at most times in the past. It is unprecedented that for decades there has been no serious threat to the democratic order in any country of the traditional West. There is no effective rival political theory, as the Marxist-Leninist vision has faded into conservative bureaucratism, corruption, and stagnation not only in the Soviet Union but also in the countries that have tried to improve upon it, from China to Cuba. Attacks on democracy almost always amount to the charge that it is not really democratic.

DEMOCRATIC INSTITUTIONS

Basic Features

The forms of the democractic state have been varied, from those of the Greek *polis* to the complex structures of modern America; and often the forms have remained while their function has changed with changing times. The American presidency is constitutionally much the same today as it was under Coolidge, although its responsibilities have been completely altered and multiplied. But there are certain fundamentals common to every democracy: freedom of opinion, expression, press, and organization; institutions whereby the people decide who decides for them— that is, elections in which voters have a free and informed choice—limited terms of political office; an independent court system and a respected legal system; minimal violence in political life; a more or less nonpolitical bureaucracy, police, and armed forces; and civil rights, including fair courts and respect for individual property.

There are other general characteristics of democratic states, such as a decentralized, market-oriented economy, free trade unions, lack of any clearly defined or officially imposed ideology, relative openness of the state, freedom to travel within the country and to depart from it, and lack of a well-defined aristocracy. All these form a well-meshed conglomerate, and all democratic governments are a good deal alike. There is not really a special American or French or Scandinavian democracy, although emphasis differs in each. Despite superficial differences, any democracy is recognizable as a democracy. The Communist states join in by promising the same things that constitute the framework of democracy—elections, freedom of speech and organization, rule of law, and so forth.

To some extent, democratic states have a strong family resemblance because they copy institutions from one another, especially from the more successful, which in recent generations have been Britain and the United States. A more basic reason is that the various traits of the democratic state go naturally together. For example, a decentralized economy is important for freedom of the press and the viability of opposition parties; these are integral to the electoral processes; the agencies of force can be kept nonpolitical only if the government has legitimacy of popular choice; a free judiciary is essential to enforce civil rights and prevent the repression of oppositions; and so on. To attack any element of the system is rightly seen as an attack on the entire system, and a wide range of interests and classes join to protest, for example, an infringement of the freedom of the press or the independence of the courts, not to speak of any direct assault on the principle of elections. This coherence is vital for the stability of the democratic order.

More broadly, the triad of democracy, freedom, and equality are inextricably bound, and there cannot be much of any one without the others. Only in a democracy can freedom be assured, and the demand for political rights is inseparable from the call for freedom. Broad political participation is the best evidence of equality. Moreover, the functioning of a democratic state requires a high degree of consensus on political values; this can be achieved only through a sense of community, to which equality contributes strongly.

Equality

Equality of political rights defines democracy as much as anything, and respect for law and legality represents respect for equality: the same rules apply to all. The basic difference between the democratic and nondemocratic state is the view of humans as equal or unequal in rights.[3] Only by adherence to the rules, moreover, can the will of the majority be made effective. However, it is important that equality be not merely legal and formal but also social and economic. In a highly unequal society, consensus is feeble and divisions may become too strong to permit resolution of problems within the constitutional framework. Democracies and parties within them differ considerably in emphasis on social-economic equality as opposed to legal-political equality, this being roughly equivalent to the Left-Right division. In particular, Social Democratic parties seek to make the state an equalizer, whereas more conservative groups stress freedom from burdens and interference by the state.

Among democracies, there are considerable differences in degrees of equality, distribution of income being much more skewed in France, for example, than in Norway. In general, however, democracies are decidedly more egalitarian than nondemocratic states based on predominantly private economies. (Comparison with communist states is difficult because in them a large part of material rewards is politically distributed.) If

---

[3]Carl Cohen, *Democracy* (Athens: University of Georgia Press, 1971), p. 258.

a society is markedly unequal, that is, has sharply demarcated and fixed classes of privilege and nonprivilege, the democratic order is precarious. This is the primary reason for the difficulty of democracy in Latin America, despite constitutions and a panoply of democratic institutions. In conditions of stress, class conflict becomes too great for the political and economic order, and the military, as residual powerholder, takes charge. Thus even such countries as Chile and Uruguay, despite long experience with democracy, were too divided to avoid military dictatorship in the 1970s.[4]

Pluralism

If equality is one of the basics of democracy, the other is pluralism. Like equality, pluralism is both cause and outcome of freedom. A society with multiple bases of authority can hardly be tyrannical; on the other hand, when people enjoy freedom they inevitably form associations or groups and develop interests that seek to defend themselves. Contrary to some contentions,[5] there is no such thing as totalitarian democracy; it is a contradiction of terms.

Most aspects of democracy derive from the nature of a pluralistic society, in which a large number of persons have and feel a share of responsibility, and partly conflicting and partly coinciding interests work within an accepted framework. Power is not monopolized but shared, in that what any group can do is definitely limited, and political weight can shift from one group to another. There is an agreement to disagree, or at least to live and let live. The state is not entirely at the disposal of any one person or group, and the sphere of the state is limited. It might

seem possible for a democracy to consist simply of the state and individual citizens. In this circumstance, however, the people would be defenseless; democracy in practice is characterized by numerous private organizations with political influence outside the state apparatus.

The modern democratic state may be regarded as a sort of federation of groups and interests, joining to maintain a social order that permits them to live freely and to carry on together the tasks which must be undertaken by the whole society. Democracy rests on an essential agreement to sustain the framework within which the parts can enjoy a degree of independence and freedom of choice. There should be no substantial class or sector that sees itself excluded from the political process.

Individualism is not necessary, as the non-individualistic Japanese have shown. In fact, an excess of individualism would make democracy unworkable. It is essential that the state have no monopoly either of truth or of organization. Freedom for organizations is more important than freedom for individuals, although the two are in practice inseparable. Groups bring together and express ("aggregate" and "articulate") the wishes of members. Interest groups, preferably overlapping and cross-cutting, are essential intermediaries between the citizen and the huge, complex modern state. They are the little powers that tell the big power what is needed; they inform, persuade, and exert pressures on behalf of their constituents. As a result, much contemporary democratic theory revolves around "pressure groups." They provide continuing input for the decision-making process wherever it is most effective, and their strength contributes to democratic stability.[6] Pluralism is important

---

[4]Robert Wesson, *Democracy in Latin America* (New York: Praeger, 1982), passim.

[5]Such as J. L. Talmon, *The Origins of Totalitarian Democracy* (New York: Praeger, 1960).

[6]This is a thesis of William Kornhauser, *The Politics of Mass Society* (New York: Free Press, 1959).

for democracy not because people are divided but because sectors and interests are capable of making themselves felt, and any group seeking power must enlist the cooperation of other groups.

Organizations of all kinds give people experience with self-government and the expectations of democracy. Clubs, most churches, labor unions, professional organizations, and the like are organized democratically in theory, if not always in practice, and their presidents and boards derive authority from consent of the membership. It is important that the elite receive political training in democratically structured organizations. The strength of private organizations is perhaps the best measure of the firmness of the democratic order. This is one reason for the fairly close correlation between economic development and political democracy; more affluent people organize more.

The loose, pluralistic order reinforces itself by developing democratic classes and placing in positions of influence persons with a stake in pluralism and democracy. Those who achieve influence in any of the multitude of private organizations are likely to favor private organizations. Labor union leaders grow powerful in the freedom of workers to organize; for journalists and writers, the staff of life is freedom of expression. There is also a large political class, persons active in and around the electoral process. In contrast, the monistic state places in positions of influence persons dedicated to the system, such as the leaders of controlled organizations, the officials of the state unions, the journalists adapted to the controlled press, and the bureaucrats who run the political apparatus.

Possibly the most influential backers of the pluralistic system are the managers and owners, for whom state control would represent a loss of values. The most important interests in most peoples' lives are economic, and the most substantial nongovernmental power is that of privately owned enterprises. If the state dominates the economy, it is doubtful whether there can be enough nongovernmental power to offset the ability of the state to impose itself on those to whom it should be responsible. History shows no example of democracies with state-managed economies; from the Athenians through medieval times and early modern Britain, democratic government and civil liberties have been rather closely correlated with economic freedom to buy and sell and to use wealth to produce wealth ("capitalism" in the modern context). Business interests favor a constitutional order, because only through rule of law is there security of property in the face of political power. They are more favorable to democracy than military, theocratic, or bureaucratic interests, although they may be angered if democratic processes lead to high taxes and restrictive legislation, and they may exercise power of their own in undemocratic ways.

Present-day Britain, France, and Italy have nationalized a substantial fraction of their economies. No advanced industrial country, however, has tried to take full control of industry, much less commerce, or to impose a mandatory economic plan. Nationalized enterprises, moreover, are to a considerable degree autonomous and so operate somewhat as private corporations whose stockholder is the state. Sweden is socialistic in that there is extensive regulation of industry and a highly evolved welfare state spends over half the national income. But production has been left almost entirely in private hands and is in many ways encouraged by tax laws more favorable to business than those of the United States. It is possible, of course, for enterprises to be managed by some form of cooperative or workers' control; the important condition is not private ownership, but autonomy from the state.

It is unclear how far countries are democratic because they have strong independent economic interests and how far they have strong nonstate economic interests because they are democratic. The political power commonly intrudes into the economic sphere in authoritarian states, even without an ideological basis for intervention. For example, a host of farms and other enterprises in Nicaragua and the Dominican Republic fell under the ownership of their respective dictators, Anastasio Somoza and Rafael Trujillo. Anti-socialist military governments frequently promote state enterprises because these offer good jobs for senior officers.

A Constitution

Whatever the social and economic context, a democracy cannot function effectively without a variety of appropriate institutions. Primary among these is a document stating and allocating the powers of the government. A written constitution is unnecessary only where the democratic system has grown up gradually and its conventions are sufficiently well accepted to prevail without a specific document. The important democracy without a written constitution is Britain. Israel also lacks a written constitution, strictly speaking. Traditionally, the first step in establishing a new democracy is a constituent assembly. Constitutions vary in length and detail; that of the United States is one of the shortest, but some are book length.

One purpose of a constitution is to register the character and purpose of the state and the fundamental relations between the state and citizens, particularly the limitations placed on the state and the freedoms or civil rights of the people. Recent constitutions also frequently stress other rights, such as the right to work and to receive education or health care. More central is the constitutional framework of the government, the principal bodies, the means by which they are chosen, and the powers allotted to them.

The constitution is more difficult to change than ordinary law. In the United States, it is much more so; and even broadly supported measures, such as the Equal Rights Amendment, may fail because of the difficulty of getting the approval of three-fourths of the states. In many democratic states the constitution can be amended simply by a larger than simple majority of the legislature, perhaps two-thirds. Frequently the legislature can in practice stretch the constitution by an ordinary enactment. Democracies generally take pride in the stability of their constitutions, which are the symbolic basis of the free political order.

The Legislature

The primary organ of government is always a parliament or legislative assembly elected by the people for a limited period. It is an old democratic idea that terms should be short to keep representatives responsive to the people; the two-year term of members of the U.S. House of Representatives is a result of this idea. It is a rather new idea, however, that all adults should participate in the election of the legislative body. Until quite modern times, the electorate was restricted in all major countries to persons who owned a certain amount of property or paid a certain amount in taxes. The theory was that the chief purpose of the legislature was to authorize expenditures and that those who contributed to the treasury were entitled to representation. In the modern egalitarian spirit, a property qualification for voting is no longer thinkable, although a few countries, such as Brazil, have a literacy test. The sex qualification lasted longer; in most countries women obtained the vote in the period between the world wars.

Legislatures in most of the democracies are *bicameral* or two-house bodies. The second or upper chamber, which nearly everywhere but in the United States has less power than the lower, is ordinarily smaller and is in many cases indirectly elected. It would probably never have been invented if the parliament had not descended from medieval assemblies in which nobles and clergy met separately from commoners. The common folk, however, were called upon to finance the king's wars; through their control of the purse strings they soon acquired the greater power. The custom remains to this day that the lower or more popular house has primary authority in money bills, appropriations, and taxation; the upper house acts as a check on possible hasty actions by the lower chamber.

In parliamentary systems, which are about two-thirds of all democracies, it is also the prerogative of the lower house to approve the government, or ministry, or possibly to overthrow it. This has come to mean that the major function of a parliament is to register the results of elections and place in office the leaders of the victorious party. This is especially clear-cut in a two-party system, as in Britain. The leader of the party winning the most seats becomes automatically prime minister and forms a government. The parliament then has something of a rubber-stamp role in legislation. Bills are drawn up and presented to parliament by the government; the majority ordinarily passes them because the members of the party in parliament share the objectives of the ministry or are loyal enough not to wish to cause trouble. They may also hesitate to oppose because a defeat for the government might bring a new election with its attendant troubles and risks

if, as is usual in parlimentary systems, a defeated prime minister can dissolve the assembly and go to the people. In the normal course of affairs the parliament passes the measures proposed to it until its term nears an end (or the prime minister for some reason calls an election). The voters are then given the opportunity to express approval or disapproval by electing a majority of one or the other party, which will form a new government.

The situation is different when the legislative body and the chief of administration are elected separately. Under the presidential system, the executive power cannot be overthrown by the legislative (except perhaps by the difficult semijudicial process of impeachment) and correspondingly cannot dissolve it. The presidency and legislature may be dominated by different parties, as has frequently occurred in the United States. This American system is less flexible and more complicated than the parliamentary system, and it has not proved successful outside the United States. The American Congress has been accused of passively accepting the initiatives of the executive, but it is unique among world legislatures for its real powers over legislation and finances.

The legislature has other functions in addition to lawmaking. Minorities may publicize their views and criticisms in the chamber, engage in delaying tactics, and sometimes lead the government to reconsider. All members generally have a right to question ministers, whose answer or inability to answer may lead to changes in policy. Members intercede with ministries or bureaucracies on behalf of their constituents. They convey popular opinion to the government. They study measures and policies in committees and commissions. Sometimes legislative committees carry on investigations of the actions of administrative agencies. The American Congress is exceptional in its powerful independent investigatory role supported by large staffs.

The parliamentary assembly should express the will of the people, and the executive branch should get things done; there must be a balance between controls and the ability to act. Government must not only heed public opinion but resolve many matters concerning which the public has little or no opinion; it should perhaps act contrary to the majority opinion of the day or to powerful interests. The elected president has, of course, a fixed number of years in which to carry out programs and endeavor to demonstrate that he has acted wisely. The parliamentary prime minister who leads a stable majority can normally count on heading the government for approximately the legal lifetime of the elected assembly, probably about five years, before he or she must give an accounting to the electorate. A prime minister who has to rely on an unstable coalition, however, may not be so fortunate. The governments of the French Third and Fourth Republics lasted only about a year on the average. Such instability means that executive leadership is weak. Decisive action is nearly impossible because the government is not likely to hold together long enough to see it through; ministers cannot become masters of their departments; and strong measures will threaten the stability of the coalition.

The Bureaucracy

The instability of governments during the French Fourth Republic meant that much direction rested with the permanent administrative staff, the experts who remained while ministers came and went. A major element of all government is a corps of administrators, or civil servants, who should implement policy. On the one hand, they are the principal source of information for the political leaders who have to determine policy; on the other, what comes out of a policy decision depends on the willingness of the civil servants to carry it out and the manner in which they interpret it.

The civil service has security of employment because of the desire to insulate administration from politics and in order to get professionals to staff departments. The institution of a civil service has also come about, one may suppose, partly because of the influence of the civil servants. In the earlier history of the United States, it was considered part of democracy to give jobs to members of the victorious party, but this was so contrary to good management that a government could afford it only in a rich land in relatively untroubled times. Reform came in the 1880s, and more and more positions were placed under the Civil Service Commission to be filled by competitive examination and to be held during "good behavior." The United States still permits a new president to change several thousand officeholders. In parliamentary democracies, on the other hand, positions almost up to the top are filled by permanent staff; a change of government replaces only the minister and a few advisors atop the bureaucracy.

Under such circumstances, even if the civil servants are loyally obedient, it may be difficult for the elected servant of the people to effect much change. Even the American president finds it difficult to carry out policies disliked by the bureaucracy unless he is strongly backed by public opinion. Civil servants are the experts and the specialists, they have been handling the problems for many years, and they know the answers and have the reasons. Moreover, in many countries (most markedly France and Japan, notably not in the United States), the top layer of the civil service is formed by a prestigious elite corps trained in the best schools and selected by rigorous examinations; they are generally better educated than the politicians, if not more intelligent.

The preferences of the state apparatus may be as important as those of civil society in accounting for actions of the democratic state.[7] The state is not merely an arena for conflicting interests by active forces. However, the civil service represents no organized structure capable of asserting power in a coherent fashion, in the way that military forces can and do; it is divided among the many government departments with links only through the political leadership. It is not closed but open on objective criteria to persons of all classes, although only a few may have the requisite educational background. If the civil service may become lofty and self-important, at least at the higher levels, it is nonetheless legalistic rather than dictatorial in mentality. It may be less than fully responsive to public opinion, but it provides continuity and expertise.

Independent Judiciary

The third essential branch of government is the judiciary, the task of which is to see that the law is impartially applied. Democratic rights have meaning only if a person may apply to independent courts for protection. The courts serve to check arbitrariness of the executive and to some extent of the legislative bodies. Judges are appointed (with few exceptions) from a well-trained professional corps by the executive authority, but they acquire independence by holding their positions indefinitely, barring grave misdeeds.

The courts are also, in some democratic countries, guardians of the constitution. The authority of courts to determine the constitutionality of acts of other branches, not only

[7]As contended by Eric A. Nordlinger, *On the Autonomy of the Democratic State* (Cambridge, Mass.: Harvard University Press, 1981), p. 1.

executive measures but also duly approved laws, is an American invention. It is quite contrary to the British tradition, whereby any act of Parliament is valid; and the European practice prior to World War II was that legislatures interpreted the constitution. Judicial review has been incorporated into the constitutions of the German Federal Republic and Japan. It is particularly appropriate for federal systems in which sovereignty is shared by central and local or regional powers; some agency must delimit the rights of the parts of the state.

Besides regular courts, various tribunals adjudicate between the citizen and the state. These range from regulatory commissions to grievance hearings and are more or less insulated from political pressures. An adjunct of democracy which originated in Sweden but has spread widely is the *ombudsman,* an official charged with investigating public complaints against the administration and publicizing the facts.

Political Parties

The constitution lays out the structure of government, but it cannot prescribe the structure of politics; most constitutions leave unmentioned a basic political institution, the *political party.* The democratic process implies a contest of competing parties. It has been asserted, particularly in respect to certain African states, that there can be one-party democracy, with broad participation in choice of leaders and decision making through a single party organization. But this is a mixture of political rhetoric and optimism. Unless the single party permits organized factions—that is, becomes virtually a plurality of parties—there is no likelihood that views opposed to those of the leadership will receive a fair hearing. The essence of the political party, as the term has been historically understood, is a competitive electoral organization; the use of *party* to designate a ruling body in a dictatorship is semantic misappropriation.

Like interest groups, political parties serve to relate the government and public opinion. In a sense they are the most encompassing and important of interest groups, with the aim of promoting a certain set of policies and placing people in office. Conceivably parties are dispensable to carry them out. Elections could be held without them, and pressure groups could urge their wishes directly on the government. Ancient Greek democracy operated well without parties. It is better, moreover, for the flexibility of democracy if parties do not identify themselves closely with particular economic or other interests. British democracy has lost some responsiveness because of the dependence of the Labour party on the trade unions. It is also better for democratic functioning if parties are themselves democratically organized; parties that are antidemocratic in philosophy are undemocratic internally. All parties, however, tend to become hierarchic and, so far as they are successful, bureaucratic.[8] The organization creates its own interests, which differ somewhat from those of the people it claims to represent.

One of the most important factors for the success of democracy, especially where it is weak, is the character of political parties;[9] and a major cause of the failure of democracy in many countries has been the inability of parties adequately to represent popular needs. In any event, parties are inevitable in the modern democracy because they serve a purpose for their members. In an electoral contest an organization is essential, and candidates with an extensive and permanent organization behind them almost always defeat those without. Parties grow up because of elections, and they persist between elections partly because it is desirable to have an ongoing body to keep in touch with voters, partly because they serve as a focus for organizing elected representatives to form a government or exert influence. And of course, there is always another election to prepare for. Another major function of parties is the recruitment of leadership; that is, they serve (more in European democracies than in the United States) as avenues of entry into politics.

In the American experience, the normal party system consists of two major parties, either of which is prepared to take the reins of government when the voters decree a change. This system theoretically provides clear accountability, which is lost if a government is formed by a coalition. It limits the people to only two alternatives—and there have been complaints that the voters have no real choice—but it makes for stability. The division of government versus opposition is natural, and it probably means an alternation of holders of power at intervals because governments grow stale and lose popularity. It also ordinarily tends to moderate divisions within society because each party can hope to win only by forming a broad coalition of interests and appealing to voters near the center. Usually two parties represent the old dichotomy of Left versus Right, those in favor of more government intervention against those opposed, those more in favor of change against those more desirous of upholding traditional ways, or those more desirous of using the state for social purposes against those who emphasize rights of property and individual freedom. The two-party system, however, is practically confined to the English-speaking nations. West Germany is not far from a two-party regime, the Free Democrats and Greens being small and rather in some danger of elimination. Canada has four

---

[8]As contended by Robert Michels, *Political Parties* (New York: Collier Books, 1962).

[9]William A. Douglas, *Developing Democracy* (Washington: Heldref, 1972), p. 59.

parties of importance, but only two are strong in any given area. Italy has two big parties and many small ones.

Another workable system consists of one party that stands at the head of the state and is challenged not by a single major opposition but by a number of other parties, the disunity of which enables the governing party to keep its position for a long time. This is the situation of the Liberal Democratic party in Japan, which has held power without interruption from 1955 to the present, although it has never received a clear majority of votes. In Italy, the Christian Democrats have headed all governments since World War II, although they have received less than 40 percent of the votes, partly because the chief alternative, the Communist party, is unacceptable to a broad sector of the Italian public. Sweden has long had a four-party system, but the Social Democrats held office from 1934 to 1976 and returned to office in 1980. Long rule by a single party intuitively seems less democratic than a fairly frequent alternation of governing parties, but it makes for continuity and cannot be seriously faulted as long as the opposition has a fair chance to contest elections and the rulership thus remains responsible to the electorate.

France for many decades was the prime example of a multiparty system. Under the Third and Fourth Republics (1870–1958), the formation of a coalition government involved bargaining among various parties over who got which ministries in return for support, and it was often difficult. When one party of a coalition decided for some reason to bring down a government in France, as in postwar Italy, it might well require six weeks to put a new alignment together. Sometimes when a new government presented itself to the parliament, it would fail to secure a majority and the process would have to begin again. Meanwhile, however, the administration under a caretaker gov-

ernment would continue as though nothing were amiss; it was merely impossible to take new actions. Multiparty coalitions usually did not last long because the circumstances that made the coalition possible changed. Continuity was greater than one would suppose, however, because ministers would return again and again. But long-range policy was difficult to plan or carry out. Since France came under the presidentially dominated Fifth Republic, the electorate has tended to divide into two camps, conservatives versus leftists, and it may be on the way to a two-party system.

A number of smaller European states have shown that it is quite possible to have stable coalition governments. Unless one party is outstandingly strong, however, multiparty systems are a less than satisfactory means of combining popular control with effective government. They are removed from the voters because no one votes for a coalition, and it may be harder for it to grapple with problems because of the need to find a common ground for several parties. In a multiparty system changes of government are seldom as clear-cut as they are in a presidential system.[10]

Multiparty politics may also be undemocratic because it is impossible to agree on policies desired by the majority of the people. Yet a multiparty system is more representative of the feelings of the electorate than a two-party system, which forces all issues into a single confrontation and blankets the true diversity of opinion.

Electoral Systems

The relation of party systems to electoral systems is a complicated question to which there are no real answers. But the system

---

[10]G. Bingham Powell, Jr., *Contemporary Democracy: Participation, Stability, and Violence* (Cambridge, Mass.: Harvard University Press, 1982), p. 180.

used in Britain, the United States, and many other countries, whereby the nation is divided into a large number of districts and each district is represented by the person who receives the largest number of votes, does hurt smaller parties. A vote for a candidate who has no chance of winning is wasted, so races are likely to be mostly between two leading candidates. Worse for small parties, there may be a penalty against those who fail to get a certain proportion of votes. A person who receives a minority of votes and may be preferred by a minority of voters can be elected. Moreover, in the country as a whole, one party's votes may be uselessly piled up in a few districts, so that a party with fewer votes overall gains more seats. This has happened in Britain, and it is possible in the United States for a presidential candidate to receive a majority of votes in the electoral college while receiving fewer popular votes than his or her opponent.

A step toward making the results more representative of the voters' sentiments is to hold runoff elections in districts where no candidate receives a majority in the first round. This procedure helps smaller parties, because votes for a candidate who has no chance of winning are nonetheless an asset for the party. They give it something to bargain with, a token of strength that can be "sold" in the second round of balloting. This has been the French system.

But this is still far from ideal, so it was widely reasoned, especially in the aftermath of World War I, that democracy required an electoral system in which the strength of parties in parliament would mirror as accurately as possible their strength in the electorate. For this purpose, the nation was divided into a few big constituencies electing a large number of representatives, the fraction pertaining to each party being approximately proportional to that party's fraction of the total number of votes received. But *proportional representation,* as this system is called, obviously facilitates a multiplicity of parties. There is no penalty for the splitting of a party, because the two parts together should get as many seats as the single party did previously. Any tiny extremist or fringe group can enter the race with hopes of getting at least a few seats and a voice on the national scene—unless there is some provision such as a requirement that a party must get a certain fraction, perhaps 5 percent of the votes, in order to be represented at all. Parties may be more like interest groups. There is no particular incentive, as in the two-party system, for umbrella parties to cover the middle ground.

By facilitating separate organization of various sectors, proportional representation accentuates divisions in society. Yet elections are more likely to bring only a shift of a coalition; the majority system, by magnifying swings of opinion, facilitates new directions. More significantly, proportional representation ordinarily means that people vote not for individuals but for party lists. Hence power goes to the party organization, which decides who gets on the list and in what order—those on top being probably sure of election; those on the bottom, sure of nonelection. In the majority system, the party organization has much less control over candidacies. Putting the choice of candidates in the hands of voters by primary elections is an American specialty, and it has much to do with the independence of Congress. Senators and representatives cannot be coerced by a threat that the party may deny them the right to run as Democrats or Republicans. They need answer only to their electors, at least if they can raise their own campaign funds.

Other devices have been proposed to improve the workings of democracy. One is the *recall,* a process whereby an official who proves disappointing may be forced to present him-

or herself to the voters for confirmation in office. It has not been widely used and has not been important even in its homeland, the United States. More significant is the *referendum*. This application of direct democracy may be required to validate certain proposals, especially local tax increases; it may also be a way for the people to pass judgment on issues placed on the ballot by voters' initiative. There is much to be said for the referendum. The campaigns it brings about are educational, and the decision of the people has more weight than any legislative vote.[11] Legislatures and ministers, however, prefer to decide by themselves; and it may be for this reason that referendums have seldom been used, except in the United States and Switzerland or when the leadership has sought confirmation of its policies, as in several French instances.

The *public opinion poll* is also a valuable aid to democracy. The frequent taking of the public pulse is a reminder to both people and government where sovereignty ultimately rests and a warning to leaders not to deviate too far from the wishes of the many.

MODERN PROBLEMS

The postwar period was very successful for the democratic states of the West. A sustained economic boom raised Western Europe and Japan from deep poverty to unparalleled affluence. Class antagonisms were softened, and the welfare state reached down to the masses. International trade multiplied dozens of times over, as barriers were brought to the lowest levels of history. Harmony among the industrial states was marred only by trivial squabbles. The issue of the place of the workers in the state, which had trou-

bled the late nineteenth and early twentieth centuries, has been largely solved, and many of the "proletariat" have become relatively affluent and conservative.

Yet if one demand is satisfied, others arise to complicate the task of government. Representative institutions that evolved to deal with political problems are faced by overwhelming social and economic problems, partly of adaption to the technological age (urban decay, environmental pollution, resource management), partly of new demands on the system for justice and welfare for all. The state causes and the state is called on to cure the ills of inflation and unemployment.

The battle for legal equality among all groups has largely been won. Yet equality is a difficult concept, and many modern controversies revolve around its interpretation. On the one hand, inequality is always present and frequently growing; to combat it requires an intrusion of the state into many areas commonly regarded as private. On the other hand, equality is an appealing concept, partly because the poor are numerous and can vote, partly because of sympathy for the deprived and resentment of the social waste of great riches. The democratic state has taken on the function—in monetary terms its greatest function—of the redistribution of wealth. No one knows how much of the differing capacities of people is due to nurture, which may (at least theoretically) be equalized, and how much to inborn capacities, which cannot be. The democracy must with difficulty decide to what extent it is fair to reward work and talent or to permit a few to raise themselves above the many. Equal rewards for unequal efforts are also unequal. And there are the costs of benefits: minimum wage laws increase unemployment, yet a democracy must have them.

It is very difficult to decide where desirable regulation turns into stifling regimen-

---

[11]Robert Moss, *The Collapse of Democracy* (New Rochelle, N.Y.: Arlington House, 1976), pp. 236–247, pleads for greater use of the referendum.

tation or when overtaxation threatens productivity. Fabulously complicated and detailed rules create incentives to find ways around them, and heavy taxation generates tax avoidance in the most honest countries. The United States has a subterranean economy estimated at anywhere from 8 percent to 20 percent of the GNP,[12] and it seems to be proportionately much larger in such countries as Sweden, Britain, and France. The Italian economy probably could not function at all if everyone obeyed the rules. The demand for services and transfer payments coincides with the expansive inclinations of the bureaucracy to raise the tax burden over 50 percent of the national product in countries such as Britain, Denmark, and Sweden. Perhaps worse than overtaxation, however, is failure to tax sufficently; democracies seem chronically and cogenitally unable to bring budgets into balance, and one result is chronic inflation with its familiar consequences.

It is a related problem of the democratic state, with its sensitivity to needs of organized groups, that established interests become vested and more or less untouchable. Many producers, having lost competitiveness, demand and receive subsidies or protection. It is politically impossible to cut off costly price supports for agriculture or shipping interests, for example, or to open the domestic markets fully to foreign manufactures. Similarly, special rights of labor unions raise costs and hold down productivity.[13] It sometimes seems to be impossible to sweep away such uneconomic incrustation within the democratic framework.

There are many other criticisms of the democratic state. Public opinion is manipulated, and money may buy elections. At least, it is a big help, although if people get the

impression that a candidate is spending disproportionately they probably vote against him. Freedom is most useful for the few, especially the rich. Government is not by the people but by bureaucrats, politicians, and interests; decisions are made behind doors, not even usually by elected officials but by irresponsible specialists. The United States has experienced the "imperial presidency" and the ever-present potential irresponsibility of executive agencies operating in secret. The democratic state is cumbersome, and the majority can never really govern. Some theorists say that democracy is no longer possible because government is too complex and that computers, not the people, must decide. The will of the people is in any case difficult to know, unstable, and uninformed, and the single vote cannot express a preference on many issues.

The general public is poorly informed regarding countless issues of foreign and domestic policy, yet there is no good way to bring public opinion into the decision-making process or to exclude it. There is no agreement about how closely a responsible government should follow a possibly volatile public opinion or seek to impose its superior wisdom. Parliaments and assemblies often seem to have abdicated their chief functions to the executive and the bureaucracy. In the United States it is an indication of some failure of the regular constitutional process that a large part of lawmaking in recent years has been the work of the courts.

The question of the limits of tolerance is always troublesome. At some point the safety or moral sense of the community must override the right of individuals to free expression or commercial exploitation. It is inherent in the nature of democracy to allow criticism; and it permits extremists of various directions to organize, agitate, and assault its institutions. Democracy can absorb much radical activism because the currents

[12]*Business Week*, July 18, 1983, p. 16.
[13]Samuel Brittan, "A Very Painful World Adjustment," *Foreign Affairs* 61-3 (1983), pp. 566–567.

are usually at odds and temporary; and extremist movements may call attention to problems and lead to new perceptions.

QUALITIES OF DEMOCRACY

Most opposition to democratic systems as they actually exist is based on the contention that they are not sufficiently democratic. The cry is for more freedom, for "people power," occasionally for order and security, rarely for minority rule. Popular will is the only recognized basis for legal or constitutional government, and "We, the people of" is the conventional beginning of constitutions. Those who would overthrow the democratic order generally claim to be its best supporters and the truest democrats. Military dictators usually present themselves as temporary trustees of power, frequently as the saviors of the constitutional order, and promise an eventual return to democracy, when the country is ready for it.

Democracy is a muddling, half-way thing, haphazard and often illogical; but it usually turns out to be less irrational than alternatives. Choices are not entirely fair and votes not adequately representative, but there is a choice and there is a vote. Public opinion cannot guide the government, but it can sometimes check the leadership and fix broad directions. It is often said that political democracy is hollow without economic democracy, but no one has found a reliable way to secure economic democracy without political.

The model democratic personality is rather flatteringly portrayed as self-confident, broad-minded, critical of authority, nondogmatic, and receptive of innovation,[14] whereas the authoritarian personality is depicted as narrow and uninnovational.[15] It gives ordinary persons satisfaction to see themselves as legally equal beings with a voice in the selection of those who are to act in their name. Only in the democratic society do people really have rights. Some sort of democratic system is the only reliable means yet devised to assure that persons outside the official power structure can criticize and demand that the rulers serve the public interest, that the government be reasonably honest and not overly self-serving. There is corruption enough in democratic politics, but there are far more possibilities of exposure and correction than in authoritarian states.

The right of free expression is necessary for the health of the state; without criticism the government is certain to be abusive. Freedom of contradiction is essential for finding truth;[16] only a democratic or a libertarian system can have the abundant flow of information necessary for good government. The government needs to be widely understood and approved in order to function well.[17] It is the essence of limited government—which in practice means democracy—that people outside the political leadership can challenge them according to rules which the leaders are not empowered to change. Democracy, then, is open politics, which opens differences up to discussion for resolution by debate and compromise. The democratic system legitimizes and organizes the political conflict that exists, no matter how repressed, in all large-scale societies.

Politics is more bitter and violent where differences cannot be settled by open discussion or submission to an agreed method of resolution; parties are separated, as in

---

[14]Alex Inkeles, "National Character," in Roy C. Marcridis and Bernard E. Brown, eds., *Comparative Politics*, 4th ed. (Homewood, Ill.: Dorsey Press, 1972), p. 17.

[15]Everett E. Hagen, *On the Theory of Social Change* (Homewood, Ill.: Dorsey Press, 1962), chap. 5.

[16]Cohen, *Democracy*, p. 133.

[17]John Plamenatz, *Democracy and Illusion: An Examination of Certain Aspects of Democratic Theory* (London: Longmans, 1973), p. 90.

Russia or the Balkans, by an unbridgeable gap of incomprehension and hatred.

The sovereignty of the elected body may be just another myth, but it is a less absurd myth and one on which most people can agree. Strong leaders may be welcomed in an emergency, but their right to power does not logically outlive the emergency. The only convincing way to demonstrate popular consent is through free elections, which not only sanction the government but also inform the leaders and indicate that their mandate is to serve the people. The democratic government enjoys a double legitimacy denied dictatorship, in that it represents the people, or a requisite fraction of them, and that it holds office by legal process. If the democracy does not fully conform to the will of the majority, this is no argument for a less democratic order; it may indeed refute criticisms of democracy's supposed proclivity to demagoguery. The fact that elites really lead does not reduce the need for responsibility and restraints on government.

An electoral system is the practical way whereby rulers may be changed by legal process. Dictatorship is self-perpetuating, and a rulership that holds power indefinitely becomes immobile and corrupt. The authoritarian government of Mexico has institutionalized a one-term, six-year presidency, lending viability to authoritarianism by applying to it an essential aspect of democracy. But this kind of constitutionalism does not seem to be generally accessible. Makers of revolution should ask themselves how the new leaders they propose to put in power are to be replaced; perhaps a new revolution is the answer. But elections accomplish in orderly fashion some of the work of revolution. In May 1968, France was gripped by an extraordinary wave presented as a revolutionary movement, although it had no program and no comprehensive organization. De Gaulle called for elections, the dis-

turbances collapsed, and the voters returned a conservative government.

In disturbed times, the problem of changing leaders may be solved by turmoil; there may be a demand for rapid and decisive action which a democratic state is unable to meet, and the sense of emergency will inspire the government. But in quiet times, the dictatorship loses ability and will to act and settles down to enjoyment of possession. The democratic order in some variant is then necessary for change and flexibility. The purpose of democracy thus is not so much equality as good government, or at least the recurrent possibility of good government. Whether or not the democratic order makes people happier we cannot properly inquire; but it seems to favor the development of human capacities, the application of intelligence to human affairs, and what is commonly called progress.

PROSPECTS

Yet the sovereign states of the world have voted, so to speak, against democracy by an overwhelming majority. In theory, nearly everyone favors it or claims to; in practice, its weaknesses seem usually to prevail. The desirability of popular participation conflicts with the divisiveness of the political struggle, with deference to superiors and scorn for inferiors, with recognition of expertise, and with unwieldiness of representative institutions. When people and groups compete merely for their special advantages, the common interest is lost. If powerful minorities are determined on contradictory policies, the state is paralyzed. If a group or class uses the state as its means of dominion, elections can no longer decide issues. Perhaps the great question of democracy is how much of it any given society can handle.

The form of government of the Western

industrial states is democratic, but the association of democracy with the West and industrial society is accidental except insofar as responsible government has favored the development of modern industrial civilization. African and Asian villages have fully appreciated the idea that leaders should be chosen by and responsible to the led. Freedom to express one's views and the right to be consulted about matters of concern and choice of leaders are universally understood ideas. Latin American slum dwellers have often elected governing committees to manage affairs on their own initiative.[18] Nowadays, representative government functions rather better in Japan, a land of profoundly non-Western culture, than in Britain, its modern homeland. The examples of postwar Germany and Japan show that democracy can overcome the handicap of alien imposition when the social structure has been appropriately reshaped by the destruction of military forces, weakening or scattering of the old aristocracy, land reform where appropriate, and democratization of education. The democratic order can then become a matter of native pride although the historic tradition was authoritarian.

Before the advent of Leninist communism and Stalinist economic mobilization, it seemed clear that representative government was virtually a condition for industrialization and modernization. For a time, Stalin seemed to prove the contrary. However, the industrializers of Russia and other Communist countries have lost momentum. It no longer appears that the Communist political system provides a faster or even a practical alternative to industrialization except under special circumstances. Nor does it appear that communism brings economic equality, because those who hold political power have the means to material advantages. Democracy permits economic exploitation, perhaps gross exploitation, but there has been devised no more reliable way of defending the interests of the poor than giving them the vote.

In 1947, when newly independent India was setting up its state, Gandhi and other leaders sought an alternative to the parliamentary democracy associated with British rule. They could find nothing. The alternatives to democracy are mystification and/or force, a doctrinal claim to greater enlightenment or the hope that a self-selected rulership will be benevolent. If most of the countries of the world are undemocratic, this implies that they are probably badly governed. And bad government is a big factor, perhaps the biggest, in low productivity or plain poverty. Antidemocratic forces are basically antiproductive. As Revel put it, "the totalitarian temptation is really driven by the hatred on principle of industrial, commercial civilization."[19] Prime Minister Desai of India took issue with those who argued that democracy is a luxury for poor countries: "I don't think that human society can ever develop to its full height without freedom. As far as my country is concerned, I would say that democracy is not a luxury but a vital necessity, and without it we could do nothing, we could not go ahead."[20]

Luxury or necessity, democracy is the possession of a small minority of countries, primarily because societies are too divided among people who feel themselves different for ethnic-cultural reasons, such as Catholics and Protestants in Northern Ireland or Afrikaaners and blacks in South Africa, or for economic reasons, as peons and landowners

---

[18]For the example of Lima, see Eric R. Wolf and Edward C. Hansen, *The Human Condition in Latin America* (New York: Oxford University Press, 1972), p. 183.

[19]Jean-Francois Revel, *The Totalitarian Temptation* (Garden City, N.Y.: Doubleday, 1977), p. 263.
[20]*New York Times,* July 5, 1977, p. 3.

in Guatemala. The very rich and the very poor have excessively conflicting claims on the state to be able to settle matters by majority vote. Democracy can expect to advance very much only as such divisions are overcome, and this can only be a slow and often doubtful process. For many countries the best that can be hoped in the near future is that more or less arbitrary rule be tempered by decency, reasonable respect for human rights, and consultation of the rulership with the citizens.

The democratic form meanwhile remains the general ideal. Better forms of government may be developed, perhaps have to be developed, although ultimately government can be improved only if people are improved. But whatever better institutions may emerge will surely include the principles of responsiblity of leadership and openness to ideas and criticism from outside, and they will probably be developed by the most sophisticated and cultured states, not as an overthrow but as an improvement of the democratic order, building on the imperfect achievements of constitutional and limited government, representative of and responsible to its people.

3

Britain

The ideas of representative government, constitutions, individual rights, legal procedures, and limited powers of the state are old and widespread. Many countries base their authority on the consent of the governed; in some, such as the Scandinavian countries and Switzerland, democracy is perhaps sounder and more thorough than in Britain. But Britain has led the modern world in the development of civil rights and a parliamentary constitution, just as it was, probably for the same reasons, the leader of the Industrial Revolution and the land of individualism and empirical philosophy.

Representative government had roots throughout medieval Europe, but in most places it was crushed by absolutist monarchy. Since the seventeenth century Britain was the chief model of representative government. The American system, although it has deviated, owes its beginning and central ideas

to its British progenitor, and most other parliamentary systems are patterned after or strongly influenced by the British. Britain, moreover, has excelled in law, justice, and freedom in the modern world. For nearly three hundred years it has been exempt from tyranny, while all major non-English-speaking powers have endured much arbitrary government.

Great Britain (England, Wales, Scotland, and Northern Ireland)—with a population of 56 million, of the same order as France and Italy, somewhat less than West Germany or Mexico—is a small country, approximately the size of Utah. But it has played an inordinately large part in the growth of modern civilization. On the eve of World War I, London was the world's financial capital, Britannia ruled the waves, Whitehall presided over the world's greatest colonial empire, and British government was the

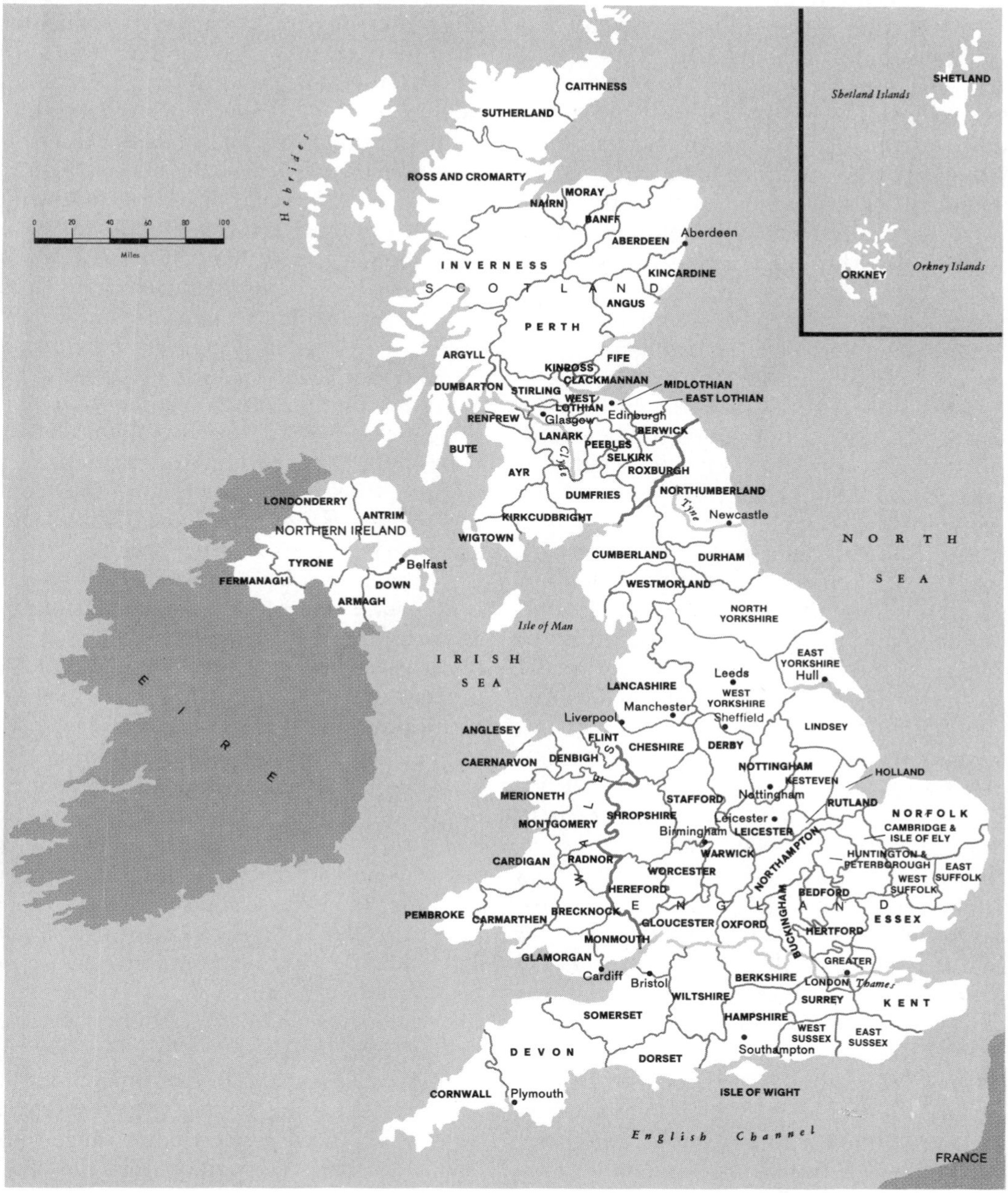
SHETLAND
Shetland Islands
ORKNEY
Orkney Islands
CAITHNESS
SUTHERLAND
Hebrides
ROSS AND CROMARTY
MORAY
NAIRN
BANFF
ABERDEEN
Aberdeen
INVERNESS
KINCARDINE
SCOTLAND
ANGUS
PERTH
ARGYLL
FIFE
KINROSS
CLACKMANNAN
MIDLOTHIAN
DUMBARTON
STIRLING
WEST LOTHIAN
EAST LOTHIAN
RENFREW
Glasgow
Edinburgh
BERWICK
LANARK
PEEBLES
BUTE
SELKIRK
AYR
ROXBURGH
Clyde
DUMFRIES
NORTHUMBERLAND
KIRKCUDBRIGHT
Tyne
Newcastle
WIGTOWN
LONDONDERRY
ANTRIM
NORTHERN IRELAND
TYRONE
Belfast
FERMANAGH
DOWN
ARMAGH
CUMBERLAND
DURHAM
WESTMORLAND
NORTH SEA
NORTH YORKSHIRE
Isle of Man
IRISH SEA
EIRE
EAST YORKSHIRE
Hull
Leeds
LANCASHIRE
WEST YORKSHIRE
Manchester
Liverpool
Sheffield
LINDSEY
ANGLESEY
FLINT
CHESHIRE
DERBY
CAERNARVON
DENBIGH
NOTTINGHAM
HOLLAND
KESTEVEN
Nottingham
MERIONETH
STAFFORD
RUTLAND
NORFOLK
SHROPSHIRE
Leicester
MONTGOMERY
CAMBRIDGE & ISLE OF ELY
Birmingham
LEICESTER
WALES
WARWICK
HUNTINGTON & PETERBOROUGH
CARDIGAN
RADNOR
NORTHAMPTON
EAST SUFFOLK
WORCESTER
WEST SUFFOLK
HEREFORD
BEDFORD
ENGLAND
PEMBROKE
CARMARTHEN
BRECKNOCK
ESSEX
GLOUCESTER
OXFORD
BUCKINGHAM
HERTFORD
MONMOUTH
GLAMORGAN
GREATER LONDON
Cardiff
Bristol
BERKSHIRE
Thames
WILTSHIRE
SURREY
KENT
SOMERSET
HAMPSHIRE
WEST SUSSEX
EAST SUSSEX
DEVON
DORSET
Southampton
CORNWALL
Plymouth
ISLE OF WIGHT
English Channel
FRANCE
0 20 40 60 80 100
Miles

model for peoples everywhere seeking political modernization.

In the seventeenth century, Britain was roughly equal in power to the Netherlands and much inferior to France. But in the next century, inventors and entrepreneurs made improvements in agriculture and manufacturing, especially textiles; and with the development of steam engines Britain led the way into the Industrial Revolution. It became by far the most productive and the richest of the powers. It was overtaken in output of coal, steel, and machinery by the United States and Germany only toward the end of the nineteenth century.

There were several obvious factors in the British success. The location of the island and its ports was excellent when overseas trade acquired importance, and since the fifteenth century England has been a trading nation. The Channel separating the island from the European continent protected but did not isolate the British culturally and commercially. Britain was spared invasions after 1066 and has intervened in continental wars only as it chose. There was no need for a standing army to burden the country and strengthen the monarch. The population, at least in its large English majority, was decidedly homogeneous. The religious controversies that troubled many nations were gotten over rather early and ceased to roil politics after the settlement of 1688, when the Catholic James II was replaced by the Protestant William and Mary. Aptly for the Industrial Revolution, Britain had coal and iron accessible to water transportation, a necessity before the advent of railroads.

Much of the credit for the rise of Britain must go, however, to its political system, which has long seemed best to combine authority with freedom, effective government with respect for rights. The British system has shown a unique ability to adapt without violence, retaining old forms and giving them new content. The last rupture of the legal order was the Glorious Revolution of 1688, an almost nonviolent affirmation of the superiority of Parliament. In modern times, the British have been extraordinarily able to adapt their institutions to new needs and new ideas within a framework of legality. Britain has maintained stability while making concessions to new forces, permitting innovation and encouraging improvement.

At the same time, the British state lay more lightly on the citizenry than almost any other. There were no large, parasitic nobility, no politically powerful army, and only a small bureaucracy. The prestige of business and trade was high, taxation was moderate, and people felt free to improve themselves by inventing ways to produce more goods, both in agriculture and industry; and they could feel confident that rapacious officials would not steal the fruits of entrepreneurship.

For such reasons, the British government is of prime interest for the understanding of constitutional, representative, or democratic government around the world. Yet unhappily Britain is no longer a convincing political model. From about 1880 it was losing ground to newer industrial powers, especially Germany and the United States. After World War I, economic woes piled up and a certain demoralization set in, one result of which was the policy of appeasement of the aggressive fascist powers in the 1930s. In World War II, Britain rallied its spiritual and material forces, held out for a time alone, and shared leadership with the United States and the Soviet Union. But after celebrating victory, Britain flagged. The immense empire was released, and Britain ceased, for the first time since the seventeenth century, to be a world power. The economy sagged; the leader became a laggard. Within the memory of living people, Britain had had the highest standard of living in Europe; now it has the lowest of major industrial countries.

The political system credited with contributing to Britain's rise must unfortunately accept some responsibility for its decline.

THE RISE OF PARLIAMENTARY GOVERNMENT

Medieval European kings were restricted by custom. They lacked the power to make laws on their own; to conscript their subjects, except as traditional obligations required their vassals to support them; or to raise taxes. Kings were expected to consult with peers of the realm and to listen to their advice. That is, they would summon men of the several estates (nobles, clergy, and burghers or commoners) to meet and advise them and to give consent to important new measures. The king especially needed the agreement of the mercantile classes for the imposition of taxes on trade; and in the later Middle Ages there were parliamentary bodies or estates of the realm in Germany, France, Spain, and elsewhere.

In England, the troubles of kings made the strength of parliaments; John, a weak king, summoned four knights from each shire to meet with his nobles in 1213. Later, the barons defeated John in battle and compelled him to agree to the Magna Carta, a charter of feudal liberties that also provided for immunity from arbitrary acts of the king. In 1295, in times of difficulties for Edward I, the Model Parliament brought together knights from the counties, burgesses from chartered towns, and upper and lower clergy, as well as high nobles under the principle, "what touches all should be approved by all."[1]

The Model Parliament long remained only a model, however. The consolidation of national states and the centralization of power

under strong monarchs meant the ebb of medieval freedoms, and representative bodies everywhere in Europe lost powers or ceased to meet. In Tudor England, especially under Henry VIII (reigned 1509–1547), Parliament lost significance, although the Commons stirred occasionally under his daughter, Elizabeth I. The Stuarts early in the seventeenth century tried to assert divine right, but the growing commercial community resisted royal levies and claimed old rights for Parliament. The clash, compounded by the quarrel of reforming Protestantism with the Catholic-leaning court, led to a bitter battle, first of words and then of armies, and then to the beheading of Charles I in 1649 and the establishment of a Commonwealth, the only republic in British history. This experiment failed. After a few years, Charles II was enthroned, but the monarch could never again pretend to absolutism. In 1688 the unpopular James II was accused of "breaking the original contract between King and people" and overthrown. William and Mary, invited from Holland to rule, acknowledged the authority of Parliament in the Bill of Rights (1689).

William made major decisions without the knowledge of Parliament. But it gradually came to be accepted that the monarch must have ministers acceptable to Parliament, and the personal weakness of the successors of William and Mary enabled Parliament to become established as the chief governing power. Queen Anne was not ambitious, and the Hanoverians who were brought from Germany to assume the throne in 1714 were at first both ignorant of the English language and uninterested in British affairs. George I seldom attended cabinet meetings and shied away from public business, and his son was little more involved.

Without pressure from a strong ruler, political institutions developed steadily. Judicial independence was established by 1700,

[1] See Bernard Schwartz, *The Roots of Freedom: A Constitutional History of England* (New York: Hill and Wang, 1967).

and it became accepted after 1703 that royal assent was never refused to a bill of Parliament. The cabinet developed as an inner group of members of the Privy Council, which had been the monarch's advisory group in Tudor times.[2] It gradually took over the government under a leader called the *prime,* or first, *minister.* For a long time it was responsible to the king only. But it became increasingly important for the government to have the backing of Parliament, especially the Commons, which controlled expenditures.

For a long time some of the old feeling remained that opposition to His or Her Majesty's government was disloyal; but Parliament, especially the elected House of Commons, sought increasingly in the latter part of the eighteenth century to control policies. The political contest gradually took shape. The Liberal and Conservative parties of modern times trace their origins to the Whigs, who favored the new succession of 1688, and the Tories, who preferred the Stuarts.[3] Through the eighteenth century, however, parties were mostly cliques, who expected places and honors when a leader achieved office, and a majority of the members of Parliament were not clearly affiliated. Government was essentially by an aristocracy of fewer than 200 persons, mostly noble landowners, broadening only late in the century as a result of the new industrial wealth.[4]

George III (reigned 1760–1820) felt himself quite British and entitled to rule. Although he was in no position to coerce or ignore Parliament, he tried to manage it by influence, bribery of various kinds, and his party of the "King's Friends." He was not unsuccessful and might well have set back the evolution of representative government. However, he insisted on prosecuting the war against the rebellious American colonies and failed. His chief minister, Lord North (1770–1782), was attacked by means of no-confidence motions in Parliament until he felt compelled to resign. The king had to accept a prime minister satisfactory to Parliament, William Pitt, who led the government from 1783 to 1801. Freed from royal meddling by the insanity of George, manifest after 1788, Pitt was the first really effective prime minister and leader of a well-organized cabinet.

From the 1780s on, the new business class nourished by the Industrial Revolution was pressing for a larger share of power. This meant reforming the electoral system of the House of Commons, which had been reasonably representative in the seventeenth century but had became badly skewed with the growth of the nation. By the end of the eighteenth century, many boroughs had few voters and the Lords or the ministry could by influence or corruption control a large part of the Commons.[5] The reforming drive was blocked by the fact that Britain found itself at war with revolutionary France more or less continually from 1793 to 1815. With the end of the Napoleonic Wars, however, economic distress led to serious unrest and a near-revolutionary atmosphere. Reform associations, preceding political parties into the arena of popular politics, conducted demonstrations, lobbied, and agitated feverishly for change.[6] The aristocracy bowed to necessity. The Reform Whigs won two elections, but the House of Lords refused its consent to changes injurious to the power of many of its members. The King, however, followed the will of Commons and threat-

---

[2]See John P. Mackintosh, *The British Cabinet,* 3rd ed. (London: Stevens and Sons, 1977).

[3]See Ivor Bulmer-Thomas, *The Growth of the British Party System,* 2 vols. (London: John Baker, 1965).

[4]Anthony Sampson, *Anatomy of Britain Today* (New York: Harper & Row, 1965), p. 3.

[5]Karl Loewenstein, *British Cabinet Government* (New York: Oxford University Press, 1967), p. 93.

[6]Samuel H. Beer, *The British Political System* (New York: Random House, 1974), p. 11.

ened to create new peers if necessary to secure a reform majority. The Lords bowed, and in 1832 the Great Reform was carried.

This measure, passed by a government of landholders, cut down the influence of landed interests and the monarch by abolishing "rotten boroughs" (those with very few voters), redistributing 141 seats in Parliament, mainly to newly industrialized areas, and regularizing and somewhat expanding the franchise. It established the principle that Parliament, or the House of Commons, based on elections in fairly equal constituencies, was representative of the nation, with an authority the hereditary monarch could not challenge. Under it, only about 7 percent of the adult population was entitled to vote; but it opened the way to further expansion of suffrage. It gave more importance to elections, and thus to electioneering and political parties. Groups in Parliament began reaching out to select and promote candidates in the constituencies, to set up local organizations, to get voters registered, and to become political parties in the modern sense.

The monarch gradually lost power. Queen Victoria (reigned 1838–1901) until the latter years of her long reign repeatedly injected herself into politics, trying to choose prime ministers, exert pressure on the cabinet, and act as broker among factions. She was decreasingly successful, however, and the middle part of the nineteenth century may be called the era of the Commons. Party affiliation was loose, cabinets fell because of shifting coalitions, and members of Commons were masters in their own right. Parliament conducted investigations, rewrote bills submitted to it, or framed its own.[7] The Whigs and Tories became Liberals and Conservatives, associated, respectively, with manufacturing and trading interests and with landholding and the Church. There began the practice of "whipping in," or sending notices requesting the vote of prospective supporters, but both parties split repeatedly.

The aristocratic system wore out with advancing industrialization. After the repeal of duties on grain in 1846, the growth of the cities continued; England was still a half century ahead of France economically. The upper classes were increasingly flooded with bankers and industrialists, for many of whom new peerages were created.[8] Education spread until literacy was general by the late nineteenth century. The Conservative government of Benjamin Disraeli in 1867 enfranchised most urban workers, partly because it was hoped that they would vote Conservative in opposition to the mostly Liberal business owners, partly because such a move seemed inevitable. Rural workers gained the franchise in 1885. Parties solidified as it became necessary to appeal to a mass electorate. The Queen withdrew from partisan politics, and the sovereignty of Parliament began giving way to the rule of parties and the electorate.

The parliamentary regime, like the British Empire, was basking in glory around the turn of the century. But a series of events began to reshape the party system. The Liberals were weakened by a split between those who favored the interests of the manufacturers or commercial interests, in the old Whig tradition, and those of more populist inclinations, who stood in the Whig reforming spirit. They failed, in any case, to absorb effectively the forces released by extension of the franchise to the masses. Trade unions had been forming since the ban on them was lifted in the mid-nineteenth century, and labor was increasingly politicized in the 1890s by the efforts of employers to use court actions against the unions. Various leftist and more or less radical and socialist groups were

[7]Mackintosh, *The British Cabinet,* p. 613.

[8]Sampson, *Anatomy of Britain Today,* p. 5.

formed, including the Fabian Society, whose members argued for gradual socialization of the economy. In 1899–1900 a number of unions, the Fabian Society, and two small leftist parties formed a Labour Representation Committee (which soon became the Labour Party) to secure the election to Parliament of persons favorable to labor, with no thought at first of challenging the big governing parties.

Previous parties had grown up in Parliament and only slowly extended themselves to organize support in the country; Labour took the opposite way. It was also a party of a new kind in that it was an organization of organizations; although individual members were subsequently admitted, they have always remained a small minority. Labour was also a political novelty in its ideological approach and its emphasis on class (despite the participation of middle-class intellectuals). But it filled a political need, and its rise was rapid. In 1906, Labour in alliance with the Liberals won twenty-nine seats, and its future was assured by a law of 1913 permitting unions to use their funds for political purposes.

The next big step was the replacement of the Liberals by Labour as the rival of the Conservatives and alternative governing party. This occurred during and after World War I because of a division of the Liberals between followers of Lloyd George and Herbert Asquith. Labour gained respectability by entering the wartime coalition, and its organization was broadened by the formation of local or constituency parties. The unions prospered and expanded, and the franchise was extended in 1918 to include men over twenty-one and most women over thirty. The country was considerably radicalized by the war, and Labour, which adopted a socialist program, was the beneficiary. Liberalism, identified with nineteenth-century individualism and free enterprise philosophy, seemed worn out. Although the Liberal Party was reunited in 1922, it could not prevent Labour from taking second place and hence becoming the prospective party of government.

The interwar years were dominated by the Conservatives, but the Depression of the 1930s and the subsequent war again tended to radicalize opinions. Labour shared in Churchill's wartime government and in the 1945 elections gained, for the first time, a parliamentary majority entitled to form a government. It proceeded to carry out a sweeping reform program, nationalizing the Bank of England (in recognition of its semiofficial character), the coal mines (in view of their bankruptcy), road and rail transportation, gas and electricity (mostly already municipally owned), and steel. The foundations of the welfare state had been laid before the war; indeed, the percentage of the national product taken by the government, which had been only 9 percent in 1890, was raised by Conservative governments to 30 percent by 1930; after the war, more social services brought it to 38 percent.[9] Labour lost power in 1951, but the Conservatives reversed little of what Labour had done. The Conservatives seemed almost as much inclined to introduce controls as to dismantle them, and the welfare state and managed economy were the new order of the day.[10]

Until 1979, not much seemed to change when a Conservative government replaced Labour or vice versa, however antithetical their official philosophies. The government of Margaret Thatcher,[11] however, undertook to change course sharply away from the

---

[9]Richard Rose, *Politics in England Today* (London: Faber and Faber, 1974), p. 55.

[10]For a summary of this period, see Peter Calvocoressi, *The British Experience 1945–75* (London: Bodley Head, 1978).

[11]See Patrick Cosgrave, *Margaret Thatcher: A Tory and Her Party* (London: Hutchinson, 1978), for a biography.

interventionist policies of the preceding decades, steering back toward a market economy. Thatcher sought to restore incentives for production, cut tax rates and public spending, reduce the nationalized sector of industry, and remove some controls from the economy. No radical changes could be made, however; the British system does not encourage quick change.

THE BRITISH CONSTITUTION

The British political system has grown by accretion over the centuries. Institutions become established, some customs disappear, and others gain acceptance. Because of this unique continuity, there has never been an occasion to put into writing many conventions and usages.[12] Britain is unique among major modern powers in lacking a written constitution. To this day British politicians, like British writers on politics, cite precedents of earlier generations as do those of no other nation.

There are constitutional documents, from the Magna Carta through the Bill of Rights to recent laws affecting the House of Lords. The right to vote, and by implication popular sovereignty through freely and fairly elected representatives, is guaranteed by numerous statutes. But there is no means of determining that any particular document is part of the constitution except by a sense of its importance. Any law can be modified or repealed by simple act of Parliament. A Parliament can even extend its own life, although to do so without a very good excuse, such as war, would be considered a gross violation of the constitutional understanding.

Many of the most important rules of the

generally understood constitution—such as that the leader of the majority party in the Commons is to be named prime minister, that he or she and the cabinet must resign or call new elections if they lose the confidence of Parliament, and that the monarch acts in political matters only on the advice of a responsible minister—are nowhere enacted but are inviolable because they correspond to the general sense of British government. The written documents, for that matter, generally claim only to define and fix established practices and rights, at least as understood by one party. The emphasis is consequently on tradition; "it has always been done" or "it has never been done" is ordinarily sufficient reason for or against a certain course. An incidental result is that obsolete institutions are adapted rather than replaced; nothing is dropped as long as it can reasonably be kept. Hence the British government, especially institutions connected with the monarch and Parliament, is a museum of antiquities, filled with rituals that once carried substantive meaning.

Government is thus conducted largely by understood norms of propriety or decency. A government that holds a majority in Parliament is restrained from tyranny and using force or changing the rules to perpetuate itself only by a sense of rightness and attachment to the values of the system. Parliament tomorrow could abolish freedom of the press or give the police unlimited powers of arrest and detention. No one dreams of doing so.

It is possible, however, only for a well-integrated and reasonably satisfied nation to get along without a clear written definition of rights and responsibilities in many areas. If conditions were less favorable, the vagueness of many rules, the possibility that a transient majority in Parliament could change fundamentals, and the lack of balancing powers might prove fatal to the democratic

---

[12]Under the Commonwealth a constitution was adopted, but it was set aside by the Restoration.

order. In the past decade there has been more serious questioning of the value and viability of the British system than at any previous time. To rely on general understanding and acceptance of conventions lends flexibility, but it requires a consensus that is no longer assured. Some Britons have concluded that they would be more secure in their liberties with written and inviolable guarantees, checks and balances among organs of the state, and judicial review of legislative measures. But no such change is in view.

ELECTIONS

The British do not vote as often as Americans or citizens of most democracies. Local, county, or borough councillors are elected triennially, but these bodies have only limited powers delegated to them by Parliament and have lost stature in recent decades. Otherwise, the British use their sovereign right only when Parliament is dissolved at intervals not exceeding five years. Sometimes a parliamentary seat is vacated by death or resignation; a by-election will then be held, which the entire country watches to discern the political trend. But the British do not vote for school boards or bond issues. The referendum was used only in 1975, when the voters approved the entry of Britain into the European Common Market,[13] and in 1978, when the Scots failed to approve by an adequate margin a bill for Scottish autonomy. The fundamental act of British democracy, then, is the making of a single mark, once in several years, on a simple ballot containing only the names of candidates and a description or affiliation in six words or less.

[13]The referendum is opposed chiefly on the grounds that it would be derogatory to Parliament. Cecil C. Amden, *The People and the Constitution*, 2nd ed. (London: Oxford University Press, 1956), pp. 301–302.

The prime minister sets the electoral machinery in motion by asking the monarch to dissolve Parliament at the moment, up to five years after its convening, that he or she deems most advantageous to the party. The royal power of dissolution derives from the fact that Parliament was originally summoned for the monarch's purposes and was sent home at his or her pleasure. It has been used when a governing majority broke up (as in 1979) or when it seemed necessary (as in the 1910–1911 crisis over the House of Lords) to secure electoral backing for an important new policy. Ordinarily, however, the power of dissolution permits the incumbent leader to choose when to meet the electorate. Parliament rarely goes to the legal limit (the average term of Parliaments since 1910 is about four years) because the prime minister wants freedom of maneuver. The fact that the government can do something to produce temporary symptoms of prosperity or that it can take advantage of a spell of good economic weather is no slight advantage for the incumbents. Their choice is somewhat restricted, however, because mid-spring and mid-autumn are, for various reasons, customary times for general elections.

The prime minister may, of course, miscalculate. James Callaghan, the Labour leader, could probably have won a fair majority in the fall of 1978, when inflation was apparently checked and the country was as prosperous as it had been for a long time. He postponed the election in hopes of further improvement and also to profit from the registration of young voters, presumably pro-Labour, in early 1979. But workers began battering the official wage guidelines, the winter was bedeviled by strikes, garbage piled up on the streets, and the dead lay unburied. Labour found itself very unpopular. Liberals pulled away from the shaky coalition keeping Labour in power, followed by the Scottish Nationalists after the failure of the devolution proposal. A no-confidence motion passed by a single vote in April, and the prime minister had to dissolve Parliament. Labour was badly beaten.

The election must be held within three weeks of the dissolution of Parliament, so nominees must be ready in advance. Candidates are picked by local parties under the supervision of central party authorities, sometimes at the suggestion of the latter, who can veto candidates but seldom do so. Ordinarily local committees make the selection, probably after meeting with several would-be members of Parliament. Anyone can present himself, and candidates no longer bear their own campaign costs. A member of Parliament (MP) is usually assured of renomination unless he or she breaks party discipline. The candidate does not have to reside among the people he or she would represent; about half do not.

Supported by a party or not, anyone with ten friends to sign a petition and £150 to put up as deposit can get on the ballot. The deposit is lost if the candidate does not receive at least one-eighth of the votes cast, and it is intended as a deterrent to frivolous candidacies. However, since the amount was fixed in 1918, the pound has shrunk to less than one-twentieth of its value. Hopes for success without the backing of a major party are slim. People vote mostly for the party, and the personal appeal of a candidate may be worth only one or two percent of the votes. One reason is that expenditures for the campaign in the constituency are limited to £4,200 ($6,720).

At the local level, the parties depend on the unpaid and generally unrecognized labor of activists. Spending for the national cause is unrestricted, however. This fact further concentrates the attention that would naturally go to the contest for leadership of the nation, which is waged mostly between the two leading parties and their champions, the sitting prime minister and the person who proposes to replace him or her. The chief contact between parties and electorate is through the press and television, in which the name of the local candidates may never appear. Their principal function if elected will be to support the government of their party or oppose that of the other party. Their political future, moreover, will depend far less on their ability to win votes than on their usefulness to their party and superiors.

The campaign has tended to become something of a contest in advertising, in which the Conservatives have a strong advantage. In 1983 they spent an estimated £20 million, in comparison to £2 million by Labour and somewhat less by the Liberal-Social Democratic Alliance. All parties, however, received free television time. More is made of the party manifestoes than of party platforms in the United States, and they represent more of an expression of party policy. However, the personalities of the leaders seem usually to be decisive, as in other democracies.

Because of the concentration of population, money, and power in London, Britain has a national press; a few newspapers with huge circulations cover the whole of England. No big papers are formally linked with a political party, but almost all of them favor the Conservatives. The government-owned but nonpolitical British Broadcasting Corporation and the independent broadcast networks give equal time to the major parties, as do commercial stations, but much less to other parties.[14]

The country is divided into 650 districts, the population of which is kept fairly even by redrawing every ten to fifteen years. Since 1970 those over eighteen have been entitled to vote; registration is easy, and a much larger

[14]See David J. G. H. Windlesham, *Communication and Political Power* (London: Jonathan Cape, 1966).

proportion of the eligible population casts ballots than in the United States—about 80 percent against perhaps 50 percent in the United States.

The results are rather unspectacular. No single party since 1935 has won a majority of popular votes, and swings are usually slight. Since 1945, the Conservative percentage of the national vote has varied only about 10 points; that of Labour, 5.7 points.[15] Ordinarily about nine-tenths of the voters vote for the same party as in the previous election. The leading parties are so close together that six out of twelve elections between 1945 and 1983 produced a change of government—a remarkable record in comparison with one-party dominance for long periods in Germany, France, Italy, and Japan. The elections of October 1974 and May 1979 gave the following results:

	Percentage of Votes		Seats	
Party	1974	1979	1974	1979
Conservatives	35.8	43.9	277	339
Labour	39.2	36.9	319	268
Liberal	18.3	13.8	13	11
Scottish Nationalists	2.9	1.6	11	2
Plaid Cymru	0.6	0.4	3	2
National Front	—	0.6	—	0
Northern Irish and others	2.8	2.8	12	13

The popularity of the Thatcher government shrank during years of bad times and steadily rising unemployment, until her approval rating was only 25 percent in March 1982. However, the British were much impressed by her resolution in the little war with Argentina over the Falkland Islands, inflation declined, and the economy improved or at least steadied. Encouraged by opinion polls, the disarray of the Labour Party, and the division of the opposition by the Liberal-Social Democratic Alliance,

[15]Rose, *Politics in England,* pp. 271–272.

Thatcher proceeded to elections in June 1983, nearly a year ahead of the deadline. The results were as follows:

	Percentage of Votes	Seats
Party	1983	1983
Conservatives	43.5	397
Labour	28.3	209
Liberal-Social Democratic Alliance	26.1	23
Scottish Nationalists[a]	1.5	2
Plaid Cymru[b]		2
Northern Irish and others	.6	17

[a]11.8 percent in Scotland.
[b]7.8 percent in Wales.

THE PARTY SYSTEM

Just as the British Parliament served as a model for parliamentary governments around the world, the British party system has influenced the formation of modern democratic parties everywhere. Electoral politics, of course, evoked the organizations needed to muster support and secure places in the elected assembly; and these naturally tended, because of the contest, to represent two basic tendencies, those more satisfied with the status quo and those more disposed to change. The British system is unusual in the degree to which this character has been retained over a long time, in the rivalry of Tories and Whigs, who became Conservatives and Liberals, then of Conservatives and Labour. Recently, however, the stability of the system has been called into question, and it may have entered a time of flux.

The Conservative Party

The Conservative Party retains something of its original character as a primarily parliamentary party, to which the mass organization is subordinate. Unlike Labour, the Conservatives have no extraparliamentary group overseeing the actions and policies of the central leadership. It is the sole purpose of the constituency parties to win elections. The center is responsible to them and their memberships chiefly in that it must secure their support at election time. The rather informally organized local parties are assisted, guided, and inspired by agents sent from the Central Office to all except a few constituencies the party has no hope of winning. The backbone of the party are the activists, a minority of a minority, correspondingly zealous and partisan.

The constituency parties are joined in the National Union of Conservative and Unionist Associations. One of its functions is to hold a yearly conference that serves as a forum for the party leadership and as an occasion for a pleasant and possibly inspiring outing by perhaps 4500 of the party faithful, a reward for toil and a chance to see, hear, and possibly touch the party great. Unlike the Labour conference, it makes no pretense of deciding anything.

The central organization, unlike that of Labour, does not concern itself with policy and carries on the party's national electoral business. It has a remarkably small professional staff of somewhat over 500 persons. This staff is permanent, unlike that of American parties which is hired for the campaign. The leader works with and must rely on persons whom he or she does not select and can hardly remove. The party chair, however, is named by and is responsible to the leader.

The leader has broad powers under little formal restraint and is personally responsible for the party program. Formerly the leader rather mysteriously "emerged" as a result of consultations among party leaders and was accepted by the Conservative MPs, candidates, and notables. When the leadership became vacant while the party was in opposition, no new leader was selected until the monarch, after proper consultations, tapped one as a new prime minister. In 1965,

however, the party adopted the rule that the leader should obtain a clear majority in a secret ballot of Conservative MPs. The leader in opposition is not subject to annual reelection, unlike his or her Labour counterpart; but party sentiment may force a resignation. Thus in 1975 Edward Heath, having lost two elections, was compelled to step down, and Margaret H. Thatcher became leader of the party. Mrs. Thatcher, daughter of a grocer and graduate of Oxford (chemistry), barrister, MP since 1959, had little experience at the top of government, having served only as Secretary of State for Education. She was the first choice of few but acceptable to most, and she appealed to the leaders of the party in opposition for her combativeness.[16]

She became the first woman ever to head a major Western political party, and she surprised the world by becoming a very strong leader. Dubbed "Iron Lady" by the Soviet press after she spoke skeptically of détente in 1976, she gladly accepted the appellation and justified it by firmness in following her convictions. With her victory in June 1983, greatly increasing the Conservative majority, she became the most dominant prime minister since Winston Churchill.

The Conservative leadership in the nineteenth century was a clique mostly of landowners and was associated with exclusive men's clubs. It has now broadened, but it remains upper class. It includes both born aristocrats and self-made people, but it is still characterized by social exclusiveness, a little snobbery, academic education, and wealth. Conservative MPs are mostly barristers, landowners, businesspeople, journalists, and retired military officers. Three-quarters of them are alumni of private ("public" in British usage) schools,[17] the largest fraction com-

---

[16]Anthony Sampson, *The Changing Anatomy of Britain* (New York: Random House, 1982), p. 44.
[17]Beer, *British Political System*, p. 93.

ing from Eton. Although it has only about 1,000 students, Eton produces about a third of bank and insurance directors as well as Conservative cabinet ministers—but almost no Labour MPs. Oxford and Cambridge ("Oxbridge") graduates, on the other hand, are numerous in the top levels of both parties[18] but strongly dominant in the Conservative Party. One-quarter of Labour MPs recently were Oxbridge alumni, three quarters of Conservative.[19]

Although Thatcher has injected more of a middle-class mentality, the party is still tinged with a somewhat archaic upperclassness; and the higher his or her economic and social standing, the more likely that a person will vote Conservative. A large majority of the upper and middle classes support the party, and the correlation of class with Conservative or Labour voting in Britain is higher than with Republican or Democratic voting in the United States. But the Conservatives must appeal to the less privileged in order to win elections, and they win about a third of working-class votes. Working-class people make up about half the party's supporters. Most of these, however, are skilled workers, among whom the Conservative party is about as popular as is Labour.[20] In the June 1983 election almost as many trade-union members voted Tory as Labour.

People seem to favor the Conservatives mostly as the party better capable of governing, whereas the Labourites appeal more on the basis of their program and the promise of economic benefits. The Conservatives are stronger in the relatively prosperous south of England; Labour is stronger in the north, with its decaying industries dependent on government support.

The bulk of the funds of the Conservative

party are raised by the constituency organizations, through members' dues, small contributions, and miscellaneous fund-raising events. About a quarter comes from donations from big business. The party has no formal connection with economic interests, and it tries to give the country what the country seems to want.

The parties differ considerably in philosophy and outlook, however. The Conservatives, who have an upper-class self-assurance in their title to power, present themselves as friends of the people and emphasize the expansion of the pie more than the way it is sliced. For generations, the Conservatives were wedded to patriotism and empire, and they still have some nostalgia for lost greatness and world destiny. They favored joining the European Common Market when Labour was hesitant. They have been more anti-Communist or anti-Soviet, although Labour governments have been faithful to NATO and the American alliance. In recent years more intellectuals have been drifting to the Conservative ranks, giving the party a more ideological flavor.

Through the postwar era, the two major parties have usually seemed to be remarkably close together in practice, despite representing opposite social classes and philosophies. The Tories often seemed nearly as attached to the welfare state as Labour. Neither party, upon a transfer of power, would repeal much legislation of its predecessor, and both accepted the mixed economy. The Tories, although favorable to business interests and private property, prided themselves on nonideological pragmatism.

Recent years, however, have seen a turn toward sharper confrontation and more ideological positions, doubtless stimulated by growing dissatisfaction and the decay of the British economy. On the Left, a strong militant minority tugged the Labour Party toward radicalism; on the Right, the Tories

---

[18]Sampson, *Anatomy of Britain*, p. 44.
[19]Sampson, *Changing Anatomy of Britain*, p. 144.
[20]Richard Rose, *The Problem of Party Government* (London: Macmillan, 1974), p. 33.

under Margaret Thatcher undertook not merely to govern the country but also to change it deeply. Thatcher sought to reduce the role of the state; cut taxes discouraging to production; reduce the deficit and consequent inflation; curb the powers of the unions; increase competition; and restore the Victorian virtues of work, saving, and discipline.[21] Her government reduced income taxes (top rate from 83 percent to 60 percent); raised taxes on consumption; eliminated long-standing controls on prices, wages, dividends, and foreign exchange; made it easy for tenants to buy municipally owned housing; and in four years cut the number of civil servants by 12 percent. Inflation declined to 4 percent from 21 percent, but unemployment tripled to 12.7 percent by 1983. The electoral victory of June 1983 encouraged Thatcher to expel from her cabinet several "wets," or less than fully enthusiastic followers. She pressed on to require union leaders to be much more responsible to members, to reconsider capital punishment, even to reduce the role of the state in medical care and higher education—an effort to turn back a generation of what were once deemed progressive changes.

The Labour Party

The Labour Party differs sharply in organization from the Conservative Party.[22] It is, peculiarly among parties in democratic countries, an organization of organizations. It was established in 1900 by trade unions and some socialistic organizations to secure representation in Parliament for labor. Sub-

sequently, constituency parties admitting individual members, like the Conservative Party, were formed, and the original affiliating organizations other than the unions nearly faded out. But the basic structure remains. The trade unions in the party provide the overwhelming majority of the membership and 80 percent of its funds, because workers in the big unions are counted as Labour Party members and contribute regular dues to it unless they specifically request to be exempted—an inadvisable move if the worker wants the goodwill of the union. Even if a member contracts out, as about a million union members do, the union can pay dues for that person and count him or her for voting purposes—or even pay dues regardless of membership in order to gain voting power.[23] Labour consequently represents a combination of middle-class reformers and organized labor, in which the former provide most of the brain and the latter most of the muscle.

It follows that Labour constituency parties are less important than those of the Conservative Party; some of them have only a dozen or so active members. Labour has central agents for only about a quarter of the constituencies. The number of individual members has declined in recent years, and there may be only about 220,000 active participants, less than half the number in 1972. Sometimes unions act as a constituency party themselves, and the local parties frequently accept nominees of unions, if only because the unions provide financial and organizational support. Candidates must, in any case, be proposed by an organization affiliated with the Labour Party; a person cannot walk in and offer himself, as one can to the Conservative Party.

The annual Labour conference brings together a smaller number than the Conserv-

---

[21]On the economic program, see "What Hath Thatcher Wrought?" *Business Week*, June 6, 1983, pp. 44–54.

[22]For a rosy view of the Labour Party, see H. B. Cole, *The British Labour Party: A Functioning Participatory Democracy* (New York: Pergamon Press, 1977). A negative view is given by Woodrow Wyatt, *What's Left of the Labour Party* (London: Sidgwick and Jackson, 1977).

[23]Sampson, *Changing Anatomy of Britain*, p. 83.

ative, somewhat over 1,000 delegates, not so much to applaud and celebrate in the manner of the Conservative conference, but to dispute and decide the party program and the composition of its National Executive Committee. Voting is by bloc—that is, the union representatives vote for their entire membership. This procedure of voting as a unit on behalf of millions of persons who have not expressed a preference in regard to the issues under consideration is hardly democratic, but it adds to the weight of the union leadership. The five biggest unions—Transport and General Workers; Engineering and Foundry Workers; Municipal Workers; Electrical and Plumbing Workers; and Ship, Distributive and Allied Workers—command a large majority, the first two alone holding 40 percent of the voting power. Over half of all union members are public employees.

The trade unions also control the National Executive Committee (NEC), which administers the party apparatus. The central staff is small, somewhat over 200, or less than half as many as the Conservative. However, while the Conservative Central Office is responsible to the party leader, the Labour National Executive Committee, with its annually rotating chair and its bureaucracy, is responsible to the conference or, for all practical purposes, to the unions. The NEC may take a different position from that of the Labour leader and the Parliamentary Labour Party (PLP), and it may seek to impose its view on them. Since 1979 it has had sole authority to write election manifestoes.

According to traditional British constitutional theory, the PLP should take orders from no extraparliamentary body but should represent the electors. It has operated, in fact, rather independently, because the MPs were fairly secure in their positions for several years and could ordinarily count on renomination by the constituency organiza-

tion. The conference in October 1979, however, decided that Labour MPs should be subject to reselection by their constituency parties, which have generally come under radical sway and are even less representative of Labour voters than are the unions. The PLP is more independent when a Labour government is in office; when Labour is in opposition, trade union support, which includes supplemental salaries for some, is more vital. The PLP can hardly stand strongly against the wishes of its organizational supporters. Labour may go against the interests of workers in order to maintain its standing with the electorate, but it can hardly be expected to oppose the unions, which could bankrupt the party on a moment's notice. The fact that the unions' enrollments have been shrinking in recent years has not lessened their grip on the party.

The leader of the party was elected, like the Tory leader, by the Labour MPs; but the 1980 conference transferred the choice to an electoral college in which trade unions make up 40 percent; constituency parties, 30 percent; and the PLP, 30 percent.[24] About a quarter of Labour MPs are trade-union officials; half of them are union-sponsored.[25] There are many teachers in the PLP and more journalists than among Conservative MPs. Labourites are also more likely to have been trained at universities other than Oxford and Cambridge. The Labourites are also older than their Conservative counterparts.

The Labour Party is more disposed than the Conservative to quarrel about programs and policies. It began as something of a movement of true believers hoping to remake society, and in 1918 it officially adopted the goal of socialism—that is, full state con-

---

[24]Samuel H. Beer, *Britain Against Itself: The Political Contradictions of Collectivism* (New York: Norton, 1982), p. 165.
[25]Sampson, *Changing Anatomy of Britain*, p. 19.

trol of the economy. The Conservative flag is the national Union Jack; the Labour emblem is the red flag, which is the subject of the party anthem:

The people's flag is deepest red.
It shrouded oft our martyred dead.
And ere their limbs grew stiff and cold.
Their hearts' blood dyed its every fold. . . .

British socialism, however, was gradualist; and movement psychology was diluted by day-to-day politics, exigencies of government, and the realization that the party has no panacea. The Left emerged much strengthened from World War II, but the experience of 1945–1951 was sobering, and the nation grew weary of many reforms without great results. Labour governments advocated nothing very radical after the mass of socializing changes enacted shortly after the war. Harold Wilson was seen as a leftist when he was elected leader in 1963, but in office (1964–1970 and 1974–1976) he turned out to be a practical administrator. His successor, James Callaghan, followed economic policies not much different from those of the Conservatives.

The pillars of Labour doctrine—public ownership of the economy, expansion of the already extended welfare state, heavy taxation to redistribute wealth, full employment, and general egalitarianism—arouse little enthusiasm among the mass of workers and none in the middle class, which decides elections. Yet the leftist sector of Labour has increasingly pushed a class approach since the mid-1970s and especially since the defeat of 1979, which embittered many activists. Trade-union officials have also turned more radical than their memberships. The so-called "militant tendency," virtually a party dedicated to revolution within the Labour Party, gained control of the Labour youth organization and many or most constituency par-

ties. Chronic squabbling between moderate and radical factions kept Labour from gaining much from the economic hardships of Thatcherism and led to the splitting away in 1981 of a section of the leadership to form a new Social Democratic Party.

Labour went into the campaign of June 1983 advocating unilateral nuclear disarmament, removal of U.S. forces, withdrawal from the European Economic Community, no restriction on unions, and a big spending program to create more jobs. Partly because of this program, partly because of the ineffectiveness of Leader Michael Foot, Labour suffered its worst defeat since its founding. Its percentage of votes, 27.6 percent, was far under the previous (1979) postwar low of 37 percent. Labour lost deposits in 119 races. It polled only 35 percent among manual laborers, and its strength lay only in decaying cities with high unemployment and aging populations.[26] In the prosperous south of England, except in London, Labour won almost no seats.

In defeat, Foot resigned. Seeking rejuvenation and a new beginning, the party electoral college chose as leader a dynamic Welshman, Neil Kinnock, age 41, who had no experience in administration. Although Kinnock had been regarded as strongly leftist, as leader he responded to the exigencies of electoral politics and tried to steer the party back toward the center. He chose as his deputy a man of the moderate-right wing, Roy Hattersley, age 50, and retreated from Labour positions on nuclear disarmament and withdrawal from the European Economic Community.

Labour continues, however, deeply divided, and a sector would prefer to lose elections rather than surrender ideological positions unpopular with the British majority. The recent organizational changes, espe-

[26]*The Economist*, June 1, 1983, p. 33.

cially the requirement of reselection of MPs by constituency parties, guarantee the strength of the left wing. Despite the pragmatism of the new leader, it may be that Labour suffers structural flaws ill fitting it for politics in a modern democracy.

The Third Party

For half a century only the Conservative or Labour parties have been able to form a government.[27] The Liberals of nineteenth-century glory have for many decades been unable to present themselves as a credible alternative, and the two-party situation has been clear and sharp since World War II. Hence Britain, like the United States (and more than any other important democracy) approaches the model two-party system traditionally praised by British and American political scientists. It seems indeed to have the virtues claimed for two-party democracy: the parties, having to court the undecided and hence moderate voters, take fairly moderate positions and enact programs within a broad consensus. Moreover, voting for a party means voting for a program and a prime minister. Responsibility is not obscured, as in the coalition politics of a multiparty system.

In the British two-party system, however, party lines are more tightly drawn around the central organizations than in the United States. There are no state parties and no state elections, and local elections are inconsequential. A British party in national defeat cannot retreat to the statehouses and from there, sustained by the power, prestige, and patronage of state office, work its way back. Yet the two-party system is less perfect in Britain than in the United States. In only six of twenty-one elections through 1979 did one party win an absolute majority in the House

of Commons, and no party has a prospect of a majority of the electorate. Many voters are obviously dissatisfied with the system. In recent years, 20 to 25 percent of the electorate cast ballots for other parties even though there was usually little chance that their candidate would be elected and zero chance that their party could form a government.

The Liberals have been the most important of the lesser parties, the only one with a tradition of government and a country-wide organization. However, having no rewards to offer its supporters, it is impoverished, loosely structured, and feebly staffed. The center has no leverage over the local organizations. The party cannot ordinarily afford to contest more than about half the constituencies, thereby confessing that its cause is hopeless. Many people vote Liberal because they are repelled by the Conservative or Labour party but are not prepared to vote for its opposite. The Liberals' support is more like the Conservatives' than Labour's—that is, mostly middle class. Their philosophy, however, is somewhat reformist-egalitarian and closer to Labour than to the Conservatives. The Liberals prefer cooperation with Labour, perhaps partly for historical reasons; they were secular opponents of the Conservatives and assisted Labour in its first steps to power.

Votes for the Liberals have varied in the postwar period from 6 percent in 1959 to 19.3 percent in 1974, but the party has never obtained more than a handful of seats because of the first-past-the-post electoral system. After the 1974 election, the Liberals gained some importance because Labour lacked an absolute majority. Although the Liberal leader, David Steel, was quite popular, he could persuade only 13 percent of the electorate to cast their ballots in 1979 for what could only be a protest vote.

The two-party system has thus seemed

[27]See Arthur Cyr, *Liberal Party Politics in Britain* (New Brunswick, N.J.: Transaction Books, 1977).

fixed, because it is impossible to become a credible alternative to the party in power without much money and organization, and it is excessively difficult to muster money and organization unless the party is already a credible candidate for power.

In 1982, however, it seemed that the travails of the Labour Party might permit a middle party to come forward. Revolt was brewing in Labour ranks from the latter 1970s, and in January 1981 a "Council for Social Democracy" was organized by dissidents under the leadership of several former Labour ministers, including Roy Jenkins and Shirley Williams. In March, thirteen Labour MPs launched a new Social Democratic Party to promote policies of moderate reform. Very little separated them from the Liberals, and the two naturally became allied. Fortune seemed to smile on the Social Democrats, and within a month polls gave them more support (35 percent) than either Labour (29 percent) or Conservatives (27 percent). By the end of the year, Gallup reported the Social Democrats far ahead, with 50 percent of the vote, to 23 percent each for Labour and Conservatives.[28] Defecting Labourites raised their representation in Commons to twenty nine. Thereafter, old patterns began to reassert themselves. The new party bickered over leadership (finally deciding on Roy Jenkins, former Chancellor of the Exchequer) and with their allies, and its support ebbed.

The Falklands war was as bad for the new party as it was good for the Tories. The Social Democrats seemed irrelevant. They had no financial base and hardly any grassroots organization; the candidate of the Liberal-Social Democratic Alliance, Jenkins, had little of interest to say, standing roughly midway between Conservatives and Labour, and a string of by-election victories came to an end as Labour recovered its balance. In the

election of June 1983, the Liberals received more votes than their Social Democratic allies, 13 percent to 11.6 percent, and won more seats, seventeen to six. With nearly as many votes as Labour, the Alliance captured one-ninth as many seats because the support of the latter was nowhere concentrated. It was small satisfaction to have been second to the Tories in twice as many constituencies as Labour.

This obviously unfair result raised the old question of proportional representation. But Thatcher firmly opposed this on the grounds that it would lead to instability of governments. Certainly neither Conservatives nor Labour was likely to countenance an innovation that would help only a third force. And the Conservatives preferred to keep Labour as the chief opposition party because it should be easier to defeat than the Social Democrats. The hope of the new S.D. leader, David Owen, was to show the party's grassroots strength by winning by-elections.

Minor Parties

Another national party is the Communist. The Communists, however, have lost most of their election deposits where they presented candidates, and for many years have had no members in the House of Commons, although, ironically, there is a Communist in the House of Lords. But the Communist movement is far stronger than indicated by the small fraction of 1 percent of the votes that it receives, because, in the intricacies and unrepresentativeness of union politics, many Communists and near-Communists have secured influential positions in various unions and hence in Labour. For the sake of respectability, the British CP has moved somewhat away from Soviet positions and has aligned itself with the more or less independent Communist parties of Western Europe.

[28]*New York Times,* December 27, 1981, p. 3.

From time to time rightist movements have sprung up, usually playing on the backlash against nonwhite immigration from former British possessions, such as Pakistan and Jamaica. They have received more publicity than votes, however, and have never achieved political importance.

The front-runner-take-all electoral system is discouraging for small national parties. It does not, however, exclude small regional parties, which have been significant in the Celtic fringes (Scotland, Wales, and Northern Ireland or Ulster). The Scottish National party, for example, can count on fairly solid ethnic support. Helped by the economic decay of Scotland and the feeling it should get more income from North Sea oil, it gathered 30 percent of the votes in Scotland in 1974 and eleven seats in Parliament. In the 1979 elections, however, in the aftermath of the failure of the Scots to give adequate support to the Labour government's proposal for devolution, it retained only two seats, and it won only two in 1983. Northern Ireland has its own concerns, and it regularly sends an independent delegation to Parliament—seventeen in 1983. The Welsh party, Plaid Cymru, took two seats in 1979. Such parties cannot hope for any share of power unless the major parties are almost equal; but they can agitate and seek concessions for their regions and their constituents.

THE GOVERNMENT

The Leader and Cabinet

If the prime minister learns from the election night bulletins that the party has lost, he or she immediately tenders a resignation to the monarch, who proceeds to name as prime minister the leader of the party that commands a majority in the new Parliament.

The monarch also names a replacement (elected by the majority party) when the prime ministry becomes vacant by death or political upset. Prime ministers may be driving chieftains (such as Winston Churchill) or inoffensive board chairmen (such as Clement Attlee). They become, in any event, the symbol of their party and the focus of its publicity. They are largely immune to open criticism from their own party because its hopes rest on them, and to attack a prime minister means practically to attack the party.[29]

Opposition to prime ministers is also impolitic because they hand out the plums to which most MPs aspire. Prime ministers decide, as freely as the political realities permit, who gets what posts and who composes the cabinet; and they can fire anyone at any time. Since it is desirable for ministers to sit in the House of Commons, a new prime minister has a rather narrow field from which to choose about a hundred colleagues and assistants— ministers, junior ministers, parliamentary secretaries, and undersecretaries. They add up to a hundred or more MPs who are not too young or too old, who are considered trustworthy, and who are interested in more work and power. It is possible to name non-MPs, but it is then necessary to bring them into the House by a by-election for a vacated seat. A few ministers are taken from the House of Lords, but it is desirable that ministers be available for questioning on the floor of the Commons. It is fairly well decided in advance of a party's taking office who its principal leaders will be, because both parties while in opposition make about fifty MPs responsible for specific departments, as a sort of shadow ministry, and a smaller number form a shadow cabinet.

The cabinet varies in size. When the pres-

[29]Peter Bromhead, *Britain's Developing Constitution* (London: Allen & Unwin, 1974), p. 31.

sure of business is most intense, as in the world wars, it has been reduced to about a dozen; it tends to expand in peacetime to accommodate influential personages. Ministers, and especially cabinet ministers, are more likely to be of upper-class background than back-bench MPs. For example, twenty of twenty-two in the 1979 Conservative government had a private-school background. Four-fifths came out of Oxford or Cambridge. More remarkable, half the members of the Labour cabinet of Harold Wilson were Oxbridge graduates.

The decisions of the government are formally taken by the cabinet, not the prime minister; but the prime minister, like the American president, may largely decide policy in both domestic and foreign affairs. Assisted by a small personal staff of civil servants, the prime minister sets the cabinet agenda and articulates its decisions. There are a dozen or so cabinet committees for legislation, defense, home affairs, economic policy, social service, and the like; and the prime minister names numerous unpublicized ad hoc committees. There is also an informal inner cabinet of a few especially trusted colleagues. Decisions of cabinet committees have the same authority as those of the full body. Under the principle of collective responsibility, all cabinet members should support the government's policies even though they may have privately disagreed. Any minister unable to do so is expected to resign.

Unlike American practice, departments are not fixed by law but can be reorganized at will by the executive.[30] Administration is coordinated through various committees, superministries, and ministers without port-folio; the Secretariat of the Cabinet, composed of permanent civil servants, keeps ministers informed and transmits decisions to the civil service. Cabinet ministers are assisted by junior ministers, and ministers have staffs of civil servants plus a parliamentary private secretary as liaison with the House of Commons. But it is extremely difficult for a hundred or so politicians to effectively direct some 800,000 civil servants. The task is especially difficult for cabinet ministers who serve both as department heads and as members of the top executive body. They must try to combine long-range planning with daily responsibilities, and it is hard to introduce changes in the face of doubts and reservations of the skilled and confident civil service. When the voters turn out a government, a hundred newcomers move in, but thousands of old hands keep things moving as before.

The Administration

Since the tenure of the minister is unpredictable and fairly short, it is orderly procedure to have permanent staff in all but the top administrative positions. Information filters up to the minister through the permanent civil servants, and orders go down through them. The idea that a new minister might bring in a new team to help push his or her policies is resisted on the grounds that there would be conflict between the assistants and the permanent advisors;[31] that this reasoning, so favorable to the professionals, is accepted testifies to their influence. The civil servants have the further advantage that they confer with colleagues of other departments to prepare positions for ministerial or cabinet consideration. The authority

---

[30]Walter C. Neale, *The British Economy: Toward a Decent Society* (Columbus, Ohio: Grid Publishing Co., 1980), p. 32.

[31]R. M. Punnett, *British Government and Politics,* 2nd ed. (New York: Norton, 1971), pp. 326–327.

of the permanent civil service is also attested to by the fact that it keeps the confidential records of previous cabinets locked away from the incumbent government. Prime ministers could in theory demand access to them but do not because they want the secrets of their own government similarly protected.[32]

The permanent civil service is influential but invisible. The permanent secretary next to the minister is anonymous and publicly silent. British bureaucrats are forbidden to communicate with Parliament or the press. A civil servant sits beside the minister responding to questions in Parliament, but the answers are given by the minister. The civil service is expected to be for or against whatever the minister is for or against, and responsibility for the actions of the department lies entirely with its political head, an arrangement that in effect shields the civil service from blame.[33] There is no probing into decision making within the government, and the public and Parliament are to note and criticize only the consequences. Indeed, the Official Secrets Act of 1911 prohibits the disclosure of any official information in principle, and civil servants are bound to lifetime silence regarding their work. There are in practice few leaks. The British administration is far more hermetic than the American or Swedish.[34]

Also, relations between the minister and the higher civil servants are easier because both very likely have similar educational backgrounds, a majority probably being graduates of Oxford or Cambridge. Half of the upper stratum of the civil service, like many Conservative ministers, come out of private ("public") schools, especially Eton, and this proportion does not diminish.[35] A large majority are of professional or managerial class origins, and they are mostly educated in such subjects as history and the classics.[36] They are generally recruited at graduation, so they have little experience of the nonofficial world and a strong *esprit de corps,* as well as a tradition of political impartiality exceptional in the world. Unlike their colleagues in France, Germany, Japan, and many other countries, they seldom seek political office but limit their ambitions to a bureaucratic career. Harold Wilson was the first prime minister with a civil service background.

Since the bureaucrats have no career stake in the outcome of programs, they are usually inclined to favor the status quo over changes that disturb routine. For this reason and because of their educational and class background, bureaucrats may incline toward the Conservative Party. Prior to the election of a Labour government in 1945, it was widely doubted that the civil service would cooperate in the execution of a Labour program. The fears, however, proved groundless; the tradition of carrying out the orders of the responsible political superior prevailed. Moreover, the Labourites soon learned that they had something in common with the civil service; namely, a propensity to extend state controls. For the Labour leaders, the civil service became the effective instrument of regulation; for the civil service, Labour reforms and nationalizations meant an expansion of their ranks and jurisdiction.

The competence of the civil service seems to be very high. It traditionally recruits bright young men (and a small but growing num-

[32]Beer, *The British Political System,* p. 39; and Sampson, *Anatomy of Britain Today,* p. 252.

[33]John P. Mackintosh, *Government and Politics of Britain* (London: Hutchinson, 1974), p. 159.

[34]Frank Stacey, *British Government 1966 to 1975: Years of Reform* (London: Oxford University Press, 1975), p. 219.

[35]Beer, *The British Political System,* p. 51.

[36]Sampson, *Anatomy of Britain Today,* pp. 259–260.

ber of young women) with a general education in the humanities. It has a dignified background going back to the Northcote-Trevelyan Report of 1853. Inspired by the Indian civil service, this report proposed impartial selection of the servants of the Crown. An open competitive examination was begun in 1870, and the civil service since then has been an almost incorruptible close-knit corps headed by intelligent and highly educated generalists. It is also highly self-protective and unionized.

The top bracket of the civil service was for many years an elite group of about 3,000, the administrative class, only a small fraction of whom came from the much larger executive class. A reform in 1971 softened this elitism by replacing the classes with a grading system for all civil servants, somewhat in the American style. The grade of administrative trainee was created as steppingstone to higher responsibilities; it recruits 250 to 300 people yearly, about half from within the civil service, by written tests and interviews. Those who prove satisfactory are rapidly pushed up the ladder, helped by training at the Civil Service College. The emphasis is still on general ability; high civil servants are expected, aside from specialties such as foreign affairs or education, to function in a large number of departments. They are in fact, often rotated to keep them generalists.

The bureaucracy is self-perpetuating because it screens its entrants (who enjoy security of employment) and selects its own upper ranks. Promotions within grades are earned by seniority and performance, and also by loyalty to the service—which helps to keep government secrets secret. Top civil servants are named on the advice of top civil servants, and the most responsible single official is the permanent secretary of the Civil Service Department. This department in 1968 assumed the directorship of the civil service from the Treasury, which for many generations was general manager of administration on the grounds that nothing was done without spending money.

The Treasury continues to be the center of the administration, because it keeps a tight grip on the budget. A minister can bring a financial proposal before the cabinet only after Treasury scrutiny; and the Chancellor of the Exchequer, as the head of the Treasury is called, prepares the budget in considerable secrecy, even from cabinet colleagues.

Because of the strength of the bureaucracy and its discretionary powers—many laws are broad and require implementation through executive regulations—British interest groups direct their attention primarily to the departments and only secondarily to Parliament. Interest groups or pressure groups of all kinds are numerous and well organized, and relatively stronger in Britain than in the United States.[37] Many are old; others have proliferated in response to the expansion of government in the past generation. Many of them are much more inclusive than corresponding groups in the United States. A much larger percentage of the British workforce (40 percent in private industry, 80 percent in the public sector, about half in all), is organized than in America, and nearly all unions belong to the Trade Union Congress. Since 1979, however, under the pressure of unemployment and an unfriendly government, unions have lost about 10 percent of their membership, the first such shrinkage in half a century. A large majority of British manufacturers belong to the Federation of British Industries, in contrast to the much lower participation of U.S.

[37]For case studies, see Richard Kimber and J. J. Richardson, eds., *Pressure Groups in Britain: A Reader* (London: Dent, 1974); and Jack Bruce-Gardyne and Nigel Lawson, *The Power Game* (London: Macmillan, 1976).

firms in the National Association of Manufacturers.

Most of the economy, despite several Labour governments, is still privately owned (about 80 percent of industry), although the government accounts for close to half of all investments. Roughly 10 percent of the labor force is in government, and a similar fraction is in nationalized industries, including electricity, road transport, railroads, gas, coal, aviation, and central banking. Nationalized enterprises are not under civil service rules but are unionized. They are neither fully government-run nor entirely guided by the marketplace and economic considerations. Operating under boards of directors appointed by a minister, they are subject to general policy directives and political interference; but they are not easily controlled. Directives to them are not easily enforced, and changing the board is politically questionable.[38] On the one hand, state enterprises are expected to make a profit (or in practice minimize losses); on the other, to conform to political and social objectives. The ambiguity causes confusion and contributes to inefficiency, as in the case of the U.S. Postal Service. And state ownership does not protect them against strikes; on the contrary, they are particularly strike-prone.

Local Administration

The departments carry out policies to a large extent through local authorities, that is, town and borough staffs responsible to elected councils. There are 65 county or metropolitan governments, divided into 453 boroughs or districts. Operating under the close direction of the central powers, which supply most of the funds, they are more like administrative units than real local governments; Britain is the most centralized of major European nations. Their responsibilities, however, are extensive, including management of social services, housing, and utilities. Although the triennial elections to the councils attract only a small fraction of the voters, they are watched as indicators of political swings. To a minor degree, the local councils give standing to the party out of power, like the American state governments. The Greater London Council in particular is something of a bastion of the left wing of Labour.

The Judiciary

The judiciary is organized in the same spirit as the civil service. The regular courts are divided into civil and criminal, and minor offenses are judged by nonprofessional magistrates. Judges, who are mostly graduates of "public" schools and Oxbridge,[39] are chosen from the elite of the legal profession, the barristers (those entitled to make pleas at the bar of the court). They are nonpolitically appointed by the prime minister or the Lord Chancellor (head of the legal branch and generally a barrister), act in isolation from national political life, and are removable only by Parliament (in practice, this never happens). The House of Lords, acting through nine specially appointed Law Lords, is a seldom-used court of last resort, over which the Lord Chancellor presides. The auditor-general is a semijudicial officer who investigates official accounts and whose independence is protected by tenure.

In conformity with British tradition, the courts pay much attention to precedent and to finding what the law has been in practice. In doing so, over the centuries they have created what is called *common law*, in contrast to the code-based civil law of continental Europe. However, all enactments of Parliament

---

[38]Max Beloff and Gillian Peale, *The Government of the United Kingdom: Political Authority in a Changing Society* (New York: Norton, 1980), p. 87.

[39]Sampson, *Changing Anatomy of Britain*, p. 157.

are equally valid for British courts. The courts may find administrative actions or regulations *ultra vires,* or beyond the powers conferred by the law under which they were taken, but they never find a law unconstitutional in the manner of American courts. Thus the courts have secondary political importance and do little for basic rights, which depend on the common sense of propriety and the disinclination of the government and Parliament to infringe on deeply held values. Also British judges, unlike American, do not make new law and do not create new obligations by reinterpreting the constitution.

The Crown

As warranted by its historical origins, the British executive acts in the name of the monarch and is called the Crown. Nearly all actions of the Crown—that is, measures adopted by the prime minister, cabinet, and governmental departments and agencies— are taken under the authorization of laws of Parliament. The government also possesses powers by prerogative, subject to no parliamentary check beyond the general responsibility of the government to the House of Commons. These include freedom to reorganize the administration in ways for which an American president would have to get the approval of Congress. They also include the making of treaties and the declaration of war.

The institution of the Crown includes the personal office of the reigning monarch, although the monarchy has shrunk to a symbol, a formal headship, nearly all of whose significant acts require the signature of a minister. Since Queen Victoria, royal participation has been almost purely ceremonial. In the nineteenth century, and a few times in this one, when there was no party leader ready to assume the prime ministership, the monarch may have had some discretion in the choice of a prime minister. However, with the regularizing of the election of the Conservative leader in 1965, the likelihood that the monarch will play a significant role in the formation of a new government is slight. The queen still has, however, the right to be consulted and informed about major decisions during a weekly audience with her first minister, and she is free to encourage or warn, just as her minister is free to disregard her advice. Her influence depends on her sagacity and knowledge, which may grow with experience and a familiarity with politics exceeding that of the transitory prime ministers. The principal function of the monarch, however, is to serve as the image of stability at the center of politics, a symbol of neutrality for the British consensus.

The monarch retains some personal discretion in the awarding of honors, although the prime minister decides on most of the names. For the most part, British royalty represents tradition and pageantry, the so-called dignified side of government, as Walter Bagehot put it—a living reminder of the glorious past. Elizabeth II is a somewhat remote personality, and the public infatuation evident at the time of her coronation in 1953 has subsided, but the royal family is popular. An overwhelming majority find the monarchy desirable, a bit of color and steadfastness in a dull and uncertain age as well as a neutral headship of state helping to stabilize the democratic order. Only a few left-Labour voices complain about the expense to the state of the palaces and servants, costing around £20 million per year, including the exemption of the queen's wealth and income from taxation.

The monarchy personifies the aristocratic background of British society and the old deference to social superiors. Even in this age of egalitarian values, the monarch has remained majestic, and the British have not followed the Scandinavian way of the democratic monarchy. If social tensions rise, the future of the House of Windsor cannot be considered assured. On the other hand, the monarch has potential influence; and a new King Charles may conceivably come to play an important role at the center of the British system.

PARLIAMENT

One primary function of Parliament, to make or unmake governments, has today been abdicated to the electorate; it is not necessary to have a vote in the House of Commons to learn who is to head the administration. No government has lost a majority of its own party since 1885, and governments have been defeated in this century only when they rested on a coalition. James Callaghan in 1979 became the first prime minister of the twentieth century to lose a vote of confidence when minor parties deserted him. The British MP is much more obedient than the American member of Congress.

MPs support the government of their party because they subscribe to its goals and because if they did not, they would be considered disloyal and would jeopardize their careers. Their chief hope of advancement is a place in the government. A defeat for the government in Parliament would mean a new election and possible defeat at the polls. If an MP is not cooperative, the central authorities have effective sanctions, including withdrawal of the whip, or exclusion from the party. Because of adverse publicity and reluctance to alienate supporters, party leaders hesitate to take such actions, but there is little impulse to rebellion. MPs are not chosen in the first place for maverick qualities, and only a handful of Labour and no Conservative members have been ostracized since 1945. And the constituency parties, which are more orthodox than the center, will put pressure on the errant member before the question of discipline arises.[40]

Concrete factors contribute to party coherence. MPs vote by marching through separate lobbies, so that a party rebel has to associate physically with the enemy. The layout of the Commons chamber, with the government facing the opposition benches, reinforces the separation of government and opposition parties; it is an overt act to cross the aisle. The fires of rebellion may flare up, as in Labour in the early 1980s; but only the Liberals, who are in fact a party of protest, retain freedom and individualism.

The government can thus count on its majority to follow instructions. The MPs are not sheep, however. Pressure from backbenchers has several times compelled the Thatcher government, despite its large majority, to modify or withdraw proposals.[41] The previous Callaghan government, lacking a secure majority, often saw its bills amended. The government could theoretically ignore the opposition. It does not do so, however, because it does not think in such terms, because breaches of custom are unseemly, and because the majority of today is aware it may become the minority of tomorrow. Both sides are more desirous of preserving the system than of seeking any particular political advantage.[42]

Much is done to preserve propriety and impartiality. The speaker of the Commons is studiously neutral. Mr. Speaker enjoys a large salary and security of office because he is by convention unopposed in his constituency. He presides according to the rule book,

[40]Ivor Jennings, *The British Constitution*, 5th ed. (Cambridge, Eng.: Cambridge University Press, 1960), p. 51.
[41]Beer, *Britain Against Itself*, p. 183.
[42]Regarding relationships and powers, see Jack Harvey, *The British Constitution*, 4th ed. (London: Harvey and Bather, 1977).

applies precedents, tries to keep debate moderate and germane, and assures the opposition a fair share of time. He rarely has difficulty in keeping order. The opposition is officially organized and recognized. The term "His Majesty's Opposition" was first used jokingly, but it has become an essential part of the parliamentary system. The opposition is a countergovernment ready to step into power when the electorate decrees, meanwhile serving as critic and check on those in power. In recognition of his services, the Leader of the Opposition receives a substantial salary beyond the parliamentary stipend. He also has a salaried assistant, the Opposition Chief Whip.

The government allocates the time of the House in consultation with the opposition, which uses more than half of it. A dozen or more whips act as liaison between the government and backbenchers and arrange parliamentary business. Debate is rather informal, because members speak from their places on the floor rather than coming to a podium and are not permitted to read their speeches. There are only benches, no individual desks, and MPs hold their papers on their laps. Even so, there is room for only about 450 of the 650 members (including 19 women in 1982). The small chamber was rebuilt unaltered after World War II, not only from respect for tradition, but also because of a feeling that its cramped layout has something to do with British democracy.[43]

Private members, those not holding office, are hardly legislators. Only about a third of the nonministerial MPs have their own small offices; others share. Unlike U.S. senators, MPs have meager staffs, and they are paid less than half as much as members of Congress (in 1983 the equivalent of approximately $24,000). Sessions, however, are longer; the House of Commons sits approximately 160 days per year. Most Conservative MPs have an outside income; most Labour MPs do not.[44] Nearly all statutes originate with the government, and it is taken for granted that they will pass essentially unchanged if the cabinet really desires. However, there is serious debate for the record and for the benefit of the country, and the government will not introduce any bill its backbenchers are not prepared to support. Debate on principles of the bill takes place on the second reading; if talk stretches out, set periods of time may be allocated to parts of the bill (the "guillotine"), and there may be cloture after the Speaker finds that all opinions have been heard. Filibustering in the manner of the U.S. Senate is impossible because of the requirement of germaneness. In debate on the budget, the opposition picks certain sections for criticism by moving a decrease of the amounts proposed. Only a minister is permitted to propose an increase. There are also other opportunities for the opposition to make itself heard. For example, after the queen's speech, in which the government sets forth its program at the beginning of a session of Parliament, the opposition has several days to attack it.

The committee system, a major source of strength of the U.S. Congress, is relatively feeble. There have been about eight standing committees of twenty to fifty members, the parties being represented according to their strength in the House. In 1979 the new Conservative government established fourteen specialized committees, each to oversee a government department, and provided them with small professional staffs. There have been select committees to investigate certain topics, but they can inquire only as

---

[43]On the work of Parliament see, for example, Mackintosh, *Government and Politics of Britain*, chap. 10.

[44]For backgrounds, see Colin Mellors, *The British MP: A Socio-Economic Study of the House of Commons* (Westmead, Eng.: Saxon House, 1978).

deeply as the government desires. Policy committees of the Conservative and Labour parties, in which members can express their views privately and freely, fill some of the gap, but Parliament does not play the investigative role of the U.S. Congress.

Congress, on the other hand, has no institution corresponding to parliamentary questioning. MPs submit questions in writing in advance to various departments on behalf of constituents. They are printed on the order paper, and the ministers' response to them is the first item of daily business. If not satisfed, the MP can raise supplementary oral questions. The Prime Minister personally submits to questioning with some frequency. Ordinarily, the purpose is less to elicit information than to make a point, and questions are usually evadable. But some 30,000 questions posed yearly[45] help to keep the bureaucracy alert, for no bureaucrat wants misdeeds exposed on the floor of Parliament. There is also a sort of British ombudsman, the Parliamentary Commissioner for Administration, who receives complaints of administrative arbitrariness submitted through MPs. However, the Parliamentary Commissioner has small powers and has achieved little.[46] In addition, MPs put in a word on behalf of constituents to government agencies; running such errands occupies a considerable part of their time.

MPs can at least congratulate themselves on standing far above members of the House of Lords. This chamber was once the more powerful, and to this day the Queen opens Parliament with her speech there. But the power of the purse early gave superiority to the Commons, and the convention was set in the seventeenth century that the Lords should not interfere with financial measures. It was established in 1712 that the monarch could create additional peers as necessary to secure a majority for any desired measure. The threat was used to pass the Great Reform of 1832 and in 1910 and 1911, to pass first a land tax to which the House of Lords violently objected (thereby violating convention), and then to reduce the powers of the Lords, leaving them only a suspensive veto of legislation and almost stripping them of power over the budget. They have some negative influence, however, because governments wish to avoid a flap in their House.

The present House of Lords consists of some 809 hereditary peers, a few archbishops, nine law lords, 26 bishops, and over 300 life peers. It is remarkable that such an unrepresentative aristocratic body should continue to play any role in British politics, especially since Labour governments have been in a position to abolish it (its membership is at least 90 percent Conservative). In fact, however, it has regained a little prestige since the reform of 1958 admitted women to its ranks and established life peerages.

Life peerages are used to reward distinguished careers, especially in government. Since few of the hereditary peers attend sessions, despite a modest per diem, the Lords have become tolerably representative of the distinguished personages of the nation. They become gradually more so, as hereditary peerages die out and no new ones are created. No real reform of the House of Lords, such as some form of election, is possible because the Commons does not wish a strong rival.

The House of Lords is sufficiently useful as a working body to justify its existence. It virtually never uses its theoretical right to hold bills up for a year (money bills for a month), even when it dislikes them. It provides an opportunity for revision and noncontroversial amendments, usually at gov-

[45]Nevil Johnson, *In Search of the Constitution: Reflections on State and Society in Britain* (Oxford, Eng.: Pergamon Press, 1977), p. 49.
[46]Mackintosh, *Government and Politics of Britain*, p. 120.

ernment request or with government consent; to abolish it would burden the Commons.[47] It passes a few useful private bills, and it carries on unhurried and occasionally interesting debates. But now that titles can be renounced, an ambitious and talented lord will certainly try to get into the Commons.

From all this it may appear that Parliament is rather unimportant and that the government, assured of its majority, does not need to pay much attention to it. The harmony of the executive and legislature in cabinet government comes at the price of subordination of the legislature. The House of Commons does not make or unmake governments, its role in legislation is limited, and its ability to control is slight. The members lack information about government operations and have inadequate means of informing themselves. The Commons has abdicated control of appropriations to the Treasury. The government has expanded much beyond the private member's ability to follow, and the committees lack support and powers. The media, especially television draw attention away from it, the unions increasingly control Labour MPs, and some decisions are removed to the European parliament in Brussels.

Yet ministers spend about a quarter of their time in Parliament, as much as in their departments;[48] and the Commons sits more than the legislature of any other major country.[49] It is an important forum of opinion, and it keeps the cabinet on the defensive, constantly forced to justify its actions. Not governments but reputations are made in it; it is the channel to high political position. Abilities are demonstrated there, to the country and to other MPs. It is the center of people who count.

THE BRITISH MALAISE

The Decline

Britain's last successful imperial drive was in the Sudan in the closing years of the nineteenth century; the later war against the Boers of South Africa was a moral failure. Britain was still the world's financial center, but it had fallen industrially behind Germany and the United States by the beginning of this century.

Since then, there has been some sense of decay, of decline of institutions and power in relation to newly rising powers. After World War I, the once sacred pound sterling crumbled, and Britain suffered severe, chronic unemployment that reached 22 percent in 1932. Per capita income grew only 5 percent from 1910 to 1932; that is, the depression brought it down virtually to prewar levels. In the face of the Nazi threat, Britain was irresolute, mobilizing effectively (and heroically) only under the shock of the defeat of France and the threat of invasion in 1940.

After World War II, Britain lived briefly in the aura of victory, but it became apparent in the 1960s and 1970s that the nation was suffering a sort of wasting disease. The leader of nineteenth-century industrialization marked time while competitors advanced briskly into the technological age. The British share of world trade declined continually; in 1955, Britain had one-fifth of developed country exports; in 1977, only one-tenth.[50] In 1939, the British standard of living was second in the world to the American and well above that of continental Europe; by 1978, it was less than two-thirds that of Germany and other Western European countries. Real income has hardly increased since 1970, and eighteen countries have sur-

[47]Stacey, *British Government*, p. 78.
[48]Beer, *The British Political System*, p. 11.
[49]Johnson, *In Search of the Constitution*, p. 54.

[50]Robin Morris, "Is Britain an Awful Warning to America?" *New Republic*, September 17, 1977, p. 24.

passed Britain in per capita product. The productivity of British labor is only a fraction of that of leading industrial powers, and British unions are notoriously strike-prone, given to featherbedding and jurisdictional disputes. Much of British industry is inefficient and obsolete.

Much of the failure is of will. In 1974, when electrical and coal strikes put Britain on a three-day work week, production declined only 6 percent;[51] that is, productivity rose under pressure by more than 50 percent. The blame for inefficiency is commonly laid on strike-happy unions, inept managers, and state interference; but Britain is generally not geared for productivity. Labor and management seem indifferent if not opposed to innovation, and security is more valued than income. The "acquisitive society" is rejected, and there is an atmosphere of skepticism about the value of individual ability and achievement. Business is generally not high class. The stimulus of competition is deplored, and genteel leisure is much prized—although not much effort is made to save labor by improved machinery. Some people would eliminate all selection by ability from the state school system. Of all the advanced Western states, Britain has the smallest proportion of its young people in secondary and higher education, and of these the smallest percentage in science and technology. The education of the gentleman-amateur is traditional in Britain, but the desire for technical education has declined in recent years, to the extent that many schools continue to function only because they are filled with foreigners drawn by the old British reputation. The prestige of engineers is comparable to that of butlers.

Since 1964, when Almond and Verba

found the United States and Britain to have the best "civic culture"[52] for a stable democratic system, there have been signs of political decay. British institutions are no longer sacrosanct, and the government no longer effectively unites the people. Since 1964 the House of Commons has registered dissatisfaction by appointing a committee every year to reexamine its procedures—a measure previously taken only at very long intervals. By most European standards, British parties are poorly organized and equipped, and they do little to enlighten the electorate.[53] Interest in national and local politics seems to have declined. Violence has increased; riots have become almost as customary as sporting matches. British crime rates, once low like Japanese, have risen to rival the American. The British are well aware of their failure to keep pace with the world; there is a pervasive discontent, evident in the desire of a large part of Britain's young people to leave their native land.

Classes and Parties

A basic reason for the British ailment seems to be strong democratic egalitarianism joined with marked traditional class differences and consciousness of status. The welfare state has not abolished class differences in psychology, occupation, and prospects. Aristocrats continue to enjoy luxury limousines, butlers, and elaborate entertainments; the poor continue half to envy, half to respect them, although the worst poverty has been eliminated and factory workers can own their cars and homes. There is considerable social mobility—the two recent Conservative leaders, Heath and Thatcher, have both come up from humble backgrounds—and this has long

---

[51]Bernard D. Nossiter, *Britain: A Future that Works* (Boston: Houghton Mifflin, 1978), p. 74.

[52]Gabriel Almond and Sidney Verba, *The Civic Culture* (Boston: Little, Brown, 1965).
[53]Johnson, *In Search of the Constitution*, p. 167.

been the case. But modern Britain takes class very seriously, and much is made of marks of distinction, such as accent and diction. Industrial managers are preoccupied not only with production but also with status. It is claimed that German managers of branches in England are much more successful in labor relations because they are more willing to treat their workers as human.[54] An inadequate and lofty British managerial class deals with a militant and alienated laboring class.[55]

Britain at the same time is less free and democratic than it might be. The British press is much more constrained than the American, for example, both by libel laws and the Official Secrets Acts of 1911 and subsequent years, under which the workings and information of the government are screened from scrutiny. The British press is much more supine than the American in accepting restrictions placed on it by the state.[56]

There seems to be no great urge for popular participation in government beyond the ballot cast once every several years. Neither party makes much pretense of representing its members or electors, which may explain the fact that membership in both parties has declined since 1953. The almost autocratic party leaders are chosen by a narrow group, subject to the need to have a person who can win an election against the other leader. More important, however, is the fact that the governing parties in Britain are exceptional among industrial countries in being class-based. The confrontation of parties is hence not far from a confrontation of classes, and the identification of parties with classes makes social restructuring difficult. An adversary relationship, with opposition for the sake of opposition, is built into the British party system.

The Conservative Party remains tied to upper-class leadership and outlook. Although it has tried with some success to appeal to working-class voters, no movement within it has ever been suspected of populist inclinations. It has never tried to forge links with trade unions or to form Conservatively oriented unions in the manner of Christian-Democratic parties on the Continent. The mere fact of a Conservative government seems to mean a duel with the trade unions, speaking for the workers;[57] and almost any economic issue takes on a political and class meaning. Virtually any measure the Conservatives may propose for the reordering of industrial relations is suspected as an attack on the working class or the unions.

The Conservative Party is less class-bound than Labour, however, and draws votes from a broader spectrum. Much of the permanence of the upper-class orientation of Conservatism may be a reaction to the fixed working-class orientation of Labour. The trade unions control the Labour party machinery through their domination of the national conference, the National Executive Committee, and central party finances. An unknown number of constituency parties also depend on union financing. Such subjection of a major party to a single set of economic organizations is unique.

It can hardly be called democratic. It does not make Labour really representative of working people, because more than half are nonunionized and only about half of the unionized are affiliated with the party. Worse, Labour is responsible not to the workers but to the union leadership, which is usually elected by a small fraction, sometimes as few

[54]*Der Spiegel*, August 1, 1977.
[55]Morris, "Is Britain an Awful Warning to America?" p. 28.
[56]Nossiter, *Britain*, pp. 217–218.

[57]Haseler, *The Death of British Democracy*, (London: Paul Elek, 1976), p. 176.

as 5 percent, of union members. Union officials cast huge bloc votes on behalf of their members in ways that many of them certainly would not prefer.

The structure of the Labour Party decrees a fixed program, condemns it to a certain sterility, and implies many economic, or uneconomic, policies. It is impossible to give up nationalized industries, no matter how wasteful, or to refuse help to failing industries, because jobs are at stake. The class division of society is in the background of all political questions, and almost any dispute may become a matter of principle. The result is immobility and inefficiency. Not surprisingly, the most efficient sectors of the British economy are agriculture and banking, both of which are little affected by unionization.

Change may be underway, however. It is not likely that Britain is immune to the homogenization that modernization generally produces in industrial societies. In recent years the British have tended to pay less attention to accent and other marks of social distinction; the young in particular are apt to be indifferent.[58] It may be that class differences are eroding.[59] The fact that the Communist Party can garner hardly any votes is strong evidence that Britain is not really divided in the manner of France and Italy, where communism has a far broader appeal. The percentage of income going to the top 1 percent of the population dropped from 11.7 percent before World War II to 4 percent by 1973;[60] attitudes eventually change to reflect this egalitarian reality. Britain is, like other advanced nations, becoming more middle class, with a growing sense of self-worth. From 1974 to 1979 the parties made remarkable progress in breaking away from class patterns: The Tories increased their

share of the working-class vote by twelve to fifteen points, and Labour improved its showing among the middle class by five points.[61] In the 1983 election, Labour retained its hold only among unskilled workers.

CONCLUSIONS

Britain led the way in the Industrial Revolution and in the application of science, or systematic reason, to the production of wealth. It has also been the prime exponent of democratic political institutions from the seventeenth century. It pioneered such institutions as trial by jury, habeas corpus, the nonpolitical judiciary, and the impartial civil service. Britain has stood for the idea of fair play, an uncommon thing in the political world. It is typically British that the leader of the opposition is paid a salary to oppose the ruling party. All over the world, Britain has come to mean parliamentary government representative of the whole people.

Britain was for well over a century the most advanced industrial country and for generations the strongest, at least on the seas, despite its relatively small size. The British political mission spread around the world, directly in the empire that held over a quarter of humanity, indirectly by the example of the power that seemed to combine riches, strength, and political virtue. Britain thus had an extraordinary role in history, and its people have justly taken pride in it. Yet success has its price. Britain, unlike France, Germany, and Japan, has not been compelled to undertake major political change.

The most burdensome of the outdated institutions that history has bequeathed to modern Britain is the structure of the two parties that monopolize the government. The

[58]Neale, *The British Economy*, pp. 21–23.
[59]Beer, *Britain Against Itself*, chap. 3.
[60]Nossiter, *Britain* p. 57.

[61]Beer, *Britain Against Itself*, p. 83.

leadership of the Conservative Party remains oligarchic, without responsibility to the rank and file or to the voters except for the need to win elections. It is hence difficult for the Conservatives not to be in some degree defensive of aristocratic privilege. The Labour Party, on the other hand, is dominated by organizations with a vested interest in class conflict. The union-dominated party was appropriate for a premodern society, with strong class divisions and built-in confrontation of owners and workers; but it is now obsolete.

The costs have been large in terms of both hindrances to productivity and loss of civility in British life. Yet adaptations and modernizations are always possible in the loose, pluralistic society. In 1973, despite the reluctance of the Labour party, Britain set aside secular pride to enter the European Common Market. In 1981, with the defection of the Social Democrats from Labour, the party system may have entered a period of flux; and the unions may reconsider the desirability of tying themselves to a single political organization. There seems to be something of a new entrepreneurial spirit and desire to change to keep Britain from falling farther behind in the competitive world, along with a revival of national feeling stimulated by the Falklands triumph. In any event, the means for change are at hand in the ancient but always flexible British political institutions.

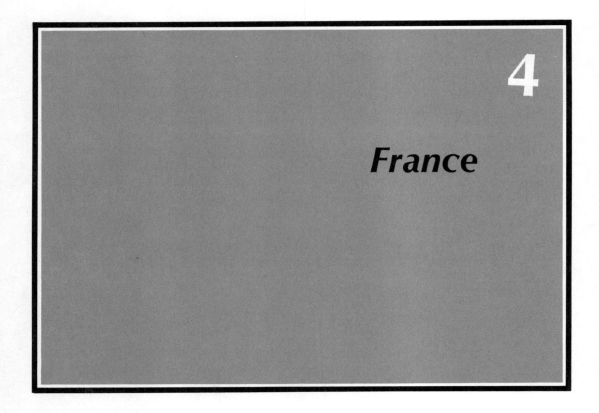

4

France

Like Britain, France is one of the nuclear nation-states of the historic West and a traditional rampart of democracy. The two nations have been leaders in the development of modern civilization and the expansion of Europe. Before postwar decolonization, the French empire was second only to the British; and France still has extensive overseas links, especially in Africa. In many ways, however, the political backgrounds of the two are opposite. Britain has no written constitution; France, since the revolution of 1789, has had thirteen: three monarchic, two dictatorial, three imperial, and five republican. Seven of these came out of the turbulence following the revolution and subsequent wars, but there were new republican constitutions in 1875, 1946, and 1958. Institutional discontinuity has been as marked in France as continuity has been in Britain. The marvel

of the Fifth Republic is that it has outlasted its founder, Charles de Gaulle.

There has also been a deep difference in political culture. French democratic tradition is more ideological and less pragmatic than the British, based more on theory and less on pluralistic reality, and concerned more with equality and less with freedom. The French have shown themselves fonder of revolutionary rhetoric, on the one hand, or attached to conservative values, on the other. French society is divided; one sector is revolutionary, egalitarian, and anticlerical; the other is traditional, aristocratic, and Catholic.[1] Changes have been slow to find acceptance, and only in the past generation can it

[1]Eric A. Nordlinger, " Democratic Stability and Mutability," in Arend Lijphart, ed., *Politics in Europe: Comparisons and Interpretations* (Englewood Cliffs, N.J.: Prentice-Hall, 1969), p. 163.

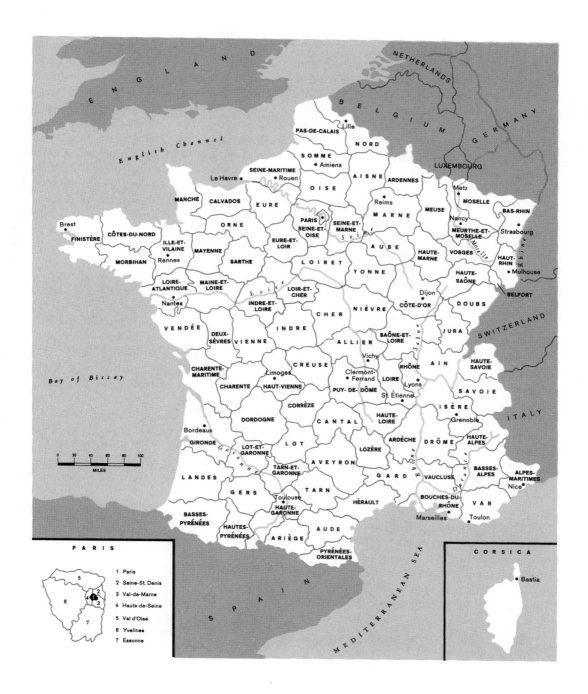

ENGLAND

NETHERLANDS

BELGIUM

GERMANY

LUXEMBOURG

English Channel

PAS-DE-CALAIS • Lille

NORD

SOMME
• Amiens

SEINE-MARITIME
Le Havre • • Rouen

AISNE ARDENNES

Metz •

MOSELLE

MANCHE CALVADOS EURE OISE

Reims •

MARNE MEUSE

BAS-RHIN

Nancy •

MEURTHE-ET-MOSELLE

Strasbourg •

Brest •

CÔTES-DU-NORD

ORNE

PARIS
SEINE-ET-OISE

SEINE-ET-MARNE

Seine

AUBE

HAUTE-MARNE

VOSGES

HAUT-RHIN
• Mulhouse

FINISTÈRE

ILLE-ET-VILAINE

MAYENNE

EURE-ET-LOIR

LOIRET

YONNE

HAUTE-SAÔNE

BELFORT

MORBIHAN
• Rennes

SARTHE

LOIRE-ATLANTIQUE

MAINE-ET-LOIRE

Loire

LOIR-ET-CHER

CÔTE-D'OR

Dijon •

DOUBS

SWITZERLAND

• Nantes

INDRE-ET-LOIRE

CHER

NIÈVRE

Saône

JURA

VENDÉE

DEUX-SÈVRES

VIENNE

INDRE

ALLIER

SAÔNE-ET-LOIRE

AIN

HAUTE-SAVOIE

Bay of Biscay

CHARENTE-MARITIME

CREUSE

Vichy •

RHÔNE

CHARENTE

HAUT-VIENNE
• Limoges

Clermont-Ferrand •

LOIRE
Lyons •

SAVOIE

PUY-DE-DÔME

St. Étienne •

ISÈRE

CORRÈZE

Grenoble •

ITALY

Bordeaux •

DORDOGNE

CANTAL

HAUTE-LOIRE

DRÔME

HAUTE-ALPES

GIRONDE

LOT-ET-GARONNE

LOT

LOZÈRE

ARDÈCHE

Rhône

BASSES-ALPES

ALPES-MARITIMES
Nice •

LANDES

TARN-ET-GARONNE

AVEYRON

GARD

VAUCLUSE

Durance

GERS

Toulouse •

TARN

HÉRAULT

BOUCHES-DU-RHÔNE

VAR

HAUTE-GARONNE

Marseilles •

• Toulon

BASSES-PYRÉNÉES

HAUTES-PYRÉNÉES

ARIÈGE

AUDE

SPAIN

PYRÉNÉES-ORIENTALES

MEDITERRANEAN SEA

Garonne

0 20 40 60 80 100
MILES

PARIS

1 Paris
2 Seine-St. Denis
3 Val-de-Marne
4 Hauts-de-Seine
5 Val d'Oise
6 Yvelines
7 Essonne

CORSICA

• Bastia

be said that the monarchists have finally given up. France remains the most unequal of major industrial nations.[2]

France invented the Left-Right antithesis. Yet both leftists and rightists have tended to look to a strong leader, rather than to the good sense of the people, to bring about reforms—de Gaulle was only the most recent example. It has taken for granted that the state manages. The French from birth are much more closely under the tutelage of the bureaucracy than Britons or Americans; it sees that they are properly cared for in the crib, educates, qualifies, certifies, fixes wages, and sets retirement conditions.[3] Except for some Church schools, nearly all education at all levels is controlled from Paris. Since the state is responsible, there is little private charity.

As former President Valery Giscard d'Estaing has written, France is weighted down under the centralization of centuries.[4] Although France is more than twice as large as Britain, with approximately the same population, it is as concentrated on Paris as Britain is on London. Italy and Germany have numerous important centers; France outside of Paris is somewhat neglected, economically and culturally. Local institutions and local government play a minor part. This is not because of lack of natural diversity. The various regions are quite different, but they have been politically welded, or compressed. To this day, France has far less patience with movements for autonomy in Brittany, Alsace, the Basque provinces, or Corsica than Britain has for the Welsh or Scots.

These differences are broadly attributable to geography and history. Continuity has been easy for Britain because it has not been invaded—and never seriously defeated—since 1066. But France has often been a battlefield, and new constitutions in 1814, 1871–75, 1940, 1946, and 1958 resulted directly from unsuccessful wars. The military played a very small part in British political development because there was no need for a standing army. The French army has intervened repeatedly in politics since Napoleonic times. The disobedience of French forces in Algeria brought de Gaulle back to the presidency in 1958 and caused crises in the next several years. As late as 1968, de Gaulle went to the army for support in dealing with nationwide unrest. France was much troubled by divisions relating to foreign affairs until recently, especially relations with the Soviet Union and the United States.

To Anglo-Saxon students of government, France has seemed paradoxical. Its ambivalence and mixture of libertarianism and authoritarianism, individualism and submissiveness, seem slightly contrary to good sense. Yet the essence of the French peculiarity, the tension between a traditional, authoritarian heritage and the desire for modernization, freedom, and democracy, is much more widespread in the world than the relatively integrated British political culture. Similar or stronger tensions have marked the history of Germany, Russia, prewar Japan, and most countries of the present-day world.

THE POLITICAL HERITAGE

Because of accidents of history, France emerged early as a strong nation from the splintered Europe of the Middle Ages. However, it was effectively unified only in the seventeenth century after the defeat of an anticentralist uprising called the *Fronde*. Under Louis XIV, the Sun King (reigned

---

[2]For a social study, see Theodore Zeldin, *The French* (New York: Pantheon, 1983).

[3]Angelo Codevilla, *Modern France* (La Salle, Ill.: Open Court, 1974), pp. 17–18.

[4]Valery Giscard d'Estaing, *La democratie française* (Paris: Foyard, 1976), p. 97.

1643–1715), France became "La grande nation," by far the strongest of the powers; its court was the model for lesser princes and its capital was the zenith of civilization. Louis made himself theoretically absolute and center of a strong, unified state. He brought the nobles to Versailles as his courtiers and servants, deprived the provinces of most of their autonomy, cultivated the arts, built up the bureaucratic apparatus, waged war for provinces and glory, and gave the French an undying pride in their nation.

The overcontrolled state decayed, however, in the eighteenth century, as the swollen upper classes became increasingly parasitic and titles multiplied. The Church discredited itself as the bulwark of the unproductive privileged classes. The middle classes, who did the work and paid the taxes, along with the growing number of educated persons outside the official establishment, became increasingly restless and frustrated. Democratic-libertarian ideas became popular, in large part as an importation from first England and then America. Montesquieu derived most of his ideas for *The Spirit of the Laws* from John Locke and the British constitution as Montesquieu understood it. Voltaire and other philosophers of the French Enlightenment were fervent admirers of British liberties. Writing under a corrupt and often unpleasant regime, they stated democratic ideals in more abstract and rhetorical terms than Britishers, who took a reasonable degree of freedom for granted.

When the profligacy of the court, the incompetence of the bureaucracy, and the resistance of the nobility to taxation brought the state to bankruptcy, the king (Louis XVI) felt he had to secure consent for new taxes. This meant convoking in 1789 the Estates-General, the old parliamentary body that had not met since 1641. Once summoned, it asserted itself; and deputies, libertarian thinkers, and the Paris mob found the absolutist state was only a hollow shell that crumbled when pressed.

For a few years the revolution deepened, radicalized by wars arising from the effort of European monarchs to come to the aid of their beleaguered brother, by the demands of the peasants for land, and by conflict over the position of the Church. At first the revolutionaries had no idea of doing more than instituting a British-style constitutional monarchy. But in less than four years the King was decapitated and replaced by a republic, and there followed a reign of the guillotine to destroy the aristocrats and "enemies of the nation." There was also an exaltation of rationalism unexampled in previous or subsequent history. Weights and measures were rationalized in the metric system, as were the calendar and timekeeping; one party wanted to establish the worship of the Goddess of Reason. But troubles piled up, revolutionary enthusiasm wore out, the Jacobin terrorists (Robespierre and his allies) were carted off to the scaffold, and a conservative semiauthoritarian Directory was set up. A successful young general, Napoleon Bonaparte, made himself dictator, then emperor. He gave France the glory the kings had dreamed of, an empire that reached almost to Russia. He also completed the centralization begun by the kings and continued by the revolution, presided over the adoption of a law code that became a model for many countries, reformed and strengthened or overstrengthened the administration, and established the principle of "careers open to talents."

When Napoleon overspent French resources by trying to conquer Russia, he was defeated and overthrown. But he committed no gross atrocities, was not the disaster for France that Hitler was for Germany, and left an enduring heritage. In 1814 the victorious coalition restored the monarchy under Louis XVIII, limited by a conservative constitution and a feeble parliament elected by a very narrow electorate. His successor, Charles X (reigned 1824–1830), tried to be a king in the old style. But the French, unwilling to accept complete reversal of the great revolution, replaced him by a prince of another branch of the royal house under a more liberal constitution. King Louis Philippe in turn lost touch with the people and was toppled by a lower-class revolution in 1848.

The Second and Third Republics

The liberal wave of 1848 brought the Second Republic and a popularly elected president. But the French showed nostalgia for pan-European hegemony by electing by a large majority the nephew of the great Napoleon, Louis Napoleon, for no good reason except the name he bore. "Napoleon the Little," as he was called, did not care to be a mere president, so in 1851 he made himself Napoleon III by plebiscite and inaugurated the Second Empire.

Napoleon III tried to emulate his uncle's conquests, and he meddled wherever he saw an opportunity. But he lacked both the opportunities and the talent of Napoleon I. The empire, with a weak and narrowly elected parliament, came under pressure to liberalize itself. It might have evolved toward representative government, but in 1870 Napoleon blundered into a war for which Bismarck's Prussia was much better prepared. The emperor was captured, and his people inaugurated the Third Republic.

In the defeat, the Parisians formed a radical government, the Commune, which Marx adopted as a model for socialism. The Commune was smashed by more conservative provincial France, but it branded into French society the fears and horror of conservatives, whereas the massacre of thousands of communards was proof to generations of work-

ers of the total evil of the bourgeoisie. The constituent assembly held after the crushing of the Commune was largely monarchist, but it set up a republic because adherents of the three different ruling houses could not agree on a candidate for the throne. This provisional Third Republic was based on no proper constitution but on three laws concerning the election of the president (by the parliament), the relationship of prime minister and cabinet to the legislature, and the composition of the Senate.

The Third Republic took its shape from practice. In 1877, President MacMahon dissolved the Chamber of Deputies after it rejected the ministry he desired. When the elections for a new Chamber went strongly against him, he resigned. The idea of the president using his legal powers to dissolve the Chamber in order to solve a political impasse was discredited, never to be revived until the Fifth Republic. Moreover, the deputies, frightened by the experience, thereafter took care to elect unambitious presidents. The presidency became a largely ceremonial office. Its chief duty (besides receiving ambassadors) was to consult after a premier was overthrown in order to pick a successor capable of mustering a majority in the Chamber.

The result was a rather ineffective government that gained France a reputation for immobility. Half a dozen or more parties had significant representation in the dominant lower house of parliament, the Chamber of Deputies. In order to find a majority for a cabinet, it was always necessary to form a coalition, ordinarily at least three parties. But the parties could never agree for very long; having come together on one issue, they would diverge on another a few months later. Moreover, there was no penalty for overthrowing a government; to the contrary, it promised many deputies a chance to earn the lifelong title of ex-minister. Cabinets endured, on the average, only eight months; to last longer was possible only by avoiding action. Instability was much less in reality than is suggested by this figure, because most of the members of a defeated government would return to the new one, and the center parties, especially the Radical-Socialists, (who were neither radical nor socialist) regularly formed a part of the government.

Since no party could hope to form a government or pursue its own program, parties merged into pressure groups. Power fell to the permanent civil service, which provided the necessary continuity of administration through all the ministerial changes and crises and gave the state most of what little direction it had.

The Third Republic was also immobilized by the persistent cleavage between those who wanted to advance the ideals of the revolution of 1789 and those who regretted the sacrifice of national greatness to violence and disorder. Rightists continued to yearn for royal or imperial authority, the true faith and national glory; it was assumed that Catholicism and republicanism were incompatible. The upper classes kept up aristocratic postures, the middle classes feared violence from the growing industrial working classes, and the peasants on their small holdings remained backward and conservative.

Recovery after the defeat of 1870–1871 was rapid, but economic growth was slow up to 1940. France fell behind its neighbors. The country fought well in World War I; thereafter, however, the political system stagnated. The economy vegetated with backward structures. In its incapacity, the parliament resorted to charging the civil service with the details of legislation. Social tensions increased. In the 1930s a Fascist movement grew up, and the Spanish civil war deepened national divisions. France stood half-paralyzed in the face of the Nazi threat. Many conservatives, including military leaders, wanted to fight against not Nazi Germany but the Soviet Union; and the Communists, on Soviet instructions, sabotaged the war effort after the Nazi-Soviet pact of August 1939.

Defeat came in May–June 1940 with merciful rapidity, thanks to which war losses were slight. The National Assembly surrendered full powers to Marshal Henri Pétain, hero of World War I. In the territory not occupied and administered by the Germans (about half of France), Pétain set up an authoritarian regime dedicated to Church, family, and nationalism, trying to save something of the French heritage while conforming to the commands of the German occupiers. The Pétain government at Vichy became more and more subservient, until it collapsed in 1944 with the retreat of German forces. The heritage of the Vichy government was the discrediting of the traditional French Right, which adhered to it in opposition to the Western Allies and the Free French movement headed by General Charles de Gaulle.

The Fourth Republic

A few French officers, led by de Gaulle, refused to accept the surrender of June 1940 and fled to England to fight on. As the war progressed toward victory, de Gaulle's Free French movement became the seed of a new government, while the underground resistance in France gathered strength. With liberation in 1944, they coalesced under the leadership of de Gaulle in a new Fourth Republic. Although for the first fourteen months it was practically a dictatorship, de Gaulle exercised his stewardship toward the establishment of a democracy. A constituent assembly was elected in October 1945.

The war had brought a strong leftward swing. The strongest party in the first postwar assembly was the Communist, which had worked effectively in the resistance because of its traditional organization and dedication; the other leading parties were the Socialists, who had been radicalized, and a semisocialist Catholic party, the Popular Republican Movement (MRP). They came into conflict with de Gaulle, who was basically conservative, and he resigned in January 1946. The draft constitution was defeated by referendum, however. A new constitution was drawn up rather like the first except that a weak second chamber was added. This was ratified by a narrow margin.

The Fourth Republic was much like the Third, and it suffered the same instability. Because of memories of Louis Napoleon and fears of the popularity of de Gaulle, the framers of the constitution provided that not the people but parliament should elect the president, and he was as weak as under the Third Republic for the same reasons. The Assembly was completely dominant. Cabinets resigned whenever they ceased to command a majority. Each ministry was under the surveillance of a committee of the Assembly. A committee was likely to mangle any controversial legislative proposal and use it as an opportunity to force a reshuffle of the cabinet. The best hope to stay in office was to avoid action, and again the civil servants or technocrats were de facto in charge.

The government was fairly effective, however. The war had brought a new unity. Rightist forces were virtually eliminated, and the share of Catholics in the resistance dampened old controversies over Church-state relations. The nation was reinvigorated by its ordeal, and economic recovery was rapid. The old France of peasants, shopkeepers, and small towns became modernized and urbanized; industry (a considerable fraction of which was nationalized) and agriculture were transformed. A welfare state was erected to provide much economic security. The Fourth Republic also achieved reconciliation with Germany and the economic integration of most of Western Europe in first the Coal and Steel Community, then (1957) in the European Economic Community.

The Fourth Republic, however, was weighed down by political burdens. One was the presence of a large Communist party which controlled about a fifth of the popular vote and the same fraction (under proportional representation) of the Assembly. It left the coalition government with the Socialists and MRP, or was expelled from it, in May 1947, when the cold war was pushing France toward alliance with the United States and hostility toward the Soviet Union, to which the French Communist Party showed total loyalty. Thereafter the Communists sabotaged everything that contributed to the Western alliance; any effort to find a majority in the Assembly had to count at the outset on a fifth to a quarter negative votes on the Left, and any effort to topple a government began with the same advantage.

The direct cause of the downfall of the Fourth Republic, however, was the effort to retain as much as possible of the colonial empire, which seemed an essential ingredient of French greatness. Military failure in the world war also made it seem more necessary to vindicate French power by force. France consequently battled vainly for seven years in Indochina until forced to withdraw in 1954. By then the insurgency in Algeria had become critical, and it was impossible simply to write off nearby Algeria like distant Vietnam. Algeria had been French since the 1830s, it was organized as an integral part of France, and its population included some 1.5 million non-Muslims of European origin.

The Fourth Republic could neither pacify Algeria nor make peace. The country grew ever sicker of the war, while the military leadership, embittered by defeats in the world war, in Vietnam, and in the Suez affair (1956), blamed the civilian government for its failure. In May 1958, when army units stationed in Algeria threatened to invade France, President Réné Coty dismissed Premier Pierre Pflimlin and named Charles de Gaulle to save the nation.

The Fifth Republic

De Gaulle was brought to power to find a way out of a war the generals were unable to win but were determined not to lose. He was accepted by the politicans in Paris because he was the only person who seemed capable of controlling the armed forces; he was accepted by the armed forces because they thought that he would support the pacification of Algeria. He took the job on condition that he have power to rule by decree for six months. He used this period for the formulation of a new constitution, largely drawn up by Michel Débré, member of parliament, lawyer, and political scientist. Whatever the qualifications of the drafters, the document seems carelessly drawn up, with repetitions (for example, the duty of the Constitutional Council to examine "organic" laws is stated twice) and contradictions (for example, the president by article 16 declares an emergency, but the Council of Ministers by article 36 decrees martial law; the president is commander of the armed forces, but the premier is charged with administering them). It was approved in a plebiscite by a majority much greater than that received by the constitution of the Fourth Republic.

The new constitution was designed to institutionalize the leadership of de Gaulle with democratic checks, providing stable yet representative government where the party system offered no basis for stability.[5] De Gaulle hated parliament and political parties; un-

[5]Stanley Hoffman, "Sucession and Stability in France," in Lijphart, *Politics in Europe*, p. 151.

able to abolish them, he severely limited their power. The president was given primary place, with authority to name the premier and to dissolve the Assembly. He was to be elected by a college of over 80,000 electors, mostly local councilors, in the conviction that this form of indirect election would favor a conservative. He was allowed the seven-year term of the presidents of the Third and Fourth Republics, which was more appropriate for a weak than a strong chief executive. Like all French presidents, he was permitted indefinite reelection, which might mean having a strong president in office for an excessive time. Among other powers, he was authorized to govern by decree in case of an emergency determined by himself after nonbinding consultations—a provision copied from the constitution of Weimar Germany despite its having led directly to the dictatorship of Hitler.

It was, in sum, a unique combination of presidential and parliamentary systems with accent on the former. Partly because of constitutional powers, partly because of the dominant personality and prestige of de Gaulle, the presidency served as the motor of government. During his period of office, 1958–1969, politics revolved more around de Gaulle himself than issues or ideology. Impatient with party politics, he disregarded even the Gaullist party formed to support him. Impatient with administration and economics, de Gaulle took foreign and domestic policy as his special province. First he had to bring the army to accept the independence of Algeria; this was achieved, at considerable risk to the life of the president, by July 1962. De Gaulle also proceeded to set free France's other African colonies. Unburdened of empire, he sought to restore French pride by staking out an independent role in world affairs. This meant stress on French national destiny, in opposition mostly to the "Anglo-Saxons," against whom he carried some resentment from wartime slights. For this reason, de Gaulle blocked the entry of Britain into the Common Market, for which he had little enthusiasm. He also withdrew France from the NATO military structure, although not from the alliance. He established closer relations with the Soviet Union than other Western powers, and he tried to make France a "Third Force" leader between East and West.

De Gaulle several times disregarded provisions of his constitution, especially in relations with the not always subservient Assembly. For example, in 1960 he refused to convoke a special session of parliament despite the fact that a majority of members requested it, as prescribed. In 1962, when the Assembly censured his premier, Georges Pompidou, de Gaulle instead of dismissing the premier dissolved the Assembly. De Gaulle liked to go over the Assembly to the people by referendum, if necessary without securing the approval of parliament, as required by the constitution.

This breach occurred in 1962, when de Gaulle undertook to amend the constitution to have the president elected by direct popular vote, because the local notables who made up the presidential electoral college turned out to be less friendly to him than he had expected. The Assembly did not want to strengthen the presidency by direct election, nor did the Senate, elected by approximately the same people who composed the electoral college for the presidency. De Gaulle proceeded on his own authority to hold a referendum, which approved direct election by a large majority.

In the presidential election of 1965, de Gaulle failed to secure a majority in the first round and was forced into a runoff with Socialist candidate François Mitterrand. The aging leader had lost his aura, and his second term was less successful than the first.

A sign of the decay of Gaullism was the odd quasi-revolution of 1968, when a student protest joined by factory and white-collar workers took control of the streets and seemed for a time about to bring down the government. It was an unexpected, almost leaderless, unorganized outburst, in which there erupted a surprising amount of general discontent. De Gaulle, having assured himself of the support of the army, cut it off by calling new elections, which ironically gave the Gaullists and their allies the largest parliamentary majority of French history.

The Heirs of de Gaulle

However, a year later, when de Gaulle staked his political life on a referendum to replace the already weak Senate (with which the Gaullists were chronically quarreling) with a weaker body, it was defeated, and he resigned. In the subsequent presidential election, the Gaullist candidate was Georges Pompidou, who had been premier from 1962 to 1968, longer than any Frenchman since Louis XIV's Colbert. He was elected because the Communists and the Soviet Union thought well of the Gaullist foreign policy and preferred a rightist opponent to a moderate who might draw part of the Left.

Surprisingly, Pompidou was as masterful a president as de Gaulle. He promoted no striking new policies, but he proved that the Fifth Republic could function without its founder. Less concerned than de Gaulle with glory and less impressed with France's special place in the world, he cooperated more with Britain and the United States, permitted the entry of the former into the European Economic Community, and downplayed relations with the Soviet Union. His administration was one of transition from personalism to ordinary politics.

Before dying of cancer in 1974, Pompidou made arrangements for his finance minister, Valery Giscard d'Estaing, to succeed him,[6] or at least made it difficult for the Gaullists to agree on another candidate. In the first round, the Socialist Mitterrand led, but in the runoff, Gaullist support enabled Giscard narrowly to defeat Mitterrand, and a crisis of leftist president against centrist-rightist Assembly was avoided.

Giscard, a product of a civil service aristocracy and a graduate of the elite École Nationale d'Administration (ENA), was the model technocrat with little political experience. Although a supporter of de Gaulle, he led his own group of Independent Republicans. He started as a rather democratic leader, as he affirmed the position of the president as helmsman of the state in the manner of his predecessors, but offered more latitude to parliament and other bodies. He sought to reduce class conflict and desired to make economic policy by consultation, not only with business interests, but also with labor and farmers. He secured a lowering of the voting age to eighteen, carried forward the educational reforms begun after the events of 1968, reformed the prison system, and broadened women's rights. He liberalized divorce and legalized contraception and abortion. He went beyond Pompidou in turning from Gaullist nationalism to cooperation with the United States and the Western alliance.

Giscard's first cabinet had five Gaullists, three Independent Republicans, three Centrists, and four nonpartisan technocrats. Jacques Chirac received the premiership as a reward for having supported Giscard for the presidency. But Chirac's Gaullist party was unhappy with many of Giscard's reform measures, especially those concerning family affairs, and Chirac sought a wider role for the premier, especially in economic policy, than the President was prepared to allow.

Hence Chirac was replaced in August 1976 by an apolitical former professor of economics, Raymond Barre, who represented no challenge to presidential supremacy. Chirac, who acquired a political base by election as mayor of Paris, dedicated himself to building up the neo-Gaullist party in opposition to both Giscard and the Socialist-Communist Left.

In view of the economic recession and the unpopularity of Barre's policy of retrenchment and austerity, it was widely believed in the year before the March 1978 elections that the Socialist-Communist alliance would win a parliamentary majority and inaugurate a program of extensive nationalization and social and economic reforms, a belief strong enough virtually to halt private investment for many months. However, the Communists turned on their Socialist allies for reasons of their own strategy. The result was a surprising defeat of the leftist forces and a victory for the conservatives, in which the Giscardians came out rather better than the Gaullists.

In his later years in office, Giscard became increasingly secluded, lofty, and even monarchic. Whereas early in his term he made a point of dining with ordinary citizens, later on he had himself served first at state banquets, where no one could sit opposite him. He concentrated power even more than his predecessors, tried to prevent criticism of himself, and used the state-controlled media for his own benefit. He undertook no more social reforms. However, he and Barre tried to reduce state interference in the economy, reduced or eliminated subsidies to unprofitable enterprises, freed prices, and pushed the modernization of industry. Political realities, nonetheless, compelled him to intervene to save jobs in the threatened steel industry. Unemployment crept up, economic growth flagged, and the leftist parties gained strength.

[6]Edwar W. Fox, "France on the Ebb Tide," *Current History* 68 (March 1975), p. 106.

Socialism in Power

By the time of the presidential elections of 1981, desire for change was strong. The Left was sharply divided. The split of 1977–1978 had not been healed, and Socialists and Communists attacked one another bitterly. The Communists apparently (with the support of Moscow) preferred Giscard to win over the Socialist candidate, François Mitterrand. The rightist parties were also at odds, as the Gaullists led by Jacques Chirac nursed their grievances against the Giscardians.

In the first round, the rightist parties led by a small margin; Giscard received 28.3 percent of the vote; Chirac, 18.0 percent; and splinters, 3.4 percent; whereas Mitterrand received 25.8 percent; Communist Georges Marchais, 15.3 percent; and splinters, 5.6 percent. In the runoff, Mitterrand had 51.7 percent to 48.2 percent for Giscard.[7] This victory was made possible by the divisions in both Left and Right; the antagonism between Communists and Socialists reduced the fears of the middle-class French that victory for Mitterrand would give the Communists great influence. Yet the Communists followed orders and voted for Mitterrand in the runoff. On the other hand, Chirac seems to have preferred Mitterrand to win, and his followers refused to vote for Giscard.[8]

Mitterrand entered office May 21, and he immediately asked the French to give him a Socialist parliament. In June, they did so, giving the Socialists 37.5 percent on the first ballot, the largest percentage for any party in this century. The Communists, who tried to identify with the leftist wave, received only 16.2 percent. The parties of Chirac and Giscard won 20.8 percent and 19.2 percent, respectively. The outcome, after the second round, was an astounding majority of 271 for the Socialists in the 491-seat Assembly. The Communists were reduced to 44; the rightist parties took 157. Mitterrand consequently had no need for Communist votes. However, he cooperated with them, giving them four minor ministries (of 44) in return for their acceptance of his program and peace in the Communist-dominated labor unions.

Thousands took to the streets to rejoice at the Socialist victory, hoping for a new order after a generation of conservative rule. True to his promises, Mitterrand loosed an avalanche of change. He nationalized a number of unprofitable industries (chemicals, electronics, aerospace, aluminum, textiles, banks), nearly doubling the state sector; he abolished the death penalty and the state security court, cut back on the nuclear program, and lowered the retirement age from sixty-five to sixty. He raised minimum wages and family allowances, while cutting the work week and lengthening vacations. He added 54,000 to the state payroll while raising taxes on businesses and high salaries. His themes were redistribution, reduction of unemployment by sharing jobs, and modernization of the economy through state control and emphasis on high technology, Japanese style. In foreign policy, he took a strong anti-Soviet stand, increasing defense spending—to the embarrassment of the Communists cooperating with his government.

Benefits, however, proved costly, and troubles piled up, compounded by the world recession. Monetized deficits produced inflation, uncertainty led to capital outflow despite controls, and high export prices led to a strongly negative balance of payments and repeated devaluations of the franc. Unemployment failed to drop but kept edging higher. The year 1982 saw the first fall in real incomes since 1945. Mitterrand turned

[7]Neill Nugent, "Strategies of the French Left," in David R. Bill, ed., *Contemporary French Political Parties* (New York: St. Martin's Press, 1982), p. 83.

[8]Frank L. Wilson, *French Political Parties Under the Fifth Republic* (New York: Praeger, 1982), p. 21.

abruptly to austerity to reduce inflation and the foreign exchange deficit; the foreign and interest costs shot up. Wage and price controls were imposed temporarily, and taxes were raised and raised again. By 1983, joy in the streets was replaced by riots, as doctors, pharmacists, students (irked by new rules favoring technical education), farmers (demanding higher support prices), grocers, and travel agents (hurt by a regulation forbidding travelers to take more than 2000 francs, equivalent to $285, out of the country) shouted their middle-class grievances. Local elections of March 1983 gave the Conservative opposition a majority of 53 percent and cost the Socialists and Communists control of dozens of local councils. Jacques Chirac swept all twenty districts of Paris and emerged as chief conservative leader. Mitterrand found himself, like Margaret Thatcher, defying the unions by eliminating jobs in deficit-ridden nationalized industry, selling shares of state enterprises, and hoping for a turnaround in the economy before the next scheduled parliamentary elections in 1986.

THE GOVERNMENT

The French political system, as though expressing the national history, is an amalgam of democracy and elitism, of freedom and authoritarianism. It also uniquely mingles parliamentary and presidential systems in a structure that has thus far functioned much better than expected but has not yet really been tested.

President and Premier

The constitution is vague and contradictory; it makes the president general supervisor and gives him power of arbitration over the government without specifying what this means. It authorizes the president to name the pre-

mier and to preside over the council of ministers, but there is no specific power to remove the premier or members of the cabinet. The president promulgates laws passed by parliament but may ask for their reconsideration; what happens if the parliament reaffirms a law and the president continues to oppose it is not clear, as the case has not arisen. The president has the same power of dissolution that existed but went out of use in the Third and Fourth Republics. However, after a dissolution the new parliament cannot be dissolved for a year, and there would be an impasse if the elections confirmed the position of the dissolved Assembly. The president has discretionary emergency powers to protect the constitutional order. There are no restrictions except that the parliament must meet and the president must undertake "official consultation" with the premier, the presidents of the Assembly and the Senate, and the Constitutional Council. He does not have to follow any advice, and it is unclear how the parliament can restrain him. This article was invoked only once, in connection with the Algerian troubles and an assassination attempt in April 1963. In the real emergency of May 1968 it was not used, probably because de Gaulle did not wish to dignify the crisis. The president is also commander of the armed forces and presides over "the higher councils and committees of national defense."

The constitution states that "the premier shall direct the operation of the government" and "the government shall determine and direct the policy of the nation." Moreover, the president appoints ministers "on the proposal of the premier." Yet presidents so far have governed as they desired, have chosen ministers at their pleasure, and have bypassed the premier and cabinet in directing individual ministries. This usage was continued after de Gaulle because the president, unlike the premier, is directly elected and because the parliamentary majority is for the president, not the premier.[9] Yet the premier has a personal staff several times larger than that of the president. Conflict has thus far been avoided only because of the deference of the premier. The premier is likely to be ousted if he is either unsuccessful or too successful, as were Pompidou and Chaban-Delmar.

The premier and cabinet, named by the president, have several times presented themselves for approval by parliament, but they are not required to do so. Cabinets have tended to reflect fairly closely the political coloration of the Assembly majority. Early cabinets were drawn largely from the civil service, but in order to have ministers capable of working effectively with parliament, the practice grew of naming deputies or former deputies, and recently nearly all ministers have come from parliament. It was intended to separate the ministry from parliament by the device of making ministerial office incompatible with membership in parliament or holding office in a business, professional, or labor organization at the national level, a provision contrary to general parliamentary custom. (Candidates for parliament run with a stand-in, who becomes deputy in case the principal dies or is named minister.) This restriction should reduce the independence of ministers; if they resign or rebel, they become unemployed. However, the incompatibility rule, like various other reforms of the Fifth Republic constitution, has become something of a dead letter, since ex-ministers find ways to return to parliament.[10]

The cabinet is not much of a policy-making body, in contrast to the British cabinet.

Its size—forty-four members in 1983—is too large for effective decision making, and plenary sessions are held mostly for ceremonial functions. There is a secretariat much like the British cabinet secretariat. A dozen or more senior ministers may confer frequently, but the authority of the cabinet or part of it is informal, except for such matters as the enactment of ordinances. The prime minister is not really the boss of the cabinet; on the one hand, the president stands over him; on the other, the finance minister, responsible to the president, can check policy.

The Civil Service

France is much more of an administered society than Britain or the United States, not far from being a bureaucratic republic whose real government is the civil service. Most of the budget, regulatory procedures, application of the laws, formulation of regulations, and to some extent even policy formation are in the hands of the able, well-trained, but somewhat exclusive and caste-like civil service. With parliamentary consent, the civil service itself may initiate major changes, such as reforms of the court system or of social security. It is a respected professional governing corps, a sort of mandarinate.

In the Third and Fourth Republics, the frequent changes of ministers left most powers in the hands of the permanent officials. Not only did a minister and advisor have inadequate time to get to know the business of the department and push long-term policies; the permanent officials knew they would not be around very long and did not have to be taken very seriously. In the frequent intervals of days or weeks between the fall of one government and the formation of another, the officials were left practically to carry on at their discretion. Under the Fifth Republic, ministers remain in place much longer,

[9]Maurice Duverger, *La monarchie républicaine* (Paris: Laffont, 1974), p. 157.

[10]Jack Hayward, *The One and Indivisible French Republic* (London: Weidenfeld & Nicolson, 1973), p. 94.

and they and their staffs (the minister's cabinet) can better guide the apparatus. On the other hand, there is less interference from the more passive parliament, and the technocratic-administrative outlook of the governments has tended to raise the role of the permanent experts.

Somewhat in the manner of the Japanese civil service, many high bureaucrats resign in midcareer to take leadership positions in both private and nationalized enterprises.[11] Graduates of the elite schools preparing for civil service examinations are in demand in business; and transfer to executive positions in industry after some years in official positions is encouraged by the fact that it entails no loss of civil service rank and seniority. Official and business elites are consequently close and work together as in Japan and unlike in Britain and the United States.

Also in the Japanese and contrary to the British and American manner, the civil service is politically involved. Civil servants are free to serve in parliament without loss of status, and many have done so in the Fifth Republic. Nearly 60 percent of the deputies in 1981 were former civil servants (many of them teachers in Socialist ranks). Civil servants can reasonably aspire to the position of minister, or even premier, as shown by the substantial fraction of Fifth Republic cabinets drawn from the civil service and the appointment of Raymond Barre. The president is free to promote higher officials as he desires, and they owe their status not merely to seniority and merit but also to political relations. The civil service is even used in a partisan manner; tax collectors, for example, are to be gentle before elections.[12]

[11]Jean Blondel, *Contemporary France: Politics, Society and Institutions* (New York: Harper & Row, 1974), p. 68.
[12]Ezra N. Suleiman, *Politics, Power and Bureaucracy in France: Administrative Elite* (Princeton, N.J.: Princeton University Press, 1976), p. 364.

The French bureaucracy is more loosely organized than the British. Until 1945, each ministry recruited its own staff; but in 1945–1946 the civil service was placed under a governing commission, the *Diréction de la fonction publique,* with hierarchical grades, standardized recruitment, and financial responsibility to the Ministry of Finance. Entrance and promotion are supposedly by impartial examination (except near the top), and there are grades much as in the British system. The elite is formed by the *grands corps,* including the Inspectorate of Finances, the Court of Accounts (*Cour des Comptes*), and Council of State, from whom the staff of ministers, ambassadors, and top officials of various commissions are drawn. The service is unspecialized in that individuals may transfer freely from one department to another. The Court of Accounts examines expenditures, doing some of the work a congressional committee might perform in the United States.

The Council of State is a high administrative tribunal, coordinator of the civil service, and adjunct of parliament in lawmaking. Descendant of the King's Council and unshaken by countless constitutional changes, it has about 200 higher civil servants, of whom about a third are councilors of state, the others subordinates. The Council of State should hear grievances and protect citizens from administrative arbitrariness. It also advises the government concerning the legality of regulations and assists in the drafting of proposed legislation. It resolves disputes within the bureaucracy, and it has several advisory sections. It is supplemented in the correction of abuses by a sort of French ombudsman, or "mediator," established in 1973. Like the British counterpart, the *médiateur* can request information and initiate action against an errant bureaucrat. However, complaints have to be transmitted by a member of parliament. The médiateur is named by the government to be checked, has a tiny staff (recently eight, including typists), and has not elicited much cooperation from bureaus called to account.[13]

Recruitment to the *grands corps* is almost entirely through the hundred-odd *grandes écoles,* including the *École Polytéchnique* and the *École Normale Supérieure,* institutions with demanding admission standards and specialized curriculums. A two-year course prepares for the exam for a *grande école,* a diploma from which is almost a necessary and sufficient condition for a good job except in some specialized professions.[14]

The top elite, however, come out of the *École National d'Administration* (ENA), an institution that is between on-job training for top civil servants and a university graduate school.[15] Except for occasional appointments of otherwise distinguished citizens, the top echelons of state are limited to *Enarchs,* as they have been called. Only 150 are admitted each year. Mostly law graduates, they are given a year of administrative experience in the field as assistant to a prefect, then return to Paris for two years of seminars in which ideas are applied to problems. Top graduates get high positions immediately; all can expect to rise rapidly. Eight members of Mitterrand's cabinet were Enarchs, including his three closest advisors.[16]

Some 2,600 Enarchs have been produced since the school was established in 1945. They form something of a meritocracy, a nobility by examination and service. They seem to be honest as well as skilled and to be generally dedicated to the public welfare as they perceive it. They mostly know one another and are selected and trained to similar manners and modes of thought. This is good for administrative efficiency; much business is facilitated by the ease with which an official can communicate with classmates and fellow alumni of ENA.

The high civil service becomes to some extent, however, a closed group, superior to ordinary mortals and disdainful of less informed outsiders, politicians, and parliament. Its entrants are overwhelmingly of upper or upper-middle class, civil service or professional background. A large majority are Parisians or have gone to school in Paris. Despite some effort to broaden the social composition by paying stipends to students, hardly any from the poorer strata manage to make the leap to the top. This situation can be changed only slightly by a provision that from 1983 places for ten entrants are reserved for persons with ten years experience in unions or local government, who will face an easier examination.

The Enarchy is not old enough to have become hereditary, but it must be expected that offspring of Enarchs will have a substantial advantage in surmounting the barriers to the ENA. The written examination is impersonal, but it is followed by oral scrutiny, which must be less forbidding for those with the correct background. However, Enarchs do not necessarily agree politically, and many of them have leftist inclinations,[17] seeing their state as the agency of progress. The bureaucracy tends toward immobility and stands for no particular policies except its own jurisdiction, and social origins have little effect on attitudes.[18]

Local Administration

The national administrative apparatus reaches down to the localities and itself carries out the policies of government, with little recourse to locally elected authorities. In

[13]William Safran, *The French Polity* (New York: David McKay, 1977), p. 219.

[14]Codevilla, *Modern France,* p. 64

[15]Don Cook, "France: The Making of an Elite," *Atlantic,* 240 (July 1977), pp. 16–19.

[16]*New York Times,* November 19, 1982, p. 4.

[17]Cook, "France," p. 19.

[18]Suleiman, *Politics, Power and Bureaucracy,* p. 111.

the ninety-five *départments*, the chief administrator is the prefect, successor of the kings' *intendant* and servant of the minister of interior. Prefects represent not only the state but also the party in power; on taking office, Mitterrand changed about half of them. The *départments* are also legal entities with elected assemblies, but these can do little beyond some bargaining with the prefects. Paris since 1975 has had an elected mayor, but there also power remains with the two prefects.

The local governmental units, the communes, are cramped by lack of revenues other than grants from the center. Their legal powers are only whatever the central government gives them, and they are mostly administrative units. The elected mayor becomes partly a state official, and his chief task is to intercede or plead with Paris. Local government is not trivial, however. There are many local questions to be decided, and the elected councils, which choose the mayor from their membership, often see lively controversy. Politicians like to be councilors or mayors; a large majority of parliament have this dignity. They have some power, moreover, in their prerogative of choosing the Senate. Mitterrand proposed to decentralize administration. Prefects became commissioners, and powers of local councils were enlarged, but it did not appear that much was really changed.

The Courts

The French judicial system is more like a branch of the civil service than the British. Judges technically are civil servants, trained by a special professional school and named by the president at the recommendation of a judicial council. They are practically irremovable, but they are subject to transfer or promotion by the minister of justice, and they conceivably shape decisions to please this official.

The accused is decidedly disadvantaged compared to the defendant in an American or British court. There is no habeas corpus, and suspects may be held during a protracted investigation; many other guarantees of the common law are absent. Usually there is no jury, the verdict being reached by a panel of judges. Instead of relying on the adversary system, judges conduct much of the trial, questioning the defendant, witnesses, and lawyers. French law is in theory straight code, in contrast to the Anglo-Saxon emphasis on precedent; but the difference is less distinct because the French judge considers precedents, whereas Anglo-American law has been largely preempted by statutes and regulations. There has been some feeling that French justice is class-bound and discriminates against the poor.

Economic Administration

Long before the Socialist regime, a series of conservative, antisocialist governments administered an economy subject to a large measure of control and nearly 30 percent directly or indirectly state-owned. Nationalization did not come for any overriding purpose. Some industrial enterprises, such as matches and tobacco, were made state monopolies generations ago for revenue. Others, such as telegraphs and railroads, were taken over as natural monopolies. Many, such as the Renault automobile works, were nationalized as punishment for wartime collaboration. Yet others, most recently steel, have been placed under state control to rescue them from bankruptcy.

Giscard did nothing to reduce the state sector, which included not only the foregoing but electric power (including nuclear power, for which France retains higher enthusiasm than most countries), gas, airlines, most petroleum, most banking, broadcasting, and a number of equipment-building enterprises. Mitterrand in 1981 carried out the biggest single wave of nationalizations in

Western Europe's history, taking in private banks, more steel, armaments, some pharmaceuticals, computers, chemicals, some textiles, glass and electronics.[19] Contrary to British practice, it has not been considered necessary to assume control of an entire industry, but public and private coexist. There is a great variety of legal arrangements, but most nationalized enterprises are rather closely run by an appropriate ministry. They usually have boards of directors with representation of labor and the public, but these have only advisory functions. Although they are supposed to be managed as independent profit-making entities, crucial decisions are probably made in the ministry. Employees do not have civil service status, but it is difficult to discharge them, at any level. It is the policy of the Mitterrand government in effect to give workers lifetime contracts. Many state enterprises require large subsidies, and they are kept in operation mostly to save jobs. Some are efficient, however, such as the Renault works; Sofretu, subway builders for the world; and military (Mirage) and civilian (Airbus) manufacturers.

The government controls an estimated 32 percent of industry, (Mitterrand having added 14 percent) but it has much influence over the entire economy.[20] The state controls 85 percent of credit, and there is a thick web of regulation, which Giscard only briefly and slightly lightened. Planning (by the Planning Commission) is not strictly compulsory, but it offers incentives for the attainment of targets, and businesses are usually glad to cooperate. There is much interaction between public and private interests in drawing up plans, and planning committees for various industries have representatives of businesses and the administrative agencies, together with a few of labor and farmers. A large majority of French companies follow government policies in their investment plans, export policies, and pricing. France is not very competition-minded. Typically, a 1973 law virtually halted the spread of supermarkets by giving local tradesmen a veto over new stores. France is the most protectionist of Western nations. It is also one of the most heavily burdened. Taxes take 46 percent of the GNP. Payroll taxes come to 62 percent. The tax system is regressive; the value-added tax, a sales tax, brings in four times as much as the income tax.

Although interest group representation is more built into the administrative system in France than in Britain, most interest groups are less well organized and have less support from those whom they represent. The French are not joiners. For example, only about a third of the farmers are organized, and these are politically divided, whereas in Britain 90 percent are in a single federation. Only a few special interest groups, such as winegrowers, have much weight; these, however, are almost irresistible. In the Fifth Republic it is futile for interest groups to work with the Assembly, and they have lost much of their interest in the parties. Their contacts are chiefly with the administrative apparatus. Perhaps it is because the French do not see much likelihood of a group effectively promoting their interests that they have been prone to resort to violence, such as wildcat strikes, the militant measures of farmers, or the semirevolution of 1968.

The trade unions have been politically active, although they are comparatively feeble. There is no checkoff of dues or union shop, unions lack funds to support long strikes, and they largely count on the government to promote labor interests in collective bargaining. Only about a quarter of the workers are unionized, 45 percent of them in the CGT (*Confédération générale du travail*), the rest fairly evenly divided between two smaller

[19]*Wall Street Journal*, October 28, 1981, p. 1
[20]*Business Week*, January 10, 1983, p. 55.

federations. Only one-tenth of the CGT membership belongs to the Communist Party, but the organization is tightly gripped by the party, which holds all top positions.[21] The other federations, the FO (*Force ouvrière*) and CFDT (*Confédération française démocratique du travail*), favor the centrists and the Socialists, respectively, but they are not party-affiliated or -controlled. They have sometimes been more aggressive than the Communist-disciplined CGT unions.

The trade unions, farmers, owners (represented by the National Council of French Employers, CNPF, or *Conseil national du patronat français*), various professional organizations, and the civil service are represented in the Social and Economic Council, a consultative group charged by the constitution with giving its opinion, when requested, on legislation and ordinances.

There is a tendency to corporatism in the French system, as the associations with which the government deals extensively, such as the physicians' organization, acquire semiofficial status and are supposed to assist in the management of their sphere of the economy. The civil service favors institutionalized consultation, and there are many consultative bodies attached to ministries. However, the officials may choose to listen or not to listen to any particular group. The influence of the petitioners is likely to be proportionate to their accommodation to government policies and philosophy, and business and professional groups were closer to the center of things under Giscard than farmers or workers; under Mitterrand the former complain of exclusion.

PARLIAMENT

The Assembly of the Fifth Republic looks outwardly much like the corresponding bodies of the Fourth and Third. About 500

[21]Codevilla, *Modern France*, p. 147.

members belonging to parties recognizably like those of forty years ago meet in the traditional semicircular chamber; and the speaker, unlike his counterpart in the House of Commons, orates from the rostrum. The life of the Assembly is five years, as previously; members are elected from individual constituencies, as in the Third Republic. In the traditional fashion, the Senate is indirectly elected by over 100,000 delegates of local councils for 9-year terms (one-third chosen every 3 years), and it is rural-dominated and conservative. The Senate, like most upper chambers, is the weaker body, with only a suspensive veto over legislation. Members of both Senate and Assembly are fairly well paid for the little work expected of them, about $48,000 in 1983.

The Assembly is hamstrung, however, by several constitutional provisions designed to protect the government from interference. For example, ordinary sessions of parliament are limited to about five and a half months per year, much shorter than the British Parliament. There are not to be more than six committees in each house in order to prevent specialization and close oversight of ministries. The Parliament has little authority over the budget. It cannot reduce revenues or raise expenditures. This provision blocks most private member bills, because nearly every measure has a monetary cost. The Assembly has only forty days to consider the budget; the Senate, fifteen; if it is not acted on within seventy days, the government can enact it by decree. Budget days are not an opportunity, as in England, for the opposition to probe all aspects of government; the Assembly can express disapproval only through a no-confidence motion. The government, proposing a bill, can exclude any or all of it from amendment and require a vote on whatever it wishes—a provision designed to restrain friends as well as opponents of the government. It may even make the bill a question of confidence, in which case it is automatically considered approved unless the Assembly passes a no-confidence motion. Giscard had to use this procedure to pass the 1980 budget.

The passage of a motion to overthrow the government is very difficult. It must bear the signatures of at least one-tenth of the deputies, who cannot sign more than one such motion per session. After the motion is presented, there is a 48-hour waiting period. Then it is adopted only if a majority of the total membership votes in favor. Proxy voting is not allowed, although in other matters it is permitted in practice despite prohibition by the constitution. The Fifth Republic has seen only one successful no-confidence motion, in October 1962, against Pompidou in protest against the proposed unconstitutional referendum for the popular election of the president. The outcome, contrary to the spirit of the constitution, was not the resignation of the government but the dissolution of the Assembly—a result that discourages future censure motions.

It is a peculiarity of the Fifth Republic that parliament can legislate only in prescribed areas, and what is not specifically permitted is prohibited. The "domain of law" covers most of the ordinary concerns of legislation, including civil rights, criminal law, taxation, the electoral system, and nationalization of enterprises. It also includes "fundamental principles" concerning the organization of national defense, local administration, education, property rights, labor questions, and state finances. Details in these areas are for the government to dispose by decree. The parliament is by implication excluded from foreign affairs (except for a declaration of war) and from the organization of administration (except as determined by the budget). The government may request decree power even in the areas specifically reserved for parliament.

The critical function of the parliament is also reduced. Previous republics had an institution called "interpellation," whereby a deputy could use an inquiry as a peg for an attack on some government action. This practice has been eliminated. Written questions may be submitted, but answers may come late or never. Friday afternoon was set aside for the question period because deputies are then usually on their way home for the weekend. Committees of inquiry are also discouraged; they can meet only privately, although their best weapon is publicity, and they are a feeble check on malfeasance.[22] When the parliament in 1973 wished to investigate wiretapping, the government declined to cooperate. Foreign affairs are discussed only in closed session. The government has managed to keep its secrets; leaks have been far fewer than in previous republics.[23] The agenda of the Assembly is set by the government, and the opposition has little access to the governing bodies and hardly any time. Private bills almost never go forward unless they have government consent, and debate has naturally been much less lively under the Fifth Republic.

The complex constitutional provisons regarding parliament and legislation invite controversy, and the framers foresightedly set up a Constitutional Council to determine constitutionality. This is a body of nine members chosen for nine-year terms, three each by the president and the presiding officers of the Assembly and Senate. Citizens or the courts have no access to it. Only those who select its membership plus the premier, or by a 1974 amendment, sixty members of parliament petitioning together, can ask for its verdict. The Constitutional Council must be consulted before the president can declare an emergency or order a referendum,

---

[22]Safran, *The French Polity*, p. 181.
[23]April Carter, *Direct Action and Liberal Democracy* (New York: Harper & Row, 1973), p. 17.

but its advice is not binding. It should ensure the validity of presidential and parliamentary elections and of referendums and scrutinize treaties for constitutionality, and it is to rule on the constitutionality of all "organic laws" (dealing with the membership of parliament) and such others as may be submitted to it. Its decisions are final, but de Gaulle showed that they could be ignored.

Supposedly the principal purpose of the Constitutional Council was to hinder any effort of the Assembly to stretch the boundaries fixed by the constitution. The old parties in the first years of the Fifth Republic indeed fought to restore parliamentary prerogatives to which they had been accustomed. They were unsuccessful, although the Assembly has gradually come to be somewhat more assertive. Under Giscard, the parliament made hundreds of amendments to government bills each session, and there have been more private bills. Mitterrand's majority, however, remained wholly docile.

Parliamentary inquiry into government operations is feeble, with neither staff nor means of extracting information. The important function of the parliament is simply to register the preferences of the people as expressed through the filter of the electoral system and the parties. A government is inhibited from doing anything very unpopular lest it be repudiated at the polls, and the possibility always exists that a hostile majority of the Assembly may force a change of government.

Elections

No French government has been without free elections since the revolution of 1789. Manhood suffrage was decreed in 1848, earlier than in any other major power, but it was not effective until 1870. Women did not receive the vote until 1945. The French believe in using their ballots: turnout is commonly about 80 percent—87.5 percent in 1981.

Members of the Assembly are elected from single-member districts, with a second round where no candidate secures a majority. Any candidate receiving over one-eighth of the votes on the first round can enter the runoff, in which only a plurality is required; but it is ordinarily more advantageous for a weak candidate to try to sell his support to a stronger one. Thus, the Assembly is not cluttered by the minor parties that might be permitted by proportional representation, yet minorities have a chance to turn votes into influence. There is pressure for parties to be less ideological and more aggressive, because their ability to make alliances is crucial.

Candidates deposit 10,000 francs, which is returned if they receive at least 10 percent of the vote. Deputies are not required to reside in their district. Voters do not seem to mind candidates being parachuted from the central office. Constituencies have not been redrawn since 1958 and have become grossly unequal in some cases. This hurts the leftist parties because they have more support where industrialization has drawn people from the rural regions. There is no limit on spending, but there is a state subsidy of 100,000 francs and broadcast time is free and rather equitably distributed.

The electoral system rewards those who can ally themselves easily with different parties. It also tends, like the British system, to turn a small advantage in votes into a larger majority in parliament. In an extreme case, in 1967 the Communists received 72 seats for 5 million first-ballot votes; the Gaullists, 234 seats for 8.5 million votes.[24]

THE MULTIPARTY SYSTEM

France has always been the land of the multiparty system, and the panorama of large and small parties has always been complex.

[24]Carter, *Direct Action and Liberal Democracy*, p. 53.

Parties have grouped around one leader or another, divided, changed names, and reunited. The constitution of the Fifth Republic has had, however, the desired effect of simplifying the party system and pushing toward bipolarity.[25] The most interesting elections are for the presidency, and although many candidates can enter, the race becomes two-sided. In view of the stability of the government, the basic division of government versus opposition appears to be imposing itself despite antagonisms within each. In recent elections nearly all the votes have gone to the four big parties, two on the Left, two on the Right.

With the exception of the Communist Party (PCF), French parties are not strongly unified, ideologically defined, or consistent regarding economic issues. None has a mass membership comparable with that of British parties. The French identify much less with a particular party (except the Communist) than Britons or most Americans because the parties are mutable, have often changed names, and in many cases have been nearly indistinguishable. It is relatively easy for a politician to change parties. For example, the former Radical premier went to the Left Socialist party; the chief of the Socialist party, Mitterrand, went through several migrations; the president, Giscard d'Estaing, shifted from conservative to center. Parties are not so oligarchically controlled as in Britain (again except the PCF). They have in many cases been little more than a group around a leader, although the formal organization is based on a congress of delegates elected by local members.

Party programs do not mean very much, and the parties in practice are usually pragmatic or opportunistic. However, French parties are somewhat class-bound. Communist deputies are likely to be workers; So-

cialist, teachers; Conservative, farmers or businessmen. In the tradition of symbolic radicalism, most parties wish to be considered leftists, that is, of the people; it is held undesirable to sit on the right in the Assembly chamber. Bitterness has mostly been between the Left and Right, seeing each other as exploitative oppressors or destroyers of national values. The standoff has led to much sterile debate and uncivil politics, in which compromise was excluded.

It may be that the experience of government by the Left will reduce tensions. Polarization, in any event, is much more of the activists and political elite than of the masses, who are not much concerned with ideology; and violence has been avoided for many years. There are many cross-cutting issues over the old dichotomy of workers versus business, and poor versus rich, such as the opposition of small shopowners and producers to the large and generally more modern sector. The farmers demand their share, often in opposition to the factory workers. Foreign policy enters: for alliance with Britain and America, for more independence, or for a pro-Soviet orientation (favored by only a small fraction of Communist voters). A divisive issue since 1789 has been the question of Church-state relations. A large majority of the French are nominally Catholic, but most are non-practicing and many are heartily anticlerical. Today the chief controversy has been over state aid to Church schools, which educate about one-fifth of French children. They were given subsidies in 1959 by the new de Gaulle government, but the Left continued to demand integration of Church schools into the state system.[26] Mitterrand refrained, however, from doing so.

In the Fifth Republic, the parties seemed to have declined along with the Assembly where they found their glory. But they have

---

[25]Wilson, *French Political Parties*, p. 7.

[26]Ibid, pp. 105, 272.

revived since the mid-1960s and have been increasing membership and becoming more coherent, finding a new role in organizing the country instead of politicking in the Assembly.

The Gaullists

The largest party during most of the Fifth Republic has been the Gaullist, the Union for the Defense of the Republic (UDR). In one or another incarnation it was at the center of power under de Gaulle and Pompidou and was close to it under Giscard. Somewhat ironically, it began as part of de Gaulle's opposition to political parties. He patronized the Assembly of the French People as an organization above parties. But it began playing the game like the other parties, and he renounced it. When de Gaulle returned to power in 1958, it was hastily reassembled as the Union for the New Republic (UNR). Originally only a personal following, this agglomeration solidified, became the second best organized party, and steadily improved its position while de Gaulle's aura was fading. The 1968 election gave the UNR (renamed UDR, *Union pour la Défense de la République*) the largest majority in French history. But the extraordinary victory reflected not basic strength but backlash against the riots and disorders, and in 1973 the UDR lost its majority in parliament. In 1974, the Gaullist candidate Jacques Chaban-Delmas trailed Giscard in the first round of the presidential election.

Under Giscard, the UDR tended to sag. But Jacques Chirac left the the premiership in 1976 to dedicate himself to rebuilding the UDR (renamed in December 1976 Rally for the Republic). In March 1977, Chirac defeated Giscard's candidate for the newly created post of mayor of Paris; from this base, he campaigned against both the Giscardians and the Left. His main theme was anticom-munism, whereas Giscard wanted to end polarization and form a centrist regime. In foreign policy, Chirac stressed nationalism and censured Giscard for excessive friendliness toward the United States.

There were some bitter contests between Gaullists and Giscardians in the first round of the 1978 elections, but they joined effectively against the Socialist-Communist front in the second. In the final tally, the Gaullists won slightly more votes than the Communists, and they gained a few more seats than the Giscardians. In the 1981 presidential elections Chirac and Giscard were half enemies, half allies. After the victory of Mitterrand, they began to cooperate more effectively and won a respectable increase in the March 1983 local elections. The triumph was mostly for Chirac, however, as he affirmed his leadership of Paris by a landslide reelection as mayor and emerged as probable Conservative candidate for the 1988 presidential election.

The *Rassemblement pour la Républic,* Rally for the Republic (RPR) may be the largest of French parties, with a claimed membership of 700,000. It is nationalistic and somewhat antiegalitarian in temper, but its social policies have been among those commonly called progressive. For example, it promoted profit sharing and worker participation in management. Its support has been highest among farmers and in small towns. Its fortunes may depend greatly on Jacques Chirac.

The Party of Giscard

The Union for French Democracy (UDF), was put together only in the course of the 1977–1978 electoral campaign. Previously, Giscard had sought merely to maintain a "presidential majority," an ill-defined grouping prepared to support his policies. Giscard's own party had been the Republican Independents, a group formed in 1962 out of a split of older conservative parties, which had been allied with the Gaullists and had usually held 75 to 100 Assembly seats. It had an ideology of deideologization, economic laissez-faire, and technocracy. The Republican Independents were joined by the leftovers of the old Radical party, an anticlerical, free-enterprise party which had played a central role in the Third Republic and had tried to revive in the 1950s and again in the Fifth Republic. Also, the liberal Catholic party, the MRP, which sprang up after World War II and became one of the biggest parties of the Fourth Republic, melted away in the Fifth Republic and dissolved itself in 1967 to the benefit of the Giscardians. The UDF then gathered up most of the other groups that felt unable to identify with either the Gaullists or the Socialist-Communist Left.

During the Giscard presidency, the UDF was of roughly similar size to the RPR, although the former had the advantage of being a channel to the power center. The UDF was somewhat demoralized and disorganized by the defeat of 1981. Giscard returned to the political fray, however; and his party made a strong showing in the local elections of 1983. Ideologically, the UDF is ill defined. It is basically an alliance of political clubs and dignitaries in the traditional French manner, a group of office-seekers who do not fit elsewhere.

The Socialists

The oldest party is the Socialist, which looks back to Fourier, St. Simon, Cabet, and other contemporaries or predecessors of Marx, thinkers of an intellectual, optimistic, and nonviolent temper. In the last decades of the century French socialism came under Marxist influence, but it has always carried syndicalist and anarchist strains. When several radical factions merged in 1905, the Social-

ists became France's first mass party. The revolutionary party was becoming deradicalized prior to World War I, and it joined in the national defense. It was radicalized by the war, however, and a majority of the members and part of the leadership broke away to affiliate with Lenin's Bolsheviks and the Russian-sponsored and dominated Communist International. Through the interwar years, the Leninists, who formed the Communist Party, represented the revolutionary tradition, whereas the Socialists became a moderate party of journalists, teachers, skilled workers, and petty bourgeoisie. Then as later, the Socialists faced the problem of how far they might cooperate with the Communists for electoral purposes despite the Leninist principles of the latter. The Socialists had a brief turn at the helm with the Popular Front victory of 1936, but this soon broke down in profound disagreements, especially over the Spanish civil war.

After World War II, the Socialists emerged as the second largest party after the Communists. They played a key part in the governments of the Fourth Republic, although their support and membership dwindled. Their position was mostly rather conservative, and they helped prosecute France's wars in Indochina and Algeria. In 1958 and afterward they flirted with rightists; as a result, a leftist splinter broke away. Excluded from power, the Socialists continued to decline. In the late 1960s, membership was down to 70,000, mostly municipal officeholders. In 1969 the Socialist candidate for president received only 8.1 percent of the vote (compared to 21.5 percent for the Communist candidate).

The Socialist Party was reorganized in 1968, and François Mitterrand, who became secretary-general in 1971, rebuilt its following. Standing for a coalition of the Left while remaining sufficiently moderate to conciliate centrists, he nearly won the presidency over

Giscard in 1974. The policy of alliance with the Communists led to the Common Program and great hopes of 1977, which were frustrated when the Communists broke away. Relations between the leftist parties continued to be strained, as each could most readily increase its strength at the expense of the other. The Communists especially found it difficult to accept the role of junior party on the Left after the Socialists surpassed them in the mid-1970s.

In the 1981 elections the Socialists received their largest percentage since 1934 and held a position of such strength that they could dictate severe terms to the Communists as the price of a minor role in the government. Mitterand put much of the Socialist program into effect in his first year, by measures of redistribution and nationalization. The Socialist Party (PS) has two fundamental and not always compatible tendencies: toward egalitarianism or social justice as usually conceived, and toward state-controlled economic development. It alone of major, modern Socialist parties lays much emphasis on nationalization and deeply distrusts market economies and capitalism. In this it upholds not so much Marxist principles as the tradition of mercantilism dating from Louis XIV. Nationalization has been viewed less as a means to build a new social order than to improve French industry, along with direction of investment to the most promising sectors. Nationalization was intended to improve productivity without political interference; as a minister put it, "state-owned does not mean state-controlled."[27] But nothing was done for workers' self-management (in contrast to the codetermination introduced by conservative West German governments), because it might complicate central direction.

The Socialist Party has usually been frac-

[27]*Business Week,* January 10, 1983, p. 45.

tious, and the congresses of two thousand or more delegates have seen much contention, as in the British Labour party, between essentially moderate reformers and those who would build society anew. A left wing of the PS, perhaps 20 to 25 percent of the membership, is strongly Marxist and not far from Communist positions. It would nationalize much more and try to insulate France from the noxious currents of world capitalism, separating from the European Economic Community, the international monetary system, and the Western alliance. Mitterrand, however, surprised and pleased Washington by the firmness of his anti-Sovietism.

The Communists

The Communist Party (PCF) has not been a party like the others but has usually represented a discordant element in French politics. It was formed in 1920 when the majority of the membership of the Socialist party accepted Lenin's conditions for adherence to the Communist International which required the party to be subversive, revolutionary, intransigently opposed to "bourgeois" society and government, and obedient to the Soviet-dominated headquarters. The French revolutionary and authoritarian traditions were joined in a single party and program.

The Communist Party through the 1920s underwent purges and splits, lost most of its membership, and elected few deputies because of its refusal to make deals with "bourgeois" parties. It revived when the economic depression began toward the end of the 1920s and when Adolf Hitler became ruler of Germany in 1933. One of Hitler's chief points being anti-Bolshevism, the Communists energetically attacked fascism. They joined a Popular Front with Socialists and Radicals and won a great electoral victory in 1936. The Communists, still inhibited from participating in a "bourgeois" government, supported the regime headed by the Socialist Léon Blum and acquired prestige as antifascists.

In August 1939, however, Stalin signed a pact of friendship with Nazi Germany. The French Communists reversed their position, opposing defense measures and sabotaging what they called an imperialist war. When Hitler invaded the Soviet Union in June 1941, they sprang to arms; and in 1944 the Communist was the strongest party on the ground. It would probably have installed a Communist government but for the presence of British and American forces and the need for economic assistance from the United States. The Communists formed the largest party in the elected Assembly and held several ministries. In the cold war, however, the position of the Communists in the government became untenable, and they left in May 1947.

In opposition, the Communists' chief task was to impede French participation in the Western alliance. Their prestige and membership dropped; shortly after World War II, Communist newspapers sold 2.5 million copies; thirty years later, only one-tenth as many. The party was rigidly pro-Soviet and Stalinist; in 1956 it supported the Soviet repression in Hungary despite the misgivings of many of its members. It was ossified in a hierarchic structure; Maurice Thorez was party boss for thirty-four years until his death in 1964. Its electoral support was more stable than that of any other party, however, and was hardly ever below 20 percent.

The constitution of the Fifth Republic requires political parties to be democratic, but this provision (unlike the corresponding position in the constitution of the German Federal Republic) has not been applied; the Communist Party was too large to be outlawed. Its structure, however, is Leninist. The Secretary-General and the Political Bureau,

along with the Secretariat, designate officials of the federations, who control the sections, which nominate secretaries for the cells. Congresses accept decisions with the same unanimity as Soviet congresses. Communist deputies turn their pay over to the party and receive a salary from it, so they are "employed" not by the state but by the party; and they deposit an advance resignation to be made effective whenever the party might require. To join the Communist Party is a commitment to a way of life.

The trump of the PCF is its domination of the largest labor federation, the General Labor Confederations (CGT). It benefits from traditions of voting leftist and the self-perception of the workers as a distinct and deprived class in a highly unequal society. The biggest reason for voting Communist, however, is to vote against the Establishment, to protest the irritations and injustices of French life. To vote Communist is to send a message of discontent to the bosses.

The PCF reached its zenith in the aftermath of World War II; since the late 1950s it has tended to lose ground. Its close adherence to the Soviet Union has increasingly become a liability, and in the 1970s it tried to identify with French rather than Russian revolutionary tradition. The PCF flirted with Eurocommunism, like the Italian and Spanish parties, but it returned to the Soviet line, supporting the invasion of Afghanistan in 1979–1980. In 1981 the PCF received its lowest percentage of the vote—15.3 percent—since 1936, and by 1983 the Communist vote was only a third of the Socialist. More and more longtime Communist local strongholds have fallen to "bourgeois" parties.

The commitment of members seems to have declined, and many are repelled by the autocratic leadership of the rather uninspiring perpetual Georges Marchais. The intellectuals, with whom the PCF was once very fashionable, have largely abandoned it because of its faithfulness to the Soviet Union, its opportunism—as in attacking immigrants from Africa[28]—and its willingness to compromise principles. The party claims 700,000 members, but the number of true believers may be less than a tenth of that.[29] The party clings to its humble place in the government for the sake of respectability and perhaps more for patronage and the opportunity to place the faithful in the bureaucracy. But it strains ideology to have to support the discharge of workers from ailing state industries, such as steel, and to countenance the stationing of American missiles in Europe.

The PCF suffers from the increasing irrelevance of its doctrine to a modern industrial state. It remains dedicated to the complete overthrow of the capitalist state but has no convincing model of what might be put in its place. The party cannot realistically hope but only daydream of gaining power with the backing of the blue collar workers only, yet it does not know how it should appeal to the middle classes. To advance, it would seem that the party must cease to be communist in the old style.

POLITICAL FREEDOMS

The French have never had a Magna Carta or Bill of Rights whereby monarchs acknowledged limitations on their powers. Instead, they produced an eloquent Declaration of the Rights of Man and the Citizen without direct legal force. Rights have always been a promise but have seldom been justiciable under French constitutions, and even when set forth have been qualified as subject to law. The Fourth Republic in its preamble subscribed to the Declaration of the Rights of Man and listed many social or economic rights, such as to employment, but these were of doubtful effect. The constitution of the Fifth Republic again in its preamble made a bow to the Declaration but otherwise ignored rights.

Legally, there is little to prevent the government from repressing expression of undesired views. A law of 1891 promised freedom of the press but made it a felony to publish statements damaging to the president or public authorities. This law largely lapsed in practice, being applied only ten times in the seventy years of the Third Republic and four times in the twelve years of the Fourth. De Gaulle, however, secured nearly a hundred convictions for "insulting the president of the republic."[30] The 1959 penal code, moreover, gives the administrative heads of *départements*, or the prefects, authorization to take whatever action they deem necessary for the security of the state. Their actions may be directed against troublesome papers, and radical newspapers have been seized on many occasions. Under Pompidou, some 1,500 journalists, leftists, and others were subjected to electronic surveillance; although this was discontinued by Giscard, there is little recourse for the victims.

An "antibreakers law" of 1970, in reaction to the disturbances of 1968, provided harsh penalties for activists and organizers of mass demonstrations leading to violence; it could be applied broadly against radicals. Persons held to be subversives in connection with the Algerian troubles of the early 1960s were tried in special courts with diminished guarantees; in 1963, a State Security Court was established to hear certain cases. The government also has facilities for presenting its own views to the exclusion of the competition. The news agency Agence France-Press

---

[28]*New York Times*, March 7, 1981, p. 7.
[29]*Time*, September 26, 1983, p. 25.

[30]Hayward, *The One and Indivisible French Republic*, p. 89.

is government-controlled and has no such nonpartisan standing as the BBC. Radio and television are under the command of the Ministry of Information and have been used rather unabashedly to present official interpretations. The press depends on the government for many favors, such as cheap newsprint; and there is some habit of self-censorship.

Civil liberties and the freedom of information that are basic to the democratic process consequently rest more on the expectations of the people and the consciences of the leaders than on constitution or laws. In 1970, for example, the government quite legally suppressed a radical Maoist paper and imprisoned the editor; but the episode proved extremely embarrassing when the writer-philosopher Jean-Paul Sartre took over the editorship. The French press is normally quite critical of the government, but its freedom is by no means so holy as in Britain, much less the United States. When the leading paper, *Le Monde,* reported that President Giscard had received gifts of diamonds from Central African Emperor Bokassa, Justice Minister Alain Peyrefitte charged its director with injury to the French judiciary, and documents relating to the gifts were seized and held secret by the courts—all without eliciting any tremendous outcry.

There has been much more controversy over the control of broadcast media, which presidents have been inclined to regard as their property to use as they please. Giscard promised to make the broadcasting independent and impartial, but good intentions were forgotten. The government has always felt obliged to show impartiality at election time and in occasional political debates; and it has given the public, unions, and the press representation on an advisory board. The state retained administrative control, however, and instructions on programming and treatment of the news came frequently from above. Employees of the broadcasting services occasionally risk their positions by refusing to propagandize. Mitterrand promised to make television independent, like the BBC; this promise was not entirely fulfilled, but an impartial supervisory board was set up, to the displeasure of many Socialists who wanted "engaged" programming.

Like his predecessors, Mitterrand refused to consider ending the state monopoly on broadcasting. Foreign radio stations aimed at selling both goods and opinions to France are correspondingly popular, as are clandestine stations that regularly pop up. From time to time the government has a campaign to confiscate them. In any event, the fact that the broadcast media are known to be partisan reduces their effectiveness.

CONCLUSIONS

When the Fifth Republic was established, it was not expected to outlive its founder. But it has functioned well and stably and has become acceptable to most of the French. Its presidents and premiers have been of high caliber. It is remarkable that only one major amendment, for the direct election of the president, has been made to the hastily drawn constitution.

The Fifth Republic has yet to prove itself, however, by the crucial test of opposition between the president and Assembly. The rules regarding relations between president and premier are complicated and potentially conflict-laden; they have worked thus far only because the one has been entirely subordinate to the other.[31]

It must be supposed that sooner or later, in the uncertainties of democratic politics, the test must come, and there has been much speculation as to the outcome. Probably the

[31]Duverger, *La monarchie républicaine,* pp. 160–164.

president would feel compelled to name a premier acceptable to the Assembly. If he dissolved a hostile Assembly without giving the opposition an opportunity to govern, he might expect the new election to return a stronger opposing majority, and he could not dissolve again in less than a year. Giscard told the voters before the March 1978 election that if they chose a leftist Assembly, they must expect the program of the Left to be enacted.[32]

By 1983, the approval rating of President Mitterrand was the lowest of any president since polling began; and the next legislative elections (not later than June 1986) may well bring a non-Socialist parliament. A president facing a hostile Assembly might become something of a figurehead, like a predecessor of the Fourth Republic. Such a president would retain the advantage of direct election, however; he, like the Assembly, could claim to speak for a popular majority. He could at least make it very difficult for a disliked premier to govern. He could hold over the Assembly a threat of dissolution, ready whenever the government found itself in difficulties. He might temporarily resolve a conflict by decreeing an emergency, although this would be a desperate remedy unless he wished to overthrow the constitutional order altogether. On the contrary, a president faced by a hostile majority might feel repudiated and resign, as de Gaulle did for less reason when his plebiscite on reconstruction of the Senate failed.

Such problems may, however, be less severe than would have been anticipated at the founding of the Fifth Republic because France has moved from confrontation toward consensual politics. Political development rests on economic development, and France has been transformed since World War II. Before it, France was the least in-

dustrialized country of northwestern Europe, but productivity has grown at one of the highest rates in the world during the past thirty years. There are still many more farmers than in Britain, but many small farms have been merged or abandoned. Those remaining have become efficient; France is one of the world's leading food exporters. There are still disproportionately many small shopkeepers, but many have been replaced by more efficient stores. The France of the small-town notable has been largely urbanized and modernized. The television culture has overlaid regionalism. Nearly every family has an automobile; secondary and higher education have been modernized and been made available to many more people; and France has become less diverse, in life-style and mentality. Inequality of income remains severe, and class differences are at least as marked as in England. But class structures have become more complex. It is not difficult to get a higher education, and education is the chief key to status: those who pass the baccalaureate examination ("*le bac*") have an open road to elitehood.

French politics has evolved toward less bitterness, less fractioning, and less ideology. The old debates over foreign policy have subsided as the fear of foreign aggression has disappeared. Colonialism has ceased to cause contention. The old issue of anticlericalism has been dissolved by tolerance and indifference. Nationalization is no longer an issue; state direction and the welfare state are accepted. The class struggle has ceased to be so urgent, and French workers have turned away from political strikes. University curriculums have been made more technical; administration has been somewhat democratized; and students have gone back to the books, more concerned to prepare themselves for a profession than to reshape society. It may be that the longterm "legitimacy crisis" hanging over France since 1789 has

[32]*Time*, February 6, 1978, p. 38.

at least been eased. The character of the state is for the first time in two centuries not seriously in question. Politics can proceed in a practical spirit to decide policies. There are many problems, and there will doubtless be many crises, but they will be of a new character and are to be met in a new spirit.

In this maturation, France shares in the evolution of the Western world. Politics has become less dissimilar in France, Britain, Germany, Japan, and the United States since World War II. Although France still suffers more class and social division than many democracies, and the idea of restraint of government is still weak, French democracy rests on a modern, pluralistic society, like that of other modern industrial powers. Its biggest problem is the same as that of the United States, Britain, and other industrial powers, the role of government and the balance between freedom and direction.

5

Germany

Germany has given the world far more than its share of poets, philosophers, and scientists; yet it has excelled in war above all other modern nations. It has produced outstanding political thinkers and legal scholars, yet it has had the most antirational government ever known in the Western world. Up to World War II, Germans had received forty Nobel prizes, compared with twenty-four for Britain, twenty-one for France, and twenty for America; yet the historical record of Germany is stained by aggression and genocide.

The political evolution of Germany in this century has been even more disjointed than that of France. It went in thirty-five years from traditional authoritarianism to democratic republic to totalitarian dictatorship to parliamentary republic. It is also an object lesson in political failure. In 1914 Germany was the world's leader in science and modern industry and was perhaps the strongest of nations, although the United States was wealthier. This standing was lost by the plunge into war in 1914. Under the Weimar Republic, Germany was well on the way to recovering much of its position; but the Nazi regime led it through continental rule to bomb-shattered defeat. Now the truncated Germany that arose from the rubble has regained by production much of what was lost by politics. Without natural resources of importance except coal, crowded on half the reduced territory of interwar Germany, the Federal Republic has become nearly as strong economically as it once was militarily. Its exports somewhat more than the United States, and its per capita GNP is double that of the British and equal to that of the United States. German industrial wages are among the world's highest, yet the German balance of payments surplus is almost as strong as that of the Japanese.

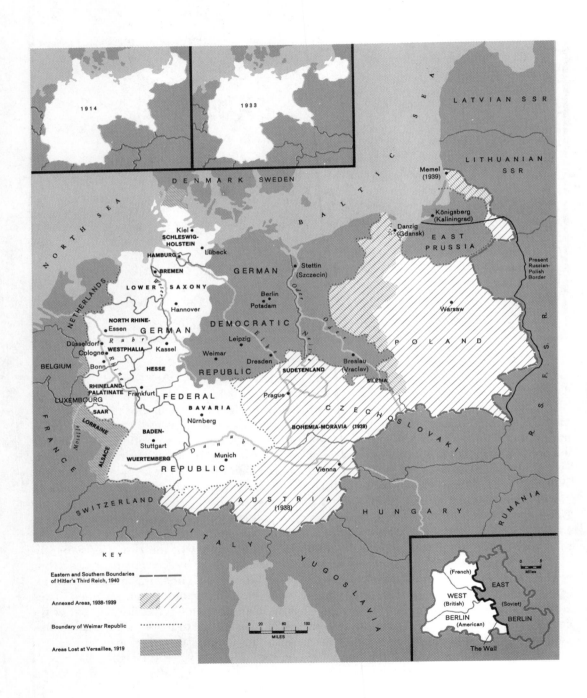

1914

1933

LATVIAN SSR

LITHUANIAN SSR

Memel
(1939)

Königsberg
(Kaliningrad)

DENMARK   SWEDEN

NORTH SEA

BALTIC SEA

EAST
PRUSSIA

Present
Russian-
Polish
Border

Danzig
(Gdansk)

Kiel
SCHLESWIG-
HOLSTEIN

Lübeck

HAMBURG

BREMEN

GERMAN

Stettin
(Szczecin)

LOWER SAXONY

Berlin
Potsdam

Warsaw

Hannover

NETHERLANDS

DEMOCRATIC

POLAND

NORTH RHINE-

GERMAN

Leipzig

Essen

Düsseldorf
Cologne

Ruhr

WESTPHALIA

Kassel

Weimar

Dresden

Breslau
(Vraclav)

BELGIUM

Bonn

HESSE

REPUBLIC

SUDETENLAND

SILESIA

U. S. S. R.

RHINELAND-
PALATINATE

Frankfurt

FEDERAL

Prague

CZECHOSLOVAKI

LUXEMBOURG

SAAR

BAVARIA

BOHEMIA-MORAVIA (1939)

LORRAINE

Nürnberg

BADEN-

ALSACE

Stuttgart

WUERTEMBERG

Danube

Munich

FRANCE

Moselle

REPUBLIC

Vienna

SWITZERLAND

AUSTRIA
(1938)

HUNGARY

RUMANIA

ITALY

YUGOSLAVIA

KEY

Eastern and Southern Boundaries
of Hitler's Third Reich, 1940

Annexed Areas, 1938-1939

Boundary of Weimar Republic

Areas Lost at Versailles, 1919

0   20   60   100
MILES

(French)

WEST
(British)

EAST

(Soviet)

BERLIN
(American)

BERLIN

The Wall

0   5
Miles

Germany has been successful insofar as it has not been violently nationalistic. But nationalism and the definition of Germany as a nation have been the crux of the German problem—the central problem of European politics from the French Revolution until 1945. Germany has never represented a clearcut entity, and efforts to form a united German nation have inevitably been incompatible with European security and the balance of power. Britain is set off by water, and France has clear-cut boundaries around most of its perimeter, but Germany is open on all sides. It has never included nearly all the peoples who might be considered German, except at the height of Hitler's conquests. The boundary with France was in dispute from the seventeenth century on, and the Alsatians still speak German. The language of Flanders and the Netherlands is a variety of Low German; most of Switzerland is Germanic, as is Austria; and there were German enclaves across eastern and southeastern Europe until they were expelled at the end of World War II.

Before 1870 there was no Germany, just a conglomeration of medium and small states, headed by Prussia, plus the German-ruled empire of Austria. The national language, based on Luther's translation of the Bible, is partly artificial, although it is taught widely and used in the media. The native dialects of Bavaria, Hamburg, and so forth, are nearly as different as the various romance languages. German nationalism has thus been somewhat synthetic, cultivated in imitation of the nationalism of more naturally coherent peoples.

Nowadays, of course, Germany does not represent a national unit. The Federal Republic of Germany (FRG) has a population of over 61 million, slightly more than Britain or France. Its territory is slightly larger than Britain, or roughly the same as other major West European powers. This is the "Germany" discussed here. Next to it lies East Germany, which calls itself the German Democratic Republic (GDR), with about half the area and under a third the population of the Federal Republic. Its politics belongs to the Communist world. An island in East Germany is West Berlin, ambiguously related to the Federal Republic and still under the protection of the United States, Britain, and France. To the south of the FRG lies Austria, the joining of which to the German Reich was Hitler's first great triumph. A result of his defeat was to affirm the separate statehood of Austria, which otherwise might be considered almost as German as Bavaria.

Defeat in World War II put an end to any idea of German expansion for the foreseeable future. The possibility of reunification of the two Germanies, West and East, was in the foreground of politics for two decades after the war. The division now seems permanent, but the longing to reduce the separation remains to complicate German foreign and defense policy.

One of the great questions of the postwar era has been whether the new, Western-oriented Germany, dedicated to economic rather than military strength, has truly and reliably turned its back on its authoritarian past. The evidence seems increasingly to justify optimism.[1]

THE WEIGHT OF THE PAST

Hitler took for his state the title of Third Reich, or Third Empire. The Second Reich was the empire of Bismarck; the First Reich was the Holy Roman Empire originally founded by Charlemagne, who was crowned successor of the Caesers (*Kaiser* in German)

---

[1]See Karl D. Bracher, *The German Dilemma: The Relationship of State and Democracy* (New York: Praeger, 1975).

by the pope in A.D. 800. It was refounded by Otto I as a basically German realm in 962. Through the Middle Ages, this proto-Germany claimed universal temporal rule corresponding to the universal spiritual rule of the pope. However, the emperor gradually lost power to the vassals who elected him and on whom he depended for soldiery. The empire became a loose conglomerate, which continued mostly as a dream until the wars of the French Revolution laid it to rest.

In and beyond its northeast corner, however, a new power was growing up in the seventeenth and eighteenth centuries. This was Prussia, a state built around an army. Prussia was the spearhead of the German push into Slavic Eastern Europe (*Drang nach Osten*), and its leitmotif was expansion and subjugation of the native peasantry. Prussia became a duty-bound society under a stern monarchy, with a stiffly disciplined army and loyally efficient bureaucracy. Prussian military prowess was converted into territorial aggrandizement under ambitious rulers, the most admired of whom was Frederick the Great (1740–1786). Prussia played a major role in the overthrow of Napoleon, and its reward was large territorial gains and a dominant position in northern Germany.

Germany remained a loose confederation, however, until the latter part of the nineteenth century. The states and statelets were generally monarchic, and the most influential political theorist was Hegel, who viewed the severe but conscientious Prussian monarchy as the synthesis of freedom and authority and the realization of the idea of history. Liberalism and republicanism were foreign imports. Nonetheless, several smaller German states adopted rather modern constitutions after 1820, and Germany was swept by the liberal-revolutionary wave of 1848, which gave rise to the Second Republic in France. Several conservative rulers were overthrown, and the Prussian monarchy acceded to a constitution that would have substantially checked royal power if it had been observed. In 1848 an elected assembly of German liberals adopted a progressive all-German constitution. But the Prussian king spat on the German crown offered him by the burghers.

Bismarck's Empire

Liberal Germany was demoralized by this humiliation and by its inability to bring about national unity. This task Prussia took upon itself under the masterful guidance of Prince Otto von Bismarck, one of the most esteemed figures of German history and the image, like Frederick the Great, of the strongman for whom might makes right. Bismarck helped his king override the constitution and legislative opposition, telling the deputies that the great issues were decided not by speeches and majority votes but by "blood and iron." Through three short wars, 1864–1870, against Denmark, Austria, and France, he united Germany, except Austria, under and around Prussia, thereby consecrating the idea of securing national goals by force.

The new or Second Reich was semiautocratic. The chancellor (equivalent to prime minister or premier) and other officials were responsible not to the elected assembly but to the kaiser. Prussia dominated the Reich by virtue of its size and strength, and the kaiser effectively ruled as king of Prussia. The kingdom was sternly conservative under the traditional oligarchic rule of king, high civil servants, military officers, and large landowners, with a growing industrial-financial elite. Representation in the Prussian parliament was based on the amount of taxes paid.

Yet the Bismarckian Reich prided itself on being a "Rechtstaat," which meant that laws were applied without prejudice by impartial courts, a compromise which gave the middle classes some sense of justice and security while leaving politics to the upper classes. Generally, people were free to speak, write, and act politically as they pleased as long as they avoided violent attacks on the authorities. The government, moreover, was somewhat restricted by the federal structure, under which the larger non-Prussian states, such as Bavaria, retained considerable autonomy, including their own armed forces and diplomatic representatives. The states were charged with the administration of federal laws, a German tradition that has continued to the present.

The states were represented in the Federal Council or *Bundesrat,* which continues today as the upper chamber of the German parliament. The lower chamber, the *Reichstag,* was the democratic organ, elected by universal manhood suffrage. Bismarck made this concession to democracy for political reasons at a time when the franchise was in few states so broad. But the Reichstag was feeble. It might hold up the budget and orate, but it had no way to challenge the government, and the chancellor could usually manage party leaders well enough to get the laws he needed.

The Second Reich was strengthened and stiffened by economic success. German industrialization was late, but after 1870 it was fast. Unlike the earlier British industrialization but like the concurrent or slightly later Japanese, it was government-fostered although carried out by private enterprise. With stress on heavy industry, its purpose was national strength as well as production for consumers. This meant protection for industry as well as agriculture, the acceptance of interventionism, and some dependence of the entrepreneurial classes on the state. Rapid industrialization also meant the growth of an industrial working class with the radical inclinations to be expected in recently urbanized labor. Lack of political participation and the rigidity of the society made the workers receptive to Marxist revolutionary theory and socialist politics, despite the welfare measures introduced by Bismarck in the 1890s. Until World War I, Germany had the largest and strongest Marxist-Socialist (Social-Democratic) party in the world.

But despite economic success, the Reich suffered strains. The democratic or liberal parties, along with the socialists, received 80 to 90 percent of the votes, but they were impotent and frustrated while the state remained politically static. There was something of the malaise of later industrializing countries in the gap between the modern and the traditional, between the advancing economy and society and the more primitive unyielding political structures. There was a sense of having been cheated in the race for world position, with compensatory cultivation of German superiority and the German soul,[2] in somewhat the way Russian thinkers about the same time claimed spiritual and moral virtues for their relatively backward country. This was mixed with racism from the long contest with the Slavs of the east. There was also more anti-Semitism than in most of Western Europe. Political anti-Semitism originated in Germany in the 1870s, partly as a weapon against socialism. From Germany it spread to Austria, Russia, and other countries.

Nationalism became more jingoistic in the years preceding World War I. German historians, seeing the power of the state as the great goal, interpreted the past in terms of striving toward a still unfulfilled destiny. Political thinking, because of lack of participation and the apparent impossibility of reform, tended to abstraction and extremism.

[2]Ralf Dahrendorf, *Society and Democracy in Germany* (Garden City, N.Y.: Doubleday/Anchor Books, 1969), pp. 8–9.

It was easy—and perhaps unavoidable—to blame foreigners, if not Jews, for the problems of modernization and the difference between Germany's position in the world and its merits as perceived by the nationalists. A catch-up race for overseas empire brought only scraps of territory in Africa and the Pacific at the cost of much friction with rival powers. The willingness of Germany to go to war in 1914 may be seen as an effort to find a way out of the impasse without sacrificing outworn structures.

The Weimar Republic

Germany mobilized fully and effectively in World War I. In the process, it became a military dictatorship; Marshal Paul von Hindenburg and General Erich Ludendorff virtually ignored the Kaiser and the civilian chancellor. But military capacity could not compensate for political errors.

It was taken for granted that defeat meant democratization. In 1918–1919 Germany was in a revolutionary ferment as new groups, some inspired by the radical revolution that had recently occurred in Russia, sought to wrest the country from the former possessors. But Germany did not have a real revolution; the state apparatus was needed to hold the country together—to keep the economy functioning and fend off starvation. The military remained because it had not been much discredited by defeat; at the end of the war Germans were fighting everywhere on foreign territory. Moreover, the moderate Socialists who found themselves largely in charge of the debacle, called on the generals to protect them from the Communists and radicals. Revolution was also truncated because the provisional government promptly held elections for an assembly to draw up a new constitution. This body, which was much less radical than the street

crowds, met in the small town of Weimar (famed as Goethe's residence) to insulate itself from the agitation of Berlin. There it drew up an exemplary democratic constitution that became a byword for the failure of democracy.

The Weimar constitution provided for full proportional representation: any party polling 60,000 votes could claim representation. There was no deterrent to starting a new party and no incentive to coalesce. In the elections of July 1932, when the Nazi party surged into the lead, there were thirty-eight parties on the ballot.

The system encouraged oligarchic authority in the parties, tended to separate representatives from electors, and contributed to the discredit of parliamentary government in the confusion of too many parties. In the fractionated Reichstag, it was difficult to hold a majority. The chancellor never had much control of the cabinet, which had to be formed with a view to which parties were supporting the government. When circumstances brought new questions to the fore, the earlier basis for agreement would be eroded, a party would desert, and the cabinet would fall, much as in the Third and Fourth Republics in France.

A more important defect was the power granted to the president, which somewhat resembled that given under de Gaulle's republic. To offset the intended supremacy of the Reichstag, the president was chosen by popular vote for a seven-year term (with re-eligibility) and was given broad lawmaking power in emergencies, which he could declare. The constituent assembly, deliberating in an atmosphere heavy with the threat of chaos, thought such a provision necessary. It would have been harmless if there had been general adherence to the democratic ideal and if the president had not been prepared to abuse it. But it was too easy to resort to emergency powers to overcome parliamentary difficulties.

It would probably not have been fatal, however, but for the personality of the war-hero marshal, Paul von Hindenburg, who was elected president in 1925 and reelected in 1932, at age eighty-four, in a desperate move to halt the Nazi march. Hindenburg, who was much more attached to Prussian junkerdom than to democracy, in 1930 inaugurated presidential rule by using emergency decrees to put into effect the economic program of a centrist chancellor, Heinrich Bruning, who faced a hostile majority in the Reichstag. Thereafter, Hindenburg used his powers more and more freely to appoint or discharge chancellors regardless of the sentiments of the Reichstag (which was seldom permitted to meet) and according to his senile whims or the suggestions of his intimates. Hindenburg thus discredited the government and the constitution he was sworn to protect, so that it appeared a triumph of democracy when, on January 30, 1933, he vested the chancellorship in Adolf Hitler, a man who had a large following in the Reichstag.

More basically, the failure of Weimar was caused by the failure to change the German social and economic order. The military forces continued under authoritarian leadership only nominally controlled by the constitutional government. The old bureaucracy remained virtually intact, as did the large estates of eastern Germany and the junker aristocracy based on them. Largely cartelized industry continued under the old ownership and management. Authoritarian structures were generally retained in the family, schools, and courts. Intellectuals mostly took a condescending attitude toward the new state, and about a quarter of the electorate never really accepted the republic. Many groups were hostile to the republic,

few were really loyal, and hardly any were ready to fight for it.[3]

The Weimar Republic, moreover, was sorely burdened. Its early years were troubled by repeated insurrections by Communists and rightists. There were grievous problems of adjustment to defeat, reparations, the French occupation of the Ruhr industrial area, and the most extreme inflation known to history, which wiped out the savings of the middle classes. There were a few years of prosperity in the 1920s, thanks to American loans, and the standard of living rose rapidly. But prosperity was not long or sound enough to give the state legitimacy. It was overtaken by the devastating depression beginning in 1929, which caused the highest rate of unemployment in the industrial world. The somewhat superficial, never thoroughly accepted young republic then proved unable to resist a determined assault assisted by an incapable president.

The Nazi Reich

The surrender of an educated and modern people to dramatic insanity remains a burden on the conscience not only of Germany but also of Western civilization, and interest and curiosity about it remain enormous. The origins, structure, ideas, organization, and leading personalities of the Nazi movement have been much analyzed; Hitler is perhaps the most thoroughly biographied man in history. There is a never-dying fear that somehow one day a similarly antirational movement might take hold in another great nation, with even worse results.

Only a peculiar crisis permitted Hitler to come to power. Prior to the Depression, there

---

[3]James Conant, "The Foundations of a Democratic Future for Germany," in Arend Lijphart, ed., *Politics in Europe: Comparisons and Interpretations* (Englewood Cliffs, N.J.: Prentice-Hall, 1969), p. 202.

was no sign that he had any real chance of success. In the late 1920s, Hitler's party seemed to shrink to a sort of club of chauvinists and Jew-baiters; it received only 810,000 votes in 1928, whereas the Social Democrats counted over 9 million and the Communists over 3 million; the Nazis were the ninth largest party. They scored their big win and became the leading party, with 37.7 percent of the vote, in the year of desperation, 1932. Hitler and his gang could even then slide into power only because the republic had been perverted by Hindenburg and the unpopular governments he had imposed. With the constitutional order already set aside, millions of respectable Germans, not only hurt by the depression but frightened by the specters of civil disorder and communism, were prepared to entrust German fortunes to a raving and disreputable but charismatic Austrian.

Yet the Germans surrendered to a ranting nonnational (Hitler became a German citizen by a technicality only shortly before taking office) who had little education and had never held a job. Austrian-born, Hitler fancied himself an artist but lived for several years in Vienna practically as a derelict. There he learned to despise Jews and other "inferior" races. The coming of war in 1914 was a release; he immediately volunteered for the Germany army. He seemed to have been a good soldier but rose only to the rank of corporal. Shortly after the war, he joined a tiny group dedicated to hypernationalism and anti-Semitism and became the leader of what was to grow into the National Socialist German Workers' Party. In the disordered situation, the NSDAP (to use its German initials) was only one of a large number of nuclei of the postwar discontented. Veterans for the most part, and frequently unemployed, they were radical in temper yet nationalistic; hence the name National Socialism aptly represented the blending of their emotions. Some of them were close to Bolshevism; in the early years there was some interchange of membership between the Nazi and Communist parties.

Hitler was a masterful speaker who knew all the tricks of persuasion and told people what they wanted to hear. He harped on the Treaty of Versailles, by which Germany acknowledged guilt for the war and promised impossible reparations, and he blamed not the leaders who had put Germany into the war and misconducted it but the democrats and socialists who had been compelled to sign the treaty. The Nazis denounced "interest slavery" and plutocracy and insisted on "socialism"—but never defined it. They claimed to be for family, community, and welfare and called for benefits for farmers, workers, and veterans; they promised protection for small business from capitalists, allegedly Jewish, and from communism, also allegedly Jewish. Hitler, who was no classic blond German, exalted the German race and promised a new community, a *Volksgemeinschaft* ruled by a heroic racial elite, free from the selfishness of capitalism and especially the pernicious Jews.

The ambiguous and contradictory program attracted the lower middle classes and white-collar workers.[4] It also drew young people, particularly university students, to comprise the shock troops of the party, which was a brotherhood of symbolism, ceremony, and dedication to a sacred cause of blood and patriotic exaltation.

As long as Germany remained prosperous, Hitler's talents counted for little; the Depression gave him his opportunity. Industrialists financed the party in hopes of rearmament orders. The unemployed flocked to the Storm Troops, which gave them an

---

[4]David Schoenbaum, *Hitler's Social Revolution: Class and Status in Nazi Germany, 1933–1939* (Garden City, N.Y.: Doubleday, 1966), p. 37.

immediate and gratifying occupation and promised to make jobs for all. The Communist Party also grew; and it helped Hitler to power by making violence customary and by joining in attacking the republic, equating democracy with fascism. Most of all, it frightened middle- and upper-class Germans, and Hitler proclaimed himself the savior of Germans from the Red onslaught.

The incessant, mostly illogical propaganda, of which most people tired in normal times, generated strong convictions in times of despair. The Nazis in 1932 became by a wide margin the largest party in the Reichstag. Hindenburg, after short-sighted and poorly informed efforts to get chancellors of his liking to conduct the government, was persuaded that it was necessary to bring in Hitler and his party. Hindenburg despised the ex-corporal, but he saw the necessity of broadening the government. In January 1933, in any case, Hitler's followers had only a small minority in the conservative cabinet, which was supposed to decide by majority vote. Yet in less than a year the Nazis were able by force and fraud to do away with the constitution.

To achieve full powers, Hitler called new elections in March 1933. In the midst of the campaign the Reichstag building burned, and Hindenburg was persuaded to declare an emergency. Whether or not it was Nazi arson is disputed, but the Nazis used it effectively to repress opposition and push through an enabling act amending the constitution. This act transferred legislative powers to the cabinet under certain restrictions, which were soon ignored. In the following months, other parties, beginning with the Communists and proceeding from Left to Right, down to the groups most closely allied with the Hitlerites, were dissolved. Union premises were occupied and strikes forbidden, equally without resistance. Press and radio were placed under the control of Josef Goebbels and the new Ministry of Enlightenment and Propaganda. In May 1933 crowds danced in the streets as bonfires were made of books by many of Germany's most celebrated writers. Eminent Germans began speaking with awe of the *Fuehrer* (leader) as the incorporation of the nation. Nazis were placed in charge of all significant official and unofficial organizations, and by December 1933 the Nazi party was declared equivalent to the state. In the following year, Hitler ordered the murder of about a thousand of his followers whose radicalism seemed threatening, plus a few conservatives. He also occupied the post of president, vacated by the death of Hindenburg, and required the army to swear loyalty to his person.

The creed or ideology in the name of which Hitler and the Nazis ruled was remarkably crude and incoherent, a mass of mysticism and prejudices. A basic theme was the superiority of the undefined German or Nordic or Aryan race, but Germans were generally considered superior to more Nordic Scandinavians. The opposite "race" was the Jewish, which was trying to conquer the world by masterful deceit. Democracy or liberalism was seen as a Jewish-supported attack on the German race, to be repelled along with communism. The natural and proper scheme of government was by the superior few, the born leaders, in particular by the high Leader himself, the trustee of the entire people. Other elements were mixed in, such as German authoritarian tradition harkening back to the Holy Roman Empire, the moral superiority of the farmers with roots in the German earth, the German mission of civilizing and colonizing Eastern Europe, and the domesticity of women. Some enthusiastic Nazis even thought of reviving the ancient Teutonic pantheon of Wotan, Thor, and so on. However, the Nazis had no catechism but a list of virtues. The good Nazi was expected to be brave, manly, self-sacrificing, and above all unconditionally and enthusiastically loyal to his superiors, ultimately to Adolf Hitler.

The only political theory was the "leadership principle" *(Fuehrerprinzip)*, according to which all authority derives from above. There was no orderly way of choosing the Fuehrer or means of replacing him if he should prove to be mortal. He was simply there, a political fact, and his arbitrary decree was law. Around him there was no stable delegation of power; a man (no woman held a political position of importance) rose or fell according to his standing in the eyes of the Fuehrer. There was no constitution and no cabinet but a sort of court in the style of classic despotism. There was not even a party rulebook; the German Nazis were far less systematic in this regard than the Russian Communists. Hitler usually let his subordinates run programs entrusted to them, intervening only as necessary to settle disputes.

Little remained of old political structures. The Reichstag met occasionally to function as a claque or sounding board, as to hear Hitler's declaration of war against Poland on September 1, 1939. There were occasional plebiscites, the announced results of which showed nearly unanimous support. Local units were reduced to administrative subdivisions under leaders delegated from the center. Independent organizations of any kind were discouraged, although not so completely forbidden as in Communist countries. Publication and broadcasting were put in the service of the party and state, although again the Nazis were less thorough than the Soviets; German papers printed much more politically indifferent material than has been the Communist practice.

The Nazi economy was not extensively nationalized (that is, formally taken from former owners) but was placed under tight party-state control. Workers were organized into a Labor Front like the trade unions of Communist countries and received flattery and symbolic concessions while wages were held down. The owner or manager was called "leader" of the factory. Competition was largely removed and profits became more secure, but owners were left little freedom of operation. Small business, which the Nazis had sworn to protect, was usually sacrificed to big business, which was more productive and easier to supervise. Nazi social policies were somewhat contradictory. Aristocrats of all kinds—generals, industrialists, bankers, bureaucrats—were highly regarded and left in place to serve the state (except for Jews). On the other hand, crude Nazi bosses were considered superior to titled bluebloods, and princes served in the labor corps alongside sons of farmers.[5]

The Nazis ruled through monopolies of organization and propaganda and through terror. Josef Paul Goebbels, an early and faithful associate of Hitler, undertook to mold opinion by any means; he was rather remarkably frank in saying that the bigger the lie the better. The Nazis were fond of mysticism and ceremony, martial music, mass exercises, sacred flags, and the like. They were successful at least in getting the masses to cheer loudly and in making millions of formerly Communist workers, who had little reason to be grateful to the regime, into its brave soldiers. The cheers were louder because the political police, the Gestapo, repressed all opposition. The death camps were constructed for the mass annihilation of Jews and others only during the war; but many thousands of Communists, Social Democrats, independent intellectuals, and others were subject to arbitrary violence from the beginning of Nazi rule. It was a dual state,

[5]Ibid., p. 77.

lawful in ordinary transactions and management of the economy, entirely arbitrary in political affairs, dealing with people according to caprice or "racial instinct."[6]

Not much terror was necessary until late in the Nazi day, however, because the Third Reich was quite successful by most standards. Many Germans, letting hope sway reason, saw Hitler's accession as the dawning of a new era of strength, prosperity, and happiness for Germany. Numerous foreigners then and later were impressed by the glowing enthusiasm of Hitler's bands, especially the young who wished to inherit the earth. Hitler came to power at the low point of the Depression; industrial production for some years rose rapidly, and the long lines of unemployed shrank and disappeared. More remarkable and fateful was Hitler's success in increasing German power in the world. Because of the passivity of Britain and France and their unwillingness to use force to maintain unilateral restrictions on Germany, Hitler was able to repudiate the Treaty of Versailles, rearm Germany, and reoccupy militarily the Rhineland. In March 1938 he fulfilled an old dream by incorporating Austria into the Reich, and a few months later he humiliated the Western powers by extorting their agreement to the annexation of German-speaking parts of Czechoslovakia. Hitler seemed to be the miracle-worker of German history.

Unsated, the Nazis, having laid aside their fierce anticommunism in a friendship pact with Stalin, went to war in September 1939. Poland was blitzed in a matter of days, and a few months later Hitler's armored divisions conquered Norway, Denmark, the Low Countries, and France. In the spring of 1941,

[6]Ernst Fraenkel, *The Dual State: A Contribution to the Theory of Dictatorship* (New York: Oxford University Press, 1941).

lightning campaigns completed German domination of southeastern Europe, Yugoslavia, and Greece. Then Hitler turned on the biggest power of all, the Soviet Union, and for a few months his armies seemed invincible, capturing millions of prisoners and territories as large as all Western Europe. His triumphs were hypnotic, so that even after the German forces began their retreat from the Volga to Berlin, there was no organized opposition. Although it became daily more obvious that the only result of continuing the hopeless battle was more death and destruction, there were no strikes, no anti-Nazi riots. Hitler had made himself the focus of the state and removed all alternative authority. Except for an attempted coup in July 1944, Germans remained suicidally obedient until Hitler killed himself as Russian forces were closing in on his Berlin bunker in the spring of 1945.

Nazism left Germany conquered and ruined. As a system of government, however, it was in the short term quite effective. It mobilized traditional German skills, industriousness, and organizational ability; the revolutionary Nazis made better use of the old elites, especially in industry and the army, than Communist revolutionaries have usually done. They were able to carry on the war with such virtuosity that the Allies, who enjoyed overwhelmingly superior resources, could drive them back only with much greater numbers.

But nazism was basically self-destructive. German science was so strong that it continued to produce excellent weapons, but many scientists were driven out, and German education was degraded not only in quality but in quantity, as university enrollment shrank. If nazism had endured, Germany would have become rather soon a technologically backward nation. The anarchic political system, moreover, was already degenerating into disorganized despotism when it was cut down by defeat.

THE FEDERAL REPUBLIC

There was no surrender until Nazi forces had been virtually destroyed, and the end of the war found Germany with no government. Even local administrations disappeared as Nazi officials vanished. The only authority was that of the occupying military forces in the zones allotted to each by Allied agreement: central Germany under Soviet rule (except the four-power control of Berlin), the northwest under the British, the southwest under the Americans, and a French sector in the west. Part of East Prussia was handed over to the Soviet Union, and the remainder of what might be called Eastern Germany was given to Poland. Some 12 million Germans were deported from these lands (and from Czechoslovakia and other countries of Central and Eastern Europe) to what remained of Germany.[7]

Millions of refugees added to the misery of a devastated land. Transportation was only slowly restored. Industrial production was less than a third of the prewar level in 1946 and rose only slightly by mid-1948. A large part of the population was undernourished, kept alive by the charity of the victors in the west, by the desire of the Russians to extract reparations in the east. A pack of American cigarettes was worth a month's wages, most of the workforce was unemployed or underemployed, and the people were stunned and demoralized. Perhaps as many Germans died during the first two years of occupation as during the six years of war.

The occupying powers had little idea of what to do with Germany except to punish

[7]For details, see Aidan Crawley, *The Rise of Western Germany 1945–1972* (London: Collins, 1973).

war criminals and remove Nazi influences— 169,000 persons were tried for war crimes in the American zone, several times more than in the Russian and British zones together. At first it was generally assumed that Germany would continue to exist as a state, and some effort was made to govern it by agreement of the four occupying powers. But the wartime alliance of the Soviet Union with Britain and the United States was replaced by the cold war. Their opposite purposes became evident early in 1947, when President Truman undertook to prevent a communist victory in Greece and proclaimed the Truman Doctrine of halting the spread of Soviet-sponsored communism everywhere. The greatest potential prize was Germany, and the desire of each side to protect its interests there was the key factor in determining the political structures that eventually emerged.

For the Soviet zone, this meant the building up of a separate communist state on the Soviet model, the basis of which was laid by German Communists who had spent the war in the Soviet Union and returned with the Soviet army. On the Western side, it meant the abandonment of ideas of deindustrializing Germany—halting the dismantling of factories of military significance and the shipment of equipment as reparation to the Soviet Union—the installation of first local and then regional *(Land)* governments, and the union of the three Western zones. A major step toward separate German governments was the issuance of separate currencies on the Western and Soviet sides in June 1948. Germany thereafter had two separate economies. The Russians furthered the division by blockading the Western sectors of Berlin, which had to be supplied by a massive airlift.

The next stage was the establishment of a government for the part of Germany under the control of the Western powers. Delegates from the parliaments of the eleven states, or *Länder*, meeting as a Parliamentary Council, drew up a Basic Law. This was not a constituent assembly drafting a constitution, because the idea of a permanent division of Germany was inadmissible. For the same reason, the small city of Bonn on the Rhine, which lacked the appearance of a permanent national capital, was made the center of government.

The Basic Law, which governs the Federal Republic of Germany *(Bundesrepublik Deutschland)* today, is long and detailed, with 149 articles; it includes many trivia, such as the requirement of the consent of certain Länder to changes of rules regarding notaries (Article 138). Unlike the postwar Japanese constitution, the Basic Law was not dictated by the Allies, although it conformed to their wishes and ideas. The most controversial question in its formulation was the degree of federalism or centralization. A compromise was reached whereby most powers went to the central government, but the Länder retained a strong role. The form of government adopted was parliamentary, with the chancellor responsible to a popularly elected house, the *Bundestag,* while an upper house represented the Länder. The position of the chancellor was fortified, however, to avoid the instability of Weimar cabinets, whereas the presidency was weakened to prevent presidential authoritarianism. The Basic Law is amendable by a two-thirds vote of both houses of parliament, and it has been patched by dozens of minor amendments.

Elections held under the new Basic Law in August 1949 produced a Bundestag which (with delegates from the Länder) chose a president. The Bundestag then by a majority of one made Konrad Adenauer chancellor. Previously mayor of Cologne, with an unimpeachable anti-Nazi record, Adenauer had spent the war in limbo and had emerged to become the dominant figure in the church-

oriented party, the Christian Democratic Union (CDU). A masterful, sometimes authoritarian character, Adenauer, who was seventy-three when elected, remained in power for fourteen years. He stamped his personality on the new state, and during his tenure it acquired a firm footing and general acceptance.

Unlike the Weimar Republic, the Bonn Republic soon achieved a legitimacy questioned only by a few extremists. One reason is that Weimar replaced the traditional and successful Second Reich; the Federal Republic followed the shameful, illegitimate, and ultimately disastrous Third Reich. The whole set of questions of responsibility for the war simply did not arise. There was never much nostalgia for Hitler's Reich, and support for neo-Nazism decreased steadily after 1952.[8] Moreover, the Federal Republic stood in contrast to the Soviet-sponsored German Democratic Republic (GDR), which most Germans saw as a Russian imposition in which lack of freedom was accompanied by a standard of living much lower than that of the Federal Republic.

The other great source of strength of the Bonn regime was its superlative economic success, long called the German *Wirtschaftswunder,* or economic miracle, an achievement matched only by the Japanese, whose experience paralleled that of the Germans. Like the Japanese, the West Germans seemed to turn their energies and talents from military-political to economic achievement. From 1950 (when the prewar level had been reattained) to 1970, West German industrial production increased fivefold, and exports increased twentyfold. War damage to equipment had been much less than commonly supposed, only about 15 percent, because of protection, camouflaging of important plants,

---

[8]John H. Herz, *The Government of Germany,* 2nd ed. (New York: Harcourt Brace Jovanovich, 1972), p. 25.

and short-sighted Allied concentration on the bombing of housing.[9] Recovery could therefore be rapid. Marshall Plan aid, 1948–1952, contributed to rebuilding the infrastructure. German labor worked diligently for relatively low wages, and there were few strikes. The lack of a military burden helped in the early years. American-supported emphasis on a market economy and decartelization may also have been useful. With the "economic miracle," civic consensus grew and made democracy more viable.

Adenauer's particular achievement, however, was to change Germany quickly from a nonsovereign international pariah into a full-fledged member of the Western alliance. He did this in the face, at first, of strong opposition of the second largest party, the Social Democrats, and others who believed that reunification was possible if Germany avoided alignment with the West, the United States in particular. Adenauer was able to push through his pro-Western policy because it became increasingly evident that the Russians would not permit a united Germany which would be free to act independently—that is, to adopt an anti-Soviet position. In 1950 the temper of confrontation was raised by the Korean war, and Germany was urged to build up armed forces of its own (under NATO command) to share in the defense of the West.

It gradually became accepted that reunification was unlikely, barring a massive reordering in international relations, and that the Federal Republic had its role to play on the frontier of the Western world. Its reward was the recovery of sovereignty. The Allied powers renounced nearly all their rights of intervention in 1955. They retained chiefly responsibility for West Berlin, partially included in West Germany (official bodies, such as parliamentary committees, meet there occasionally) but permanently in need of Allied protection. Germany remains under a few restrictions, particularly the prohibition against nuclear weapons.

The cutting off of East Germany made it easier for the western areas to have a new political birth. It had the unintended desirable consequence of reducing West Germany to a population comparable to those of Britain, France, and Italy, making it easier to fit Germany into the NATO alliance and the European Economic Community. In 1951 West Germany, France, Italy, the Netherlands, Belgium, and Luxembourg formed a steel and coal community, which was expanded to become the Common Market in 1958. The enthusiasm of the 1950s for European federal union faded in the face of multiple difficulties, but the EEC became a permanent reality and gradually acquired more importance not only for free trade in manufactured goods but also for capital flow, monetary management, agricultural controls, and the free movement of labor. Through it Germany tied its life firmly and apparently irrevocably to the West.

With domestic and international success, Adenauer attained great popularity. In the Bundestag election of 1957, the CDU (with its Bavarian affiliate, the Christian Social Union, or CSU) obtained the first one-party majority in German history. But in time Adenauer's charm wore thin, and his arrogance increased. He came to see himself and the party he dominated as virtually equivalent to the state and found opposition intolerable. In 1963, at age eighty-seven, he was induced to resign in favor of his economics minister, Ludwig Erhard.

Erhard's "social market" policies (laissez-faire and incentives for production plus benefits for workers) were very successful, and he was at first highly popular. But he lacked

---

[9]Fritz Crone, *Die deutsche Tradition: Uber die Schwierigkeiten Demokratie zu leben* (Opladen: Westdeutscher, Verlag, 1975), p. 31.

the steel to make an effective chancellor, and his position disintegrated. By 1966, losing credit in a minor recession, he resigned to make way for a "great coalition" of the CDU-CSU with the principal opposition party, the Social Democrats (SPD). Kurt Georg Kiesinger of the CDU became chancellor, seconded by Willy Brandt, former mayor of Berlin, of the SPD. Under this arrangement parliamentary opposition practically ceased, and the Bundestag lost significance. The opposition, lacking expression in parliament, grew into an "out-of-parliament-opposition" (*Ausser-parlamentarische Opposition,* or APO) of radical, mostly leftist, forces who indulged in more or less violent activities.

The lack of opposition in the Bundestag, together with the economic slowdown, also led to a brief resurgence of rightist politics. A party that called itself the National Democratic Party of Germany (NDP) and claimed not to be anti-Semitic or pro-Nazi but seemed rather Nazi in spirit gained a few seats in several *Land* parliaments. (It failed to enter the Bundestag, however, and within a few years had virtually disappeared.) The important service of the "great coalition" was to facilitate a democratic transfer of power by permitting the SPD to show itself responsible and capable of government and giving some of its members experience in ministerial office. The 1969 election gave the largest number of votes to the CDU-CSU, but the SPD plus the small liberal Free Democratic Party (FDP) held a majority, and the FDP saw a greater role for itself as ally of the SPD than of the CDU. A new coalition was formed with a slim majority in the Bundestag, and the CDU-CSU went unhappily into opposition. The Bundestag again became active and important.

The accession of Willy Brandt to leadership of the SPD-FDP government in 1969 marked a maturation of German democracy and the beginning of a new era. Brandt had gained celebrity by his defiance of Communist pressure as mayor of West Berlin. He was untainted by nazism, having spent the Nazi years in exile and in opposition. (His predecessor, Kiesinger, had served the Nazis.) With a clean and trustworthy image, Brandt stood for the new generation. His chief interest, like Adenauer's, was foreign policy; but Brandt looked rather to the East, undertaking to normalize German relations with the Communist world while maintaining ties with the West. This *Ostpolitik* took Brandt to Moscow and to Warsaw, where he made an immortal gesture by kneeling before a monument to murdered Jews. Ostpolitik achieved the opening of diplomatic relations with the GDR and treaties providing for improved relations and recognition of the territorial status quo. The division of Germany was slightly eased at the price of surrender of the Federal Republic's claim to be the sole legitimate representative of all Germans and virtual abandonment of the dream of reunification.

Brandt's opening to the East won him a Nobel Peace Prize. Some in his own party, however, were uneasy about what they considered excessive concessions to Communist powers, and a few FDP deputies crossed over to the CDU to erode his slender majority. In 1972 he had to call new elections; the Bundestag was dissolved prematurely for the first time. The results confirmed the coalition in power, but Brandt's prestige waned. Attention turned to domestic affairs, which he seemed less competent to handle. In 1974 Brandt wearily resigned.

Helmut Schmidt then took the reins. Former leader of the SPD group in the Bundestag and finance minister, Schmidt was tough, pragmatic, and chiefly concerned with economic stability. Under his leadership, Germany affirmed its world role as a leading economic power, and Schmidt did not mind giving the United States monetary advice.

The mark became one of the world's strongest currencies, and the balance of payments became a much hotter issue than reunification.

At length, however, the recession of 1981–1982 came to Germany also, although its economy continued to be among the strongest in the world. The uneasy alliance between the SPD and the FDP broke down, as the latter feared being dragged down by the growing unpopularity of the former. The FDP allied itself with the CDU, and the leader of that party, Helmut Kohl, was chosen chancellor. He brought about an election on March 6, 1983. The victory of the CDU-CSU was interpreted as something of a victory for the United States and the Reagan administration, which had backed the conservatives as strongly as it discreetly could, while the Soviet Union had done its best for the SPD.

President and Chancellor

The architects of the Basic Law deprived the president of the powers Hindenburg misused. The president is elected not by the people but by the Bundestag plus an equal number of delegates from the Länder; thus weakened, he is allowed only five years of office instead of seven. He has been, as intended, a nonpartisan head of state, rarely called upon to make political decisions. The election of the president has usually been noncontroversial, but partisan politics came to the fore in the choice of the strongly conservative and one-time Nazi Karl Carstens in May 1979. As Bundestag president from 1976 to 1979, however, Carstens had showed himself to be above partisan politics.

The president has the privilege of proposing a chancellor to the Bundestag, but it elects whomever it pleases by secret ballot. Under certain circumstances, especially if the chancellor should be defeated in the Bundestag and no successor is chosen, the president can dissolve the Bundestag. Other official acts must be countersigned by the chancellor or a minister. It is not clear whether the president could refuse to sanction a measure decided by the cabinet or decline to name a minister desired by the chancellor. The case has not arisen; indeed, there has been no real conflict between president and chancellor. It is the president's prerogative to have a representative at cabinet meetings. He is subjected to impeachment by either the Bundestag or the Bundesrat.

It may be that the president could have been more aggressive or might be in some future emergency, instead of remaining little more than a figurehead. But the chancellor, on the other hand, has such a strong position that the political system can only qualifiedly be called parliamentary. He is protected from parliamentary overthrow somewhat like the premier of the Fifth French Republic, but unlike the French premier he is master of the government. He can be ousted only if the opposition in the Bundestag agrees on a successor and elects a new chancellor by a majority. In view of party discipline, a chancellor can normally expect to remain in office for the full term of the Bundestag. It is not certain, however, that constitutional provisions would really protect a chancellor who had lost his majority in the Bundestag but whom it could not replace. He might well surrender. This occurred often in the French Third and Fourth Republics as premiers gave up—as they were expected to do—in the face of a hostile chamber without being under constitutional compulsion to resign. It is also conceivable that a hostile majority in the Bundesrat could block legislation and make it impossible for the chancellor to govern.

The German chancellor, like his British counterpart, can ask the president to dissolve the Bundestag if it refuses a vote of confidence. This occurred in 1972, when defections cut away the slender SPD-FDP majority of Willy Brandt. The CDU-CSU tried to elect its leader as the new chancellor, but he failed by two votes in the secret ballot. A few months later, the president proceeded, at Brandt's request, to dissolve the chamber after a no-confidence vote and call new elections, which gave Brandt a workable majority. Kohl became chancellor by a constructive no-confidence vote. Shortly afterwards, in order to strengthen and legitimize his government, he arranged to lose a no-confidence vote, after which he could ask the president to dissolve the Bundestag and call elections.

The chancellor has full freedom to name and change the cabinet, and he is the national leader, beside whom the president is a figurehead and the Bundestag a debating society. He is also the effective symbol of his party.

Administrative Apparatus

There is no requirement that the chancellor and ministers belong to the Bundestag, but they ordinarily do so. Cabinets have customarily been small, from fifteen to twenty or so, and the number of strictly political positions is minimal. A minister has no cabinet, only a parliamentary state secretary, who is a sort of junior minister concerned with relations with the Bundestag, and a permanent state secretary who heads the bureaucratic apparatus of the ministry. The latter is a civil servant selected by the minister and serving at his pleasure. About ten top civil servants in each ministry are subject to transfer by the minister, but any removed must be given a new position commensurate with his or her status.[10] When the Kohl government ended the thirteen-year SPD tenure, very few changes were made.

There is no tradition like the British of a politically neutral upper civil service, and permanent officials engage in party politics. They are free to enter the Bundestag without loss of status, and they make up about a third of the membership of that body.[11] They continue to receive salaries while serving as members of Landtage, filling up to half the seats in them. As a consequence, they also form a large part of the Bundesrat. The potential influence of the civil service is thus obviously enormous.

The senior bureaucrats seem to have a strong *esprit de corps* based on the German tradition of highly competent, principled, and respected public servants. Entrance, as in France, is mostly through training and competitive examinations. Only about a tenth are employed by the federal government, 80 percent by the Länder, and 10 percent by local authorities.[12]

In the past, the bureaucracy was authoritarian in mentality and contributed to the breakdown of the Weimar Republic. It has been extremely rank-conscious; a suitable title was a life's ambition. Officials are unionized and have security (they can be dismissed only for grave cause by a court of their peers), good pay, and prestige. The upper civil service is something of a caste standing above the society it regulates. Civil servants draw up the laws, help to pass them, formulate implementing orders, and execute them. Perhaps half the upper ranks come from civil service families. In one respect, however, the German civil service is less narrow than the French. Entrants come from a large number of universities under the jurisdiction not of the central government but of various Länder.[13]

---

[10]David P. Conradt, *The German Polity* (New York: Longman, 1979), p. 163.

[11]Herz, *Government of Germany*, p. 112.
[12]Conradt, *The German Polity*, p. 168.
[13]See Renate Mayntz and Fritz W. Scharf, *Policy-Making in the Federal German Bureaucracy* (Amsterdam: Elsevier, 1975).

The Law and the Courts

The German legal and judicial system is rather similar to the French. It relies on code law, ultimately based on the Roman tradition. It is the duty of the courts to administer the law. German judges, like the French, devote themselves to the judiciary from the beginning of their careers. They are named and promoted by the ministers of justice and form, not a separate branch of government but a branch of the civil service with independent status. Land and federal courts are a single system, in which regular tribunals are under the state and federal tribunals hear appeals. The corps of prosecutors forms a parallel hierarchy. Judges conduct trials and examine witnesses, and decisions are made by panels of judges with a few jurors. Again like their French colleagues, German judges are said to be inclined to assume the prisoner is guilty.

The Constitutional Court has special political significance. The idea was, of course, an innovation in German and European practice, imitative of the U.S. Supreme Court. The sixteen judges, forming two panels, are elected by the Bundesrat and a Bundestag committee proportionally representing the parties. A two-thirds majority is required, so the appointments are probably nonpartisan. Judges need not come from the bench, so there is some diversity of backgrounds. They serve a single twelve-year term.

Like the U.S. Supreme Court, the Constitutional Court has the power to declare laws unconstitutional and void, and it has done so freely. Unlike its U.S. counterpart, it advises on the constitutionality of legislation under consideration, thus shortening legal battles. It has had the task of deciding the legality of allegedly antidemocratic parties. It adjudicates disputes between Länder and the federation and between organs of government; it may, for example, be called on to determine whether a particular piece of legislation requires the assent of the Bundesrat. Like the U.S. court, it is the guardian of civil liberties—which, in contrast to Britain and France, are enshrined in the Basic Law and are enforceable in court.

Federalism

West Germany is one of the world's very few successful federal systems. In the reconstruction of Germany, the United States favored federalism as an impediment to dictatorship, but the federal structure grew naturally from the formation of the West German state. The Allies established regional governments after the war before much thought had been given to a central government. Nearly all the new units were artificially carved out, with only occasional resemblances to the old semisovereign German states, and they have not (with some exceptions, such as historic Bavaria) enjoyed as much loyalty as Americans give states such as Texas or Ohio. But the Länder soon became organizational entities with their own momentum and vested political interests. Bonn has never become a real focus of German life, and elites are dispersed among numerous centers—Hamburg, Frankfurt, Stuttgart, Munich, and the Rhine-Ruhr cities.

The Basic Law was drawn up by delegations from Land parliaments, and it was ratified not by plebiscite but (unlike the French constitution) by the component states. The Länder are represented at the federal level more closely than American states are represented in the Congress. The Bundesrat, in the German tradition, consists not of elected representatives but of delegates from the Länder, each of which has three to five seats according to population. This system implies inequality of popular representation; Bremen, the smallest Land, has three seats and a population of 700,000; Nordrhein-West-phalen has five and 16.5 million people. A further concession to the federal principle is that votes are cast as a unit according to the instructions of the Land government. Delegates to the Bundesrat are usually Land cabinet ministers or civil servants, not politicians, and they may be replaced at any time.

In the distribution of powers under the Basic Law, the Länder are less favored than American states. The federal government has not only the powers regularly vested in a federation, such as defense and foreign affairs, but also concurrent and prevailing jurisdiction in most other matters. The Länder have residual powers in education, culture, religious affairs, police, and local government. Even in these areas, the federal government may intrude; the expanding cost of higher education, for example, has made it necessary to call for federal assistance and consequently to accept federal controls. But the Länder are in another way stronger than American states, because they are charged with the administration of federal laws. They thus may be able to block federal policies by noncooperation. The federal and Land administrations, closely intertwined, share revenues. Some taxes go entirely to Bonn and some entirely to the Länder, but most are divided. Of public revenues, 40 to 50 percent are spent by the central government, about a third by the Länder, and the remainder by local government.[14]

The Länder have parliamentary governments, with varying party complexions, like the federal government in miniature, except that all but Bavaria have unicameral legislatures. Parties out of power in Bonn hold office and responsibility in various Land capitals, just as an out party in the United States can maintain itself in a number of state-houses. Different parties keep up the practice of working with one another, and the national opposition party can show its ability to govern. Elections are held at least every four years in each Land. Occurring at odd times between federal elections, they add to the interest of politics, are weathervanes of national trends, and keep changing the political scene.

THE PARLIAMENT

German parliamentary government lacks the historical associations of the British House of Commons, not to speak of the picturesque traditions. No German representative body has ever played a very hallowed role; German history has nothing to compare even with French Assemblies. Premodern German parliaments were defeated, the Reichstag was shackled in Bismarck's Reich, and the Weimar Reichstag was reduced by the Nazis to a chorus. In the Bonn republic, the federal parliament has usually been dull and rather bureaucratic, and its debates have served less as a means of political education than those of the House of Commons. However, since 1969 the Bundestag has been a livelier and more effective body, and its importance seems to be increasing.

The Bundestag has 496 members, who get a reasonable salary (equivalent to $38,000 in 1983) plus considerable expenses. A few deputies are associated with unions or other interest groups. Many, about a third, are civil servants on leave; like their French and unlike their British counterparts, civil servants are allowed to run for and occupy legislative office without loss of official status. Few—recently under 10 percent—are women.

The Bundestag chooses its president, who regularly comes from the largest party (the CDU except for 1972–1976) and who is not

[14]Günther Kloss, *West Germany* (London: Macmillan, 1976), pp. 16, 31.

expected to be so politically neutral as the Speaker of the British House of Commons. The president has important functions in handling the business of the Bundestag, along with the Council of Elders of twenty-seven members drawn from the parties proportionally to their strength. Among other things, this steering committee selects Bundestag committees and their chairs and sends proposed legislation to appropriate specialized committees. There are about twenty of these committees, and most of the work of the Bundestag is done in them. Much of the real work of the house is also done within the *fraktion,* as the party group is called. Any fifteen or more deputies can constitute a fraktion and hence claim representation in the Council of Elders and committees; in practice, the fraktion is equivalent to a deputation of a party. The fraktion has a leader and several assistants, who act as whips and coordinators, and it adopts a position on current questions. With rare exceptions, the deputies support the agreed position, as they must under penalty of expulsion and probable political death, because party support is virtually indispensable for reelection. A fraktion has some half-dozen sections specializing in foreign or defense matters, cultural affairs, economics, finances, and the like; a deputy ordinarily progresses by becoming a specialist in some area and thereby preparing for a leadership position.

The German parliament fulfills the normal parliamentary functions—legislation, examination of the budget, checking on administration, and education of the public regarding issues and alternatives. Its procedures are fairly conventional. Bills may be proposed by fifteen members of the Bundestag or the Bundesrat or by ministries and cabinet. If by the latter, they go first to the Bundesrat for examination by Land representatives. Then they go to the Bundestag, where the bills are considered mostly in com-

mittee and usually without publicity. Passed by the Bundestag, the bill goes back to the Bundesrat. If the Bundesrat rejects it, the Bundestag may override in about half the categories, comprising about half the legislation. Bundesrat concurrence is required, however, for constitutional amendments and many matters affecting Land governments or finances.[15] If the two houses are at odds, a committee may try to negotiate differences. In regard to the budget, Germany has the same rule as Britain and France that no proposals to increase spending can originate in the parliament. To avoid possible deadlock between the chancellor and a Bundestag hostile to him but unable to choose another, the drafters of the Basic Law devised a "legislative emergency," in which, with restrictions, bills rejected by the Bundestag may be passed by the Bundesrat alone. This procedure has never been needed.

In its control and education functions, the Bundestag has not been exceptionally successful. A defense commissioner to assist the parliament in overseeing the military—an office established as a reaction to the autonomy of the army under the Weimar government—has had little to do. There is also a committee to protect the interests of the parliament when it is not in session, a response to the failure of parliament to meet for long periods in the last pre-Nazi years. The committees on foreign affairs and defense are also permanently in session. The Bundestag can establish investigatory committees, which are entitled to summon members of the government; it must establish them at the demand of a quarter of its members. However, such committees have been inadequately staffed and lack the power to require information. They are controlled by the majority

---

[15]Ibid., p. 23; Frank Pilz, *Einführung in das politische System der Bundesrepublik Deutschland* (Munich: C. H. Beck, 1977), p. 53.

party, and in the strict discipline of German parties they amount to the government investigating itself. Officials may decline to give information, and information obtained may be held in secret.[16]

Questioning of ministers may be initiated by petition of at least twenty-six deputies; a dozen or so of these are held yearly. The government must reply, and the reply can be briefly debated. At the beginning of each day's, session there is a question hour when a deputy can ask up to three questions (submitted at least three days in advance); but they are usually trivial and have drawn little attention. More significant is the "topical hour" begun in 1965. Held at any time at the request of thirty deputies, it provides for five-minute speeches and has been devoted to ventilating opinion on issues of the moment.

The principal function of the Bundesrat is the coordination of federal legislation with its execution by the Länder. But it is an important body in its own right. Minister-presidents of the Länder hold the presidency by rotation, and delegates to it are Land ministers or their deputies, assisted by civil servants. The delegations serve as conduits for decisions made by the Land governments, which decide how the votes are to be cast. In practice, the Bundesrat serves to a large extent as a channel for bureaucratic influence on lawmaking.

Elections

The Bundestag has a term of four years, unless dissolved sooner because a cabinet loses its majority. This has occurred only twice in the history of the Federal Republic, although it befell all but one Reichstag of the Weimar years.[17] Candidates are nominated

in theory by conventions of delegates elected by party members, in practice mostly by regional or local party functionaries. There are no primaries. Candidates need not reside in their district or Land, but most of them do. There is no limit on electoral spending, but the federal government provides a subsidy for campaign purposes, recently DM 3.50 per voter in the previous election (there are also subsidies for Land and local campaigns). Parties also receive free television time corresponding to their previous voting strength. The voting age is eighteen, and turnout is a credit either to interest in democratic politics or to a sense of duty; it has regularly been well over 80 percent of the electorate.

Deputies are elected by a system of modified proportional representation that has been in effect since the founding of the Federal Republic. Half the seats are assigned to 248 electoral districts (half the number of members), and in each of these a deputy is elected by a simple plurality of votes, in the British and American style. But voters also choose a party, which presents a list of candidates within the Land. When the votes are added up, the seats won directly are subtracted from those to which the party would be entitled by list votes. The result is personalized proportional representation. The number of seats a party receives corresponds closely to the percentage of votes for its lists in the Länder, whereas voters have the pleasure of casting ballots for half the members of the Bundestag as individuals, and deputies can win election in their own name. As in England and France people vote mostly for the party and its candidate for chancellor, who is elected by the deputies of the party in the Bundestag.

The proliferation of small parties is avoided by the provision that a party must obtain at least 5 percent of the votes nationwide or directly elect members from at least three districts in order to benefit from the

[16]Pilz, *Einführung in das politische System*, p. 64.
[17]See Tony Burkett, *Parties and Elections in West Germany: The Search for Stability* (London: Hurst, 1975).

proportional provisions. Small parties are also discouraged by the fact that they must have at least fifteen deputies to form a fraktion and take part in the organizations of the Bundestag. The results of recent elections were as follows:

Party	1972	1976	1980	1983
CDU-CSU	44.9%	48.6%	44.5%	48.8%
SPD	45.8	42.6	42.9	38.2
FDP	8.4	7.9	10.6	6.9
Other	0.9	0.9	0.5	0.5
Green			1.5	5.6

Number of seats corresponds closely to percentage of votes.

THE PARTIES

The freedom to organize brought a flurry of party formation in the early days of the Bonn government; in 1949, eleven won places in the Bundestag. By 1953, however, only six were represented, and since 1961 only three (the CDU-CSU being counted as one), until the Greens managed to get over the 5 percent barrier in 1983.

The Basic Law recognizes parties as an essential part of the democratic process, and they are regulated by law. Party organization must be at least nominally democratic. The supreme organ is a party congress of delegates elected by members, which chooses high party officers. Parties tending "to harm or abolish the basic libertarian democratic order or to endanger the existence of the Federal Republic" are subject to proscription. A Communist party has been permitted since 1968, however. The two big parties stand against one another somewhat like the Republican and Democratic parties in the United States, both rather broad, the one more conservative and more representative of business interests, the other more reformist-statist and more associated with labor interests. The victory of neither represents a threat of revolutionary change.

Although other parties present candidates, all but the largest suffer the indifference of the masses. The CDU-CSU and the SPD have memberships in the range of a million, the FDP less than one-tenth as many. Germans are not much inclined to affiliate personally with parties, and membership is low in proportion to the population. The Constitutional Court outlawed official subsidies to the parties except for campaign purposes, and for the SPD and CDU-CSU the largest single source of income is membership dues; contributions are nearly as important for the conservative party, much less so for the leftist.

CDU

The Christian Democratic Union, together with its Bavarian affiliate, the Christian Social Union, has won the largest number of votes in all national elections except in 1972, when the SPD inched ahead. The CDU was organized soon after the war, and it gathered parts of all the pre-Nazi conservative and moderate parties into a broad coalition. As the successor of the old Catholic Center party, originally formed to oppose Bismarck's anti-Catholicism, it has something of a Catholic orientation in a country with slightly more Protestant adherents; and most practicing Catholics favor it. A substantial majority of CDU voters and deputies are Catholic. But it makes a strong effort to be nondenominational, balancing Catholics and Protestants in leading positions. It has a broad appeal among owners and workers, especially white-collar; in industrial cities and rural areas; and among farmers and small businesspeople. Women are more likely to support it than men.

During its entire formative period, Adenauer was the autocrat of the CDU. He remained chairman for two years after relinquishing the chancellorship, finally retiring at eighty-nine in 1965. Since then, the leadership has been ineffective, especially since the party went into opposition in 1969. The CDU is in power in most Länder and can consequently oppose the SPD-FDP government through the Bundesrat. In policies, the CDU is basically conservative. It long used the slogan "No experiments," and this has remained its feeling. Aside from unequivocal anticommunism, it is divided on both social and foreign policy. The Kohl government was less ideologically conservative than that of Reagan and Thatcher, but it likewise sought to reduce the role of the state, encourage private investment, check welfare spending, and promote traditional virtues of industry and patriotism.

CSU

The CDU is relatively decentralized, little more than a league of Land organizations. The Christian Social Union was originally organized autonomously to permit it to compete more effectively with a Bavarian regional party; but after the demise of that party, the CSU maintained its distinctiveness under the permanent leadership of Franz Josef Strauss. Its dominance in one of the largest Länder gives it special importance for the conservative leadership of Germany. It is a more authoritarian and centralized party than the CDU, more Catholic, more nationalist-rightist and anti-Communist. From 1969 and the beginning of Ostpolitik, it has led the opposition to concessions. There has been some friction with the CDU, which CSU leaders find too complacent and com-

promising. However, its leader, Strauss, was chosen to head the alliance in 1979. Despite failure in 1980, he remained influential and seemed to be an important mentor of the Kohl government in 1983. The CSU received 10.6 percent of the vote in the 1983 election, to 38.2 percent for the CDU; the former was rewarded with three places in the cabinet of eleven.

SPD

The Socialist is the oldest German party; it goes back to 1863 and the Association of German Workers found by Ferdinand Lassalle. It became the first German mass party. In the 1890s it adopted the ideology of Marx and Engels and talked of proximate and violent revolution. But as the revolution failed to appear and the workers became more prosperous, the SPD grew pragmatic and moderate in practice. In 1914 the SPD supported the war effort instead of the workers' international movement. At the end of the war, a majority of the party helped to stabilize the basically capitalist society, although a minority broke away to promote revolution as the new Communist party. During the Weimar period, the SPD was democratic-reformist.[18]

After World War II, the Socialist party in East Germany, where it probably represented a majority, was compelled to merge with the Communists. In the more conservative West, its advocacy of general nationalization was not very popular, and it was in the minority from the beginning of the Federal Republic. Perhaps stung by Nazi charges of being unpatriotic, it tried to outflank Adenauer by appeals to nationalism. It stood

---

[18]See Douglas A. Chalmers, *The Social Democratic Party of Germany: From Working-Class Movement to Modern Political Party* (New Haven, Conn.: Yale University Press, 1964).

for German reunification and opposed tying Germany to the West in the hope that the Soviet Union might permit a neutral Germany to reunite. This policy became increasingly unpopular, however, and was abandoned in 1959.

In that year the SPD, adopting the Bad Godesberg Program, discarded Marxism and the principle of class struggle. The party accepted the basic ideas of the CDU-led republic and the market economy, advocated nationalization and controls only for definite needs, and proposed nonclass welfare policies. Socialism was no longer to be a religion; indeed, Brandt declared that he was not a Socialist but a Social Democrat. After this metamorphosis, the SPD gradually but steadily gained ground until it formed a government in 1969 and became the largest party in 1972.

The renunciation of revolutionism has had its cost. The SPD has changed from a militant movement to a party of politicians. It is largely controlled from the center by a self-perpetuating group of functionaries, trade union officials, and elected and appointed government personnel, who manage the local party organizations and effectively decide nominations. The apparatus is stronger because the SPD is, more than other parties, a business, owning much real estate, presses, and securities; its income from property is more than double that of the CDU. Most workers vote for it and the chief labor federation is friendly to it, but there is no organizational tie to trade unions like that which binds the British Labour party. In Germany, political socialism antedated strong trade unions; the latter did not create the party but came to its support.

The SPD is free to take moderate positions because, unlike the French and Italian Socialist parties, it is not flanked by a strong Communist party competing for the workers' vote and drumming on radical slogans. After Brandt, the party became even more centrist; Helmut Schmidt, representing its conservative wing, seemed as devoted to traditional economics as most American presidents. The SPD, however, has long had a radical sector, especially among the youth; and the party has been pulled to the left by losses of many members of the antiestablishment Green party. Going into opposition to the Kohl government, the SPD took a semi-neutralist position, proposing a moratorium on new missiles and greater efforts to reach agreement with the Soviet Union, while promising public works spending to create jobs, a shorter work week, and other benefits.

FDP

The Free Democratic Party has shared in nearly all the governments of the Federal Republic because its relatively small delegation has been necessary for one of the two big parties to form a majority. The FDP has consequently held a number of ministries out of proportion to its voting strength—in the Kohl government it had three of eleven, including the foreign ministry, held by its long-time leader, Hans-Dietrich Genscher. It has no faint hope of forming a government or even becoming a major party in any foreseeable future. To the contrary, it has not won a majority in a single district since 1961, and it remains on the scene only because of proportional representation. It lives under the perennial fear of falling below the 5 percent necessary to remain in the Bundestag, fearful that if it once lost its strategic position it would be deserted.

Ideologically, the FDP stands slightly apart from the CDU and the SPD. It is less conservative than the CDU in regard to church-state relations, civil rights, and relations with the East. On the other hand, it is even more favorable to free enterprise than the CDU. It has seemed to ally with either of the two big parties with equal ease.

The Greens

A new party made a sensational entry to the Bundestag in April 1983, carrying potted plants and wearing beards, sweaters, and tennis shoes. The Greens, a coalition of environmentalists, antinuclear activists, pacifists, students, teachers, civil servants, dropouts, and the generally disaffected, became a national party only in 1978. In 1979, they caused a sensation by winning 3.2 percent of the votes for the European parliament, and they soon had places in six of the eleven Landtage. They campaigned energetically and picturesquely against pollution, big construction projects, nuclear power, and above all, nuclear missiles. The outstanding personality, Petra Kelly, was educated mostly in the United States, where she learned the politics of protest during the Vietnam war. The party is very democratic, trying to settle issues by general discussion and changing leaders every two years.

The Greens include a number of Marxists, and they use Marxist vocabulary. They generally regard the United States as more dangerous than the Soviet Union. But the party purveys much more modernized German romanticism than communism. The Greens protest not so much capitalism as materialism; they would rather undo industrial civilization than socialize it. When the 1983 Bundestag opened, the Greens were offered seats on the left; they demanded and received a place in the middle. The Greens suffer a basic weakness in that they have no program for managing the economy. After entering the Bundestag, the party was seriously divided over playing the regular po-litical game and reaping the benefits of participation, or standing on principles, refusing to cooperate with the system, and conserving their purity of rebellious faith.

Minor Parties

The Federal Republic has been inhospitable to both leftist and rightist extremists. In the first years, there were several regional parties, but they faded out, except for the CSU, which survived as a branch of the CDU. A party speaking for the millions of refugees from the East disappeared as they merged into German society. There have been some right-wing parties (which have denied Nazi affiliation), but their appeal has diminished steadily, partly because of the firmness of the Federal Republic, partly because of the succession of generations.

On the Left, the Communist Party of Germany (KPD) had some strength immediately after the war because of traditional appeal, Soviet prestige, and miserable conditions, but it declined as East Germany became an antimodel and the West prospered. In 1956 the KPD was outlawed by the Constitutional Court in the atmosphere of the cold war and confrontation. In the changed atmosphere of 1968 a new German Communist Party (DKP) was permitted—not because the law had changed but because the fear of communism had subsided. It is closely tied to and dependent on the East German government, and it has faithfully followed the Soviet and East German line. However, it has not prospered despite its support and recently has received only a small fraction of one percent of the vote. The far Left, in any case, is split between pro-Soviet Communists, anti-Soviet Maoists or Trotskyites, the unattached New Left, and anarchists. The terrorists of the latter 1970s were apparently liquidated by efficient police action.

GERMAN SOCIETY: AUTHORITARIAN OR DEMOCRATIC?

For many years, support for democratic institutions has been maturing, and German values have evolved away from the traditional past.[19] The old awe of authority, instinct for obedience, and reverence for uniforms seems largely to have vanished, at least among the younger, more modern, and more prosperous sectors of the population. A large majority have known only the Bonn republic, and the generation unscarred by the Nazi era is a much less respectful breed of individualists. With the disappearance of Prussia, the Prussian tradition has become irrelevant. The Protestant and Catholic churches were both rather authoritarian and linked to the state, and as late as the 1960s the Catholic Church was advising people how to vote (for the CDU-CSU). But in recent years, the trend has been away from both churchgoing and denominational schooling, although most Germans pay the voluntary 10 percent income tax surcharge for their church. It is possibly significant that the German language is thoroughly infiltrated by English and that the Germans, unlike the French, are not concerned.

Psychologists would consider especially significant the changes in sexual and family mores. Although German women still mostly accept traditional feminine roles and German society is still strongly male-dominated, especially in government and politics, women have begun to take jobs from which they were previously excluded, and there is a strong women's movement. Sexual freedom and pornography are almost up to Scandinavian levels, a marked change from the old Germany. West Germany has the lowest birthrate ever recorded in any nation in peacetime, under ten per thousand, far below the replacement level; school entrants in the early 1980s were only half as numerous as in the 1970s. A major Nazi program was to produce as many new Germans as possible; the new Germany seems bent on racial suicide. And much of the old spirit of domination has gone out of husband-wife and parent-child relations; there have been strong drives for permissive or antiauthoritarian education.[20] These changes have been greater in the more educated and wealthier sectors of society, whom the less educated follow.[21]

Decreased respect for authority and status is correlated with increased social mobility. Germany has hardly been internally divided into two nations in the way of France, and class conflict arising from industralization was considerably mitigated from an early date by social security and state paternalism. But class differences were rigid in the Second Reich, and they were not much eased during the Weimar period. The mobilization policies of the Nazis had an egalitarian effect, as did the universal sacrifices required by the war. The flood of refugees from the east also mixed and leveled.[22] Recent surveys have found less class consciousness in the Federal Republic than in England, France, or Italy.

Because of the cost of higher education and the inherited advantages of the children of the upper classes, university education was formerly practically limited to the well-placed; status thus perpetuated itself. The number able to enter the universities was very small,

[19]Kendall L. Baker, Russell J. Dalton, and Kar Hildebrandt, *Germany Transformed: Political Culture and the New Politics* (Cambridge, Mass.: Harvard University Press, 1981), p. 25.

[20]John Dornberg, *The New Germans: Thirty Years After* (New York: Macmillan, 1976), p. 123.
[21]Herz, *Government of Germany*, p. 26.
[22]Charles E. Frye, "Parties and Pressure Groups in Weimar and Bonn," in Lijphart, *Politics in Europe*, p. 225.

only about 4 percent in the mid-1950s, and graduates were assured good positions. In recent years, however, over 20 percent of young people have gone on to the higher learning that was an elite privilege a generation ago; now the proportion of young people receiving advanced instruction is comparable to that in other European countries and the United States. Universities are tuition-free, and subsidies are granted to nearly half the students. In view of high factory wages, there is no economic reason why working-class children cannot receive an education corresponding to their abilities. An increasing number of students, although still only a minor fraction, are women. The diploma, however, no longer guarantees a good job.

Status also depends on income, and income distribution in the Federal Republic is about as equal, or as unequal, as in the United States. Moreover, income in the postwar period has depended to an encouraging extent on effort. The old rich mostly survived defeat in World War II—although not so well as they survived the loss of World War I—but they have been joined by a host of new rich. The economy was rapidly built up, and fortunes, or at least good incomes, were made on the way. Following wartime destruction and postwar privation, a good life was to be gained by personal effort. Society and state encouraged everyone to make money and hence improve one's status. Germany made an ideology of economic success,[23] and economic success meant social fluidity.

The backbone of German stiffness was agricultural East Prussia, whose large landholders, the so-called Junkers, constituted a sort of nobility ruling a passive peasantry. They are no more, but rural areas in the

postwar period have been strongholds of conservatism and have given the most support to rightist movements. Agriculture has now receded to occupy less than a tenth of the labor force. Farmers stage protests for higher support prices, but they are too few to dominate the state. The government is seeking to reduce their numbers further by encouraging mechanization and the consolidation of holdings.

German industry has been at least potentially an authoritarian influence because of concentration and cartelization for price maintenance and market sharing. After the war, there was some effort, especially in the American zone, to break up huge enterprises and monopolistic combinations, but it was not very successful. For the most part big business came through the upheavals unhurt, and business interests are powerfully organized and close to governing circles. In recent years the Federal Cartel Office has been trying to curb combinations and break up at least some cartels.

The power of business has not prevented the institutionalization of a labor voice in management, by representation on a supervisory board. This "codetermination" grew out of the works councils of Weimar times, which were empowered to consider grievances and other matters of interest to workers. The system was instituted in 1951 in the coal and steel industries, in which workers and owners are equally represented on the board; in most other industries workers are allotted a third of the seats. Partly because the big unions are basically conservative, this measure has justified neither the hopes of sponsors nor the fears of opponents, but it has brought a modicum of democratic relations to industrial management. In 1976 workers were empowered to elect half the supervisory boards of companies with over 2,000 employees—a not inconsiderable step

[23]Jane Kramer, "A Reporter in Europe: Hamburg," *New Yorker*, March 20, 1978, p. 72.

toward industrial democracy, although in case of a tie the board chairperson, a management representative, has the deciding vote.

The press is subject to concentration of control similar to that of industry. There are several highly respected papers in various centers, in contrast to the way those of London blanket Britain. But many are under a single ownership; the conservative Springer chain controls about a third of the total circulation. For the most part, papers are moderate and unaffiliated with political parties. They tend to conservatism, although several are liberal, and there is no important strongly leftist paper. The broadcast media are publicly owned, but by the Länder, not the federal government. The federal government once tried to establish a network of its own, but the Constitutional Court quashed it as an infringement on the right of the Länder to manage cultural affairs. Radio and television are noncommercial, generally informative in discussion of current affairs, and as impartial politically as can be expected.

The army was a mainstay of nationalism in Weimar times, although it was not responsible for putting Hitler into power but long remained rather aloof from him. After the war, it was at first assumed that Germany would be demilitarized indefinitely. Because of the cold war, however, German rearmament was hesitantly undertaken. Much was done to democratize the army, and it seems generally to have been successful. The distance between enlisted men and officers was reduced. Courts-martial were abolished, and soldiers were permitted to unionize, although not to strike. The new *Bundeswehr* was made something of an organization of civilians in uniform; its long-haired soldiers would have caused a Prussian general apoplexy. A parliamentary overseer was established. The effort to infuse a new spirit seems to have been successful, although pockets of pro-Nazi and anti-Semitic sentiments remain.[24] But the prestige of the officer and of the military career is not high, and the young men drafted for fifteen months' duty plead conscientious objection in alarming numbers.

There is little place for militarism because the issues to which military power was relevant have receded. An army can bring little if any glory; it is useful only for defense against a possible attack from the east and perhaps hardly for that. Germans see security much more in terms of the American nuclear shield than their own ground forces. The intellectual and emotional world of the Third Reich is almost as dead as the Holy Roman Empire. Germany is no longer the cockpit of world politics, as it was from 1870 to 1945. Resentments coming out of the war, the bombings, and the misery of the first postwar years has been fairly well washed away by prosperity. Germany is the best supporter of the European Economic Community. A significant gesture was to issue its citizens European instead of German passports.

CONCLUSION: THE GERMAN PROBLEM

Recent German political theorizing, so far as it exists, tends to pragmatism; it is reformist and moderate rather than leftist or conservative. The prewar past has little importance for the majority of the population, born since the fall of Hitler. Yet the Nazi period has left scars. Trials of war criminals have continued into recent years, to remind people of realities of the past. The statute of limitations has been repeatedly extended. In 1978 the minister-president of Baden-Württenburg resigned because of his involvement in

[24]*New York Times*, February 23, 1978, p. A-2.

death sentences thirty-three years before. There has been much talk of "coming to terms with the past," but until recently there has been a tendency to ignore it. History taught in schools typically ended with the Weimar period. In the late 1970s, however, there was a flurry of writing about Nazi times, and books on Hitler—generally truthful— were very popular. The Nazi aberration was explained as a result of many factors, but not excused.[25] There remained much sensitivity and concern for the world's perception of Germany, and anxiety lest the French and the Italians continue to see traces of nazism.

The Nazi experience and its failure probably have made Germany not more but less susceptible to the totalitarian temptation and lures of glory through strength than other nations. It may be recalled that the only consequential party of postwar times dominated by former Nazis, the NPD, felt obliged to call itself "democratic." There are neo-Nazi terror groups, some formed as a reaction to anarchist-leftist terror, but those involved are probably fewer than 1,000.[26]

The concerns and passions of German youth are new, and they have led to something new in German history, radical terrorism. The leftist undergound, which was estimated to involve some 1,500 persons, came out of the leftist and student protest movement of the late 1960s and early 1970s. It reached a climax in 1977; subsequently, police methods became more effective. Youthful radicalism in Weimar times was mostly Nazi; recently it has been leftist and anticapitalist, although hostile to Soviet-style bureaucratic communism; and it has followed the worldwide pattern of such movements from the United States to Japan. Its murders

of members of the establishment bore no relation to a political program; indeed, there was no political program except terror. To some extent, it seemed a rebellion against material satiation that has left young people without goals; most terrorists came from upper-middle-class, or upper-class families.

Terrorism caused civil liberties to be questioned. In 1976–1977, for example, laws provided that propaganda for violent acts against that state should be punishable as the acts themselves, and that persons suspected of terrorism could be held incommunicado.[27] The government has also faced demands that such materials as Hitler's speeches and Nazi tracts be censored. In 1972, the right to civil service employment was generally denied to members of organizations held to be subversive, particularly the Communist Party, but the law was softened in 1978. In 1968 the state gave itself broad, although carefully restricted, emergency powers that could be employed to suppress an opposition.

Freedoms, however, rest mostly on the temper and expectations of the people, and they are generally as well observed in Germany as they are in Britain and France. Apparently the German people can distinguish legitimate criticism and political opposition from antidemocratic, violent, and subversive actions; and any effort by a government to use special powers to protect itself from legitimate attack would be counterproductive. In 1962 the then minister of defense, Franz Josef Strauss, bludgeoned the newsmagazine *Der Spiegel* with arrests and seizures in response to exposures of malfeasance. The resulting furor strengthened civil rights, and the episode was not repeated. There is some tolerance for police methods, such as wiretapping, that would be regarded as im-

[25]Dahrendorf, *Society and Democracy*, pp. 17–18.
[26]*New York Times*, May 1, 1978.

[27]Kramer, "A Reporter in Europe," pp. 46–52.

proper in the United States. However, it was a demonstration of sensitivity that the 1983 census was delayed and modified because of fears that it could be used to supplement police controls.

Much depends on economic conditions. If there were long lines of near-starving unemployed, both Nazi and Communist doctrines would be much more alluring. Through most of its existence, however, the Federal Republic has had full employment and a shortage of labor; as many as 2 million foreign workers, *Gastarbeiter,* were recruited, mostly from southeastern Europe. Only in 1974, in the international recession, did unemployment become a problem. The importation of Gastarbeiter was halted, and many were sent home. Combatting inflation had top priority, and Germany has in this regard been one of the most successful countries of the Western world. It has also been phenomenally successful in maintaining a large balance of payments surplus despite the high cost of imported fuel. Growth has slowed, but Germany has continued to prosper sufficiently for confidence in the future.

With economic success, Germany seems to progress toward political maturity, the politics of compromise. Postwar leadership has been generally of high caliber, and there have been no difficult crises. After a period of uncontested CDU domination, politics has become lively and interesting, and the Bundestag has taken on the appearance of a genuine parliamentary body. The apathy of the early postwar years, the reluctance to become involved in politics after the loss of Nazi illusions, has passed. In the moderation of politics, Germany seems to be coming close to a system of two aggregative parties, both accepting the fundamentals of the state. The contrast with the party system of Weimar is total. Then, farmers pressed their demands through three political parties; now, they are represented by a single Farmers' Union,

which promotes their cause as a pressure group.

People shy away from party affiliation and vote for strong figures like Adenauer and Brandt. There are more independent voters and ticket splitters. The importance of such issues as ecology and nuclear power is a new phenomenon in German history. The extremists are no more numerous than in other industrial nations, and the governing parties are legalistic and moderate. It seems fair to conclude that Germany, like France, is well on the way to leaving behind its authoritarian past and that German leaders have some justification for seeing their country as a model. By ordinary criteria, Germany, with its imported democratic institutions, has been an outstanding success.[28]

Germany remains, however, caught up in uncertainties that can be dispelled only by a fundamental restructuring of the world power system. Germany lies on the forward edge of the Western world, facing Soviet power—a large army stationed just across the eastern border—like no other Western nation. Germans are deeply fearful that any major East-West conflict would probably begin in their country, which would become a prime nuclear battlefield and might well be totally destroyed. On the one hand, the Germans are strongly anticommunist, and they are willing hosts to the bulk of American overseas forces. On the other, they are of all peoples the most obviously worried by nuclear armaments and the most desirous of their limitation. They are also heavily engaged in trade with the Soviet Union and the Soviet bloc, especially East Germany, in hopes that increased pacific interchanges must result in lessened hostility and danger.

Germany is at the same time the only di-

---

[28]Edwin Hartrich, *The Fourth and Richest Reich: How the Germans Conquered the Postwar World* (New York: Macmillan, 1980), sees the Federal Republic as a model for the United States.

vided great power. The issue of reunification has receded, but it does not fade away, and fears of conflict mingle with hopes of overcoming the artificial division of the German nation. For this reason, the Federal Republic heavily subsidizes the faltering economy of the German Democratic Republic.

In 1983, the chief of German cold warriors, Franz Josef Strauss, turned around to push rapprochement with East Berlin.

As in the past, Germany's destiny rides on foreign affairs; but now Germany is not the villain but the victim of the world constellation.

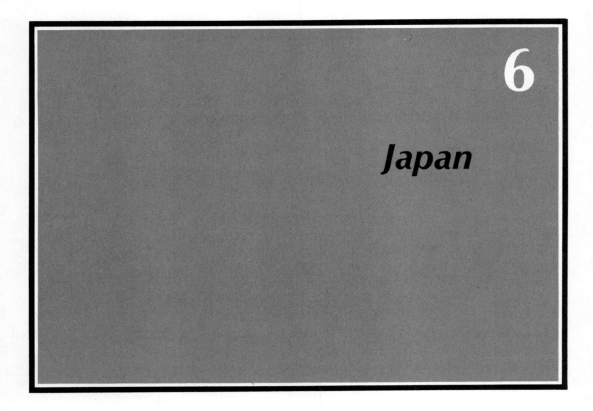

6

Japan

Of the major industrial powers, Japan came last to democracy. France has a more authoritarian background than Britain, Germany than France, and Japan than Germany; even more than Prussia, traditional Japan was a land of warriors. Japan and Germany, more than most industrial nations, mix modern technology with old modes, combining the traditional with the scientific-industrial. But the amalgamation is much more striking in Japan than in Germany. It is also remarkable that the economic success of these four nations in the last generation is roughly proportional to the newness of their democratic parliamentary institutions. France has prospered better than Britain but has been left behind by Germany. Germany, on the other hand, has been outdone by Japan, economically the best performer in the world. Japan, with 115 million people crowded into an area about equal to Montana and much more mountainous, with no raw materials of consequence except modest deposits of coal and copper, has raised itself from wartime ruins and total poverty to a level of prosperity like that of Western Europe and the United States. Its industry is in many ways the most modern of all; it alarms the world by its productivity. For example, a Japanese worker produces twice as many cars per year as an American worker. Japan has most of the world's industrial robots; and its industrial production is greater than that of the Soviet Union and next to that of the United States, twice as populous and many times as rich in resources.

There are obviously various causes of this prosperity. Defeat is one; the Japanese, like the Germans, rose from the rubble with a new leadership plus new, more rational institutions and with a determination to achieve by peaceful work something of what they

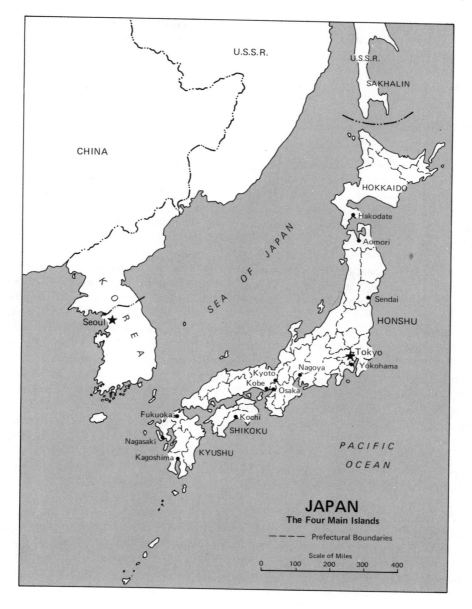

JAPAN
The Four Main Islands

– – – – Prefectural Boundaries

Scale of Miles

0   100   200   300   400

failed to achieve by arms. Certain factors have been unique and unrepeatable (obviously, other countries of the non-Western world must have lacked Japan's historical advantages), but this is equally true of Russia, America, or any other state that might be taken more or less as a political model. The Japanese success is evidence that the chief handicaps of the poorer countries are social-political and that these handicaps can be overcome. The Japanese have been diffident in advertising their ways, at least since their essay in empire failed; but countries desiring to industrialize and develop more effective institutions might well take lessons from the Japanese. So, for that matter, might the United States.[1]

THE JAPANESE HERITAGE

Japan is an exceptionally, indeed uniquely homogeneous, well-defined nation. Its history has been marked by continuity and, until 1867, relative isolation. From prehistoric times until 1945 the islands were never successfully invaded. The Japanese occasionally reached outward as traders, pirates, or invaders of adjacent lands; and they borrowed abundantly from abroad, chiefly from China, the most highly civilized land with which they were in contact. But they were mostly self-contained.

The patterns of the Japanese state and much of its culture came originally from Tang China (618–907), especially the bureaucracy and administration that were so well elaborated in imperial China. The exaltation of the emperor was also derived from the Chinese example. However, whereas Chinese dynasties collapsed or were destroyed after a century or so (the mandate of heaven being withdrawn), Japan has never known an attempt to overthrow the monarchy and seldom to replace the monarch. The imperial house has maintained continuity since legendary times, although the emperor has had little real power since the ninth century.

The mountainous islands of Japan were difficult to govern as a unit. Feudal warfare among the rulers of nearly autonomous fiefs was endemic for centuries. At the beginning of the seventeenth century, however, an outstanding general, Tokugawa Ieyasu, crushed his opponents at the battle of Sekigahara (1600) and consolidated his power, nominally under the emperor, as *shogun* (generalissimo). The shogunate reduced the local lords, the *daimyo*, to dependents, compelled them to reside part of the year at the capital, regulated their marriages, kept their families hostage, and forbade them to communicate with one another.

The shogunate also closed Japan. In the sixteenth century Western ships, first Portuguese and then Dutch, had entered Japanese ports, as had European missionaries. European weapons contributed to Ieyasu's victory. But Westerners brought not only Western technology, which was mostly welcome, but Western ideas, which were not. Christianity spread rapidly and seemed to threaten the social order. The shogunate drew a curtain around its domain. Foreigners were expelled, and Japanese were forbidden on pain of death to leave or reenter the realm. Only the Dutch were allowed to maintain a small trading station on an island in Nagasaki harbor, on condition that they do no proselytizing.

In peace and isolation for two centuries, Japan codified a strict class system and a highly deferential social order. The base was formed by peasants and artisans. On top were the warriors, the *samurai*, who became administrators and intellectuals when there was no more fighting. In a somewhat doubtful position were the merchants, who stood at the bottom of the Confucian scale but who grew increasingly wealthy and influential with passing generations. They began to intermarry with the increasingly impoverished samurai class and so to acquire status.[2] The samurai themselves were divided by rank: Some enjoyed hereditary princely status, but others were lesser retainers, proud but often

---

[1]As contended by Ezra F. Vogel, *Japan as Number One: Lessons For America* (Cambridge, Mass.: Harvard University Press, 1979) and many books on Japanese management.

[2]Richard Storry, "Change in Tokugawa Society," in Jon Livingstone, Joe Moore, and Patricia Oldfather, eds., *The Japanese Reader: Imperial Japan, 1800–1945*, 2 vols. (New York: Pantheon, 1973), p. 20.

in debt to merchants. The class structure, with its strict legal distinctions and regulations regarding residence, occupation, and dress, plus enormous differences between the very rich and very poor, would not seem conducive to modernization. Japanese society, however, remained somewhat pluralistic and more open than, for example, the Chinese. The many measures taken by the shogunate to ensure the obedience of the feudal lords were necessitated by the potential for disobedience. The clans under the daimyo remained largely self-sufficient and autonomous, and the tradition of independent power centers was aided by the rugged character of the country. Below, the villages were substantially autonomous; at the top, the shogun could not claim absolute power because of the formal superiority of the emperor.

Probably because of the real looseness of the formally hierarchic society, Japan was by no means lethargic in isolation. Commerce developed, until by the early nineteenth century the country was economically united. Cities grew as centers of trade, industry, and administration. The state apparatus was improved, so that when a new ruling elite determined to modernize after midcentury, it had a corps of civil servants to carry out its decisions. Moreover, ability and knowledge took precedence over birth in the selection of officials, at least in the lower ranks.[3] The groundwork was thereby laid for the efficient professional bureaucracy of modern Japan. Education was broadened; by the time of the Meiji Restoration in 1868, Japan was one of the most literate countries of the world, with about half of the boys receiving schooling outside the home.[4] In 1720, the shogunate had begun the importation and translation of "useful" books from the Dutch, so the Jap-

anese were not ignorant of Western technology or world events—particularly the fate of China in the face of Western penetration.

When the American naval commander Matthew Perry came with gunboats in 1853–1854 and insisted that Japan open itself to intercourse with the world, he encountered not a frozen society but one feeling its way toward change, a society with a sense of nationhood, a functional bureaucracy, worldly attitudes, and respect for merit and achievement.

Modernization: Meiji Japan

Late in the eighteenth century, the Russians sought to establish relations; they were rebuffed, as were British overtures a little later. But in 1853 Commodore Perry entered a Japanese harbor with four steamships and presented a demand for a commercial treaty—partly because of desire for trade, partly to aid shipwrecked sailors, partly because the United States believed it was right to spread the blessings of civilization. Later he returned with ten ships, which so impressed the Japanese (who were forbidden to build large seagoing vessels) that they agreed to open two ports and make other concessions. England, France, Russia, and the Netherlands demanded and received equal treatment. Commercial treaties were negotiated, and Western powers secured extraterritorial rights for their citizens and control over Japanese customs.

Knowing the humiliations China had suffered, the Japanese were alarmed; there arose a ferment of discussion about how to save the nation. They quickly began purchasing arms from the Dutch. The ossified shogunate, however, seemed incapable of dealing with the situation, and it was blamed for the unavoidable concessions to the foreigners. Happily, the legitimate emperor was a potential alternative focus of national identity.

[3]T. C. Smith, "Japan's Aristocratic Revolution," in *The Japanese Reader,* vol. 1, p. 93.

[4]Nobutake Ike, *Japanese Politics: Patron-Client Democracy,* 2nd ed. (New York: Knopf, 1972), p. 5.

The discontented elite, mostly unemployed or underemployed samurai, could consequently make a revolution by proclaiming the traditional rights of the universally respected emperor. A brief civil war sealed the transfer of power. The restoration of the Meiji emperor was a calculated move to bring about a national renewal. It meant not imperial absolutism but a young new oligarchy—the average age of thirty top leaders in 1868 was slightly over thirty[5]—dedicated to change for the sake of conserving essentials.

The first slogan was "Expel the barbarians," but the leaders soon perceived that it was necessary to learn from them. From the early 1860s, the government began sending study missions to Europe and the United States. Soon foreign experts were imported, until by 1890 there were about 3,000 in Japan, not only technicians but scholars, artists, teachers, managers, and administrators.[6] They were kept under supervision and were to train Japanese replacements as rapidly as possible. A growing number of foreigners who took up residence in Japanese ports for business purposes also provided a conduit for Western technology and thought.

From the outset, industrialization was oriented toward heavy industry and military production. In many cases, it was necessary for the government, because of the shortage of native entrepreneurs and the wish to avoid foreign investment, to start industries itself; but the plants set up were (except for those of military importance) eventually sold cheaply, in many cases to former samurai. Government-business cooperation, which is conspicuous in contemporary Japan, began with the official sponsorship of industrialization in the nineteenth century. The chief service of the government, however, was to provide stability and a sound taxation and monetary system; private light industry led the way.[7] Silk was the first major export. Cotton textiles followed, and these two provided the greater part of Japanese exports until World War II. Industrial growth continued to be very rapid; production rose about 10 percent yearly from 1893 to 1908—a rate fantastic for that age—and only slightly more slowly, 7.5 percent yearly, until 1937.

Japanese leaders hoped at first to limit Westernization to technology, and their slogan was "Japanese soul equipped with Western learning."[8] But more and more had to be copied, not only machines but also business practices such as accounting, administration, and incorporation, plus legal codes and civil courts. In each case the modernizers tried to find the best model. A legal system was established to deprive the Western powers of their excuse for extraterritoriality; this was also a reason for adoption of a constitution in 1889. Administration was reformed; the national administrative apparatus was remodeled and enlarged. Agrarian relations were revised; taxation was shifted from rice to land, a measure designed to encourage production at some cost in social justice. In 1872 a system of general primary education was begun, and secondary and higher schools were opened. After Tokyo University was established in 1877, a university education became the principal key to advancement, as it has remained.

The modernizers hoped to preserve the essential Japan by adopting tools from the barbarians; modernization should not conflict with traditional society but protect it. However, the Restoration brought centralization and an end to traditional social dis-

---

[5]John Whitney Hall, *Japan from Prehistory to Modern Times* (New York: Delacorte Press, 1970), p. 269.
[6]Ibid., p. 287.

[7]Edwin O. Reischauer, *Japan: The Story of a Nation* (New York: Knopf, 1970), p. 134.
[8]Osamu Muro, *Introduction to Japan* (Tokyo: Asian Economic Press, 1968), p. 54.

tinctions. The various clans and daimyo were fused into a single Japanese state, and restrictions on the several classes were swept away. The way was opened for boys of any class to rise as high as talent permitted. The daimyo surrendered their domains in return for indemnities, and samurai received stipends in compensation for the loss of feudal revenues. The stipends were replaced in 1876 by lump payments, which contributed to the capitalization of the new industries. The samurai class abolished its own special status.[9]

There was deep uncertainty about how far change should go, an ambivalence like that which gripped nineteenth-century Russian intellectuals and troubles many in the Third World today. Antipathy toward the whites who showed up Japan's weakness and backwardness and haughtily imposed their will on it mixed with admiration, an extraordinary willingness to learn, and sometimes a desire to be like them. While the government thought in terms of seeking only technology, a "modernist" pro-Western movement grew up among the people. Fascination with Western culture and science sometimes seemed to get the better of native values. In the late 1870s and 1880s, many were disposed to cast Japanese culture overboard, perhaps adopt Christianity, and possibly even discard the Japanese language in favor of English. But the state exalted the emperor and refurbished traditional Shinto, a loose faith based largely on nature worship. After 1890 the pendulum swung back to the superiority of Japanese values.

The first decades of modernization were hard for samurai, artisans, and especially the peasants, who, as usual in such circumstances, were called on to pay most of the costs. The government was confronted with economic crises, unrest, conspiracies, even some armed resistance because of increased tax burdens and social dislocations. It was able to survive in large part because after 1873 it had a growing conscript army, in which young men were trained and indoctrinated to repress peasant riots and restive samurai.

By the end of the nineteenth century, Japan was striding onto the world stage. In 1871 it began positive diplomacy with the appointment of a foreign minister (aided by an American advisor). By 1875, it had begun a career of Asian imperialism, forcing on Korea an unequal treaty like those the Western powers had forced on Japan. Through the 1880s and 1890s, Japan was freeing itself of the unequal treaties, although it did not recover complete control of tariffs until 1911. In 1894, Japan easily defeated China and harvested a solid indemnity and some Chinese territories, chiefly Formosa (Taiwan). In 1902, Japan entered an alliance of equals with Britain. In 1904, it went to war with Russia over Korea and Manchuria and thrilled Asia by victory over that huge power. Between 1914 and 1918, Japan participated in the Allied war against Germany and Austria-Hungary and was richly rewarded, although it failed to make China a colony.

Toward Parliamentary Government

Along with imperialism, the period from 1875 to 1930 saw liberalization and movement toward responsible government. Although the government was strengthened in the 1870s and 1880s and gained a powerful instrument of coercion in the mass conscript army, the demand for more popular participation waxed along with the admiration for Western ways. A written constitution was deemed a source of strength indispensable for a modern state[10] and a basis for respectability.

[9]Reischauer, *Japan*, p. 126.

[10]Muro, *Introduction to Japan*, p. 54.

The leaders of liberalism were, not surprisingly, samurai excluded from power; their insurrections having been defeated in 1870 and 1877, they became a political opposition demanding representative government.

A dozen years after the Restoration, the conservative rulers came to believe that it was better to grant a conservative constitution as an imperial favor than to wait until public opinion forced the adoption of a radical one. In 1879–1880, local assemblies were elected; in 1881 it was formally promised that Japan would receive a constitution; and in 1885 a modern cabinet system was established with a prime minister. The commission to study Western constitutions visited various countries in 1883, but it paid attention chiefly to the German system. In part, the Japanese were impressed by the rapid rise of Bismarckian Germany; more crucially, they picked the German as a scheme for retaining power in the hands of the traditional rulers while making the indispensable concessions to modern demands.

The constitution of 1889 was conceived not as a democratization of the state but as a regularization and modernization of the oligarchic regime. It was promulgated without public discussion in the name of the emperor, and it legalized him as a sacred power above the government, to which the prime minister and cabinet were responsible. The emperor's household was independent of the constitution, and he had authority to issue ordinances. The lower chamber of the Diet, the House of Representatives, was elected by one percent of the population, persons paying certain amounts in taxes. The upper chamber, the House of Peers, was based on a new peerage created in 1884–1885 by the issuance of patents to leading oligarchs. Regular legislation required the consent of both houses. The chief power of the lower house was to reject the budget; but the government had the recourse (borrowed from the Prussian practice) of continuing the previous year's budget.

The constitution did not give the oligarchy the expected stability, however. From the opening of the new Diet in 1890, the political leaders (who were of the aristocracy) strove to wrest as much as they could from the government. Elections regularly gave the opposition a majority in the House of Representatives. The prerogative of the Diet to refuse authorizations proved to be real; in the rapidly expanding economy, the previous year's budget was never enough. So the government found it advisable to bargain with parties and elected leaders, to bribe them or to secure their cooperation by admitting some to a share in the government. It was at first only a nuisance to have to cajole or pressure the Diet, but there gradually grew to be some recognition of responsibility to the elected representatives. The Diet provided an arena for political controversy, and the electoral campaigns and elections gave a feeling for representative government.

If the Meiji constitution failed to conform to the expectations of the oligarchs, they could not scrap it. It contributed, as desired, to the international respectability of Japan; and it was no more than enlightened opinion expected of a modern country, perhaps somewhat less. The concessions to democracy, however, were offset by authoritarian tendencies. Having set up a nationwide school system, the government quickly proceeded to use it for indoctrination. The idea of the nation as a great family under the father-emperor was inculcated; every Japanese committed to memory the 1890 "Imperial Rescript on Education," which idealized the throne and the duty of obedience. In 1900 it was established that only generals and admirals on active duty were qualified to head the service ministries: the armed forces were thereby given veto power over the formation of cabinets.

Under these conditions, liberalization was slow and uneven. While some cabinets were closer to the Diet, others were more "transcendent" or dependent on those around the emperor. There was no simple ideological cleavage; individuals and factions, chiefly the military, personal advisors of the emperor, and top bureaucrats, contested for power. A small group of elder statesmen, the *Genro,* wielded great influence. The civil service gained prestige because it was recruited from university graduates at a time when the new learning was of supreme importance in the remaking of Japan. Moreover, the civil service became increasingly a meritocracy in the 1890s, because the number of qualified graduates exceeded the positions available and selective examinations were used to recruit the ablest.

After World War I, in which Japan participated on the side of the democratic powers led by Britain, France, and the United States, democratization made more headway. When riots in August 1918 forced the resignation of the government, there emerged the first party cabinet headed by a premier who was the leader of the majority party in the Diet. There followed a series of party cabinets almost unbroken until 1932. In the general atmosphere of liberalism, naval limitation treaties were signed with the United States and other leading powers. The army was reduced in numbers. The old leadership was gone, and the elite had lost its solidarity. The bureaucracy was as quietly powerful as ever; but power spread to the parties, to the new middle classes, and to the giant financial combines, whose ability to subsidize parties, factions, and candidates became a major political factor. In 1925, the franchise, which had been somewhat broadened in 1919, was expanded to all men over twenty-five, more than tripling the electorate, from 4 to 14 million (women received the vote only in 1946).

Mobilization and War

Democratization was superficial. Although Japan could no longer be ruled in the old oligarchic way, the elite was not prepared for real popularization. The cities were fairly liberal, but the bulk of the population lived in the conservative countryside; its sons went into the army to be made dedicated servants of consecrated authority and unflinching nationalism. The government was frightened, after the Russian Revolution, of proletarian agitation as the number of industrial workers climbed; and indeed communism and other radical tendencies secured a following among intellectuals in the early 1920s. A labor movement grew up, although it never organized more than a tiny fraction of nonagricultural workers.[11] Repression increased; the expansion of the electorate in 1925 was accompanied by a Peace Preservation Law forbidding criticism of the social-economic order. In 1928 the death penalty was decreed for "dangerous thoughts," and in 1928–1929 some 65,000 Japanese were arrested for that crime.[12] The Communist party was destroyed by repression in the 1930s.

The world depression beginning in 1929 reduced markets for the exports on which Japan increasingly depended and also discredited the Western democracies. In the early 1930s the country energetically and successfully promoted exports, but the response of the Western powers was to raise new barriers. Nationalists saw this as proof of the failure of the liberal approach. At the same time, the Japanese were feeling increasingly cramped on their islands. Famine and infanticide had kept the population stable at 28 to 30 million for generations prior to the mid-nineteenth century, but by 1925 it

[11]Ike, *Japanese Politics,* p. 45.
[12]Albert Axelbank, *Black Star Over Japan: Rising Forces of Militarism* (New York: Hill & Wang, 1972), p. 119.

had doubled to 60 million and was increasing by 3 percent yearly. The peasants were ever more crowded on the land, half of which was under tenancy by 1920.[13] The gulf between city and country was wide and growing, and the benefits of industrialization were diluted by population growth.

The nationalistic-militaristic spirit was growing even as parliamentary government seemed to advance. The cumulative effects of schooling in emperor worship, military virtues, and chauvinism overtook the liberal thinking borrowed from the West. The discontent of the peasantry, which furnished the bulk of recruits, helped to radicalize the army. Resentment against the influence of concentrated big business was translated into anticapitalism and, because of the electoral influence of money, into antiparliamentarianism, while venality weakened and discredited the parties. From the point of view of traditionalists, Japan was sick from the importation of decadent and immoral Western customs and ideas. Politicians and capitalists were evil; austerity and discipline were the means to national regeneration.

Relations with the Western powers cooled. The 1919 Paris Peace Conference refused to write racial equality into the peace treaty, and a little earlier sundry U.S. laws had discriminated against the Japanese with regard to landholding and immigration. Trade barriers were raised specifically against Japanese goods. The old idea of Asian expansion grew with the rising need for markets and raw materials. Profitable wars in 1894, 1904, and 1914–1918, along with political gains achieved in Korea, Manchuria, and China, encouraged the idea of empire-building, both to solve economic problems and to show Japanese equality with the Europeans and Americans and superiority to the Chinese.

In an atmosphere of tense nationalism and repression of dissent, as the world was sinking into depression in 1931, Japanese forces in southern Manchuria undertook to conquer that Chinese province. The Japanese had important holdings and concessions in Manchuria, which was semidetached from China but which the Chinese, stirred by a national revival, were trying to reintegrate. The Japanese had to choose between surrendering their gains of many years and seizing the richly endowed but sparsely populated territory. The army moved, and the civilian government felt compelled to support it.

Easy conquest of the territory, over twice as large as Japan, brought nationalistic euphoria. Many new jobs were created[14] as the army began building up the new domain. Military force, even more than modernization, seemed the way to success. The influence of the armed services mounted as they took advantage of their direct access to the emperor and the general reverence for him to set themselves above the civilian government. Political leaders who refused full cooperation with the army were assassinated by jingoistic firebrands; and after the murder of a civilian prime minister in 1932, Admiral Saito formed a "supraparty" government. Party rule seemed to have failed, and Japan reverted to something like the semimilitary rule that had prevailed for centuries.

Young officers mounted a mutiny in 1936 and killed several leading politicians in the name of power for the emperor, but senior officers suppressed the insurrection. The army moved, however, toward dictatorship. As Hitler was making grand boasts and chalking up bloodless victories, and Mussolini was conquering Ethiopia over the impotent protests of the Western democracies, fascism seemed the means of modern suc-

---

[13]Hall, *Japan: Prehistory to Modern Times*, p. 312.

[14]Muro, *Introduction to Japan*, p. 71.

cess, just as liberalism had earlier—and the former was the more consonant with Japanese tradition.

By 1937, it was possible to form a government without party figures; the Diet and the parties that controlled it were powerless. The emperor became a living god, and Shinto was made the official cult. The people generally supported the military, as did the bureaucracy and the big business combines, the *zaibatsu*, which came to an accommodation with the military for mutual benefit. The four zaibatsu that dominated the Japanese economy up to 1945 (Mitsui, Mitsubishi, Sumitomo, and Yasuda) were giant conglomerates, the power of which was increased in the war as the government and armed forces worked with the strongest firms to produce munitions and to build up and exploit the expanding empire. Militarism, anticapitalist in temper, became entwined with the Japanese variant of capitalism.

This government was trapped by its forward drive. Japan had assumed responsibility for "peace in East Asia" and had laid its stakes on an empire on the mainland. But the Chinese, under the leadership of Chiang Kai-shek and the Nationalists, were no longer willing to bow to European foreigners, much less to the despised Japanese. The Japanese had always to go forward or face the loss and humiliation of retreat. Having nibbled at North China for many years, in July 1937 they undertook to swallow the main body of that immense country. The generals expected quick victory, but the war was unwinnable. Even if Chiang and his Nationalists would have compromised they could not, because Mao and the Communists had raised the banner of national resistence.

The war led Japan toward full mobilization, centralized economic planning, and a political "new structure." In 1940 the political parties were dissolved. An all-embracing Imperial Rule Association was established, with organization down to neighborhoods, to suppress all dissidence. Yet there was no fascist-style leader, only the most nebulous ideology, hundreds of patriotic societies instead of a single mobilizing party, and no real totalitarian system.

Believing the Nazis were winning the war, the Japanese became allied with them in 1940, a step designed to deter the United States. It had the opposite effect of increasing American resolve to stop the concerted aggression of the Rome-Berlin-Tokyo Axis. The United States moved to cut off sales of essential raw materials, particularly oil, and insisted on Japanese withdrawal from China. Again Japan faced the necessity of moving rashly ahead or accepting a costly and humiliating setback. Pearl Harbor, December 7, 1941, was the outcome. The Japanese fought capably and valiantly; the first months were gloriously successful. Japanese youths adhered to the tradition of never surrendering, and when the struggle grew desperate, many gladly offered themselves as guidance systems for sacrificial bombing planes.

But the "Japanese spirit" which the leaders promised would inevitably prevail was overwhelmed by American material superiority. In June 1945 the emperor, asserting himself as a leader for the first time in a millennium, called on the Supreme Command to seek a way to end the war. After the atomic bombings of Hiroshima and Nagasaki proved the futility of resistance, he personally made the decision to accept Allied terms, and an era was closed.

The New Japan

American forces undertook to remake and democratize the Japanese nation, and they succeeded beyond all reasonable expectations. It was a unique and almost uniquely successful operation, comparable only to the parallel remodeling of West Germany. There were various reasons for success. The Occupation was purely American; no interference by the Soviet Union or other powers was permitted. General Douglas MacArthur, who became de facto emperor, acted vigorously and efficiently to implement reforms. The Japanese, accepting defeat, turned from fanatical resistance to complete conformity with the wishes of the victors. Humbled and bewildered by the defeat, for which they had no preparation, they were ready to welcome almost whatever the Americans brought. About a third of all housing had been destroyed; food production was down by nearly a half and industrial production by four-fifths. The people were near starvation, and per capita income was reckoned at an incredible seventeen dollars in 1946.[15] The only hope for survival was to do as the victors said. The Japanese followed orders and became democrats.

The Occupation demilitarized and reformed. The armed forces were dissolved, although the government continued to function; Japan, unlike Germany, was never ruled directly by occupying forces. Seven leaders were hung as war criminals, and a few resorted to suicide. Several thousand were imprisoned, a small number compared to those punished in Germany. Some 186,000, mostly army officers, were disqualified for public office; the desired effect was to bring in new people to implement new policies. Political prisoners, including Communists, were released. State Shinto was abolished, and nationalistic organizations were dissolved. Labor unions, forbidden since the late 1930s, were organized. The zaibatsu, blamed for aggression, were dismantled; fortunes were confiscated and an antimonopoly law was enacted. Farm tenancy was ended by land reform because rural discontent was regarded

as a cause of militarism, and a limit (7.5 acres) was placed on holdings. Secondary and higher education was broadened. Control of education, because of its possible use for indoctrination, was given to localities. The powers of local government were enlarged, and the police were decentralized.

Soon after the surrender, discussion of a new constitution began, and in due course the Japanese government submitted drafts to the MacArthur headquarters. The Japanese proposals were found too conservative and too little changed from the Meiji constitution, so in February 1947 the headquarters drew up its own draft in a mere six days. The Japanese accepted, under some duress; it appears that Occupation authorities threatened to appeal to the people and hold a referendum. One reason for the haste in accepting, as for the haste in drafting, was to avoid possible Soviet interference. Japanese leaders also wished to avoid public controversy that might lead to a still more radical document and elimination of the emperor.[16]

The new constitution left the emperor in place, as had been permitted by the conditions of surrender, but only as a symbol, not even as formal head of state in the British style. He had earlier renounced the family claim to divine origin; his remaining position, stripped of the once-powerful Imperial Household and Privy Council, rested on the will of the sovereign people. The constitution began, "We, the Japanese people." The British parliamentary system was adopted instead of the American presidential system, which has hardly anywhere been imitated successfully; government was by prime minister and cabinet responsible to the lower chamber of the elected Diet. The constitu-

---

[15]Reischauer, *Japan*, p. 244.

[16]Ardath W. Burks, *The Government of Japan* (New York: Crowell, 1961), p. 28.

tion, drafted not by Washington but by MacArthur's staff, was decidedly liberal.[17] Most controversial was the unique Article 9 renouncing war and the maintenance of armed forces. This innovation was perhaps General MacArthur's contribution, although he said that Premier Shidehara originated it.[18]

There was little friction between the Japanese people and the occupying forces. The war trials and purges caused no great sensation; the Japanese, unlike the Germans, felt little guilt because there had been no industrialized death camps. There was no revolutionary ferment, and the restructuring required by new conditions was contained after 1945, as it was after 1854, within the elite. Although willing to learn, the Japanese did not rush to abandon their ways; the postsurrender flurry of conversions to Christianity soon leveled off. However, parties and politics were fluid for a few years, with groups frequently uniting or splitting. Elections in April 1947 made the socialists the strongest party; for nearly a year, June 1947 to March 1948, there was a socialist premier. Since then, governments have been moderate-conservative with little ideological change.

After 1947, the basic policies of the Occupation had been carried out, and the presence of a foreign power gradually became more burdensome. Moreover, with chilling relations between the United States and the Soviet Union turning into the cold war, American authorities lost interest in demilitarization and came to regard Japan as a potential ally against the new Communist foe. Antizaibatsu measures were halted to permit

industrial reconstruction; policies became more favorable to business, less favorable to labor and unions. As a result, the Japanese Left became and remained anti-American. But in the elections of January 1949 the Japanese socialists lost most of their seats to the conservatives, with whom the United States found it easy to cooperate. Command had already been giving way to consultation, and the Occupation was gradually wound down. It was formally ended by the treaty of peace, which, drafted without Soviet concurrence in September 1951, took effect in April 1952.

The treaty, delayed for several years by Soviet objections, was not punitive: it deprived Japan of the empire but imposed no permanent restrictions. It was coupled with a security treaty that placed Japan securely under the American nuclear umbrella and tied that country to American military policy. A small American force remained to man bases in otherwise demilitarized Japan.

Set free, the Japanese undid only a few Occupation policies. The decentralizations of education and police were reversed because they had no basis in Japanese custom and local authorities lacked adequate funding. Most of those purged regained political rights. In 1950, in the face of the Korean conflict, a small military establishment was initiated, called "police" in deference to the constitutional prohibition. Most important, the zaibatsu were permitted more or less to put themselves back together. But the new combines were less monopolistic and more diversified in ownership, much less family or clan enterprises.

Rapid economic growth became the great national objective. Up to 1950, recovery had only begun, per capita income in that year being calculated at only $132.[19] But growth thereafter was extremely rapid, the GNP ex-

---

[17]Regarding the drafting, see J. A. A. Stockwin, *Japan: Divided Politics in a Growth Economy*, 2nd ed. (London: Weidenfeld and Nicholson, 1982).

[18]J. A. A. Stockwin, *Japan: Divided Politics in a Growth Economy* (New York: Norton, 1975), p. 179.

[19]Reischauer, *Japan*, p. 244.

panding in real terms about 10 percent a year over a long period, while exports grew at the rate of 14 percent and productivity at 8 percent—rates unparalleled in the world. Growth was mostly industrial, but agriculture was also improved.

The war in Korea suddenly created a huge demand for many Japanese products. A stable, moderate government collaborated actively with business to raise production. Taxes were low, partly because defense spending was insignificant, partly because the state wished to foster private capital formation. Wages were low and rose less rapidly than productivity; unions were fairly weak and unaggressive. The free trading atmosphere and the relative openness of the American market, by far the most important to Japan, encouraged the indefinite expansion of exports. The Japanese people, having been humiliated by American wealth and technology, resolved to catch up and to restore their self-respect by the only means at hand, economic success. Nationalism turned from imperial to industrial glory.

Nationalism was not entirely focused on better and cheaper cameras or color televisions; much of it was directed politically against the United States. The Occupation became unpopular in its last years, and the security treaty that replaced it seemed to consign Japan to a permanently inferior and unfree condition, with the danger of involvement in wars of no interest to Japan. It also conflicted with the deep pacifism and "nuclear allergy" caused by the war and the unique Japanese experience with atomic bombs. Questions revolving around political relations with the United States, the security treaty, the American bases, and the Japanese defense forces dominated Japanese politics for a generation, along with related matters, such as policies toward trade unions and in education. Through the 1950s, ironically, pro-American government parties were tending to dismantle Occupation reforms, including the constitutional ban against maintaining armed forces, whereas the anti-American parties fought to keep them intact. Opposition to the security treaty came to a climax in 1960. Premier Kishi began negotiations for renewal with revisions favorable to Japan in 1958; despite the clamor of opponents, he rammed it through the Diet by dubious procedures in May 1960 in preparation for a June state visit by President Eisenhower. The disorder was such that the government felt unable to guarantee the safety of its guest and canceled the trip.

The uproar, however, subsided fairly soon and the Japanese gradually lost interest in the security treaty. The leftist vote, which had been on the upgrade since 1949, rose to about 40 percent in 1963 but failed to rise further or ever to make a socialist government seem a real possibility. It fell in 1967 and 1969; the young people, ever the mainstay of opposition, seemed to be turning away from the chief opposition party, the Japanese Socialist party. The student revolt of 1968–1972 was directed against conformity in general, like similar movements in Paris, Berlin, and Berkeley, and seemed to have little political impact. The return to Japan of Okinawa, a Japanese-inhabited island which the United States had found useful as a naval and air base, dissolved a potential cause of contention.

The Liberal Democratic Party (LDP) has continued to run the government under Premiers Sato (1964–1972), Tanaka (1972–1974), Miki (1974–1976), Fukuda (1976–1979), Ohira (1979–1980), Suzuki (1980–1982), and Nakasone (1982–   ). Tanaka was forced out of the premiership because of involvement in the Lockheed scandal, leading to his conviction (but not imprisonment) in 1983. Intrigues related to this scandal also cost Miki his position. Fukuda failed renomination because Tanaka turned against him. Ohira died in office on the eve of the 1980 election. Suzuki resigned because of unpopularity.

The LDP remained remarkably stable, and pressure for a leftist turn tended to diminish. China lost attractiveness as a model with the failure of the Great Leap Forward (1958–1960), the eccentricity of the Cultural Revolution (1966–1970), and the subsequent admission of economic failure by Mao's heirs. The Soviet Union is generally disliked because of an abiding Japanese dislike for Russia, because the Soviet Union insists on holding several small islands to the north of Japan which the Japanese consider to be theirs, and because of the Soviet military presence in the area.

Extremists of the right, ultranationalists, are hardly visible, although occasionally violent.[20] The militarism that was feared in the early 1970s has not materialized. Military expenditures have increased, but only in proportion to overall growth, remaining slightly under one percent of GNP. Political violence, which was largely related to foreign policy, has subsided as foreign policy has ceased to be controversial. Radicals took up such causes as trying to block the new Tokyo airport.

Most frictions with the United States, the power that continues to dominate the Japanese horizon despite the opening of full relations with China, revolve around nonviolent issues of monetary policy and trade barriers. On the one hand, American protectionist moves trouble the Japanese. On the other, American unions and Congress have become increasingly disturbed by the ever larger share of the American market captured by Japanese wares in many cate-

gories. Such difficulties are the outcome, to a degree unavoidable, of Japanese economic progress. The growth of the Japanese economy in the 1970s, although no longer quite so spectacular, has continued stronger than that of any other major power. It came temporarily to a halt in 1973–1974 when the price of oil, all of which Japan must import, quadrupled. But the ability to surmount that crisis, check inflation, and continue earning huge surpluses on the payments balance was the best evidence of economic soundness. The predictions of the late 1960s—made by Western experts and joyfully received by the Japanese—that Japan would be the prime economic power by 2000 were hasty, but time may yet prove them realistic.

THE GOVERNMENT

If Japan is exceptionally capable of meeting the challenges of the postindustrial age, it will be partly because of a political system more purposefully put together than any other. Just as in the days of the Restoration the Japanese shopped around for suitable institutions, they have endeavored in the postwar period to plan their state for maximum effectiveness.

They have had to shape their institutions within the framework of a constitution foisted on them hastily and in controversial circumstances, but it has proved flexible enough, despite the fact that the constitution has never been amended and is politically unamendable. The formal requirement is fairly stiff, the concurrence of two-thirds of the membership of both houses of parliament plus a referendum, and there has never been agreement on prospective changes. More particularly, the Left has always had enough strength to block amendment, and it has maintained a stance of no amendment lest

[20]Axelbank, *Black Star Over Japan*, pp. 87–88.

any tampering with the constitution opens the door to infringing on democratic rights and Article 9 prohibiting armed forces.

The Prime Minister and Diet

The constitution provides for a conventional parliamentary system. Unlike most parliamentary governments, Japan has no formal head of state to provide continuity and to nominate a new prime minister. It does not seem to matter; the civil service, extending almost to the top, provides continuity, and the House of Representatives elects the prime minister on the nomination of the largest party. He is consequently always a person of long experience in the national government, quite unlike U.S. practice.

The prime minister names his ministers, perhaps twenty, balancing factions of his party. He also removes ministers, rather frequently responding to pressure by reshuffles. The majority of the Cabinet must be members of the Diet; in practice, nearly all have been. The Cabinet is rather like the British. It acts by consensus and as a unit. There are various councils and a Cabinet Secretariat headed by a minister. The minister of finance is most important after the prime minister. Ministers spend a good deal of time in the Diet, where they are subject to questioning. A peculiarly Japanese institution is the Conference of Civil Servants which heads ministries directly under the minister and coordinates relations between the administration and the cabinet.

Basic authority to legislate is vested in the elected House of Representatives of 511 members (including recently 25 women). There is also an upper chamber with limited powers replacing the abolished House of Peers. The House of Councilors has 252 members, of whom 152 are elected from prefectures, 100 from the nation at large by proportional representation (since 1983),

permitting many small parties to enter the chamber. Half are chosen every three years for six-year terms. If there were a major difference (as there has never been), the lower house can override the upper by a two-thirds vote. If the House of Councilors fails to act on the budget within thirty days, it is considered passed as approved by the House of Representatives. If the House of Representatives should vote no-confidence, the prime minister may dissolve it and call new elections. This has not happened since 1954 and seems unlikely except in a period of turmoil. The maximum life of the Diet is four years, but it has usually been dissolved earlier at the option of the prime minister.

The House of Representatives is organized much like the British House of Commons. The drafters of the constitution, mindful of the role of U.S. congressional committees, gave the Diet committees extensive power of investigation. There are eleven standing committees, in which the parties are represented proportionally to their strength in the House, plus special committees. Japanese ministers spend much time testifying before them, and they offer the opposition many chances to make itself heard.

The Diet in practice exercises much less authority than the American Congress, although rather more than the British House of Commons. Most legislation is initiated by the government—that is, ultimately by the bureaucracy. Backbenchers of the governing party do not vote against government bills; at most, they may abstain. They spend most of their time doing errands for their constituents. The pay of Japanese legislators is the world's best; in 1983 roughly equivalent to $120,000 to $140,000. Their facilities, however, are much inferior to those of U.S. members of Congress, and Japanese legislators are expected to spend heavily helping their constituents. The opposition parties can seldom do more than delay action; this may be effective, however, because sessions are rather short, business is not usually carried over, and it is not deemed proper simply to override the opposition by majority vote. All interested parties should be taken into account, and government should be by consensus as well as by majority.

Most bills are passed without opposition. In the exciting times of twenty years or so ago, the opposition sometimes resorted to withdrawal from the Diet session. The government could still pass bills, but action by an incomplete house meant loss of face for the cabinet and was an affront to Japanese feelings. In 1960, opponents of the renewal of the security treaty, mostly socialist deputies, tried to block action by forcibly preventing the Speaker of the Diet from taking his place. Their removal by the police lost the government considerable public support.

Elections

The several-member district system for elections to the House of Representatives is not new—it was established in 1925 when the suffrage was expanded—but it is unique. Each of 130 constituencies elects three to five members, but each voter can vote for only one. The three to five persons (as the case may be) receiving the largest number of votes are elected. This amounts to a compromise between single-member, one-round elections, as in Britain and the United States, and proportional representation. A minor party capable of polling even less than 20 percent of the votes in a five-member district has a good chance of electing a representative by concentrating its votes on a single individual.

The leading party may elect more candidates than indicated by its share of total votes, but not nearly as many as in single-member districts, where all votes for other than the leading candidate are wasted. It is not easy for a party to decide how many candidates to enter in any given district. If too few, they will receive more votes than needed; if too many, they may divide the votes going to the party and cause fewer of its candidates to be elected. Moreover, if the candidates are uneven in popularity, one may take away votes needed by others. Prime Minister Tanaka proposed in 1973 changing to a mixture of single-member constituencies and proportional representation, but the suggestion was dropped because of strong opposition.[21]

The support of local party organizations is generally necessary in order to gain nomination, and the individual's appeal seems to be based mostly (in the case of the governing party) on services to constituents. Nearly all candidates are native to their constituencies, and it is essential to have a personal following. This obviously favors incumbents and persons with good connections in the government, perhaps high civil servants. Socialist candidates hope mostly to have the backing of trade unions. Hardly any women, it may be noted, are elected to the Diet, although more women than men vote.

There are many rules about the conduct of campaigns that limit expenditures, numbers of speeches, newspaper advertisements, and so on. Contributions by individuals and firms are legally limited and subject to disclosure. Stringent rules are bendable in practice: some candidates reportedly spend a million dollars or more over the legal limit of $50,000. The rules tend to make it more difficult for persons without good organizational backing to break into the charmed circle.[22] Television, which is partly state-owned, partly private, maintains impartial-

[21]For a detailed study, see Gerald L. Curtis, *Election Campaigning Japanese Style* (New York: Columbia University Press, 1971).

[22]Stockwin, *Japan*, pp. 87–88.

ity; it has become increasingly important and has contributed to the personalization of politics. Postwar electoral turnout has been regularly about 75 percent. The number of votes required to elect a candidate varies as much as four to one. Since districts were drawn up in 1947, urbanization has brought about marked overrepresentation of the rural areas. In 1976, the Supreme Court declared the electoral districting unconstitutional because of unequal representation, but not much has been done about it because the LDP, with its greater strength among farmers, is reluctant to remedy this situation fully.

The Parties

The Japanese constitution, like the American, says nothing about political parties; but these are central in the political process. The Liberal Democratic party has remained at the helm, in effect, since November 1955, when it was formed by the merger of two conservative parties. This is in marked contrast to the frequent turnover of the prewar party governments, 1918–1932, and also to the instability of the first postwar years.[23]

The LDP. The LDP is primarily supported by business interests, which provide funds; by farmers and many of the middle class, who furnish votes; and by bureaucrats, who administer the state headed by party leaders. It is basically conservative in spirit, rather like the British Conservatives or the German Christian Democrats. It rejects ideological directions. It belongs to the traditional and respectable sectors of Japanese society, yet it is enlightened and pragmatic enough to see need for change, which it does not oppose on ideological grounds.

[23]See Nathaniel B. Thayer, *How the Conservatives Rule Japan* (Princeton, N.J.: Princeton University Press, 1969).

The organization of the party is rather complicated, with central staff and local branches. The president until 1978 was elected by LDP members of the Diet plus representatives of the prefectures; now he is chosen by a two-stage process. Dues-paying party members (over three million) in prefectures vote in a sort of primary, and the Diet members choose between the two top candidates. The party president is automatically its candidate for prime minister. In the first all-party election in 1978, the party secretary-general, Masayoshi Ohira, received more votes than the premier, Takeo Fukuda; the latter withdrew without contesting the runoff. The party president is elected for a three year term, reelection being allowed only once. This system in effect limits the terms of the prime minister to six years, but none has held on more than three since 1972.

The most important party body is the Executive Council, including fifteen members from the House of Representatives, seven from the House of Councilors, and eight appointees of the president of the party. There are also yearly congresses including Diet members, four delegates from each prefectural branch, and representatives of affiliated organizations. But this large body, like Conservative conferences in Britain, serves mostly as a meeting ground and rubber stamp. The membership of the LDP, formerly small and almost limited to office-holders, grew greatly because of the transfer of the power to choose the party president (the prime minister) to the ordinary members. The chief power of local party organizations is to select candidates, whom the center ordinarily approves, and to manage the primaries for the presidency.

The LDP spans a spectrum, from a few rightists who want nuclear armament and restoration of the position of the emperor through strong conservatives to moderate liberals, and it has little means of disciplining deviants. Because it is dedicated primarily to holding and using power, it is divided by competition for power but united by the need to hold together in order to keep it. As a result, the LDP is a conglomeration of six to eight somewhat fluctuating factions. The largest recently with 60 members has been that of former Prime Minister Tanaka, the old-time party king-maker. Despite his conviction in the Lockheed scandal, Tanaka came strongly through the December 1983 election. The Suzuki faction in 1984 had 49 members; Nakasone, 40; Fukuda, 40; Komoto, 28; Nakajawa, 7; 26 deputies were unaffiliated.

The political contest actually takes place more within the LDP than between it and the opposition; that is, electoral contests are sometimes more between rival LDP candidates in a constituency than between the LDP and another party. Factional maneuverings decide who is to become party leader and hence prime minister, and the cabinet must be put together to make an effective coalition of factions. Thus, the 1984 Nakasone cabinet included six of the Tanaka faction, three Nakasone men, four each of the Fukuda and Suzuki factions, and two of the faction of Toshio Komoto.

Factions have regular meetings, headquarters, known membership, and their own discipline.[24] Ordinary party members also affiliate with factions. A faction ordinarily lasts at least until the leader retires or dies, whereupon it breaks up or a new leader takes over. Rank order within factions is informal but depends on seniority, electoral successes, and services rendered. Only within a faction can a politician hope to rise, perhaps to cabinet office. Political progress must be gradual and conformist, based to a large extent on seniority. Moreover, businesses donate to factions, usually more than one, so only by affiliation with a faction is a would-be candidate likely to get adequate support for a campaign. The fact that LDP candidates compete vigorously against one another in the constituency races also contributes to factionalism; rival candidates belong to different factions.[25] But factionalism does not extend to the Diet, where all vote the party line or, rarely, abstain.

The existence of such parties within the party means much politicking and possibly unedifying deals, if not corruption. In order to secure election, the prime minister must bargain with various factions and form a coalition. On the other hand, the factions, although not dogmatic, often stand for conflicting policies and approaches. They make differing views heard in the highest councils, and they restrict the power of the prime minister and make him removable. Every three years, the factions lie in wait to overthrow the ruling prime minister.

Partly because of the faction system, LDP rule has been remarkably stable. If a cabinet is discredited or worn out, it is replaceable not by an opposition party, but by a different coalition of the LDP. Thus adaptable, the party has kept voter support, although the LDP vote has tended to decline from its high point soon after the formation of the party. The Occupation land reform—a reform no conservative party could have undertaken—provided the conservatives with the solid backing of a large class of small landholders, and LDP votes in the rural areas have held up well. Support in the cities has been less stable, but the LDP has managed to hold nearly half the total electorate at all times.

In 1976, its seats in the House of Rep-

---

[24]Ibid., p. 15.

[25]Concerning factions, see Haruhiro Fukui, "Factionalism in a Dominant-Party System," in Frank P. Belloni and Dennis C. Beller, eds., *Faction Politics: Political Parties and Factionalism in Comparative Perspective* (Santa Barbara, Calif.: ABC-Clio Press, 1978), pp. 43–72.

resentatives sank to 249 and it had to recruit independents to muster the necessary majority.[26] In 1979, the LDP won fifteen out of fifteen governorships contested; and Premier Ohira held early general elections in hopes of increasing his majority. The LDP share of votes rose from 42 to 45 percent, but it won only 248 seats. However, in the premature election of 1980, it won 289 with 48 percent. In local and House of Councilors elections in 1983 the LDP slightly improved its position, while the opposition was more divided. The conviction of former prime minister and faction leader Tanaka for bribery forced another early election in December 1983. The voters punished the LDP by reducing its share of the votes to 46 percent and its seats to 250. Nakasone had to rely on a few independents and the eight deputies of the New Liberal Club to form a majority. The New Liberal Club is a splinter that broke away in 1976 to protest the party gerontocracy and the involvement of Tanaka in the Lockheed affair. Its leader entered the government in December 1983 and it seemed quite close to the LDP.

Party	1980 Seats	1980 Votes	1983 Seats	1983 Votes
LDP	284	47.9%	250	45.8%
JSP	107	19.3	112	19.5
Komeito	33	9.0	58	10.1
DSP	32	6.6	38	7.3
JCP	29	9.8	26	9.3
NLC	12	3.0	8	2.4
Independent	11	3.5	16	4.9
Minor	3	.9	3	.8

The best hope of the opposition would seem to be a division in LDP ranks, but the pragmatic party leaders will certainly endeavor to avoid this. The LDP is too much

[26]Margaret A. McKean, "Japan's Beleaguered Ruling Party," *Current History* 75 (November 1978), pp. 158–164.

entwined with the bureaucracy and business leadership of Japan to be easily dislodged unless the economy suffers serious setbacks.

Opposition Parties. Extreme rightists are few; the opposition has always been largely leftist, or more or less radical-revolutionary. This derives partly from tradition. In prewar Japan, those out of sympathy with the ruling elite, prevented by repression from working for reform within the system, saw no chance for peaceful change. Only revolution seemed to offer hope, and the only visible hope of revolution was through class conflict. By corollary, they became and remained more or less Marxist.

Marxism, a philosophy at once modern and anti-Western, is an attractive vehicle for the sentiments of those at odds with the capitalist-supported LDP government and the leading capitalist power, the United States, with which that government has been allied. But Marxism has contributed to the futility of the opposition, for it has fueled ideological disputes. By its dogmatism and propensity to violent positions, it has tended to disqualify the leftists for majority support, to encourage extralegal methods, to exclude compromise, and to harden the conservative stance.

The leading opposition party is the Japan Socialist Party (JSP), which was formed by the merger of two socialist parties in October 1955. There had been repeated realignments earlier, and since 1955 there has been continued disagreement on tactics and the correct Marxist interpretation of Japanese development. The JSP reached its electoral high tide in 1960 when it captured 145 seats in the House of Representatives. In that year, however, a moderate sector split away to form the Democratic Socialist Party (DSP). The JSP won 107 seats in 1979, and the same number in 1980. In 1983 it gained five seats but only a tiny fraction in votes.

The Democratic Socialists, who had advanced to 35 seats in 1979, fell to 22 in 1980 but came back to 32 in 1983.

The membership of the JSP is very small, but the expansion of the LDP has compelled it to seek a mass basis. The party depends heavily on the major trade unions affiliated with it; about half the JSP deputies in the Diet are trade union officials. The party seems too closely tied to a particular sector of labor and trade unions and too doctrinaire to hope to gain a majority and qualify for national power. The JSP is composed of factions much like those of the LDP except that, unable to aspire to material rewards, they are more ideological.

The Japanese Communist Party (JCP), originally founded as an affiliate of the Soviet-dominated Comintern in 1922, was illegal and repressed in the 1930s. It prospered for a few years after legalization in 1945. But it suffered from American hostility in the cold war, and in 1950 leading Communists were purged from political life on security grounds. In 1952 the JCP lost the few seats it had held in the Diet. Thereafter, it took a militant anti-United States position but suffered confusion and divisions and was very weak until the early 1960s.

By 1964 the JCP was badly torn by the Sino-Soviet split. It tended to side with Peking but tried to bridge the gap between China and the Soviet Union, only to please neither. Pro-Soviet and pro-Chinese minorities defected to form splinter parties of their own, while the main body remained neutral. Although the JCP would probably have preferred alliance with the Chinese party, it was alienated by the pretensions of the Chinese, and Mao's Cultural Revolution cost his party most of its attractiveness to the Japanese.

The Japanese Communist Party thus became independent, somewhat in the manner of the Italian Communist Party but more fully so, long before Eurocommunism was invented. In 1971, at the Twenty-Fourth Congress of the Soviet party, it made the strongest plea for the autonomy of Communist parties. It has since endeavored to modernize and shed the old revolutionary-conspiratorial image. Well before the French party, it claimed to stand for democracy in the ordinary sense of the word, including freedom of opposition parties in a Communist-governed state. The Japanese party newspaper was made more popular and less ideological. Perhaps most important, the party structure was loosened and some dissent was permitted, although it has sufficient discipline to exclude organized factions.[27] The party formally renounced Marxism-Leninism in 1976. However, it is still linked in the public mind with the Soviet Union and suffers from disputes with that country over the northern islands and fishing rights. It holds nearly 10 percent of the electorate.

The other major opposition party is more idiosyncratically Japanese. In the early 1970s, the most striking feature of the political landscape was the Komeito, or "Clean Government" Party. It was formed in 1964 by a neo-Buddhist proselytizing sect, Soka Gakkai, which furnishes its chief backing, although the organizations are formally distinct. The Komeito entered the House of Representatives elections in 1967. It surged forward again in 1969, and in 1976 became the third largest party; it won fifty-eight seats in 1979, and the same number in 1983. Komeito is a party of protest, given to fairly extreme rhetoric, but basically conservative and anti-communist as well as antiestablishment. It may conceivably be a candidate for a coalition if the LDP should be unable to govern alone. It has commonly allied itself with the leftists against the LDP; in 1979, however, it stood with the LDP against the JSP and JCP.

[27]Fukui, "Factionalism," p. 52.

There are various splinter groups and some special interest parties, such as one demanding reduction of taxes on salaries and another pushing for more welfare benefits. Japan, however, has seen nothing like Germany's Green protest.

The opposition parties continue to exist, despite their frustrations, because many people have views and interests contrary to those of the governing sector. In Japan, these are primarily trade unionists, at odds with the basically pro-business orientation of the government, and critics on grounds of principle—students, intellectuals, and much of the well-informed, influential, and uninhibited press. The larger opposition parties, especially the JSP and the JCP, have something of a base in local government, much like the French Communist Party. Socialists and Communists are strongest in the cities, especially in rapidly growing suburban communities.

The mostly leftist opposition is hopelessly divided ideologically and organizationally, and no single party represents a credible alternative. The best hope of the opposition parties is to take enough votes from the LDP so that it will have to form a coalition with one or another, which will thus gain a toehold on the ladder of power. It is remarkable how little the opposition parties were able to profit from the discredit and disarray of the LDP because of the Lockheed scandal (1976–1978). One basic difficulty of the opposition lies in the fact that 90 percent of the Japanese consider themselves middle class.

Opposition parties cannot make policy but only criticize and obstruct, and perhaps prevent the ruling party from undertaking anything very unpopular or force the modification of proposals. This is a genuine function in a democracy, although it is different from the classical British-derived image of opposition as alternative government prepared to transfer power to new hands with new ideas when the people weary of the party in power.

The Bureaucracy

Only about 9 percent of the Japanese labor force is employed by the government.[28] Yet nowhere in the democratic world is the bureaucratic apparatus more important than in Japan, where it not only executes decisions but also largely originates them and probably most policy, in accordance with the consensual process. Although a minister may shift high civil servants for his own reasons, he has only one political appointee by his side. At the top of each ministry is a small coherent group, the membership of which is constantly in flux.

A sector of the bureaucracy, the Ministry of International Trade and Industry (MITI), is closely entwined with business through consultation and advice, through multifarious regulations, and through governmental control of the credit on which Japanese firms rely very heavily. A number of public corporations date from the years when the Meiji government was establishing industries, including the national railway, which coexists with private railways, salt and tobacco monopolies, telecommunications, and some banks and financial institutions.

Opposition between the public and private spheres is much less marked in Japan than in the United States; private corporations, like public ones, are expected to conform to national purposes. MITI plans export production for maximum efficiency, and a multitude of official and semiofficial advisory councils and boards oversee all aspects of the economy. The government relies much

[28] T. J. Pempel, *Policy and Politics in Japan: Creative Conservatism* (Philadelphia: Temple University Press, 1982), p. 20.

less on legislation than administrative guidance, much of which is by suggestion or even a "lifted eyebrow" but is nonetheless effective.[29] The bureaucracy is understandably the chief target of pressure groups, because it is the heart of the Japanese system.[30]

People have more respect for the civil service than for politicians; it is as nearly a meritocracy as exists in the world. Entrance, since late in the nineteenth century, is by rigorous and honest examinations administered mostly by individual ministries under the supervision of the National Personnel Authority, the equivalent of a Civil Service Commission. Most entrants come from Tokyo University, which acquired preeminence from its headstart in the Meiji era; a much smaller fraction, from Hitotsubashi or Kyoto University. These three provide over three-quarters of the senior civil service.[31] Prior to World War II, those who passed the written test were subject to qualifying oral examinations, at which examiners could prefer graduates of their old school. At one time, over 90 percent of the higher bureaucracy were alumni of Tokyo. Even without favoritism, however, the dominance of the elite universities is self-perpetuating because they draw the best students and the best instructors. The leading universities also provide outstanding personnel in law, science, and business—top firms limit their recruiting to the top universities. In nearly all cabinets, Tokyo has provided a plurality of ministers.

Entry to the elite thus depends on mental prowess; every year, hundreds of thousands of graduates of secondary schools go through "examination hell," as their intellectual accomplishments are rigorously tested. To succeed, they must demonstrate enormous knowledge and general preparation; this doubtless favors memorization, but it rewards genuine ability. There seems to be no favoritism, although a higher-class background is inevitably some advantage. University training is free in the public institutions: Tokyo University receives students of all strata (except the few unable to afford the requisite schooling) and places them, by virtue of their talent, among the nation's elite.

Competition begins with the parents' efforts to enroll children in the best kindergarten and continues through elite preparatory school. Once the student has leaped the barrier into the university, the road is easier; but it is still necessary to pass an intensely competitive examination to enter a prestigious ministry. After admission to the civil service, promotion depends partly on seniority, partly on peer evaluation, which induces more conformity and cooperation than individualistic ambition. The most promising, never remaining long in one spot, rise rapidly, perhaps to section chief or even vice minister.

A bureaucrat spends his entire career within a single department, because ministries have been decidedly self-contained since the days when each was separately responsible to the emperor. There is much rivalry among them, in contrast to the group feeling of the Indian Civil Service. The Ministry of Finance has enjoyed the most prestige, as in France and Britain, but status changes. The Foreign Ministry, for example, improves its standing as Japan becomes more active in world affairs.

A career probably does not last long enough for the bureaucrat to grow stale. The capable civil servant retires when no more positions are open above him, about age fifty or a little after. This means that high civil

---

[29]Jeffery M. Lapon, "Administrative Guidance in Japan," *Fletcher Forum* 2 (May 1978), pp. 139–141.
[30]On decision-making in Japan, see T. J. Pempel, ed., *Policy Making in Contemporary Japan* (Ithaca, N.Y.: Cornell University Press, 1977).
[31]Stockwin, *Divided Politics*, p. 130.

servants are probably in their forties. There is a continual turnover of personnel, with new people bringing in new ideas from the leading universities.

Early retirement also means there is a continual supply of highly intelligent men in early middle age with high-level government experience. Upon "descent from heaven," as retirement is called, ex-civil servants mostly go into business, probably in a branch related to their official career. They may be recruited by firms desirous of their expertise and also the contacts they retain in the ministry. They may have arranged a place in advance in return for assistance rendered while in public office—the borderline between ordinary practices and corruption is indistinct. Ministries with close relations with business, such as MITI, Finance, Construction, and Transport, are naturally most likely to place retirees in public or private corporations. It is to be noted that the movement is from government to business, not the reverse, as frequently occurs in the United States. There may be some value in a system whereby the public servant does not see government work as the entirety of life, and early retirement of high bureaucrats may be one ingredient of the Japanese success.

Many ex-bureaucrats also go into politics, generally into the Liberal Democratic ranks. About a quarter of the members of the Diet have been veterans of the civil service, half to two-thirds of the ministers, and all premiers except Suzuki, Miki, and Tanaka. Only by election to the Diet can a civil servant hope to reach top rank in the government. Here again relations are self-reinforcing: those "descending from heaven" crowd into the LDP because it is the way to power; consequently, the LDP is better qualified to govern, has close relations with the administrative apparatus, and has a firmer grip on power. The administrative, business, and political elites cohere, and the outsiders remain out—except insofar as their children can leap the examination barriers.

Judicial System

The Japanese court system has secondary political significance, as in European countries. It is not, however, virtually a branch of the civil service but a coordinate branch of government consecrated in the constitution. Following American practice, a Supreme Court was established as guardian and interpreter of the constitution, but it has not gained prestige comparable to that of its American counterpart. Its fourteen members plus a chief justice are appointed by the cabinet for life. They are subject to decennial recall, but this has thus far been only a formality. Unlike the German Constitutional Court, the Supreme Court rules only on specific cases under adjudication. For a long time it was rather unwilling to declare laws invalid, but since the mid-1970s it has done so more freely, and it has acted several times to protect rights guaranteed by the constitution.

Lower courts are administered by the Supreme Court. Their judges likewise have life tenure and are subject to the formality of a referendum every ten years. As in European practice, the judge mostly conducts the trial, often without the help of lawyers. The outcome of criminal cases is almost always conviction, because prosecutors do not prosecute unless they feel confident of the case. Judges, prosecutors, and lawyers are recruited by competitive examination of law school graduates; those who pass receive two years of training in a special institute. The three groups are consequently close in mentality.

The courts have much less work in Japan than in the United States because crime rates are far lower—there were recently 280 times as many armed robberies in New York as in

Tokyo[32]—and because the Japanese are not inclined to litigation. As far as possible they prefer to settle disputes by informal procedures. The number of lawyers in Japan is a minute fraction of those in the United States, and whereas in the latter country the law is the broadest road to politics, in Japan lawyers are usually mere specialized professionals.

Local Government

The Meiji regime was fully centralized. The American-drafted constitution and the Occupation, in the interest of pluralism, tried to set up autonomous local administration with substantial powers. This system was too contrary to tradition to be permanent, but something of local self-rule remains.

The country is divided into forty-seven prefectures; they, and the cities, towns, and villages in them have an elected governor or mayor and an elected unicameral assembly. The term of the former is four years, but he can, in a parliamentary way, be forced out by the assembly unless he dissolves the assembly and calls new elections. Local autonomy is less in practice than in theory because of lack of resources; about half the funds of the local units is supplied by the center. However, the local administrations have some importance, like German Länder, as agencies on which the central authorities rely for execution of policies.

The greater political importance of local government, however, is that it gives opposition parties opportunities to clutch crumbs of power. Most local offices are held by independents, predominantly of conservative persuasion,[33] but the opposition at least gets an opportunity to show itself as a potential governing force. For example, a candidate backed by the Socialists and Communists was mayor of Tokyo from 1967 to 1979. Local elections are closely watched as a political barometer, and occasional victories help the morale of those shut out of the national administration.

Interest Groups

Although the rights of all are reasonably respected, it is fair to say that Japan is primarily governed by a tangled network of Liberal Democratic politicians, civil servants, and big business, highly concentrated in Tokyo. There are all manner of factional groups and cross-linkages in all directions. The financing of LDP factions by business interests is a major channel of influence. There are also contributions to the party and electoral campaigns, and this symbiosis of money and politics is a major grievance of the opposition. Not many businessmen go into politics, however. Perhaps a fifth of LDP Diet members have a business background, but these come predominantly from medium and small firms.[34]

National, regional, and local business associations are highly organized and very effective.[35] Several business associations, headed by the Federation of Economic Organizations (*Keidanren*), work with the bureaucracy and the LDP. The most effective economic power, however, is represented by the six big conglomerates, headed by Mitsubishi and Mitsui, reborn after the postwar breakup. They represent economic power, along with seven major corporations, including Hitachi, Toyota, Nissan (Datsun), and Matsushita (Panasonic), with many links of ownership, supply, marketing, credit, and management.

[32]Robert C. Christopher, "The Changing Face of Japan," *New York Times Magazine*, March 27, 1983, p. 86.

[33]Robert E. Ward, *Japan's Political System*, 2nd ed. (Englewood Cliffs, N.J.: Prentice-Hall, 1978), p. 170.

[34]Ike, *Japanese Politics*, p. 87.

[35]Vogel, *Japan as Number One*, pp. 102–103.

Organized labor, in contrast, stands outside the sphere of leadership, although it is neither silent nor impotent. One reason labor has less access to political decisionmaking is its affiliation with opposition parties. The larger federation, *Sohyo*, with some 4.5 million members in 1977, is allied with the JSP, for which it supplies funds and organization. The lesser *Domei*, with 2.2 million members in 1971, has supported the DSP. *Churitsoren*, with 1.3 million members, is unaffiliated, as are over 8 million members of nonfederated unions.

Sohyo is composed mostly of workers in the public sector. These are legally forbidden to strike and at least partly for that reason are more militant than most workers in private industry; they can push their goals only by political action. Their wages have tended to lag; and there has been more labor disorder in public than private enterprise.

The fraction of Japanese workers unionized is about one-third, smaller than the British, larger than the American, about equal to the German. Large enterprises are much more unionized than small, and the unions are organized not by trade but by workplace. They are less aggressive and class-conscious than European unions because workers identify much more with the firm. However, Japanese unions remain political because of suspicion of the government; the importance of political decisions regarding taxes, inflation, wage policies, and the like; and the fact that many are employed by the government.

Various other pressure groups, such as professional and consumer unions, play a part and may well exert great influence on decisions of particular concern to them. The reliance of the LDP on the rural vote has been noted; as a consequence, the farmers have more clout with the government than the trade unions. The farmers' concern is for support prices, secondarily for protection from imports, and there is an annual bargaining in which agricultural are weighed against consumer interests.

The press, agressive, well-informed, and well-staffed, is especially important. Mass newspapers like *Asahi, Mainichi,* and *Yomiuri Shimbun* have national circulations of many millions—newspaper readership is nearly twice as many per million population as in the United States.[36] They also have a mission to criticize the governing elite. A government cannot ignore them, and it engages in doubtful practices only at a risk of exposure.

JAPANESE SOCIETY: SUCCESS AND CONSENSUS

Many reasons have been cited to explain the phenomenal ability of the Japanese to modernize and then to recover so rapidly after World War II. Lists[37] are not very helpful, because many less successful countries have had equal access to raw materials, modern technology, the American market, cheap labor, undervalued currency, and exchange controls. Some of the Japanese advantages are obviously wearing out. Wages are no longer low, and increases sometimes outpace productivity. Many industries, including the Japanese specialties of shipbuilding and textiles, suffer from the competition of the cheaper labor of South Korea and Taiwan. Technological borrowing is no longer so easy now that Japan has come to the front rank of the advanced countries and exports nearly

[36]Pempel, *Policy and Politics in Japan,* p. 25.
[37]Such as given by Brzezinski, *Fragile Blossom* (New York: Harper & Row, 1972), pp. 38–41. See also Edward F. Denison and William K. Chung. *How Japan's Economy Grew so Fast: The Sources of Postwar Expansion* (Washington, D. C.: Brookings Institution, 1976): and Vogel, *Japan as Number One.* In distribution, where the pressure of international competition is feeble, Japan is inefficient. The price of an imported article to the consumer may be ten times its cost to the importer.

as much technology as it imports. It was a recent Japanese concession to permit the export of military technology to the United States. The Japanese are technology- and production-minded. There may be 200 to 300 titles on "total quality control" in a single bookstore near Tokyo station.[38] The productivity of labor in Japanese television factories is double the American. More basically, Japanese children spend about twice as much time studying as American. Over 90% of young Japanese graduate from high school, compared with 77% of Americans, and the Japanese high school graduate has knowledge comparable to the average American college graduate.[39] The Japanese work harder and more willingly and save five times more of their income than do Americans.

The Japanese had the good fortune to start from scratch after the war; their industrial plant is much more modern on the average than the American one. But it is more important that Japanese standards of quality and reliability are higher than those of Europe and America. A study of quality of air conditioners showed seventy times as many defects in American as in Japanese models.[40] The Japanese manage more effectively, and relations between government and business and between employers and employees are better than in the United States.

Many observers have surmised, perhaps wishfully, that these characteristics of the Japanese, arising supposedly from the feudal background and the needs of impoverishment, cannot be permanent. They reason that the Japanese must succumb to the ills of the modern consumption society as the waves of modernization erode their some-

what primitive character. The young in Japan are especially susceptible, as they tend, like youth everywhere, to reject the values of their parents and are caught up by world fashions; television, even more universal in Japan than in the United States, breeds a consumer mentality. Japanese workers take more days off, and the fascination with statistics of economic performance wears off.

Japan, moreover, has had to shift attention from conquering markets to catch up on neglected social services, housing, and infrastructure. The aging of the population is a problem as in other industrial countries. But it is not clear that marked decadence is the outcome. Competition in education seems to be as intense as ever. The low Japanese crime rates have not been converging toward the American but declining. The robbery rate is 125 times lower in Japan than in the United States. As society changes, the position of women, formerly very low, has improved. Better diet and health are making a physically stronger race and raising Japanese life expectancy above that of Sweden. Pollution was a terrible problem, as production had priority; but Japan has coped with it more effectively than any other nation.

The Government-Business Link

The Japanese have shown an unparalleled ability to work together for common goals— government with business, management with workers, and managers with one another. Japanese business generally welcomes government leadership and is ready to accept guidance and sometimes to subordinate the profits of the day to the needs of the nation. Corporate executives consult with officials regarding major decisions and take government intervention for granted. The Japanese in this sense are still a little like a family set apart from the rest of humanity. Bureaucrats, politicians, and business leaders—

[38]*Business Week*, July 18, 1983, p. 38.
[39]*Christian Science Monitor*, October 27, 1983, p. 20.
[40]*Christian Science Monitor*, September 15, 1983, p. 23.

all of similar education, probably from the same university—get together to plan for their joint success, the greater glory of Japan, Inc., and the national prosperity, which is close to that of their own organizations.

The chief agency of government-business cooperation is MITI, which seeks to direct investment into the most promising lines. It nurses new industries and eases the demise of the losers.[41] In the 1950s it helped the fledgling automotive industry; lately it has targeted computers and related lines, funding, for example, research into artificial intelligence. However, the role of MITI has probably lost importance as the corporations have gained maturity and strength; and the hand of the state has not always been helpful, in Japan as elsewhere.[42]

One concrete aspect of cooperation is that taxation is designed to encourage production rather than to discourage it. The proportion of national income taken by the government is only about half that in major European nations and the United States. Credit is used more freely for expansion than in most Western countries. Government support does not necessarily underwrite inefficiency; firms that cannot justify themselves go bankrupt—18,000 in the recession of 1977. Nor does it imply monopolies; Japanese firms are oriented toward the world market and compete vigorously among themselves not only for profits but also for market shares. The concentration of ownership in Japanese industry is less than that in the United States and Europe. The government is not the servant of business; the relationship is mutual. Bureaucrats and political leaders have been committed to national development since the Restoration, and

they seek not only to satisfy their clientele but to promote their ideas of national welfare.

The Employer-Employee Link

The ability to see common interests with or above personal interests is equally a strength of the Japanese corporation. American executives often work extremely hard because they identify with the firm; in Japan, lower personnel do so also. Many stories are told of workers running instead of walking on errands or declining to take vacations to which they are entitled. They sing the company song before going on shift, and the company is their "economic family." The big modern firms, in compensation, offer many paternalistic benefits, even to helping workers find mates. They regard their workforce as a major asset, and their duty to it ranks with their duty to the stockholders.[43]

The major firms guarantee lifetime employment, which is a uniquely Japanese practice. Lifetime employment owes something to the feudal custom of mutual and permanent obligations between superiors and inferiors, but it has grown stronger since World War II. It was reinforced by the shortage of qualified labor in a rapidly expanding economy and by the desire of enterprises to hold employees whom they trained.[44] Workers ordinarily start at low pay and work up by seniority and merit. The fact that one's future career is clearly laid out and offers indefinite prospects motivates effort and self-improvement. Poor performance, unless exceptionally bad, is not usually cause for dismissal; it means undesirable assignments and no promotion.

[41]See Chalmers Johnson, *MITI and the Japanese Miracle* (Stanford, Calif.: Stanford University Press, 1982).

[42]Toshimasa Tsurate, "The Myth of Japan Inc.," *Technology Review* 86 (July 1983), pp. 43–48.

[43]On the Japanese firm, see Rodney C. Clark, *The Japanese Company* (New Haven, Conn.: Yale University Press, 1979).

[44]Chio Nakane, *Japanese Society* (Berkeley, Ca.: University of California Press, 1970), pp. 15–16.

Workers loyal to the firm in which they expect to spend their working life, which provides multiple benefits and upon whose fortunes their fortunes hang, can welcome the rapid introduction of the latest technology. Here the contrast with many American and British craft workers is sharp. Most Japanese trade unions are focused on the enterprise, although they belong to national unions and federations. Hence the union also identifies with the firm while protecting the interests of its members, including permanent employment. The system introduces rigidities, but they are less serious because protected tenure is not for everyone. Firms keep the workforce somewhat flexible by hiring temporary workers. They also contract out production to smaller firms, of which there are many: Half a million little shops employ fewer than 200 workers each. Nearly half of all Japanese workers are thus outside the corporate framework, self-employed or in family businesses.[45]

The Consensual Style

The "family style" of Japanese business fits the general social outlook; much in Japanese society may be seen as an extension of the paternalistic, tight-knit family. The powerful achievement ethic is more collectivist than individual; individualism is regarded as nihilistic and selfish. Privacy is neither feasible nor desirable, since it means separation from the group. Loyalty is supremely important. Despite much consciousness of rank, the leadership style is low-key; the democratic way of Japanese managers contrasts markedly with the hauteur of their British counterparts. Preferred leaders are those who are worthy of trust—good members of the group who help their followers. They lead not by

extremism but by avoiding divisions and taking moderate positions.

The Japanese want decisions by consensus rather than majority rule, if the latter leaves a discontented minority. For this reason, it is felt to be wrong for the majority party to push through laws to which the minority strongly objects. In practice, legislation has usually been fairly well agreed on between the LDP and other parties. The search for consensus may lead to immobility and timidity of opinions; the Japanese notoriously avoid giving offense and may seem to say yes when they simply are too courteous to say no. Responsibility may be excessively diffused, but every effort is made to maximize communication within the group. Views are thoroughly aired, so all concerned are committed to whatever position may be reached. Since top officers do not expect to give orders, policies frequently originate at lower levels and filter up. Japanese managers spend much more time consulting with their employees than do American or European managers. This not only improves morale but also encourages underlings to think and ensures that views other than those of the leadership come to the fore.[46]

Japanese Democracy

Japan is far more rule-bound and less individualistic than the United States.[47] Yet Japanese democracy is successful in the terms in which the success of a government is ordinarily measured. It keeps order, improves the material well-being of its citizens, and

[45]Ike, *Japanese Politics*, p. 9.

[46]Vogel, *Japan as Number One*, p. 144. For impressions of Japanese psychology, see Robert C. Christopher, *The Japanese Mind* (New York: Simon and Schuster, 1983).

[47]For impressions of the Japanese, see Frank Gibney, *Japan, the Fragile Superpower* (New York: Norton, 1979); and Robert C. Christopher, *The Japanese Mind* (New York: Simon and Schuster, 1983).

raises the standing of the nation in world affairs. It would be difficult to disprove that Japan is actually run by a small number of big businessmen, high civil servants, and LDP politicians. Yet if the country is run by capitalists, they do not form a coherent group but are strongly competitive among themselves, and they have not prevented the rise of workers' real wages. If the bureaucrats are not populists, they, like business interests, are disunited and have no overall goals except the broad national interest. They are not dictatorial but dedicated to the rule of law and general improvement. Most important, the distribution of income is probably more egalitarian than in any other country, and there is little class consciousness. There is much social mobility. Persons of undistinguished origins can rise to the top in both government and business. Bench workers can reasonably aspire to rise to management positions. In the old society, everyone's place was fixed by birth; in the new, status depends most of all on the competitive examination system and education. Students from low-income families have good chances of entering top universities, and their occupational aspirations are higher than those of American students of comparable background.[48] The merit system is self-perpetuating, in the sense that those who get to the top by talent want the same criteria applied to others.

Japan, then, is something of a meritocracy tempered by democracy. Far more than the American, Japanese government is dominated by trained professionals, under a very few elected or appointed leaders. Elections serve the purpose not of transferring power or bringing many new persons to the top but

[48]Nathan Glazer, "Social and Cultural Factors in Economic Growth," in Hugh Patrick and Henry Rosovsky, eds., *Asia's New Giant: How the Japanese Economy Works* (Washington, D. C.: Brookings Institution, 1976), p. 840.

of keeping the rulers responsible and responsive to the wants of the people, giving them legitimacy to govern while restricting their actions. It is prima facie undemocratic that a single party holds office continually, but the prime ministership changes frequently with political currents.

Democratic institutions are not a Japanese specialty. Before World War II one would say that the Japanese showed rather a gift for totalitarianism, with their receptivity to emperor worship, repression of individualism, arrogance of powerholders, and docility of the masses. But defeat discredited the old order and made a much more equal and fluid society, which modified the democratic institutions pushed upon it. It is a happy demonstration that it is possible for a society without democratic traditions to become thoroughly democratic in a brief period with institutions and values rather different from those traditionally associated with Western democracy. Moreover, so far as the democratic qualities of Japan have to do with its spectacular economic rise, it appears that industrial growth does not have to be at the expense of equality but may prosper from it.

JAPAN IN THE WORLD

The Japanese are strongly ethnocentric and have a more marked sense of identity than perhaps any other nation; the universe is populated by Japanese and non-Japanese. To be rightly Japanese, one must be born such; and even Japanese who have lived too long abroad, or have been educated at foreign schools, may find themselves excluded. Racially indistinguishable Koreans who have lived in Japan for generations are subjected to intense social prejudice. Japaneseness rests in part on a difficult and unique language. Few foreigners learn it, and few Japanese manage to acquire more than rudimentary English, despite its utility in foreign relations and business. The linguistic curtain is a real barrier to Japanese participation in world affairs.[49]

Yet the deeply insular Japanese are fully aware of their dependence. Because the nation can produce no important fraction of any needed raw material, reliance on imports is complete. Under these conditions, there is no question of a return to insularity or empire. On the contrary, Japan has pioneered a historical experiment as a great power almost without armed forces. In a nuclear age, war for Japan would be a catastrophe. So it has a simple but sensible foreign policy: to get along with everyone—not only the United States but also Vietnam; not only Mainland China but also Nationalist China; not only oil producers and sources of raw materials but European buyers as well.

Japanese relations with the United States are especially important. Considering the depth of cultural differences, they have been remarkably smooth and advantageous for both sides. Many frictions are due to the fact that it has been difficult for the United States, like the parent of an adolescent, fully to take account of the fact that the former inferior and dependent has grown up and wishes to be treated as an equal. There has also been a suggestion of racial prejudice; the United States has been loftier in dealing with the Japanese than with the French or the Germans. Yet Japan has acquired stature and general respect, and it is America's strongest economic ally. It is also a very important political ally, and Japanese security depends on the American shield. Political frictions of the past seem to have been largely left behind,

and the security treaty is no longer controversial. When a U.S. aircraft carrier docked at Sasebo in 1983, the antiwar demonstration greeting it was a tiny reminder of the protests against a visit in 1968.

There are two sources of friction. One is the American demand that Japan spend more for its defense—a demand that is ironic for those who remember Pearl Harbor. Pro-American Prime Minister Nakasone has moved to raise the military budget, but this is not popular and change is slow. The other and sorer point is the Japanese invasion of U.S. markets and the large U.S. deficit in trade with Japan. Much is said of Japanese barriers to American exports, mostly non-tariff. They certainly exist; in Japan as in the United States farmers and other producers whose livelihood is jeopardized by imports raise loud protests, which the LDP cannot ignore. However, Japan is not really protectionist; if it were, it would not be so efficient. More important than trade barriers is the overvaluation of the dollar, which in effect imposes a duty on Japanese imports and gives a bounty to Japanese exports. But the basic problem is simply Japanese productivity. The more positive American response is to learn from the Japanese, and never has the United States tried so assiduously to adopt methods of a foreign country—in many cases methods originated by Americans and better applied by Japanese.

China is also vitally important for Japan. It is the greatest source of Japanese culture, and despite age-old rivalry, there is an affinity between the two peoples. China also represents protection for Japan from possible Soviet pressure, a supplement to the American security umbrella. And with its wealth of undeveloped raw materials and potentially gigantic market, China represents great economic possibilities for industrial Japan, the state best situated to utilize them. Japan is now the chief agency in the

---

[49]Roy A. Miller, *The Japanese Language in Contemporary Japan* (Stanford, Calif.: American Enterprise Institute, 1977), p. 19; Edwin O. Reischauer, *The Japanese* (Cambridge, Mass.: Harvard University Press, 1977), chap. 37.

Westernization of China, and the character of their relations will be fateful for both.

Despite Japan's distinctiveness, it must inevitably become more a part of the world. It cannot exclude foreign ways and does not try to do so. English words find their way into the Japanese vocabulary in ever growing numbers. More and more Japanese travel; and Japanese investment abroad grows steadily, mostly in the Third World. Some comes to the United States, where Japanese managers have shown themselves able to make failing businesses profitable. In the growing interaction, much that is distinctively Japanese may be expected to disappear. On the other hand, the Japanese, who were long diffident about their success, are coming into a new and merited pride. Japan will probably have more and more influence on the way the world goes.

7

Third World Politics

Political ills mostly arise from inequality. This is obvious within states. Not only is it impossible fully to square unequal gifts with equal rights; parties, classes, races, or elites of some description hold superior power and privileges that the inferiors resent. The conflicting values and goals of the rich and poor, powerful and weak, are the greatest cause of difficulties for democracy in most countries. Similarly, on the world scene many of the problems of international relations arise from the fact that a small group of nations, the so-called advanced industrial states, are vastly more productive and wealthier than the much larger number of "developing nations," or less hopefully, "less developed countries." The gap between the economic levels of the richer and poorer is so great that in many ways they live in different universes, and their values and demands on the international community inevitably conflict.

The distance between societies in which high school students expect to own automobiles and those in which a family is fortunate to have a bicycle can be bridged only by superhuman understanding and good will.

The predominant characteristic of the Third World is poverty and a sense of lagging behind. The term was coined in the cold war to designate a group of nations, mostly recently freed colonies, that chose nonalignment in the struggle between the West (then called the "Free World") and the East, or the Soviet bloc. Since the 1960s the term has become more ambiguous, because the Communist states and the "Free World" have both lost coherence and the boundaries of the Third World have become blurred. Here, however, we will include in it all non-Western states except those, particularly China, that have clearly placed themselves in the category of Communist.

The advanced industrial states are those that participated in the scientific-industrial upsurge of Western Europe after the Middle Ages and especially in the last two centuries, plus overseas lands peopled by their descendants (the United States, Canada, and Australia). This group of countries is often called collectively the "West," despite its geographic scatter. Japan must be added to the group because it has assimilated their ways of production so successfully as to be more advanced than many countries of the geographical West. The countries of Eastern Europe, the Soviet Union and its client states, plus Albania and Yugoslavia stand apart. Their industrial development is well ahead of a large majority of Third World countries, although it is uneven; some, especially East Germany, Czechoslovakia, and Hungary, are not far from the level of productivity of most of Western Europe. Their political life, however, is shaped more by their Marxist-Leninist institutions than by their economic level. Various other states on the fringes of the industrial world—Portugal, Greece, and Turkey in particular—occupy an intermediate position, as do some smaller rapidly industrializing states of East Asia, such as Taiwan, South Korea, and Singapore. Some, such as Argentina and Uruguay, were once prosperous by European standards but have slipped back.

Some of the countries with the world's highest per capita incomes, such as Saudi Arabia, are still considered to be part of the Third World because of their background and social forms. The Third World, however, is primarily characterized by low income. The industrial countries have a per capita product in the vicinity of $10,000. The less developed range widely, the average for Latin America being about $1,800; for Africa, $700; and for South Asia, about $300. A number, mostly in Africa, have less than $200; the bulk of their people live virtually outside the market economy. There are various other correlates. The Western countries are characterized by high literacy. They have fairly adequate health care and diet, low infant mortality rates, and long life expectancy. They are well housed (probably a room per person), and they have telephones, electric appliances, and automobiles in abundance. Being industrial, they are mostly urbanized. They are uniformly democratic. The Third World states generally suffer illiteracy, high infant mortality, and lower life expectancy; they have poor medical services and poor diet. They are ill housed (probably a family per room), and except for the better off, do without telephones, electric appliances, and automobiles. Their populations are mostly agricultural and rural; multitudes have increasingly been flooding into the cities, but the masses of humanity in the new slums hardly form a city in the traditional sense. They lack a politically informative press, and their elections, if any, rarely give an opposition a real chance to contend for power.

Thus, there exists a world that has assimilated and gained by the scientific-industrial revolution and one that has (except for enclaves of industrialization) gained very much less. There are no satisfying answers for why this situation should persist when knowledge, technology, and even capital are readily transferable. It seems plausible that the rich are rich and the poor are poor because wealth has been transferred from the latter to the former, the implication being that the remedy is a reverse transfer. Reality, however, is more complicated. The societies of the present-day Third World were, generally speaking, stagnant and unproductive before the Western onslaught. Modernization has generally raised material well-being, although reduced death rates and consequent population growth have swallowed up much of the new surplus. It is not true that the Third World is falling ever further behind. The middle-income countries, from Kenya to Singapore, have substantially increased their percentage of world production. It is the very poor, led by India, and most of Africa, whose share of world output has shrunk in the past generation.

HISTORICAL BACKGROUND

Throughout the historical record, there have always been differences of economic level, relatively wealthy centers of civilization and poorer and less cultivated regions without. Probably this was true from the time humans first began making many useful inventions. It clearly was when the Sumerians were building the first considerable cities about 5,000 years ago. In the fifth and fourth centuries BC, the Greeks stood far above most other peoples not only in literature and philosophy but also in manufacturing. From about the tenth century, the Western world was ahead of the non-Western peoples in arts of war. Medieval popes forbade (futilely) the selling of weapons to the heathen, somewhat as the West tries to prohibit militarily useful exports to the Soviet Union today. The First Crusade, AD 1095 was a technological tour de force, as a small expedition successfully invaded distant Palestine and maintained itself for generations against a far more numerous native population.

The material capacities of the West were obvious by the fifteenth and sixteenth centuries, when Portuguese and Spanish adventurers looking for gold and spices explored the seas, easily defeated native peoples, and built up huge colonial empires. In many places, the peoples they encountered had only meager crafts and were called savages; others, as in India and China, had a sophisticated civilization and levels of wealth not grossly disparate from Western standards.

But they were militarily weak, in part for political reasons.

From the latter part of the seventeenth century, the growth of Western capabilities began to accelerate markedly because of scientific and technological discoveries, while the non-Western world moved slowly if at all. The Industrial Revolution that took shape in the eighteenth century overwhelmed the nineteenth; the twentieth century has seen an almost unbelievable outpouring of inventions, particularly in chemistry and electronics. Especially since World War II, growth rates have risen to levels that would have seemed fantasy to an earlier age. A 2 percent increase in per capita production annually was an excellent rate in the nineteenth century; this meant that incomes doubled in thirty-five years. But since 1945, many countries have shown rates of 5 to 7 percent, implying a doubling of production in ten to fifteen years. Consequently it has become ever harder to catch up, and the old problem has become far more acute. If three hundred years ago the average person in the Western sphere may have had three or four times the material goods of those outside it, the ratio nowadays is ten to a hundred times.

There are other reasons why the gap worsened until recently. Technology has become vastly more complex and hence harder to assimilate. It was not difficult to copy simpler inventions, even the manufacture of simple firearms, for example. But modern industrial production is a product of exceptional conditions; and an exceptional effort, perhaps including the restructuring of society, is required to assimilate it. The gap, moreover, has become more of a political problem because there is much more contact, communication, and mutual awareness. Africans and Indians see American and European life as represented (or misrepresented) by movies and television, and the number of travelers has multiplied enormously. At the same time, most of the educated world has adopted an egalitarian outlook that regards inequality as inherently unjust and reprehensible. Hence the poor countries have at the same time and over a few short decades found themselves relatively far poorer than in previous generations, have become much more aware of the fact, and have learned to resent it as wrong and unnatural.

The non-Western world has not been entirely passive, of course, but has been moved to self-defense for a century or more. Japan reacted rapidly and successfully to the threat of foreign gunboats in the mid-nineteenth century. The relative dominance of Europe in the world reached its height in the latter part of the nineteenth century; most of the globe not yet appropriated was then carved up by colonial powers, Latin America (mostly freed from Spain early in the century) and China being spared. But from around the beginning of this century, there were anti-Western or anticolonial stirrings in many countries of Asia, as peoples with ancient cultures began questioning their exploitation by Europeans. World War I was a grievous blow to the prestige of the West, and numerous independence movements began soon afterward. World War II set the stage for the end of the colonial empires and the appearance of a host of new nations. On the one hand, the colonial rulers were weakened or beaten and had lost the will and power to dominate vast overseas territories; on the other, the steadily rising demand for self-determination made dominion uncomfortable and unprofitable not only economically, but also politically.

The West thus gave up its original ambition to remake Asian or African societies in the European image, and it set the colonial territories free with varying but mostly quite inadequate practice at self-rule. Arbitrarily carved-up colonies were told that it

was up to them to behave like sovereign nations—nearly all of Africa became independent, as forty-odd states, in the decade after the Gold Coast became free Ghana on March 6, 1957. Raising a new flag, however, did not solve basic problems. Only the top crust of the Third World society was Westernized, and usually only superficially; and there was no easy way to forge an effective economic, social, and political order. The old power relationships remained; if colonialism was broken, the ex-colonies found themselves in a less overt dependence they called "neo-colonialism."

Thus nations of the Third World, mostly under European political dominion until a few decades ago, are formally free but in fact little better off materially and unsure how to use the sovereignty they possess. They admire and resent the wealthier and stronger powers and would like to come up to modern standards, yet they fear to lose their character and culture. Above all, they are frustrated, unable to understand why there are such great and persistent, sometimes growing differences between the sated and the hungry.

THE PROBLEM

Economic and Social Factors

From the fifteenth century on, European explorers carried guns, clocks, presses, and a myriad of intriguing and useful inventions around the globe, proudly displayed them, sold them for gold or native wares, and willingly instructed peoples in the use and manufacture of these devices. Yet even Chinese emperors and Indian potentates, who had many skilled artisans at their disposal, seldom copied the European marvels or did so only randomly. Only occasionally and belatedly was there any effort to copy Western industrialization; and most such efforts, as in China, were more costly than successful. Since the nineteenth century, and especially in the last twenty years, many countries have partially emulated Japan and have, generally with foreign technicians and capital, installed efficient industrial plants. But the fundamental situation remains. There is available a huge store of productive technology, all but the very newest of which is readily available; yet in most countries the productivity of farmers and workers is ten to a hundred times lower than in North America and Western Europe.

Some causes are geographic. For example, the climate is unfavorable in the majority of less developed countries that are tropical. In lowland tropics, heavy physical work is difficult. Hygiene is much more difficult than in cooler climates, and debilitating diseases and parasites thrive. Tropical soils are fragile, and hot-climate agriculture presents special problems. Highland tropical countries are more fortunate, but here too it may be that lack of seasonal change is unstimulating. Yet such geographic determinism has limited validity. Albania and Afghanistan have brisk climates, but they remain relatively backward. Argentina, Uruguay, and Chile, which have agreeable and healthful climates, have fallen further behind in recent years after promising development in the first part of this century.

Shortages of natural resources also impede development. Much has been made of the dependence of the industrial countries on the raw materials of the less developed, but most of the latter are in fact rather poorly endowed. The oil deposits of the Near East are exceptional, and they benefit relatively small numbers of people. Only a few countries, such as Chile and Zaire (copper), Jamaica (alumina), or Nauru (phosphate), have the good fortune to have large revenues from minerals; and mineral exports have yet to finance a real transformation of the economy. The most precious natural resource is good agricultural land, and in this regard the situation of most Third World countries is deplorable. Family plots in South Asia and the more crowded lands of Africa are apt to be in the range of one acre, and frequently less. Vast regions are virtually empty, but they are too mountainous, too dry, or otherwise unsuited for cultivation.

Another simple yet almost intractable difficulty is the notorious population explosion. When population is increasing 3 to 4 percent yearly, as it is in most Third World countries, it is very hard to increase output rapidly enough to make a dent in poverty. Africa is the most afflicted. The poorest of continents, it also has the most rapidly growing population, and per capita income may be lower in 1990 than it was in 1960.[1] It is especially difficult to raise agricultural production rapidly enough to keep up with the number of new mouths, and in most countries per capita food production has diminished in recent years. This means an even poorer diet or importation of foodstuffs instead of the capital goods needed for modernization, and increased dependence and economic instability. Not only does rapid population growth increase the number among whom the national pie must be divided, it also raises the proportion of dependents the working population must support. In many Third World countries, half the population is under the age of 16, with corresponding unfilled needs for schools and medical services and demands on parents' scanty resources.

Some countries, such as Brazil, impressed with their open spaces, are unworried; many others, such as Egypt, are in desperate straits: About 45 million people live on 5.7 million

[1]Carol Lancaster, "Africa's Economic Crisis," *Foreign Policy* 52, Fall 1983, p.149.

acres of agricultural land, and every year a million are added. A secondary disaster from population growth is the destruction of soils and the environment, as hard-pressed farmers clear hillsides and woodgatherers make deserts.[2] At least half the arable land of Mexico, for example, has been ruined or nearly ruined.

Differences tend to accentuate themselves: The relatively prosperous Third World countries, and the more prosperous sectors within individual countries, generally have more moderate birth rates; the least prosperous sectors and countries are the least disposed to limit families. This fact increases the gap between countries and between classes within countries in health, education, and welfare. Moreover, poverty keeps birth rates high because poor countries have no funds for social security and people need children for support in sickness and old age.

With poverty and overpopulation go malnutrition and disease. The physical and also mental capacities of most peoples of the Third World are cut down by inadequate nourishment. Indian nationalists used to see the difference between their people and the British in the fact that the latter ate meat. Over a billion persons are afflicted by chronic disease—some 500 million by malaria, 400 million by hookworm, 200 to 300 million by filariasis (elephantiasis), 200 million by schistosomiasis (flukes). Such pandemic ills hamper both work and learning. Many children never start school; most who do, drop out before properly acquiring the art of reading or soon forget it. In the face of unavoidable hardship, people become fatalistic; status is valued over achievement, and rhetoric takes the place of action. Acculturation to modernity causes anxiety and confusion.

Higher education, more for elite status

than for the acquisition of useful knowledge, creates an alienated intelligentsia of the half-Westernized. Many of them are unemployed; it is often impossible for more than a small fraction of university graduates to find jobs corresponding to their diplomas. Many who have useful skills are drawn away to lands where they are better rewarded and working conditions may be more favorable. The brain drain of scientists, engineers, physicians, and other highly trained persons from countries where they are badly needed (but perhaps unemployed) to richer countries is constant.

Most Third World societies are poorly integrated. Few have been solidified by deeply felt shared experiences like the history of common endeavor and shared causes that forged the nation-states of Europe. At best, the state stands for an anticolonial struggle now long past. Most countries are a mélange of languages and ethnic identities representing dozens, perhaps a hundred or more, groups that differ in language, food, clothing, folklore, and social customs. In Kenya, for example, the Kikuyu and Masai, living side by side, have totally different ways of life. Many states, particularly those of Africa, lack a national language and for communication have to use the language of the former colonial masters—English, French, or Portuguese. Even Swahili, which Kenya and Tanzania have taken as their official language, is only partly native. In many countries, such as Nigeria and Pakistan, English is the language of administration and of the elite. To know only a local language in Africa and most of South Asia is to be ignorant of the world.

The use of a world language widens the gulf between elite and masses, and this is the worst of the divisions within Third World societies. Malnutrition, disease, and illiteracy accentuate the separation of the majority from the small sector that has benefited from

[2]James S. Packer, "Slash and Burn below the Border," *Smithsonian* 4 (April 1973), pp. 67–70.

modernization and contact with the industrial world. The well-to-do in India, the Philippines, Nigeria, or Mexico enjoy amenities like those of affluent Americans or Germans, while the Indian farmer or Mexican peon is a world away from the American or European farmer. Inequality of income, the basis for differing life-styles, is far greater in the Third World than in the West, and its effects are harsher: The gulf between the person who has an automobile and the one who can hardly afford a bicycle is much greater than the difference between the person who has a Cadillac and the one who has a Honda. A Nigerian trained as an engineer wants to earn what engineers on the international market and those hired from abroad earn, but this is about a hundred times the average Nigerian income. Third World elites are also separated culturally from the masses; their children go to elite schools, and perhaps are educated abroad.

Most Third World societies also have a feeble work ethic. The educated are likely to feel they are entitled by virtue of their superior learning and background to a fairly easy and comfortable life with limited mental and no physical exertion. Political leaders speak of the urgency of modernization and economic progress for the relief of poverty, but one cannot assume that the wealthy and educated agree on this priority. Social classes are frequently most concerned for their own standing, and part of the standing of Third World elites is their height above the multitude. Thoroughgoing modernization would threaten their comfortable way of life. There is pressure for industrialization to provide jobs for the educated, and intellectuals often feel anger or shame at the poverty of their lands in comparison with industrial countries, but elites are likely to be skeptical of any changes injurious to their interests. Landholders in Latin America not only resist land redistribution but underutilize large estates and keep labor in surplus. For similar reasons, there is ambivalence about population control and the spread of good public education.

The Political Crux

The woes of the non-Western world operate together and reinforce one another, and almost any might be picked out as primary—lack of managers, lack of capital, poor health, poor education, and the like. But they mostly have a political or social aspect, and the most obvious bar to attacking them is the ineffectiveness of organized political mechanisms. For example, the emigration of scientists and engineers is ascribable not only to higher pay abroad but also to the rigidity of university systems, lack of research funds and facilities, nepotism in employment, lack of appreciation for science and scientists, and similar frustrations. Foreign-trained Filipinos come home to encounter endless petty regulations and unappreciative employers, and many then reemigrate. One of the chief causes of low productivity, as well as mass misery, is unemployment; it may be that less than half the workforce has regular employment. Massive unemployment (with little or no relief for the jobless) implies structural defects in the society. On the other hand, some Third World countries without special advantages or natural resources have shown very high growth rates in the past generation; manufacturing has boomed at record or near-record rates in Taiwan, South Korea, and some other countries. This proves that if a government can provide stable conditions, minimal interference, legal order, and moderate taxation, relative cheapness of labor can provide a basis for rapid growth.

Usually governments cannot provide such conditions or possibly do not strongly desire to do so, and productive enterprise is hamstrung by multiple costs and obstacles. Much of the difficulty can be summarized as corruption, by which we mean the misuse of official position for private benefit. Corruption includes bribery, extortion, nepotism, and venality, and is the scourge of all but a few Third World countries. It changes government from an agency of order to an agency of disorder. It introduces high costs and uncertainties into business and rewards political more than economic success; it becomes more important to have official connections than to be an efficient manager. Instead of the government collecting taxes to be spent for public welfare, officials collect payoffs to be spent for private luxury. Nepotism, which is in some places almost mandated by family structure, not only places incompetents in office, but also discourages honest ambition.[3]

Corruption means that bureaucrats respond to wealth, so it is conservative in its implications. It increases inequality because the wealthy profit from it, and it creates new riches. It extends from high to low. Governmental agencies employ ten people to do the work of one in order to make jobs for the newly educated; salaries being entirely inadequate, taking bribes is a necessity. Police officers, for example, may be paid almost nothing; it is assumed that they make a living from their little sliver of power. Even schoolteachers may expect to supplement their salaries by giving good grades to appropriate children. Permits are needed for almost anything, and their issuance needs lubrication. Here and there leaders inaugurate campaigns against corruption, usually more against low-level than high-level profiteering, but no campaign can have more than momentary success without a change in basic attitudes.

The extent of corruption is quite varied.

Possibly it is worst in some African countries; in Zaire, apparently, nothing moves without grease. President Mobutu's personal take was estimated at $4 to $5 billion.[4] In many countries a large fraction of trade is smuggling, necessarily with the connivance of officials. For example, in Burma most consumer goods are illegally imported for the black market. Illegal drug traffic (cocaine and marijuana) brings Colombia several billion dollars yearly and is the largest earner of foreign exchange. The best initiatives are thwarted; for example, in Indonesia, officials pocket the compensation allotted to displaced peasants. Petty bureaucrats may merely make a decent wage by charging for their services, but high figures, such as President López Portillo of Mexico, may siphon off hundreds of millions of dollars.

Corruption goes with inefficiency; it is easier to steal because in many countries accounts are carelessly kept and the government may not know where money is going. The importance of position and personal relations implies that material rewards are to be gained politically rather than economically, that is, by unproductive rather than productive effort. The primacy of politics at the same time impedes the growth of strong independent groups interested in honest government. Corruption also thrives on controls; the more regulation of the economy, the more rules to bend for a consideration or to charge for applying them.

Corruption means bad government; and bad government, at least from the point of view of modernizers, is part of the cultural background of most Third World countries. The political order discourages faith in the power of reason and individual self-assertion, while it rewards dishonesty. A country is backward not only because its economy is backward but also, in the words of a disil-

[3]Anthony Downs, *Inside Bureaucracy* (Boston: Little, Brown, 1967), pp. 156–157.

[4]*Christian Science Monitor*, October 8, 1982, p. 13.

lusioned Third World writer, because its very nature is backward.[5] It is impossible to build a modern productive society while clinging to ancient ways. Yet the situation of relative poverty and weakness tends to perpetuate the essence of the difficulty, which is the authoritarianism and inequality of Third World societies. They suffer the curse of inadequacy and insignificance, which produce paralyzing anxieties.[6] Destiny is made abroad and by strangers, and good things are foreign. People do not feel themselves movers of the world they live in but its victims.

Contact and communication only increase the economic, social, psychological, and political effects of inequality. Although political imperialism is gone, Third World peoples complain with some justice of an oppressive "neocolonialism." Economic inferiority makes economic dependence. The less developed country opens the door to foreign corporations for material reasons but finds foreigners managing key sectors of the economy; the host country is at the same time desirous of having the rich, alien corporation and resentful of its power and status. "Cultural imperialism" is even more benign. Popular movies and television programs from the West are cheap and modish; native culture is drowned by a flood of imports, and the Third World country becomes a cultural colony. But even as the West turns benevolent and tries to give assistance and good advice, it is still in a sense imperialistic: charity is the ultimate expression of superiority, and the one most difficult to deal with. It is easy to oppose a colonial government, but only fanatics reject charity.

One of the major effects of the relative weakness and dependence of the Third World is to reinforce basic patterns of hierarchy and inequality, giving power to those who have become more or less Westernized and to those who deal with the more powerful outside world, either seeking its favors or defending against its encroachments. Those who enter into the culture and economy of the modern world become more prosperous and more powerful; those who continue in the old ways become relatively poorer. A spirit of inequality permeates relations, as those on top look up (probably without admitting it) to outside powers and compensate by scorn for inferiors, just as in the typical hierarchic order an official bows low to superiors and walks over those below. This situation, and awareness of it, have brought a variety of attitudes toward and reactions to the West and the pluralist-capitalist system.

The Dilemma of Modernization

The countries of the Third World wish to defend themselves, their independence and national integrity, against the West and also to have the material benefits of industrial development and modern technology. These desires, or needs, present the people, especially the intellectuals, with a series of extremely difficult questions.

There are three phases of the problem. First and easiest is to acquire technology. This is in theory rather simple. A country can import machines, operating manuals, and production instructions; bring in technicians to train native managers and workers (or send students abroad); construct the necessary buildings, roads, ports, and lines of communication; and proceed to produce steel or textiles. If the situation is at all promising, it can secure foreign capital to finance much of the operation.

However, for an economy to function with

[5]J. R. Sinai, *The Challenge of Modernization: The West's Impact on the Non-Western World* (New York: Norton, 1964), p. 57.
[6]Lucian W. Pye, *Politics, Personality, and Nation Building: Burma's Search for Identity* (New Haven, Conn.: Yale University Press, 1962), p. 287.

tolerable efficiency, a series of institutions are necessary: an organized market (or a substitute in some control authority), labor regulations, financial and trading arrangements, educational facilities, and so forth. To set these up in good working order is far more difficult than installing machine tools.

The third requisite is still more difficult. A productive economy requires not only the institutions directly supporting it but also a political order that gives a stable protective environment, provides incentives for production, protects the economy from destructive political interference, and permits long-range economic calculation. It is easy for a government to be persuaded that it should promote the construction of industrial facilities, the modernization of agriculture, and the like. It is not hard to decide that the necessary facilities should be provided or permitted for the economy to adjust output to needs, to gear together the factors of production, marketing, and so forth. But it is not in the nature of a political system to change itself purposefully into a different system. Holders of power wish to strengthen their position by developing the economy but not to put different kinds of people in their places, renouncing the standing and privileges of power. Moreover, to change the social order profoundly means, or seems to mean, sacrificing the national personality. Hence, modernization is limited. It is natural to want modern means of production, but non-Western countries wish—quite naturally—to have them without much change of social order.

The Japanese have obviously been the most successful in borrowing and adapting Western technology. It should be recalled, however, that they do not deserve the entire credit. Purposeful borrowing from 1870 to 1930 raised national production most satisfactorily, but it did not come near solving the political question. Japan's feeble parliamentary experiment gave way to military rule that would certainly have checked economic growth eventually if the country had avoided international adventures. But political failure led to catastrophe, which turned into a blessing as the defeated nation was gifted with a modern political system. In other cases, economic growth based on revolutionary inspiration has been checked by political institutions basically unfavorable for economic modernization. Thus the Soviet Union, following the Stalinist model of forced-draft industrialization and collectivized agriculture, showed good results for several decades; but it no longer seems that the Soviet system is capable of promoting a sophisticated modern economy. China showed political failure more dramatically when the Great Leap Forward cut short a period of rapid improvement, and then the Cultural Revolution truncated the recovery getting underway. At present it is fair to doubt the long-term economic prospects of South Korea and Singapore, successful as they have been, unless more responsibility is built into their political systems.

Thinkers and leaders of the non-Western world are thus faced with the question of what they should or can adopt from the West and what of native tradition can well be retained. It might be fairly logical, if a country wants to emulate the economic development of the West, to adopt Western ways and values—individualism, pluralism, representative government, a basically market economy—and all that these imply. Here and there, people have advocated this course or something like it. For example, in the latter half of the nineteenth century, when Russia was obviously poor, weak, and vulnerable in relation to its neighbors, some proposed throwing the old ways overboard, adopting a constitution, perhaps ditching the obscurantist Orthodox Church. But such an approach is psychologically inadmissible. The Russians, masters of a huge empire, were not prepared to admit general inferiority, and in various ways they disliked the neighbors whom they envied. Consequently, the majority, while acknowledging a certain (undeserved) technological superiority of the West, exalted the Russian soul and idealized native ways, more or less accepting and rationalizing the autocratic government. In the years preceding World War I, as Russia grew industrially, mostly from private enterprise, it seemed that the government might evolve toward parliamentary forms, and in 1917 it briefly seemed that the Westernizers were victorious. However, in the situation of war, defeat, political disorder, and economic hardships, the Leninists turned Russia back to an anti-Western position, covered with an outwardly Western political theory.

In a hundred variations something like this conflict seethes in all countries of the non-Western world. On the one hand, they want the power and material capacities generated by Western modernization; on the other, they resent the intrusion of Western influences and do not want to make themselves into mere imitators of the intruders. Even Eskimos and Native Americans suffer this ambivalence: they find it painful to give up traditional ways and values in order to have the full benefits of modern society. Nowhere has the contradiction come more vividly to the fore than in Iran, where a monarch bent on drastically and very rapidly Westernizing the country without diminishing his own autocratic power was succeeded by a fundamentalist regime desirous of taking the country back to a purer and simpler age—without giving up television and jet aircraft. At the same time, even if many or most people would adopt Western political ways, they cannot do so, or can do so only superficially. There are usually no means to install a democratic government, and still less can a pluralistic society be achieved by merely wishing.

Difficulties of Democracy

Representative, more or less democratic government has for over a century and a half been associated with power and material progress, as well as with rights and freedom, and the feeling has slowly and irregularly grown that to be modern it is necessary to have a constitution, elections, legislature, and all that goes with these. Traditional and semifeudal ideals have here and there reasserted themselves, and new ideologies have raised a challenge. But fascism is too crude and narrow to offer a real alternative, and the appeal of communism has been shadowed by its reliance on class struggle, dogmatism, and denial of freedom. The appeal of democracy, on the other hand, rests not only on its philosophic virtues but also on its association with prosperity; only very large oil resources produce wealth comparable to that of the Western democracies, including Japan.

Hence democracy is considered the desirable form of government everywhere that people can freely express their opinion, and many a tyranny—from the "People's Democracies" of the Soviet sphere to the pseudoconstitutional dictatorships of Latin America—claims to incorporate it. Yet it has proved difficult to establish and more difficult to sustain in the world outside the sphere of West Europeans, their overseas offshoots, and Japan. Aside from some small islands, the democracies of the non-Western world consist of several Latin American countries, and India and Sri Lanka in South Asia.

Generally speaking, the causes of low productivity are equally causes of the failure of democracy. More specific is the lack of a basis in the popular consciousness. Nowhere did European explorers encounter democratic countries, except in tribal societies or on a very small scale. The Spanish and Portuguese gave Latin America the experience of three centuries of exploitative monarchic-colonial rule. Even where, as in British colonies, there were consultative councils and a degree of autonomy, the approach was thoroughly elitist. Colonial rule in Africa and Asia was in effect one-party government, which made it seem more natural to revert to one-party systems after independence.

Not only was democracy absent from the native cultures, there was seldom much notion of individualism or rule of law. Even the educated have found the idea of impartial adjudication and application of rules without regard for the results difficult to grasp. The popular demand, then, has been less for a form of government, or democracy, than for concrete benefits and satisfactions which an authoritarian party can plausibly promise. Moreover, whereas in the traditional culture there were probably institutions and mutual obligations moderating despotism, in the modernizing, disrupted society, people have fewer means of resistance, and tyranny may be more oppressive. Old forms are degraded, new ones fit badly, and government may more than ever rule by force alone.

Most countries of Asia and Africa lack the basic unity essential for an orderly democratic structure. Africans still generally belong more to ethnic or tribal groups than to the artificial nations that appear on the map; and such countries as India, Pakistan, and Indonesia have scores of languages and countless groups separated by religion and way of life. In most places, if political parties are permitted they become representative of particularistic groups—that is, they are almost inevitably divisive and may threaten to tear the state apart. To mitigate disunity, Ghana and the Ivory Coast prohibited not only ethnic parties but also marks of ethnic identification such as facial scarification. Even if there is a single generally understood language, there may be little basis for unity and common loyalty. Free and open political competition then spells disorder.

The gulf between upper and lower classes, which is a major obstacle to development, is an even greater hindrance to democracy. Modernizing societies are inevitably divided. They were aristocratic before, and they become more so as those who have advantages become the beneficiaries of modernization. Some live and work at more or less the level of America or Western Europe; others may become poorer than their ancestors because of crowding on the land or degradation in urban slums. The fact that the poor are undernourished and disease-ridden makes it harder for the aristocrats to think of them as theoretically equal citizens. Where people are in effect surplus, the democratic postulate of the value of the individual has no meaning. The poverty-stricken masses, on the other hand, are alienated from the state, which they regard as the possession of the bosses. The right of the majority (that is, the poor) to make political decisions seems tenuous. For leaders to offer the masses the opportunity to rob them of power and possessions by mobilizing votes is to expect a great deal. The chasm between upper and lower classes in Western Europe was never so great, but even there many generations of controversy and contest were necessary before aristocracies formally permitted the masses equal participation in the political system. For the poor, on the other hand, the rhetoric of democracy is hollow as long as class differences remain great.

Third World elites often have a theoretical commitment to democracy, but they are not likely to push theory to the point of endangering their way of life. The primary holders of power—army officers, bureaucrats, businessmen, and large landholders—control the political system to their advantage and resist changes that would make it more responsive to workers or peasants.[7] When democratic politics seem to endanger the social order, the middle and upper classes will welcome a military coup, as they did in Brazil in 1964 and in Chile in 1973.

The loose order of the poorly integrated democratic state may provide opportunities for enrichment, so that the poor see themselves as cheated by the politically influential rich. In the Philippines, before the Marcos dictatorship, members of congress in the service of the rich oligarchs thrived in an atmosphere of lawlessness and gangsterism and blocked social and economic development; peasants were reduced to sharecropper bondage by debts. The desire to curb the rich families was a principal excuse for Marcos's institution of martial law and one reason that it was widely acceptable. That the dictatorship has raised a new class of profiteers and has minimally benefitted the masses is incidental.

The spread between the privileged and the common folk is accentuated by the weakness of the middle class and private entrepreneurship. There are many little businesses, but larger and politically more significant undertakings are likely to be foreign-owned and managed, held by a few rich persons with close connections to political power, or controlled by the government itself. There is thus not much basis in the economy for political pluralism. The situation is self-reinforcing: the private sector being weak, the government adopts policies hostile to it and fails to provide it with the security necessary for growth.[8]

A new intermediate class of technicians and white-collar workers has been growing in most Third World countries, persons of some education and aspirations to modern life, but without capital or high status. But these bureaucrats, engineers, journalists, and managers hardly constitute a middle class like the classic European bourgeoisie, because they depend on the government for income and status. Thus they are hardly a force for democracy but are subject to manipulation by the political leadership. However, they are numerous; the government is always by far the biggest employer, often the only big employer.

Along with a small independent middle class, the less developed countries usually have only a feeble press. Newspapers are seldom able to carry out much of their normal function of criticism, and they are often venal and subject to pressure from the authorities. A common means of restricting freedom of the press without frank censorship is through official control of the importation and distribution of newsprint; the government is also probably the biggest advertiser. Freedom of the press is something of an alien concept, less readily understood than voting. Much news is of foreign origin, and control of news may be presented as anti-imperialism; in the 1970s, less developed countries were making great attempts to "liberate information and the mass media from the colonial legacy," which seemed to mean placing them under government control.

In Europe, industrialization proceeded largely autonomously in a favorable climate; the state was called on to play only a sec-

---

[7]For the Latin American case, see Robert F. Adie and Guy E. Poitras, *Latin America: The Politics of Immobility* (Englewood Cliffs, N.J.: Prentice-Hall, 1974).

[8]Peter T. Bauer and Basil S. Yamey, *The Economics of Underdeveloped Countries* (Chicago: University of Chicago Press, 1957), pp. 164–168.

ondary protective role. In later industrializing states, Germany and Japan in particular, the role of the state was more vital, as it purposefully fostered industry for political as well as economic purposes. In the less developed countries of today, it is likely to seem even more necessary for the state to undertake the role of modernizer because of the anxiety to catch up and also because of the shortage of domestic capital. The alternative is to invite the foreigners inside the gates—and to give them what may seem decisive power over the economy.

If the government is at once the maker and beneficiary of economic development, democratic politics becomes problematic. A contest among parties then means a contest for public funds, and the possessors are not easily persuaded that they should surrender their livelihood and standing by a process called "election." In the most honest state, political power is valuable; in a corrupt state controlling most of the national production, political power is indefinitely remunerative. To relinquish it signifies not only loss of income and status for a major fraction of the educated classes but also exposure to prosecution for malfeasance. Because of fear of reprisals, repressive governments cannot suddenly turn virtuous and yield office to an opposition favored by the people.

In many situations, then, representative government seems incapable of managing the demands and coping with the monumental problems of developing nations. Modernization and the revolution in communications give people an awareness of countless things that others have and they want, and there is no ready explanation for why the deprived should not have a great deal more. Hence any group that secures influence in the democratic system feels justified in calling on the government to provide for its welfare, and excessive demands

cause breakdown of institutions.[9] Labor unions want benefits that may impede industrialization less by the direct raising of labor costs than by uneconomic regulations that reduce whatever benefit entrepreneurs derive from relatively low wages. Bureaucracies, moreover, form the most potent pressure group next to the military; but bureaucracies want security, even for incompetence or indolence, and the state is expected to provide employment for all who deserve it. There is no real idea of the limited capacity of the government to provide, and claims on its resources are infinite.

A formidable problem that may be beyond the capacity of a democratic government is the limitation of population. It is not popular among the masses of the peasantry to say that they should have only two or three children when children mean additional income and security. Under the semidictatorship of Indira Gandhi, the Indian government moved energetically to curtail reproduction, carrying out in its final year millions of sterilizations. The unpopularity of this coercive program contributed greatly to the loss of the 1977 election, and Gandhi's more democratic successors radically cut back the program of population control. Restored to office, Gandhi did not attempt to revive it. Communist China is the outstanding example of rapid and radical lowering of the birthrate by authoritarian means unavailable to less sternly ruled societies.

Despite all the difficulties and problems of democracy, frank despotism is backward, and elites see themselves diminished as citizens of an unfree state. Indians, especially those traveling in the West, take pride in

---

[9]S. Huntington, "Political Development and Political Decay," in *Politics in Traditional Societies,* Harvey G. Kebschull, ed. (New York: Appleton-Century-Crofts, 1968), p. 59 and elsewhere develops this basic thesis.

belonging to the world's most populous democracy and see in this a superiority to their rivals and neighbors in Pakistan. For small, weak Costa Rica, democracy is the national pride.

FORMS OF GOVERNMENT

Just as the states of the Third World are extremely varied in geography and resources, they differ extremely in political institutions, from settled constitutional democracies, respectful of legality and rights, to the most repressive despotisms, which might realistically be called gangs of thugs holding a nation hostage. Most occupy a middling position with some pretenses of constitutional rule and a fair degree of freedom, at least for those who refrain from opposing the powers above.

Democracy

The fortunes of democracy in the Third World have risen and fallen repeatedly over the past half century. In the prosperity prior to the Depression of the 1930s, there seemed to be a tide toward political freedom in the countries of the Third World that were then free, particularly in Latin America, where the old-style *caudillo* rule was clearly in retreat. The bad times of the 1930s and the victories of fascism reversed this trend; dictatorship came into power in many countries, led by Argentina and Brazil. In the wake of World War II, there was a resurgence of democratic politics. Then, when the colonial empires crumbled, the new states were almost all born with democratic political forms. The United States gave the Philippines a close copy of the U.S. constitution and set the islands loose to govern themselves soon after the expulsion of the Japanese. The British had long been introducing elements of self-government into their colonies, progressing by degrees from nominated to elected legislative councils, native ministers, and a native prime minister under the British governor-general. When the British flag was lowered, native leaders finished occupying the constitutional framework. French colonies were less well prepared, but there too liberation generally came to a regime copied rather closely after that of Paris.

The colonial empires became independent because there was no way to deny them the application of democratic theory, and for the most part the leaders of independence movements were well acquainted with the axioms of democracy, attacked colonial rule in democratic terms, and had extensive experience in competitive politics. The new countries of Africa and Asia nearly all had at birth a sovereign parliament elected by adult suffrage, a prime minister responsible to it, a formal head of state as an element of stability, an independent judiciary and civil service, and a nonpolitical military establishment.

The parliamentary order soon yielded to dictatorship. Within five years of independence, nearly all the new states of black Africa had a single-party regime or a clear tendency toward one, and a few years later the majority had outright military governments without freedom of opposition. To date, black Africa has never had a political overturn by constitutional means. Botswana and Gambia, both under a million in population, may be considered democracies by virtue of permitting opposition parties, but there is no indication of what might happen if the opposition seemed to become a threat to the governing party. Democracy for a few years seemed to have much more reality in Nigeria, but the coup of December 31, 1983, showed its fragility.

It was to be expected that many or most of the former colonies should, on becoming independent, cast off institutions inherited from colonial powers. However, Latin America, which had copied American constitutional forms and political vocabulary since obtaining independence early in the nineteenth century, also inclined toward a dictatorship. Only Costa Rica, formed by a small, relatively homogeneous population, remained constantly faithful to democratic traditions. Argentina succumbed to the semifascist populist dictatorship of Juan Perón in 1944, and it has been unstable under a succession of military dictatorships alternating with attempts to return to civilian rule ever since. Uruguay fell into deeper and deeper economic trouble until a long democratic tradition was ended by military control in 1973. As a result of tensions and divisions in Chile, a Marxist, Salvador Allende, became president in 1970; growing chaos led to a stern military dictatorship in 1973. In a situation of mounting disorder, the Brazilian military swept aside a leftist government in 1964. By the late 1970s there remained only two governments in South America that could reasonably be called democratic: Colombia, where the two major parties ruled oligarchically by agreement, and Venezuela, where oil revenues make it possible to keep both military and masses reasonably satisfied despite tremendous inequality. After 1978 the tide turned, as Ecuador and Peru went back to elected civilian government, Brazil undertook a step-by-step return to constitutional government, and the military rulers of Argentina stepped back in 1983 from the center of the stage. Yet this seemed merely another swing of the pendulum, and the military is the residual if not the actual holder of power in all Latin America except Mexico and Costa Rica.

Lebanon, the only democracy of the Arab world, fell victim to Arab quarrels in 1975. Morocco tried democracy from 1963 to 1965, but King Hassan ended the experiment when it seemed to be getting out of control. Democratic governments established under American sponsorship in South Korea and the Philippines were both ended in 1972 when the respective presidents, General Park Chung Hee and Ferdinand Marcos, declared martial law and scattered or jailed their opponents. It was a major blow when Indira Gandhi in June 1975 declared an emergency and made India a semidictatorship. Her authoritarian rule was overthrown in elections she rashly permitted in March 1977, but the coalition that defeated her broke up in disorder and she was reelected in January 1980. She has since ruled constitutionally, perhaps because the opposition presents no threat. Pakistan held elections in 1977 but got a military dictatorship. A populist and libertarian as well as religious upsurge toppled the long firm throne of the Shah of Iran in December 1978, but he was succeeded by a theocratic dictatorship. Recent trends are mixed, but overall it is difficult to expect much improvement in political institutions unless economic and social progress is sufficient to mitigate discontents. On the other hand, it is unlikely that there can be much economic progress without the growth of open, legal, and responsible political institutions.

Military Government

If more or less liberal democracy seems impractical, the most frequent alternative is military government—rule by those who have been entrusted with armaments to defend the nation and keep order. This mission is extended by military leaders to the management of the state, and they have adequate title to power in the fact that no one is in a position to oppose them. Sometimes other groups that feel threatened by a disorderly situation welcome the military seizure of power, but the initiative usually comes from inside the barracks. The officers volunteer to save the country.

The variations of military rule are many. It ranges from direct government by a clique of professional officers through civilian administrations installed and supervised by the armed forces to regimes in which the military leadership quietly retains the substance of power while permitting civilian politicians to act as they see fit, provided that the interests and basic policies of the military are not contravened. In the absence of strong attachment to a constitution or a charismatic personality, it is almost inevitable that the army should exert at least residual power.

Yet military government is not traditional in the Third World; it is a modern phenomenon resting on the power of modern weapons and the fact that the military represents a modernized sector in a premodern society. In Latin America there were numerous dictatorships by generals in the nineteenth century, but they were personal followings based on loyalty to a boss rather than military regimes as we understand them today. In the past, the prestige of the military has been rather low in African and Asian cultures.

No one, including the army officers, seems to have had any idea of the potential of military government when colonies were first becoming states; it was assumed that the Westernized intellectuals in the forefront of the liberation struggle would continue to guide the new nations. But army dissatisfaction emerged in 1963 in the murder of the president of Togo and in 1964 in a mutiny that Julius Nyerere of Tanzania could suppress only with the assistance of the British. In 1965 army elements took charge in the Congo (later Zaire) and in 1966 in the Central African Republic, Upper Volta, Nigeria, and Ghana; and in 1967, in Togo, Congo (Brazzaville), and Mali. The idea was contagious.

In the weakness or absence of other viable institutions, it is perhaps surprising that military takeovers have not been more general. Civilian governments may be discredited because they cannot keep order, because the nation may be in danger of falling apart, or because problems are intractable and results are far below expectations. Armies are relatively easy to create, following models left behind by the colonial power or readily borrowed from abroad. They do not have to be very good because their mission is seldom to fight a comparable opponent but to coerce civilians. The army, moreover, has advantages beyond physical force. It can offer direction and purpose for many persons, especially the young; and it provides a promising career far superior to anything a man can hope for in the native village. In many countries the officers are better trained than most civilian politicians, and they may be more honest. The military is an exponent of nationalism and focus for loyalties even if it has no mission for conflict. It has the additional advantage of firm organization; no other group is likely to be able to command comparable obedience. In this way, the military can function a little like a Leninist vanguard party.

The reasons why armies or parts of armies take power are various.[10] Ordinarily, a coup is provoked by some clear failure of civilian leadership; the generals seldom move against a legitimate and effective government. Inflation, economic woes, or riots may undermine the civilian government. If the politicians violate the constitution or political norms, as in falsifying elections, the army is likely to feel impelled to act as the guardian

[10]See Eric A. Nordlinger, *Soldiers in Politics: Military Coups and Governments* (Englewood Cliffs, N.J.: Prentice-Hall, 1977).

of order. If the government is excessively and openly corrupt, the officers may undertake to clean house. But the most common cause, or at least the most common immediate provocation, is probably that the army perceives a threat to its corporate interests,[11] economic or political; and an almost invariable result is a boost in military pay. An odd case is that of Suriname. A group of officers attacked the civilian government in 1980 because of a dispute over pay; finding themselves in possession of a country, the soldiers proceeded to rule it and found the task so pleasant they resolved to stay on whatever the cost.

The generals, having taken power primarily for their own interests, are usually guided mostly by their own interests in formulating policies. However, the military is ordinarily reformist in relation to traditional oligarchies because officers are usually of middle-class origins. The poor lack sufficient education to enter the military academies that are the gateway to a career; aristocrats look down on it (although power has raised the prestige of the profession in societies that formerly deprecated it) or do not want to begin at the bottom of the ladder. The officers may therefore be egalitarian with relation to large estateholders or the very rich, but they support the status quo against mass politics. If an army undertakes social change, as in Peru or Iraq, the mission does not last long. The military establishment, because of its hierarchic structure, is inherently conservative.

In the early and mid-1960s, when democratic institutions were evidently not prospering in the Third World and military regimes were taking the place of incapable civilian governments, observers tended to place their hopes on the military as a force capable of dragging countries out of a swamp of poverty and backwardness.[12] The military was viewed as less corrupt, more oriented toward modernization, even more socially democratic in its lack of class bias. Military regimes seemed better qualified to pull a country together, lay the basis for the industrialization necessary for modernization, and thus make themselves obsolete. No one is more aware of the importance of technology, and the organizational structure of the military should facilitate the formation of public policy. Army leaders have reason to know the problems of poverty, ignorance, and backwardness, all of which mean weakness.

Cognizant or not, they have not been able to do much about these ills. Military rule has proved as disappointing to political scientists of the West as to those more directly affected. Officers may be technically trained and in tune with modernization; in the beginning they frequently promote national unity, urbanization, and the building of an economic infrastructure, especially roads, communications facilities, and the like. But military power means devoting more resources to the military, the police, and probably the bureaucracy, leaving less for productive investment.[13] The army is not likely to have a good grasp of the real problems of economic and social change, and it is poorly equipped to guide modernization. Only the Brazilian forces seem to have come near setting up a rational technocracy, thanks to high educational standards and adherence to the rules for advancement and retirement. The military copes no better than civilian regimes

[11]Samuel Decalo, *Coups and Army Rule in Africa* (New Haven, Conn.: Yale University Press, 1976), p. 19.

[12]John J. Johnson, *The Military and Society in Latin America* (Stanford, Calif.: Stanford University Press, 1964); and Lucian W. Pye, "Armies in the Process of Political Modernization," in J. J. Johnson, ed., *The Role of the Military in Underdeveloped Countries* (Princeton, N.J.: Princeton University Press, 1962), pp. 69–89.

[13]Decalo, *Coups and Army Rule in Africa*, p. 30.

with corruption, which probably grows as the holders of power settle down to the advancement of their own interests.

It is not even clear that a military government is more stable than a civilian one. The man on top is apt to scatter his attention in the unrewarding effort to manage the whole state, and thus loses contact with his power base. When discontent grows, another general may remove him just as he removed the preceding civilian leader. Or the military may wearily recognize that it cannot properly manage the country and opt to return to the barracks—without, however, relinquishing the power to intervene again. It seems that most Third World regimes are likely to continue to be military-dominated if not military-run for a long time.

Varieties of Authoritarianism

Most Third World governments are more or less dictatorships, but they range over a wide spectrum in regard to arbitrariness, concentration of power, and social policy. Some, such as the one-party government of Mexico, leave people rather free to mind their own affairs, even to criticize the rulers. Others, such as the Marxist government of Sékou Touré in Guinea, seek in principle to control all activities. Some rulers are ignorant, crude, and cruel; others are reasonably enlightened and benevolent.

An example of arbitrary and destructive dictatorship was that of Idi Amin in Uganda. It is ironic that from 1962 to 1966 Uganda seemed to be one of the most successful pluralistic states in Africa; but after Amin seized power in January 1971, he became a buffoon on the world stage and a scourge to most of his people. The number killed on his orders is said to be from 100,000 to 300,000 in a population of about 12 million. Extortion, police banditry, and free-ranging corruption largely demodernized the economy and reduced the people to subsistence farming. Another ruler careless of his subjects' welfare was Jean-Bedel Bokassa I of the Central African Empire, who lavished the resources of his very poor country on a $25 million coronation. He seemed to fancy himself as a new Napoleon.[14] Typically, Bokassa built a television station for an audience of forty receivers. Yet despite frequent murders, Bokassa did not weigh so heavily on his subjects as Macias Nguema, president of Equatorial Guinea. Ostensibly a Marxist, Nguema seemed intent on exterminating everyone with any education or standing in the community who did not directly serve him. It was reported that tens of thousands were murdered and a fourth of the population was harassed into exile, nearly a record for modern times. Perhaps such despotism is injudicious; however, all these egregious tyrants have been overthrown and disgraced.

The better dictators feel the need to do useful things, from education to roadbuilding, either as a justification of their authority or from idealism. Many leaders, especially those coming out of independence movements have refrained from abuse of power. One example was Jomo Kenyatta, the father of Kenya. Never in danger of losing his preeminent position, Kenyatta permitted far more freedom than he had to; the Kenya press was among the most informative in Africa. In 1975 he even let a parliamentary majority form in opposition to his government on the question of corruption, although he subsequently had some critics detained and warned that there was a limit to his tolerance.[15]

President Felix Houphouët-Boigny of the Ivory Coast exercised similar restraint and succeeded in building up the economy of his naturally poor land far beyond that of his

[14]*Newsweek*, December 19, 1977, p. 42.
[15]*New York Times*, January 25, 1978, p. 5.

neighbors. Tax incentives and reliable and nonextortionate government have drawn foreign investment, especially French; commercial agriculture is encouraged; administration is relatively honest; and the annual economic growth rate has been 6 to 7 percent since 1960. Houphouët-Boigny is criticized, however, although the standard of living of the Ivorians has risen dramatically, for having in effect turned the country over to the French, who are several times more numerous than in colonial times.

By contrast, the regime of Mobutu Sese Seko of Zaire is chaotic and ineffective. Graft is so customary as to have largely lost the taint of illegality; it is simply the way of doing business. Using the semiideology of "authenticity," Mobutu changed the name of the country and its main features and decreed the Africanization of all personal names, including his own; at the same time, he has his children educated in Belgium. The extravagances of the leader are legendary, including his 747 jetliner and eight or more European residences. The real value of agricultural production declined, it is said, by 75 percent from 1960 to 1977,[16] and a large part of the population is reportedly chronically undernourished. Only copper, cobalt, and other mineral exports, plus foreign loans, keep the economy afloat.

In North Africa, the Moroccan monarchy attempted to defuse discontent by various concessions, but mostly by seeking technical solutions for problems—for example, by trying to apply fertilizers as a substitute for land reform. The rich become more opulent, the poor struggle to survive, and the government promises that the next election will be more honest. Tunisia's Habib Bourguiba, on the other hand, has been little troubled by opposition to his paternalistic

[16]Ibid., April 29, 1977, p. A-31; *Los Angeles Times*, October 19, 1983, p. 23.

and generally enlightened rule, the chief problem of which is the age of the ruler (born 1903). The energetic young leader of Libya, Muammar Qaddafi, has been eager to change an unsatisfactory world order. One of his policies, or perhaps avocations, has been the support of international terrorists, on whom he has spent hundreds of millions of dollars of his country's oil revenues. Torn between the desire for modernization and the desire to protect the Arab personality, he has subsidized industrialization, decreed that only Islamic law should prevail, and called for the destruction of the books of infidels. In 1973 he launched a consciousness-heightening People's Revolution somewhat like Mao's Cultural Revolution of a few years earlier.

Most of the monarchies of the Near East have been brought down by military coups; those remaining have taken the lesson not of sharing power with popular representatives but of seeking popularity by improving the conditions of the people. Saudi Arabia, Kuwait, and other states awash in dollars have been able to mitigate opposition by welfare policies and opportunities for the ambitious in the expanding economy. There has thus far been little pressure against these theocratic, absolutist monarchies, but it can be assumed that the skies darken as growth slows and expectations overtake achievements, long before the exhaustion of subsoil treasures brings inevitable crisis.

A somewhat different category is that of the East Asian countries which, with little or no mineral or agricultural resources, have enjoyed phenomenal economic growth. These are Singapore, Taiwan (Republic of China), and South Korea, to which might be added Hong Kong, a British crown colony. The political problems of the last are solved by British administration. The other three are dictatorships; yet the cultural background and international situation of each are such that government is moderate and purposeful. Singapore is a well-run little island state, with a single party and a single leader, Lee Kuan Yew, since it became independent in 1965.[17] Its per capita income is over eight times larger than that of neighboring Indonesia, which is infinitely more fortunate in natural endowment. There have been fairly honest elections, but criticism is generally not tolerated. Thanks to an energetic birth-control program, population growth is approximately zero, and the country faces problems of affluence as well as scarcity.

South Korea has shown almost unparalleled industrial expansion in the last two decades: Real wages in recent years had been growing at 10 percent annually until the 1982 recession. Exports increased 120 times in fourteen years to 1977 (in current dollars), and peasants expect to have television. Much the same may be said for the better-known economic miracle of Taiwan. As the Chinese civil war neared its close in 1949, the remnants of the Nationalist armies, government personnel, and others afraid of the Communists, about 2 million in all, took refuge on the island. They made themselves overlords over the native Taiwanese, four times as numerous; but to sustain hopes of return to the mainland they had to modernize. Economic progress, as in the case of Japan, was made a surrogate for military success. The GNP grew at 9 percent a year for two decades and more, making Taiwan the wealthiest country of Asia after Japan and Singapore. Foreign trade increased by eighty five times from 1951 to 1976, from $183 million to $15.7 billion, substantially more than that of Mainland China, with fifty times the population. An extensive land reform relieved poverty in the countryside, and social friction was minimized by compensating landowners with stock in industries taken from the for-

mer Japanese rulers. The birthrate has been reduced by intelligent programs to near-European levels, and life expectancy is approximately the same as in the United States. Sooner or later, however, it must be expected that the present competent oligarchic rule will either decline into corrupt dictatorship or be compelled to implement the democratic forms of the constitution.

ANTI-WESTERNISM AND SOCIALISM

Most less developed countries almost instinctively reject capitalism, the economic system of the industrialized West. One African writer states, "Any politician in Africa or the West Indies who publicly championed capitalism, which in many minds is associated with imperialism, would certainly lose his job."[18] The opposite of "capitalism" is "socialism," and the colonial experience and association of capitalism with foreign domination is ample reason to oppose it. The prominent and irritating capitalism of the postcolonial period is also foreign, and populist-radicals unite with native business interests against it. Aristocrats in less developed countries relieve their own consciences by blaming the West for the poverty of the masses, which benefits the upper classes but is not to be blamed on them. Political leaders likewise lay the responsibility for difficulties and failures on the industrial nations, especially the United States. It is axiomatic that the economically powerful states are practically omnipotent; what happens is therefore their fault. This is the essence of the "dependency theory," a doctrine explaining the economic and political condition, especially of Latin America, as the result of external capitalist domination.

Anti-Westernism also supports the de-

---

[17]Willard A. Hanna, "Singapore: From Survival to Sophistication," *Common Ground* 2 (April 1976), p. 45.

[18]K. Nyamayaro Mufuka, "The Jamaican Experiment," *Current History* 74 (February 1978), p. 72.

mand for "reparations" for past exploitation, which saves self-respect by turning more or less charitable aid into debt repayment while encouraging a transfer of resources beneficial to the less developed country and especially its elite. There has been some tendency in the West to accept moral responsibility for much or most of the sufferings of the less affluent majority of mankind. This view is not only morally satisfying and basically flattering to Western power; it also suggests that the remedy for the momentous problems of the Third World is at hand and fairly simple, merely to end the wrongdoing and transfer a modicum of wealth to those who need and deserve it.[19] More broadly, Western society has lost much of its élan and self-confidence, its faith in individualism, work, and reason; if it is modish for Western intellectuals to decry values formerly associated with the rise of the West, the intellectuals of the non-Western world echo the lament and find confirmation of the deeper virtues of the native society.

Anti-Westernism means anticapitalism, which means socialism, which implies a controlled economy and authoritarianism. "Socialism" is at least outwardly egalitarian, but in practice it seems to turn out more like the old authoritarianism supported by modern social and political theory justifying the overwhelming role of the state.

There are many reasons for its attractiveness. People expect improvement from the state, which represents modern power. Economic development is a necessary part of the mystique of nationalism.[20] State socialism is the ready answer to the problem of fixing long-term goals and allocating resources most effectively for rapid growth. Capitalism is disorderly and stands for antisocial competition, the philosophy of "dog eat dog." Capitalism means inequality and exploitation; socialism is a synonym for the justice that means most to the poor—economic justice. It is the watchword of anti-imperialism. Nationalization has the perhaps decisive merit of providing more jobs for the educated. Socialism also offers, or seems to offer, a means to unity over tribal or ethnic divisions, whereas a privately oriented economy seems to promise schism. Central control of the economy is a potent bond.

Authoritarian government is more natural for the less developed countries because the obvious need is not for innovation but for purposeful borrowing, and the state apparatus seems better equipped to do this. If it is assumed that there is a choice between development or freedom, the choice is not in doubt. Socialism then becomes a means to modernization without basic cultural change. It is usually joined, at least initially, with charismatic leadership, which arises in fluid situations because of the lack of accepted traditional authority and the need for a new focus for the new nation. A program of economic rights is a substitute for political rights, and it is difficult for an opposition to put forward a credible alternative.

Modern authoritarianism is incomplete without dogma or doctrine. The doctrine is frequently a variant of Marxism, which served the Russian rebels well at the turn of the century. Strictly traditional societies lack ideology in a narrow sense, but under modern conditions, ideology is a sort of statement of purpose and self-justification which may be naive but which satisfies the requirement for an official answer. Fascism found some adherents in the Third World before World War II, among military men of Argentina and Chile, for example; but it was thoroughly discredited by the German defeat. Only an occasional somewhat aberrant fig-

[19]As discussed by P. T. Bauer, "Western Guilt and Third World Poverty," *Commentary* 61 (January 1976), pp. 31–38.
[20]Jean Y. Calvez, *Politics and Society in the Third World* (Maryknoll, N.Y.: Orbis Books, 1973), pp. 295–296.

ure, such as Idi Amin of Uganda, confesses an admiration for Hitler. Third World ideologies are varying mixtures of socialism, democracy, nationalism, traditionalism, anti-Western utopianism, militarism, Marxism, and Leninism. But the Marxist component is commonly strongest.

Marxism was brought to the Third World mostly by the Russian-led movement and in the shape given it by Lenin and his successors—a vision of a party-managed order legitimated by the right of the workers, or as reshaped for the less developed countries, the right of the poor and exploited peoples. Its emphasis on mass action, moreover, suits regimes seeking to build a new nation and to modernize as rapidly as possible by mobilizing the abundant resource, people. It fits anti-imperialism into a broad, modern philosophic framework and makes the struggle of the weaker states for recognition and equality part of a grand historical process, in which victory is certain. It makes the rich into evil losers, the poor into virtuous winners. The Marxist approach, in which the division of the pie is more important than its enlargement, suits the mentality of those who regard themselves as cheated in the division of the world's goods. Marxism gives a cause overriding the national or ethnic heterogeneity which afflicts most Third World states, an excuse for demanding common allegiance to the cause; it can substitute for nationalism. That Marxism, at least in the Leninist version, is elitist does not repel people because this is the reality of the non-Western society. Marxism promises a miracle: to overcome backwardness while supporting essential nativism. It stands for equality, for which there is an emotional demand, but equality less for individuals than for the group, the nation striving for equal standing in the unequal world. Finally, it answers or pretends to answer or shows a way to answer all social, economic, and political questions.

To these attractions must be added the moral, political, economic, and military support of the Soviet Union. From the outset, that country has undertaken to spread its doctrine and politics to all peoples, partly from pure messianism (especially in the early years), partly for political gain. Its zeal for the revolutionizing of the Third World has been particularly stimulated by the Leninist conviction that profits from colonial and semicolonial areas were the sustenance of capitalism in Europe. In the first decades after the Russian revolution, the impact of the Communist International was not strong except in China. But after World War II, particularly since the death of Stalin in 1953, the Soviet leadership made a concerted effort to bring Third World countries within its philosophic and political sphere, seeking to enlist not only Communists but also many "bourgeois" nationalists. In recent years it has advanced in the Third World mostly by giving military assistance to revolutionary or anti-Western forces, as in Mozambique, Angola, Ethiopia, Yemen, and elsewhere.

Socialism is framed in modern, scientific terms and facilitates social changes. It rationalizes strong authority and control over all aspects of life and the economy. It justifies censorship, applied particularly to information and ideas from the capitalist West. It promises employment and power for the educated. It justifies a party monopoly of authority, and it provides a basis for unification. It explains backwardness and holds out a utopian future. It has the prestige of a great modern movement patronized by a superpower.

In view of such attractions, we might suppose that the Third World would be solidly socialist. But socialism has prospered much less in fact than in theory. Only a few states come close to following the Soviet model, and a number once rather closely aligned with the Soviet Union, such as Egypt and

Iraq, have fallen away. The reasons are many. The Soviet image of rapid economic growth has been clouded by the inability of the Soviet Union to supply the needs of countries disposed to lean on it and by the fact that the Soviet economy has stagnated. Third World countries find themselves relying willy-nilly on Western trade and technology—as does the Soviet Union itself to a large extent. For practical reasons, over nine-tenths of their trade is with the West. The evangelical appeal of communism is much reduced by disharmonies among Communists; the violent antagonism between China and Russia makes it less plausible that either holds the keys to heaven.

Marxist ideology is also less than satisfactory. It makes some sort of dialectical philosophical sense only in terms of the destiny of the industrial proletariat, but Third World countries have not proletarians but peasants, for whom Marx had all the scorn of a thorough urbanite. Marxism-Leninism is also burdened with atheism, and there is too much religiosity in the Third World, especially Africa, for it to be broadly acceptable. At the same time, communism, in the Marxist-Leninist style, is also something alien, another white man's creed.

Moreover, communism means a thorough overthrow of the old structures, and this is seldom possible without a war. In some countries where there has been war—in Vietnam, Laos, Cambodia, and the former Portuguese possessions in Africa—strong regimes have been set up as nearly on the Marxist-Leninist model as seems consonant with their extreme backwardness.[21] But for the most part elites have come to power without mass mobilization of the population or extensive armed struggle and without a strong mass-based party. The "revolution" is largely rhetoric; there is no overwhelming popular demand for change. In fact, local elites, landholders, merchants, and traditional powerholders, have strongly resisted change. The extremism of communism is hard to achieve unless a violent defense is needed against a violent threat. It is easy enough to install a merely authoritarian regime; to build and mobilize a penetrating regime with an effective mass party requires favorable circumstances.[22] Hence, socialist or Marxist theory far exceeds its practice, and the social revolution usually remains something of a masquerade. Most Third World countries that call themselves "socialist" rely in fact on private enterprise.

The greatest reason why the socialist blueprint has largely remained on paper is that it has not turned out well where ambitious leaders have tried to implement it. One of the most hopeful experiments was Ghana, first (1957) of the African colonies to become independent. Its leader, Kwame Nkrumah, did away with the parliamentary-democratic institutions carried over from colonial days, made his party the sole ruling group, semi-deified his own person as "Liberator," nationalized as much of the economy as possible, and tried to mobilize the people under an adaptation of Marxism called "consciencism." The result was disaster. The big trade surplus became a large deficit, and real incomes fell sharply from 1958 to 1965. Oppression and mismanagement led to Nkrumah's overthrow by a military junta in 1966 and his exile in disgrace. The best that can be said for the socialist period is that the country has not been much better off since a military government took over.

The allegedly socialist regime of nearby Guinea has been more successful only in re-

---

[21]President Samora Machel of Mozambique said, "Armed struggle is a wonderful university." *New York Times*, March 2, 1977, p. 7.

[22]Eric A. Nordlinger, ed., *Politics and Society* (Englewood Cliffs, N.J.: Prentice-Hall, 1969), p. 117.

taining power.[23] The first sub-Saharan French colony to become independent, it adopted an anti-Western stance from the outset, with the support of the Soviet Union and its allies. The independence leader, Sékou Touré, set about establishing total rule by the Democratic Party of Guinea, abolished open opposition, nationalized industry, tried to plan economic development, set up control institutions on the Communist model, and largely isolated his country from the West. For a few years after independence (1958) things did not go badly, despite confusion and corruption, but since the early 1960s the economy has stagnated. Bungling and embezzlement have thwarted planning, agriculture has largely reverted to subsistence, and the economy hobbles along thanks to the 80 percent of exports produced by foreign-managed capitalist mining enterprises. It is testimony to an extraordinary degree of misgovernment that about a fifth of the population of a nation with relatively abundant land and mineral resources fled the country. Sékou Touré, however, took steps backward and shifted away from Soviet alignment from 1978. On his death in 1984 the army denounced his tyranny.

The experience of a third West African exponent of socialism, the Congo Republic, Brazzaville, has been slightly less discouraging.[24] There the leadership declared a People's Republic in 1969, and the country has taken on some of the appearances of a Marxist-Leninist state under the monopolistic Congolese Labor party. A bloated bureaucracy governs the economy, as far as possible, and consumes three-quarters of the budget. Because of the lack of incentives, the principal crops—cacao, coffee, peanuts, and bananas—have declined sharply in recent years. Like Guinea, the Congo is kept afloat by foreign capitalism, economic aid mostly from France, and the French and Italian oil companies that supply two-thirds of the national revenues.

The model socialist country of East Africa, Tanzania, has been more open and humanistic, less dogmatic, and more inclined to at least the appearance of democracy and dialogue. The ideology of its leader, Julius Nyerere, is Africanism, a generalized anti-capitalism with demands for reparations from the West, mixed with egalitarianism and communalism. Tanzania became the favorite African recipient of not only Chinese but also Western foreign aid, especially from the Scandinavians, who hoped to see a successful example of African socialism. The country of some 16 million with a very low per capita income (about $250 in 1979) receives yearly some $300 million in foreign aid, which comprises a sixth of the budget and the bulk of development funds.

The great enterprise of Nyerere was to relocate the primitive peasantry, which makes up over nine-tenths of the population, into more or less modern *ujamaa* (familyhood) villages. These villages were to provide communal facilities while land is worked by individual farmers, although at the highest stage cultivation is to be collective. The program began in 1967; with some use of force, it relocated the majority of the population by 1977.[25] Tanzania also embarked on a program of industrialization through state corporations, mostly supported by foreign aid. But nothing seems to have worked very well. Agricultural production failed to keep up with population growth, and many persons

[23]See Claude Rivière, *Guinea, The Mobilization of a People* (Ithaca, N.Y.: Cornell University Press, 1977).

[24]See Decalo, *Coups and Army Rule in Africa*, pp. 123–159.

[25]On the program, see Frances Hill, "Ujamaa: African Socialist Production in Tanzania," in *Socialism in the Third World*, Helen Desfosses and Jacque Levesque, eds. (New York: Praeger, 1975), pp. 216–246.

reverted to subsistence farming. The state-run factories lost large amounts of money, some were reduced to operating part time, and some were abandoned. Roads and buildings have decayed, and there are shortages of almost everything.[26]

The most socialistic country of non-Communist Asia is Burma. For a decade after independence in 1948 Burma was a parliamentary democracy of sorts, but military intervention began in 1958 and led to the installation in 1962 of a dictatorship under the command of Ne Win, chairman of a revolutionary council of army officers. Ne Win set up a single-party regime with a vague ideology of Marxism, socialism, Buddhism, and xenophobia. The government took over private enterprise and land ownership, a step made possible by the fact that many owners were Indians or Chinese, and placed the entire economy, education, the press, and government services under direct army rule.

The result has been something close to demodernization of the economy. Formerly the world's leading rice exporter, Burma has become barely self-sufficient. Production has remained at a low level, whereas population has grown steadily. Unable to own land, farmers have no incentive for improvements; and most of the harvest is sold illegally. Burma's distinction is the world's most prevalent black market. State stores are nearly empty, and if they have something desirable, a bribe is required. Almost everything must be obtained through smugglers or dealers in appropriated state property. Teak and cattle are illegally exported to Thailand. Smugglers are efficient; one can order a piano and expect delivery in two weeks. A major occupation is to try to buy something in order to resell it; civil servants spend a large part of their time supplementing meager incomes on the black market. Employees of the state bakeries typically divert eggs and sugar and send tasteless cakes to state stores. It is estimated that 70 percent of commerce is illegal.

Per capita income, $150 in 1979, has declined in real terms over the past twenty years. Public transportation is mostly inoperative, cities built in colonial times slowly crumble, and few buildings go up except for officers' villas. The nationalized enterprises are held by army officers (the higher the rank, the more important the enterprise), and down to the lowest ranks the army forms a privileged class with its own shops and other facilities.

A number of other Asian states have inaugurated partly socialistic systems with less spectacular results but with no very marked successes. India avowed socialism to be its objective from the time of independence (1947) to the defeat of Indira Gandhi (1977), but this meant only nationalization of some industries and a great deal of regulation. For this or whatever reason, India has fallen economically and technologically farther behind the world average.

Sri Lanka under the leftist government of Srimavo Bandaranaike nationalized foreign tea plantations, placed state corporations in charge of the economy, and tied up the country in restrictive regulation. Government programs provided enough social services for the nation to receive a high "quality of life" rating despite its relative poverty. But high taxes, low productivity, and inefficiency led to so many shortages that the nonsocialist United National party won a landslide electoral victory in 1977. Its leader, Junius Jayawardene, adopted capitalist policies and welcomed foreign investors.

A number of Arab countries, including Iraq, Syria, Egypt, South Yemen, Libya, and Algeria, have inaugurated "Arab socialism," in all cases under military leadership. Egypt

[26]Leonard Levitt, "Tanzania: A Dream Deferred," *New York Times Magazine,* November 14, 1982, pp. 138–156.

under Nasser nationalized most industry and large-scale trade, leaned on the Soviet Union, and gave Nikita Khrushchev hope that it was drifting toward communism. It did not prosper, however, and under Anwar Sadat policies were reversed to relax controls, favor private business, and invite foreign capital. One result has been a much more conspicuous gap between rich and poor. Socialism in Algeria has been associated with declining agricultural production, and mass unemployment is a serious problem. Shortfalls are compensated for by petroleum revenues, but it remains to be seen whether they can provide a sound basis for the economy.

For Somalia, socialism was associated with foreign policy and the claim to Somali-inhabited parts of Ethiopia. A coup in 1969 brought General Siad Barre to power. A few foreign-owned businesses were seized, the Somali language was put into writing, labor was mobilized, and the country was declared a "democratic republic," with an ideology of "scientific socialism." The United States at the time was supporting the archenemy, Ethiopia, ruled by the aged emperor Haile Selassie; Somalia therefore requested Soviet help. Arms and advisors came on a large scale. Then Selassie was overthrown by self-styled Marxist officers and Ethiopia switched its allegiance to the Soviet Union, which armed Ethiopia even more energetically than it had armed Somalia. In response, Somalia ejected the Russian advisors. turned to the West, and deemphasized socialism in its conflict with its neighbor.

Cuba, to the contrary, was converted permanently to a fully socialized or sovietized economy and state. It has been a political success, partly because of the driving leadership of Fidel Castro, partly because the United States has made Cuba a David standing against a widely unpopular Goliath. The principal achievements claimed for revolutionary Cuba are the extension of health care, the promotion of literacy and mass education, and the elimination of the direst poverty. On the other hand, over a tenth of the population has fled the country despite difficulties. The economy has been virtually stagnant during most of Castro's rule, and it continues to float thanks to the world's greatest subsidization, the equivalent of several billion dollars per year from the Soviet Union.

In the Western hemisphere, the best example of a socialist or socialistic state, aside from Cuba, has been Peru. A military group, taking power in 1968, expropriated U.S. oil companies, set up national corporations to manage major industries, established workers' cooperatives, and turned plantations over to Indian peons. It worked badly, and in 1975 leftist President Velasco Alvarado was replaced by the moderate Morales Bermúdez. The latter relaxed censorship, returned newspapers to owners, slowed down socialist programs, and invited foreign oil companies to come back to prospect. The military gave up running the country and permitted free elections and a return to civilian government in 1980.

The early socialists, including Karl Marx, were probably right in regarding socialism as an aspiration for the most developed countries. If socialism is a possibility, it would seem to be so only at a higher level of economic development and under optimal social and political conditions. Possibly socialism is feasible for a Sweden, but the planned economy requires more sophisticated information and organization than the unplanned. At a lower level of sophistication and in less well-ordered societies with a shortage of educated personnel and much corruption, it seems more difficult to replace the automatic guidance of the marketplace by human direction. But the political utilities of socialism promise it a secure future in the Third World.

TRENDS AND PROBLEMS

In some long term it may be assumed that if civilization continues its course, the whole conglomeration of states of the earth must rise or fall, succeed or fail together. The direction of technology is toward annihilation of distances and local differences. But for the present, which probably means a generation or so, the trend is toward diversification. The more modern and prosperous Third World countries modernize and grow richer; the poorer and worse governed become poorer and more backward.

The performance of the better-off Third World states has been good enough to actually narrow a little the overall First World-Third World gap.[27] On the other hand, a number of countries have gone backward or downward in political, economic, and cultural levels; and various governments have acted energetically to demodernize their countries. In nearly all African countries, per capita food production is going down. The regression of Burma has already been noted. The economies of Zambia, Zaire, Ghana, Uganda, Guinea, and others have been brought near collapse. In such countries as Equatorial Guinea, Guinea, and Uganda, most of the few educated persons have been murdered or driven out, and the new generation is growing up with almost no general education and less technical training. A number of other countries have seen no material progress over a long period. For example, in Chile, leftist and rightist regimes have left the people poorer than a decade or so earlier. Argentina and Uruguay a half-century ago were up to Western European material and educational standards, but now political disorder has overcome technological improvement. Prosperity is no more, al-though life is still reasonably comfortable; cultural centers have decayed, and promising universities have been emptied of scholars.

Even if production rises, the next generation of leaders may be in some ways less qualified than the present-day rulers. The quality of universities in Latin America has gone down over a long time, although enrollments have soared. The number of newspapers in black Africa declined by more than half from the early 1960s to the late 1970s from 240 to about 100—a tiny number for such a huge and populous region—and their quality is commonly lamentable. The "brain drain" continues, as able and ambitious people are discouraged by poor prospects in their native countries and seek more rewarding and fruitful lives where conditions are more encouraging. And the effect is circular. The more the talented intellectuals of a country such as Argentina go abroad, the less attractive the country becomes for others and the less capacity it has for training new talent.

There is a principle of concentration. Advanced centers have capital, talent, education, communications facilities, and so on, and they draw more capital and brains. Research and development are done in the most advanced areas, and management operates from major centers. The best students and teachers go to the best schools and make them still better unless others make a special effort to compete. The less developed countries, if they are to catch up, must strive especially to attract capital and talent.

Yet under the impact of an ever-growing volume of communication, travel, and trade, the world is growing together and becoming culturally homogenized as never before, with inevitable economic and political implications. Transistor radios bring instant news and national politics to jungle peoples; and many things, such as birth control, become

[27]According to the World Bank, *Wall Street Journal*, September 18, 1977, p. 10.

at least less impossible. In Africa, newspapers decline but radio spreads. There is only one copy of a daily paper per 210 persons but a radio for every 20; and many people listen to foreign broadcasts. Television is appearing in once-isolated Asian villages and giving visions of an undreamed-of existence. The lowliest of people, Indian outcasts, hear speeches on radio and learn to regard themselves as legal equals of the Brahmins. A whole new universe of existence greets peasants migrating to modernizing cities, and all values are called into question, in Bahia (Brazil) as in Lagos (Nigeria). More and more people travel and compare, and they return home with new ideas and standards of conduct.

Within the Third World, modernization flows primarily to the cities and the capitals, seeping outward from them into the countryside. Cities everywhere grow more and more alike; there is little to distinguish new buildings in Chicago, Rio de Janeiro, or New Delhi. Life in the city also becomes more alike for elites everywhere, who enjoy many of the same luxuries. But the countryside looks up to the city, and the masses to the elites, for values and modes, and the elites adopt Western ways not only because they wish to belong to the great world but also because they thereby affirm their superiority over the masses.

Contrary currents of modernization and decay thus flow across many countries; yet humanity seems to be moving toward a single destiny. Unless the advanced industrialized countries can fairly well surmount their major problems, they can hardly lead the Third World forward; on the other hand, unless the troubles of the Third World can be overcome, it will be difficult for the industrial West to maintain its momentum.

But it seems impossible for the less developed states to increase productivity and meet the demands of their citizens unless they can develop more effective political institutions. No program can be expected to have long-term beneficial effects unless it brings changes in the social and political order.

Yet there is little agreement concerning what constitutes political development. There was much writing on the subject in the 1960s, mostly in rather sociological terminology of institutionalization, mobilization, penetration, and the like, underlaid by a general idea that developing societies should become more like the United States and Western Europe. There should be greater differentiation of functions, and the state should establish a well-articulated professional structure to administer the rationally formulated political will, in accordance with generally accepted rules. The state should reach down into the lives of the people while the people were brought into the process of decision making through political parties and elections. The state should acquire the capacity to tax, control, and invest—that is, to modernize the economy. Traditional elite structures should be swept aside in favor of equality of opportunity and allocation of power according to function. The concept of political development, according to von der Mehden,[28] should include a basic consensus on goals, national integration, adequate communication between people and leaders, an effective civil service, occupational mobility, well-developed interest groups, widespread participation in political life, constitutional government, well-defined political institutions, and civilian control of the military. This all added up to a fairly good description of the United States, or what the United States would like to believe of itself, with the implication that political development would grow out of economic and cultural modernization.

[28]Fred R. von der Mehden, *Politics of the Developing Nations* (Englewood Cliffs, N.J.: Prentice-Hall, 1969), pp. 5–6.

It soon became evident, however, that modernization was not proceeding as smoothly as expected. In Huntington's view, social and economic change, arising from the contact of traditional societies with the West, preceded political change, the failure of which held back general modernization. The awareness of people of themselves and the state and their participation in politics rose, and concurrently there arose demands for services and material improvement which the state was unable to satisfy. Popular participation, outrunning political institutionalization, brought not modernization but political decay. The state, overwhelmed by needs, reverted to cruder forms; unworkable parliaments were replaced by dictators who could check or ignore popular demands.

Whether or not this analysis is realistic, it is clear that the political evolution of the less developed countries is far from being a straight path. It is unlikely that the majority of less developed countries should be governable in ways that are fairly successful in the more homogeneous and self-assured nation-states of the West. It is utopian in most less developed countries to expect in the near future a free contest of political parties to decide through the ballot who shall have control of the state. Conceivably, trying or pretending to be democratic when the society is not prepared for it causes more confusion than progress. Yet it is not clear how else nations can satisfactorily govern themselves. There is not likely to be much political progress unless there is social as well as economic progress toward more just and better integrated societies.

Government in the Third World reflects the enormous diversity of human culture and personality. Yet there are many common problems. These include the questions of what is to be admitted from the modern world and what is to be rejected, what is to be retained of the native ways and what is to be sacrificed to necessity or the desire to increase material well-being or to catch up with the more powerful. The problem of the control, allocation, and transfer of power is even more crucial and difficult than in the industrial states. Disunity is a grave burden, and the inequality of the few rich and powerful against the poor and impotent masses is especially troublesome. Government in a large majority of countries is dictatorial, usually shaded by oligarchy; but dictatorship is seldom an answer and never a permanent solution.

The future of the Third World is to a large extent the future of humanity, because about nine-tenths of the babies being born today are in the poor countries. The industrial countries, especially the United States, still have enormous influence, however; and the future will be much brighter if this country learns better how to aid its less fortunate fellow nations.

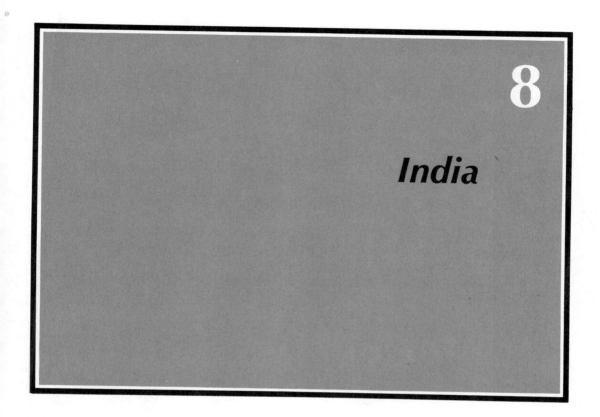

8

India

Four-fifths of the roughly 730 million people of India live in half a million villages and laboriously coax miserable yields from the earth. It is a land of hunger and religion, a world unto itself, with ethnic diversity greater than that of all Europe. It is the home of one of the world's greatest cultures, the one most alien to our own. Nearly naked holy men sit permanently cross-legged, foreheads smeared with ashes, and the welfare of starving sacred cows is a major political issue; more organized charity is dedicated to their relief than to that of humans. Rats consume enough grain to feed tens of millions of people, and sacred cobras kill tens of thousands yearly. Indian mysticism is not vibrant or joyous but resigned and passive; its goal is only an end of suffering. Much of the sense of Hinduism and the Indian so-

cial order is the consecration of defeat and want.[1]

Hinduism is not one religion but a group of faiths with countless gods, although through it run a few simple ideas—reincarnation, *karma* or spiritual merit, and *dharma,* or the moral law. They are all bound up with the dominant institution of caste. Every Hindu is born into one of an almost indefinite number of castes or subcastes, except those so unfortunate as to be below regular caste, the Untouchables, who are about 15 percent of the population. Caste lines are very complicated, but the most important element is profession; they are somewhat like hereditary endogamous trade unions. In a

[1]See Clark Blaise and Bharati Mukarjee, *Days and Nights in Calcutta* (Garden City, N.Y.: Doubleday, 1977), for a picture of Indian society.

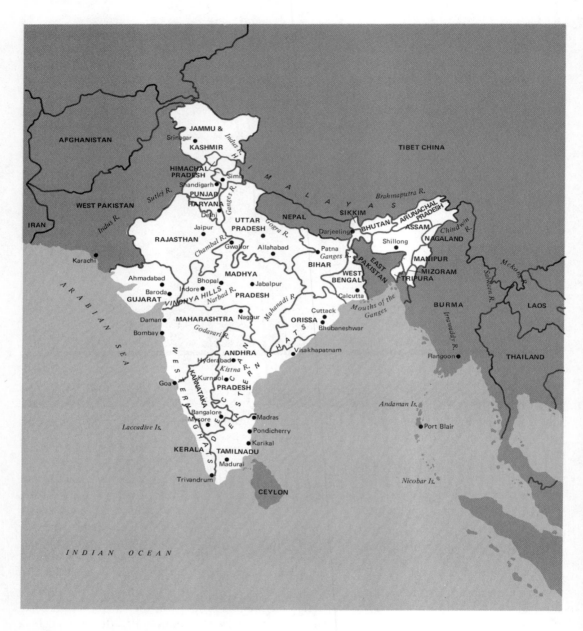

simple village there may be a half dozen to twenty or more castes, differing in customs, manner of speech, dress, and food. Castes are graded hierarchically according to the purity of the occupation with which the caste is identified, with the priestly Brahmins at the top and ordinary laborers at the bottom. Below are the Untouchables, who remove the excrement left in the streets by their social superiors, take away cadavers, and skin cows for people who would be polluted by such work.

The institution of caste has been somewhat eroded by modernization in the fluid cities but much less so in the traditional villages. It is the essence of immobility, reinforced by the belief that one's station in life results from the merits and demerits acquired in a previous incarnation. Everyone, moreover, is superior to someone else and so has an interest in the caste system, except the Untouchables ("scheduled castes," or Harijans). Yet the caste structures seem to be a major factor in the viability of Indian democracy.

The origins of the system are to be found in the Aryan conquest of India several thousand years ago. The fair-skinned victors wished to remain rulers, and they accordingly restricted intermarriage with their subjects. On top were the Brahmins, who rationalized the layering of society; they were followed by the Kshatriyas or warriors, the Vaisyas or merchants, and the Sudras or farmers and craftsmen. These were called *varnas* or "colors," the higher being lighter in complexion. From them developed thousands of subgroups and a complex institutionalization and rationalization of inequality. Much of the sense of caste rests on the idea of pollution, which is like fear of disease. Many rules turn around the preparation of food; anyone can eat a Brahmin's cooking, whereas only an Untouchable can eat dishes prepared by Untouchables. The latter have the occupations most subject to contagion in a hot and unhygienic land.

India was once a land of civilization-building like classical Greece and preimperial China; but it has been repeatedly conquered and oppressed, subjected to a series of repressive tyrannies. It has produced superb architecture, painting, and literature; but its tradition has long since been reduced to formalism. Now its poverty reduces capacities. Per capita GNP was a little over $200 in 1980, and 290 million people had less than $6 per month.[2] India ranks fifteenth in GNP of the world's 160 countries. Probably nine-tenths of its people are malnourished. Most children are stunted, and not a few are mutilated to make them more pitiable beggars. Poverty is compounded by ignorance and superstition. Prime Minister Indira Gandhi is said to follow the guidance of astrology, like almost all her compatriots. There is a sense of futility and passivity; the spirit of enterprise is feeble, civism is thin, and few identify with their nation.

Yet India is also a land of growing modern industry. It is a regional military power, with one of the world's largest armies and air forces. It has an expensive atomic program, and in 1974 it tested a nuclear device. It has its rebellious youth and idealistic reformers. Although most villages have no electricity, in 1980 India launched a satellite. Most remarkable of all, it has managed, since achieving independence, to govern itself in a fairly legal and democratic fashion, and in 1977, after a two-year lapse, to restore constitutional government through an election. That this huge country, in which children are rented out for a dollar or so per month, and which has all the problems of the less developed world from illiteracy to ethnic heterogeneity, is democratic is a fact that deserves more study than it has received.

In the 1950s and 1960s many Americans regarded India as a land of hope, the progress of which should demonstrate the superiority of democratic institutions over the totalitarianism of China, the great nation in similar circumstances. But growth lagged, and

[2]*New York Times*, May 26, 1981, p. 10.

India became increasingly critical of the United States and friendly to the Soviet Union; in 1970 and 1971, American policy tilted toward Pakistan for strategic reasons. China became more popular as a model, and interest in India declined. In post-Mao times, however, Americans have come to look less sanguinely upon China, while India has moved away from the fringes of the Soviet orbit. It remains to be seen whether the more structured China or more anarchic India will be the better model for the Third World.

COLONIAL INDIA

India, like China, the Near East, and Egypt, was the birthplace of one of the world's great civilizations. Its fabled riches drew Alexander the Great to its fringes in the fourth century BC. But India was repeatedly conquered and over the centuries fell into decay, technological backwardness, and weakness. From the end of the fifteenth century, European adventurers and traders, first Portuguese, then Dutch, French, and British, were lured to India, the greatest goal of the seafarers of that age. The government of the Moguls (Mongols, descendants of Central Asian conquerors) was too corrupt and disunited to offer much resistance; and European powers gained footholds at various sites around the subcontinent. The British East India Company entered in the seventeenth century and gradually extended its domination of the country to completion in the latter part of the eighteenth century. Victorian England took pride in its civilizing mission, and in 1835 English became the language of government. The British congratulated themselves on bringing free institutions to India, although this purpose was always qualified by the interests of the ruling administrators and mercantile houses.

In 1857, resentment against the alien intrusion culminated in the Sepoy Mutiny, in which part of the British-led army turned against their masters. As a result, the government of India was transferred from the East India Company to the British Crown. Moreover, the British turned away from ideas of changing Indian society, relying instead on the old elite of rajas and zamindars, hereditary tax gatherers.

The Sepoy Mutiny represented the last gasp of the old India. During the remainder of the nineteenth century, the British could rule India comfortably and proudly with a minimum of European troops, because Indian society was divided between Muslim and Hindu and into countless sects. Nationalism was feeble. The British built railways and irrigation works; by the end of the century, India had one of the world's largest railway networks, and the periodic famines had been largely ended. The British hardly changed Indian customs and social order, although they outlawed some of the more repugnant practices, such as *suttee*, the self-immolation of the widow on her husband's funeral pyre. But they founded schools, fostered local government, and permitted the beginnings of modern industry.

To educate and modernize, however, was to create a new India increasingly difficult to rule within the parameters of the British political and legal system. Demands inevitably grew for Indian participation in government, for autonomy, and eventually for independence. The first leaders of the new national movement were from the upper middle class; the old upper class was largely involved with the British administration. Educated in the British system and finding a new unity through their education and knowledge of English, they applied to themselves ideas of legal equality and representative government. They also became aware of the glories of the Hindu past, brought to light mostly by British and German scholars. As elsewhere in Asia, nationalism did not arise from popular discontent or a mass outcry for improvement but from the resentments of middle-class intellectuals.

An anti-British movement took shape as a protest against discrimination in the upper civil service. It had been official British policy since 1833 to permit equal access to civil service careers regardless of race, and there had been some Indian participation at the upper levels since 1858. But it remained difficult in practice for Indians to get responsible positions, and disappointed applicants called on the British Raj to fulfill the neglected promise. In 1883 a bill was introduced to place British and Indian applicants on the same footing, but the pained outcry of British administrators in India caused it to be withdrawn. The anger and humiliation of educated Indians, no longer convinced of their own inferiority, brought about the meeting of the first Indian Conference in 1883 and the Indian National Congress in 1885 (on the initiative of an Englishman, A. O. Hume). This was the first of many such congresses, which grew into the prime organization of the independence movement and, after independence, into the Congress party, which ruled India for the first thirty years of its nationhood and a branch of which still rules today.

The nationalists of the 1880s admired British culture and government and wanted not to sever the bond with Britain but to secure equal rights for Indians within that relationship. With faith in British democracy, they politely called attention to injustices and humbly presented petitions. Some British supported them as a desirable opposition party.[3] But the colonial authorities

[3]B. R. Nada, *The Nehrus, Motilal and Jawaharlal* (Chicago: University of Chicago Press, 1974), p. 45.

were generally insensitive and often arrogant, and the pleas went unanswered. Indian leaders became disillusioned and more vociferous. Almost from the beginning, the Congress was divided between moderates and at first a few, then more, extremists. After 1900, the talk turned more and more to *swaraj*, or independence. The victory of Asiatic Japan over half-European Russia in 1904 thrilled and encouraged the nationalists. In 1906, the Congress for the first time adopted swaraj as its policy. Meanwhile, the British, more for convenience than principle, gradually associated more Indians with the administration of their country. Reforms of 1909 provided for the election, with a very restricted franchise, of some members of local and provincial councils.

The two world wars greatly accelerated the independence movement. The Britain that called on India for help no longer seemed omnipotent, and the million Indians who fought for it in World War I saw less need to be colonial subjects. The promises of freedom and democracy in the name of which the Allies fought both wars, the visions of Wilson and Roosevelt, were obviously applicable to India as well as to victims of German aggression. And the wars sapped the British resolve to hold other peoples in subjection by force.

In World War I, the British viceroy made vague promises of greater freedom in return for Indian help. Fulfillment was meager. In 1919, a reform was promulgated whereby most of the central parliament was elected, but the governor-general kept a veto over its actions and retained control of the instruments of order. Under a dual system, or "dyarchy," in the provinces, elected legislatures could have jurisdiction over most matters, but the governor kept in his hands the maintenance of order and the revenues. This law could not satisfy anyone, and agitation, controversy, and intermittent disorder did not cease until independence in 1947.

In 1919 also, one of the striking figures of history, Mohandas K. Gandhi, entered the political scene. Born in 1869, the son of a minister in a small Indian state, Gandhi received a legal education in England. Going to South Africa as a young lawyer, he pleaded the rights of the Indian minority in that British colony, acquired an antipathy for Western civilization, and sought in Hindu ethics the moral power by which the physically weak could resist oppression. In 1907 he conducted his first civil disobedience campaign against discriminatory laws in South Africa. He earned an extraordinary reputation and the title of Mahatma ("Great Soul"). Upon his return to the holy ground of India in 1915, he was already a revered leader. In 1919 he began nonviolent resistance against abuses and emerged as the spiritual patron of the independence movement.

Gandhi inspired the movement and uplifted it spiritually. He also brought the masses into the agitation, which had been virtually limited to the wealthier classes and intellectuals (although only a very small percentage of the population was ever involved). The most important organizers of the movement were the Nehrus, Motilal and, from 1929 on, his son Jawaharlal; the saint was Gandhi. A totally religious man, he was broad and humane. He condemned the cruelty of Untouchability, called Untouchables *Harijans,* or "People of God"; and he made the greatest effort to unite Muslims and Hindus, who were already in the 1920s moving toward the separation that was to lead in 1947 to separate countries, Pakistan and India. Gandhi mixed these causes and the drive for independence with a striving for simplicity and purification. Rejecting the industrial world, he made the home spinning wheel the symbol of the Congress party, as it has

remained. By hand labor, his followers should at once make themselves worthy of swaraj and free themselves from dependence on the products of British factories.

In 1930, Gandhi led thousands of peasants in a 200-mile March to the Sea to extract salt in defiance of the British monopoly. Uniting moderates and radicals by his nonviolent revolutionism, he organized many strikes and peaceful demonstrations and was repeatedly imprisoned. He insisted that civil disobedience be uncontaminated by violence. One of his weapons was to fast; the British feared to allow him to die lest the country dissolve in an uproar. Two worlds met when the wrinkled little man, barefoot and wearing only a loincloth, conferred with the ornately uniformed British viceroy.

Through bitterness and violence as well as nonviolence, India gradually moved toward self-rule. The Government of India Act of 1935 inaugurated provincial self-governments elected under a broadened franchise—which was, however, still under one-fifth of the adult population. At the center, the British governor-general retained broad residual powers, but the legislative assemblies gained much authority over nonsecurity affairs. The Congress became a broadly representative political party by successfully contesting provincial elections in 1937 and forming ministries in most provinces.

World War II finally set events in motion. The viceroy announced that India was at war without consulting the Indians. Gandhi and the Congress refused to cooperate unless India was given independence. The British refused, although in 1942, chastened by German and Japanese victories, they offered a constituent assembly and full dominion status at the end of the war. Nehru favored acceptance, but Gandhi rejected it and called on the British to leave India. He and all other important Congress leaders were jailed, and independence had to await the end of the war.

INDEPENDENT INDIA

The defeat of Winston Churchill in the election of July 1945 brought to power Clement Attlee and a Labour government committed to Indian independence. If British India had been reasonably homogeneous, it would undoubtedly have become independent soon thereafter. But the great schism that once facilitated the imposition of British rule, the violent antagonism between the Hindus and the Muslim minority, made agreement difficult. At the beginning of the independence movement, Muslims and Hindus cooperated in the Congress; but as soon as the party entered electoral politics, the Muslims began to pull away lest they be swamped by the Hindu majority. They demanded a separate Muslim electorate. The Congress leadership regarded such a division as unbearable in what they wished to be a secular state.

The split hardened into an unbridgeable division as each side built an organization around its positions. The Congress asserted itself as representative of all the people; the Muslim League insisted that it represented a separate group and from 1940 a separate nation. The Muslim leader, Muhammed Ali Jinnah, made his goal an independent Muslim state, to which the Congress was bitterly opposed.

The British at first rejected any settlement unacceptable to the Muslims; however, in February 1947 the British government declared that it would leave India not later than June 1948. The Congress leadership reluctantly, over the opposition of Gandhi, accepted the principle of partition and the independence of Pakistan. The various states and principalities ruled by native rajas under British hegemony were allowed choice of adherence.

The problems of division filled the next year. Hundreds of thousands died in Hindu-Muslim rioting; some 20 million streamed out of Hindu and Muslim areas to the side of their coreligionists. In most cases, the rajas' choice of India or Pakistan was noncontroversial; but Hyderabad had a largely Hindu population under a Muslim prince, and the decision for India was made by the Indian army. In Jammu-Kashmir, a Hindu prince reigned over a Muslim majority; Indian forces occupied a majority of the territory, Pakistanis a minority. The confrontation led to armed conflict in 1947–1948 and 1965 and kept India and Pakistan near war for twenty-four years.

Jawaharlal Nehru, idealistic, Westernized, and internationalist, became the effective leader of the new Indian nation after Gandhi was assassinated in January 1948. The Parliament elected in 1947 by the provincial assemblies became the constituent assembly of the new India; 70 percent of its membership were members of the Congress party. The constitution it drew up went into effect on January 26, 1950.

This long document (over 250 pages) set the patterns of Indian democracy. One important decision was that English should be the language of the central administration along with Hindi, the language of 30 to 40 percent of the population, mostly in North India. Many patriots had wished to make Hindi the national language, but South Indians objected because this would place non-Hindi speakers at a disadvantage. Although the controversy has continued, English remains the administrative language and seems to have been gaining in popularity. Its use has kept India open to foreign ideas and helped to perpetuate Western legal and political patterns. In number of books published and newspaper circulation, English outranks Hindi. A second decision was to reject Gandhi's idea of a decentralized, non-industrial India based on the village and village councils, or *panchayats*. Nehru and the modernizers wanted a strong India, with a modern, centralized government.

The basic form of government, a parliamentary democracy, was never in question. The main structures were simply continued from the colonial period, during which Congress leaders had acquired considerable parliamentary experience. Most of the constitution was taken verbatim, or nearly so, from the Government of India Act of 1935. The organizational structure of the state, the legal system, and the civil service were British and only slightly and gradually changed.

Unlike the Japanese constitution, the Indian constitution had been amended forty-two times up to 1977. Amendment is rather easy, but rules differ for different articles. Some require only an ordinary majority of Parliament for amendment; most require a two-thirds majority of both houses, and for some, ratification by at least half the states is also necessary. The ease of amendment means that the letter of the constitution is no bar to arbitrary power.

Universal suffrage was boldly adopted for a population 80 percent illiterate. Civil rights were duly enumerated, not only those traditional in Western constitutions—such as freedom of speech, press, and religion and habeas corpus—but also rights of equality, education, welfare, and cultural freedom. Untouchability was outlawed. Equality of religion was guaranteed in the officially secular state, although cow slaughter and alcoholic beverages were prohibited.

Rights, however, were considerably restricted by broad emergency powers the president could invoke at his discretion, subject to confirmation by parliament within two months. From the little war with China in 1962 until the electoral defeat of Indira Gandhi in 1977, some kind of emergency was in effect almost continually. Emergencies were frequently invoked to repress disorders unrelated to the original crisis. Preventive detention, the arrest of suspicious persons, and confinement without trial, customary under British rule, were authorized by the constitution and sanctioned by an act of 1950 directed against leftist guerrillas. This power was used only moderately, mostly as a weapon against banditry and large-scale subversive disorders, until 1975. But the protection of civil rights depended, and still depends, more on forbearance and accepted ideas of propriety than on specific constitutional guarantees.

THE GOVERNMENT

Legislature

The Indian political system, like that of Japan, represents an implantation of Western institutions on alien soil. But conditions in India are much more adverse, and the Indian system is less eclectic and less well devised than the Japanese. It functioned rather well as long as leaders were satisfied to carry on approximately in the British style. With the fading from memory of colonial times, and the passing of the leadership formed under British rule, the state entered a period of instability, the outcome of which is unpredictable. The constitution rested its authority on the will of the people, and basic powers were vested in the bicameral parliament. The lower house, the *Lok Sabha*, to which the prime minister and cabinet are responsible, is directly elected from 542 single-member constituencies like the British House of Commons, with a maximum term of five years, extendable in emergency (only in 1976 was the period actually extended). Like the British Commons, the Lok Sabha can be dissolved, but this is potentially disastrous for members, who wish to remain in office for five years in order to qualify for pensions. Almost a fifth of the seats are reserved for "scheduled castes and tribes"; that is, only Harijans and members of tribal groups can be candidates in the respective constituencies. The upper house, the *Rajya Sabha,* has 250 members, 12 nominated by the president (to permit the placing of distinguished citizens in the legislature), the remainder elected by the assemblies of the states, with smaller states having somewhat more representation than proportionate to their population. The term is six years, one-third being elected every two years, and the Rajya Sabha cannot be dissolved.

The upper house cannot censure and overturn the government, and it is much weaker than the Lok Sabha. If a money bill, which must start in the Lok Sabha, is rejected by the Rajya Sabha, the Lok Sabha may repass it. There is provision for a joint meeting to decide differences between the houses, which gives the deciding voice to the lower house. Until 1977, however, the composition of the two houses was similar, both being dominated by the Congress party.

Procedures in the Indian parliament have been patterned after those of the British House of Commons. Bills are referred to appropriate committees and undergo three readings, as in the Commons. Since they are mostly drafted and introduced by the government, Parliament's work has usually been rather perfunctory. Members get low pay and have no staff and few facilities. Until the Congress party split in 1969, no other party had sufficient members (10 percent of the total) to qualify as official opposition. However, the cabinet has always felt it necessary to pay some attention to parliamentary debates, which have been a major source of publicity. Opposition members of parliament, however outnumbered, can make points by written or oral questions to ministers, who spend much time on the floor.

Leaders

In the Indian system, the president takes the place of a constitutional monarch. His constitutional executive powers are very broad, but it is expected (although not expressly so stated) that he will exercise these powers on the advice of his ministers. He can, among other things, hold up legislation (except money bills) and return it to parliament to be repassed; and he can promulgate ordinances when parliament is not sitting (to be confirmed within six weeks of its reconvening). At times, the president, unlike the British monarch, has spoken out on policy, and he may have discretionary authority in doubtful situations. If at some future time no single party is dominant, he may have a choice in the selection of the prime minister. But generally the president has acted as a nongoverning head of state, as intended by the framers of the constitution.

The president is elected for five years by a large electoral college consisting of members of parliament and members of state assemblies, in which each MLA (member of a legislative assembly) has a vote roughly proportional to the number of persons in his constituency, and the MPs together have a total equal to that of the MLAs. The vice president is chosen by parliament in joint session; his chief importance has been that he several times has succeeded a retiring president.

The president names a prime minister, who has the support of the Lok Sabha, that is, the leader elected by the majority party.

The prime minister is the chief of the government and leader of the nation, who sets the main lines of domestic and foreign policy. He or she speaks for India, dominates the news media, leads the majority party, and holds a position similar to that of the British prime minister or the German chancellor.[4] The prime minister in turn chooses ministers. They, like the prime minister, must be members of parliament, preferably of the Lok Sabha.

The ministers compose a council, but it never meets and has little collective responsibility. The inner circle of a dozen or more of the more important ministers meet as the cabinet to formulate and oversee policy. Most of the work of the cabinet is handled by small committees. The cabinet is chosen at least in part to represent different groups, communities, and factions in the parliamentary party, often persons of disparate views. Its members are formally ranked on the basis of seniority and perceived importance, but ranking does not really indicate political power. At times, the prime minister has relied heavily on a small Public Affairs Committee of the cabinet for guidance on major issues.

Elections

In India, voter registration is simple and automatic. In view of the prevalent illiteracy, voters can choose their party by its symbol—a cow and calf for the old Congress party, a plowman for Janata, a hand for Indira Gandhi's party. Until 1962, a voter had to put the paper ballot in the box marked with the symbol of the party; thereafter, for secrecy, the voter has marked the choice of candi-

[4]See L. N. Sharma, *The Indian Prime Minister: The Office, Its Functions and Powers* (Columbia, Mo.: Smith Aria Books, 1971).

dates on a paper placed in a general box. A finger is marked with indelible ink to prevent repeat voting. Parties have observers at polling stations to ensure honesty, and the entire process is under the control of the nonpolitical Election Commission, the head of which has the tenure and status of a judge. Candidates are picked by parties and registered by the Election Commission. They do not have to reside in the district. To discourage frivolous candidacies, a candidate must deposit 500 rupees ($50), returnable if he or she receives at least a sixth of the votes. Most candidates lose their deposits.

Campaigns are festive occasions, with processions, meetings, dancing, and speeches. There are strict regulations, including low limits on expenditures (about $12,000 for a campaign for a place in the Lok Sabha). This limit is quite unenforceable, and actual spending on behalf of a candidate may be much higher. Financial support comes mostly from businesses that need assistance in dealing with the bureaucracy or protection from legal or tax problems. Despite poverty and ignorance, participation is high: in recent elections between 55 and 61 percent of the eligible voters went to the polls, a turnout similar to that for American presidential elections. Sometimes, however, thugs hired by landowners have kept Harijans from the polls.

The Bureaucracy

The cabinet is assisted by civil servants of the central secretariat, headed by a cabinet secretary. Top personnel, up to the minister, are also members of the civil service. There was originally some distrust of the civil service because it had served as the arm of British authority. However, the Indian Civil Service was too competent and useful to be discarded, and the government of independent India continued it with little change as the Indian Administrative Service (IAS). Charged with executing laws and policies under the direction of the political ministers, it has naturally become a major political force and a bulwark of legality and stability.

Most of the millions of civil servants are petty bureaucrats of the state or central government services, such as employees of postal and revenue departments. They also include workers and administrators of state enterprises, including steel, petroleum, coal, and electric production plus the largest banks, many engineering firms, and numerous miscellaneous enterprises owned by either federal or state governments. At the top, about 2,000 officers (out of some 10 million government employees) of the IAS occupy top posts in administration, both at the center and in the states. Most serve state governments, although they rotate between the federal regime and the state to which they are attached. Entry is by competitive academic examination open to university graduates from twenty-one to twenty-four years of age. Only about a hundred are admitted annually. They are mostly from urban professional or civil service backgrounds, although a number of posts are reserved for scheduled castes and officials promoted from state services.[5] Nearly half are sons of government officials. About a quarter formerly came from the southern state of Tamilnadu because of the extensive use of English in that Tamil-speaking state (the written examination until recently was given only in English).[6] Tenure is permanent; promotion and transfers are based partly on merit, mostly on seniority. As may be imagined, the IAS has high morale and an elitist mentality. Much

attached to status and privileges, it is often lofty and unresponsive. Its quality seems to have declined since independence, partly because of the lowered standards of the universities.

The civil service is powerful not only because the permanent secretary may virtually run the ministry but because so much goes through its hands. Multiple government agencies oversee the organized sector of the economy, and permits or licenses are needed for almost everything. Not only imported but Indian-made goods are widely allocated, wages and prices are regulated, and investments are directed.[7] There are thus endless opportunities for private profit to supplement the bureaucrats' poor pay, and it is assumed that papers are stalled in the apparatus unless their way is lubricated.

Parallel with the civil service is the court system. Lawyers with at least three years' experience are eligible for a competitive entrance examination; upon appointment as judges, they acquire career tenure. Seniority is important in promotion, and the president customarily names judges of higher courts from the lower benches. The president also names justices of the Supreme Court (on the advice of the prime minister), but is supposed to consult with the Chief Justice and should follow rules of seniority. The Supreme Court is the designated guardian of the constitution, with authority to declare laws and official acts unconstitutional. It has not hesitated to do so, and its verdicts have been accepted. For example, in 1970 it declared the nationalization of banks unconstitutional because of the lack of adequate compensation. It struck down repressive acts of the 1975–1977 emergency regime until the government by constitutional amend-

---

[5]H. H. Hanson and Janet Douglas, *India's Democracy* (New York: Norton, 1972), p. 147.

[6]Robert Hardgrave, Jr., *India: Government and Politics in a Developing Nation*, 3rd ed. (New York: Harcourt Brace Jovanovich, 1980), p. 72.

[7]Stanley A. Kochanek, *Business and Politics in India* (Berkeley: University of California Press, 1974), p. 293.

ment deprived it of the power of review of basic constitutional changes. The independence and integrity of the courts are a major strength of democracy; India is one of the few countries of the Third World where one can sue the government and hope to win.

Federalism

Like the constitution and civil service, the federal system derives from the 1935 act of the British Parliament and its allocation of limited powers to the provinces. Indian states continue to be so inferior to the central government that the propriety of calling the government federal may be questioned. Unlike traditional federal unions, the Indian system did not arise by a joining of parts but was set up by the central authority because of the practical difficulties of direct government. In the lists of powers reserved to the union, those given to the states, and those held concurrently, the federal government has much the best of it; it can even alter the boundaries of a state or abolish a state by ordinary law. States do not have their own constitutions but are subsumed in the central constitution. The federal government may issue directives to states or, by decision of the Rajya Sabha, assume authority over areas constitutionally reserved to the states. Taxation is mostly in the hands of the central authorities, and the states are dependent on conditional grants to supplement their limited powers of taxation.[8] The president, on the advice of the prime minister, appoints a governor for each state. In relation to the state government, the governor occupies a position like that of the president in the federal government. But the governors, although normally expected to act on the advice of their minister, have more power locally than

the president has nationally, and they have not felt bound to act impartially. Their role has been great because the party situation in many states has been fluid and uncertain.

The inferiority of the states is underlined by the authority of the president (in effect, of the prime minister) to find that a state government is unable to act in accordance with the constitution, set it aside, and impose "president's rule." This power does not come into practice as long as central government and states are in the hands of the same party. During the long dominance of the Congress party there was only one federal intervention prior to 1967, when the president saw a breakdown of legality under the Communist government of Kerala in 1959. However, when center and states are ruled by antagonistic parties and when states have difficulty in forming stable governments, the temptation to set aside an inconvenient state regime is strong. After the 1967 elections, when the Congress party lost control of many states, presidential rule was frequently decreed for political purposes without the justification of a real breakdown of order. However, president's rule is normally for no more than six months (which may be extended by parliament), and it is supposed to lead to new elections. In 1983 emergency rule was imposed on Punjab after violence arising from the Sikh autonomy movement, with the approval of all major parties.

The government of the states is practically a copy of the federal government on a reduced scale, with the governor appointing a chief minister, who names a ministry of a dozen or more. The ministry is responsible to the legislative assembly, which may have from 60 to 520 members elected for a five-year term and subject to dissolution. The MLAs are generally less educated and less Westernized than MPs, but also more representative of their electors. Some states have

[8]Hanson and Douglas, *India's Democracy,* p. 42.

a smaller upper house with restricted powers. Approximately a fifth of about 4,000 constituencies are reserved, as at the national level, for Harijans and tribal peoples. There is no separate state court system.

Frequent defections from parties and changes of party front have made state politics unstable. The state divisions of the Congress party had some ability and inclination to go their own way when the Congress party ruled nationally, and it was not easy to coerce them. Since 1967, other parties have governed in various states, including Communists in Kerala and West Bengal, and they have pressed for more autonomy. The states have also been influential in parliament, because candidates have been selected at the state level or below; MPs owe their positions primarily to the state, not to the national party organization.

It is a strength of the states (and hence of federalism) that they have the linguistic and cultural solidarity the federal government lacks. The original twenty-seven states of the union were simply continuations of colonial provinces and princely holdings, and their boundaries had little ethnic significance. After independence there was agitation for the redrawing of boundaries to unite people who could communicate with one another, but the Congress leadership strongly resisted this idea. It had made a point during the long struggle for independence of cultivating a single Indian nationality to embrace the enormous diversity of languages and cultures in the subcontinent. To recognize diversity by giving various language groups their own states seemed a step backward. However, the biggest political controversy between 1953 and 1956 was the question of redrawing state boundaries. In 1956, the State Reorganization Act satisfied most of the demands by providing for fourteen states and ten union territories; and in subsequent years,

eight more states were carved out. A number of separatist movements still remain unsatisfied, and any minority that forms a local majority can assert its claim. However, their rough correspondence with ethnic or linguistic boundaries gives the states significance and vitality.

Their obvious weakness, including the possibility of being set aside, is inevitably rather demoralizing for state governments. They are, however, actually important, and India is closer to genuine federalism than one might think. The center depends (like the West German government) on the states' administrative apparatus for the implementation of federal policies; in India language differences makes it less practical for the central government to administer the country directly. The civil service is organized mostly around the states, although the IAS, the police, and several technical services are centrally recruited. Twenty percent of the IAS officers in any state are to be promoted from the civil service of that state. The state governments rest on elections, and when they have made a clear mandate, it is unwise for the central government to ignore or abuse them. The assemblies being closer to the people than parliament, elections to them arouse more interest; and most government–people interaction takes place at the state level. When the central government was paralyzed (1977–1979), much authority gravitated to the states.

Local Government

States are subdivided into districts with a population of a million or so, under "collectors" named by state governors. Cities have elected assemblies, but the chief officer again is the commissioner chosen by the state. Villages elect *panchayats*, councils of some twelve to fifteen members, including representatives of Harijans and women. Rules differ in different states, but higher-level panchayats for local areas are indirectly elected; chairs of these higher panchayats meet at the district level. The panchayat is an ancient Indian institution that had mostly fallen into disuse by the eighteenth century. The British did something to revive it; and Indian nationalists, especially Gandhians, tended to idealize it as true democracy. The naive idea of turning government, except for a necessary minimum of central functions, over to the village panchayats was rejected, but the constitution mandated the states to organize panchayats and endow them with suitable powers.

The panchayats were rather inactive in the first years after independence, but new life was injected into them in the early 1960s when it seemed necessary to secure more popular involvement in the community development program. The panchayats were not successful[9] in reviving that program, but they acquired an important role in the supervision of development funds. They also have charge of elementary schools, local roads, and the like; and they settle minor civil disputes.

It was at first assumed that local elections would be nonpartisan, but they became politicized as factions appealed to parties for support. Generally, the panchayats seem to be dominated by the traditional powers of the village and the larger landholders, but these at least have to appeal to or bargain with the poorer sectors; and local self-government has raised the political consciousness of the peasant masses. Some 3 million local leaders look to elections as a way to power. The panchayats not only serve as the bottom rung of political recruitment but also support the notion that leaders hold office by the will of the voters.

PARTIES AND POWER

The Nehru Period

Since independence, India has gradually grown into its democratic constitution, and the ruling organization, the Congress party, slowly lost the enormous strength acquired during the struggle. The Congress gradually became less a movement, and more an interest group and a personal following of the prime minister. Opposition parties slowly gained vigor and pulled sectors of the Congress away, and every general election through 1977 (except 1971) was more strongly contested than the preceding one. A Congress victory in 1971 seemed to reverse this trend, but in 1975 Prime Minister Indira Gandhi declared a national emergency and arrested her critics in order to sustain her position, only to fall in the elections of 1977 and rebound in a personal victory in 1980. There has been a corresponding change in the character of the leadership from the Westernized intellectuals who raised the banner of freedom to native politicians dealing for advantages. Each election has also seen a decline in the average educational level of both parliament and the state assemblies and in the number of English-speaking representatives.[10] Groups formerly relatively indifferent to politics, especially landholders and businessmen, along with professional bosses, entered politics and the Congress party, eventually to make it mostly theirs, while the idealists abandoned it.

The first fifteen years after independence were filled with hope and optimism; India

---

[9]Ibid., p. 200.

[10]Hardgrave, *India*, p. 64.

seemed to be successfully combining economic development, a large dash of socialism, and political freedom unusual in the Third World. India was proving that democracy could work in a very big and very poor non-Western country. It was also held up, or held itself up, as a successful exponent of nonviolence and the pacifist leader in a world of ideological stress, violence, and threat of war.

Yet nonviolent India itself was chronically in a state of near-war with Pakistan, mostly over Kashmir, the Indian-held part of which was annexed in 1957. There were also insurgencies like the Communist guerrilla movements that accompanied the retreat of Western power in such countries as Malaysia and Burma. Peasant uprisings, mostly led by the left wing of the Communist movement, occurred now and then from the late 1940s into the 1970s; but the government proceeded ruthlessly against them, and they never constituted a serious threat. The Communists gradually accommodated themselves to the constitutional system.

The first period of Congress rule was dominated by Jawaharlal Nehru, who shared power with the less charismatic and less visible Sardar Patel, chief of the party executive, until Patel's death in 1950. Thereafter Nehru stood alone, master of the party organization as well as the government. He could doubtless have made himself dictator without difficulty, but he wanted a free India.

Nehru was a cosmopolitan nationalist. A close friend of Gandhi, he was born of Brahmin lineage and to great wealth; the family residence was princely. His political outlook was shaped in the 1930s by British democratic socialism.[11] He vaguely subscribed to

[11]Frank Moraes, *Nehru: Sunlight and Shadow* (Bombay: Jaico Publishing House, 1964), pp.18–19.

Marxism and sympathized with the Soviet experiment and later with Chinese Communism, but he was repelled by their violence and totalitarianism and deeply pained by the 1962 border clash with the Chinese. Nehru saw the liberation of India as part of the liberation of Asia and Africa, a liberation he hoped would lead to freedom with economic justice—that is, socialism.

Nehru consequently gave the Congress party a vague commitment to socialism, which represented not only justice and welfare but also liberation from the capitalist colonial past; but he did not try to impose a revolutionary program. Socialism remained a dimming aspiration. Its principal incarnation was in the Five Year Plans, which succeeded one another from 1951 on. Copied after the Stalinist invention but far less rigid, they ran counter to Gandhian economic philosophy in their emphasis on heavy industry, especially steel and machinery, as the basis for future prosperity. The new industrial plants, the "temples of modern India" in Nehru's phrase, were to produce a surplus for reinvestment and so cause Indian productivity and world influence to spiral upward.

The plans were partly successful; the second (1956–1961) especially saw good growth. But they were always at the mercy of the monsoons, and increases in national income depended more on the weather than on the bureaucracy. The third plan, 1961–1966, was set back by the diversion of resources to the military after the 1962 conflict with China. Afterwards enthusiasm waned, as it became obvious that plans could not bring an economic revolution, and that nationalized industries were not much better than private ones and usually much less efficient. Land reform in the 1950s greatly reduced tenancy, but agricultural programs seemed to help the more prosperous peasants who could take advantage of them, and consequently increased inequality in the villages.

Nehru, a poor judge of character who increasingly relied on yes-men, overstayed his abilities; by the time of his death in May 1964, shadows were falling over his vision. In 1963 there had been the beginnings of a split between the Congress party in the central government and the organization outside. Under the guidance of K. Kamaraj, an informal "Syndicate" of powerful leaders of the Congress in individual states was formed to keep control of the party apparatus.

The party organization chose as Nehru's successor Lal Bahadur Shastri. But Shastri died in January 1966, less than two years after taking office. The Syndicate and most of the party organization this time supported Indira Gandhi, daughter of Nehru and widow (since 1960) of a minor Congress leader, Feroze Gandhi. Indira Gandhi had come into political life as her father's aide. In deference to him, she had been made president of the party in 1959; and in Shastri's cabinet she had the secondary post of minister of information and broadcasting. The party bosses regarded her as a docile character, under whose reign they could rule.

Rising Opposition

The preeminence of the Congress party, with about three-fourths of the seats in the Lok Sabha (although it received only about 45 percent of the votes) for nearly thirty years was rather like that of the Liberal Democrats in Japan. Both parties had no serious contenders for power, despite the support of a minority of the population, because of the splintering of the opposition. And both were often divided by factionalism. There were differences, however. While opposition to the Japanese ruling party was almost exclusively from the Left, opposition to the Congress came from both conservatives and radicals. It was one of the strengths of the Congress party that it, like the Mexican ruling party, stood squarely in the middle. It also profited from the winner-take-all electoral system, which enabled a minority of votes to be translated into a majority of seats. On the other hand, the Indian federal structure favored a loosening of the party system. Opposition parties could gain control of the state governments or at least participate in a ruling coalition, thus gaining some share of power and making themselves credible alternatives.

Until independence, the Congress represented a broad amalgamation of forces agreed on a national goal; as soon as the goal was reached, the coalition was certain to loosen and divide. The earliest opposition group, however, was the Communists, who had had their own organization since 1928. The most ideologically oriented of Indian parties, they had followed Soviet directives in support for the British war effort from 1941 on and had opposed Gandhi and favored the Muslim League. In 1948 the Communist party of India (CPI) turned to violence, stirring up strikes, urban disorders, and peasant movements in the hope of creating a revolutionary situation. In the 1950s, after the death of Stalin and Khrushchev's proclamation of "Peaceful Coexistence," it turned to "constitutional communism," supporting the Congress party and government as long as it was "progressive." In 1957, it made Kerala the first state to have a non-Congress government. The Communists ruled in Kerala until divisions and rioting gave the central government, which feared that the CPI might solidify its power there, an excuse for intervention in 1959.

Deepening conflict with China gravely hurt the party and caused it to divide in 1962 between Moscow-oriented conservative

Communists and determined radicals. In 1964 the leftists formed the pro-Peking revolutionary Marxist party, the CP(M). In due course, the extremists became dissatisfied with this party, rejected the electoral approach of both the CPI and the CP(M), and seceded (1969) as the Marxist-Leninist Communist Party, the CP(M-L). The CPI remained faithful to the Soviet Union, to which it owed financial support, and for a few years prospered in alliance with the government of Indira Gandhi, only to share her fall in 1977. The CPI, however, has retained its firm strength in Kerala. The CP(M), which turned from Maoist to neutral in the Sino-Soviet dispute, gained control of Calcutta and West Bengal, which have been its fortress through the turmoil of recent years.

The Indian Communist parties—except the antiparliamentary CP(M-L)—have been relatively democratic in their organization and have never been able to impose the discipline characteristic of Communist parties elsewhere; even Leninism cannot overcome the Indian propensity to division. The leadership has consisted of middle-class professionals—lawyers, teachers, and doctors. The Communists have never attained much strength in the Hindi-speaking heartland of India but have to some extent represented a reaction to North Indian domination. From 1952 to 1967 they were the second largest faction in the Lok Sabha, although they never received more than 6 percent of the vote.

The CPI in Kerala and the CP(M) in West Bengal have behaved rather pragmatically and have administered their states capably. The CP(M), for example, wants to attract foreign capital to Calcutta. In 1980 the CP(M-L) had disappeared, but the CP(M) was the third largest party in the Lok Sabha with thirty-five seats; the CPI held ten.

The Socialists were the first opposition group to emerge from the independence co-alition. At first they formed a faction within the Congress movement devoted to a more radically egalitarian program. Some withdrew after the death of Gandhi to form a Socialist party, but it was crushed in the 1952 elections, receiving only 2.5 percent of the vote and twelve seats. The party then merged with a group of Congress dissidents to form the Praja Socialist party. Its outstanding figure was Jaya Prakash Narayan, who withdrew from active politics in 1954 to dedicate himself to the "land-gift" movement of Vinoba Bhave, but returned later to lead a popular movement against Indira Gandhi.

Indian socialism has been torn by ideological uncertainty; it has wavered between different interpretations of Marxism, Western European democratic socialism, and Gandhism, with its emphasis on the peasants, equality, and simplicity. It has been decidedly anti-Communist in temper. Lacking ideological coherence, it has undergone various schisms with a loose and fluctuating membership and has ceased to play a significant role.

On the Right, there have been a number of movements favoring a more religious or more nationalistic course. The most important and enduring of these was Jana Sangh, which gathered strength election by election to surpass by 1967 both Communists and Socialists with thirty-five seats and over 9 percent of the popular vote. The Jana Sangh wanted a united Hindi-speaking India that would dominate the subcontinent. It favored nuclear arms and Hindu orthodoxy. At the beginning the Jana Sangh derived organizational strength from a Hindu revivalist group, but it officially claimed to be nonsectarian. Most of its support came from the cities of northern India.

The Swatantra (Freedom) party was founded in 1959 to oppose the socialistic tendencies of the Congress government; it promoted "farm and family" and economic freedom. The party received support from business interests, landowners, and many others fearful of or irritated by the power of the central government. It preferred friendship with the United States over the Soviet Union. In 1967, Swatantra became the second largest party in the Lok Sabha, with 8.5 percent of the vote.

Several opposition parties have been local. The anti-Hindi southern party, Dravida Munnetra Kazhagam, had its strength principally in Tamilnadu, where it won a majority of seats in 1967. Defectors from the Congress after 1967 under the leadership of Charan Singh formed a personalist party in Uttar Pradash, the Bharatiya Kranti Dal, a middle-class group. Another regional party of importance was the Akali Dal, representing Sikhs in the Punjab. There have been many other smaller parties, mostly parochial or ephemeral—as many as sixty or seventy participating in some elections.

INDIRA GANDHI AND THE DECLINE OF CONGRESS RULE

By the late 1960s, the Congress aura had worn thin, although it still made the most of the names of Mahatma Gandhi and Nehru. Having retreated from the old goals of equality and social reform, the party responded more to pressures than it promoted change. It had become a conglomerate of many disparate interests, dependent mostly on petty landlords, the village potentates who had replaced lawyers as the most numerous class among Lok Sabha deputies. Democratization implied conservatism, at least initially, as influence gravitated from nationalist reformers to rural bosses. Businesses became the financial mainstay of the Con-

gress; they gave to the party that could help or hurt them. The factions that asserted themselves after Nehru were mostly personal and local. The Congress's position seemed secure because it alone was well organized throughout the country and in every state, with a structure parallel to that of government at all levels.

India, however, was suffering a growing malaise. The Congress government, responsive to the landowners and more prosperous peasants, increasingly alienated the more numerous poor and landless. The Five Year Plans brought some expansion of industry but little improvement in standards of living in either city or country. Rather, they increased inequality; some, better able to take advantage of modernization, prospered; many more were hurt by the concomitant inflation.

The 1967 elections consequently brought the Congress party near to defeat. Its vote declined from 46 to 41 percent, and its seats in the Lok Sabha went down much more, from 73 to 54 percent, because the opposition parties for the first time joined forces for better electoral effect. The Congress still had a sufficient majority to govern, and no other party held as much as the 10 percent required for official recognition as opposition in the chamber. But the Congress was no longer the only way to political advancement. It was crushed in several states and lost control of nine. The opposition could not rule effectively, however, as defection and redefection became the mode in the state legislatures. President's rule was temporarily imposed on most of North India.

The setback of 1967 resulted in a crisis in the Congress party in 1969 and its splitting and reorganization. Party leaders, grouped around the Syndicate, found themselves at odds with the government headed by Indira

Gandhi, who had proved unexpectedly self-assertive.[12] Concerned that the party was losing the young, the poor, and the illiterate—that is, the large majority of voters—Gandhi undertook a program of change, a new commitment to socialism. She also wished to build a personal following that would enable her to gather the reins into her own hands and reassert the prime minister's superiority over the party organization that her father had enjoyed.

In July 1969, Gandhi sent to the Working Committee of the party, the body charged with policy scrutiny, a memorandum urging nationalization of major banks, effective land reform, ceilings on urban property and incomes, and curbs on large industries. This led to a struggle between Gandhi and the conservatives in the party, led by Morarji Desai. As a result of the ensuing split, about a quarter of the Congress MPs seceded to form a new opposition party in the Lok Sabha, the first to have official status, and Gandhi proceeded to nationalize the large banks.

Gandhi's populist turn, the nationalization not only of banks but also of various other enterprises, and the stiffening of tax collection revived the flagging Congress party. In 1971, Gandhi, seeing her popularity high, held a general election a year before it was required. Her party won two-thirds of the seats in the Lok Sabha, while nearly all the opposition parties lost ground even though they had formed a loose alliance. Late in the year, attention shifted to foreign affairs as East Pakistan, which had been East Bengal, rebelled against the alien rule of West Pakistan. India entered the conflict and soon defeated the Pakistani army in the east, permitting East Pakistan to become independent Bangladesh—and removing Pakistan as a serious threat to Indian dominance in the subcontinent. The popularity of Gandhi was confirmed by state elections in March 1972, when the Congress party recovered the ground lost in 1967 and won in all the important states.

These victories gave Gandhi mastery of what appeared to be the sole important political organization. Lacking her father's tolerance of diversity, she set the old hands aside and made a monolithic leadership party of servants and sycophants.[13] Whereas Nehru had worked with leaders of state Congress committees, Gandhi selected them and expected them to be loyal to her. Increased unity permitted growing authoritarianism. The party was now more impatient with individual and property rights; to "abolish poverty" took priority over private ownership, and the courts became the refuge of expropriated landholders. There was an increase in political violence, including disruption in the Lok Sabha.

The popularity of the government began to sink as the poor suffered more from the stagnation of the economy than they benefitted from its programs. Food production increased more slowly than population; although the GNP rose about 3 percent yearly, the standard of living perceptibly declined. Inflation worked incredible hardship on the urban poor. The year 1973 was especially bad: The Congress party seemed to disintegrate, and several states were placed under president's rule when Congress governments fell apart. In 1974 inflation reached a rate of 30 percent, and the monsoon was poor. Charges of official corruption became more insistent. As the Congress party weak-

[12]There are many biographies of this leader, for example, Dom Moraes, *Indira Gandhi* (Boston: Little, Brown, 1980).

[13]Zareer Masani, *Indira Gandhi* (London: Hamilton, 1975), p. 294.

ened, the opposition drew together; Swatantra and six other parties amalgamated to form
the Bharatiya Lok Dal, the People's party.
Indira Gandhi became more dictatorial. In
May 1974 she ended a national railway strike
by arresting tens of thousands of strikers,
alienating much of her most faithful following. Student violence surged on, sometimes
even toppling state governments, fueled by
the fact that huge universities turned out
graduates unqualified for technical and
managerial work but disqualified for ordinary jobs by diplomas in law or humanities.
The explosion in 1974 of a nuclear device
was only a costly little lift for national pride.

The Emergency

Troubles began coming to a head late in 1974.
In Gujarat, legislators suffered *gherao,* the
Indian improvement on the sitdown strike
in which managers are imprisoned in their
offices. The state government resigned.
There were strikes, food shortages, and riots;
and the Socialist elder, Jaya Prakash Narayan, came in to preach boycott and "total
revolution against corruption." The opposition defeated the Congress in elections in
Gujarat, and the state of Bihar was paralyzed
by Narayan's followers. The High Court in
Gandhi's home district in Allahabad found
her guilty of electoral offenses and disqualified her from holding office for six years.
The crime was minor, the use of some government officials to assist her campaign in
1971; but other members of Parliament had
been disqualified for similar transgressions.
The opposition announced a civil disobedience campaign.

This was an obvious emergency for the
career of Indira Gandhi and those around
her. Accordingly, on June 26, on advice of
the prime minister, the president declared
a state of emergency. The idea was old; there

had been "emergencies" in the conflicts with
China and Pakistan, and emergency powers
had been used not only to meet external
threats but also to keep order. But it was
new for the government to decree a state of
emergency to frustrate legal process.

Thousands of oppositionists, including the
aged Narayan and Desai, were rounded up
and carted away to jail. Eventually, perhaps
100,000 people, including parliamentary
opposition leaders, and friends and colleagues of Gandhi's father, were imprisoned. Many were held without trial until the
relaxation of the emergency in January 1977
or its end in March. Gandhi viewed the opposition campaign as an illegal subversion of
a duly elected government, which it was
proper to uphold by whatever means necessary, so she claimed to be a democrat while
imprisoning tens of thousands for political
offenses. She seems also to have believed that
by putting a lid on agitation and criticism,
ending strikes and disorders, and acting
ruthlessly against lawbreakers, she could
promote discipline and work (which became
her chief motto), and thereby increase productivity and abolish poverty as she had
promised and failed to do. She saw her power
as good; impediments to it—the free press,
nonpolitical courts, and the opposition—were
therefore evil.[14]

The emergency regime was consequently
a mixture of repression and an effort to move
the economy forward by authoritarian techniques. The press, with which Gandhi had
long been interfering, was totally muzzled,
although it had not been restrained in genuine military emergencies. Journals were
closed, newspapers printed official reports

[14]R. K. Murthy, *The Cult of the Individual: A Study of
Indira Gandhi* (New Delhi: Sterling Publishers, 1977).
For a sympathetic view, see Mary C. Carras, *Indira Gan-
dhi in the Crucible of Leadership* (Boston, Mass.: Beacon
Press, 1979).

and propaganda, and news services were merged into a government controlled agency. The intelligence services infiltrated newspapers and other organizations; those not jailed were subject to surveillance. The government of the two states controlled by the opposition, Tamilnadu and Gujarat, was assumed by the central authorities. The courts were subjected to pressure and deprived by constitutional amendment of some power of judicial review.

Gandhi coupled political action with a popular program. Speculators were castigated, and prices were fixed or reduced; after the grievous inflation of the preceding year, the price level actually declined slightly for a number of months. Students were sent back to their books. Crime was cut sharply, since police could arrest freely and legally valid evidence was not needed. Smuggling halted or became inconspicuous. Trains ran on time, more or less. Business was relieved of strikes, and wages were frozen. Bureaucrats went to work. Moreover, troubles were not publicized; not only opposition activities but also reports of drought were kept out of the papers. The government, in possession of plenary powers, also attacked the population problem, chiefly by vasectomy. It became the policy to seek sterilization of all fathers of two or three children. Local administrators, pressed to fill quotas, dragooned masses of defenseless men onto operating tables.

The dictatorship tended to intensify. Before 1975 Gandhi had been building up the police and intelligence apparatus as the bulwark of her government; the Research and Analysis Wing (RAW), India's CIA, had expanded from foreign intelligence operations to the surveillance of politicians, judges, journalists, and even high government officials. Gandhi now relied heavily on it. Actions became increasingly arbitrary; for example, twelve inspectors were imprisoned because they found irregularities in textile exports by the mother-in-law of Gandhi's son Sanjay.[15]

India was bathed in newspeak, almost like a totalitarian state. There developed a cult of the prime minister, seen as a mother goddess. Young Sanjay, who became her chief advisor, was "the rising sun of India." Hundreds of books and films glorified them. Late in 1976 Gandhi seemed, in defiance of the tradition surrounding the name she bore, to be moving toward a regularized authoritarian state. The party was centered on her alone, and the cabinet had become like a royal court. The prime minister gave herself power to amend the constitution, and there were reportedly proposals for drawing up a new constitution to place power even more firmly in the hands of the executive. There were moves to make India a sort of corporate state, with "apex" bodies standing over reorganized professional associations and groups of producers to coordinate their subordination to the government.[16] Respect for democratic norms, however, was sufficient that Gandhi had at all times to affirm that she was acting legally and democratically. She never felt able to rule as a despot. She did little to infringe the rights of the states. She did not imprison judges who acted contrary to her will; at most she transferred some of them against their wishes.

She lacked an organization reaching down into the villages that might have enabled her to remake Indian society.[17] She was hardly a dictator by temperament but often inde-

---

[15]*New York Times,* November 6, 1977, p. 4.

[16]Lloyd J. and Susanne H. Rudolph, "India's Election: Backing into the Future," *Foreign Affairs,* 55 (July 1977).

[17]Francine R. Frankel, *India's Political Economy 1947–1977* (Princeton, N.J.: Princeton University Press, 1978), p. 547.

cisive and ineffective.[18] Hence she could not do without Parliament and put off elections indefinitely. If she had lost the claim to govern legally by popular mandate, in all probability the military would have removed her.

Back to Democracy

The elections to be held in early 1976 (Indian elections are held in the spring for reasons of weather) were postponed a year, the first time since independence that a Parliament had extended itself. In November 1976, they were postponed another year. But in January 1977, the prime minister suddenly announced elections for March. The economy was in fair shape and crops had been satisfactory, but difficulties were accumulating, and it probably seemed a good time to renew the electoral mandate. All groups were evidently compliant or passive, and the opposition was crushed and fragmented. Gandhi was, in any case, kept unaware of sentiment in the country by censorship and the sycophants around her.

In order to make the elections properly convincing, Gandhi "relaxed" (without revoking) the emergency. Many opposition leaders were released, and censorship was lifted. Almost immediately, the principal opposition parties, the old Congress from 1969, the Jana Sangh, the Bharatiya Lok Dal, the Samyutka Socialists, and some smaller groups gathered together what remained of their forces into the Janata ("People's") party, with which the larger Communist party, the CP(M), allied itself. Since the mid-1960s these parties or their predecessors had been trying to unify the opposition; they were able to do so in 1977 because of the shared experience of prison and repression and because of their fear for the survival of the democratic order.

[18]Masani, *Indira Gandhi*, pp. 293–295.

The Moscow-faithful CPI supported the Congress party without enthusiasm. It had earlier been alienated from Gandhi, despite her long flirtation with Moscow, because of her conservative, antilabor policies and also because Sanjay was violently anti-Communist.

The Congress presented itself as the party of Nehru and Mohandas Gandhi, and it had not only abundant money and the old party organization but also government resources. The hastily thrown together Janata party had almost no money and little organization, and its leaders were old and feeble—Narayan was an invalid and Desai was eighty-one. The press was unchained, but it was still under pressure; editors were aware that they could be punished if Gandhi retained power. Although some held back, others opened fire on the ruling party. There was no freedom of the air; the All-India Radio ignored the opposition and poured out government propaganda through the millions of transistor radios that were the chief source of news in the villages. Gandhi did not hesitate to use other assets of incumbency. Many concessions and favors were handed out when it appeared that the election was in doubt. Government workers received bonuses, opposition workers were harassed, and air force helicopters were available for Gandhi and her party. Some 200,000 police and paramilitary forces were ordered into the countryside, perhaps to intimidate people by their presence.

But Janata rallies were packed and enthusiastic; those summoned to greet Gandhi were thin and apathetic, sometimes hostile. Nonetheless, the world was unprepared in mid-March for the stunning defeat of the government. Nearly every important minister and advisor of Indira Gandhi was beaten. In some of the big Hindi-speaking states of north India, the Congress party failed to secure a single seat. Janata secured 270 seats with 43 percent of the ballots, nearly the same percentage as the Congress received in 1971. Votes for the Congress were down to 35 percent, which brought 153 seats in the Lok Sabha. The Congress was saved from obliteration by south India, where the emergency was felt less than in the north; there it fared rather better than in 1971. It was also helped by some disunity among the opposition; in over a hundred races the opposition vote was divided.

The fall of Indira Gandhi's regime was ascribable to many grievances. Most important was the coercive sterilization program. In 1976, vasectomies were done at the rate of a million per month, and the masses equated the operation with emasculation or considered it religiously injurious. Harijans particularly saw themselves as victims. Another well-intended but ruthlessly executed program was slum clearance; hundreds of thousands were forcibly removed from shantytowns with little care for their subsequent housing and livelihood.

Many were alarmed by the rise of Sanjay. "The Boy," whose chief passion was for cars, which he undertook to produce in India without success but at great expense to the state, became his mother's heir-apparent. Although Sanjay's four-point program (for family planning, tree planting, literacy, and the abolition of dowries) was sensible, he was generally detested not only for nepotism but also for his arrogance. Indira Gandhi was also hurt by the frictions and injuries of the emergency. Many ordinary people were politicized by the repression. Lawyers and journalists saw their professions, as they had known them, endangered. Villagers learned the meaning of democracy and dictatorship from the constable, and the urban poor were educated by arbitrary police. Finally, the civil service made an opposition victory possible. In many countries the state can "win" elec-

tions, whatever the popular sentiment, by the use of force and chicanery. Indira Gandhi's government could not do so because the civil service was professional and, in the Indian Administrative Service, independent. Balloting, overseen by the Central Electoral Commission, might be influenced but could not be falsified. Moreover, the nonpolitical army seems to have declined to intervene when Gandhi apparently requested its help in forestalling defeat.

As returns came in, showing defeat turning into catastrophe, India rejoiced. As one paper wrote: "We Indians can hold our heads a little higher today."[19]

The Janata Government

The new government under Morarji Desai ended censorship, restored civil rights and parliamentary immunities, allowed foreign correspondents to return, and repealed the emergency. Officials made themselves accessible to the public. In state elections, opposition parties had time on the state radio, and Desai stated that the government would give up control of radio and television. The press had a field day exposing the malpractices of the emergency. But few malefactors were imprisoned. Indira Gandhi was allowed to stay for months in the official residence; and she, Sanjay, and her ministers remained free pending the outcome of investigations. The enthusiasm for liberties was less than total, however. In 1979, there were between 500 and 1,000 political prisoners, mostly leftists. The government retained some leverage over the press, the apex organizations stayed in place, and the RAW seemed to be a permanent fixture.

Whatever unity the Janata had rested on

[19]*Time*, April 4, 1977, p. 31. See also Anirudha Gupta, *Revolution through Ballot* (New Delhi: Ankur Publishing House, 1977).

the personality of Morarji Desai, a follower of the Mahatma although of authoritarian temperament.[20] Devoted to a somewhat eccentric and very strict diet, Desai was more of a moral crusader than administrator or party leader. The Janata movement was an agglomeration of five parties plus a few independents,[21] who agreed on nothing except dislike for Indira Gandhi. They began pulling apart the day after the election. Many of the new rulers were as greedy, ignorant, and corrupt as the acolytes of Gandhi whom they denounced.[22]

The Desai government was more Indian in background; few spoke English easily and none were educated abroad. Its policies were also more Indian. It favored the Hindi language and Vedic medicine. The Janata approach to economic development was Gandhian, decentralization to states and villages and agriculture rather than industry. It proposed that production should be as far as possible in the home, in small industrial plants if necessary, and in large plants only as a last resort.[23] Industry should be labor-intensive, and large industry producing consumer goods should not be expanded. Hundreds of articles were to be made only in rural areas, in hopes of slowing if not stopping the human tide moving to the cities. The vasectomy program was abandoned.

Whatever the merits of such policies, the incoherent Janata government seemed incapable of action. Little was actually done for the peasants. Disorders, repressed under the emergency, became chronic—strikes, Hindu-Muslim clashes, and student riots. In July 1979 Desai had to call on the army to quell disturbances. Crime surged, and black markets and smuggling thrived. Inflation swelled, and the government could not meet wage demands. The Emergency years became the good old times.[24]

In the face of mounting discontent, Janata disintegrated. It was never able to develop any real organization, and it could not formulate any generally acceptable programs. Many were alienated by the Hinduist tendencies of the leadership. There were defections and splits and totally unprincipled alliances and maneuverings, in a parody of parliamentary democracy. Desai quarreled violently with the second man in the coalition, Charan Singh, ostensibly over the alleged misdeeds of Desai's son Kantilal. Factions battled, confident they no longer had to fear Indira Gandhi.

Gandhi, however, remained very much a force for reckoning. A few months after her defeat, she returned boldly to politics, split the Congress organization again, and set about rebuilding her political machine and popular following. Her party won several local victories in 1978, and she was returned to parliament. The investigations of alleged abuses during the emergency limped along.

With the help of Gandhi and her seventy-two deputies, Charan Singh, leader of the Lok Dal, brought down the Janata government. He replaced Desai as prime minister; but Gandhi, having helped him against Desai, was not prepared to support him in office. No one could muster a majority in the Lok Sabha, so President Sanjiva Reddy dissolved the parliament and elections were scheduled for the first days of 1980.

[20]As appears in his autobiography, *The Story of My Life* (Delhi: Macmillan, 1974).

[21]C. P. Bhambhri, *The Janata Party: A Profile* (New Delhi: National Publishing House, 1980), p. 1.

[22]Ved Mehta, *A Family Affair: India through Three Prime Ministers* (New York: Oxford University Press, 1982), p. 52.

[23]*New York Times*, October 30, 1977, p. E-3.

[24]Balraj Madhok, *Stormy Decade* (Delhi: India Book Gallery, 1980), pp. 217–218.

Return of Indira Gandhi

In the ensuing campaign, the chief contenders were Jagjivan Ram, heading what remained of the Janata after the withdrawal of Desai; Charan Singh, representing his basically lower-middle-class Lok Dal party; and Indira Gandhi, leader of Congress I (for "Indira"). Two Communist parties, the South Indian Dravidian party and the Sikh party, were also in the running, together with many hundred independent candidates. Gandhi, speaking to as many as ten rallies per day, made no apologies for her period of authoritarian rule but promised a return to order and prosperity. The press, having apparently forgotten censorship, seemed inclined to welcome her back. Opposition parties mostly played up the abuses of Gandhi's emergency with no program of their own.

From the beginning it was evident that Gandhi was in the lead, and enthusiasm for her seemed to grow as she stood out for forcefulness despite the fact that she had no particular program or philosophy beyond love of the people. Politicians hastened to support her as soon as it seemed she might win: there was a rush for certificates attesting to imprisonment in Janata times. The masses were apparently weary of instability and hopeful that restoration of firm government would bring economic improvement.

The magnitude of Gandhi's victory, however, was quite as startling as that of her defeat less than three years earlier. She won 350 seats in the Lok Sabha, a two-thirds majority enabling her to amend the constitution without the need for allies. Her party's share of the popular vote went back up to 43 percent, about the same that the Congress had received in the old days; most of the huge swing in seats came from the complete fragmentation of the opposition. No other party received the fifty seats necessary to form a recognized parliamentary opposition. The Lok Dal won forty-five; the CP(M), thirty-five; Janata was humbled with thirty-one. Two-thirds of the new Lok Sabha were picked by Sanjay.

Gandhi named a cabinet of mostly new faces, drawn from her faithful supporters, in contrast to the factionalism of the Janata regime. She consolidated Congress I control of state governments. Three state legislatures changed allegiance, as politicians sought to save their jobs. Those of nine others were dissolved, following the precedent set by Desai in 1977. Elections then completed Congress control except for regions of Communist strength, Tamilnadu, Kerala, and West Bengal.

A major setback was the loss of the new general secretary of the Congress party, chief lieutenant and heir-apparent, Sanjay, in a stunt plane crash in June. There was an orgy of adulation for the young deceased, but Sanjay's group was ignored after his departure. For some months, Indira Gandhi was semiparalyzed with grief. However, she turned to her older son Rajiv, who seemed to have been happy to be an airline pilot. Pressed to go into politics, he became his mother's aide; and in 1981, aged thirty-six, he ran for Sanjay's vacant seat and assumed the leadership of Sanjay's youth organization. In February 1983 he was named one of four general secretaries of the party, and it was assumed that he would carry on the Nehru dynasty in India's unique melding of monarchy and democracy. Maneka, Sanjay's widow, tried to claim the succession for her infant son, but this led only to an angry break with Indira Gandhi. In 1983 Maneka launched a new party, the National Sanjay Forum, several of whose candidates were victorious in state elections.[25]

[25]*New York Times*, March 27, 1983, p. 6.

The Congress I party seemed to be nothing but a personal following with no idea or direction but the will of the aging leader (born 1917). Seared by the defections of 1977, Gandhi wanted no strong characters around her, made loyalty the chief virtue, and allowed no dissent. The old popularity of the Congress and its penetrating organization seemed to have been largely lost, as Gandhi lost touch with her political base. Corruption rose to new height and breadth.[26]

Perhaps because the opposition was ineffective, or because Sanjay was replaced by the easy-going Rajiv, Gandhi showed no inclination to return to a dictatorship. There was no atmosphere of fear, and the press was critical. However, again she was sometimes called a goddess, and she secured a new preventive detention law, permitting anyone to be jailed (with certain judicial safeguards) for a year without trial for "acting in a manner prejudicial to India." The government was also empowered to ban strikes. Thus Gandhi arrested 6,000 union leaders before a threatened strike and 20,000 more as the strike began.[27]

Gandhi claimed, in effect, that India was not to be governed democratically. The country was torn by multiple conflicts—between higher castes and Harijans, between Muslims (12 percent of the population) and Hindus, and among ethnic groups. The Assamese massacred Bengali immigrants, and the warlike Sikhs demanded self-rule. Indian democracy lumbered forward, however. State elections in January 1983 left the Congress I in control of only fifteen of twenty-two states, but people did not seem generally to translate dissatisfaction with conditions into dislike of Indira Gandhi. Chandra Shekhar

of Janata formed a coalition of five opposition groups to fight the next general election, but its unity was fragile.

INDIAN DEMOCRACY

Problems

Events of 1975–1981 showed the weakness of Indian democracy. It is a flower in the desert, apparently too fragile for its harsh environment, that nevertheless clings to life. India utterly defies the well-known correlation between democratic government and modernization, standard of living, and education. Illiteracy of adults is in the range of 70 percent, and only about 2 percent of Indians are literate in the principal language of administration, English. Most children enroll at some time in primary school, but less than 30 percent finish fifth grade; at the present rate illiteracy will not be reduced below 50 percent in fewer than thirty years. Higher education is not much more promising, although a relatively large proportion of the relevant age group (about 8 percent, compared to 1 percent in China) attend. Standards have declined markedly since independence, and few graduates acquire productive skills. Students in Bihar went on strike for the right to cheat on examinations, and won.[28] Student unrest is chronic, and the graduates are natural recruits for antidemocratic movements. Huge universities with dull curricula, mechanical learning, and unresponsive administration create a class of unhappy, frequently unemployed young people, made superior beings by their diplomas and knowledge of English.

Half the population is below what Indians consider a bare subsistence level, and there has been little visible improvement in the

[26]Ved Mehta, "Letter from New Delhi," *New Yorker,* August 3, 1981, p. 52.
[27]*Newsweek,* February 1982, p. 49.

[28]*Los Angeles Times,* January 17, 1982, p. 8.

decades since independence. Grain production, vulnerable to the fluctuations of the monsoon, has barely kept pace with population, and other crops have declined. Unhappily, this cannot be reckoned as part of the price of industrial growth, which has also been poor. In 1950, India was the twelfth worldwide in industry; in 1983, twenty-second; in exports, India dropped from nineteenth to forty-sixth place.[29]

Urban problems have become ever graver. Multitudes stream in from the countryside and overwhelm facilities, yet large-scale industry can employ only 5 percent of the labor force. Unemployment is high. If South American slums are eyesores, Indian slums are cesspools. Inequality is enormous and has worsened since independence.[30] The very wealthy of India are wealthy by anyone's standards; they live behind guarded walls in polished elegance, oblivious to the starvation beyond their gates. Swank hotels are built by men who sleep among the bricks, and some people pay $100 or more for theater tickets while landlords disregard the legal minimum wage of eighty cents per day.

The governmental apparatus is inefficient, top-heavy, self-seeking, and corrupt. About half the organized nonagricultural workforce is employed by the state, most of it without benefit to the public; rolls expand because of the infinite need for jobs and the desire of those in authority to help their extended families, friends, and caste brothers. Management is so inefficient that electric output is less than half of capacity despite chronic shortage.[31]

Paperwork is so slow that a year may be required for a noncontroversial import permit and four years for the license necessary to start a new business. Baksheesh is the rule

in relations between officials and the public or business.[32] The commonest form is a tip to expedite action; if a paper has to be signed by a bureaucrat, his signature is valuable and should be compensated. Much minor corruption is relatively harmless, but bribery enters into the awarding of contracts and their fulfillment, the issuance of licenses, and the collection or noncollection of taxes. Jobs are for sale. Family connections are everything, and nepotism is sanctioned by caste and custom.

Opportunities for corruption are multiplied by a heavy web of regulation and cumbersome controls. Industrial establishments must be licensed and are subject to endless regulation by various committees and ministries.[33] On the other hand, government licenses are almost patents of monopoly for inefficient producers. It is the general assumption that private enterprise is unscrupulous and hence must be regulated by the state, no matter how incompetent or corrupt the latter, whereas the need to cope with state controls requires business to be unscrupulous.

An essential part of democracy is the structure of interest groups through which people interact with the state. In India these are few and weak. There are some 3 million trade union members among 21 million employees of firms or government. The trade unions are militant and often violent; but they are fragmented, unrealistic, and ineffective and are frequently led by politically ambitious outsiders from the middle classes.[34] Business and agricultural interests are weakly organized or not at all. Most modern business and industry are owned by members of

[29]*Los Angeles Times*, May 30, 1983, p. 8.
[30]Masani, *Indira Gandhi*, p. 305.
[31]Ibid., January 10, 1982, p. 12.
[32]See Ronald Segal, *The Crisis of India* (London: Jonathan Cape, 1965), chap. 6.
[33]Stanley A. Kochanek, *Business and Politics in India* (Berkeley: University of California Press, 1974), p. 81.
[34]Hardgrave, *India*, p. 133.

the traditional trading communities, such as Jains and Parsis, and are regarded with a traditional dislike. The most effective interest groups (aside from castes) are landowner associations. The chief political means of the masses, and the only one to which the government has been attentive in the past, is the semiviolent mass campaign. The Indians have specialized in mass protest from the Mahatma's time—processions, road blocking, gherao, sitdowns, hunger strikes, and showdowns. The Indian administration in principle distrusts interest groups as narrow, selfish, obstructive, and contrary to good administrative order.[35] The common public attitude, on the other hand, is to avoid contact with the government.

Political parties function less as representatives of popular interests than as cliques of job seekers, the hangers-on around the chief. The older elite, trained to democratic government, has given way to less-educated and unprincipled manipulators. Loyalties are thin; delegates reportedly switch parties readily for a modest sum of money, and leaders are discredited by defections. Indira Gandhi remains the only leader with a national following across class, caste, and regional lines. The government revolves around her, and it is assumed that her offspring will follow her. India has been governed by the Nehru family for all but four of the years since independence, and the brief, unhappy Janata years did not encourage the belief that there was any alternative.[36]

In the atmosphere of corruption, bureaucratization, inequality, oppression, and senseless conflicts, the ideals of the Mahatma of nonviolence, hand industry, and spiritual fulfillment have withered to a cliché.

Conditions of Democracy

Amid growing disorder, there are calls for authoritarianism. Some say that Indian democracy is of and for the upper classes, while radicals have called for economic change impossible within a constitutional order.[37] Yet India has continued, for all its difficulties, to be almost uniquely democratic (along with Sri Lanka) in the immense Afro-Asian world, with a considerable degree of freedom, legality, and constitutional political process, only briefly infringed by the emergency.

In large part, this persistance may have been possible because of the unique Indian religious and social system. Nowhere else (except in Sri Lanka) is there anything really comparable, and in India it pervades everything, even reaching from its Hindu base into the Muslim and Christian communities. It is easy to conclude that Hinduism and its mentality are deeply antidemocratic. It bespeaks withdrawal, passivity, and self-centered spirituality rather than engagement in the community; the Hindu is responsible only to oneself in the ascent to salvation.[38] Yet the patience and tolerance of Hinduism are probably favorable for democracy, as is the nonconformism of the Hindu ethos.

Caste is also ambivalent. It consecrates hereditary inequality and hierarchy; nearly everyone has superiors and inferiors by birth. Castes give security when life offers little, but they isolate people within their particular occupational and marriage groups; there is little need for Indians to concern themselves with persons of other castes. Caste divisions can be barriers to modernization and cooperative action; for example, an irrigation ditch may be held up by the irreconcil-

---

[35]Ibid., p. 115.
[36]Madhok, *Stormy Decade*, p. 218.

[37]Frankel, *India's Political Economy*, p. 435.
[38]V. S. Naipaul, *India: A Wounded Civilization* (New York: Knopf, 1977), p. 116.

able claims of various castes. Politics at the local level turns from issues to bargaining among castes and the formation of caste alliances, which upon victory claim their spoils in favors and jobs.

However, castes provide a basis for the organization of parties at the lower levels, and much of democratic politics centers on caste issues. Castes teach democracy in that they are commonly organized on basically democratic principles; the ideas of discussion, consent, and popular choice of leaders are not strange to the Indian villagers. Peasants in remote villages react well to arguments about civil liberties, fundamental rights, and the independence of judges.[39]

The caste, binding a group in a close and well-understood body under the guidance of the elders, gives individuals a focus of action and a means of interaction with the state. India is poorly endowed with interest groups of the conventional Western type, but castes take their place and help structure the population. Party lines cut across castes, as they cut across occupations in other democratic countries. Political parties cannot afford to identify with any one caste because no single caste approaches a majority. But castes, and particularly the caste associations formed expressly for political purposes, are an important means of integrating the masses, especially those who are illiterate, into the democratic process.[40] Caste associations work to get members elected and seek not domination but advantages within the democratic framework; they make the democratic process meaningful for their members. The states are the prime arena of action, because

caste influence is limited by linguistic boundaries.

The fact that caste consecrates inequality is antidemocratic in the usual sense, but it tends to moderate the demands of the masses. The elite, sure of its position, is less fearful of democracy than in many African and Latin American countries. Caste moderates demands; the lower classes do not unite to clamor for radical change.[41] There is room for bargaining and accommodation; there is also a system of accepted rights and duties that favors orderly government, which in the contemporary context means democratic government. The mentality of caste professionalism probably deters generals from entering politics and stiffens judges' resistance to dictation.

History has also been propitious for Indian democracy. Thanks to long British rule, the party system was institutionalized before independence, and a British-educated elite set the democratic system in place and presided over it until parliamentary government was well established. The impartial court system was also a British gift, vital for the preservation of a constitution. The legal profession, in India as elsewhere, has a strong interest in the democratic system.[42] Such personalities as Nehru and Gandhi, who drew values from their British educations, gave India a good start on the democratic road. Democracy inspired the independence movement.

India entered independence with a relatively large number of well-educated persons to staff the new state. Many of them were civil servants, and the nonpolitical civil service, with entrance by impartial examination, tenure, and esprit de corps, has been

[39]Frankel, *India's Political Economy*, p. 576.
[40]L. J. Rudolph and S. H. Rudolph, "The Political Role of India's Caste Associations," in Eric Nordlinger, ed., *Politics and Society* (Englewood Cliffs, N.J.: Prentice-Hall, 1969), pp. 254–258.

[41]Frankel, *India's Political Economy*, p. 577.
[42]*New York Times*, June 14, 1977, p. 2.

a mainstay of the legal order. The civil service may be stiff and haughty, authoritarian in dealings with the people,[43] but it is legalistic and opposed to arbitrary action. It has maintained its own integrity, and any government needs its cooperation. Because of its standing, the ruling party, whatever its majority in parliament, cannot control the counting of votes.

The armed forces of India are exceptional by Third World standards for political neutrality—a noninvolvement contrasting with the domination of the military in Pakistan. The British tradition of nonpolitical professionalism has been maintained, and there was no apparent inclination to intervene even in the various wars and emergencies; the command, moreover, is regionally divided to make extralegal action more difficult. Only in the time of the emergency of Indira Gandhi were there rumors of possible military intervention.

However the causes may be weighed, democratic engagement has been high since multitudes joined Mahatma Gandhi's campaigns, and popular pressures have brought down many state governments. Illiterates are eager to mark the preferred symbol on their ballots. Campaigns are lively and colorful, and the villagers are aware of the possibility of changing something by their vote. The villages have been politicized by the panchayats, with a consequent increase of turnout in the countryside. Elections are orderly, and the results are accepted with little protest.

It is sometimes said that democracy is of no value for the poor, but the poor of India are well aware that their numbers count. The vote is the chief power the poor possess against wealth and position. It gives strength to castes in proportion not to their standing but to their numbers; upper castes have to solicit the support of lower classes and Harijans. Political rights have meaning, especially when they are taken away. As an old peasant said before the crucial elections of March 1977: "Just because a man is poor and maybe cannot read does not mean that he cares nothing for his human rights. The Congress Government has tried to shut my mouth this last year and one-half, and therefore the Congress loses my vote."[44]

The Outlook

It may be that the democratic experiment cannot progress. But India is not changeless. The village has a schoolhouse, transistor radios, and perhaps a cinema or a communal television. It sells its produce, buys some manufactures, and participates in government development programs. It cannot be like the isolated village of the past. The country is fueled not only by cow dung but also by uranium. Astrology is as strong as ever, but India has the world's third largest pool of trained scientific personnel. Many laws and programs favor Harijans, and they are increasingly aware of their rights. The status of women is improving steadily. Divorce and abortion have been made easier, and the dowry and child marriage are decreasing. The literacy rate of women is rising more rapidly than that of men, and the few who manage to get a higher education are entering professions. Although India added 15 million mouths in 1982, the rate of population growth has slowed somewhat, despite the recent setback to family planning programs. Life expectancy increased from thirty-three years in 1947 to fifty-two in 1981.

Yet economic performance has been me-

---

[43]Walter L. Weisberg, "Determinants of Indian Politics," in *Dynamics of the Third World: Political and Social Change*, Charles Schmitt, ed. (Cambridge, Mass.: Winthrop Publishers, 1974), pp. 56–57.

[44]*New York Times*, March 3, 1977.

diocre, as industry has failed to keep pace with the world in either quantity or quality. Efficiency is far away; to place a local telephone call in Calcutta takes an average of thirty-three minutes.[45] Agriculture remains miserably backward; each farmer feeds two people on $1\frac{1}{3}$ acres of cropland. Although grain production has tripled since independence, per capita caloric consumption has dropped slightly.[46] However, Indian farmers are fully capable of modern production, as exemplified by the huge and highly successful Anand dairy cooperative.[47]

India may thus be engaged in a race to determine whether modernization and the development of democratic institutions can proceed rapidly enough to offset increasing tensions and the political disorder that has set in with the passing of the generation of the independence movement. If authoritarianism prevails, under the governance of Indira Gandhi or some other leader, or the military establishment finally moves to assert itself, it cannot be expected to function better than in most Third World dictatorships. On the other hand, India has open political processes and an informative press, which makes a scandal of abuses such as payoffs to a government more or less responsible to its citizens. India may conceivably find ways to the future within the framework of its pluralistic society. If so, it will be of the utmost importance for the majority of humankind.

---

[45]*Los Angeles Times,* May 30, 1983, p. 8.

[46]Marcus Frande, *India's Rural Development* (Bloomington: Indiana University Press, 1979), pp. 55–63.

[47]Ibid.

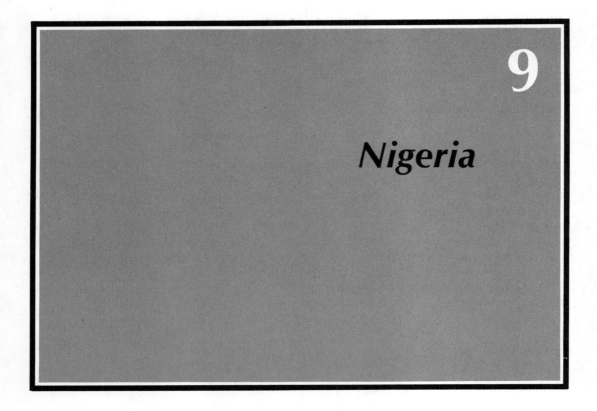

9

Nigeria

Although India has upheld its democratic-constitutional order through almost the entirety of its independent existence, Nigeria has twice shifted from democratic to military government. Since becoming independent in 1960, it has been ten years under civilian rule; during this time it was the outstanding democracy of Africa. Changes have had something to do with economics. The successful restoration of democracy in 1979 owed much to oil wealth, and misery brought by reduced revenues provoked the generals to foreclose democracy at the end of 1983. Nigeria is thus more typical of Third World politics than India, although Nigeria is much more democratically inclined than most African states and more like the Latin American republics that swing irregularly between democracy and dictatorship.

Although Sudan and Zaire exceed it in size, Nigeria is big, substantially larger than Texas. Having very roughly 100 million inhabitants (there has never been a good or generally accepted census), it is by far the most populous country of Africa, with a quarter of the people of the continent. It regards itself as Africa's natural leader, and its statesmen have been active in African causes, especially opposition to white rule in southern Africa. The Nigerian claim to leadership is strengthened by economic power. Until recently it was a very poor country, with a per capita GNP estimated at $73 as late as 1964–1965. In the 1970s, however, oil production rose rapidly and incomes leaped tenfold, only to fall back as the petroleum scarcity gave way to a glut. Nigeria is still a basically poor country with some expensive modern ornaments, less stable and less capable of feeding itself than before the golden tide came over it.

The unity of Nigeria derived originally

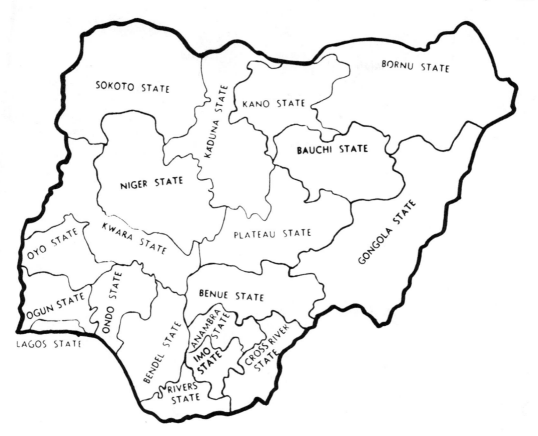

only from the framework set up by the British colonial administration. Like other countries of black Africa, it is an ethnic patchwork of more than 200 tribes. English, the official and unifying language, is the native tongue of a minuscule minority. Three principal groups comprise over half the total population: the Hausa-Fulani in the semidesert North are the most numerous; the Yoruba dominate part of the southern coastal region; and the Ibo, the southeastern area. Many other peoples are scattered between and around these three, especially in a middle belt between the North and South.

The basic split is between North and South, which are not only inhabited by distinct groups but also have different cultures and climates. The North, where scrublands merge into the bleak Sahara, is pastoral and agricultural. It is Muslim in religion and culture, having been converted to Islam between the twelfth and sixteenth centuries. It is conservative, hierarchic, and relatively little changed by modernization. In the South, excessive rainfall generates dense, unhealthy forests. The peoples of the South, because of more receptive cultures and more contact with Europeans, are more educated, largely Christianized, more affected by Western ways, and more open to change. In the North, women are still kept in seclusion and polygamy still prevails; the women of the South own and operate most of the shops and booths in the bazaars. Northerners have long been

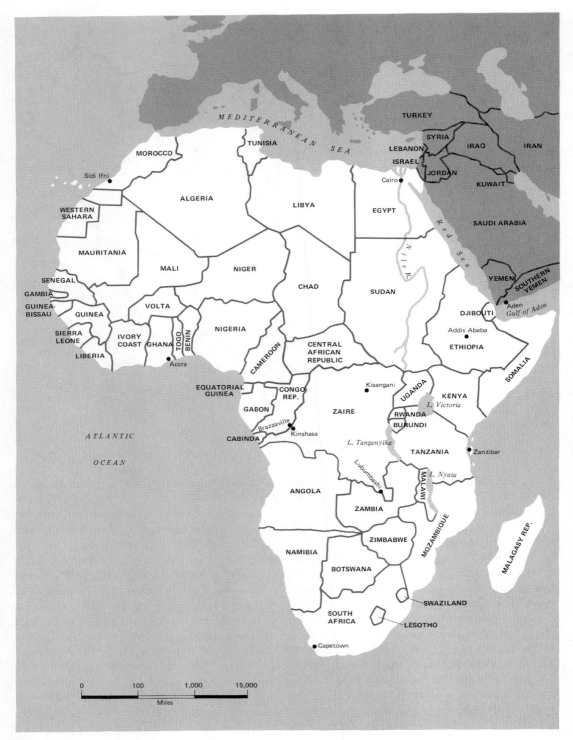

afraid that the Southerners (especially the Ibo) would dominate and exploit them because of their superior education and skills; the Southerners (especially the Ibo) were afraid that the cruder Northerners would crush them by weight of numbers. This was the chief reason for the failure of Nigeria's democratic constitutional federal system in 1966 and for the ensuing civil war.

THE COLONIAL BACKGROUND

Nigeria, along with Ghana (formerly the British West African colony, the Gold Coast), seemed exceptionally well prepared for self-government upon achieving independence on October 1, 1960. Thanks to British education there was, by African standards, a relatively large number of persons capable of staffing the new government. And because British rule had long been mostly indirect, Nigerians had considerable experience in handling their own affairs.

In the seventeenth and eighteenth centuries, the region that became Nigeria was a major center of the slave trade. In the nineteenth century, the British government moved to halt the slave trade, and British merchants increasingly penetrated West Africa. They called on their government for protection when they came into conflict with local potentates, and protection evolved into domination. The British presence began with the annexation of Lagos, the principal port and present capital, in 1861. British power, exercised by a trading company, was extended over the numerous emirates, kingdoms, and tribal states through the following decades, gradually developing into a settled colonial administration in the 1890s.

The British were rather reluctant colonialists, and they asserted ownership to a large extent because of rivalry with the French and the Germans. In 1900 the British government assumed the company holdings and established three protectorates, corresponding to the Northern, Western, and Eastern regions. These were partially amalgamated into a single Nigerian entity in 1914, but it was British policy to rule as much as possible through traditional authorities, and the colonial political structure was never centralized. In deference to the Muslims, Christian mission schools were excluded from the North; as a result, fewer northerners learned the English necessary to qualify them for civil service positions, and the relative backwardness of the North was accentuated.

As in most of Africa, the colonial experience was too brief to work fundamental changes in Nigerian society. However, the development of communications, transportation, education, and government proceeded rapidly after 1918. The British built roads and railways—to bring the groundnuts of the north and the palm seeds of the south to market—and schools to train administrators. Europeans were not allowed to own plantations, so no white settler class like that of East Africa developed. Nigerians acquired some familiarity with the ways and ideas of the colonizers and began to criticize the colonial administration and seek more rights. World War I was educational for the Nigerian soldiers who served alongside Europeans, and there was scattered political agitation from 1918 on. Ethnic associations began to lobby for roads and schools for their districts, and discontent gradually matured into a call for independence. The Nigerian National Democratic Party was founded in 1923. Nationalist agitation gained strength in the 1930s, and political parties coalesced along ethnic lines in the 1940s, with the Ibo in the lead. The press, quite free under the British, helped to organize the discontent. The leaders of the independence movement from the 1930s on were Nnamdi Azikiwe in the East and Obafemi Awolowo and S. L. Akintola in the West, all of whom became principal figures in the politics of independent Nigeria.

World War II carried forward the educational work of World War I, as Nigerian troops fought against Europeans in the name of freedom and gained a sense of nationhood in the process. The British bowed to the gathering pressure and step by step yielded power—first local, then regional, and finally national. A partly elected council had been instituted in 1922, but progress was slow until after World War II. From 1945 to 1960 there were five constitutions, with the South, as usual, leading the North. Unlike other African countries, Nigeria had no single independence movement to dominate the new state. From the first national elections in 1954, each region had its own dominant party, which endured until military rule preempted civilian politics in 1966. The 1954 constitution, which was largely the work of Nigerians, was truly federal, granting restricted powers to the central government. The regional bureaucracies were stronger than the federal, and top figures in the respective parties mostly remained in regional capitals, delegating lieutenants to act for them within the federal government.

By 1957 a Nigerian federal prime minister was installed under a parliamentary system copied after the British, with a governor-general taking the place of the monarch. After the general elections of 1959, the North held a majority of seats in the Federal House (elected on the basis of population), 173 of 312 seats. An indirectly elected Senate with restricted powers was expected to protect the interests of the smaller regions. In the regions, similar parliamentary-style governments ruled, with British and later Nigerian regional governors as "heads of state." These officials became figureheads during the 1950s. Independence came with minimal friction and maximal hope under a constitution based on that of 1954. On October 1, 1960, Azikiwe became the first Nigerian head of state as governor-general.

FROM DEMOCRACY TO MILITARY RULE

Independence: Disappointed Hopes

Nigeria's transition to independence was perhaps the best prepared of all the new African states. The government was parliamentary both at the center and in each of the three regions (a fourth, the Midwest, was carved out in 1963). Political power resided mostly in the regions, each strongly dominated (to the extent of perhaps 90 percent of the seats in the assembly) by a regional party: in the North, the Northern People's Congress, headed by the Sardauna of Sokoto, Ahmadu Bello, and Abubakar Tafawa Balewa, who became federal prime minister; in the West, the Action Group, headed by Awolowo and Akintola; in the East, the National Council of Nigeria and the Cameroons, representing the Ibo. Each party, however, tried to develop a minority following in other regions. The federal government, a shaky coalition, was relatively weak despite extensive enumerated powers and the right of intervention in the regions in case of emergency. The administration was almost entirely in the hands of the civil service; only the top man (the "commissioner") was a politician.

Regional governments were also parliamentary in form, with an elected House or Assembly, an upper House of Chiefs to check it, and premier and ministers. Below the regional level, some localities were governed by hereditary chiefs, some by more or less elected councils. At the base, villages had hereditary heads, sometimes with elected councils, to collect the head tax and the cattle tax, settle disputes, repair roads and wells, and represent the people to the local authority and the local authority to the people.

In the early 1960s, Nigerians seemed to be politically involved, moved by aspirations and fears for their country perhaps more strongly than, for example, Brazilians or Indians. But strains on the constitutional structure grew rapidly after independence, which brought little of the expected prosperity. Party cadres, having gained independence, seemed to want only to enjoy the fruits of office. The private interest groups that seem to be essential as intermediaries between people and government in a democracy were virtually lacking. Farmers were unorganized; trade unions were weak, divided, and ineffective. Business interests were for the most part foreign-owned and staffed at the upper levels. Nearly three-quarters of the capital of firms worth over $70,000 was foreign, half being British; and nearly all banks were foreign.[1] The most powerful interest group was the bureaucratic apparatus itself; government consequently served to a large extent as a means of extracting revenues for the benefit of officeholders. Under cover of democracy, it might be said that the feudalists of the North with the politicians of the West organized a "kleptocracy," or rule of theft, in Andreski's term. Nigeria became a model of the failure of a well-structured Third World democracy, although political decay came not from the excessive expectations of the masses but from misbehavior at the top.

The chief cause of tension was the conflict between the North (Hausa-Fulani) and the East (Ibo); the West (Yoruba) held an intermediate position. The three chief components were too few for workable federalism; they were also too unequal, both in culture and in population. The Hausa-Fulani, a plurality of the population, could theoretically dominate the federation, although the dissidence of smaller peoples in the middle belt

between North and South reduced their influence. English, a necessary means of communication, was far more widely taught in the South than in the North, and the inequality of general education promised to continue the disparity. As late as 1966, when 62 percent of the children of the Eastern (Ibo) Region were in primary school, in the North only 8 percent were enrolled, despite ambitious programs for expanding primary education.[2] Ibo society, moreover, was relatively adaptable and receptive to modernization, whereas Northerners were more traditional. Educated Ibo with modern ideas, unable to find adequate employment in their own region, drifted to the West and North, where their superior attitude caused them to be warmly disliked. There was no satisfactory sharing of power between the more educated and the more numerous, and a quota system giving Northerners half of all civil service appointments after independence (they had only 1 percent in 1960) seemed unjust to the Ibo. Modernization and education over the previous decades had intensified rather than moderated antagonisms.

In 1962, the basic ethnic conflict took on an ideological flavor as one party, the Action Group, took up African socialism. It sought to eliminate what were seen as remnants of colonialism in order to promote a different, African, and anticapitalist social order. Awolowo, the first important agitator for independence, took the lead, making an issue of the defense pact signed with Britain in 1960; through his efforts, it was abrogated in 1962. The Action Group in the Western Region then split, because Akintola wanted to form an alliance with the conservative Northern Peoples Congress, and Awolowo, who favored a socialistic program, was opposed. Awolowo secured a majority in the assembly and tried to remove Akintola from the pre-

---

[1]E. Wayne Nafziger, *African Capitalism: A Case Study in Nigerian Entrepreneurship* (Stanford, Calif.: Hoover Institution Press, 1977), p. 56.

[2]John M. Ostheimer, *Nigerian Politics* (New York: Harper & Row, 1973), p. 155.

miership. Violence was followed by federal intervention, and Awolowo was tried for treason and sentenced to ten years' imprisonment. The trial revealed enormous government corruption and generated widespread disillusionment with democratic politics.

The difficulty of managing the country constitutionally was shown by what should have been only a technical problem, the taking of a census. A 1962 census surprisingly showed a majority of the population to be in the South (the Eastern and Western Regions). In view of the protests of the North, it was set aside, and a recount in 1963 gave the North a substantial majority. With the acquiescence of the West and over the objections of the East, this census was used as a basis for representation in parliament. In this somewhat confused situation, opposing coalitions conducted a bitter campaign in the 1964–1965 elections. The dominant party of the East led a coalition against the parties dominant in the federal government, the principal Northern party and its Western allies. Claiming harassment, the Eastern opposition called for a boycott, hoping that President Azikiwe, an Ibo, would postpone the elections. But the prime minister refused and was supported by both the Chief Justice and high military authorities. The elections were held, but they were clouded by bribery and terrorism.[3]

Disorder was growing. A rebellion of the Tiv, a middle-belt people, in 1964 cost thousands of lives. Most of Nigeria's urban workers went on strike in a mass protest against inflation and corruption, while politics seemed to have degenerated into a ruthless battle of ethnic groups for public revenues.

Coup and Civil War

The army had been politicized by the re-

[3]John Hatch, *Nigeria: A History* (London: Secker and Warburg, 1971), pp. 228–229.

placement of British officers with Nigerians, mostly Ibo. The Nigerian military had been taught civilian supremacy in the British tradition, but they saw the civilian government as corrupt, cynical, and disposed to use force illegally, as in the 1962 intervention in the West and in the electoral crisis of 1964–1965. They were also encouraged to act by a series of military coups in 1965—in Algeria, Dahomey (Benin), the Central African Republic (called Empire) and Upper Volta—that began the trend to military rule in Africa.

On January 15, 1966, Ibo junior officers attempted a coup, killing federal Prime Minister Balewa, Northern Premier Bello, Western Premier Akintola, and a few Northern army officers. They seem to have been motivated by fear that the federal authorities were planning to use the army to support the discredited Akintola regime and to eliminate Ibo opposition. The conspirators supported the imprisoned Awolowo; they wanted to establish a socialist state and end the domination of the federal regime by the Northerners.

Because of disillusionment with the civilian government, the coup was not unpopular, and non-Ibos were generally willing to follow their Ibo officers. But it failed in the capital, Lagos, where Commanding General and Chief of Staff J. Aguiyi-Ironsi made himself supreme commander. The rebels gave up, and Ironsi was welcomed as the bringer of order. As an Ibo, however, he soon caused apprehension about Ibo domination. He relied mostly on Ibo for advice, worked to centralize the government, and in May 1966 decreed a unitary state and a unified civil service in which Ibo could claim jobs everywhere on the basis of their education. Riots in the North against the proposed new unitary constitution turned into a pogrom in which thousands of Ibo were killed. There was talk of secession. Tension grew and rumors spread, until in July a countercoup killed Ironsi and a number of other Ibo officers. In the disorders, Lieutenant Colonel Yakubu Gowon, from a minority tribe, emerged as the leading commander.

Gowon promised to return to a federal structure and civilian rule. But the conflict of the Ibo against the Northerners was not resolved. In September–October 1966, Hausa-Fulani took the establishment of the new regime as authorization to attack the Ibo; in a second and much more terrible wave of massacres, some 30,000 Ibo were slaughtered in the Northern Region. Over a million Ibo fled back to their native territories from the North and West; no longer seeing any point to the federation, they pushed for independence.

For several months there was near chaos, as the military forces fell apart. Troops returned to their native regions, leaving the federal police responsible for holding the country together. Federal authority ceased to exist in the Eastern Region after October 1966. The Eastern military leader, Colonel Odumegwu Ojukwu, saw no reason to submit to the authority of Gowon, who had been installed by no one but himself. There were a few months of negotiations, during which federal leaders made far-reaching concessions to the East. Ojukwu, however, refused all compromise; the East declared its independence as the Republic of Biafra on May 30, 1967.

The hope of the Ibo was to gain the support of the West against the North. The West, however, opted for the federal side because Northern leaders agreed to give Awolowo, now released from prison, a prominent place in the central government and also to defuse the North-South issue by dividing the old regions into twelve states, six of them carved from the Northern Region. This move was made possible by the desire of the northern emirs for autonomy. It also represented a concession to the smaller tribes of the North, which had been slighted in the tripartite division. If this step had been taken sooner, Nigerian federalism might have been more viable.

Fighting began in July 1967. The federal government had an enormous superiority of manpower and resources; it also had the advantages of legitimacy; international recognition; and aid from Britain, the United States, and the Soviet Union. The Biafrans had better morale as defenders of their homeland. Most other African countries opposed their attempt at secession because of fears for the unity of their own ethnically divided states. Biafra was kept alive after the summer of 1968 mostly by a trickle of aid from France. But the blockade by the federal forces was decisive. Biafra was choked for lack of munitions, and millions starved until its last centers were occupied in January 1970.[4]

Military Government

General Gowon was as unvindictive in victory as he had been in the conduct of the war. The Ibo were permitted to return to public life without further punishment and rather soon regained most of their former standing, although for several years they remained almost completely excluded from top levels of government. War damage was rapidly repaired as oil revenues began pouring in. The war settled the secessionist issue. Nigerian integrity is no longer in question, and the new elite adhered to "one Nigeria."

Gowon promised a return to civilian government by 1976, but it was much more difficult to terminate than to institute military rule. Not only were there fears of new disorders and a reluctance on the part of the generals to surrender power, but the army was unmanageable. Before the civil war it

[4]On the civil war, see A. H. M. Kirk-Greene, *Crisis and Conflict in Nigeria: A Documentary Sourcebook, 1966–69,* 2 vols. (London: Oxford University Press, 1971).

had been small for the size of the country—518 officers and 10,500 enlisted men in January 1966.[5] It emerged huge and powerful, about 250,000 men, a force capable of overriding all political interests. Its power was reinforced by control of public revenues, mostly from petroleum export. The general assumption was that there should be a return to civilian government after the end of the war. But the soldiers, whose minimum pay was eight times the per capita income, had no desire to be demobilized; and the government saw no point in creating a pool of bitter ex-soldiers. Only those who found acceptable civilian jobs were released, and demobilization brought the armed forces only down to 210,000 by the beginning of 1979. The army consequently was the overwhelmingly dominant pressure group.

Politicians were removed from power after 1966, but the military authorities did not undertake to administer the country themselves.[6] Chiefs recovered some of their previous powers. More important, the coup shifted power to the bureaucracy, which was largely relieved of the pressures of parties and to some extent those of interest groups.[7] After 1966 the heads of ministries were civil servants, replacing politicians as decision makers below the supreme military command. Although they had no autonomy, the new states served as useful administrative units, closer to the people and more homogeneous than the old regions. Ethnic groups other than the Ibo, Yoruba, and Hausa-Fulani played a larger role. Since 1967, the largest number of army troops and officers and most of the leadership have come from the smaller tribes.

[5]Ostheimer, *Nigerian Politics*, p. 119.

[6]For this period, see Oyeleye Oyediran, *Nigerian Government and Politics, 1966–1979* (New York: St. Martins Press, 1979).

[7]Margaret Peil, *Nigerian Politics: The People's View* (London: Cassel, 1976), p. 27.

After the civil war, there was a strong move to reduce foreign participation in the economy. Antiforeign feelings had been aroused during the war; the officers in charge were less associated with foreign business than many of the ousted politicians; and the climate had turned to anti-Westernism in the Third World. Many types of businesses were required to be purely Nigerian-owned by a decree of June 1971, while others had to have at least 40 percent Nigerian equity—a rule that meant easy profits for many Nigerians willing to act as fronts. Not only Europeans (principally the British) but also Near Easterners (mostly Lebanese) were squeezed out. Oil production rose rapidly. Previously generous in its concessions, the government after 1970 began demanding an ever larger proportion of the rapidly growing profits. The government acquired more and more of the producing companies' shares, and oil companies were required to train and promote Nigerians to replace foreigners. By 1971–1972, oil provided the bulk of revenues, giving the nation a capacity unique in black Africa to promote its people's welfare and economic growth. Oil money, however, generated inflation and worsened inequalities.

More than any of his predecessors, Gowon sought to curtail corruption, but it continued to proliferate. The military government gradually lost popularity. Repressive laws played a part: decrees of 1968 and 1969 restricted and then abolished the right to strike, prohibited the publication or broadcasting of anything tending to cause unrest, and gave the police powers of arbitrary detention. Leading journalists were driven away, and the government established an official news service. All radio stations—the chief source of news for the majority of the population—were placed under official control. A 1973 decree gave the authorities the right to ban unions.

Despite these measures, Gowon did not

have a firm grip on the country. Nigeria continued to be sufficiently pluralistic that politics bubbled beneath the surface, and criticism was not long or thoroughly repressible. The press remained among the most outspoken in Africa. Although editors were often arrested, they took on the duty of speaking for the public in the absence of a legislative assembly, even though in some cases their papers were government-owned. They harped on private wealth-seeking in public office, criticism Gowon rightly saw as an attack on the military government and himself. A new census of 1973, which showed an incredible gain for the North, caused skepticism and indignation, because revenues were apportioned to the states largely on a basis of population.

There were other grievances. Congestion in the port of Lagos, caused by overeagerness to spend oil revenues and bureaucratic incompetence, hurt many businesses and caused shortages. Transportation and communications were exasperatingly inefficient. Telephone, electricity, and water services were unreliable at best. There was an embarrassing shortage of petroleum products. An effort to draft students for a term of civil service led to largely successful protests, although a National Youth Service outside one's native state was subsequently implemented. Although subject to repression, unions, especially those of federal and state employees, troubled the government as the only major organized political power aside from the army.[8] A commission's report in September 1974 recommending large wage increases for civil servants set off a wave of slowdowns and strikes by those who saw themselves less favored. Wages were as much as doubled, inflation accelerated, and the unions in and out of government were strengthened.

[8]Victor A. Olorunsola, *Soldiers and Power: The Development Performance of the Nigerian Military Regime* (Stanford, Calif.: Hoover Institution Press, 1977), p. 64.

By 1975, the press was calling for the replacement of the military governors of the states, whose enrichment was notorious but whom Gowon felt unable to remove because they belonged to the top circle of military commanders. In October 1974 Gowon retracted his pledge to restore civilian government by 1976 on the grounds that sectionalism was still too strong. Many people continued to urge new elections, and papers were attacking Gowon by name. Nearly everyone outside the government seemed to be critical of it. It was therefore no surprise when a group of officers headed by General Murtala Muhammad took advantage of Gowon's trip to Uganda to depose him on July 29, 1975, the ninth anniversary of his accession to power. The coup was quiet; Gowon accepted it philosophically and went to England to study political science.

The new regime was headed by a Supreme Military Council composed of officers in their thirties and forties, under the leadership of Muhammad, assisted by a Federal Executive Council and a cabinet of commissioners (ministers). Military governors were installed in the states. Muhammad immediately began a reform program. The civil service was purged and some ten thousand officials lost their jobs, although hardly anyone was prosecuted for malfeasance and many found lucrative new positions. Commissioners and governors were removed, many senior officers were retired, and illegally acquired property was subject to confiscation. These people were replaced by officers directly under Supreme Headquarters and not members of the Supreme Military Council. Seven more states were formed to strengthen the center; the heartlands of the Hausa, Yoruba, and Ibo were split to reduce further the influence of these groups. The 1973 census was canceled, and the government returned to the 1963 census as the basis for allocation of funds to states. To assuage popular dissatisfaction, import duties on many mass consumption items were reduced; and the traditional cattle tax, made obsolete by oil revenues, was abolished.

The reformist activity of the new government was punctuated by an attempted countercoup in February 1976. A few officers managed to kill General Muhammad, but the uprising collapsed because the military oligarchy held together. Gowon's complicity was claimed but not proved. Muhammad, who had not been in power long enough to lose his aura, became a hero figure of the revolution. His second in command, General Olusegun Obasanjo, a Yoruba, became head of state. His chief of staff was Shehu Musa Yar'adua, a Fulani. Rule was not by a strongman but by an oligarchy, including representatives of various ethnic groups. Very little has been divulged concerning the inner workings of his leadership. It was nonideological and relatively mild: criticism in the press was permitted, and the leading universities enjoyed considerable freedom of expression. Traditional and local institutions continued to function.

RETURN TO CIVILIAN RULE

Rarely in Africa has the army relinquished power to civilian authorities. Muhammad, however, restored Gowon's promise of elections and a return to civilian rule and this promise was reaffirmed by Obasanjo for 1979. Although many of the middle-ranking officers enjoyed the advantage of power, the senior generals mostly adhered, at least in theory, to the tradition of military professionalism and civilian political supremacy in which they had been trained by the British. Moreover, running the government was frustrating because officers became involved in political matters for which they were not prepared, and the unity of the armed forces

was strained. More important, however, was the feeling that self-respect required constitutional, elected government. Nigerians wished to prove wrong the South Africans who claimed that blacks were incapable of decent self-government.

The country moved step by step, as carefully planned by the military, toward civilian rule.[9] Debate on a new constitution began in 1976. At the end of that year there were local elections, and in August 1977 a constituent assembly was elected. The new federal constitution abandoned the British model and was patterned rather closely after that of the United States. It provided for a House of Representatives of 430 members and a Senate of 95 (5 from each state). The president and vice president were limited to two four-year terms. Most powers were given to the federal government, including concurrent jurisdiction over agriculture and education. The constitution was made amendable by a two-thirds vote of both houses with ratification by two-thirds of the states. Several special features were designed to mitigate ethnic divisions. The president must receive at least a quarter of the vote in at least two-thirds of the states. Political parties were required to have headquarters in Lagos and chapters in at least thirteen of the nineteen states. The president must have a person from every state in his cabinet. An independent federal commission was established to ensure impartial elections. The president could be reelected only once, as in the United States. State governments were patterned after the federal.

Voters were registered throughout the country, and new political parties were organized; of the dozens that appeared, five were accredited. The important leaders from the earlier republic included Awolowo, aged

[9]On the transition, see J. Bayo Adekson, *Nigeria in Search of a Stable Civilian-Military System* (Boulder, Colo.: Westview Press, 1981).

seventy, who headed the mainly Yoruba United Party of Nigeria (UPN), and Azikiwe, aged seventy-four, a lawyer-journalist, who led the mostly Ibo Nigerian People's Party (NPP). The other three licensed parties were North-based: the business-oriented National Party (NPN) of Nigeria, led by a moderate conservative, Alhaji Shehu Shagari; the Great Nigerian People's party, which split off from the National Party, led by Alhaji Waziri Ibrahim, member of a smaller tribe and one of the richest men in Africa; and the socialist-oriented People's Redemption Party (PRP). The parties were generally moderate in outlook, little concerned with foreign or ideological issues. Like their predecessors before the civil war, they were mostly organized along ethnic lines. Only the NPN was a really national party.

From July 7 to August 11, 1979, Nigerians trooped five times to the polls to elect a federal Senate, a House of Representatives, state governors, state legislative assemblies, and finally a president. The good order maintained contrasted markedly with the uproar and violence of the previous general elections, fourteen years earlier.[10]

In the July 1979 elections for the federal Senate and House of Representatives, state governorships, and state assemblies, some 8000 candidates were in the race after the Federal Electoral Commission disqualified about a thousand, mostly on grounds of corruption. The NPN of Shehu Shagari won most places, about one-third in the Senate and House, followed by Awolowo's UPN and Azikiwe's NPP, as voters stuck fairly close to the old ethnic patterns. The plurality for the NPN in the congress foreshadowed the victory of Shagari in the following presidential election.

Awolowo and Azikiwe won solidly in the Yoruba and Ibo areas, respectively, but Shagari was first or second in all states except Lagos.

The Shagari Government

Shagari[11] seemed not far from the ideal president. Born in 1926, a Hausa-Fulani, he was raised in the Muslim North—some of his close relatives are said to be still unlettered nomads. He became a school teacher and entered politics at age twenty-eight, winning a seat in the federal House of Representatives. He held seven cabinet portfolios, 1959–1975, including finance and internal affairs. Modest in manner and pragmatic in approach, he made no move to promote a cult of his personality. He was the only leading Nigerian politician to rise above ethnic interests to a national view. It was his great merit that he divided oil money equitably among states of different political color—the states receiving 31.5 percent of federal revenues and local governments 10 percent, allocated mostly according to school enrollment.[12]

Shagari, in order to forge a working majority in the congress, had to form an alliance with Azikiwe's NPP. However, in July 1981, Azikiwe's group withdrew, allegedly because they wanted more "lolly." The government had to lobby for its measures, and lobbying frequently implies material incentives. Cross-voting was common, and there was not much party discipline, although the constitution prohibited elected officials from changing jobs. Most of the parties suffered splits in the first years of the Shagari presidency, and in various states it was not clear what party was dominant, if any. In view of the requirements of the constitution, all parties tried to spread over the country, but the old division

---

[10]On the return to civilian government, see Jean Herskovits, "Democracy in Nigeria," *Foreign Affairs* 58 (Winter 1979–80), pp. 317–325.

[11]For a biography, see David Williams, *President and Power in Nigeria: The Life of Shehu Shagari* (Totowa, N.J.: F. Cass, 1982).

[12]Ibid., pp. 185–186.

of Ibo, Yoruba, and Hausa-Fulani remained central to politics.

The residual political power, the military, receded from sight after installing the civilian regime. Obasanjo went back to his farm and took a university post, and those who shared the government with him also retired from active duty. No one could be mustered out unless a job, generally in the government, was found for him; but the army was reduced to 140,000 men, whom Shagari tried to keep satisfied with modern weapons, good pay, and active training. In July 1981 Shagari had to call on the army to put down disturbances in the northern capital of Kano, but there were no further consequences. Shagari earlier had settled a border clash with Cameroon peacefully despite pressure from the military and general awareness that at any time the soldiers might come out of the barracks again.

The Shagari administration was marked above all by the surge and ebb of petrodollars. In 1979, prices and income more than doubled, and oil came to provide about 95 percent of foreign exchange and 75 percent of government income. This wealth enabled the country to undertake all manner of public works (including a subway system for Lagos), to put billions of dollars into agriculture, to build new universities, to start construction of a new capital, Abuja, in the central highlands, to launch a program of universal education, and to import much of the paraphernalia of a modern society. But oil wealth had the same pernicious effects on Nigeria as on other producers, from Iran to Mexico. The national currency, the naira, was highly overvalued, making imports cheap and exports difficult. Vast sums went for luxury imports, while agricultural exports came almost to an end. The small holders who had provided nearly all the exports of cocoa, palm oil, peanuts, cotton, and so forth of pre-oil times were put out of business. The country,

with 70 percent of the population engaged in agriculture, became dependent on food imports, largely from America, from wheat flour to frozen chickens. Millions of people moved from the countryside to the cities, where the oil money was.

Oil money also led the country into something near bankruptcy. Spending, encouraged by visions of indefinitely rising revenues, outran income, and Nigeria ran a deficit, like most other OPEC nations. Overspending caused inflation, and the country went into debt—by no means so heavily as Mexico, about $14 billion in 1983. Oil money further gave the idea that a lot of wealth was waiting to be privatized, and corruption reached even greater heights.

In two years, however, the situation changed radically. Oil became surplus in the world, and prices began to crumble in the latter part of 1981. Nigeria held stubbornly to a high price of $40 per barrel, only to see buyers depart; production fell from 2 million barrels per day to under half a million. Oil revenues went down from $26 billion to $10 billion a year. The government belatedly lowered prices to market levels, and sales and production climbed back, but it was necessary to cut back sharply on construction projects, ban luxury imports, and be satisfied with a modest rate of growth.

In August 1983 a second set of elections was held on schedule. The three leading candidates for president were the incumbent, Shehu Shagari of the NPN, and the old-time leader, Obafemi Awolowo of the mostly Yoruba UPN, followed by Nnandi Azikiwe of the mostly Ibo NPP. The campaign was conducted with much verve, singing and dancing seasoning the speechmaking, as candidates toured the villages. Radio stations and newspapers, mostly operated by the states or the federal government (and hence mostly pro-Shagari) contended with high partisanship. There was some violence, about a hundred persons reportedly being killed. Shagari's party was general conservative, pro-business, and pro-American. Awolowo's UPN was moderate-leftist in the Social Democratic tradition. Azikiwe's NPP promised not greatly different policies but better government. A minor party pledged to rid the country of rats, mosquitoes, and "blood-sucking politicians."[13]

Over 25 million voters thronged to 150,000 polling places to put thumbprints on ballots carrying symbols as well as names of the candidates. Shagari received 47 percent of the total votes—12 million—or 4 million more than Awolowo. Shagari met the requirement of breadth by garnering 25 percent or more in sixteen of the nineteen states. Tribal loyalties proved still the largest single factor. Although Shagari was able to expand his following, his strength was mostly in the Muslim North and among the smaller peoples of the central regions. Awolowo and Azikiwe carried their ethnic constituencies but showed little support elsewhere.

Shagari's party won 263 of the 400 seats in the House of Representatives, whereas the NPP took forty-eight; the UPN, forty-one; and the PRP also forty-one. The NPN overwhelmed its rivals in the Senate races, taking fifty-five of eighty-five contested seats. In state elections held a week after the presidential election, Shagari's party captured thirteen of nineteen states. There was more violence and apparently more fraud than in the national elections; in two states where Awolowo was strong, the elections had to be postponed.

Electoral victory thus relieved the NPN of any need to seek coalition partners and put it in a position to work its policies alone. This raised the question whether the ruling party might not in the future use the powers of the state to eliminate effective opposition, in

[13]*New York Times,* August 5, 1983, p. 5.

the manner of various nominally democratic African states.

Nigerian democracy was at the same time strained by economic woes. Unemployment was rampant. The trade deficit continued, and the foreign debt piled up. Import restrictions seemed to exclude needed equipment, spare parts, and raw materials but not luxury goods. Shagari, who had been unable to make a dent in corruption during his first administration, established a Ministry of National Guidance to watch over the honesty of administration, kept only seven of his previous forty-five ministers, and had his nominees for office screened by a Senate committee. But it was impossible rapidly to change the system in conditions of great economic stress.

Military Government

The position of Shagari seemed fairly solid in late 1983 because of his strong electoral victory. Dissatisfaction increased, however, with growing financial chaos. It was brought to the fore when he announced on December 29 a harsh austerity program, cutting imports by 40 percent and government expenditures by 30 percent.

On December 31, General Mohammed Buhari declared himself commander of the armed forces and head of a new military government, "to save this nation from imminent collapse." He accused the Shagari government of corruption and ineptness, suspended the constitution, banned political parties, and replaced state governors with army officers. A Supreme Military Council, like that of the years before 1979, took the place of the cabinet. Shagari was arrested, and many high officials were charged with shameless self-enrichment.

The chief reason given for the coup was the endemic corruption, but it was ironic that the chief victim was the exceptional leader never charged with corruption. It was also alleged that the August elections had been dishonest, as they certainly were to some extent; but no one seems to have doubted that Shagari was the choice of the voters. The biggest factor in the downfall of Africa's only democratic government was evidently the state of the economy. Soaring inflation pushed necessities out of reach and made people generally welcome change, although General Buhari had no specific remedies.

General Buhari, born in 1942, is a career soldier with British training. He was prominent in the military regime that replaced General Gowon in 1975, and he served first as a state governor, then as chief official in petroleum affairs.[14] His approach was pragmatic and moderate. There was no stern repression; the press was left fairly free, and civil rights were generally observed. However, there was no promise of new elections or return to constitutional government.

CONCLUSION

That Nigeria could remain a democratic exception in Africa was inherently unlikely unless oil revenues could assure a stable prosperity. When the economy turned down, the shallowness of democratic roots permitted the constitutional structure to be toppled almost without protest. The structure of Nigerian society has always been highly unfavorable for democracy. The chief pressure groups are the oversized army and bureaucracy. Trade unions are divided and weak, partly because of chronic unemployment, partly because of the dominance of official employment. Farm, labor, and professional groups are far less active than in the Western world. The class structure of Nigerian society is also negative for democratic govern-

[14]*New York Times,* January 2, 1984, p. 1.

ment. Inequality is immense, and it tends to grow with modernization, economic growth, and urbanization. Status no longer derives from lineage but mostly from education and wealth, although traditional elites are still strong in the North. At the top levels of society there is an elite trained abroad or at the leading university, that of Ibadan, which is for Nigeria somewhat like Tokyo University is for Japan. Those who are fortunate enough to tap government funds or oil revenues are ipso facto wealthy; yet the large majority profits very little. Top civil servants are paid at European or American levels, while ordinary laborers receive African wages, a hundred times less. Elites insist on imported shoes and clothes; the masses have very little use for either. Palatial mansions have high fences and are guarded day and night. Not far away, people slosh through mud-filled streets to stinking hovels. Neither rich nor poor are troubled by the frequent power failures, the former because they have standby generators, the latter because they have no use for electricity. The best to be said is that the money-making spirit has generated an assertive new business class, and young persons from modest backgrounds can rise to elite status through education and employment in the bureaucracy or the army, although the overwhelming majority are left far behind.

Difference of language contributes to, or is an expression of, the inequality of elite and masses. As in a majority of Third World countries, administration, prestigious occupations, and education above the primary level are conducted in a foreign tongue, which is the unifying means of communication among the elite. Most Nigerians have a smattering of English, at least in the cities and in the southern part of the country, and its use is spreading. But to use it fluently and correctly is a prerequisite for social position. The upper elite, many of whom have received their education abroad, indulge in linguistic snobbery and cultivate an Oxford accent.[15] The North is still a world away, dependent on peanuts instead of oil, with a Hausa-speaking elite ruling in feudal fashion. The federal public service, despite the outcome of the civil war, is still 90 percent Southern.[16]

Problems of inequality are accentuated by a rate of population growth among the world's highest.[17] No one really knows how many Nigerians there are, and when a count is made or a school is opened there always seem to be more than expected. As elsewhere in the Third World, the main cities have mushroomed. Lagos grew from 600,000 to 2.8 million in ten years, and its metropolitan area now has perhaps 10 million inhabitants.

In such a divided and unequal society, corruption is a major scourge. It is generally taken for granted; "dash" is regarded as a form of commission, a cost of doing business, for which appropriate sums are budgeted. Civil servants expect inducements for almost any service; government contracts imply graft; money buys positions and bends justice. Dash is payable to board a plane, to get an appointment, to occupy a hotel room, or to placate a traffic policeman. Rakeoffs take perhaps 40 percent of government revenues.[18] Thievery is a related disorder; ships in Lagos harbor may be boarded several times in one day by gangs that hold the crew hostage and unload portions of the cargo. About half of textiles, half of batteries, and a third of cosmetics imported into the country were estimated to be smuggled.[19] This is more difficult to combat because government personnel are involved and many persons profit as goods go through many hands.

There are exhortations to honesty, but few of the elite give a good example. Minor sinners are sometimes punished, big ones rarely. Persons making denunciations are more liable to be jailed than those denounced. Corruption is endemic at the universities, part of the lives of the elite from their youth. It undermines public ethics and creates cynicism about the motives of everyone in government. Happily, however, Nigeria has never been looted by its rulers in the manner of Zaire, the Central African Empire, or Zambia, whose presidents have built stupendous palaces or otherwise spent a large part of the national income on themselves. But graft and inefficiency are costly; $3 billion spent on an agricultural program was said to be entirely wasted. Under a series of five-year plans, large sums have gone not only to graft but also to show projects such as grandiose and uneconomic steel plants. Efficiency does not come easily; businesses rely on motorcycle messengers instead of telephones. Papers move with glacial slowness; it may take two to four years to receive an import permit. Poor planning has been a major factor in the economic setback of 1982–1983, forcing austerity and borrowing on world markets. Nigerians will be very fortunate if the development plans can provide the basis for self-sustaining economic growth after the oil has gone, in thirty years or so at present rates of extraction.

The Nigerian economy still depends to an uncomfortable degree on foreigners, and oil has markedly increased dependency. Most public sector construction and many projects are carried out by foreign firms, and European agribusiness manages state farms.[20]

[15]Piere L. van den Berghe, *Power and Privilege at an African University* (Cambridge, Mass: Schenkman, 1973), p. 59.

[16]Paul Beckett and James O'Connell, *Education and Power in Nigeria* (New York: Holmes and Meier, 1978), p. 167.

[17]See Dupe Olatunbosun, *Nigeria's Neglected Rural Majority* (Ibadan: Oxford University Press, 1975).

[18]*New York Times*, March 14, 1981, p. 4; August 29, 1981, p. 19.

[19]*Newsweek*, August 8, 1983, pp. 45–46.

[20]*Wall Street Journal*, November 25, 1981.

By 1975 the government had acquired a majority interest in the oil companies, but it lacked Nigerian experts to manage them fully and had to rely on foreign corporations to handle distribution. Pressure for indigenization is continual. There are many regulations regarding the hiring of foreigners, and various kinds of businesses are subject to quotas for Nigerian employment and ownership. Some, such as real estate, buses, and retail trade, must be entirely Nigerian. On the other hand, Nigeria badly wants investment by multinational corporations to increase employment and build up the economy; rules are bent for this purpose. Recently about 50,000 expatriates, two-thirds of them British, have been employed on contract in Nigeria, considerably more than were there before independence.

Perhaps mostly because relations with Britain were always fairly amicable, and also because of the influence of the conservative North, Nigeria has been little attracted to the socialistic politics and economics that have captivated many states in Africa and Asia. The sense of inferiority from colonialism was less acute in Nigeria than in most colonized lands, and it seems to be ever more left behind. There is a leftist sector led by university students, labor organizers, elements of the bureaucracy, journalists, and frustrated intellectuals. However, the business community, the small but growing professional groups, and most of the military leadership have been more conservative. In foreign policy, Nigeria joins Third World causes, regarding itself as the natural leader of Africa; and it has promoted a West African economic community. It identifies with Africanism and negritude and stresses the native cultural heritage in arts and theater. The struggle of blacks for equality in southern Africa is the chief concern of Nigerian foreign policy. It is suspicious of Western motives and critical of Western ways, which seem to threaten moral breakdown. Yet it is eager to do business with the West, and its relations with the United States have been good.

The decades of independence have been sad for Africa, filled with frustration and disillusionment. The new nations, whose boundaries were drawn in European chancelleries in the nineteenth century, remain economically dependent, some of them on personnel from the former colonial power. In many, per capita income has declined over the past decade, per capita food production in almost all. Governments are mostly harsh, some very brutal. Censorship is almost everywhere, and corruption is a general miasma. Here and there one sees something that may be called progress, as new skyscrapers break the horizon, but cities exploit the rural majority, and the military-bureaucratic elite exploits everyone. In many places roads are overgrown with weeds, and abandoned schools rot. Socialism, democratic forms, party dictatorship, and military rule have all been tried and have all failed.

In this gloomy picture, Nigeria is a less dark spot, despite the military's taking of power. Nigeria alone has a substantial democratic tradition, with habits of informative journalism, independent courts, local self-government, more of a middle class than most African countries, and a relatively good educational system, both elementary and advanced. Much of Africa's hope must rest with it.

10

Mexico

No other Third World country has an impact on the United States comparable to that of Mexico, with its migrant workers, debts, poverty, and potential riches. Independent over a century and a half and on the edge of the Western world since the sixteenth century, Mexico suffers all the problems of the Third World. The country is largely desert and mountains or tropical jungle; there is only about one acre of arable land per capita. Large oil resources were the greatest hope for relief of poverty, but they have not sufficed. The population (of about 78 million in 1984) is ethnically and racially diverse. About 10 percent of the 78 million Mexicans speak one or another Indian language, and about 20 percent are culturally Indian. These form most of the depressed classes. Persons of European (mostly Spanish) background, who predominate in the upper classes, constitute approximately 10 percent of the population. The remainder are *mestizos,* or racially mixed.

Literacy is optimistically estimated at 78 percent, but in the countryside it is not over 50 percent, and about half the peasants do not wear shoes. Agriculture, still the occupation of nearly half the people, contributes less than one-sixth of GNP. Population is growing at about 2.4 percent per annum, implying a doubling in thirty years. Half of the people are under sixteen. Each year, some 900,000 enter the labor force, competing for about 350,000 new jobs. Half the labor force is un- or underemployed.

As in other Third World countries, people flock to the cities, especially the capital. Two-thirds of the population is now urban; and Mexico City, with 14 million people in 1982, is projected to have 30 million by the end of the century, thus becoming the world's largest megalopolis. Located in a once beau-

259

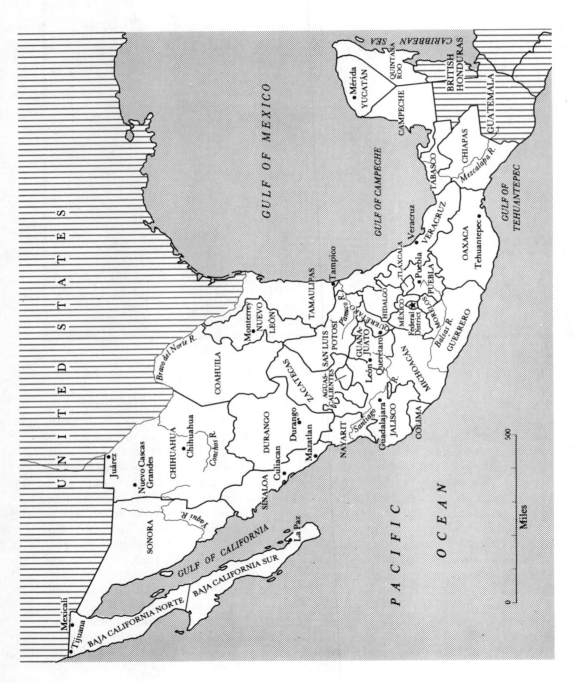

MEXICO

tiful valley at 7,800 feet, it has acquired perhaps the world's worst smog blanket and traffic snarls surpassed by none. As in other Third World countries, national life is centered on the capital, the commercial, industrial, financial, and cultural as well as political hub.

Society and government in Mexico are, as in most Third World countries, hierarchic and authoritarian. Despite a revolutionary tradition inequality is even greater than elsewhere in Latin America: the Mexican business executive earns 50 percent more than an Argentine counterpart, while the Mexican worker receives only about half as much as the Argentine. The very rich have private jets, whereas nearly a third of the population has less than the minimum diet for reasonable health, and a majority of children are said to be undernourished.

Mexico lives in the shadow of the United States politically, culturally, and especially economically. Mexico is the third largest trade partner of the United States (after Canada and Japan) and since 1982 the leading oil supplier. About two-thirds of the foreign news in Mexican papers comes from U.S. agencies and about half of the motion pictures. The shoppers of Mexico City buy many of the same brands as those of Los Angeles in similar supermarkets.[1] Over half the industrial investment is from the United States, American capital dominates the largest and most modern corporations, and much of Mexican politics revolves around the question of whether to invite foreign capital to build up the country or to check it for the sake of national independence, and a strong state is regarded as necessary to protect the economy from capture by foreign (especially American) interests.

[1]*New York Times,* January 13, 1982, p. 7.

Nonetheless, the Mexican political system has been possibly the most successful of Latin America. The revolution early in this century, although ultimately falling sadly short of its goals, achieved more of a social upheaval than any other in Latin America except Castroism. Almost alone in Latin America, Mexico has avoided military politics since 1929, and the military share of the budget is the lowest in the hemisphere except for Costa Rica. The constitution of 1917 is still in effect. The succession of presidents, each serving out a six-year term, has been regular and orderly since the inauguration of Lázaro Cárdenas in 1934, a record unique in Latin America and rare in the world. Industrialization and modernization are frequently considered primary goals of relatively poor countries, and in this regard Mexico has done well, at least until the 1982 deluge of capital flight, collapse of the exchange value of the peso, hyperinflation, falling incomes, and inability to cope with gigantic debt. Mexico has been considered one of the Third World countries with the best chances of entering the company of the advanced industrial nations. Its annual increase of GNP of about 6 percent yearly between 1940 and 1981 was the best in the Third World over that period; only a few countries of East Asia, such as Taiwan and the Republic of Korea, have enjoyed higher rates over a shorter time.

This considerable success has been achieved under a sui generis system of limited authoritarianism. It contains much more show than reality of democracy, but it has provided stability and security for producers. Its key feature is a single six-year term for a strong president, who must submit himself to the formal approval of the electorate. The government thereby escapes the vices of decadent dictatorship and feels itself firm enough to permit a fair amount of healthy freedom.

HISTORICAL BACKGROUND

Before the Spaniards came in the sixteenth century, the central part of present-day Mexico was ruled by the loose Aztec empire, which possessed an impressive although somewhat grotesque culture. Spanish rule, which lasted three hundred years, was grossly exploitative. A Spanish aristocracy took most of the land as feudal estates, government was a tangle of corruption and parasitic privileges, and the brutalized population shrank.

Nineteenth-Century: Turmoil and Tyranny

Independence came slowly and painfully. In 1810 a priest of Mexican-born Spanish (*criollo*) origin, Padre Miguel Hidalgo, raised the Indian poor against the criollos and Spanish. He was defeated and executed by conservatives, but civil war dragged on. Independence came in 1821 when a royalist general, Augustín de Iturbide, turned against the liberal government that had gained power in Spain. He joined with the leader of the rebellious forces and ended Spanish rule. The liberals were satisfied because this meant independence; the conservatives, because it sustained the privileges of the Catholic Church and established a monarchy.

Emperor Iturbide I, however, lasted only a year. The antimonarchist leader was Antonio López de Santa Anna, a dubious character who dominated Mexican politics until 1855. During this period politics was a running contest between two broad coalitions, conservative and liberal. The conservatives represented mostly the wealthy, the landowners and merchants along with the powerful clergy and the traditional military, persons generally of Spanish background and Spanish colonial tradition. The liberals represented the *mestizos* and the middle classes, such as there were. They found inspiration in the French revolution and the republicanism of the United States and especially disliked the immense wealth and power of the Church.

After 1855 the liberals, led by a lawyer of Indian origin, Benito Juárez, one of the most inspiring characters in Mexican history, and by the Lerdo de Tejada brothers, managed to abolish ecclesiastical courts and attack Church landholdings. This reform led to intermittent civil war, punctuated by a French effort to establish an empire under Prince Maximilian of Hapsburg (executed in 1867). Juárez returned to power, but he died in 1872. In 1876, a military hero, Porfirio Díaz, declined to accept electoral defeat and made himself president. With a slight interruption he held the reins until 1911, giving Mexico a prolonged period of peace and economic construction.

The rule of Díaz was ruthless and effective. He crushed banditry partly by hiring the bandits as police. Oppositionists were repressed, bought off, imprisoned, or murdered if necessary. Roads were built, and the modernization of the economy was pushed with the assistance of foreign capital, which by 1910 amounted to two-thirds of nonagricultural and nonhandicraft investment.[2] Díaz prided himself on rationalism and surrounded himself with persons of a rationalistic, supposedly scientific cast of mind, the *científicos*. A rather dark mestizo, he whitened his face with talcum powder.

His program of order and progress through foreign investment worked well for some years, producing a growth rate comparable to the modern achievement. But the Díaz regime was for the elite. Nothing was done to educate the masses; the illiteracy rate remained about 80 percent. Only the wealthiest benefitted materially; while the GNP went up, the real wages of peasants and workers

[2]J. Kautsky, *Patterns of Modernizing Revolutions: Mexico and the Soviet Union* (Beverly Hills, Calif.: Sage Publications, 1975), p.16.

went down. A tiny minority owned most of the land. Holdings of Indian villages since Aztec days were seized for the benefit of Mexican or foreign estate owners, and the rural masses were held in peonage or debt slavery. Corruption became ever more massive. Political power was in the hands of a small group of septuagenarians and octogenarians who feared change in principle.

The Revolution

Despite rising discontent, the power of Porfirio Díaz seemed unshakable as the 1910 presidential election approached. But the eighty-year-old dictator made the error of telling an American newsman what Díaz knew the American public wanted to hear, that Mexico under his tutelage had attained political maturity permitting free elections. This suggested to Mexicans that there might indeed be a real election. A mild-mannered, idealistic aristocrat, Francisco I. Madero, wrote a book on the subject and became a presidential candidate on a platform of "effective suffrage and no reelection." Madero was imprisoned, and Díaz proclaimed himself reelected. Madero, released for a bribe, went to Texas and raised the banner of revolt on October 25, 1910.

Risings sprang up all over the country, the dictator's army collapsed from incompetence and venality, and Díaz fled. But Madero was unable to govern. Inexperienced in politics, too trusting and idealistic, he was attacked by radicals who wanted more change and by conservatives (supported by the American ambassador) who wanted none. He was betrayed and murdered by a counterrevolutionary general, Victoriano Huerta, in February 1913. The country, torn by civil war, was often close to anarchy and banditry. Among the contenders was Francisco ("Pancho") Villa, known in American history for his raid into the United States and General Pershing's vain pursuit. A charismatic and colorful figure, Villa was a political failure. Emiliano Zapata in the south, expressing the anger of the dispossessed peasants, broke with Madero and injected a note of radicalism and egalitarianism, which was strengthened by his murder in 1919. The more conservative strain in the movement was headed by one of Madero's generals, a landholder of northern Mexico, Venustiano Carranza. He restored order and formed a government, which he headed until 1920. Carranza's greatest achievement was the calling of a constitutional convention. The constitution it produced in 1917 followed the populist, liberal, anti-Church lines of the constitution of 1857 but was revolutionary in its social concerns.

The tumultuous decade of 1910–1920 cost the lives of over a million persons, one-tenth of the population, and impoverished the land. It was a social revolution in that it largely destroyed the previous ruling class. But the Mexican revolution was amorphous, guided by no simple "truth" or ideology. Madero's principle was "effective suffrage [free elections] and no reelection," ironically a slogan Díaz had once raised against Benito Juárez. Others who rebelled at the same time as Madero were less concerned with political institutions and more with the plight of the masses, especially the Indians. There was a strong strain of nationalism in reaction to Díaz's subservience to foreign interests; Carranza in particular was determined to stand up to the United States. Anticlericalism was prominent because Díaz, a one-time liberal, had ended up promoting the power and prerogatives of the Church, by far the largest landholder. Land reform was a major goal, consecrated in the constitution and on the agendas of Mexican presidents from Carranza (a hacienda owner) on. There were also ideas of anticapitalism, socialism, and workers' rights, which were likewise placed in the constitution. Egalitarianism merged into Indianism, a turning away from the Europeanization of the previous four centuries toward the exaltation of the precolonial past and the Indian as the true representative of the Mexican nation. Never systematically woven together, these generally populist goals formed the basis of a revolutionary coalition and constituted the legitimation of the new government.

Consolidation

After 1917, the Mexican system gradually settled into its modern shape. Carranza, only theoretically a revolutionary, hardly made a beginning toward carrying out the social promises of the constitution. Contrary to the spirit of "no reelection," he attempted to continue his power past his term by imposing an unpopular successor. His generals, led by Alvaro Obregón, the outstanding military figure of the revolution, deposed him; he was killed in flight in 1920. Obregón, president from 1920 to 1924, worked to pacify the country. He engaged in controversy with the United States over the subsoil (oil) rights of American companies, theoretically annulled by the 1917 constitution. He made a serious start at redistribution of estate lands; and with his blessing, organized labor became a major political component of the political system, as it has remained. In 1923, with the backing of popular forces, he crushed the last serious attempt at a military coup.

Obregón was succeeded in 1924 by another general, Plutarco Elías Calles, who turned his attention to economic modernization. His administration also saw backsliding from revolutionary ethics to conspicuous consumption. But Calles emphasized anticlericalism, attacked the Church, deported alien priests and nuns, and forbade the wearing of religious garb in public. (The clergy went on strike, and rightists and fervent Catholics raised the "Cristero" rebellion. It failed, and the clerical issue receded.) Obregón wanted the presidency again in 1928. Calles at first was opposed but yielded to Obregón's superior forces. The constitution was amended to permit reelection after an intervening period, and Obregón was duly elected. Then Obregón was assassinated by a religious fanatic before he could take office, a fortuitous event that saved the principle of no reelection.

Calles was now the strongest figure on the scene. He was not able to succeed himself as president, however; he hoped to command from behind the scenes, through a puppet president. This worked rather well for a series of three weak presidents from 1928 to 1934—the constitution had been amended again to forbid reelection and to lengthen the term from four to six years. But Calles had problems. In 1928–1929 some fighting was necessary to impose his choice, and he felt obliged to bring together the peasant and labor groups upon which (in addition to his standing with the army) his position rested. In 1929 he organized the National Revolutionary Party (PNR) as an amalgamation of organizations supporting the goals of the revolution and Calles personally. At first a loose umbrella grouping, it soon became the inclusive official political organization. It was backed in numerous ways by the state, and it had a strong financial base, since federal employees were required to give it at least one week's pay per year.

For the presidential term beginning in 1934, Calles accepted the candidate favored by the left wing of the party, Lázaro Cárdenas, a faithful Calles follower. But Cárdenas campaigned extensively, built up his following, and placed his people in key positions. He won the loyalty of the peasants by more land distribution, sometimes expropriating holdings of Calles' followers, and he organized the peasants and workers. By

1936 Cárdenas could expel Calles and his principal allies. He also completed the institutionalization of the revolutionary order. He distributed twice as much land as his predecessors had since 1915 and promoted the *ejidos,* semicommunal villages in the Indian tradition revived by the Zapata movement in the turmoil of the revolution. At the end of his term, half of the peasantry was in these collectives, which mixed family landholding with cooperative ownership.[3] Although a general himself, Calles largely ended the power of the military. Obregón had begun the demilitarization of politics by repressing many generals after the attempted coup in 1923. Calles, fearful of his own position, made a point of separating generals from troops personally loyal to them. Cárdenas armed workers and peasants, excluded the military from local elections, and continued the reduction, begun in the late 1920s, of the military share of the budget. He asserted Mexican nationalism by insisting that capital, especially foreign capital, must serve the national interest; and he applied the consitution to expropriate foreign (practically speaking, U.S.) landholdings. He supported a strike of oil workers; and after the companies refused to accept an arbitration verdict, he nationalized the oil industry in May 1938, to the applause of Mexicans and the shock of British and American business.

Cárdenas also reshaped his political base, the party. He separated the peasants from the labor confederation and organized them as the National Peasant Confederation (CNC), to which all ejido members belonged ex officio. He reformed the labor organization, the Confederation of Mexican Workers (CTM), and made them another "sector" of the party. Peasants' and workers' dues added to the contributions of government employ-

ees. Cárdenas also made the military a sector of the party, giving them a formal political role but actually reducing their influence by placing them with the peasants and workers. These three sectors, along with a fourth catchall "Popular Sector" including government employees, professionals, and business people, formed the renamed ruling party, the Mexican Revolutionary Party (PRM). Although Cárdenas kept power securely with the presidency, he made the party, which had previously been rather conservatively oriented, the vehicle of his reformist-egalitarian politics. By virtue of his identification with the masses, his popular measures, and his unwavering (anti-American) nationalism, Cárdenas became a national hero. Possibly, he could have continued as president if he had desired. However, he stepped down in 1940 with his laurels green, and his self-restraint reaffirmed the no-reelection rule.

The Revolution Halted

The period of rapid change ended with the replacement of Cárdenas by Ávila Camacho in 1940, and conservative politicians inherited the revolution. Ávila Camacho declared an end to the war with the Church by avowing himself a believer and permitting the Church to regain much of its influence, although not its property. Land reform did not stop entirely, but he presided over the rebuilding of an economy battered by strikes and land redistribution. In 1946 the party was renamed the Institutional Revolutionary Party (PRI), as it has remained, aptly suggesting the completed institutionalization of the revolutionary state.

The most significant change in the party was the abolition in 1944 of the military sector, sealing the political decline of that force. Although as late as 1938 military men had held about half the top positions in the government, they had little corporate feeling,

[3]Vincent Padgett, *The Mexican Political System* (Boston: Houghton Mifflin, 1976), p. 41.

and they left politics without protest or joined the popular sector as individuals. The president after Ávila Camacho, Miguel Alemán, a lawyer by profession, was the first civilian since Benito Juárez to serve a full presidential term (1946–1952). All succeeding presidents have also been civilians trained in administration.

Under a rather placid succession of capable but uninspiring presidents—Adolfo Ruiz Cortines (1952–1958), Adolfo López Mateos (1958–1964), Gustavo Díaz Ordaz (1964–1970), Luis Echeverría Álvarez (1970–1976), José López Portillo (1976–1982), and Miguel de la Madrid (1982–   )—there have been no grand new departures or sensational policy changes. Continuity has been virtually guaranteed by the fact that each new president has been a member of the cabinet of his predecessor. Alemán stymied land reform by giving landowners the right of appeal. He also turned the country's attention from reform to economic development, and this has retained top priority. Bureaucrats, professionals, and business people have replaced workers and peasants as the mainstay of the ruling PRI. The revolutionaries settled down to the enjoyment of power and possessions; the "class struggle" of Cárdenas's day was replaced by "harmony of classes for the sake of Mexico." Corruption has sometimes been rampant, sometimes more subdued. Antigovernment violence has surged from time to time, as in the wave of strikes and peasant land invasions of 1958–1959; but it has been competently handled by a mixture of heavy-handed force and concessions. Distribution of lands from holdings above the legal limit (basically 100 hectares per person) has continued; an impressive total of well over 50 million hectares has been turned over, it is claimed, to somewhat over 2 million families, which makes an unrealistic 60 or so acres per family. However, much land fell into the hands of bureaucrats.[4] Well before the 1970s population growth began to overtake available land and bring a decline in real incomes in the countryside.

Official policy has tended to swing from the populist-egalitarian-interventionist, emphasizing social justice, to the conservative and probusiness, emphasizing economic growth and the hope for betterment through increased production. The administration of Díaz Ordaz, which tended toward the Right, saw the most serious antiregime violence since the 1930s. The climax was the 1968 massacre of Tlatelolco. After a series of confrontations between police and students of the huge National University, a crowd of young protesters, many armed, thronged through the streets in defiance of an official ban, breaking the political mores by insulting the person of the president. The minister of interior, Luis Echeverría, permitted the use of force, and hundreds were killed.

Upon becoming president Echeverría set out to be a populist and the champion of the people.[5] He instituted obligatory profit-sharing in industry.[6] He decreed general wage increases, placed legal ceilings on profits, and put more banking under government management. He attacked foreign corporations and tightened the rules for Mexicanization.[7] He pushed public investment at the price of deficit financing and inflation. He promoted education; at the end of his term he boasted that 100 percent of the six- to twelve-age group was in school, expenditures on education had increased five times in six years, the number of technical institutes had in-

[4]Kenneth F. Johnson, *Mexican Democracy: A Critical View* (Boston: Allyn & Bacon, 1971), p. 30.

[5]Salvatore Bizzarro, "Mexico's Government in Crisis," *Current History* 72 (March 1977), p. 102.

[6]Susan Purcell, *The Mexican Profit-Sharing Decision: Politics in an Authoritarian Regime* (Berkeley: University of California Press, 1975), pp. 145–146.

[7]Giorgio Perissinotto, "Mexican Education: Echeverría's Mixed Legacy," *Current History* 72 (March 1973).

creased from 289 to 1,301.[8] Just before leaving office, he turned a million acres over to peasants. In foreign policy, he stressed ties with countries other than the United States. He tried to make Mexico a leader in the struggle of the Third World for concessions from the industrial West, and incidentally aspired to be secretary-general of the United Nations.[9] He had greater success in making himself wealthy.

Echeverría named his lifelong friend and finance minister, José López Portillo, as his successor, but López Portillo swung the tiller rightward. The courts, with presidential acquiescence, annulled the last-minute generosity of Echeverría to the peasants. Facing problems of mounting unemployment, peasant unrest, severe inflation, and the devaluation of the peso, López Portillo sought to create a favorable climate for productive enterprise, including foreign investment. He signed a pact with 140 major companies to coordinate public and private investment policies, hold down prices, and restrict government spending and the expansion of government-controlled industry. The officially controlled labor confederation agreed to a 10 percent limit on wage boosts, much less than the loss of value of the peso. López Portillo looked to modernization in agricultural production instead of to land reform, which often created inefficient dwarf holdings.

The biggest story of the López Portillo administration, however, was written in terms of oil. Mexico had been a petroleum producer from the early part of this century, but production had lagged for many years prior to the mid-1970s. Then, because of higher prices, exploration was increased, and enormous fields, among the world's largest, were discovered in time to profit from the second price rise of 1979–1980. The bonanza gave Mexico four years of the most rapid growth of its history, 8 percent per annum; provided jobs for the first time for the new entrants to the labor force; and promised a prosperous future Mexico.

The seemingly ever-rising exports of oil with ever-rising prices also encouraged borrowing large sums from foreign banks, and spending even more than the government took in. Chronic habits of waste and corruption went into a general splurge. Many, including the president and his family, became extremely rich. But in mid-1981 oil began to become a glut, and prices weakened. The Mexican monopoly, Pemex, like the Nigerians, found it hard to accept that prices had to be lowered, and exports and receipts shrank drastically. More billions were borrowed to keep up programs and to sustain the overvalued peso. By early 1982 that had become impossible. Capital fled the country, the peso collapsed, and inflation exploded. Blaming the banks and those who sought financial security abroad, López Portillo nationalized the banks in September 1982, thereby winning laurels as a populist and shifting Mexico far toward a state-run economy.

Meanwhile, López Portillo had named as his successor Miguel de la Madrid Hurtado. Born 1934, son of a lawyer, de la Madrid studied law at the elite Mexican National Autonomous University (UNAM) and earned a master's degree in public administration at Harvard—a fact that he kept quiet. He rose in the state bank and Pemex, following López Portillo upward, and became the President's chief planner in 1979. Uncharismatic and rather conservative in temperament, he was as friendly to the United States as any Mexican president was likely to be.

De la Madrid, taking office on December 1, 1982, followed the usual practice of swinging mildly away from the policies of his pred-

[8]Ibid., pp. 115–116.
[9]George Grayson, "Mexico's Opportunity: The Oil Boom," *Foreign Policy* 29 (Winter 1977–1978), pp. 65–89.

ecessor and benefactor. He excluded the left wing of the party from his appointments; reassured private enterprise; and undertook an austerity program to reduce imports, deficits, and inflation. However, he made no move to denationalize the banks—which was perhaps politically impossible—or even to divest the countless enterprises held or controlled by the banks. He did act against the old problem of corruption, setting up an anticorruption ministry, ordering officials to make disclosure statements, promising to punish enrichment in office, and prohibiting the police from taking bribes.[10] But the police protested the attack on their incomes by ignoring traffic violations.[11] The people remembered that López Portillo had once campaigned against corruption and waited to see whether big profiteers of the previous administration would be touched. To the general surprise, one, former Pemex Director Jorge Díaz Serrano, was jailed on charges of misappropriating $34 million—out of some $4 billion that seemed to have evaporated from Pemex accounts.[12] But no move was made to touch the huge fortunes of the López Portillo clan.

De la Madrid's biggest problem, however, was Mexico's towering foreign debt, rising inexorably past $80 billion. This he confronted ably, imposing an austerity program, balancing Mexico's foreign trade account, and securing new loans and restructuring of old to postpone the pressure. The cost, nonetheless, was dire—shrinkage of the economy, cutting the real income of the middle class by nearly half, greatly increasing the already intolerable unemployment (leaving only 40 percent of the workforce with full-time jobs) and raising dangers of serious political unrest.

[10]*Christian Science Moniter,* January 24, 1983.
[11]*New York Times,* December 29, 1982, p. 2.
[12] *New York Times,* April 27, 1983, p. 2.

THE GOVERNMENT

The Mexican political system has copied its constitutional forms rather closely from those of the United States, but it has given them a very different authoritarian content through the effectively monopolistic political party. The result is a compromise between democracy and dictatorship.

Centralized Power

The Mexican president is elected directly by popular vote. There is no vice president; Congress elects a successor to an incapacitated president. Congress has two houses, the Chamber of Deputies, elected from districts roughly equal in population, and the Senate, with two senators from each of thirty-one states and the Federal District. The term of deputies is three years, that of senators six years, with reelection possible only after an intervening term. The states have a parallel apparatus of a governor elected for six years and a unicameral legislature elected for three years, immediate reelection in each case being prohibited. On the local level there are municipalities, with elected mayors and councils. The court system, however, is entirely federal.

The constitution means little. Power in Mexico is far more centralized than in the United States; and the president, in the Latin tradition, is much more of an autocrat. He initiates almost all legislation and never needs his veto power; laws are usually passed unanimously or opposed by only a small minority. Congress does not even have a significant voice in the budget, and the prohibition against reelection prevents the legislature from developing a corporate feeling. At best, Congress is a forum for the opposition deputies permitted in it for the sake of democratic appearances, and it has become livelier after the reforms of 1978 increased the representation of the opposition. It also provides dignified sinecures for important politicians.

The president can remove state governors or other officials at will, either by pressure or legal intervention, pending new elections. The power is used: Echeverría ousted two governors in 1975. The governor is more an administrator for the central government than a political figure in his own right, and little can be done on the state or local level without the concurrence of federal authorities. In practice, the state governments are allowed to manage their affairs, barring major problems.[13]

Police in the states are under federal commanders. The states collect only about 11 percent of government revenues, compared to the 75 percent that goes to the federal treasury.[14] The old *caciques,* the traditional quick-shooting bosses, have disappeared except in a few isolated areas, replaced by the party man and servant of the president. The municipalities are at the mercy not only of federal but of state authorities. The governor can depose their officers almost at will, and they have almost no funds, except whatever is allotted to them from above. There is no real separation of federal, state, and municipal apparatuses;[15] all are at the service of the president. No tradition of local self-government provides a basis for democracy.

The only part of the government with a little independence is the courts. Justices of the high courts, particularly the Supreme Court, are named by the president with life-time tenure; they are removable only by Congress and only for misconduct. The Supreme Court has ruled in some cases against the government, or at least against a ministry, particularly in cases of expropriation; but it is possible for a minister simply to ignore the ruling.[16] There has never been an executive-judicial confrontation.

The president is thus a magistrate without checks or balances. He is inevitably subject to multiple pressures from economic and social groups and forces, and he can execute policies only insofar as they are acceptable. Yet legally he is something of an autocrat. He is not even restrained by a cabinet. There are no regular formal cabinet meetings, only consultations with individual ministers or with specialized committees, which are formed and dissolved with little or no publicity. In the government, only the president expresses an independent opinion, and he avoids giving the appearance of yielding to pressure.[17] In 1982 López Portillo nationalized the banks, not only without authorization in law or action by Congress, but without consulting his cabinet or his treasury or finance ministers or his already elected successor.[18] With justice, the president receives credit for all decisions. He is also sole commander of an enormous bureaucratic apparatus, including hundreds of agencies.

He commands the party apparatus. This is entwined with the state—party figures often have sinecures, even multiple sinecures, in the bureaucracy[19]—and has a hierarchic structure of its own, decisions flowing down from the top. The president of the party is installed by the president of the state and remains at the pleasure of the latter, usually only a fraction of his term of six years. The formally supreme National Assembly, a body of around a thousand delegates from the three sectors, is supposed to represent the

[13]Martin C. Needler, *Politics in Mexico* (New York: Praeger, 1982), p. 91.

[14]Padgett, *Mexican Political System,* p. 204.

[15]Merilee S. Grindle, *Bureaucrats, Politicians, and Peasants in Mexico; A Case Study* (Berkeley: University of California Press, 1977), p. 47.

[16]Padgett, *Mexican Political System,* p. 203.

[17]Needler, *Politics in Mexico,* p. 91.

[18]*Washington Post,* September 12, 1982, p. 26.

[19]Johnson, *Mexican Democracy,* p. 68.

people. It has theoretical power to fix party statutes, select the party president, and nominate the party's candidate for the presidency; in fact, it acclaims the proposals of the president. A smaller body, the National Council, which includes the party president, the secretary-general of the party, presidents of state party committees, and fifteen representatives of each sector, is supposed to represent the party organizations of the states. It has some function as a coordinating body, but it could affect decisions only in case of a rupture in the top leadership.[20]

The governing body of the party since 1929 has been the National Executive Committee (CEN), which is somewhat like the politburo in Communist countries and which holds similar powers over the party apparatus. Its president is the party president, who also presides over the National Council. It includes the secretary-general, chiefs of the sectors, and representatives of the Chamber of Deputies and the Senate.[21] The CEN convokes the National Assembly and National Council and dictates how delegates to these bodies are to be chosen. It approves party rules and programs; and it has rights of intervention in lower party bodies, including the removal of officers. The party president, in turn, is boss of the CEN. He convokes it, controls its budget, oversees the fulfillment of its decisions, and exercises its powers in case of emergency.

To monitor and manage party activities, the CEN has a set of secretariats suggestive of those of Communist governments—one for each sector and others for political action (to coordinate with the government), political indoctrination, press and propaganda, party finances, and social action (education, community development, and so on). There are also divisions devoted to electoral action, adjudication, sport, and administrative services.[22] The CEN supervises party nominations to elective posts below the governorship. Candidates for higher offices are chosen directly by the president without benefit of any fixed party procedure other than the cheers of the appropriate assembly. For lower officials there are nominally democratic forms, although the rules have been altered from time to time. Sometimes the precampaign seems quite open, with several candidates pleading their case with the party membership; but the PRI organization steps in to make the choice, who may be someone not previously mentioned. The delegate of the CEN participates in the selection. The CEN then ordinarily approves the candidate, who will have formally promised to fulfill the plans, programs, and directives of the PRI. Popular or not, the candidate picked by the party apparatus is invariably acclaimed by the assembly formally charged with making the nomination. It is even possible for the CEN to change candidates without the formality of an assembly. As a concession to democracy, the PRI membership may be given a choice of several candidates for local councilor.[23]

In 1965–1966, the party president, Carlos A. Madrazo, undertook to infuse more spirit into party elections by having candidates chosen by vote of party members. This step, however, was anathema to the bosses, local and national, and was rescinded before it was ever applied. Madrazo also tried to curb corruption; the result was his dismissal. In 1971–1972 party rules were modified in the directions desired by Madrazo (who had in the meantime been killed), providing for a secret ballot in sectoral elections and giving young people and women more voice in the

[20]Padgett, *Mexican Political System*, p. 78.
[21]Johnson, *Mexican Democracy*, p. 63.

[22]Padgett, *Mexican Political System*, pp. 81–82.
[23]Robert Furtak, *El Partido de le Revolución y la Estabilidad Política en México* (Mexico City: Universidad Nacional Autónoma de Mexico, 1974), pp. 124–135.

party. The effect, however, was insignificant.[24] Procedural changes depend for their substance and implementation on the top circle of leadership; as long as this is under no great pressure from below, it is not likely to diminish its power voluntarily.

The lower structure of the party is a complex interlocking arrangement of hierarchies of party and sector organizations. There are party assemblies and executive committees at each geographic level, each with a secretary designated by the party organization above it. The sectors also have regional and local organizations, with subsidiary and component groups. The assemblies are composed of delegates from the sectors in proportion to their memberships.

The feeblest sector is CNC, a complex aggregate of peasant leagues, to which ejido members automatically belong. The peasants, mobilized to vote for PRI candidates, receive in return only driblets of credit and other favors.[25] They lack the power to press demands, and the upper echelons of the organization are occupied not by peasants but by lawyers, named by politicians.[26]

The labor sector likewise serves more to control labor than to channel its demands on government; neither the agrarian nor the labor sector acts as a pressure group for its membership. Most of the unionized workers, about 3.5 million, are in the CTM (Confederation of Mexican Workers), headed since the times of Ávila Camacho by Fidel Velásquez. There have been many splits and secessionist movements, and Mexican labor has never been fully unified, but the unions are generally government controlled. The minister of labor has broad powers over the unions, including the power to authorize or forbid strikes. Trade union leaders, al-

though named from the top, are ordinarily acceptable to the workers unless they are excessively greedy and prone to take payoffs from management or appropriate union funds. They are in reality virtually government functionaries, and they are often compensated with party or elective jobs. The influence of the CTM declined steadily after Cárdenas, but in the early 1970s Echeverría turned to it for support and permitted it to contribute to shaping economic policy.

Unlike the agrarian and labor sectors, the National Confederation of Popular Organizations (CNOP) has no ministry of its own. But it has considerably more influence than these two together, because it represents much more independent power and it supplies the largest number of high officials. The number of representatives it sends to the national Congress is more than double that of the labor sector. The CNOP is a collection of many groups, large and small, including federal workers, state and municipal employees, teachers, small businesses, cooperatives, and small landowners. Most of its members are government workers. Military men and others may be members as individuals. The clergy are still excluded, a holdover from the anticlericalism of earlier years. Businesses employing more than five persons are not admitted because they would contradict the populist image the CNOP wishes to convey. Manufacturing and trading companies, however, must belong to their respective confederations, with which the government deals. There are also informal associations, the most important of which is the Monterrey Group of conservative industrialists, which is close to the right wing of the PRI.

The PRI is thus a ruling party with the task of keeping the people aligned with the leadership and assisting in the fulfillment of the policies formulated at the top. Founded in 1929 to stabilize politics and end the regimen of coups and assassinations, it has suc-

---

[24]Padgett, *Mexican Political System*, p. 88.
[25]Grindle, *Bureaucrats, Politicians, and Peasants in Mexico*, p. 142.
[26]Padgett, *Mexican Political System*, p. 151.

ceeded admirably. It keeps close to the political mainstream and tries to satisfy labor, peasant, and business interests. It is philosophically broad, including Marxist socialists and advocates of free enterprise. It is leftist principally in foreign affairs for the sake of its revolutionary image, with little cost at home.[27] It is a meeting ground for elites in government and around the country, who have to find common positions within its framework. Its chief practical business is to manage elections, and it has been popularly called the "ministry of elections." It also channels information and demands up and down in the hierarchy.

The PRI performs many of the functions of the Communist party in the Soviet Union and other Communist countries and has much in common with the Soviet party. Both have democratically structured but ineffective assemblies and a solid framework of professionals under the command of the top. In both, candidates are designated by, or at least approved by, higher authorities and ratified by the membership. In both, personal relations at the top are decisive. In Mexico as in the Soviet Union, the party intermingles with the state that supports it and provides the basis of its strength. The Mexican party, however, is inferior to the state. Lenin's party existed before the Soviet state, and it has kept decision making in party bodies; the Mexican party was formed as an adjunct of the state and has remained so. The Soviet leader is first of all secretary general of the party; the Mexican leader rules the party by virtue of being president of the state. Membership in the Mexican party is open, even obligatory; the gates to the Soviet party are narrow and closely guarded. In sum, the Mexican PRI is a compromise between the democratic and the totalitarian, like the Mexican political system.

[27]Needler, *Politics in Mexico*, p. 2.

Elections

Candidates for elective positions are chosen with some concurrence of the party masses at the lowest levels, little at the middle, and none at the top. Nominees are presented to assemblies and hailed. With rare exceptions, they are in due course overwhelmingly chosen by the people. The only election of much interest and importance is that of the president.

The means of selecting a new president is simple: the incumbent names the person to succeed him. He may, from conviction or courtesy, consult his wife, high officials of the party, or elder statesmen or ex-presidents. He presumably seeks a nominee broadly acceptable to the party and the country. He does not want to antagonize too many people, and he wants the electorate to show enthusiasm for his choice. The candidate, who has regularly been of middle-class origins, usually from a populous central state, has always been a faithful servant in the cabinet of the outgoing president and a loyal follower and party man in a system that blesses loyalty.[28] But he has rarely had an important position in the party apparatus.[29] The top leaders wait anxiously and indulge in guessing games, but the choice is the president's. In 1975, party, government, and interest group leaders favored Mario Moya Palencia; but when Echeverría tapped José López Portillo, all joined in his praise. Politicos were said to be unhappy with the choice of de la Madrid, but it was no matter.[30]

A party organization is given the honor of making the public announcement. Heads of the party's three sectors call on the candidate to inform him of his selection. Then a chorus of groups and associations hails the beloved

[28]Daniel Cosío Villegas, *El Sistema Político Mexicano* (Mexico City: Joaquín Mortiz, 1973), p. 18.
[29]Furtak, *El Partido de le Revolución*, pp. 139–140.
[30]Alan Riding, "Getting Mexico Moving Again," *New York Times*, July 4, 1982, p. 17.

son of the people whom the president has graciously bestowed on them, and a grand convention unanimously confirms the nomination. Before de la Madrid was announced, only 6 percent of Mexicans had heard of him; two days later, nearly everyone seemed to believe he would be a good president.[31]

The cabinet minister nominated must leave his post, according to the constitution, at least six months before the election. This rule, ostensibly to preclude the use of official power to sway the election, frees the nominee to carry on an energetic campaign. He makes speeches, meets with a host of political figures, and travels the length and breadth of the country, visiting as many as possible of the 15,000 villages. De la Madrid campaigned 218 days, traveled 55,800 miles with a suite of 300, and attended 1,287 meetings.[32] The candidate shows himself and gets acquainted with the country that is to be his for the next six years, mixing image-building with education. He does not spell out new policies, because this could be disrespectful to the man who picked him.

After a strenuous campaign, he can retire early on election night. Probably most of the people are genuinely convinced that he is the best-qualified person, or at least that there is no realistic alternative. There are, if necessary, ample means of shaping electoral results as desired. The PRI controls the electoral commissions, and fraud is easy in country districts, although more difficult in the cities. Ballots can be placed in boxes without having been touched by voters; PRI men may be trucked to the polls while the opposition is kept away; errors may be made in counting, which opposition parties are seldom able to oversee. The PRI is suspected of rather regularly padding its majorities.

Some states have reported 99 percent of all votes for the PRI candidate, presidential or gubernatorial; and the PRI has never lost a race for senator or governor. In the presidential contest it receives around 90 percent. In 1970, Echeverría got only 84 percent of the vote. In 1976, López Portillo obtained 94.4 percent because the opposition failed to present a candidate. In 1982 de la Madrid had to be satisfied with 74 percent of the votes of the 75 percent of the electorate voting. The rightist National Action Party (PAN) got 16.4 percent; the leftist coalition, United Mexican Socialist Party (PSUM), 3.6 percent; and three small radical parties, 3.5 percent.

As in Communist countries, the elections are a demonstration of solidarity. Ironically, the party gets the most support from the poorer classes, who benefit least from its policies, while most opposition comes from the middle and upper classes, who benefit most. There are many nonvoters although voting is formally obligatory; abstention may indicate opposition or indifference.

Regime spokesmen hail shutout victories as proof of "political maturity and democratic advancement." Lack of a real contest, however, generates cynicism and frustrates the purpose of the elections, to mobilize public support. Consequently, the opposition candidate may be "assigned" a suitable percentage of the votes.[33] Moreover, democratic appearances have been served since 1940 by allotting opposition parties a few seats in the Chamber of Deputies by proportional representation. This seems to have worked well, because the number of opposition deputies increased in 1972 to almost 20 out of 219, and in 1978 to 100 out of 400. The Chamber of Deputies thus looks and sounds like a genuine legislative body without troubling the government.

---

[31]*Wall Street Journal,* June 20, 1982.
[32]*Time,* July 12, 1982, p. 48.
[33]Lorenzo Meyer, "Historical Roots of the Authoritarian State in Mexico," in José Reyna and Richard Weinert, eds., *Authoritarianism in Mexico* (Philadelphia: Institute for Study of Human Issues, 1977), p. 11.

The Opposition

Defeat of the PRI would be a cataclysm for tens of thousands of worthy or eminent persons. They have little cause to fear, however. The PRI has a financial base no other party can approach, and it has the use of government facilities. The party controls jobs and benefits. It associates itself with the revolution and the nation; it and only it uses the national colors. For most people, loyalty to Mexico means loyalty to the PRI.

The last real challenge to the official candidate for president was in 1940; since then, opposition has been feeble, and after 1952 mostly symbolic. In the PRI view, "there are no real opposition parties in our country."[34] Some people keep trying, however. Through 1952, disappointed would-be PRI candidates for president tried to mount a challenge to the official nominee. Since then, various political tendencies have kept small opposition parties functioning as a means of securing a hearing for themselves, state a case, or gain a place in the system. The PRI wants a challenge to encourage electoral turnout, keep local bosses on their toes, and make Mexico look reasonably democratic.

The chief opposition party since the settling down of the revolution has been the National Action Party (PAN). Its beginnings go back to the contest over the presidency in 1929, when Calles imposed a rather unpopular puppet. It gathered force as a conservative protest against the leftist policies of Cárdenas. In 1940, a popular general, Juan Andreu Almazán, frustrated in his presidential aspirations, seceded from the PRI and formed his own party to wage a bitter battle against Ávila Camacho, the official candidate. The PAN joined him, but he failed, principally because his hopes of military intervention proved vain. In 1952, another

general challenged the PRI, with predictable futility; the PAN made a demoralizingly poor showing.

Since 1952, the PAN has continued to field presidential candidates but has lost militancy. It has occasionally harvested local victories—for example, in 1968 it won elections in the two main cities of Baja California, Tijuana and Mexicali, both on the U.S. border; but authorities canceled the elections on specious grounds.[35] In other cases, local PAN victories have been allowed to stand but not to be repeated. The PAN and other opposition parties are rarely victorious except at the local level, and they control fewer than a hundred municipalities. The PAN was proud of receiving 14 percent of the vote in 1970, 34 percent in the Federal District. In the 1973 local elections, the party got 16.5 percent, 40 percent in the Federal District. Almost all PAN votes are in cities. It hoped to continue this positive trend, but in 1976 it could not agree on a presidential candidate, and its convention broke up in disarray. In 1982 it may have really received 20 or 25 percent of the vote, much more in the urban centers.[36]

Opposition parties, mostly the PAN, won thirteen of 105 local elections in July 1983, scoring well in the northern states where U.S. influence is strongest. The opposition thus came to control the mayorship in five of thirty-one state capitals. The anti-PRI vote, which was mostly in better-educated middle class areas, was viewed as largely a protest against economic hardships. Leadership of the PRI seemed uncertain whether to tolerate electoral defeats in the name of democracy or to resort to traditional means of assuring desired results of balloting. In the southern town of Juchitán, the PRI demonstrated

[34]José G. Guerra Utrilla, *Los Partidos Políticos Nacionales* (Mexico City: Editorial América, 1970), p. 228.

[35]Kenneth M. Coleman, *Diffuse Support in Mexico: The Potential for Crisis* (Beverly Hills, Calif.: Sage Publications, 1976), p. 15.

[36]*Business Week*, September 12, 1982, p. 106.

firmness, perhaps because of proximity to Guatemala. The state governor simply removed the leftist mayor and replaced him with a PRI man.[37]

The PAN has been partly tamed and brought into the official sphere. It no longer attacks the PRI as a form of communism but remains a principled critic and advocate of a more liberal-democratic order. It calls for separation of the PRI from the state apparatus, impartial elections, free trade unions, and municipal autonomy. It favors religious education in schools. Its support is essentially conservative, from classes that formed the backbone of the conservative party in the nineteenth century, the adherents of the Church, landowners, and businessmen, plus a minority of intellectuals who criticize the PRI from the right rather than the Left.[38] The PRI spokesmen characterize the PAN as reactionary and counterrevolutionary, an attempt of the rich to take the government from the masses. This view is realistic in that only wealthy persons, lacking the financial support the PRI gives, can afford to be PAN candidates. It could rationalize repressing the PAN if there seemed any danger of its success. The PAN serves the PRI by validating the latter's claim to represent the Revolution and the people.

There are several smaller opposition parties. The older two, the Authentic Party of the Mexican Revolution (PARM) and the Popular Socialist Party (PPS), have been entirely subdued or "coopted" by a mixture of pressures and rewards. The PARM, like the PAN, stands to the right of the PRI. It was formed in 1958 by a general to support his anti-PRI candidacy. It continued to operate powerlessly, representing mostly old generals and their cliques; since 1970 it has

backed the PRI candidate. The PPS, which began in the late 1940s as a vigorous leftist protest, has suffered the same fate. It has almost become a branch of the PRI since its dynamic founder, Vincente Lombardo Toledano, died in 1968.[39] One of its functions is to attack the PAN on behalf of the PRI. Both the PARM and the PPS supported the PRI in 1982.

In 1978, the López Portillo government, having relaxed the previously stringent requirements for the legalization of new parties, recognized three more. One of these was the Socialist Worker's Party, a leftist group close to the PRI. Another was the Democratic Party, a rightist splinter intended to draw support from the PAN. This party represented remnants of an old semi-Fascist movement, the Sinarquistas, who stood for anticommunism, anti-Semitism, and hypernationalism, while favoring Church, family, and Latin-style authoritarianism. López Portillo also legalized the Communist party, at the very time when he was severely repressing extreme leftists. The Communist party, illegal for forty years, earned recognition by stressing independence from the USSR, in the manner of the Spanish Communist party. In 1979 it received 14 percent of the vote in Mexico City. In 1981 the Communists joined half a dozen other radical leftist groups to form the United Mexican Socialist Party (PSUM). Independent leftists remained aloof, however, and the Left continued to be divided in the 1982 election. The economic crisis of 1982–1983 seemed to add little to the popularity of the PSUM, despite hardships, falling wages, and unemployment. To the contrary, the PRI was strengthened by the nationalization of the banks.

The opposition cannot unite. Some want more active government intervention, oth-

[37]*New York Times,* July 29, 1983, p. 3; *Time,* August 22, 1983, p. 28.

[38]Salvatore Bizzarro, "Mexico's Government in Crisis," *Current History* 72 (March 1977), p. 103.

[39]Franz A. von Sauer, *The Alienated "Loyal" Opposition: Mexico's Partido Acción Nacional* (Albuquerque: University of New Mexico Press, 1974).

ers more freedom from government; the cause of democracy or political liberty does not suffice to bring them together. At the same time, the governing elite manages judiciously, not so much repressing opposition as depriving it of a political base. The opposition is institutionalized and given seats in the Chamber of Deputies (5 for any party gaining 2.5 percent of the vote, 100 of the 400 seats being reserved for the opposition parties regardless of their strength), without permitting it to endanger the power structure.[40] On the contrary, it provides useful criticism and occasionally ideas, informs the government about causes and the extent of discontent, and injects a little life into the ostensibly democratic but well-orchestrated political system.

Opposition leaders, if they are willing to be sensible and bend a little, are given jobs and an opportunity to become influential, just as Porfirio Díaz hired bandits to be policemen. Student radicals usually wind up as government bureaucrats. Echeverría offered jobs to the leaders of the disturbance he so forcefully repressed.[41] The alternative to grasping the outstretched hand is wandering in the wilderness. Dissidents are even taken into the elaboration and execution of decisions that they have opposed.[42] The PRI thereby shows itself as the only possible government. Opposition parties, unable to offer practical benefits, are driven to simplistic solutions, exaggerated attacks, negativism and panaceas. With reason, President Díaz Ordaz in September 1969 warned young rebels against rejecting the system. An opposition vote, then, is not so much for an alternative party or program as a protest against corruption, poverty, and the PRI monopoly.

Most of the unregistered extremists are on the Left, persons who see the PRI (with some justice) as having abandoned the goals of the revolution. For the most part, however, Mexican radicalism is disjointed and given to sporadic and futile violence—by invading peasants, illegally striking workers, shouting students, or armed rural or urban guerrillas. In 1959 and after, many Mexicans were hoping that Castroism might be the answer, but this gradually lost its luster. The radicals' only hope seems to be to stir things up so that something can happen, any change being potentially an improvement. The only thing the various groups have in common is enmity for the United States. They thereby condemn themselves to impracticality, because it is impossible for Mexico really to oppose its powerful neighbor.

THE REVOLUTIONARY FAMILY

The loose and shifting but rather small elite group of about 200 persons that stands at the head of the PRI and the state apparatus, the "revolutionary family," has ample means of ensuring its control, as it has done for sixty years. It uses elections to prove, every three and six years, that it is preferred by the people and hence legitimate. It gives the opposition opportunities to express itself, thus demonstrating that Mexico is free and democratic, without permitting anyone to mount a serious threat to the regime. Independent groups may be freely formed, but to progress they must obtain government support—that is, join the system. For example, in the early 1960s an unofficial peasant organization gained some strength in Baja California; but before it could become dangerous, the PRI offered positions to some of the leaders and met a few of the peasant demands.[43] The movement wilted. Dissident leaders are bought out, or their lieutenants

---

[40]Needler, *Politics in Mexico*, p. 32.
[41]Needler, *Politics in Mexico*, p. 79.
[42]Purcell, *Profit-Sharing Decisions*, p. 139.

[43]Coleman, *Diffuse Support*, p. 14.

if those on top are stubborn. Repressive measures may be selectively applied to demonstrate the folly of rebelling against the system, sops are tossed to the discontented to remind them that benefits come from the PRI, and alienated groups are divided. The PRI steers near the center, with about as much opposition on the Left as on the Right.

The PRI, "party of the workers," claims to represent all Mexicans and to be the only guarantor of order and progress. It is the visible custodian of the revolution and its heritage, and is naturally confused with the government in the popular mind. The legitimacy of the state, representing continuity and law, blends with the legitimacy of the revolution, representing Indianism, nationalism, and social justice. Nationalism has always been a predominant theme of the revolutionary tradition, and the PRI makes itself the bearer of the national traditions. Legitimacy also rests with the exalted father figure of the president; the good comes from him, the bad from evil advisors.

Control of Resources

The PRI is the only party that reaches down to the people everywhere, especially in the countryside, where it takes care to manage ejido elections.[44] Do you need fertilizer or a tractor? The PRI provides. For the workers, it is sane and sensible to cooperate with authorities. Independent labor movements are possible, but unions must be registered and the ministry of labor can decline to register a union or veto union acts. Unauthorized strikes and rebellious unions invite police action. The large majority of labor disputes are settled by the government,[45] and good standing with the PRI avails more than militancy. Profit sharing gives the authorities another lever, as they can reward or punish

[44]Padgett, *Mexican Political System*, p. 161.
[45]Ibid., p. 231.

at will by changing the entitlement of a group of workers. Instead of making legally based demands on their government, Mexicans petition it for favors; receipt of favors requires reciprocal support.

The solid basis of PRI power is control of resources. An ambitious Mexican probably thinks of a job in the apparatus; almost everyone of importance has been on the enormous government payroll, or at least has had close relatives benefitting from a bureaucratic position. In the Spanish tradition of economic interventionism, paternalism, and controls, the state runs railroads, electrical production, and the petroleum industry, plus a wide range of manufacturing industries and banking. Where it does not participate it regulates, and it can cripple any large enterprise by denying permits. Many industrialists are of rightwing persuasion, but it is much better business to work with the PRI than with the PAN, which they would philosophically prefer.

The regime also has substantial control over the dissemination of ideas. Thousands of intellectuals in and outside the universities depend on the state. Young Mexicans learn the correct interpretation of the revolution and the PRI's role, since all elementary education is state-controlled, as is nearly all secondary and higher education—although there are Catholic schools, despite their constitutional prohibition. Radio and television are in the hands of the government, although other parties are permitted a little time. Book publication is rather free.

The nominally free press snipes at the government, especially for local abuses, mostly from the Left. But criticism seldom touches the ruling party as such and is virtually never aimed at the president. In the electoral campaign, the press gives very little coverage to the opposition. The government controls the supply of newsprint, gives or withdraws official advertising, and may occasionally apply various other pressures. There are subsidies for the cooperative, whereas uncooperative papers may find themselves paralyzed by a strike. For example, a Tijuana paper that attacked the state governor was taken over by union action and the staff was replaced. Another example was the quashing in 1976 of the independence of a leading newspaper, *Excelsior*. Its editor, Julio Scherer García, broke away from the otherwise nearly universal fawning of the capital press, began investigative reporting in the American style, and ventured to criticize institutions. The government of Echeverría counterattacked. Several hundred persons were brought to stage a sit-in on newspaper property, and a meeting of the governing cooperative of the paper was bulldozed into firing the editor. *Excelsior* was then taken over by a corporation owned by President Echeverría, which already controlled two leading newspaper chains. Scherer was able to start a newsmagazine using black-market newsprint, and after his personal friend, López Portillo, became president, his problems faded. He started a new daily in November 1977, with the encouragement of some high officials—but he could not get *Excelsior* back.

Shortly after taking office, de la Madrid proposed a law ostensibly to promote responsibility in journalism but which could lend itself to censorship. The press protested, but it was suggested that its indignation may have been aroused mostly by the cutback of subsidies under the austerity program.[46]

The government is thus hesitantly and usually nonviolently repressive. It can use stronger means, however. The regime has a panoply of laws available to use as desired to coerce business, the Church, labor, peasants, or intellectuals.[47] It has been accused of holding varying numbers—not over a few hundred—of prisoners on political grounds. The accusation is denied, but from time to time opponents of the state have been beaten or have mysteriously disappeared. How far the state would or could use force if it really felt itself endangered one can only guess, but there is no reason to suppose that it would shrink from bloodshed. It did not shrink in the 1968 massacre, when the principal threat was to the success of the Olympic Games. The revolution only modernized the authoritarian order.[48]

Ways of Power

Two decades ago, many observers of the Mexican system were inclined to be optimistic about its democratic elements and confident of Mexico's future as a modernizing society. But the most obvious change over the past thirty years has been the waning populism and revolutionism, which live on only as rhetoric, and the conversion of the PRI into an instrument of privilege. The party is less a means to bring the needs and wants of the people into politics than an agency of control. The successful bureaucrat is not the one who innovates but the one who keeps things running smoothly.

Land-hungry peasants were the strongest force behind the revolution, and for a decade they were a major force in politics. But since Cárdenas, the agrarian sector, once in the vanguard of change, has become a stronghold of bossism, with the same old bureaucrats holding onto their posts. The CNC has come to serve not so much the peasants as the professionals who staff it.[49] The formerly aggressive labor movement has similarly lapsed into bureaucratic lethargy, and the official

[46]*New York Times*, December 29, 1982, p. 2.
[47]Needler, *Politics in Mexico*, p. 74.
[48]For an interpretation of Mexican authoritarianism, see Kenneth E. Johnson, *Mexican Democracy: A Critical View* (New York: Praeger, 1978).
[49]Padgett, *Mexican Political System*, p. 163.

unions do so little for the workers that under a quarter of urban labor is unionized.[50]

The Mexican system is as opaque as the Kremlin, but it is clear that decisions are made at the top, with little or no public debate and not much input from outside. The PRI does not favor grassroots participation in the implementation of its programs; in its paternalistic view, popular organization is undesirable.[51] Higher positions in party and government are generally for persons of upper-class origins. University education, which is almost inaccessible to the poor, is more than helpful for a government career—not only for the prestige of the degree but for the useful contacts one makes in the university.[52] The UNAM in particular is the breeding ground of political leadership.

As in the Mexican tradition and all authoritarian regimes, politics revolves around personal relations. The apparatus of intermingled party and state is made up of countless cliques, and people relate not to an office but to a person. Relations are mostly vertical, between chief and subordinate; the chief gives positions and chances for advancement, and in return, requires the full support of subordinates. The system is held together by rewards for personal loyalty, the chief virtue. To get a start, aspiring youths should know someone with influence to whom they can be useful; much depends on sagacity in judging who offers the best possibilities, because once one joins a clique it is not easy to change. Cliques are not only patron-client groups; they also form horizontally, as people who are in a position to help each other join for mutual promotion. They may be held together by *compadrazgo*, or godfather kinship. Cliques may simply grow up, as exchanges between individuals develop into commitments, mutual aid, and alliances. They may be formed quite deliberately as people seek others with whom to make a useful political association. This means, incidentally, that only in the capital can one cultivate the necessary relations to make a real career in politics. This kind of politics is not diminished by modernization, although it becomes somewhat more sophisticated. Personalism in Mexico seems quite as strong among highly educated young people as among the older generation.[53] Everyone in politics is a client of someone except the president.

The clique system means loyalty to family and close friends but implies unscrupulousness toward others, who are competitors, if not enemies. It is based on the use of position for advantages, which may be material as well as political. It is hard to attack abuses, if anybody is so inclined, because officials, sharing not only strong loyalty but also an interest in corruption, protect and cover up for one another. Hence, because of the cliques as well as the common vices of monopolistic power, the Mexican state is riddled with all manner of corruption. Costs of projects are mercilessly inflated. To be a traffic policeman is to have a commercial position that compensates for low pay. The new police chief of Mexico City in 1982 could not halt payoffs because he could not get funds to give compensating salary increases.[54] Supervisors allegedly forced police to be grasping by charging fees for the use of a motorcycle, uniform, revolver, ticket book, and so forth.[55]

Gratuities erase infractions of all kinds at all levels. Farmers pay large tips to get grain accepted at government receiving posts.[56] Authorities like to have trade controlled by quotas rather than fixed tariffs, because quo-

[50]Needler, *Politics in Mexico*, p. 62.

[51]Grindle, *Bureaucrats, Politicians, and Peasants in Mexico*, pp. 144–161.

[52]Ibid., p. 52.

[53]Ibid., pp. 38, 176.

[54]*Christian Science Monitor*, July 12, 1983, p. 7.

[55]Flavio Tavares in *O Estado de Sao Paulo, World Press Review*, August 1983, p. 27.

[56]Johnson, *Mexican Democracy*, p. 106.

tas require importers to negotiate with the officials.[57] The quickest and easiest way to wealth is through bureaucratic position, not so much by outright stealing as by influencing contracts and countless insiders' deals. It is reasonably safe. Occasional investigations hit only the small fry, and the maximum penalty is likely to be the return of loot. It is virtually impossible to clean up, because this would require punishing everyone at the top and destroying the system.

There are also many ways to improper gain short of outright bribery. Laws are flexible, there are no conflict-of-interest rules, and officials are free to accept gifts. Businesses cope with regulations and labor troubles by paying appropriately. Many jobs are artificial; Mexicans suspect that as many as a million phony positions were created in the López Portillo administration. López Portillo named many relatives to high-paid positions. In Pemex and other state enterprises, jobs are the gift of union bosses, who profit thereby. The oil workers' union also has a right to half of Pemex contracts, which give it a virtual economic empire. Not surprisingly, Pemex has three times as many workers as the Venezuelan state petroleum producer, for a similar level of production. This inevitably causes tremendous waste, and corruption is both unequalizing and demoralizing.

No Reelection: The Sexenio

Despite corruption, the clique-ridden system has a good record of economic growth and stability. Personalist politics and methods of control may be turned not only to selfish but also to national goals, and there exist well-motivated and sensitive officials who do their best for local communities, although they do not advocate a redistribution of power. The way to achieve some good is through the ap-

[57]Grindle, *Bureaucrats, Politicians, and Peasants in Mexico*, p. 39.

paratus; and the common view of the PRI as a successful agent of modernization, integration, and legitimation has some realism. Moreover, the Mexican elite is by no means closed; a poor boy without connections who makes himself useful to the party or to a rising politician may rise indefinitely—although the doorway may be too narrow for the large majority, especially because of the grave shortage of public secondary schools. The system is not vindictive; former oppositionists who are willing to serve the party and state may attain the highest office.

The vices of the government, moreover, are not demonstrably worse in 1984 than they were in 1929. Corruption and bossism have always existed; Calles and his crowd were as shameless profiteers as López Portillo. The saving grace of the Mexican system is that it has escaped the usual decadence of dictatorship because it does not permit power to stay very long in any one set of hands. In effect, there is a new government every six years, with a change of personnel more thorough than a change of administration in Washington.

This peculiar Mexican institution came about by a series of historical events. Many Latin American countries have been well aware of the danger of a president using his office to reelect himself and make himself dictator, and constitutions have prohibited the president from reelection or have required that he remain out of office for a term. But almost everywhere such provisions have been overthrown; only in Mexico has the principle of no reelection been combined with a strong presidency and a one-party system. This is evidently the most abiding achievement of the revolution. The Porfiriate broke down not because it was oppressive but because it had no way of renewing leadership; the revolutionary state somewhat accidentally developed a means.

The principle of no reelection was proclaimed by Madero at the beginning of the revolution in 1910. It had often been proclaimed previously, but by 1910 it had acquired special importance because it had been so grossly violated. It was strengthened by the admirable character of Madero, who made it his theme. Then his murder prevented his breaking the rule and left his image unblemished by abuse of power. Nonetheless, Carranza sought in 1920 to retain power. His death in the attempt reinforced the no-reelection rule. Obregón was not prepared to seek reelection at the end of his term in 1924; but after the Calles term, in 1928, he did so. The constitution was changed correspondingly. His assassination, however, prevented the breach of the rule.

Calles in 1928 was inhibited from seeking reelection but believed he could govern through puppets. At the same time, the constitution was again amended to prohibit reelection. The term was also lengthened to six years, giving a president a reasonable period to put his program into effect. Calles was probably satisfied to act as boss behind the scenes and thought he could continue to do so with Cárdenas as front man. Cárdenas was very popular, but he declined to seek reelection. His example and his influence in retirement served to discourage following presidents from trying to extend their terms, although Alemán apparently had such thoughts near the end of his term (1952). Since Cárdenas, the principle of no reelection has become a fixed part of the Mexican political culture, a sacred constitutional rule, and almost the only part of the constitution that has real importance. There is fear that to violate it would be to invite civil war. Díaz Ordaz rejected a move to permit reelection of deputies to the Chamber (who serve three years) as a possible step toward reelection of the president.[58] The principle is more compelling because it has been made general for all elective offices—governors, federal and state legislators, municipal councilors, even presidents of ejidos.

A corollary institution is the massive turnover of personnel every six years. Lower-level bureaucrats have job security by collective contract, but there is no regularized civil service and no tenure. With each new presidential term, some 50,000 officeholders are replaced at municipal, state, and federal levels. Elective officials go into the administration by the thousands, and party and government bureaucrats take elective posts. The president places his personal followers in power on top, and they bring their followers in turn, so desirable jobs (except in the court system) are reallocated among the deserving.

The disadvantages of this sexennial instability are obvious. It is a nightmare from the point of view of classical bureaucracy, and it is possible only because the one-party system gives reasonable continuity. It lacks the basic traits of Weberian bureaucracy: it does not have regular career ladders, with advancement by merit or training; and it lacks security, fixed chain of command, impartiality, and clearly defined duties. It is characterized by personalism and irregular lines of authority. A person may go from almost any job to almost any other. The system reinforces patron-client relations and makes cliques essential, because hiring is done on a personal basis and the only possible assurance of making a career is to know the right people. Moreover, since officials have a limited term beyond which they may be unemployed, the temptation is overpowering to seek financial security as rapidly as possible. The well-placed politician may put aside enough in six years to live comfortably forever;[59] a lucky few come out of the sexenio as multimillionaires.

[58]Furtak, *El Partido de le Revolución, p. 137.*

[59]Frank Brandenburg, *The Making of Modern Mexico* (Englewood Cliffs, NJ: Prentice-Hall, 1965), p. 11.

Lack of continuity is also an impediment to accomplishment. When the ministers and their deputies have taken office at the beginning of the new term, they take about a year to put their staffs together, during which time the initiatives of the preceding administration are forgotten or abandoned. Another year is spent in reshaping the agency and getting new programs underway.[60] There may be some three years to do whatever they propose to do. By the fifth year, impending change is in the air; the bureaucrats become cautious in preparation for seeking a new job under the new president. High-placed figures start guessing and maneuvering to attach themselves to the most likely candidate, to some neglect of their performance for the waning administration. There can be little planning beyond the six-year period and each term must repeat mistakes of its predecessors.

The advantages, however, balance the drawbacks. Dictatorship is most productive when it is fresh; in Mexico it does not last long enough to become stale and oppressive. Every six years a new president brings in new ideas and new collaborators, and they cannot become senile in office. Two-thirds or more of those occupying the top 180 to 200 positions in each administration are new, and very few serve in more than two administrations.[61] Opposition does not become desperate, because everyone knows that the present government will not last long and can hope that the next will be better. By the time discontent has built up, the term is waning, and talk turns to the succession. Blame is not for the party of the revolution, in any case, but for individuals who misuse its power;

they can be endured for a few years. This undercuts not only popular but also potential military opposition. The generals have less incentive to set aside a president who faces a fixed terminus.

The fixed period means the regularization of authoritarianism. The office of president is effectively institutionalized, so that it confers broad powers that do not attach to any personality. The president himself is exalted as near perfect, wise, energetic, and devoted to the people; only when his term ends is it admitted that he was less than perfect so that his successor can be seen as an improvement.[62] The ex-president, however, is never held accountable for misdeeds.

The system of limited dictatorship also places fairly competent men in charge. It seems that outgoing presidents want credit for choosing a capable successor, and they pick a man who has been thoroughly tried in administration. Mexico gets capable, not charismatic, leaders; and each president redresses the imbalances of his predecessors.

The sexennial renewal, contrary to what might be expected, also produces a fairly competent bureaucracy, perhaps one of the better, despite its propensity to corruption, in Latin America.[63] Organizations are most effective when they are new; and reshuffling at the top permits widespread reorganization every six years in a fashion impossible for an American president, who is faced with an irremovable and hence almost unmovable apparatus. New people want to make their mark in the allotted time with new programs. All are on trial, because after six years they will have to look for a new position. In part, this means not only working on political connections but also doing a job for a

---

[60]Grindle, *Bureaucrats, Politicians, and Peasants in Mexico,* p. 165.

[61]Peter H. Smith, *"Continuity and Turnover within the Mexican Political Elite, 1900–1971,"* in James W. Wilkie, Michael C. Meyer, and Edna Monza de Wilkie, eds., *Contemporary Mexico* (Berkeley: University of California Press, 1976), pp. 170–173.

[62]Meyer, "Historical Roots," p. 12.

[63]Richard S. Weinhart, "Introduction," in *Authoritarianism in Mexico,* José Luis Reyna and Richard S. Weinhart, eds. (Philadelphia: Institute for the Study of Human Relations, 1977), p. x.

boss who ultimately is called on to perform for a president aware of pressing national needs and desirous of making good marks in history.[64] In one sense, the sexennial turnover makes it difficult to carry through a program; on the other hand, it makes the apparatus flexible and responsive. In many democracies, the bureaucrats can quietly laugh at the political chief who walks in with dreams of changing things; they were on the scene long before he was and will be there long after he departs. The reshuffling of positions keeps most of the old crowd on hand, albeit in new jobs. But new people come in. There are always opportunities created by movement from one position to another, and officials undertaking new responsibilities bring their own sets of aides. On the municipal level, this adds to social mobility; positions are refilled every three years, and many of the lower classes have a chance to get a foot on the political ladder.[65] The juggling of positions also makes it easier to coopt outsiders or former antagonists; every few years many plums become available.

It seems paradoxical that the apparatus should be subject to frequent change under the rule of a single party, whereas in multiparty states the civil servants are impregnable in tenured status. However, only under the rule of a single party, with essential continuity of philosophy and of the political elite, would it be possible to shift officeholders so massively and so frequently. Within this limitation, the ability to change personnel gives much of the flexibility and regular renewal of rulership that are among the virtues of democracy. There is stability because of the real and continual although limited competition of elites, none of which has a permanent title to any particular part of the state.[66]

Impermanence of position thus brings an element of pluralism into an authoritarian society. Not only can officials be less assertive of authority that is only temporarily theirs; the "corporatist" authoritarianism depends on a degree of popular participation and is minimally repressive.[67] A change of presidency thus restored the discharged editor of *Excelsior* to journalism. A democratic process is necessary to legitimize the new government and enable it to make a fresh start. For this it is not necessary, of course, that elections be genuinely free, but the party needs a good facsimile in order to have a convincing mandate. Hence opposition parties are tolerated, even encouraged. The government must take into account the mood of the people, and there is far more of a contest than is permissible in the Communist system. The limitation of official tenure also tends to restrict state management of the economy. Officials have less interest in building up bureaucratic power that will not long be theirs, and they want a private sector to which they may go if necessary, although the overlap of political and business elites is much less than in Japan.[68] In sum, the regular circulation of ruling personnel offsets many of the vices of authoritarianism, lends the Mexican system stability through flexibility, and makes viable the domination of the state bureaucracy.[69]

PROBLEMS AND PROSPECTS

The Mexican system has shown great ability to ride with, absorb, and overcome opposition movements without sacrifice of power.

[64]Grindle, *Bureaucrats, Politicians, and Peasants*, p. 51.
[65]Ibid., p. 44.
[66]Johnson, *Mexican Democracy*, p. 72.

[67]Weinert, "Introduction," p. xiii.
[68]Peter H. Smith, "Does Mexico Have a Power Elite?" in Reyna and Weinert, p. 147.
[69]It is not to be imitated. The question, "Is Mexico the Future of East Europe?" asked by Melvin Croan, in *Authoritarian Politics in Modern Society*, Samuel P. Huntington and Clement H. Moore, eds. (New York: Basic Books, 1970), pp. 451–480, must be answered negatively. Cf. Needler, *Politics in Mexico*, p. 133.

Major strikes have been met with repression and/or concessions. Peasant discontent has surged up from time to time, but land invasions and marches send only minor tremors through the government. Terrorist groups and sensational kidnappings are troublesome, but they tend to discredit the opposition. The student masses are perennially agitating or on strike, but their protest reached its bloody climax in 1968. They have, in any case, little to offer as a political alternative. It is wholly probable that the ruling group will use whatever force it feels necessary to preserve order—its order. Thus far, not much has been needed.

Yet the Mexican system faces most of the problems of the other Third World countries, and it may be overwhelmed by them. The population problem is acute and only slightly eased by large-scale illegal migration to the United States. The number of Mexicans has quadrupled since World War II, an increase no country can properly cope with. There is no possibility of providing industrial jobs for more than a small fraction of those who enter the labor force each year. Statistically, economic growth has kept well ahead of population growth, except for a few recent years. However, after fifty years of land redistribution, in 1965 there were more landless agricultural workers than in 1915, when Carranza issued the first land reform decree.[70] The rural population swells while the number of jobs shrinks. Of 28,000 *ejidos,* four-fifths are too backward, inefficient, or poor to be self-supporting.[71] There have been illusions of transplanting masses of peasants to the wet tropical lowlands, but very little has resulted from large expenditure. Agricultural production per capita has steadily declined in recent years, and diet has apparently grown poorer; perhaps five-sixths of Mexicans are inadequately nourished.[72] The poor, with no future on the land, increasingly crowd into immense urban slums, especially around the overcrowded, polluted, chaotic capital, where they present a potential for radicalism. Eighty percent of the rural workforce earns less than $25 per month, largely because of high unemployment.[73] A majority of the active population is still functionally illiterate.[74]

Until 1972, official policy favored population growth; but in that year the government, perhaps persuaded by the overcrowding of the capital and employment problems, reversed itself and inaugurated a family-planning program. López Portillo pushed this program energetically, and the population growth rate is reportedly down to 2.4 percent; but this still means doubling every 30 years. The goal is to reduce the rate of increase to 1 percent by the year 2000. But the large rural population, the low employment rate of women, and the persistence of the social values of a traditional society keep the birthrate high.[75]

Mass poverty continues, despite the statistical tripling of the per capita GNP since 1910, because the benefits of economic development are unequally distributed. Forty percent of the population is little if any better housed, clothed, and nourished than in the days of Porfirio Díaz, while the top 20 percent has made the largest relative gain.[76] Whatever equalization was brought by the revolution has been erased, and inequality has become ever sharper. Some say the poor are poorer than in 1910, or at least worse

---

[70]Padgett, *Mexican Political System,* p. 265.
[71]*New York Times,* December 13, 1977, p. 2.

[72]Marvin Alisky, "Mexico's Population Pressures," *Current History* 72 (March 1977), p. 131.
[73]*Christian Science Monitor,* January 16, 1978, p. 14.
[74]David Felix, "Income Inequality in Mexico," *Current History* 72 (March 1977), p. 113.
[75]Ansley J. Coale, "Population Growth and Economic Development: The Case of Mexico," *Foreign Affairs* 56 (January 1978), pp. 415–429.
[76]Felix, "Income Inequality," p. 111.

nourished. Economic inequality is a heavy burden on politics in most Third World countries, but behind its revolutionary-populist rhetoric, Mexico is among the most unequal. The Mexican rich live very elegantly by the standards of the world's jet set.

There is a large potential for discontent and political conflict. For a long time the national product was expanding rapidly and providing resources to placate most demands or at least to give hope of improvement within the system. But now Mexico has to live not with growth but with unaccustomed austerity.

There were signs of trouble in the early 1970s, but oil seemed to solve the problem. Oil income, which represented three-quarters of export earnings, doubled yearly from 1976 to 1981. But imports, both of capital and consumer goods, rose even faster. The foreign debt was $11 billion in 1982. The budget went into chronic deficit, which increased to $16^1/_2$ percent of the national product by 1982. Inflation spiraled up, and the effort to combat it by subsidizing prices only hurt the economy.

Mexico was proud not to have devalued the peso in dollar terms from 1954 to 1976, but as it lost purchasing power, it became increasingly attractive to buy imported goods or travel abroad and to convert money into dollars, for profit if not for safety. After the 1976 devaluation, the peso was again held up artificially, thanks to even more borrowing, until the dam burst in 1982 because of the severe drop in oil revenues. To try to halt the panic flight of capital, exchange controls were instituted—a series of confused, conflicting, and changing regulations that showed poor coordination at the center of the government. The banks were blamed and nationalized, and dollar holdings in Mexico were in effect confiscated—a blow to confidence not soon to be overcome.

The government adopted an austerity program as required by the International Monetary Fund (IMF), wages fell far behind inflation, unemployment rose to perhaps 50 percent (with underemployment), and inputs were severely reduced. Oil exports were increased. The peso was allowed to fall to 150 for the dollar, an almost sixfold depreciation. All such measures were insufficient, however, to enable Mexico to meet payments due without large additional bailout loans, rollovers, and restructuring; the best that could be hoped was to slow the rule of the outstanding debt. Meanwhile inflation went to about 100 percent, threatening the peso again.

Behind the acute distress of the battered economy lie serious structural problems. It is not clear how a political system geared to material benefits for its members can expect to achieve sound financial management, without which it is problematic for strong growth to return. It is hard for a kleptocratic regime to manage an economy wisely, and the costs of mismanagement rise as the state sector of the economy increases. The government's share of the economy crept up from 20 percent in 1970 to nearly 50 percent in 1981, and nationalization of the banks (with their assets) raised it much more. The gross inefficiency and corruption of the biggest state enterprise, Pemex, are not encouraging.

It may be that the Mexican system, which worked well in the past, is not competent to guide a modern economy. There are signs, too, that the system is narrowing and decaying. The political elite seem to become more closed. They stand somewhat apart from the industrial elite centered in Monterrey, and ties to the private sector are a political handicap. The children of the latter are not recruited to high political posts. Neither, of course, are workers or peasants, as the hereditary element grows stronger.[77] It is notable that presidents and their cabinets come

[77]Needler, *Politics in Mexico*, p. 79.

increasingly from the capital (which has half the national income for one seventh of the population), without experience of the provinces, as do a large fraction of the bureaucracy. The elite receive fresh blood at their discretion.

If the governing circle becomes increasingly self-regarding and tends to isolate itself from the country—as the López Portillo clan certainly did in the last years—the long-time stability may come to an end. Then a popular revolution will be much less likely than military intervention in the Latin American tradition. At present, the military are not conspicuous on the political stage, but they are not absent. High officers often occupy party and elective office, and the party president has several times been a general.

The army decayed in the 1950s and 1960s, but it has since become more of a professionally trained corps with a corporate identity. Echeverría built a huge, modern military academy in 1976, and military spending has tended to increase, rising to 2.3 percent of the GNP in 1982. The last attempted coup was in 1935, and the fact that officers share the honors and riches of the sexenio system helps to keep them quiet. Also, as a precaution, the president has a guard of 5,000 under his personal command. Nonetheless, there have been recurrent rumors of a possible coup, and if the government came to seem excessively incapable, such rumors would doubtless multiply, conceivably to the point of converting themselves into reality.

The weakness of the PRI is its tendency to concentrate power with minimal concessions to outsiders, while the idealism formerly associated with its rule has been washed away. It is a dictatorship, although a qualified one, and like any dictatorship is self-centered and unreceptive to criticism; it can shut off feedback from outside almost at will. It is therefore no longer attractive to the young and the intellectuals; opposition is strongest in the most modern and progressive parts of the country and among the most educated people.

Yet the system is elastic, and we have no idea what its limits may be. Conceivably, assuming that the no-reelection rule is maintained, it may be able to undertake any necessary reforms if pressure becomes very strong. It has maintained continuity for more than sixty years, and it may be able to adapt itself well enough so that no alternative can displace it. Whether it can continue to lead Mexico into modernity and prosperity is less clear.

11

Communist Systems

Although the states of the world range along a continuous spectrum from the most democratic to the most authoritarian, the democratic countries of the Western tradition, with representative government and loosely controlled economies, form a fairly welldefined set. Likewise, the set of countries ordinarily known as Communist and selfdesignated as "socialist" can usefully be considered as a single group despite their great diversity.

Logically, Communist systems might well be considered together with the many states we call the Third World. Except where communism has been externally imposed, the states called Communist are of non-Western background and mostly were parts of the former colonial or semicolonial world. They are all concerned with economic development and industrialization, like most Third

World states. In foreign policy, Communist powers support the majority of Third World countries on most issues. Moreover, a number of Third World, especially African, states stand somewhat ambiguously on the margins of communism. Guinea, Angola, Mozambique, Ethiopia, Congo, Guinea-Bissau, South Yemen, Nicaragua, and a few others proclaim their dedication to Marxism or Marxism-Leninism and "scientific socialism."[1] The boundary is unclear. Moreover, it is only in the Third World that Communist or Soviet influence has advanced in recent years. In western Europe and other parts of the industrial world, Communist parties have generally lost a good deal of whatever standing they had a decade ago.

A basic characteristic shared by the Com-

[1] Bogdan Szajkowski, *Marxist Governments, A World Survey* (London: Macmillan, 1981).

munist states with nearly all Third World countries is elitism. Despite declamations in favor of the poor and the oppressed, Communist states place authority unequivocally in the hands of a self-selected and self-perpetuating leadership; the inequality of power is quite as effective as the inequality of wealth. The basic difference between Communist and dictatorial non-Communist states is that in the former the concentration of power is more absolute, better organized, and rationalized by an egalitarian ideology. There are Third World states fully as ruthless as Communist states, and dissent has been more dangerous in recent years in Guatemala, Argentina, or Uganda than in Poland or Hungary. But Communist rule is more coherent, purposeful, and total than that of tyrannical Third World states. It is the specialty of the Communist system to bring together control of the economy and dissemination of information in order to reinforce well-engineered and elaborately organized political control backed by coercive force.

In this regard, the Soviet Union, its East European allies (Bulgaria, Czechoslovakia, East Germany, Hungary, Poland, and Romania), its Asian satellite (Mongolia), Yugoslavia (with qualifications), Albania, China, North Korea, Cuba, Vietnam, Laos, and Cambodia form a reasonably well-defined group. They are the contemporary examples of the totalitarian or near-totalitarian state with a modernly organized monopoly of political power. They form a political category only. In economic level and cultural background they are utterly diverse, from East Germany and Czechoslovakia, industrialized and historically Western, to Cuba, agricultural and tropical Latin American, or Korea and Vietnam, relatively poor and backward and nourished by the Confucian tradition.

One reason for treating these diverse states together is that they characterize themselves as belonging to a special political order. All are governed by parties that call themselves "Communist" or in some cases, as in Poland, Hungary, and Albania, "Worker" or "Labor" party, and they are or once were affiliated with the Soviet Communist Party. For the most part, they regard one another as "family." China and Albania, which since the early 1960s have found the Soviet Union and its allies "revisionist" or worse, previously accepted Soviet leadership. Yugoslavia declared its independence in 1948, but counts itself one of the "socialist" states. All see themselves as representatives of a new and better social order. The Communist states, in other words, possess a common ideology—Marxism as adapted by Lenin to the needs of the Russian Revolution (Marxism-Leninism), and as further adapted by Stalin to the needs of absolutist party government in a relatively backward country. There are variations, especially in China and Yugoslavia, but the central message is everywhere the same; the right of the party, perhaps of an exalted leader, to govern in the name of the proletariat and with collective ownership of the economy. This is all to be achieved against the opposition, perhaps violent, of the outworn class of the capitalists, or "bourgeoisie," and the "imperialist" states, which the Communists claim to surpass immeasurably in freedom and democracy.

The Communist states also are alike in basic political forms. Each has a monopolistic political party which uses the official state apparatus as its administrative arm. The party comprises a small fraction of the population and selects its own membership; careers are made through it. Its structure is, with a few exceptions, almost the same in all Communist countries. The official state apparatus is also similar, with a formally parliamentary system. Except in Yugoslavia, factories are run by governmental organs, mostly central ministries, and agriculture is generally collectivized and state-directed.

In all Communist countries, the media are wholly at the service of the party or state, which has a monopoly on political organization; the political police play a large part; the courts are dependent; the government is contemptuous of elections in principle; and terms of office are indefinite—in sum, the characteristics of the democratic state are reversed to make a coherent recognizable form.

Similarity of ideology and political structure results in part from borrowing from the Soviet Union. Constitutions ordinarily have been copied, as have party rules and institutions. Cuba, after a non-Communist revolution in 1959, turned to the Soviet Union for support and eventually modeled itself on the Soviet pattern. Other Communist states started out in the Soviet mold because they were established by Soviet agents or by parties affiliated with the Soviet-dominated Communist International (founded by Lenin in 1919, formally dissolved by Stalin in 1943). The Mongolian People's Republic was founded in 1924 under the aegis of the Soviet Red Army. The Soviet Army oversaw the communization of Eastern Europe, except Yugoslavia, the Communist party of which was a faithful adherent of the Comintern, and Albania, which began as a satellite of Yugoslavia. The Chinese and Vietnamese parties were likewise obedient to the Comintern, which was godfather if not father to them.

Another common factor among Communist states is origin in war and violence, which make it easier to clear away old upper and middle classes and establish totality of control by a political party previously excluded from power. The Soviet state arose from defeat in World War I and economic breakdown. Lenin's coup was made possible by the loss of legitimacy of the previous governments, and a civil war hardened the Bolshevik monopoly of power. The Chinese party came to power by twenty years of fighting, assisted by the Japanese invasion and World War II. That war not only brought Soviet forces into central Europe but removed old institutions and left an open field for the Communists. War also brought Communists to power in what had been French Indochina. The nearest to an exception is Castro's Cuba, in which a non-Communist revolution was launched against an unpopular dictator in peacetime. But the communization of Castro's revolution went forward in the tense and occasionally violent confrontation with the United States; communization coincided with military mobilization. War is the great teacher of communism; its virtues are primarily the military virtues of organization, obedience, and dedication to a cause.

Communist states are further alike in that they rest (except Czechoslovakia) on an authoritarian political background. The extreme authoritarianism of communism can be imposed on an open society by force, as the example of Czechoslovakia demonstrates; but habits of strong government, centralization, and hierarchic order made it much easier for traditionally authoritarian societies to adjust to the Communist state. Moreover, all states voluntarily embracing communism were rather backward economically. Prerevolutionary Russia was by no means so poor as the Bolsheviks have claimed, but its economy was devastated by the civil war, from which the Leninist state really takes its beginning. Communist revolutions succeeded in China and Indochina at preindustrial levels and in the most backward parts of Europe—Yugoslavia and Albania. When Castro took over, Cuba was fairly rich by Latin American standards, but it was rather primitively agricultural. The Third World states most prone to Marxism-Leninism are also among the poorest, from Mozambique and Angola to Ethiopia.[2]

Finally, Communism has been one reaction of non-Western societies to the assault of the industrial West. In Russia, China, Vietnam, and Cuba, it has served as a means of mobilization against Western intrusion, of renewing and strengthening the self-respect of those treated as inferiors, while holding out a utopian vision of future happiness. Its strength is unity and self-reliance, and its motif is anti-Westernism rationalized as anticapitalism.

Fundamentally, the Communist states are alike because the elements fit together and reinforce one another, just as do the elements of the democratic system. Lack of any of the pillars would call into question the stability of the whole edifice: freedom of expression would undermine ideology, independent courts would encourage political independence, a competitive economy would tend to undermine bureaucratic authority, and so forth.

Consequently, the Communist states form a group to be usefully studied together. Our interest in them is in part practical; they are opposed in principle to the liberal, pluralistic, or Western way of government. The Communist countries are also of theoretical interest as the political opposites of the pluralistic societies, with their maximization of controls over all aspects of life and minimization of external inputs into the political center.

HISTORICAL ROOTS

The idea of the political party holding all

real powers of decision, ruling by a somewhat scholastic doctrine, and using the other organizations of society as its levers belongs to the modern age. The main features of communism, however, have appeared in many societies of the past. The idea of joint property has probably been common from the dawn of humanity. There is much sharing in primitive societies, and in emergencies humans are instinctively collectivist. Many—perhaps most—religious societies find virtue in the nonownership of material goods; monasteries, Christian or Buddhist, are organized on principles of economic communism. The philosophers of utopias from Plato to Aldous Huxley depict propertyless communities. Intellectuals of all ages have found private ownership a distraction and a blemish on the social order.

The authoritarian-bureaucratic side of communism had ample precedent in the great universal or near-universal empires of the past, such as the Roman, Chinese, and Russian. Organizationally, such empires had characteristics reminiscent of modern Communist systems. The ruling class was bureaucratic rather than hereditary; a large part of the property of the realm, especially land, and perhaps everything in theory, belonged to the state or the emperor; and there were extensive controls over the economy. The claims of the empire were universalist, and it was given to xenophobia and introversion. It upheld a more or less obligatory official creed to legitimize the rulership and its exercise of power. For example, Confucianism in the old China set forth the necessity of hierarchic order, headed by the emperor, to whom the people owed obedience in return for his care for his people.[3] Empires also

---

[2]See Peter Wiles, *The New Communist Third World* (New York: St. Martin's Press, 1982).

[3]See Robert Wesson, *The Imperial Order* (Berkeley: University of California Press, 1967), p. 186.

exalted loyalty, discipline, and subordination of the individual to the collectivity, in much the same manner as Communist states. They blessed service in the supreme cause and devotion to the ruler. They were nominally egalitarian, because all subjects were supposedly equal in submission to the exalted ruler. Great emperors, from Hammurabi of Babylonia to Constantine or Peter the Great, referred to the common people as their children and assumed the duty of helping the poor. The emperor opens careers to all classes; he may prefer persons of humble origin, because they, owing everything to him, should be most reliable. One example of imperial egalitarianism was the Chinese examination system, under which any young man might in theory attain the highest rank by passing a series of examinations.

The model Communist state, however, looks more like the ideal empire than the reality usually found in history. In practice, as an empire aged, the powers of the ruler decayed, and local powers began to manage their own affairs while professing obedience. A few accumulated great wealth; egalitarianism and the concern of the ruler for the masses became a sham. Under such conditions there have sometimes been political movements, much like modern communism, that aimed to restore equality, deprive and punish the illicit hoarders of wealth, and turn over the goods of the earth to all the children of God or the emperor. Then envy and quarrels would be laid aside, and all would live in happiness and equal justice. This is essentially the vision of modern communism: to restore, with modern methods, the virtues of the ideal autocracy. It is consequently not surprising that communism should have taken shape in a deeply troubled autocratic empire.

THE GROWTH OF COMMUNISM

The Beginnings in the Russian Empire

For several reasons, the modern Communist movement had its start in Russia in the nineteenth century. Because of geography, contacts between Russia and the West were especially intense, and the humiliation of comparison was felt early and deeply. At the same time, the high educational level of a few Russians made it possible to borrow a well-developed ideology and make use of Western political forms. The Russian empire was huge and powerful; it was also multinational, so a philosophy of renewal had to be universalistic. Russia was a semi-Asiatic empire of basically European racial and religious background, accustomed to taking from the West technology and techniques necessary for its strength. When it borrowed ideology and political forms suitable for the restoration of the authority of the decadent tsarist empire, it developed Leninist communism.

The Russian empire, like the Soviet state, was absolutist. Autocracy was seen as the bar to anarchy and as indispensable for unity, as party rule is today. The will of the tsar was equivalent to law, like the will of the party or its leader. The ruling class was a self-selected bureaucracy. Private property was little respected, and the state intervened widely in the economy. There were censorship and control of movement, as there are now. The empire exalted itself as the bearer of order and justice based on an official truth (Russian Orthodoxy), and it assumed an endless struggle for self-preservation and expansion, just as the Soviets have.

Virtually from its inception, however, the Russian empire was troubled by the ambiguity of its relations with the West. It wanted technology, especially military; modern administrative organization in order to rule effectively; and modern social institutions in order to feel equal to the most advanced countries. Yet it abhorred the political philosophy of individualism and limited government that made possible in the West the growth of new technologies and appropriate institutions. In the sixteenth century, for example, Ivan IV imported Western technicians but terrorized his nobles, in part to root out the infection of Polish ideas of constitutionalism. Peter the Great compensated politically for massive material Westernization by increasing the obligations of everyone and reaffirming his despotic power. But by the eighteenth century, aristocratic Russia was becoming ever more Western in manners and styles, and there were flickers of dissent among the elite.

In the nineteenth century, the problem of reconciling autocracy and Westernization became acute. With the onset of the Industrial Revolution, borrowing became more necessary and more difficult; while Russia, in order to function at a modern level, had to become a modern, complex society. The autocracy was solidified by victory in the Napoleonic wars, but at the death of Alexander I in 1825, some officers infected by service in France attempted a constitutionalist coup. Frightened, Nicholas I put an "iron curtain" around Russia for thirty years. The cost was weakness and backwardness, demonstrated by defeat in the Crimean War (1854–1856). Defeat opened the gates to intensified relations with the West, reform, and modernization. But the reforms—including an unsatisfactory liberation of the serfs; the establishment of weak, aristocrat-dominated organs of local self-government; slackening of censorship; and improvement of the court system—were half-hearted and raised more expectations than they satisfied.

In the West meanwhile, the advancement of science and industry was accompanied by an upsurge of economic and political liberalism, individualism, democracy, and nationalism—all sentiments poisonous to a multinational autocracy. There was also growing up in Russia an educated class, many of them un- or underemployed and embittered, that did not fit into the tsarist order and whose expectations could not be satisfied. Hence the latter part of the nineteenth century saw a remarkable ferment of political discontent and radical speculation, as a new "intelligentsia" searched for ways to save the country.[4]

This new class emerged first in Russia because of its relations with the West but has its counterpart throughout the Third World today. It was composed of persons sufficiently affluent to obtain an education, mostly students or ex-students, teachers, journalists, lawyers, and the like, who were educated to disharmony with the traditional society without being truly Westernized. Their mentality was basically authoritarian because of their background. Although they perceived the faults of the autocracy and hated it for its weakness and injustice, they sought salvation from a good ruler guided by a just philosophy. They wanted to help the people, but they had no idea that the people should be consulted. They were preoccupied with Russia's relations with the West and with ways of modernization. Longing to be as modern as possible, they laid naive hopes on science and eagerly grasped the latest intellectual modes.

There were many cross-currents and a variety of ideas, as there are in the Third World today, but two fundamental positions emerged: the Westernizers and the nativists,

[4]See James H. Billington, *Fire in the Minds of Men: Origins of the Revolutionary Faith* (New York: Basic Books, 1980).

or Slavophiles. The former took the fairly logical point of view that the way to meet the danger was to adopt Western ways; throw out unserviceable native institutions and values, perhaps even the Orthodox Church; and make Russia something like a copy of the successful Western powers. A policy close to this was, of course, adopted by Meiji Japan in a somewhat parallel situation. But Japan could do this better than Russia, partly because the Japanese self-image was less inflated than the Russian, partly because Japan was effectively united by race and culture. For most of the Russian intelligentsia, the idea of patterning Russia after Western society was unacceptably humiliating. Moreover, full acceptance of Westernization placed in doubt the status of Russians and the integrity of the imperial domain. If individualism, commercialism, political freedoms, and "bourgeois" representative government were to prevail, Ukrainians, Balts, Poles, Georgians, and a host of other nationalities would clamor for equality, and the whole structure would come crashing down.

Consequently, a majority of the vocal intellectuals took the more satisfying position of denigrating the West and exalting Russia, at least the idealized Russia that should exist. They were particularly inclined toward "socialism," a vague concept with connotations of progressiveness, rationalism, and economic justice. Socialism was much more interesting than freedom, which meant economic inequality and hardly seemed applicable to Russia because of its backwardness. Socialism was also anticapitalist, and capitalism was hateful, not only because it represented the irritating power of the West and non-Russian values, but because the greater part of Russian industry was foreign-owned or at least foreign-managed. The Russians, moreover, congratulated themselves that they might move more easily to

socialism than the arrogant Western "bourgeois" powers. There was a good deal of sharing and egalitarianism among the peasantry which formed the bulk of the population—exaggerated by publicists who idealized peasant institutions without knowing much about them. Russia was therefore supposedly purer and less corrupted than the commercialized West, and hence readier to leap to the higher state of socialism. Humiliating poverty thus gave Russia, as they saw it, superiority over the money-grubbing West. Long before Lenin, Russian writers were finding servitude, inequality, and misery in the West, and seeing the potential for achieving the opposite in despotic, unequal, penurious Russia.

As the intelligentsia became more numerous and more desperate in the last decades of the nineteenth century, they began looking to turn ideas into reality. The most obvious means was to convert the people, who by their numbers should bring down the old order. Missionary efforts, however, were shattered by peasant incomprehension and police action. Some turned to terrorism, but their great triumph, the assassination of Alexander II in 1881, brought only more repression. The perplexity of the intelligentsia increased also as it became apparent that Russia, far from leaping into socialism, was actually becoming industrialized in capitalist fashion. At this point a grand new theory, Marxism, arrived from the West.

Marxism found little response in England, where Karl Marx and his collaborator and financial mainstay, Friedrich Engels, lived and worked most of their lives. In semiauthoritarian Germany, however, it was taken up as the ideology of the labor movement. In Russia it became, especially in the 1890s, the new revelation for a generation of intellectuals. Its basic virtue was that it put in scholarly language with a metaphysical (Hegelian) basis precisely what the intellectuals of a proud but semibackward empire passionately wanted to believe: that the detested West was decadent and its lofty bourgeoisie doomed to destruction, that the capitalism they hated was outmoded and had to be replaced, that poverty was a virtue, and that the poor would be the builders of a higher order of society.

Marxism blended mystic faith with a materialistic-scientific outlook, to the pleasure of Russians who renounced religion as outmoded but whose spirit was fundamentally religious. That Marxism was dogmatic and intolerant was of no matter in an intolerant atmosphere, while Marx's utopia was akin to age-old peasant dreams of the land of milk and honey, with no conscription and no taxes. His stress on class struggle harmonized with Russian messianism. His internationalist creed also suited perfectly an empire increasingly threatened by the growing self-consciousness of Poles, Balts, Ukrainians, Caucasians, and others. Marxism united all under the banner of the proletariat.

There were logical drawbacks. Marxism laid its hopes on the factory proletariat as the class of the future, but Russia had about forty times as many peasants as industrial workers. However, the radicals felt disillusioned in the peasantry and ready to turn to a new tool of revolution, and it was also possible to stretch the concept of "proletarian" (as Lenin did) to include landless peasants. More serious was the secondary place Marxism assigned to such a feebly industrialized country as Russia. Marx foresaw socialism coming out of capitalism in the most advanced countries, such as Britain, France, or Germany. Russia, in the regular sequence of history, could only expect to go through the horrors of capitalism and emerge to the glory of socialism far behind the others. Some Russian Marxists held to the conviction that

Russia could advance to socialism only after a long capitalist development. Such Marxists declined to press for power in 1917 and by their self-denial facilitated the seizure of power by Lenin's Bolsheviks. The latter had no such scruples, mostly because they were activist power-seekers less sensitive to philosophical niceties, partly because Lenin developed a rationalization for an immediate socialist revolution in Russia: the colonial and semicolonial countries were exploited by finance capital of the industrial countries so that these could buy off their workers and prevent revolution while the colonial countries became a sort of proletariat. The honor of starting the world socialist revolution could therefore fall to the Russian workers.

Lenin, born Vladimir Ilich Ulianov in 1870, did the most to adapt Marxism to revolution in Russia and thereby shaped the basic ideology of the Communist movement. After a term of exile in Siberia, he went abroad in 1900 and spent nearly all the years until 1917 in Western Europe, chiefly in France and Switzerland. There he tried to build up a political party according to his interpretation of the needs of the socialist revolution. Marxism had passed its zenith as an intellectual vogue; Lenin sought to save it and give it practical strength by organizing a party of dedicated revolutionaries. As he set out in his most important tract, *What Is to Be Done?*, the workers, lacking political consciousness, had to be led by a tightly organized group of persons trained in Marxism, who happened to be almost entirely of middle- or upper-middle-class origin. In this concept lay the germ of totalitarianism: the party knew the right way and stood for the working class, so opposition was not permissible. A further corollary was that the leader, despite some democratic forms, was supreme within the party; the true doctrine was in practice what the leader said.

The Russian Revolution

From 1903, when Lenin organized his faction within the Russian Social Democratic (Marxist) Party, until World War I, the movement did not seem to pose much threat to the imperial government. It was a small group of emigré leaders, with a few thousand followers within Russia; and Lenin and his fellows spent most of their energies in polemics with fellow radicals. Their hopes rose in 1905 when the government nearly collapsed because of its incompetence and defeat in the war with Japan. Lenin returned from exile but took little part in the turmoil. The tsar made some concessions, promising civil rights and a sort of parliament, and the regime regained its hold. After 1906, the revolutionary movement was at a low ebb. The idea of revolution had lost its allure, and the liberals or constitutionalists offered the greater threat to the empire. Russia was prosperous; a growing private economy and a modernizing society presented opportunities for the educated. Russia seemed to be following the path of Westernization, with a partly free press and freely functioning, although largely impotent, political parties. Leninism in reality represented an earlier generation, and a destructive war was necessary to bring it to power.

The war that began in 1914 soon strained Russian resources, and by 1917 the economy was breaking down. Still worse was the incompetence of the government, headed by a weak and foolish tsar, who listened to his neurotic tsarina, who followed the advice of an eccentric monk, Rasputin. In March 1917 rioting in the capital over a shortage of bread became a revolution. The tsar abdicated, and Russia was headless.

To carry on the government and the war, a Provisional Government was set up by members of the old parliamentary body, or Duma. There were also established councils, or "soviets," of representatives of factory workers and garrison forces, on the model of the strike councils of the 1905 revolution. These exercised a sort of negative power, checking the "bourgeois" government but assuming little responsibility. Public opinion had been radicalized by the war, the defeats, the large number of casualties, the loss of territories, the influx of refugees, inflation, and food shortages. Most people were, or claimed to be, socialists. Yet there was at first a great euphoria of freedom, and the people rallied around the Provisional Government. For seven months Russia had, for the only time in its history, a wholly free press, uninhibited political controversy with many competing parties, and full civil liberties. The Westernizers seemed to have won.

In this situation, Lenin called for an immediate socialist revolution. Having been in Switzerland since 1914, he returned to Russia across Germany and set about forthwith to convince his own party and increasing numbers of the masses that they should fight not the Germans but the capitalists at home. At first, his message was unpopular; but the war went badly, the economy deteriorated more rapidly under the liberal regime than it had under the autocracy, and disorder grew. Peasants carried out their own anarchic land reform; increasing numbers of soldiers deserted and flocked to the capital, ready converts for Bolshevism. Workers eager for socialism made factories unmanageable. Minority peoples, such as the Ukrainians, moved toward autonomy or independence. Popular support for the government sank. Rightists afraid of too much change split from leftists who wanted much more change; anarchists threatened socialists. Hardly anyone really stood by the moderate Provisional Government, which could not cope with any of the big issues. The Bolsheviks, who called for immediate peace and promised bread and land right away and utopia tomorrow, won more and more followers. By November, the Bolsheviks were able to persuade the garrison of the capital that the government might send it to the front. Not class-conscious workers but war-weary soldiers put Lenin in power. On November 7, 1917, Lenin leaped from fugitive to head of the world's largest state.

Many reasons may be cited for Lenin's victory. His ideas appealed to an increasingly desperate people. His was a well-organized, tightly knit organization dedicated to the conquest of power. His second-in-command, Leon Trotsky was a good manager (Lenin himself, accused of being a German agent, spent several months before the coup off-stage in hiding). Other parties, irresolute and unaware of what a Bolshevik victory would mean for them, made no determined effort to prevent it and fought among themselves up to the end. Lenin had the benefit of German financing,[5] which enabled his party to sustain a large press, a well-staffed organization, and paramilitary units beyond the capacities of other parties.

With the sanction of a Congress of Soviets meeting immediately after the coup, Lenin set up a new government with "commissars" as ministers and then sent the Congress home. Refusing to form a coalition with other socialist parties, he proceeded as rapidly as possible to construct an authoritarian state. Censorship was brought back, and within a few weeks, a political police. Land was turned over to the peasants (who already held most of it), and factories were placed first under workers' and then under state control. A flood of measures put marriage, inheritance, the church, and courts on a new basis.

The revolution was completed by the civil war, which began shortly after Lenin's peace with the Germans in March 1918 and lasted until late 1920. It was a chaotic struggle, in which the Leninists were more than once on the edge of defeat. It eliminated non-Bolshevik socialists and moderates as well as conservatives; and the conflict, augmented by hunger and massive terrorism, completed the destruction of independent classes and social forces. It crushed competing parties and local autonomy and led to full government control of the economy, since rationing and the allocation of goods in the interest of military mobilization virtually eliminated money. It also gave bolshevism a military cast and washed out what Social Democratic humanitarianism there had been in Lenin's party.

Victory in the civil contest gave the Leninist party confidence and the conviction of right. Because their enemies had been helped by a rather desultory intervention of the Allied Powers, the Bolsheviks saw it as a triumph over world capitalism. But the European revolution the Russian revolution was supposed to spark failed to ignite. As fighting came to an end, the Bolsheviks, would-be leaders of the universal revolutionary tide, found themselves rulers of the Russian empire (except for a band of territories lost in the west). They faced the old problems of governing and modernizing the huge realm; but they had a new legitimizing faith and mission, a new leadership party, and a vigorous new class of governors.

Chinese Communism

The revolution led by Lenin failed to spread beyond the Russian empire (which became

[5]The German investment in the Bolsheviks is documented in Z. A. R. Zeman, *Germany and the Revolution in Russia 1915–1918* (London: Oxford University Press, 1958).

the Soviet Union), and Communist regimes established in the confusion of 1918–1919 in Hungary and Bavaria were quicky suppressed. However, the Soviet party and government undertook, eagerly at first, to spread the Leninist system through affiliated parties, the Communist International, and other organizations. The first major success came in China, like Russia a great autocratic empire injured and irritated by the West.

In China even more than in Russia, the power of the ruler was unquestioned, and the state was administered by a class selected, like a Communist party, for moral qualities and learning. Yet the ruling dynasty was far along in the historical cycle from vigor to decadence when in the nineteenth century the Western powers began making inroads, demanding concessions, and humiliating perhaps the proudest people in the world.

The Chinese state, unlike the Japanese, could not pull itself together to assimilate Western techniques for its defense. In 1911–1912 the dynasty collapsed and a Western-style democratic republic was set up, but it rapidly sank into warlordism and dictatorship. A small but growing class of intellectuals searched for an answer to China's woes. A nationalistic reaction surged, partly against the Western powers, which had been treating China somewhat as a colony, partly against the Japanese, who were trying to acquire an empire on the mainland. The young Soviet state, interested in China both as a counter to Japanese power and as an arena for spreading revolution, stepped in; it first helped organize Sun Yat-sen's Nationalist movement and then sponsored the formation, in July 1921, of a Chinese Communist party.

The Communists, like the Nationalists, were fundamentally concerned with the restoration of China; they differed in believing that social revolution and mobilization of the masses were the first requirement. The Chinese Communist Party expanded rapidly after it became allied with the Nationalists in 1922. It grew strong enough to seem threatening, and in 1927, Chiang Kai-shek, Sun's successor in the leadership of the Nationalist movement, turned violently on his radical allies and nearly destroyed the city-based party.

One of the Communist leaders, Mao Tse-tung, was determined to make the peasantry instead of the urban proletariat (industrial workers were few indeed) the vanguard of revolution.[6] He managed to establish a guerrilla base south of the Yangtse River, and there a Soviet republic was proclaimed in 1931. The Communists were then besieged by Nationalist forces; in 1934 they broke out to make the famous Long March to northwestern China, where they would be more secure. This was the crucial time of Chinese Communism, and the Long March became an epic and legendary feat. During it, Mao became the accepted head, and the leadership was solidified; nearly all important figures in the party for the following thirty years were veterans of the Long March. It also set the independence of Chinese communism. Mao had already gone against Soviet theory in stressing the peasantry as the revolutionary class; during the Long March, the Maoists were quite on their own and for long periods unable to communicate with the Comintern.[7]

The Long March was a military disaster, however; about 90 percent of the party and

[6]James C. Hsiung, *Ideology and Practice: The Evolution of Chinese Communism* (New York: Praeger, 1970), p. 61. For a biography, see C. P. Fitzgerald, *Mao Tse-tung and China* (London: Hodden and Stoughton, 1976).

[7]James P. Harrison, *The Long March to Power: A History of the Chinese Communists 1921–1972* (New York: Praeger, 1972), p. 243.

its forces were lost. The party was revived and enabled to attain power by the Japanese invasion. Japan had been encroaching on China since the seizure of Manchuria in 1931, and the war became serious and general with the Japanese entry into central China in 1937. The Nationalist government, forced to fight the Japanese instead of the Communists, was driven far into the interior and weakened. The Communists moved in as guerrillas and leaders in the irregular fighting at which they excelled, and they mobilized the peasants more in a national than a social-revolutionary cause.

For some years, Nationalists and Communists more or less collaborated, but the more purposeful and better-organized Communists gained. By 1945, they had several millions in regular and irregular forces and rather easily won the civil war that broke out after the defeat of the common Japanese foe.

On October 1, 1949, Mao Tse-tung proclaimed the People's Republic of China, not in the republican capital of Nanking (now Nanjing), but in the ancient imperial capital, Peking (now Beijing). As in Russia, at a time of national upheaval and foreign invasion the ideologically best cemented, best organized, most militant, and most consistently anti-Western party became heir to an outworn autocracy.

Eastern European Communism

World War II brought Communists to power in eight states of eastern and central Europe: Poland, East Germany, Hungary, Romania, Bulgaria, Czechoslovakia, Yugoslavia, and Albania. In all these except Czechoslovakia, Communist parties before the war were prohibited and very small. For the first five, the Soviet army was the direct mover of the Communist "revolution."

The process of communizing or Sovietizing these countries[8] varied according to local conditions, but its essence was the replacement as rapidly as feasible of non-Communists in positions of influence (anti-Communists were excluded from the outset). Leaders in the first instance were old Comintern hands, reliable Stalinists who had spent the war in the Soviet Union. They usually formed a "patriotic front" or coalition with socialists or moderates, taking for themselves the key positions, especially control of police and information. Presumably mostly for reasons of foreign policy, Stalin did not incorporate the occupied countries into the Soviet Union. But in a few years they were virtually copies of the Soviet state, each with its apparatus of persuasion and coercion and nationalized economy modeled on that of the Soviet Union, each ruled by a little Stalin—Ulbricht in East Germany, Dimitrov in Bulgaria, and so forth—wholly obedient to the great Stalin.

However, conditions other than the presence of Soviet forces—which were not entirely an asset because of their behavior—contributed to the triumph of communism in Eastern Europe. The old governments and governing classes had been destroyed by the war, and Communists led resistance movements almost everywhere. In demoralized societies, the Communists stood out because of their purposefulness; they promised progress and a new way of life when other ways seemed to have failed.

In the case of Czechoslovakia, the Red Army swept across the greater part of the country but then withdrew, leaving Czech Communists, who had led the anti-Nazi resistance, in a strong but not commanding position. In free elections the Communists

---

[8]It is summarized in Thomas T. Hammond, ed., *The Anatomy of Communist Takeover* (New Haven, Conn.: Yale University Press, 1975).

gained a plurality, although not a majority, and a coalition government was formed. For a few years, Czechoslovakia, under a Communist premier, was a unique example of the collaboration of Communists and democrats, with a free press and competitive party politics, an East-leaning bridge between East and West. But by 1947, the popularity of the Communists was visibly declining, and polls indicated that they would lose in the elections scheduled for 1948. The party reacted by advocating single-slate elections, undermining other parties, and tightening its grip on the police. Non-Communist ministers resigned. In a showdown, the Communists organized demonstrations, threatened civil war, and demanded full powers. Faced with Soviet troops on the borders and Communist control of police, army, and communications, the non-Communist president, Eduard Beneš, named the Communist leader, Klement Gottwald, premier. Czechoslovakia was rapidly Stalinized and became indistinguishable from other Soviet satellites, although it was not militarily occupied until 1968.

Communism came still more independently to Yugoslavia, which was to become in 1948 the first rebel against Soviet leadership. Josip Broz (Tito) was one of the very few high Yugoslav Communists whom Stalin allowed to live through the purges of the 1930s. After the Nazi attack on Russia in June 1941, Tito launched a guerrilla movement against the German forces that had occupied Yugoslavia a few weeks earlier. The Titoist partisans won out over rival guerrilla groups through a long and difficult war. They had better leadership and organization; they alone were all-Yugoslav, whereas other movements represented particular nationalities; and they lacked scruples. Others were deterred from anti-German actions for fear of the massive retaliations the Germans

promised and sometimes carried out. The partisans did not hesitate, and hence acquired a reputation as the most active and consistent anti-Fascists.

At the end of the war, Tito, with the country at his feet, proceeded to adopt a copy of the Soviet constitution and to Sovietize the land. Yugoslavia seemed the most Stalinist of the satellite states. But frictions rose between Moscow and Belgrade over economic priorities (was Yugoslavia to industrialize or concentrate on furnishing materials for the Soviet Union?), foreign policy (was Tito to act as a leader in the Soviet bloc?), the interference of Soviet police inside Yugoslavia, and other issues. Tito, having come to power largely on his own, was not disposed to subordinate himself and his people. In 1948, the quarrel came into the open. Stalin thought he could overthrow Tito by anathematizing him, but Yugoslav Communists proved better Yugoslavs than Communists. Relations between the Soviet bloc and Yugoslavia were cut; and the West, especially the United States, came to the economic assistance of the country. Yugoslavia undertook to construct its own brand of communism, claiming to fulfill Marx's ideal of a true workers' state. It has since stood out among Communist states for worker control in industry, a relatively free market economy, and a genuine federal structure, all without sacrificing the basic leadership of the Communist organization.

The communization of Albania was an echo of that of Yugoslavia. A national resistance movement arose in Albania, which had been an Italian colony since 1939, after war came to the Balkans in 1941. A few Communists got together to form a Communist Party, but it operated under the guise of a national liberation movement with a democratic program. As in Yugoslavia, Communists fought against non-Communist resistance forces as well as Axis occupation forces;

they were victorious, with a little material assistance from the Western powers and the guidance of their Yugoslav comrades. In 1944, under the leadership of Enver Hoxha (who remains leader of his party today) they formed a Communist government. Albania was a vassal of Yugoslavia until Tito's break from Stalin offered Hoxha an opportunity to purge the pro-Yugoslav section of the party and become an independent ally of the Soviet Union. In 1960, the developing Sino-Soviet split enabled Albania to distance itself from Moscow with Chinese support. Finally, in 1977–1978 Albania disengaged itself from a China that had turned away from Maoist radicalism. Albania became in its own estimation the one true Communist country, and its capital, Tirana, became the beacon for many extremist left-wing splinter parties disillusioned by Moscow and Beijing.

Outlying Communist States

North Korea. In the last days of the war with Japan, Soviet forces occupied the northern part of Korea in agreement with the United States. The Soviets proceeded to set up a Communist government where there had been virtually no Communist movement. Soviet troops were withdrawn in 1948, but North Korea, or the Democratic People's Republic of Korea, seemed to remain for several years, like China, a faithful satellite of the Soviet big brother. However, the Korean state, under the leadership of Kim Il-song, began moving toward independence even before the Sino-Soviet dispute enabled it to go its own way in the early 1960s. Adhering to neither side in the split, the Koreans have usually stood closer to China.

Korean communism has been outstanding for dedication to the nationalistic cause (concretely reunification), for thoroughness

of repression, and for the hyperbolic cult of the leader. No country is more militarized, and there is virtually no pretense to democracy. Despite relatively small size and poverty, North Korea has been a leader in the export of revolution, dispatching cadres to assist radicals in the Near East, Africa, and Caribbean region.

Indochina. The formation of the Vietnamese Communist party was chiefly the work of Ho Chi Minh, who left his country, then a French colony, in 1912 at age twenty-two to spend many years abroad. After the Russian Revolution, he was attracted by the anticolonialism of the Leninists and became a professional worker in the Communist International. He brought together a number of leftist organizations to found the Indochinese Communist Party under Comintern direction in 1930 in Hong Kong.[9] But it made no substantial progress until the Japanese invasion and occupation in 1940–1941 ended French prestige and military capacity.

In 1941, Ho set up a broad patriotic front in which the Communists were submerged but dominant. As the Allied victory neared, Ho's was the only functioning nationalist organization; in September 1945, he proclaimed the Democratic Republic of Vietnam. French forces, however, entered Indochina in March 1946, and by the end of the year war had begun. It extended over twenty-nine years. The long guerrilla conflict against French (1946–1954) and American forces (1961–1973) hardened the regime. A repressive land reform (1953–1956) virtually completed the elimination of opposition elements and consolidated its Communist character.

[9]Douglas Pike, *History of Vietnamese Communism, 1925–1976* (Stanford, Calif.: Hoover Institution Press, 1978), p. 10.

The Communist regime established in North Vietnam by the Geneva agreement of 1954 never gave up the goal of reunification, which was finally accomplished by the conquest of South Vietnam in 1975. A side effect was to give victory to allied Communist parties in Laos and Cambodia. The Cambodian Communists proceeded to establish the most extreme Communist system yet seen, emptying the cities; putting people to work under armed guard for subsistence rations; exterminating educated persons; and abolishing money, medical care, schools, and the like. They turned against their former Vietnamese comrades, and border conflict became war late in 1977. In 1978–1979 the Vietnamese occupied the country and installed a government favorable to themselves.

Cuba. Mao, Tito, and Ho showed that a peasant revolt could be turned to communism. Fidel Castro showed that a charismatic leader, under conditions of tension, could turn a country to communism with no popular uprising at all. The decisive factor in Cuba's becoming Communist, rather than Third World socialist like Algeria or Iraq, was the personality of the dynamic Jefe Máximo.

Castro was a youthful rebel against the dictatorship of Fulgencio Batista. After a brief prison term for an attempt at armed subversion, he went abroad to prepare a new assault. With a few followers, he landed on the Cuban coast in December 1956. Most of them were lost in their first encounter with the army, but about fifteen reassembled to hike away to the mountains and start a guerrilla struggle. They had a program of democratic rights and restoration of the constitution set aside by Batista, and they received no support from the Cuban Communist party until near the end of their fight. As the dictatorship became increasingly demoralized, its armed forces fell apart, and Castro rode to victory on January 1, 1959.

In his first months of power, Castro was or seemed to be a practical, nonideological reformer. But he soon began gravitating to anti-American and pro-Communist positions. He rejected democracy by declining to call elections or have a constitution. Relations with the United States suffered, as Castro resented American criticism and confiscated American landholdings. The quarrel escalated, the United States did its best to isolate Cuba, and Castro began looking to the Soviet Union for support. Anticommunism was forbidden. Castro began socializing the economy, and the Communist party was the best available organization to help manage it.

Violent confrontation with the United States motivated or furnished a rationale for instituting a full-fledged Communist state. At the time of the Bay of Pigs invasion, April 1961, Castro spoke of his revolution as "socialist," which in Leninist terminology meant "Communist." The emergency permitted wiping out most resistance or potential resistance, and victory encouraged the implementation of revolutionary plans. Large numbers of anti-Communist Cubans had emigrated, and the cessation of trade with the United States and most other hemisphere countries made Cuba dependent, as it still is, on Soviet trade and aid. Leaning on the Soviet Union, desirous of totally transforming Cuba, and able to make the Communist party entirely the instrument of his will, Castro adopted the Communist system in all its essentials. Despite profound differences in origins; personality of the leader; and economic, cultural, and international environment, the Communist political form imposed itself as the best way of fortifying total power.

Nicaragua. The overthrow of the American-supported Somoza dictatorship in Nicaragua in 1979 led to the establishment of a semi-satellite of Cuba in Central America. Resentment against the United States, desire for fundamental change in a country with a long history of political misfortune, the Marxist-Leninist ideology of the Sandinista leadership, the antagonism of the American administration, and the availability of Cuba as model and source of trained cadres all combined to the communization of the country. The private economy was taken over or reduced to impotence, the press was subjected to censorship and near-total control, opposition parties were excluded from influence and most activities, the Church was severely pressed, and nearly all activities were placed under Sandinista guidance. This would hardly have been possible, or would have been much slower, but for the help of several thousand Cuban advisors, teachers, doctors, technicians, military and police trainers, and so forth—a relatively large influx into a small country and a novel way of spreading the Marxist-Leninist system.

African Near-Communist States. In the 1970s the Marxist-Leninist system seemed to have spread to several states of Africa, particularly Angola, Mozambique, and Ethiopia. In each case, the Soviet Union extended military assistance to people engaged in a difficult military contest, and those favored by Soviet aid adopted what they could of the Soviet political pattern. In Angola and Mozambique, guerrillas fighting against the Portuguese colonial power set up near-Communist states on gaining independence; in the case of Ethiopia, a revolutionary government fighting against Somalia over disputed territory took on a Communist character.

These states were too poor and weak, however to be able to copy effectively Soviet structures. To a large extent their Marxism-Leninism remained rhetorical. It was not clear whether it was a permanent commitment in the face of their need for economic assistance from the West.

THE COMMUNIST IDEA WORLD

Anyone who tried to understand Communist systems by reading Marx and Engels would be badly misled. What is taken from the Marxist classics has been reshaped in practice; some of the phraseology has been retained, but it is used to develop other themes. Communism is authoritarianism, and it shares traits with other mobilization-type regimes, statism, nationalism, and militarism. But the Communist states are special because of their ideological base, the canons of Marxism-Leninism.

Much in the Communist way is typical of strongly authoritarian states, for example, fondness for parades and mass demonstrations, physical sports,[10] sloganeering, and awe-inspiring constructions and ornaments. Pictures of the leader were omnipresent in Perón's Argentina, Hitler's Germany, and numerous other non-Communist as well as Communist states. Authoritarianism commonly implies heroics, a cult of leadership and violence, and emphasis on will and character over intellectual ability or achievement; unity and loyalty are its supreme virtues.

Nationalism is also characteristic of the authoritarian system, understandably because the strong state asserts itself in relation to other states. This political imperative wholly overrides the internationalism of Marxism.

[10]The Olympic excellence of Nazi Germany and of the German Democratic Republic is notable.

From the point of view of Marx, nationalism was associated with capitalism; the workers were naturally internationalist, and in the era of socialism national differences would disappear. Lenin was a true internationalist, or at least antinationalist, as he showed by working for the defeat of Russia by Germany. But nationalism soon began creeping back into the supposedly internationalist movement, and Russianism was already prominent in the 1920 war with Poland. Under Stalin, the Soviet Union set about building socialism on its own ("socialism in one country"), losing interest in international communism except as an instrument of foreign policy. The Russian past again became respectable, and Soviet patriotism was exalted. World War II—called by the Soviets the Great Patriotic War—was fought in the name not of the proletariat but of the motherland. After World War II Stalinist Russia engaged in a virulent campaign against "kowtowing to the West."

In its subsequent extensions, communism became still more nationalistic, taking on the mission of freeing countries from foreign domination as in China, Indochina, Yugoslavia, and Cuba.[11] The national cause and values led Yugoslavia and China to declare their independence of the Soviet Union. Nationalism has become virtually a religion for Romania. Old princes, previously denigrated as cruel tyrants, were glorified as national saviors, and the special merits of Romanian culture were exalted. Maoist China carried self-reliance to the extent of depriving China of needed foreign technology. North Korea minimized contacts with all foreign states, including the Soviet Union; cultural imports were limited to what was strictly necessary for technological purposes.

[11]See Peter Zwick, *National Communism* (Boulder, Colo.: Westview Press, 1983).

In Communist states, travel outside the national borders is severely restricted or prohibited (except in the case of Yugoslavia and to some extent a few other East European countries). Foreign publications, even nonpolitical ones, are restricted or banned. Foreign trade is usually viewed as a necessary evil. The Maoists went to absurd lengths to prevent the slightest contact of foreigners with ordinary Chinese; for example, if a foreigner wanted to eat in a restaurant, Chinese were whisked away from neighboring tables. Movement even among closely allied Communist states is not free and is largely limited to officially sponsored and controlled traffic.

Closely akin to the nationalistic bent is the militaristic propensity of Communist states. As noted, all independent Communist states have been formed, or at least tempered in their beginnings, by military struggle, and the Communist system is better designed for war than anything else. The party is like a well-organized army, hierarchic, anti-individualist, antiproperty, and idealistic. The controlled economy, censorship, and repression of political deviance are aspects of the warring state, considered acceptable in the West in connection with military emergency.

With strong, purposeful organization and subordination of the individual, Communist states have excelled in combat. Although it suffered staggering losses at first, the Soviet Union turned back the Nazi invasion even before receiving substantial assistance from the West. Mao won the civil war despite American help for his enemies. Communist forces in Korea and Vietnam held off or defeated armies much superior in firepower. The Soviet civilian economy stumbles from shortage to shortage while excelling in military production. Cuba has great difficulty supplying the people with oranges, but its armed forces play a major role in Africa.

Marxism-Leninism

The most characteristic feature of these states is their claim to be inspired by a specific set of interpretations and goals, usually summarized as Marxism-Leninism. As Shafarevich put it, "socialism is not just an economic system, as is capitalism, but also—perhaps above all—an ideology."[12] Although various states have diverged from the Bolshevik ideology, central themes of Marxism-Leninism are axiomatic for all Communist states. All use the Marxist political lexicon, stressing "proletariat," "workers," "class," "class struggle," "bourgeois," "capitalist," "imperialist," "feudal," "contradictions," and the like, just as the party is always the "vanguard" of the workers, although meanings may be altered. For example, "proletarian" and "revolutionary" become synonymous with good, and "bourgeois" or "capitalist" with bad. In China any deviant could be called "capitalist roader."

Marxism-Leninism in its details is an elaborate scholastic edifice;[13] the fundamentals, however, are suitable for sloganeering and mass indoctrination. The basic proposition is that political history derives from relations to means of production and has an economic basis, the class struggle. Society advances through stages dependent on forms of ownership, from the feudal order ruled by landowners to the capitalist order dominated by the owners of industry. These in turn are destined to be overthrown by the workers, who will become the new ruling class. The proletariat, rightfully ruling by virtue of its overwhelming majority, will establish a higher form of society, socialism, which will grow

into the perfect condition of communism. This will be a utopian order of free and voluntary labor, with harmony and sharing of material goods, the climax of history and the redemption of humankind. The agent of progress is thus the proletariat, industrial workers in the usual understanding. But the mass of untutored workers, although anointed by destiny, is unprepared to act politically. So Lenin insisted that the revolutionary party must assume its rights and responsibilities—the party consisting of those indoctrinated in the true philosophy, whatever their background (which is nearly always middle class), and hence devoted to the true interests of the workers—that is, to the welfare of society as a whole.

The broad claim of this doctrine is egalitarianism, the right of the poor over the rich. The cheated and misused workers are to receive their due. This is a pervasive modern ideal, associated with freedom, democracy, and progress; it is also ancient ("Blessed are the poor"), based on sympathy for suffering and hatred for those who enrich themselves at the expense of others. It assumes the virtues of poverty, both of the deprived masses and the poorer nations. The poor are morally purer and greater of soul, so the future rightfully belong to them. The attack on the old society as the bulwark of unequal privilege was joined with the promise of a new order of brotherhood, compassion, and abundance for all.

The original function of the ideology was to make possible a social revolution in the name of the workers but managed by the party. It gave the Leninists the coherence to form an effective organization and the self-confidence to demand power for themselves and to appropriate the palaces of the tsar. After the Communists secured power, Marxism-Leninism became the guide and rationale for its consolidation and the trans-

[12]Igor Shafarevich, "Socialism in Our Past and Future," in Alexander Solzhenitzyn et al., eds., *From Under the Rubble* (Boston: Little, Brown, 1975), p. 29.

[13]It is summarized, for example, in Gustav A. Wetter, *Soviet Ideology* (New York: Praeger, 1962).

formation of society, the justification for social and institutional changes to fulfill the revolution and make irreversible the shift of power. Thus, ideology is reason enough to destroy potential opposition by nationalizing industry, expropriating landholders, and collectivizing the peasantry. Without an ideological justification, it would have been difficult for Stalin to remove everyone of independence through purges presented as defense of the revolution.

When the revolutionary reconstruction has been completed and the party's need changes from transformation to stability and the enjoyment of power, the ideology must obviously evolve to fill this new requirement. It began as a revolutionary creed, but revolution is no longer desired, perhaps not even abroad. It is egalitarian when there is no need to tear down an old ruling class but to sustain a new one. It is freighted with internationalism when the state has become nationalistic. Communist ideology must therefore be turned inside out to make it a defense of an established order. This is done almost invisibly, by changing meanings instead of words. The main propositions, even the radical language, are retained; and it is never admitted that ideology is being revised. "Revisionism" is a term of contempt; the party admits only to the "creative development" of Marxism.

Functions of Ideology

The basically outworn ideology is sustained with great efforts, the intensity of which is perhaps proportional to the loss of revolutionary spirit. To spread and inculcate the word is one of the chief tasks of both party and state. Except perhaps in such countries as Hungary, where indifference seems to prevail, or in skeptical Poland, communism may be called government by propaganda.

No non-Communist states come close in this regard; even Hitler's Reich lagged well behind.

To some extent, ideology stays in place by inertia, the fact that leaders are accustomed to it and that it is always easier and safer to go on using the same phrases. The old revolutionary themes also continue to be useful in regard to the outside world even when inapplicable at home. Although few Communist regimes today display much desire to spread the revolution, the mission of supporting socialism, the oppressed masses, and national liberation is still appropriate. There is little evidence that the foreign policy of the Soviet Union or other Communist states has been much shaped in recent years by ideology, as opposed to more conventional motives of prestige, power, and security; but there is also no real conflict. Marxist-Leninist goals are elastic enough to be interpreted to coincide with state goals.

A stronger use of ideology than the rationalization of the use of power abroad is its legitimation at home. If all governments have a philosophy to give rightness to might and make obedience a virtue, Communist regimes have a triple need. They demand much more of their citizens and impose sterner controls. They not only expect that people pay taxes and contribute to the national defense, but restrict their expression, movement, and activities. Moreover, absolute rule by a self-selected elite without an electoral basis needs rationalization. The party asserts its right to rule by calling itself the representative of the working class, which in the Marxist analysis is the maker of the socialist revolution and consecrated heir of the future. The party, a group supposedly selected for character and ideological dedication, is, in the common Soviet slogan, the "wisdom, honor, and conscience of the people." All government in Marxist thinking is class government. Hence the virtuous government is that of the virtuous and historically sanctioned proletariat, the future if not the present majority. But the workers themselves obviously cannot actually rule, so the Communist party rules for them with their support and assumed consent.

In the Marxist picture of class struggle, the revolution is never finished (at least, as long as there remain capitalists anywhere). The dictatorship of the proletariat must continue, and opposition is counterrevolutionary and beneficial to the narrow, backward capitalist class. There can be no doubt of the class character of the Communist government; since the capitalist class was overthrown, the new rulers can only be the proletariat, whose dominance is best realized by the party. The workers being an unpropertied and unselfish class, party rule is necessarily for the benefit of the people. The socialist state, unlike the capitalist, cannot possibly be exploitative; to oppose it is to oppose the building of a better future for all.

Many things follow. Communist citizens in working for the state are working for themselves. Factories produce not to make a profit but to serve the people, so workers must not strike against their own factories. There can be no legitimate opposition, because political conflict represents class interests, and the right of the working class is supreme. Any dissidence must be motivated by alien class interests, probably attributable to foreign "bourgeois" powers. The party is morally right, because morality is a product of class interests; "Morality was always a class morality."[14]

The position of the ruling party is intellectually reinforced by the scholastic side of

Marxism, dialectical materialism, which claims the prestige of modern science. "Scientific socialism" furnishes answers as eruditely as need be and enables the leadership to profess certainty about many uncertain things. Only the elite trained in this supreme science can grasp the deeper meaning of political affairs. Since they possess the key to truth, disagreement is indefensible.

Ideology serves not only the relations of elite and masses, but the self-image of the elite and relations among them. It relieves them of the sense that democracy is necessary and upholds their self-confidence by explaining and justifying their status. The subordination of theory to practice ("praxis") in Marxism facilitates taking success for truth. All are educated to common values, modes of thought, and euphemisms—any Communist knows the meaning, for example, of the "class approach." The understanding of the old school tie in Western societies is a very feeble counterpart.

The Marxist-Leninist world view morally isolates the nation, setting off progressive socialism from backward capitalism, the faithful from the heathen. It glorifies the defense of the community against the nefarious influences of individualism (greed equals capitalism) and "bourgeois nationalism." The polarization of the universe into the controlled and hence virtuous inside and the uncontrolled and sinful outside is extended into the Communist state: critics or dissidents are identified with the "capitalists," accused of being bought and hence damned for capitalist greed. Condemnation of the heathen world encompasses nonconformist culture from modern art to popular music.

Marxism-Leninism is thus a rationalization for censorship. It is also an inspiration and guide for censors (and writers and editors) in sensing the limits of the allowable.

---

[14]Friedrich Engels, *Anti-Dühring* (New York: International Publishers, 1939), pp. 109–110.

There cannot be detailed rules to cover everything, although the censors' instruction book runs into hundreds of pages; ideological guidelines enable writers to avoid most errors. The doctrine also acts as a sieve, permitting the importation of useful technology while barring undesirable political or philosophical ideas. Otherwise expressed, the Communist state wants commercial relations, including credits, and technological imports; but it cannot admit a free flow of ideas, which would amount to "ideological coexistence." Ideology helps to screen the flow.

While excluding poisonous ideas, the official doctrine provides a single unifying creed. Although drier than a religion, it can be taught to people of any creed or nationality as a science, backed by an array of facts or supposed facts, like chemistry or geography. This is most helpful for states troubled by ethnic divisions, such as Vietnam, Czechoslovakia, Romania, Yugoslavia, and the Soviet Union. The overarching creed of "scientific socialism" provides a common framework and language for Russians, Central Asians, Poles, East Germans, and so forth, as well as a vehicle of communication for all Communists. As shown by Marxism, nationalism is a "bourgeois" fiction, designed to divide and weaken the workers and "proletarian internationalism." Class interests are inestimably superior to national interests. The imperative of "proletarian internationalism" is especially important as the ideological basis for Soviet domination of eastern Europe.

Marxism supports collectivism at all levels and discourages individualism by its emphasis on society and class; in the Communist state people should regard themselves as members of collectives, from the school classroom to the nation, to which they owe devotion and loyalty and from which they can expect support. Among the most important collectives are the units of production. The enterprise is subject to the larger collective, the state. The vesting of all property in the people as a whole is further guarantee of unity.

Turning from the Past to the Utopia

The philosophic mandate for conformity derives its emotional justification from the program for change and renewal of society, and a marked break from the past is practically a defining characteristic of Communist as distinguished from other authoritarian states. Although respect for the national past grows after the state settles down, as has happened in the Soviet Union since the mid-1930s and in Romania and other countries of Eastern Europe since the 1960s, time is still divided into before and after the revolution and the inauguration of Communist power. In China, the repudiation of the traditional culture was particularly strong, probably because it was associated with shameful weakness. A positive aspect of the commitment to social change is the emphasis on the liberation of women in order to break up conservative social structures and to bring them into the labor force, although women are as much excluded from positions of power in Communist as in other societies.

A concomitant of casting overboard old ways and traditional institutions is the anti-church or antireligious stance that sets off Communist states. Policies differ, although all Communist states regard religion as a hostile force to be combatted at least by education. In Poland, for example, the government would like to abolish religion but is in no position to do so, and on occasion, solicits the cooperation of Catholic leaders. Yugoslavia is fairly tolerant. Albania, on the other hand, claims to have done away with organized religion; and various other countries, such as China and North Korea, virtually ended open religious observances. Marx was an atheist before he was a revolutionary, and both he and Lenin pushed atheism beyond the logical requirements of Marxist doctrine or politics. Communism wants no philosophical competitor.

When the Communist state settles down, the privileged wish to retain privileges, like their counterparts elsewhere; and major social change becomes undesirable for the only persons who have the authority to impose it. However, the idea of continuing progress toward a perfect society is one of the best means of reconciling people to the imperfections of the present. So conservative Communist states are at least ostensibly goal- and future-oriented, holding up a utopia as the reward for present sacrifices and the reason to serve the party, which alone can bring the new Jerusalem. It is more suitable to hold out a wonderful distant goal than to promise a modest near-term benefit; the former can always be postponed.

The utopian vision has been seen by many observers as the distinguishing characteristic of Communist societies.[15] The reward of present sacrifice is to be a life relieved of the burden of private property; people will take joy in cheerfully contributing their best to the common welfare. Coercion will be unnecessary, except in cases of abnormality, because crime is generated by inequality and ownership. The state, as Engels foresaw, is to wither away. Culture will flower in unprecedented richness. People will be perfect not only morally but as was promised by Krushchev's 1961 Party Program, physically as well. The vision is ancient, but it is per-

suasive because it is based on systematic and allegedly scientific analysis and the laws of social development.

When Lenin was calling for a coup in 1917, many of his followers assumed that the seizure of power by the proletariat, or its party, would bring about the ideal state in a few months. During the civil war, it was to arrive with or soon after victory. Since then, it has only receded. Stalin expected miracles of the transformations he undertook, but he had no liking for the withering of his state apparatus. Khrushchev mildly tried to revive the utopian spirit, and his 1961 programmatic statement solemnly promised that his generation of Soviet citizens would live under the higher condition of communism. The Chinese in 1958 saw themselves leaping ahead to communism by the Great Leap Forward and the People's Communes. But it no longer seems to be expected that any social transformation will bring utopia closer.

On the contrary, the increasingly vague utopian goal is to be achieved by economic construction, the benefits of which to the consumer may be distant because of the preference for heavy industry. This preference has hardly diminished through ten Soviet Five-Year Plans and has been emulated by the countries of the Soviet bloc and by China prior to the split. Fulfillment of the plan is a value per se, proof of modernization and warrant of abundance at some future date; abundance of goods, in the Marxist scheme, is to be translated into the building of the new society.

Education is the other leg on which the state strides. It at once teaches proper values, raises skills and productivity, and reaps gratitude for turning peasant youngsters into engineers or managers. Equally important, it remakes character, bringing forth the New Man, the flawless character prepared to study, work, and fight for the true cause. Ideology

[15]For example, Richard Lowenthal, "Development of Utopia in Communist Politics," in Chalmers A. Johnson, ed., *Change in Communist Systems* (Stanford, Calif.: Stanford University Press, 1970), pp. 33–116.

thus upholds an extreme work ethic (much stronger in theory than in practice). One should strive diligently without thought of personal reward, less for material than for moral incentives—honor and recognition as a devoted member of the collective, symbolized by tributes, diplomas, and medals. Stress on such incentives commends itself not only because symbolic rewards are inexpensive but also because they accord with the antimonetary spirit and the intended direction of society. For a Communist state to increase economic incentives and differences of pay is a retreat from central goals.

Labor is the true glory of humankind in the Marxist view, an attitude appropriate not only for the future but for getting over the traditional scorn for labor of the authoritarian society and for attacking intellectual individualism. Bourgeois values, on the other hand, are despised; desire for money is seen as mean and uncouth. The disparagement of individual enrichment also helps officials to refrain from using their positions for personal gain or at least to keep it inconspicuous. In pluralistic societies, a tightly controlled economy is feasible only in the unity and dedication of war; in the Communist state it requires an ideological underpinning.

It is a corollary that the good Communist should be rather ascetic. Although the Bolsheviks, like many radicals, inclined to free love before attaining power and in the early days of tearing down the old society, Communist regimes have a puritanical bent. The ideal party member has little time or thought for love; at best, he or she will form a working partnership with a fellow-worker of the other gender. Sex is hedonistic and individualistic, to be kept out of sight and mind (however freely practiced in private). For many decades, no kiss sullied the Soviet screen; and in China, the Soviet Union, and most other Communist states, amorous manifestations in public are still subdued, if permitted at all. The less rigid East European states—Poland, Hungary, and Yugoslavia—are more relaxed in this regard. In Cuba communism has most compromised with eroticism.

In sum, the Marxist-Leninist ideology at once justifies the rulership and seeks to mold the perfect citizen of an authoritarian state: dutiful; selfless; unquestioning in loyalty to the collective, the government, the party, and its leadership. The utopian-directed ideology of present struggle and future peace is a pillar of the Communist system, along with the political monopoly of the party and the state monopoly of the economy. Although the ideology has been put together ad hoc, it has great strength. It is definite and yet indefinitely flexible. Communists have been able to retreat in good order, as when Lenin in 1921 permitted private enterprise or when the Chinese gave up the Great Leap Forward in 1960. Firm conviction in ultimate rightness permits concessions without much loss of morale. Otherwise stated, ideology has enabled Communists to act unscrupulously without being cynical. They have been able to maneuver, to give words unaccustomed meanings, and to remove people as convenient, all with a sense of virtue in the service of the party. Elites wedded to Communist ideology have never let it go. The Communist system wavered in China's Cultural Revolution of 1966–1968, but it came back.

The ideology is for both masses and leaders. To the people, it holds out respect, formal equality, and a role in the supreme cause. If communism uses people, it may be that they are happy to be used as parts of the great collective, given a psychological as well as economic security in return for submerging their individualism. Equality is a difficult concept; but communism offers at least theoretical dignity for the poor, some concern for subsistence welfare, and perhaps opportunities to rise through education, work, and skill to positions of prestige and authority. The revolution is a great leveler, elevating new leaders, at least when the movement is fresh, from the ranks of the people. Often the most trusted young activists are children of the underprivileged, who may be expected to be the most grateful and hence the most loyal. For this reason, Communist states have favored access of the children of workers and peasants to higher education. This has been especially the practice where the Communists feel most hostility, in East Germany and Czechoslovakia.[16] Communist leaders have recently been rather lofty and secluded, but Mao and Tito shared hardships with their soldiers, and Castro and his cabinet cut sugar cane.

Marxism-Leninism offers the elite inequality of power, which is less offensive than inequality of wealth and more satisfying. It makes them responsible in theory to the class that is most manipulable and requires that the workers serve the elite in the name of the people. Whereas the Communist utopia spells future equality, harmony, and happiness for the masses, to the rulers it means the perfectly governable society. In it, all are perfect servants of the state. It is unnecessary to ask whether the leadership believes in the ideology or uses it for its purposes. The ideal inspires the rulers, justifying the sacrifices accepted or imposed; and the ideal is the excuse for holding and using power. The two aspects are inseparable. The rulers are at once the devotees and the beneficiaries of the cause. Communism melds together selfless idealism and unscrupulous self-seeking.

[16]For the Soviet practice, see Dmitri Pospielovsky, "Education and Ideology in the USSR," *Survey* 21 (Autumn 1975), pp. 24–25.

INSTITUTIONS OF RULE

The Party and Its Leadership

Ideology and political institutions are correlated, and the states that share Marxism-Leninism have generally similar political institutions. The model was the Soviet Union, whose forms other Communist states have accepted or imitated. The parties of the Comintern were directed to organize themselves after the pattern of the Soviet party; and where Soviet armies imposed communism after World War II, they established institutions like those they knew. The Soviet example has also been adopted by choice. It has the prestige of success, and those who desire to rule in a Communist fashion do well to adopt proved structures and methods, as Castro learned after a decade of experimentation. That political institutions should be similar in such varied countries sharply contradicts the notion of a political superstructure arising from the infrastructure or the correspondence of economy and culture with politics. It is understandable, however. The Communist structure everywhere serves the same basic purpose.

The central institution of the Communist state is the party, the instrument on which Lenin concentrated. The party may be composed largely of peasants, but the leadership is always mostly or almost entirely of middle-class origin. Inside the party, origins do not matter; the party itself is the "class." As Lenin desired eighty years ago, the party is a select group, a sort of club whose members call one another "comrade." Members are theoretically the best workers, always selected by the party itself, generally by local groups with the concurrence of higher officials. Membership is a privilege, a condition of careers that have anything to do with political affairs—and nearly everything in the

Communist state is touched with politics. In non-Communist authoritarian states, a ruling political party will be open to all who care to join, but Communist parties are always restricted to a minority, ranging from about 3 percent of the population in China and Cuba to more than 12 percent in North Korea. In North Korea, however, there is a "core," or party within the party.

Party members everywhere have special privileges and opportunities; they are those in whom the leadership places trust. In return for status, they are expected to be model workers, lead blameless lives, and demonstrate unquestioning loyalty. Members of the North Korean party, for example, "find their identity and indeed their purpose in life only by striving to fulfill the leader's directives."[17] To have individual thoughts is to court trouble. Members are likely to be called on to give much of their time to party work, and they must accept whatever duties the party gives them. On the other hand, devoted members can count on advancement, support in trouble, and security. Expulsion is unusual.

At the base of the party organization are cells or primary groups, in which the membership of up to several hundred meet fairly frequently. Attached to the primary organization is more or less of an apparatus, a secretary who acts as president, and one or more committees, perhaps an "activist" section or the equivalent. If the group is large enough, the secretary will be a full-time professional party worker—that is, he or she will belong to the inner core of the party apparatus. There are equivalent organizations at district, city, provincial, and regional levels, with periodic conferences or congresses of delegates, secretaries, committees,

and professional administrative staff. At the top there is a general congress, which ordinarily meets only once every several years (every five years in the Soviet case), but which is formally the supreme authority of the party. It elects, or in practice acclaims, the top leadership.

Inner party affairs are generally cloaked in secrecy. Relations among the several levels of party organization are in most cases obscure; they have been described in some detail only in the Soviet case. Theoretically, the members elect secretaries and delegates to conferences and congresses, which in turn elect secretaries and guiding committees; but so far as elections are actually held, the results are subject to confirmation by higher authorities and candidates are probably nominated from above. For example, in Vietnam, elections can be suspended and committees are appointed by higher committees.[18]

The higher organization of the parties is better known. The national congress of hundreds, or thousands in the Soviet and Chinese cases, sanctions a Central Committee of a few score to a few hundred individuals. This is in theory the supreme party body, except for the occasions when the congress meets, and decisions are promulgated in its name. But it holds sessions only a few days a year and so cannot be an operative ruling body. Attached to it, however, is an administrative apparatus headed by a secretariat, typically composed of six to a dozen secretaries, headed by a general secretary or first secretary, who is head of the party. The most powerful policy-making body is the executive committee of the Central Committee, the political bureau or *politburo*, as it is usually called. Typically composed of twelve to fifteen full members plus fewer alternates,

[17]Chong-sik Lee, *The Korean Workers' Party: A Short History* (Stanford, Calif.: Hoover Institution Press, 1978), p. 134.

[18]Pike, *History of Vietnamese Communism*, p. 136.

the politburo overlaps with the secretariat, a large fraction being members of both. It also brings together the chief officers of government and administration.

The essence of the pattern is centralization and unity. "Democratic Centralism," invented by Lenin, is the prevalent principle. Its chief precept is the submission of the minority to the majority and of lower to higher bodies, that is, the central authorities. Commands go from the top down; from the bottom there can be suggestions and queries. Unity is felt as indispensable for the party and all who depend on it; in its name, those who command inferiors defer to superiors for the good of the party. The logical result is that there must be a single will at the top of the pyramid, a personality capable of reaching final decisions and acting as arbiter of conflicting claims. Consequently, although the Communist parties subscribe to Marxism and the economic interpretation of history, which downgrades the role of the individual in relation to economic and class forces, they have been preeminently leadership parties dominated by overshadowing figures, such as Lenin, Stalin, Mao, Kim Il-song, Tito, Castro, and Ho. Leaders have been virtually irremovable; the ouster of Khrushchev in 1964, because he seemed threatening to the oligarchs, and of Gomulka in 1970, because he could not keep order in Poland, have been notable exceptions. Stalin clung to power through the 1930s despite policies of collectivization and forced industrialization that cost millions of lives and reduced the standard of living by about half for several years. Mao survived the collapse of the Great Leap Forward and the madness of the Cultural Revolution. Castro admitted failure when his grand campaign of a 10-million-ton sugar harvest fell short in 1970, but he did not resign.

After the demise of a strong leader, there has been some feeling for collective rule; thus after the passing of Lenin, Stalin, Khrushchev, Mao, Ho, and Tito, there was a period of government without any one dominant personality. However, there is a penchant for building up a leader, or permitting him to build himself up, as a father figure and symbol of the state and party authority. Thus Leonid Brezhnev received adulation far beyond any apparent accomplishments. Yuri Andropov was able to step into his shoes with exceptional rapidity, and soon his words were quoted daily and his pictures took the place of Brezhnev's, although he had been virtually unknown to the Soviet people. Similarly, on the death of Andropov, Chernenko was elevated to the honors, although he had been known only as Brezhnev's handyman. Kim Il-song, without apparent genius except for getting rid of his opponents and no recorded deeds or ideas of outstanding merit, is practically deified, receiving far more veneration than ordinarily given to God in Christian countries. Even in Poland, acolytes chanted the name of Gierek, a capable but not signally successful head of the party, as though he were emperor. In Communist states, publicity focuses on one chief, although it may be unclear whether he really has great power of personal decision or must heed a group of near equals in the politburo, among whom he might conceivably find himself in the minority. The Vietnamese party alone seems to have genuine collective leadership. China deviated in the 1980s, when Deng Xiaoping, although clearly the dominant personality, did not claim the top position.

If the image of the chief is inflated while he is on top, it is correspondingly deflated after he is gone. Stalin was denounced by Khrushchev, and the Brezhnev government virtually erased the name of Khrushchev from Soviet history. It was assumed that Walter

Ulbricht, who presided over the formation and growth of the East German state, was the grand figure of his party, but soon after his death he was found unworthy. Romania's Ceausescu similarly condemned the man who patronized his rise to power. Brezhnev, exceptionally, has been respected although neglected by his successors.

In the Stalinist past, the purge was almost a hallmark of Communist rule, and it was theorized that it was a necessary part of the political style, totalitarianism being maintained by terror and insecurity. This is no longer the case; security of office during good behavior, like the status of judges in democratic societies, seems to have become the rule. The purge in the Chinese party after Mao's death and the overthrow of the Gang of Four (1976–1978) were exceptional in the Communist landscape of recent years. Yet the Communist parties have not become bureaucracies in the Western sense. There is no formal tenure that would permit functionaries to feel independent, and there are no regular rules for entry or promotion. Careers depend on the will of superiors.

If the party is not strictly a bureaucracy, it amounts to a supergovernment. Ceasing to be a party in the Western sense by removing competition, it raises itself over the state and assumes the responsibility for decision making and policy direction. In Western political systems, the leadership of a party may organize and staff a government, but policy formation is in the hands of the state. In the Communist system, the state serves as administrative agency for decisions reached in the politburo or other party body, perhaps with the advice of administrators. The apparatus of the state, with its ministries and bureaucracies, is a servant of the party for the purposes within its competence, just as the police and military forces (directly under party command) are the strong arm of the

party, the labor unions are its agency for handling labor affairs, and the youth organization is its auxiliary for dealing with the young.

This "party-state" seems to be necessary, since all Communist states have maintained it, despite tendencies, in Romania and Yugoslavia in particular, to shift some decision making to governmental bodies. It seems desirable for the prestige of the party and its authority to command the state apparatus. Moreover, party supremacy facilitates arbitrary action. The state, as a legitimate institution functioning on a basis of regularity and legality, should serve as a predictable and reliable framework for economic activity; the party retains the freedom to move as it sees fit. It is logical, moreover, that if the party incorporates the will of the forward sector of society and not that of the people as a whole, then responsibility for guidance should rest with the party, not the government, which is representative of the whole of society. The rule of law must be kept subordinate to the will of the party. This accords with the Marxist theory of the state as the instrument of the ruling class.

Some strong leaders have restricted primary decision making to themselves and their personal entourages, but party primacy has always been vindicated. Under Stalin, party bodies were largely removed from decision making. But after him, the party was revived and strengthened. After Mao shattered the party in the Cultural Revolution, it was rebuilt and fortified. Castro found that he needed the party apparatus to govern effectively when the revolutionary drive slowed.

There is no competing political party—shadow parties kept up in East Germany, Czechoslovakia, China, Poland, and Vietnam are little more than agents of the Communist Party. Moreover, no independent organization, political or otherwise (except some tolerated religious groups), is permitted lest it take on political meaning and become potentially subversive. A literary society, for example, could deviate into political questions. By the same token, there are no organizations of independent standing (with the partial exception of Yugoslavia). It is even undesirable for leaders (except the highest) to be independently popular; authority should flow only from the party and with its sanction.

The State

In Communist systems, the line between the governing party and the official state is blurred. The party makes pronouncements in its own name and works closely with governmental organs at all levels. The real governor of the province is the party secretary. High officials are party members, and it is often unclear when they are functioning in a party and when in a state or official capacity. The party is financed by the state, although it has revenues of its own (chiefly from members' dues); the numerous party functionaries are paid from general revenues. The degree of fusion of party and state varies. In Yugoslavia, the party is more detached, more broadly supervisory, and less administrative. In Romania, on the other hand, the party has been merged with the state. Central Committee departments are joined to the corresponding ministries, and the local party secretary is regularly head of the local government council.

The original intention of the "dictatorship of the proletariat" as proposed by Lenin was quite different from the structures that have resulted. So far as a blueprint was drawn up, it was to be based on an idealized version of the government of the Paris Commune of 1871. The workers would assemble in the factory and choose one of themselves to act on their behalf in a council; this body, made up of regularly employed proletarians, would be legislature and executive combined. Something like this was attempted in the soviets (councils) that sprang up in Russia after the fall of the dynasty, and Lenin's revolutionary motto (except for a few months) was "All power to the soviets." When he made his coup in 1917, Lenin sought the approval of the Second Congress of Soviets, a large body of delegates from soviets all over Russia; and what legitimacy the new government had was based on the authority of this body, which had been indirectly elected by workers and soldiers.

It was a "soviet" government only nominally, however. The Congress was sent home, and Lenin set up a rather conventional government, except that ministers and ministries were called "people's commissars" and "commissariats." (The title of "minister" was restored after World War II.) The general structure of Communist governments has ordinarily been formally parliamentary, with theoretical responsibility of the ministry, headed by a prime minister, to the formally elected legislative body. There are a president or head of state, ministers, state commissions and committees, and a court system, as in a parliamentary state. On regional or local levels there are corresponding bodies, elected councils or congresses, and executive bodies formally responsible to them. There are also local or village councils, in which a considerable number of citizens participate in the execution of policy. The structure is regulated by a written constitution, which for the most part reads much like the constitutions of Western parliamentary governments.

Considerable effort is made to give the Communist governments (especially in the West) the appearances of democracy. The constitutions include most or all of the freedoms and civil rights common in Western constitutions, plus others such as the right to work, to rest, or to health care. There is no juridical means of invoking the rights proclaimed in the constitution, however; and they are balanced by or conditional on performance of duty to the state or society, as defined by the party. The "right to work" becomes in practice a duty to engage in "productive labor." And the constitution consecrates the supremacy or "guiding role" of the party. But the sovereignty of the people is formally set forth, and authority is based theoretically on elections. Much is made of "socialist democracy," something far superior to "bourgeois democracy." The Supreme Soviet of the Soviet Union, called "the Soviet Parliament," is held up as the true representative of the Soviet peoples because it has sheepherders and steelworkers (although a large majority of the deputies are party functionaries).

Some Communist governments do not bother to hold elections. China had none for many years and has held only a few local elections in recent years. On North Korean ballots there is no provision for choice or a negative vote. Cuba had no elections from 1959 until the regularization of the state in the early 1970s and has not bothered to hold more since. In most Communist states, however, elections are held, usually every two years, with the trappings of popular democracy, except that there is no choice of candidates. A slate of party nominees is presented to the voters, who are pressed to appear for the ceremony of casting ballots, with announced results of near-unanimous approval. This principle is generally observed also in trade unions and other party-dominated organizations in order to avoid a possibly disruptive contest. Voters have sometimes been permitted a choice between candidates, mostly at local levels, in Poland, East Germany, Hungary, Yugoslavia, and North Vietnam. In all cases, however, the candidates are picked or at least approved by the party.

The councils or assemblies thus chosen have no political stature, despite the fact that their composition is wholly controlled. Generally speaking, at the local level they meet more and have more business, but their task is merely the local application of superior orders. The top legislative body has a slight reality in a few countries, particularly Poland and Yugoslavia. The Polish Sejm has frequently amended and sometimes even rejected bills,[19] and Catholic deputies make it a forum for some mildly critical remarks. But usually the legislature is a purely acclamatory body, meeting only a few days a year to hear official reports and laudatory speeches and to approve unanimously whatever is put before it. The body has no home, and the deputies have no offices. They are amateurs, mostly worthy party and government functionaries, who are honored by being chosen to represent the people.

Closely related to what may be termed "pseudodemocracy" is the use of formally democratic mass organizations as "transmission belts" for the party, in Stalin's phrase, to fit people into the party-directed system without inviting them to share power. Transmission belts include trade unions, women's groups, paramilitary associations, and youth leagues. They are "preemptive organizations"[20] in the sense that they stand in the way of independent organizations. A host of party-controlled groups, from hobby circles for schoolchildren to societies for pensioners, are supposed to fill all social

[19]Peter Vanneman, *The Supreme Soviet: Politics and the Legislative Process in the Soviet Political System* (Durham, N.C.: Duke University Press 1977), p. 229.
[20]Johnson, "Introduction," in *Change in Communist Systems*, p. 19.

needs; such "social organizations" are stressed more when the regime feels insecure.[21] Non-Communist authoritarian states also make use of officially sponsored economic, political, and recreational organizations; but the exclusion of independent organizations is unique to Communist states.

Economic Management

The Communist states call themselves "socialist" on the grounds that the economy is publicly—that is, state—owned; its supervision and management is the chief business of the state apparatus. Centralized control of production fulfills the Marxist mandate and traditional concepts of socialism, makes possible (in theory) rational direction of resources and rapid growth, and is supposedly a means to economic justice. It also removes possible material support for an opposition. Everyone must work for the state and is consequently psychologically as well as economically bound. Centralized management of the economy makes jobs the gift of the party, and it means that everyone in a position of authority has a stake in the system.

For these reasons, Communist states carry the exclusion of private or uncontrolled enterprise much beyond economic needs and economic rationality, even when the state is unable to fill wants. To buy lemons in the Caucasus where they are abundant and sell them in Moscow is a crime. It may be forbidden to produce something for sale even with one's own hands, although peasants are usually allowed to dispose freely of the produce of garden plots. To repair leaky faucets for pay is likewise prohibited in the Soviet Union, although tolerated because of the inadequacy of state services. In several East

European countries, small-scale private businesses are allowed, even with a few hired hands. Hungary, which ended central planning in 1968, has gone farthest toward a market economy, permitting many private service occupations, private taxis, even private construction firms—in effect legalizing the "second economy."[22] Cuba, Vietnam, and North Korea (like China until 1980) permit almost no private business; Castro nationalized even shoeshine boys.

The means of management are complicated in detail and somewhat different from country to country. In principle, however, they are fairly simple. Trade, industry, and more or less of agriculture are under the jurisdiction of appropriate ministries, assisted by a variety of subsidiary controlling organs. Production facilities are grouped into enterprises, which have budgets, charge expenditures against income, and buy from and sell to other enterprises. It is desirable for enterprises or firms to make a profit, but this is generally not the primary consideration; the principal objective is to fulfill the plan. The national economic plan, nominally made for five-year periods in countries of the Soviet bloc and some others, is broken down into targets for industries, regions, and single plants, and even for shops within plants and for individual workers. Supposedly if everyone produces what is planned and interchanges goods as predetermined, the economy will function efficiently and output can be raised abundantly.

The difficulty of directing anything so complex as a modern economy from a single center defeats the theory. It has always been necessary for producers to go outside the plan to meet unforeseen needs, and it is impossible adequately to define objectives to motivate managers correctly. For example,

---

[21]As noted by Huntington in Samuel P. Huntington and Clement H. Moore, eds., *Authoritarian Politics in Modern Society* (New York: Basic Books, 1970), p. 38.

[22]*New York Times*, November 10, 1983, p. 4.

if the goal is to produce a certain number of shoes, the factory makes the cheapest kind; if the goal is to produce the maximum tonnage of machinery, it is made as heavy as possible. There also enter the typical rigidities and vices of monopolies.[23] Consequently, as economies become more complex and moral incentives lose force, Communist economies have shown increasing waste and inefficiency.

Growth rates of Communist states have tended to decline, and for the most part they are currently below world average. Most marked has been a decreasing rate of return from investments, perhaps only half what it was twenty years ago. Successive plans have been less ambitious; in view of the inflation that troubles planned as well as market economies (although in somewhat different ways), claimed modest growth of output may represent actual decline. Where they have been able, consumers have shown their discontent; in Poland in particular, workers in 1980 were so unhappy that they deserted the official unions, formed their own *Solidarity*, and would doubtless have brought down the Communist government but for the threat of Soviet intervention. Queues, often blocks long, are a regular feature of shopping in nearly all Communist countries; people are said to make a living by standing in line and selling their place as it comes near the goal.

Industry has generally been more successful than agriculture. Peasants have been collectivized in all countries except Poland and Yugoslavia (where the party officially looks to eventual collectivization but does very little to promote it)—that is, deprived of their land (except for small household plots) and made in effect employees of huge corporate farms covering thousands of hectares.

Sometimes these are frankly state enterprises, like factories; sometimes they are nominally cooperatives owned and governed by the members and their elected officers. It makes little difference, because the party and state officials rule in any case; and they are generally cumbersome and inefficient. Only in East Germany has collectivized agriculture seemed successful; its well-mechanized farms are quite productive.[24] The failures are notorious; and the need for formerly grain-exporting countries to import large quantities is both embarrassing and costly. Incredibly, in the Soviet Union the household plots, with 1 percent of the acreage, produce (with some assistance from the collectivized sector) about a third of the nation's food.

Control of Opinion and Dissent

The Communist state rests on the monopoly of organization and political action (backed by police and military forces), the near monopoly of the economy, and the attempted guidance of minds. By assuring "right thinking," the party should be able to prevent wrong action.

Censorship in some form is universal. It may exclude not only political criticism but anything considered slightly unpleasant. For example, crime is not reported except in some cases where there has been exemplary punishment. Industrial and other accidents are taboo; with less reason, so is news of natural disasters, such as floods, unless notoriously calamitous. A general cloak of secrecy covers not only almost everything of political interest but also much that would seem quite harmless. Citizens of Communist countries are never informed factually about their own armed forces or their foreign aid programs,

[23]George R. Feiwel, *Growth and Reform in Centrally Planned Economies: The Lessons of the Bulgarian Experience* (New York: Praeger, 1977), p. 159.

[24]Jonathan Steele, *Inside East Germany* (London: Jonathan Cape, 1977), p. 190.

although the information is in the world press. There is nothing of differences of opinion among leaders unless a faction is expelled from power; even then, explanations are likely to be scanty. The Soviet people, for example, were never really told why Khrushchev was ousted, and subsequent demotions have generally remained mysterious. The leading cadres have no personal lives, as far as citizens know. Various Asian countries keep secret even the names of high officials or the meetings of bodies supposedly representing the people. They publish hardly any solid data, not even favorable, about the economy or anything else. The extreme case was Kampuchea (Cambodia), where the workers for a time knew only the person of their immediate commander, behind whom stood the anonymous Organization.

Censorship and a penchant to reveal no more than necessary are ordinary traits of authoritarian states. It is the Communist speciality to make maximum use of all means of communication to convey positive messages, from respect for leaders and gratitude for the benefits of the system to proper work habits and enthusiasm. Merely authoritarian states set limits that writers must not transgress; Communist states instruct writers as to what they should say. Communications, moreover, should be purposeful. If a story were merely entertaining, it would be slightly subversive. There are concessions to pure entertainment, and the less truculent states of Eastern Europe are more relaxed in this regard, but there should preferably be a positive message and no frivolity. One extreme was the prohibition, for the several years of China's Cultural Revolution, of almost everything except Mao's Thought and commentaries thereon.

Ways to control opinion are many. Writers and artists are organized in guilds, exclusion from which means exclusion from the profession. At the same time, writers who produce approved materials have status and luxuries without much work. It is not easy, however, to produce works that are interesting and reasonably original within the confines of official canons, called "socialist realism" in the Soviet sphere. This requires a rather simple realistic presentation and themes inspirational for the building of socialism and the formation of the "new man." There should be no "arty" art, unrealistic painting, or unconventional music. Most Communist governments have gone to considerable lengths to suppress Western-style modern music; Czechoslovakia has even decreed that musicians must pass political theory examinations. But authors find it difficult to treat their own society because there should be no real conflicts within socialist society, and the perennial topics of sex and individualistic deviations are more or less disapproved.

Probably the most important way to form attitudes and the one hardest to resist is the educational system. From beginning to end, ideological training is required, from kindergarteners who learn about Grandfather Lenin's love for them to university students who must master the dialectics to qualify for a degree. In addition to obligatory instruction in Marxism-Leninism, all courses, even arithmetic, should convey something of the message. All university instructors are expected to show ideological preparation; physics professors must have Marxist-Leninist attitudes. It was a sign of liberalism in Hungary that it could be debated whether it was really necessary that physicists prove their ideological rectitude.

The press also carries on the struggle for minds. Only persons considered well qualified, generally party members, are admitted to journalism. Its effectiveness, however, is limited by the exclusion of most of what would be called news in the West, personal or controversial items as well as anything that might conceivably have a negative impact. Fortunately, there exists a black outer world of capitalism, the crime, poverty, and general degradation of which can be freely elaborated. The typical Communist newspaper is only four or six pages and rather stereotyped, with reports of official actions, occasionally long speeches by leaders, accounts of successes in production, and the like. The papers, in fact, are rather similar from one year or one decade to the next. The interest and liveliness of the press varies inversely, of course, with the intensity of the system; Polish papers are less dull than Soviet, and the Yugoslav press approaches that of a Western country.

Radio and television are equally used as a means of forming opinion, and they are perhaps more effective than the printed media. Their message can be absorbed passively by the weary citizen. Radio has a grave drawback, however, in that Western shortwave broadcasts cover the Communist sphere, and those within a few hundred miles of foreign lands can tune to middle-wave broadcasts. Western television is accessible to Soviet Estonia; to East Germany; and to most of Czechoslovakia, Hungary, Yugoslavia, Albania, and Bulgaria, in many cases in understandable languages. Jamming is only a partial answer to the electromagnetic invasion.

How effective lifelong exposure to the official truth may be one can only guess. Humans are often refractory, and the imposed message is largely ignored. Moscow has probably the world's greatest grapevine. Indoctrination has not been sufficiently successful for any Communist government to risk free elections. After twenty years of Soviet control, peoples of regions occupied by the Germans in World War II seem generally to have greeted the invaders warmly until repelled by their brutalities. Numerous surveys of East Europeans traveling in the West with the intention of returning to the homeland have shown large majorities desirous of a different form of government. According to an East German dissident group, "First Ulbricht's and then Honecker's effort to replace the need for a national identity with love for the Soviet fatherland has achieved the opposite: growing repugnance for everything that comes out of Moscow and often uncritical admiration for the glittering German West."[25]

It may be assumed, however, that most persons in Communist countries, genuine intellectuals excepted, seem generally to accept the official version and are certainly unwilling to do much against their governments. It appears for the most part that people accept that the basic aims of their state are good, even though plans are poorly carried out. They assume there is nothing to be done about it anyway and perform the obedient motions as required.

But there has always been a minority, usually very small, prepared to speak or act against the Communist state in defiance of its overwhelming power. For this reason, Lenin restored the political police a few weeks after he took power. It has been active in pursuit of "counterrevolutionaries" ever since, and all Communist states have security organizations. The severity of repression has varied from time to time and country to country, but it has never ceased entirely. The barbarism of Stalin's destruction of the class he most disliked, the less impoverished peasants, or *kulaks,* and of all those whom he suspected of possible opposition has been exceeded only by the Kampuchean madness

[25]*Der Spiegel,* January 2, 1978, p. 21.

of the 1970s. Generally, Communist states have been most brutal early in their lives, as they sought to eradicate classes more attached to the previous regime.

The latitude of dissidence permitted in recent years has ranged from almost nil in North Korea to sometimes surprisingly great in Hungary or Yugoslavia. In the Soviet Union private criticism seems frequently allowable, but authorities attend quickly to public manifestations of discontent. Guilty persons may be merely intimidated and warned; repeaters are subject to loss of jobs, cancellation of residence permits, forced labor, perhaps confinement in psychiatric prison-hospitals, or in a few cases, exile abroad. Czechoslovakia, Romania, and Bulgaria handle protesters much like the Soviet Union, with a mixture of soft and hard pressures. People talk as they please in Hungary, and religious instruction is permitted in schools, but the media are kept ideologically correct. Yugoslavia has no problem of defiant uncensored writing because the borders are virtually open, Western writings are obtainable, and the press is sometimes remarkably critical.[26] The number of opponents jailed is only a few hundred, not enough really to inhibit the population but enough to intimidate most intellectuals.

It seems reasonable to guess that most Communist states are much more severely conformist and repressive than necessary for the maintenance of power. This may be ascribed to a sense of insecurity and the fear that any tiny opposition might grow dangerously, like a spark in a dry haystack. It may likewise represent arbitrary exercise of power by the police or be related to simple dislike of criticism. Those who enjoy torrents of adulation and are often told how the people love them might well resent the effrontery of a handful of eccentrics and wish to erase this blemish on their state.

Who Rules?

It is an intriguing occupation of political analysts to try to determine where power really lies in a system. There are usually answers at hand—presidents, prime ministers, their colleagues and collaborators, general secretaries, and the like. But it is always possible that people wield more power than is formally assigned to them, or less; there are figureheads and powers behind thrones.

This peering behind the screen in the most powerful Communist countries is important. If we can learn who really rules, policies may become more understandable and perhaps predictable. The effort goes in two principal directions. One is kremlinology, a sort of refined journalistic approach that seeks to analyze in terms of personalities through various hints about status and attitudes emerging to public view.[27] The other is a more sociological approach, an effort to discern the influence of various groups in the society through detailed, more or less statistical studies.[28]

In Communist states there is no admitted politics at all; everyone supposedly is moved only by zeal, and public statements are framed to show only unanimity. The Communist states themselves usually declare to the world who governs; the party, the central committee, the politburo, and the general secretary or equivalent; and from time to time

[26]*Los Angeles Times,* October 7, 1983, p. viii–4.

[27]Examples are Michael Tatu, *Power in the Kremlin: From Khrushchev to Kosygin* (New York: Viking Press, 1970); Robert Conquest, *Power and Policy in the U.S.S.R.: The Study of Soviet Dynamics* (London: Macmillan, 1961).

[28]An example is H. G. Skilling and F. Griffith, eds., *Interest Groups in Soviet Politics* (Princeton, N.J.: Princeton University Press, 1969).

there are published lists (as at party meetings) that can be taken as rank orderings. Supposedly references in the Soviet press have some relation to the importance of a given body; rather frequent mention of the politburo, for example, indicates its standing. The Central Committee cannot ordinarily be important as a decision maker, but membership in it appears to be equivalent to top elite status. Yet sections of the Central Committee, almost never mentioned in the press, seem to be very influential. On the other hand, the much-publicized parliamentary organs are showpieces.

How much power the leader himself has is somewhat conjectural and is not to be judged solely by his personality cult. It seems that Brezhnev was rather less decisive than indicated by his cult, and Chairman Hua gave the impression of being somewhat of a figurehead. In the 1940s it was widely conjectured that Stalin was more or less subject to his politburo, but it has become clear that he was very much the boss. One can be certain that Kim Il-song is not only the living god of North Korea but its boss, because he has remained steadily at the top while personages around him have changed kaleidoscopically. The power of the dictator depends, however, on keeping subordinates divided. Stalin could have been set aside if conspirators had been able to secure the concurrence of the police and/or military forces. This was precisely what he was determined to prevent, as he alternately terrorized and rewarded.

In any large organization there must be pressures upward and downward, those on top responding as well as commanding, even though little is allowed to appear on the surface. In regard at least to Soviet politics, there has been much discussion of the antithesis of two obviously important groups, the party apparatus and the state bureaucracy. Such an antithesis was evident in 1953–1954 when Khrushchev, head of the party, and Malenkov, chairman of the Council of Ministers, were jousting for Stalin's mantle. This was an exceptional situation, however, because Stalin had downgraded the authority of the party and used other groups (army, police, and state apparatus) to offset it. Khrushchev reasserted party superiority, and there has since been little evidence of a real dichotomy of power. The official state is not integrated. The Council of Ministers does not act as a unit—if it indeed even convenes—and does not control its own personnel. The party, representing the principle of unity, manages individual ministries and branches of government separately.

It appears that the political police in the Soviet Union, Poland, and elsewhere have to a limited extent pursued their own interests. Economic managers also form a potentially powerful group whose interests in some ways are at variance with those of the party managers. Various specialized groups, such as educators, jurists, and the like, have been able at times to express mildly divergent views. In all groups, however, the leading positions are held by party members whose first loyalty should be and probably is to the party, the organization on which their careers depend. The leadership listens to expert opinion and is (we assume) influenced by it. But the party leadership is free to listen or not, and it decides whose opinions it will hear.

The armed forces stand out for their potential influence. From shortly after their revolution, the Bolsheviks, aware of the precedent of Napoleon's usurpation of the French Revolution, were obsessed with the danger of a military seizure of power. The army has been the sole organization capable of taking power away from the party not only because of its possession of arms but also because of its coherence and command structure. The Soviet party and others following its example have therefore taken extraordinary precautionary measures. There are multiple lines of control to preclude any possibility of the army rising against the party. Officers are party members subject to party as well as military orders, and the party has a hierarchy of political officers through the forces parallel with the line officers. A military coup would seem possible only if the party system had already virtually broken down.

This does not contradict the fact that military commanders have been or are very influential in the upper echelons of the party. In Yugoslavia, for example, generals hold many positions near the top of the government and party. At times in Cuba and China, a majority of the central committee and politburo have had a military or guerrilla background. The military ethos of the system and the emphasis on heroics and wartime glories must suggest to high officers that they could direct the state as well as the political bosses. If the civilians should appear to be incompetent, in particular unable to furnish the army what it needs, the military leaders might well assert themselves. In Poland, it is not clear to what extent the party leadership called on General Jaruzelski and the army to save them or the generals undertook to save the country from a breakdown of order and probable Soviet invasion.

THE EVOLUTION OF COMMUNISM

The revolutionary state is a little like a baby born in stress and bloodshed, and like the baby it changes in two basic ways. On the one hand, it grows up, matures, and gains adult strength; on the other hand, it loses the capacity for change and growth. The naive hopes of childhood give way to realism and disillusionment, and vital energies begin to decline long before senescence.[29]

The Soviet state had the burden of developing the Communist state. Before the revolution, no one had any idea what the "proletarian" state would look like, except perhaps that enemies of Lenin freely predicted tyranny as a result of defying the rules of Marxism. The Leninists took over the old state, as mobilized for war, and built on it, extending rather than replacing it. Stalin collectivized agriculture and thoroughly centralized control over the entire economy. The system as it came through his purges has lasted, with minor adaptations, to this day. Other Communist states, especially those under Soviet influence, have proceeded much more rapidly and directly to the goal of a Soviet-style system.

Institutionalization

The first step in the institutionalization of communism is the elimination of bases of non-Communist power. Nationalization removes the class of large-scale business owners. Land reform does away with the landowners. Collectivization means the end of the peasantry as an independent class. Centralization of the economy eliminates the independence of small business. Concurrently, writers, artists, journalists, and so forth, are mobilized. There should remain no social ground from which to attack the system and hardly anyone with the independence to turn against it.

At the same time, the system continually pounds its message into the people. The doc-

---

[29]See Robert Wesson, *The Aging of Communism* (New York: Praeger, 1980).

trine that seemed strange at first becomes the only one people know; the rulership becomes the only one imaginable. At first it struggles to find reliable schoolteachers; eventually, the teachers themselves have been taught by persons who have never known any other government. It is not possible to convince everyone that the state is good; too many abuses and broken promises contradict the propaganda. But it may be possible to convince a large majority that the premises of communism are true and that there is no choice. Expectations of stability and paternalism are created that only a Communist government might be able to provide—for example, guaranteed employment.

Perhaps most important, the mature Communist system nourishes a large class of persons for whom it means career, station, and the purpose of life. This is obvious in regard to the party apparatus, whose status is equivalent to that of the party, and the hordes of controllers who would be unqualified for another job if the controls were abolished. The political police would fear retribution from a non-Communist regime. And it is not to be supposed that Soviet enterprise managers want much more operational freedom. They adjust to the numerous reins upon them, and to be set free would add to their responsibilities and their worries. Furthermore, they enjoy the priority given so long and insistently to producers over consumer goods. The sellers' market is comfortable for the seller; when there is a ten year waiting list for cars already decades outdated, factories feel no pressure to improve models. The journalists adapt to censorship, and their life would be much more demanding without it. The published and approved writers are protected from the competition of the more creative and orig-

inal. Even those engaged in cheating the system have an interest in its continuation; elimination of artificial shortages would force them to seek new professions. The Communist system is thus strong to the extent that security is more precious than freedom.

The movement has also solidified itself by spreading and forming an international system. Lenin and his colleagues were convinced at the outset that their revolution had to spread indefinitely or it would be choked. They did not succeed in extending it beyond Russia until long afterward, but much of its strength now resides in the fact that some twenty states subscribe to Marxism-Leninism. The Soviet Union regards itself as the general guarantor of "socialism" everywhere. It intervened in Hungary (1956) and Czechoslovakia (1968) and retains forces in those countries to convince people of the impossibility of change. Communism in the Soviet Union likewise draws strength from dominion in Eastern Europe. This is the badge of Soviet prestige; any patriotic Russian must be aware that without the overlordship of seven states, influence over others, and leadership of the world movement, all based on party power and Marxism-Leninism, Russia would be much reduced.

For Communist states outside the Soviet bloc as well, the sense of belonging to a grand universal movement is an essential part of their legitimation and confidence. Yugoslavia has many differences with the Soviet Union and is threatened only by that power, yet it takes comfort in belonging to the socialist company. Even China and Albania, although hostile to the Soviet Union and hence to the Communist majority, derive some moral support from the global Marxist-Leninist movement. This may explain the otherwise almost incomprehensible fact that they, while vilifying current Soviet leadership and policies, retain two past Soviet leaders, Lenin and Stalin, as major heroes and authorities.

Stabilization and Decay

Upon seizure of power, a revolutionary movement becomes an established government. The desire for violence gives way to the desire for order, and the needs of state building and management are opposite to those of making revolution. Doctrinaire intellectuals, persons of words and ideals, are replaced by administrators concerned with career and power, for whom commitment to doctrine must be pragmatic. The critical give way to the uncritical. Proletarian values of equalization turn around to bourgeois values of status and possession. The system becomes dedicated, perhaps after some years of turmoil, to self-maintenance.

A major social transformation such as the Russian or Chinese revolution promises the universe, and many persons dedicate themselves with enthusiasm to this goal. But the new dawn is more gray than rosy, and instead of enjoying a new abundance, people struggle to keep up a modest standard of living. The promise can be postponed on the Marxist ground that the industrial base for socialism has to be laid, but the joys of building an ever-receding utopia diminish with passing decades. As late as the early 1960s, Western writers could see the Soviet Union and other Communist states as working toward a new and better way of life; but now the sluggishness of their economies and multiple troubles make it difficult to sustain such faith.

Probably few people in the Communist world today have any real faith in the Marxist-Leninist vision, although they apply the vocabulary and concepts they have learned; it is intellectuals in the non-Communist world who cling to Marxism and socialism as the alternative to capitalism and imperialism.[30] Everywhere, from Vietnam to Hungary to Cuba, more non-Communist, materialistic incentives are offered. The living tissues of ideology fall away, leaving the bones of self-interest.[31] Many in the Yugoslav party do not consider themselves Marxists.[32] Religion thrives in many Communist states. The Polish government seems to have given up the fight against the Catholic Church and hopes for its cooperation in maintaining order. Everywhere it becomes harder to ask citizens to sacrifice for the future, and Communist states increasingly call on traditional values—the family, nationalism, and self-interest. The elite themselves seem largely to have lost the earnest conviction of earlier days. Their fondness for Western styles and goods is notorious, and it appears that large numbers in the Soviet Union and elsewhere listen to foreign broadcasts. Trotsky believed the Communist state must inevitably decay if it gave up its mission, but it no longer has a clear mission at home or abroad beyond the maintenance or pursuit of power.

Part of the ideological and political decay of the Communist states is the decline in social mobility and the growth of a new possessing and governing class. Any ruling class cherishes and defends its privileges. A capitalist class is ordinarily unstructured, ill-defined, internally competitive, and open to anyone who can make money. A Communist elite, on the contrary, is structured for coherence, unity, and self-protection; competition is for the favor of superiors; and entry

[30]Robert C. Tucker, "The Deradicalization of Marxist Movements," *American Political Science Review* 61 (June 1967), pp. 343–358.

[31]Wesson, *The Aging of Communism*, Chap. 2.

[32]David A. Dykes, "Yugoslavia: Unity or Diversity," in Archie Brown and Jack Gray, *Political Culture and Change in Communist States*, (New York: Holmes and Meier, 1977), p. 80.

into the select group is controlled by the group. From the point of view of Communist officials, there is no reason why they, having risen by their merits, should not enjoy the fruits of power that their peers are enjoying, that their children should not have at least as much. The revolution becomes the possession of the holders of force.

Outstanding workers and persons of special talents are still recruited into the party, and parties boast of the large number of worker entrants. But it also seems clear that the parties are being deproletarianized, and the apparatus is upper class; party secretaries above the lower levels in the Soviet Union and Eastern Europe must generally have a higher education. With no external checks, nepotism is inevitable; the top leadership in several countries, particularly North Korea, Romania, and Albania, has set an example. Even apart from the restricted nature of party elitehood, social mobility seems to be diminishing markedly with the slowing down of economic change. The prospect for a worker's children to enter the intelligentsia is small.

The privileges of the elite are great and growing. They have special access to almost everything, including imported goods. The top bracket live in a world of their own, closed to ordinary mortals. Ranking Chinese cadres are as secluded from the masses as the mandarins of old. The new elite do not so much own as enjoy; they are entitled by rank to vacation villas and fine limousines, places at the theater, allowances of hard currency, and tickets to special stores, all of which would be lost if they should prove disloyal. As long as they are loyal, however, the apparatus protects its own. If incompetence or even malfeasance forces removal of a manager from a Soviet plant, he or she will probably not be disgraced but quietly transferred to an equivalent position elsewhere.

The long-term results for Communist society are only to be guessed at. The revolution that was to produce perfect equality has instead brought more rigid inequality than any known in the West; the falsification can only be demoralizing. Social advancement has been a major appeal of communism. Peasants became urban workers, workers became intelligentsia, and their children moved into management positions. This has to a considerable degree compensated for poor living conditions, and if this satisfaction disappears, discontent is likely to spread. Workers increasingly demand better wages even if they have no particular ideas of political change. But a demand for meat has political implications; the Communist society that is reoriented toward satisfying consumer demands will be a different kind of society.

Much of the vigor and success of the new Communist state may be due to the fact that the incompetents of the old regime, who held positions because they had the right parents and associates, were cast out. The deadwood was replaced by dynamic, mostly young people, selected for ambition and ability in the scramble of revolutionary politics. But first the idealistic intellectuals tend to drop out or are purged, and then the one-time revolutionaries or their successors grow old and tired. Their children may inherit some of their ability and drive, but their grandchildren are likely to have less. The competence of the closed ruling group is certain to decline. This means not only lowered quality of leadership, but more isolation of the elite. The natural reaction of those who regard themselves as entitled to power but feel insecure is to close ranks. But this defense only worsens the basic problem, which is most acute at the summit of power. At the same time, as the system becomes solidified, it is increasingly difficult to remove aging oligarchs. So the top bracket ages steadily, and as it ages it becomes less hospitable to new blood. The senescence of the Soviet politburo is notorious; the average age of full members for a number of years has been about seventy as older members occasionally pass on and are replaced by youngsters in their fifties or sixties. Aging is general throughout the apparatus. The average age of those on the Central Committee is only a few years younger than that of its superior, the politburo; and the postmature hold sway in ministries, regional administration, the high command, and so forth, as the old stay on and block avenues of advancement.

A secondary reason for reluctance to rejuvenate the oligarchy is the camaraderie and mutual confidence of a group that underwent a traumatic formative experience together. The Soviet rulership consists of men shaped and advanced by the rigors of Stalinism, especially the great purges of 1936–1938. Until the death of Mao, the Chinese Communist leadership was made up almost entirely of veterans of the Long March, which was almost concurrent with Stalin's purges. In other parties with a guerrilla past (in Yugoslavia, Albania, Vietnam, and Cuba), the rulers are a band of ex-guerrillas who age together. The Vietnamese politburo is thus of the same average age as the Soviet, and the Central Committee is only a year younger.[33]

Decline of ideological commitment, rigidification of society, and lowered quality of leadership result in less effective control of society. Decreased ability of the party to put its policies into effect has become apparent in many areas. The slowing of economic growth has been marked; modest plans are generally unfulfilled even in reports of dubious accuracy.

[33]Pike, *History of the Vietnamese Communist Party*, p. 149.

The Czech Communists inherited the most modern industrial plant of Central or Eastern Europe; by now it is obsolete or obsolescent. East Germany, formerly the economic star of the Soviet bloc, has also subsided into near stagnation. Vietnam has ironically gone downhill since the end of the fighting deprived it of its unifying mission. The Soviet Union has spent huge sums on science, and it claims to have several times as many scientists as the United States; but the results have been disappointing. Dependence on the importation of Western technology, much of it via the KGB, seems to grow steadily. A substantial proportion of the Soviet economy is illegal or semilegal, although more or less tolerated; this is also generally the case in the East European countries. In fact, the black market is generally essential to the functioning of the planned economy. There is a huge demand for legal and illegal imports from the West, for example, pop records and blue jeans, at amazing prices. West German marks are the second medium of exchange in East Germany, and American cigarettes are sub-rosa currency in Romania. Having slightly opened up after the demise of Mao, the Chinese have admitted black markets and other shortcomings.

Social policy and the formation of the new society have been equally unsuccessful. Despite profamily and natalist propaganda, the Soviet divorce rate rivals the American, and the birthrate is even lower in the cities. Alcoholism is a grave problem, especially in the Soviet Union, Czechoslovakia, Poland, and Hungary. Crime is known to have increased, although no solid information has been released. Soviet speakers sometimes claim that crime hardly exists in the Soviet Union, but it can no longer be said that Soviet cities are safe for nocturnal strolling. Even Castro has admitted a rise in crime in Cuba. Most politically significant is the general growth of corruption. Bribery and the bending of laws for personal advantage is part of the cultural tradition and background of almost all the Communist countries; repressed by the puritanism of the revolution, it has been creeping back, or oozing down. Lower ranks find themselves able to do more of what upper ranks have done since shortly after the seizure of power—namely, to use position for personal advantages and comforts. Tito lived in more luxury than bygone kings of Yugoslavia; his servants emulated him as far as they could by the means at their disposal.

Compliance is no longer so reliably humble. The growth of Soviet dissent and underground literature has been much publicized; there are tendencies in the same direction in most Communist countries. The police can jail outstanding dissidents and keep illegal publications in bounds, but they cannot silence everyone. It seems that people generally talk more freely, tell political jokes more openly, and respect the authorities less. The Polish government has lost the power to coerce people fully in the ordinary manner of the Communist state.[34] Even the formerly passive Romanians have indulged in strikes and demonstrations in protest against poor living standards and have been rewarded by promises of more goods.

Pressures

The Communist state, then, seems to be subject to internal decay. Its situation is complicated by influences from the Western world, to which the original Communist revolution was a reaction and which no state, however large and powerful, can fully exclude. Even before the civil war ended, Lenin began opening trade with the "class enemy" powers. It was a principle of Stalinism to

[34]Peter Osnos, "The Polish Road to Communism," *Foreign Affairs* 56 (October 1977), pp. 209–220.

shut out foreign influences, but a price was paid in backwardness. Since Stalin's time, especially since about 1970, trade and other contacts with non-Communist states have grown enormously in volume and in importance. Not only do Communist states look to the West for a wide range of imports, but they are compelled to relax controls to some extent to permit exporting enterprises to compete in the world market, and they have acquired a stake in the health of Western capitalism. There are, moreover, scores of Soviet and East European enterprises operating abroad, most of them in the West and many in partnership with Western "monopolies." Thousands of Communist officials make their careers in dealings with capitalists in a manner totally at odds with the original concepts of Leninism.

In many other ways as well, the influence of the West is corrosive of Communist ways and mentality. Travel abroad by Communist citizens cannot be freely allowed without loss of control and sacrifice of stereotypes; its denial causes resentment. Official exchanges can be used primarily to obtain technical information, but scientists cannot be blind and be good scientists. Foreign radio and television may not convert many people to opposition, but they sow doubt.

The evolution of the Communist state past its period of building and growth may properly be called decay because it is change contrary to the purposes of the revolution and the precepts of the party. Decadence is the regular affliction of authoritarian states. Long-lasting Latin American dictatorships have invariably become corrupt and inefficient. Mussolini's fascism at first brought discipline and efficiency—he allegedly made the trains run on time—but seventeen years after its inception, it was a corrupt and pompous fraud. German nazism would have followed a similar course if it had not been brought down by defeat. Despotic governments of premodern times could hold off decay much longer, partly because they could more effectively isolate themselves, partly because they did not usually try to regulate all activities. Modern absolutism is more vulnerable because it tries to manage too much and so destroys needed feedback; it cannot isolate itself in an age of advancing technology without unbearably weakening itself, and in an age of rapid communication it must constantly justify itself.

Social change is necessary for the legitimation of the unlimited authority of the party; when communism ceases to be revolutionary, it thereby ceases to be legitimate. Controls are effective when new; in time, people learn both to evade and to profit by them. Unless the Communist state can go forward rapidly enough to make its claims reasonably believable, it must go backward.

Yet political pluralism is very distant. The Communist system has undertaken to destroy all bases of organized opposition, and it has broadly succeeded. The party is the sole political organization. It holds all the levers and controls, not only the means of force, but the economy and media of information; it holds society together. Change is likely to be through it rather than against it; dissidents usually speak in terms of softening or persuading the party, not displacing it. The only obvious way to pluralism would be through a division of the party along territorial or functional lines, but the organization is designed to prevent division. Dissidents hope vaguely that some event may cause the hollow system to collapse, but that hope is faint. Most persons apparently see no alternative; they are perhaps more afraid of a possible breakdown of the system than they are desirous of change.

Change does come, but it is gradual and swings toward more relaxation as pressures rise, and toward more repression as elites become fearful. The inefficiency of the controlled economy is compensated by some slackening or neglect of controls and more leeway for uncontrolled activity. But Communist states could make many concessions and greatly reduce their administrative burdens without surrendering party rule. Hungary and Yugoslavia have shown that freedom of travel and of expression, without active censorship and with prohibition only of attacks on the regime and its principles, reduces tensions. Released from the compulsions of the plan, enterprises produce for the market and fairly well satisfy it. Yet the party's political monopoly is unimpaired. The relaxed Communist state seems to be under no great strain (except, in the Yugoslav case, from minority nationalism) and may well be able to make adjustments as they become unavoidable.

Communist states were able under conditions of violence and conflict to set themselves up as entities apart and distinct from traditional forms. With the passing of time, and in peaceful conditions for which the Communist form is less well suited, inherent flaws come to the fore. Marxist-Leninist states lose the power either to achieve great transformations or to tyrannize very thoroughly; they become less intense, less total, and more like conventional uninspiring strongarm government.

The Soviet Union

The mother of communism, the Soviet Union, is an authentic superpower. By far the largest of states, with a sixth of the world's land mass, it has an area two and one-half times that of the United States or Canada. It has immense mineral resources, although much of its natural wealth, including oil, is located in the less agreeable northern and eastern parts of the country. With about 280 million citizens, it follows China and India in population and is the most populous of the industrialized states. It consists of a huge multinational empire, with Russians comprising about half the population, Ukrainians about 20 percent, and scores of diverse nationalities making up the remainder. For centuries Russia was a sort of European-Asian hybrid, a state facing Europe and ruling a largely Asian domain, a member of the European state system yet deeply alien to it.

The Russian political tradition has been starkly autocratic since the Tatar conquest of the thirteenth century; when the Tatars were pushed back, Muscovy became heir to the despotic and universalist Tatar empire. Russia has always been a little mysterious, but since Stalin's departure, enigma has largely evaporated, leaving only secrecy.

THE SOVIET POWER, 1917 to 1984

The mass of Russia in the nineteenth century seemed to hang menacingly over Europe, and Karl Marx warned vehemently against the Russian danger. After the revolution of 1917, Russia took on a new shape and a new mission as the Soviet Union made itself the champion of social revolution and acquired new power through modernization and industrializa-

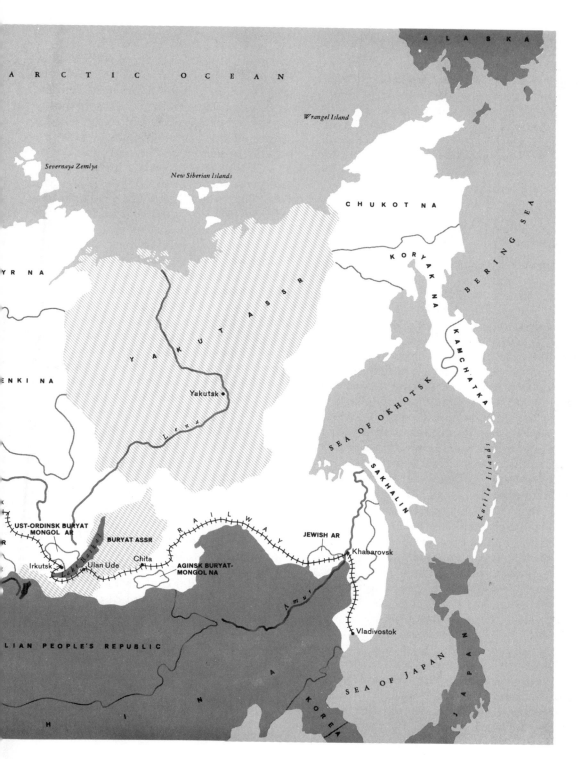

ARCTIC OCEAN

ALASKA

Wrangel Island

Severnaya Zemlya

New Siberian Islands

CHUKOT NA

YR NA

KORYAK NA

ENKI NA

BERING SEA

KAMCHATKA

YAKUT ASSR

Yakutsk

Lena

SEA OF OKHOTSK

SAKHALIN

Kurile Islands

UST-ORDINSK BURYAT
MONGOL AR

BURYAT ASSR

R A I L W A Y

JEWISH AR

Irkutsk

Lake Baikal

Ulan Ude

Chita

AGINSK BURYAT-
MONGOL NA

Khabarovsk

Amur

Vladivostok

LIAN PEOPLE'S REPUBLIC

C H I N A

KOREA

SEA OF JAPAN

J A P A N

tion. Since World War II the Soviet state is the only country that poses a visible threat to the vital interests or physical survival of the Western world. It almost alone is the reason for the enormous American and NATO defense budgets. It makes world communism a significant political movement. Russia, the Soviet Union, whatever its successes or failures, is the other and contrary superpower.

Lenin's State

Perhaps Russia was always destined to be great; even anti-Soviet Russians seem to agree that Russia is and should be the center of the universe. Conceivably it might have become quite as great today if no man born Ulianov had ever called himself Lenin. But it was Lenin and his followers who gave Russia a new political system and hurtled it into the twentieth century, turned a mostly peasant country into the world's second economic power (which recently has fallen behind Japan to take third place) with a gigantic industrial plant and collectivized agriculture, won the greatest victory of Russian history in World War II, acquired an imperial domain in Eastern Europe, and ultimately built up military power roughly equal to that of the United States. This they achieved through the renewal of the social order. They junked the incrustations of many generations of bureaucratic rule; a new, energetic, uninhibited corps of leaders took charge. They were mostly in their twenties and thirties—Lenin at forty-seven was the "old man"—and they undertook to construct a wholly new order not only for themselves but also for all peoples.

Victory in the civil war, which ended late in 1920, strengthened the convictions and the confidence of the Bolshevik or Communist party. Several times on the edge of defeat, they had overcome their numerous opponents supported by the world's leading powers; victory was proof of rightness. On the other hand, the condition of the country was indescribably bad. The cities were mostly emptied, as people went out to the villages in hope of eating and keeping near a fire through the winter, and industry was almost at a standstill. Discontent was high; even victory could not make the Bolshevik government popular with peasants compelled to surrender their crops without return and with workers whose standard of living was far worse than it had been in living memory.

Moreover, many persons remembered that the revolution had been made in the name of freedom and the rights of the people; now that the war was over, they called on the Leninists to permit democratic government. Although Russia had an authoritarian tradition, hopes for liberty had been widespread, and many understood the general ideas of democracy not only from awareness of elections and constitutions in the West but also perhaps from the village assemblies in which opposing views were freely aired and decisions were reached by majority vote.

In 1921 the Leninists reacted to unpopularity by tightening their grip in all ways. An insurgency of sailors at the Kronstadt base, demanding political freedom, was mercilessly crushed. The non-Bolshevik leftist parties, which had been tolerated for their usefulness in the civil war, were liquidated. Local soviets and local branches of the party were brought under central rule. At the top of the party, the freedom of discussion that survived from the old leftist tradition was gradually eliminated. A rule adopted in March 1921 forbade factions—that is, organized promotion of any policy not approved by the central leadership. There were purges of the party, first to exclude unsuitable characters, but soon to remove inconvenient persons. Dissent was narrowed year by year.[1] The authority of the professional party staff, headed by Stalin as general secretary from April 1922, became overpowering.

Lenin was largely responsible for the formation of the Soviet state and its chief features—supremacy of the centralized party, repression of opponents, censorship, and state control of the economy—although he was active head of the government for little more than a year after the end of the civil war. In that time, however, he made a major retreat from socialism, permitting a large amount of private enterprise to rebuild the country. He also lightened the obligations of the peasants and invited them to produce for the market. Toward the end of his life, Lenin seems to have had second thoughts about the results of his revolution; if he had been in command longer, it is not impossible that the Soviet Union would have taken a more moderate course. But he named Stalin, who already had several strategic positions in the apparatus, to the post of general secretary, soon thereafter had a stroke, and was more or less incapacitated until his death in January 1924. In the following years, Stalin intrigued all rivals to political destruction, made himself feared as Lenin never had been, and brought the Soviet system to completion.

Stalinism

Lenin's communism was still tinged with the spirit of social democracy; Stalin's stern despotism leveled and compressed. Lenin allowed most people to live their own lives; Stalin made all into servants of his state. Lenin was an internationalist; Stalin, although a Georgian from the Caucasus, was a centralizer and Russifier. Lenin favored social change; Stalin whipped society into subjection to his design.

For Lenin, terror was a means of defense; for Stalin, it was a means of rule.[2]

Yet Stalin seemed to be a rather reasonable man before he attained supreme power. One reason for his victory in the contest for the succession was that he appealed as a moderate. According to Khrushchev, his democratic manners contrasted with the haughtiness of many others.[3] He worked hard for the party. The other oligarchs thought him relatively harmless and certainly less to be feared than Trotsky, chief strategist of the 1917 coup and the civil war commander.

In 1929–1930 Stalin stepped out of his role as moderate and compromiser to inaugurate programs of forced collectivization of the peasantry, who formed a large majority of the country, and of rapid industrialization under state planning. He exceeded the most extreme proposals, brought the countryside close to civil war, destroyed half of Russia's livestock, set agriculture back for decades, and ground even the favored city workers down. Yet it was accepted by the Bolsheviks, who were no friends of the peasants, as a leap toward modernization; and it made the Soviet state the all-controlling organization that it has remained. With reason, Stalin's successors, even at the height of de-Stalinization, always credited him with these great achievements.

The liberal classes of the old Russia had largely succumbed to revolutionary terror or civil war or had emigrated. Stalin, in the interest of his own power, replaced the edu-

---

[1] On the political compression, see Leonard B. Schapiro, *The Origin of the Communist Autocracy: Political Opposition in the Soviet State, 1917–1922* (Cambridge, Mass.: Harvard University Press, 1977).

[2] Adam B. Ulam, *Stalin, the Man and his Era* (New York: Viking Press, 1973); Robert C. Tucker, *Stalin as a Revolutionary, 1879–1929* (New York: Norton, 1973); Bertram D. Wolfe, *Three Who Made A Revolution* (New York: Dial Press, 1948); Ian Grey, *Stalin, Man of History* (Garden City, N.Y.: Doubleday, 1979); Anton Antonov-Ovseenko, *The Time of Stalin* (New York: Harper & Row, 1981); Roi Medvedev, *Let History Judge: The Origins and Consequences of Stalinism* (New York: A. A. Knopf, 1971).

[3] *Khrushchev Remembers* (Boston: Little, Brown, 1970), pp. 27–28.

cated, partly Westernized Bolsheviks of Lenin's party with homegrown bosses loyal to him, unsophisticated and ruthless. At the same time, there was a sense that socialism could not fail; ideological conviction was still intense. An American writer in late 1927 believed that miners earned more than Stalin and that the leaders were moved above all by the universalist Communist ideal.[4] Stalin proposed to fulfill the promise of the revolution by socializing agriculture and by the instant industrialization of the country.

Stalinism was made possible by the Russian background: the tradition of submission to the autocrat, the total monopoly of political power, and the belief in the uncontestable mission. Moreover, Stalin could undertake harsh measures, as Lenin could not, because by 1929 the party organization had built up a strong corps of administrative cadres to implement the decrees of the dictator.[5]

At a cost of millions of lives, the peasants were placed in collective or state farms, where they had to work for the state, although households were allowed to keep small plots. The errors, waste, and bungling of planning were slowly overcome, planners and managers gained experience, and Soviet industry—chiefly heavy and defense—was built up at a rapid tempo. These developments meant the concentration of all economic power in the hands of the party headed by Stalin; potential support for any opposition was abolished.

There remained, however, some freedom of dissent. Until the early 1930s, Russians, especially those belonging to the party, felt entitled to talk fairly frankly and to discuss policy within the framework of the accepted ideology. But Stalin terrorized and cowed the Soviet people and his own party as perhaps no people in history had been terrorized before. That Stalin had such a purpose when he began large-scale terrorism at the end of 1934 seems unlikely. The murder of a potential rival of Stalin, Sergei Kirov, apparently at Stalin's instigation, in December 1934, may have set the grand purges in motion; to cover up, Stalin blamed long-since defeated oppositionists and took the opportunity of liquidating them physically. Having done so with success, he went on to strike at individuals and groups who seemed in any way dangerous to his suspicious mind.

The purges surged to a horrendous climax in 1937, tapered off in 1938, and were declared finished late in that year, although executions continued and labor camps held millions to the end of Stalin's life in 1953. About 13 million people lost their lives by a bullet in the head or from the cold and hunger of the labor camps.[6] The dimensions of the disaster may be judged by comparison with the approximately 35,000 victims of the famed Terror of the French Revolution. The purge snowballed, as everyone was called upon to denounce saboteurs and spies. The police demanded that victims name their accomplices, and these in turn became victims forced to denounce their accomplices. Anyone with the faintest foreign connection, such as receiving a letter from abroad, was suspect, as was anyone of whom it could be said that he or she had expressed doubts about the wisdom of the leader of the party. Peasants were shot for having taken a handful of grain. Generally, the more influential the person, the more endangered. It was difficult for industrial managers to escape accusations of sabotage, and a large majority

---

[4]Theodore Dreiser, *Dreiser Looks at Russia* (New York: Liveright, 1928), pp. 16–25.

[5]See Adam B. Ulam, *Stalin*, chaps. 8, 9.

[6]For an account of the purges, see Robert Conquest, *The Great Terror*, 2nd ed. (New York: Macmillan, 1968). The camps and procedures are eloquently described by Alexander Solzhenitsyn in the three volumes of *The Gulag Archipelago* (New York: Harper & Row, 1976–1979).

of them were caught up. The bulk of the supposedly supreme party body, the Central Committee, were killed. The military, the only force capable of opposing Stalin, was struck with special violence. About half the officers were removed and shot, as were nearly all the top ranks.

This madness was made possible by ideology, the concept of class war, dedication to the revolution, and the myth of party infallibility. Stalin acted in the name of the party of the proletariat; to oppose him was to oppose history and to favor reactionary capitalism against the revolution and the new world in gestation.[7] Revolutionary idealism gave the police the conviction of doing their duty and prevented potential victims from acting in their own defense; neither, of course, had much idea of the magnitude of the disaster. The purges also became possible because the naive new cadres raised up by Stalin, uneducated or trained only crudely and professionally, took his word as gospel and obeyed the authority that raised them to power. The extremism of the purges also owed much to the amorality and indifference of Stalin and to his paranoia, nourished by the fact that he, a man from the Caucasus, stood atop an increasingly Russian state. The purges were idiosyncratic; no other Communist state except Kampuchea (Cambodia) has suffered a similar nightmare. There has been annihilation of real or supposed class enemies, such as the Chinese elimination of the landlord class; but Stalin's purges were unique in murdering the party elite, including countless high figures who desired above all to serve the party, its leadership, and Stalin. The purges were also folly for the dictator himself. For a time, the state was gravely weakened, and Stalin was certainly endangered by the miasma of fear. In the long

run, however, they served him well. They made room for a new class of bosses and managers who owed their advancement to him and were well aware that their careers and safety depended on total loyalty. As the purges ran down, the Soviet elite was the youngest of all major states. The survivors learned to hide dangerous thoughts, better, not to think them. Fawning became internalized, and Stalin forced his people to believe that they loved him—and they wept at his death.

It is arguable that these achievements, the gathering of the peasantry into party-controlled collectives, state-managed industrialization, and the suffocation of dissent both within the party and outside, could have been brought about with much less pain, suffering, and waste of human and material resources by a more tactful and gradual procedure. Communist countries subsequently promoting collectivization have done so by stages and with more concessions to peasant feelings, and nowhere have the results been so disastrous as in Russia. The frantic pace of the First Five-Year Plan was economic folly; common sense dictated a methodical advance as capital and experience accumulated. The purges likewise were far more severe than necessary to intimidate critics. Stalin could have picked off and made an example of a hundredth of the numbers whom he destroyed, somewhat as the contemporary Soviet state keeps dissent manageable by bullying or arresting not millions but thousands.

Yet Stalin deserves credit for fashioning the totalitarian Communist state. For this, his ruthlessness was essential. If collectivization had been carried out via voluntary cooperatives, it would probably have halted with a mixed or looser system and without the total party control imposed by violence. If industrialization had been promoted ra-

[7]Seweryn Bialer, *Stalin's Successors* (Cambridge, Eng.: Cambridge University Press, 1980), p. 43.

tionally, it would probably never have seemed desirable to destroy small-scale private production, and Russia would have retained a more productive system somewhat like that of present-day Hungary. But by evoking an ideologically powered storm, Stalin thrust his country all the way to what may best be called totalitarianism and put in place a huge apparatus with a vested interest in keeping it there.[8]

Stalin thus completed the work of Lenin. He built up the party-state apparatus and rewarded generously those who served him well (and whom he trusted). He cast revolutionary egalitarianism to the winds, paying qualified engineers as much as a hundred times more than unskilled workers. He raised up a new kind of ruling class, technically trained but uneducated in a broader sense, dedicated to the party and its leader, grateful for having ascended from the peasantry and proud of new status and grandiose works. Stalin was a centralizer who deprived the minority nationalities of the small degree of autonomy Lenin had allowed them. He was a Russifier who declined to speak his native Georgian, and he oversaw the gradual Russification of the party—not from any special love for Russian culture, but because rule from Moscow meant rule by Russians. His was an essentially nationalistic dictatorship; and he restored the past. The Russian empire was found to have been "progressive" in its expansionism. The armed forces were built up and glorified; officers recovered the privileges lost in revolutionary days. Women were urged to bear many children for the nation.

Stalin fed his people a simplistic Marxism-Leninism (which became Marxism-Leninism-Stalinism) of clear goals and simple solutions. His deified person became the chief article of faith, although he was an unexciting speaker with no flair for mass politics. He incorporated the destiny of Russia and of the proletarian socialist revolution; the chief virtue was eager and absolute obedience to his wishes. Propaganda, incessant and inflated, replaced information; disclosure of almost any fact became a crime. To regularize his rule, Stalin gave his subjects, just as the purges were moving toward their climax, what was called (and widely believed to be) "the world's most democratic constitution," providing for supposedly free elections and guaranteeing an impressive list of civil rights.

With the end of the purges, the tumultuous era of the Russian revolution was finished, a little more than twenty years after the taking of the Winter Palace. There was, however, a reinvigorating storm, the Great Patriotic War. During the struggle, after the shock of early defeats had been absorbed and the people realized that the Nazis intended to enslave them or worse, the Stalinist system was infused with the determination to survive. Marxist ideology was replaced by patriotism and party hacks by doers. Censorship was relaxed. Generals were sent from labor camps to command posts. Stalin made peace with the Orthodox Church and formally dissolved Lenin's beloved Comintern, although he kept its staff intact eventually to aid in the administration of Eastern Europe. The Great Patriotic War became a glorious and uniting chapter in the mostly uninspiring and divisive history of the Soviet state.

With victory and expansion into eastern Europe, however, the Soviet state brought back Marxist-Leninist indoctrination, the ideological world picture, and strict dictatorship. The people hoped for relaxation as reward for sacrifices, but Stalin called for more sacrifices. Buoyed by victory, the state

[8]For a general treatment, see Ulam, *Stalin.*

settled down to stern rule by the new elite and the godlike leader. Stalin continued enough quiet terrorism to keep his aides filled with fear, but not enough to risk shaking the state. Intellectual creativity was more stifled than ever. Minimizing foreign contacts and denigrating Western culture, Stalin tried to de-Europeanize Russia.[9] The dictatorship became more capricious and personal as his distrust grew while his capacities declined in old age. The top bodies of the party, the Congress, the Central Committee, and even the Politburo, fell into disuse; Stalin governed through his court.

Khrushchev

At the beginning of 1953, Stalin was evidently preparing a major new purge; but he opportunely had a stroke and died on March 5. Within a few days the name of the genius-leader nearly disappeared. At first, leadership in the new government fell to Georgi Malenkov, Stalin's closest assistant. He seems to have preferred the post of chairman of the Council of Ministers to that of secretary of the party, possibly believing the party had become less important than the state apparatus. Malenkov made some moves toward greater satisfaction of consumer wants. Meanwhile, the leading party secretary, Nikita Khrushchev, undertook to restore the supremacy of the party. He attacked Malenkov as too soft and forced him from office in February 1955. Khrushchev's victory, however, was not of a policy but of the party. Once on top, Khrushchev carried on the Malenkov program of moderate relaxation.

Khrushchev, a thorough Stalinist as long as the boss lived, seems to have been imbued with a certain idealism from his wartime experiences. He wanted to release his country from the suffocation of Stalinism, to return to what he viewed as the purer revolutionary ethos of Leninism, and to reinvigorate the party as an instrument of the great cause. For this purpose or to strike at his rivals, more closely associated with Stalin than he was, he denounced the dead demigod, the murder of thousands of loyal Communists, and the outrageous "cult of the personality." Khrushchev first struck in a sensational "secret speech," but he later brought much of the shame of Stalinism into the open. Neither then nor later, however, did the Soviet leadership rehabilitate the revolutionary leaders, from Trotsky down, whom Stalin murdered or denounce the persecution of Lenin's friends and widow.

Unlike Stalin, Khrushchev mixed with the people. He permitted more foreign trade and admitted tourists. Recognizing that in the nuclear age war could no longer be considered inevitable, he espoused "Peaceful Coexistence" as a drive for the supremacy of Soviet socialism by nonviolent means. He continued curbing the power of the secret police, and he released most remaining political prisoners. Defeated rivals were merely eased from power.

In some ways, Khrushchev was harsh. He closed most of the churches Stalin had allowed to operate, he applied the death penalty for economic crimes, and he took measures to exile "parasites" from major cities. But in many ways he turned away, albeit slightly, from Stalinist rigors. He tried, unsuccessfully, to decentralize control of the economy to regional councils. He eased discipline over writers and artists, although he occasionally shouted at them and imprisoned a few. He reduced income differentials in the name of egalitarianism and offended the new class by requiring youths to have work experience before higher education.

[9]Ivar Spector, *An Introduction to Russian History and Culture,* 5th ed. (New York: Van Nostrand, 1969), p. 461.

Hesitantly and inconsistently, Khrushchev tried to turn from regimentation to participation, from a strictly party state to a popular state. But he brought about no loosening of the party's rule, and he enjoyed an impressive cult of his personality.[10]

Brezhnev

The party bureaucracy did not take kindly to Khrushchev's reformism, and annoyance at his disturbance of their lives plus fear that he might weaken the authority of the party seem to have turned the new top echelon against him. He was ousted legally by a conspiracy in October, 1964, the first case in the history of Russia of the orderly removal of a sovereign ruler. The new oligarchs, led by First Secretary (later General Secretary, in the Stalinist tradition) Leonid Brezhnev, seemed determined to eschew adventures and avoid sharp policy changes. At first they apparently promised more freedom, but after consolidating their position they allowed rather less. They sought to rationalize the economy to revive industrial and agricultural growth, and they enacted a sensible reform to give managers more authority to exercise their judgment and produce useful goods. But this reform was lost in the gradual application. Nothing more was done to purge the Stalin legacy, and in the latter Brezhnev years, Stalin reappeared as a true Soviet hero in literature.[11] The cult of Lenin

was inflated as never before, and he became a symbol not of revolution but of order and authority. Conventional ideology was reemphasized. Khrushchev's egalitarian measures were mostly undone, and the role of the party and its apparatus was strengthened.

Brezhnev at first seemed only slightly above his fellows, and his name was coupled with that of Alexei Kosygin, chairman of the Council of Ministers. But Brezhnev gradually and quietly replaced potential rivals by friends and backers until the Politburo majority was behind him. In 1970 he made the huge celebration of Lenin's birthday virtually his own show, and in 1971 he dominated the Party Congress much as Stalin had done. By 1976, quotations from his mundane works had largely replaced those of Lenin in the papers, books were written about him, and documentary films glorified his deeds. More than 7 million copies of his works were sold, far more than those of Khrushchev.[12] In 1977 Brezhnev crowned his glory by removing the formal head of state, Nikolai Podgorny, and assuming a presidency with enlarged powers. Stalin and Khrushchev had assumed the premiership, but Brezhnev became the first Soviet leader to combine headship of the party with formal and real headship of the official state. In his last years, before 1982, the personality cult became ever more inflated.

The Brezhnev years were anticlimactic. The revolutionary drama was played out, and the hope of Stalin's day, that harsh measures would bring the new society, had faded. Brezhnev used a new term, "developed socialism," but it only expressed a hope of modernization and an excuse for the failure of the utopian society to be born as pro-

[10]See Edward Crankshaw, *Khrushchev: A Career* (New York: Viking, 1966); Carl A. Linden, *Khrushchev and the Soviet Leadership 1957–1964* (Baltimore: Johns Hopkins University Press, 1966); and Roy Medvedev, *Khrushchev* (Oxford, Eng.: Basil Blackwell, 1982). An inside view is given by Khrushchev in his memoirs, *Khrushchev Remembers* (Boston: Little, Brown, 1970) and *Khrushchev Remembers: The Last Testament* (Boston: Little, Brown, 1974).

[11]Victor Zaslavsky, *The Neo-Stalinist State* (Armonk, N.Y.: M. E. Sharpe, 1982), pp. 1–15.

[12]Bialer, *Stalin's Successors*, p. 69.

grammed.[13] The principal development was stabilization, the solidification of party institutions, and the growing fixity of elites under Brezhnev's policy of "trust in cadres." There was no more threat of unpleasant reforms, and there was no pretense of reducing the role of the party. Officials stayed in place indefinitely. Battles must have gone on beneath the surface, but there was no public controversy among high figures; speeches by politburo members were impersonal and almost interchangeable. Terrorism was replaced by less dramatic repression. Dullness was the order of the day. Soviet society had become essentially conservative, with great respect for protocol, distinction, and tradition.

Andropov

The people whom Brezhnev put in place apparently wanted him to stay, and there was no sign of disaffection as long as he was vigorous. By 1982, however, it seemed that he had not long to live. After the death in January, of the long-time chief ideologist and kingmaker, Mikhail Suslov, several Brezhnev loyalists were removed, accused of corruption. In May, the KGB chief, Yuri Andropov, was promoted to the Secretariat, thereby holding the memberships on Politburo and Secretariat that have been requisite for top office since Lenin. It appeared nonetheless that Brezhnev's preference was for Konstantin Chernenko, an apparatchik of exceptional mediocrity whose only important asset was his usefulness to the boss. Whatever the revered leader desired ceased to be relevant after his sudden demise on November 10. With the support of the military and the KGB, Andropov was almost immediately elected general secretary.

Unlike Stalin, Brezhnev was mourned only in an organized fashion, as buses brought groups to pay their respects. Brezhnev portraits quickly came down, and his name almost vanished from the press, but there was no purge of Brezhnev followers, even of his relatives in high positions. There was no pretense of collective leadership, as there had been after Stalin and Khrushchev, and the papers began greeting Comrade Andropov. He did not immediately take Brezhnev's other major title, that of head of state, but he received it in June 1983—formally acquiring in seven months what had taken Brezhnev thirteen years.[14]

Andropov was the first general secretary to have risen not through the party apparatus but through the KGB; he was its chief for fifteen years, during which it gained markedly in capacity and influence. What remained of the dissident movement was almost completely crushed in 1983. Andropov also attacked slackness and corruption in the party and called for discipline in labor. For a few weeks in January 1983 police went around checking documents of people in stores, theaters, and so forth during the day to learn why they were not working,[15] and new laws stiffened penalties for economic crimes. But soon daytime shopping and absenteeism were back to normal.

There were moves to improve economic performance by giving managers more control of budgets, investments, wages, and profits; to reward innovation; and to measure

---

[13]Donald R. Kelley, "Developments in Ideology," in *Soviet Politics in the Brezhnev Era,* Donald R. Kelley, ed. (New York: Praeger, 1980).

[14]On the rise of Andropov, see Zhores A. Medvedev, *Andropov* (New York: Norton, 1983); Arnold Beichman and Mikhail Bernshtam, *Andropov* (New York: Stein and Day, 1983); and Vladimir Solovyov and Elena Klepikova, *Yuri Andropov, a Secret Passage into the Kremlin* (New York: Macmillan, 1983).

[15]*New York Times,* January 31, 1983, p. 3.

performance more realistically, measures like those which had failed in the past.Not much was changed, and from mid-August Andropov was not seen in public. It was said that he had a cold, and from time to time statements were made in his name or he was reported carrying on party business while convalescing. In February 1984, however, he died of kidney disease.

Konstantin Chernenko, who had been left in second place by Andropov, was promptly elevated to the top position he had failed to get on the death of his patron. He had made his entire career as Brezhnev's handyman, and he brought back the calmer atmosphere of the Brezhnev era. The old guard stayed on, the bosses relaxed, and change awaited a new generation.

THE PARTY

The Soviet constitution calls the Communist Party "the force directing and guiding society." One organization holds together and guides all the institutions comprising the Soviet system, the state apparatus, trade unions, military, police, professional organizations, and so forth, and puts them all in the service of a single cause, its own. The Communist Party is the largest of all organizations, with about 16 million members, supposedly carefully selected and trained and bound to obedience to the central authorities. The party holds the entire society firmly in its grip, and there is no reason to doubt that it can continue to do so as long as it stands united.

Holding itself to be the vanguard of the working class, the party has endeavored to recruit authentic proletarians. From the point of view of the party leadership, it is desirable to have worker members because they are less troubled by doubts, are more impressed by the honor, and are readier to check the vagaries of the more educated. According to official figures, in 1982, 42 percent of the 17.8 million members were workers. However, party membership is more useful and attractive for administrators and managers, and 45 percent were classified as "white-collar workers and others" (the remainder being collective farmers).[16] Members must pass a probationary period, and some are expelled, mostly for such faults as drunkenness or laziness. They are supposed to set an example as workers and citizens. They also should give freely of their time for party activities, such as checking on performance in the factory or conducting meetings. Their rewards are partly material, such as extra pay, better housing, and educational and career opportunities. Benefits are also moral and political: prestige, access to information denied ordinary citizens, and the sense of belonging to the class that counts.

Many persons in responsible positions, such as industrial managers, high bureaucrats, army officers, and the like, virtually have to be party members in order to hope for a career. The true political elite, however, is the regular party staff, whose numbers are guessed to be around 200,000, a little over 1 percent of the total membership. These form a self-contained and self-selecting group. Positions are theoretically filled by elections from the bottom; members of primary organizations choose their secretaries, delegates, and so forth, and these choose higher officials, committees, and so forth, up to the top. In practice, candidates are nominated from the top down; secretaries at any level choose the secretaries below them. Forms of elections are followed, but the tenets of "democratic centralism" (in-

[16]For details, see T. H. Rigby, *Communist Party Membership in the USSR* (Princeton, N.J.: Princeton University Press, 1968); Robert Wesson, *Lenin's Legacy* (Stanford, Calif.: Hoover Institution Press, 1978), pp. 279–283.

cluding the principle of unqualified obedience of lower to higher organizations) exclude any challenge from below.

Organization

Primary party organizations usually center on the workplace, by tradition from revolutionary times and because of the emphasis on production. Secondary organizations correspond to the administrative divisions of the state, with committees, bureaus, secretaries, and so forth, from villages, cities, and provinces to the "republics" of which the Soviet state is formally a union. At each level conferences and congresses are held periodically, but with decreasing frequency, up to the Party Congress that meets in Moscow for a few days every five years. There is also an administrative bureaucracy, increasing in size and complexity as one rises in the hierarchy. The main chain of command is through party secretaries, each the virtual commander of lesser secretaries within his or her jurisdiction. The bureaucracy also serves as a channel of authority, as departments at one level command those beneath them.

The party apparatus consists of elites within elites within elites, layered according to confidence and responsibility. The upper upper class might be said to consist of about 6,000 persons forming the *buros* of provincial central committees plus their superiors. The top aristocrats are the slightly over 400 members of the Central Committee—provincial first secretaries, leaders of major organizations, ministers, a few generals, high party figures, and the like.

The central organs of the party are headed by the Party Congress of about 5,000 delegates. They listen to speeches, enjoy the sights of Moscow, acclaim the guidelines of the Five-Year Plan, and approve the new Central Committee presented to them. The Central Committee is theoretically the supreme authority when the Congress is not in being, or all the time. In its closed sessions it may hold lively discussions of policies. However, it meets only several times yearly and may be decisive only when the top leaders are divided. For example, in 1957 the Central Committee supported Khrushchev against the majority of the Politburo (then called the Presidium) who wished to demote him; in 1964, it sanctioned his removal.

Much more important in ordinary affairs than the Central Committee is the apparatus centered on it. There is a Secretariat of eight (in 1984), headed by the general secretary; they are the commanders of the apparatus. There are also some twenty departments attached to the Central Committee, most dealing with branches of the economy, others with party affairs, propaganda, foreign relations, and so forth. Their activities are unpublicized, but they seem to act as a sort of supergovernment, overseeing ministries or activities in their respective fields.

About half the secretaries are also members of the Politburo ("policy bureau"), the most influential body, roughly corresponding to the cabinet in a typical parliamentary government. Before the removal of Khrushchev, this body varied somewhat in size and saw much flux in membership. Since 1964, however, it has been fairly stable, about fifteen regular members and about a half-dozen nonvoting or "candidate" members, the importance of whom is unclear. It has also been remarkably stable in personnel; Politburo members seem to be assured tenure as long as they are inoffensive. There are no published rules as to who should belong to it, but it seems to be made up of those whose cooperation is deemed most important. The politburo brings together not only secretaries of the Central Committee but also the chairman of the Council of Ministers; first

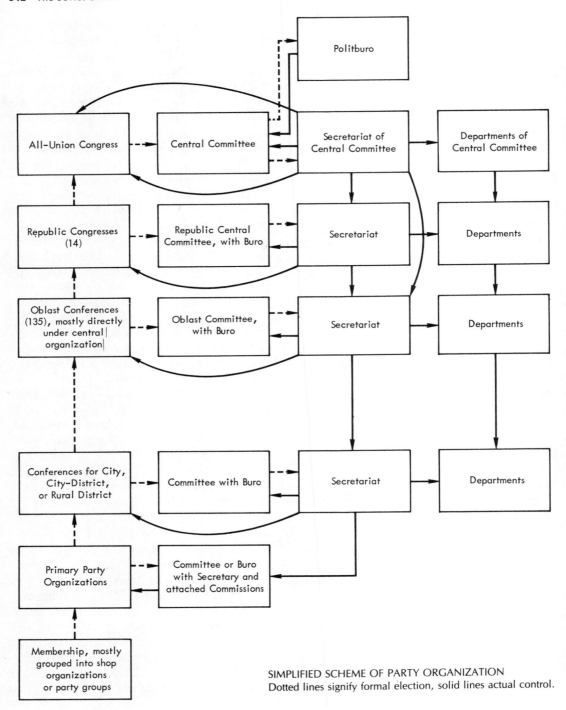

SIMPLIFIED SCHEME OF PARTY ORGANIZATION
Dotted lines signify formal election, solid lines actual control.

secretaries of the most important non-Russian republics; Leningrad and Moscow first secretaries; foreign and defense ministers; and heads of the political police (KGB), Party Control Commission, and trade unions.

The Politburo seems to meet weekly or oftener. In the early part of the Andropov era, newspapers sometimes published Politburo agendas. It was not divulged who was meeting, when, or what was decided; but it appeared that the politburo took up such secondary issues as the price of women's coats, traffic regulations, and work hours of television repair shops.[17] Some Politburo members are evidently senior. Those who stood nearest Brezhnev in the latter part of his rule were Mikhail Suslov, the chief party ideologist; Andrei Kirilenko, the organizational secretary; and Konstantin Chernenko, Brezhnev's assistant. In Andropov's year of rule, the general secretary was followed by Chernenko; Dimitri Ustinov, armaments chief, closely linked with the military; and Andrei Gromyko, in charge of foreign policy. Under Chernenko, the old hands, Ustinov, Gromyko, and Chairman Tikhonov of the Council of Ministers remained near the top; but it appeared that the second-in-command was Mikhail Gorbachev, secretary in charge of agriculture, far the youngest of the top echelon at age fifty-three.

At the top stands the general secretary, who seems now entitled to the presidency of the state. To what extent decisions are made by the general secretary or by the Politburo is not clear.[18] Stalin reduced his Politburo to a nullity. Khrushchev gained a clear ascendancy, but he could not override it freely; he may have been ousted partly because he

tried to do so. Brezhnev's acceptability rested in large part on his pushing nothing to which any group was much opposed. Although he had the advantage of KGB powers, Andropov's authority was never very strong, because he had no opportunity to replace Brezhnevites on the Politburo. Chernenko, not a very self-assertive personality, seemed to be only an unthreatening first of equals.

The entire structure is designed to concentrate and hold power at the center. Its unity is both organizational and ideological; it would be hard to manage such a vast and complex structure if party members and especially the leaders were not thoroughly indoctrinated in the purposes of the party and the necessity of conformity. There is some feedback from below, with rights of criticism theoretically protected in order to check abuses by the middle ranks. The structure has weaknesses, however, which may in the long run outweigh its strengths. The problem of replacing leaders with indefinite terms of office is insoluble. High positions are held into senility; there inevitably result incompetence and discontent among the younger cadres who see their upward progress blocked. To get ahead, one must be coopted from above by possibly insecure superiors; passivity is more promising than dynamism. As a diplomat put it, "The problem with the leaders is that you have to be very gray to emerge. You just can't get to those posts without being gray."[19]

Party Management

The party has many means, formal and informal, of securing its supremacy and obedience to its will, or the will of its center. First, it acts as a direct supervisory mechanism. Departments of the Central Committee oversee ministries and other organiza-

---

[17]*Christian Science Monitor*, May 19, 1983, p. 1.

[18]See Archie Brown, "The Power of the General Secretary," in *Authority, Power, and Policy in the USSR*, T. H. Rigby, Archie Brown, and Peter Reddaway, eds. (New York: St Martin's Press, 1980), chap. 8.

[19]*New York Times*, February 18, 1978, p. 2.

tions, and this principle is observed at all levels. The provincial or local administration is under the scrutiny and guidance of the corresponding party secretary and apparatus. The factory manager is supposed to make managerial decisions, but the party secretary should check performance and perhaps improve it. The result is a vast hierarchic party apparatus parallel with governmental and economic organizations and impinging on them at each level. Policy decisions and orders go down through parallel channels from the Central Committee apparatus and from the ministry (or other nonparty authority). The system appears cumbersome, prone to confusion of responsibility and waste of energies. But it gives a double control and a means of overcoming the inertia or possible unwillingness of the bureaucratic apparatus by enlisting as overseers a corps of loyal persons not themselves responsible for administration.

A still more diffuse means of guidance is the party fraction. Within any nonparty organization, such as a trade union, the Academy of Sciences, the Writers' Union, or even a government office, party members are supposed to form a group, a sort of caucus, to make sure that the organization follows guidelines, elects the proper persons to the leadership positions, and operates according to party policy. This they can probably do by persuasion and the fact that they alone have a well-formulated program. No less important, they convey an understanding of what the party wants in the particular instance and what it finds tolerable; few will care to propose a contrary course.

Perhaps a more fundamental means of guidance is the control of staffing of all positions of importance, from brigade leader on a collective farm to chairman of the Council of Ministers. Staffing is systematically organized. Lists of posts are farmed out at various levels, the *nomenklatura* of the respective district; the corresponding secretaries are responsible for placing suitably reliable and qualified persons in these positions. This is as true of nominally elective positions, such as the chairman of a collective farm, as it is of frankly appointive positions, such as the director of an institute. Even minor jobs, such as tractor driver on a collective farm, too trivial to be on the nomenklatura, are subject to party control. Very high positions are subject to the Central Committee, that is, to one of its departments or the Secretariat. A person who has once received a nomenklatura post qualifies permanently, assuming reasonably good performance; position becomes almost a species of property. Any career of consequence, except in professions of special skill (such as athletic activities), requires the approval of the party; it is not enough merely to be inoffensive.

The party has other means at its disposal, of course, including the command of agencies of force. The political police, which is very large, efficient, and adequately ruthless, is closely welded to the party system. The party is also an agency of propaganda, not only through its control of information media but also directly through its membership. Party members should spread the word among their friends and co-workers, using the most effective means of propaganda, personal persuasion.

In principal, the party wishes to control all organized decisions of any importance, and in practice it is apt to get into the most detailed matters of economic, cultural, and social management.[20] The party goes increasingly outside its ranks to consult experts, but it selects the experts and admits

[20]Theodore H. Friedgut, *Political Participation in the USSR* (Princeton, N.J.: Princeton University Press, 1978), p. 53.

no compromise of its monopoly of decision making.[21]

THE STATE

A fundamental promise of the socialist revolution, as conceived by Marx and Lenin, was to make the coercive state unnecessary. Lenin claimed in *State and Revolution,* written shortly before he came to power, that the operations of government could be performed by ordinary citizens, so that a formal bureaucracy would be unnecessary under the dictatorship of the proletariat. But the new Soviet government rapidly built up a huge bureaucratic apparatus, and the organs supposedly representative of the workers were made instruments of the party leadership.

The Soviets

The legitimacy of the state theoretically rests on its approval by the Supreme Soviet, successor to the Congress of Soviets that assisted Lenin in setting up his government in 1917. Elections are held regularly to demonstrate the democratic nature of the state and the eager unanimity of popular approval for the party and its leaders and policies, biennially for local soviets, quadrennially for the Supreme Soviets of the fifteen constituent republics and that of the Soviet Union. Candidates are nominated formally by "social organizations," but in practice by the party. Most candidates are party members, especially for the higher soviets. There is no contest, but the electoral campaign is made the occasion for many speeches and much exhortation. Since only one name appears on the ballot, the voter can at most cross off the

name of the candidate; but this means making an overt gesture of disapproval. Sometimes in local elections the nominee is so unpopular that more than half the voters cast negative ballots, but the announced results for elections to the higher soviets are in the neighborhood of 99.99 percent in favor, the long-term tendency being toward unanimity.[22]

It is an honor to be a representative to a soviet, especially the Supreme Soviet. An effort is made to select worthy workers and peasants for perhaps a third of the seats, the remainder being filled by party or government officials and white-collar or professional people. As a reward for their labor and merits, they have junkets to the capital and a chance to meet bigwigs, at a cost only of having to sit through long speeches and reports.

The higher the soviet, the greater the honor and the less the work. The Supreme Soviet, composed of about 1,500 deputies in two chambers, meets ordinarily twice yearly for three or four days each session. Its powers in theory are total. Formally, it is a parliament, with the prerogative of approving the government, passing laws, and authorizing taxes and expenditures. In fact, it approves unanimously and with never a recorded abstention all proposals placed before it. Even when measures have been announced by surprise, the deputies have been completely and unquestioningly obedient. There are not, in fact, many laws to consider, because most matters are handled by decrees. Deputies may sometimes put in a plea for another bridge or school for the home district, and the party people who head commissions of the Supreme Soviet may well do some lobbying behind the scenes. Its chief function, however, is symbolic. Secondarily,

[21]Robert W. Siegler, *The Standing Commissions of the Supreme Soviet* (New York: Praeger, 1982) pp. 18, 261, 266.

[22]See Friedgut, *Political Participation,* chap. 2.

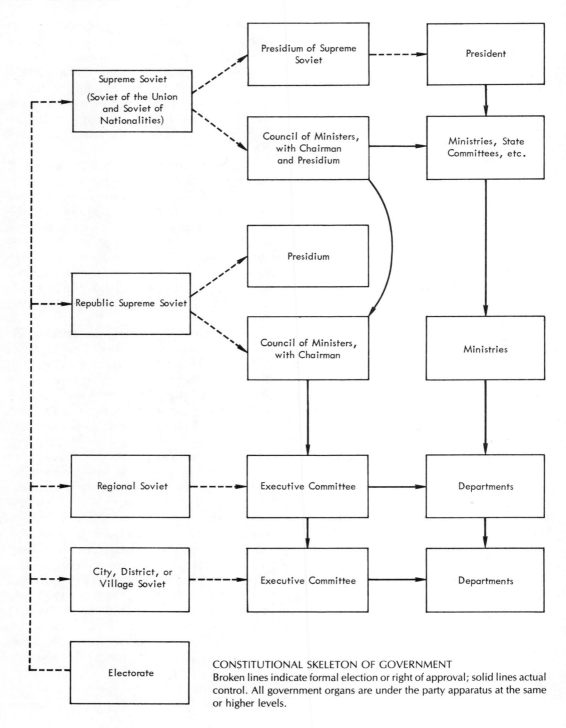

CONSTITUTIONAL SKELETON OF GOVERNMENT
Broken lines indicate formal election or right of approval; solid lines actual control. All government organs are under the party apparatus at the same or higher levels.

it serves as a means of liaison of the center with the provinces. Deputies may carry something of the sentiments of their electors to the bosses in Moscow, although they are unlikely to utter anything disagreeable. They are expected, after their outing in the capital, to explain party policies to the folks back home.

A remarkable fact about the Supreme Soviet is the little use made of it. Since it stands for popular sovereignty but is totally controlled by the party, it would seem useful to keep it in session a large part of the year, to make it a major forum and to use it both to sanction and to explain policies. That it is not so used but sent home before the deputies can really begin to communicate with one another testifies to the party's anxiety lest decision-making take place, even to a small degree, in public view and with the concurrence of outsiders, however closely selected. A show institution must be purely show.

There has been speculation about whether the Supreme Soviet and other pseudodemocratic institutions might evolve toward more genuine democracy. There is not much to encourage this view. If the Supreme Soviet has any legislative function of revision or amendment, it is through committees that meet secretly and whose relation to the Supreme Soviet is nominal. In recent years there has been no visible trend toward longer meetings or more debate in the reported sessions. The Supreme Soviet cannot lead; if government should become more representative, the movement will have to come from elsewhere.

The Supreme Soviet has a collective presidency or Presidium, recently with thirty-nine members, including the chairmen of the Supreme Soviets of the republics. It is permanently in session and under the constitution exercises the powers of the Supreme Soviet when this body it not in session, or nearly all the time. It issues decrees with the force of law, sometimes jointly with the Central Committee. The president of the Presidium is the chief of state for ceremonial and protocol purposes. For many years, this position was held by a nonentity, as though to underline the superiority of the party over the state. When Brezhnev went from the Secretariat to the state presidency in 1960, it was a demotion. However, he strengthened the position; and a senior Politburo member, Nikolai Podgorny, held it from 1965 to 1977. Brezhnev then took the presidency for himself and apparently invested it with some importance. However, the Soviet state managed well enough without a president from November 1982 to June 1983, when Andropov assumed the office.

Lower soviets meet longer and more frequently than the Supreme Soviet. Although there is little pretext that they enjoy much authority, they are meshed with local administration. Deputies are considered responsible and prestigious persons, who are called on for many tasks, ceremonial and other, as representatives of the state. They are supposed to mobilize citizens for civic duties; they should also help citizens in battles with red tape and bureaucratic indifference. Over 2 million strong, their members are an important link between the administration and people. The party encourages popular participation in local government partly to save salaries, partly, it seems, because local activities occupy energies that otherwise might be misdirected.[23]

Each of the fifteen republics also has its Supreme Soviet, with a first minister and Council of Ministers as well as corresponding party bodies. In theory the Soviet Union is a federal system, and the subdivisions of various nationalities (Russian, Ukrainian, Georgian, Uzbek, and so forth) are de-

[23]Ibid., pp. 6, 22.

scribed as sovereign by the constitution. The revolution promised freedom to the minorities of the former empire, and Lenin thought of separate states joined by the international party. The formal union was established only late in 1922, after Lenin had been partially incapacitated; and to this day the peoples of minority republics are assured by the constitution that they are free to secede—although any such suggestion is treason. In practice, the republics amount to little more than administrative subdivisions, with rights to use the local language. Real federalism is difficult in any case, because about half the population (and over half the territory) is in the Russian republic, which in turn contains over two dozen "autonomous republics," "autonomous regions," and "national districts," all of which have the honor of representation in the House of Nationalities of the Supreme Soviet.

The Administrative Structure

The administrative structure parallels the soviets, with ministries at the top level and an "executive committee" with its departments attached to the local soviet. The central Council of Ministers, headed by its chairman and deputy-chairmen, has nearly a hundred members and a presidium, the functions and membership of which are unpublicized. The chairman of the Council of Ministers, usually called the premier in the West, is the chief officer of the administrative system and has usually been very high in the hierarchy. Stalin and Khrushchev took that office as well as the top position in the party, but Brezhnev never did so. Its current occupant, Nikolai Tikhonov, seems to rank not far from the top of the hierarchy. He has several deputies, whose importance is unclear.

Some of the central ministries operate with and through the corresponding ministries of the republics, decentralizing minor decision-making. The mixture of direct and delegated administration extends to local levels. The result is a multiplicity of lines of authority. A small industrial plant may find itself subject to the supervision of the city's executive committee while under the orders of the relevant Moscow ministry and that of the republic, not to speak of various planning authorities and a number of party agencies, in a confusing maze of dozens of overlapping responsibilities and jurisdictions.

Instruments of Force

As a necessary backup to administration and persuasion, the armed forces and the political police (KGB, "Committee of State Security") looms large. The proportion of the GNP invested in defense is estimated at about 14 to 16 percent, although the difficulty of putting a price on Soviet inputs means that the best estimate is a rough approximation (the U.S. defense budget is about 6 percent of the GNP), and in terms of real value it may be higher. It is widely rumored that a majority of industrial plants have military functions.[24] Military preparation begins in secondary school, and youths are drafted for two years service. After discharge, officers remain in the reserve and are subject to recall to age fifty. This is an effective means of control; those who make political trouble are likely to find themselves sent for a two-year stint to northern Siberia.[25]

The party is like an army and the army is like a party, with political officers alongside regular commanders. Much time is given to political education in Marxism-Leninism;

[24]Boris Rabbott, "A Letter to Brezhnev," *New York Times Magazine*, November 6, 1977, p. 60.
[25]Zaslavsky, *The Neo-Stalinist State*, p. 19.

"proletarian internationalism" (the superior right of the proletariat of the world, as represented by the CPSU); and Soviet patriotism, the mixture of duty to the motherland and to the cause. The army is also an instrument of Russification. Draftees of various minorities are mixed with Russians, and Russian is the sole language.

Party controls in the military forces are elaborate and multiple. They include a dual hierarchy, with political officers responsible for morale and indoctrination alongside regular officers; an antisubversion police network; and party organization, whereby officers, almost always party members, are subject to party as well as military discipline. Perhaps most important is control over careers; an officer must have the approval of party authorities in order to advance. Such checks should be more than sufficient to assure subordination, at least in normal times.

There is little reason for the armed forces to seek political power, in any case, and there has been very little indication of political ambition on the part of the marshals. They get about all they could ask for except freedom. Only Marshal Georgi Zhukov, when a member of the Presidium (Politburo) in 1957–1958, was accused of trying to reduce the role of political officers and the time spent on political talk. But his dismissal was probably due more to the fact that he wielded political power that Khrushchev perceived as dangerous.

Enjoying high priority, the military forces seem far more efficient than the civilian economy. Unlike most Soviet-made goods, Soviet guns and tanks are of high quality. The peacetime armed forces are not exempt, however, from difficulties which trouble the Soviet system in general. The gap between accomodations, perquisites, and pay of officers and men and between higher and lower officers is far greater than in Western forces and certainly affects morale. Officers are said to brutalize their men and holdovers maltreat new recruits. There is interethnic friction, especially between Russians and Central Asians. The forces are so rule-bound that training seems to have suffered. Latitude for initiative is virtually nil. Much equipment is reportedly defective, and the authorities rationalize poor food and miserable accomodations as preparation for what may be expected in war. Alcohol is apparently the chief diversion.[26]

The Soviet army is designed not only to fight a possible war but also to keep order in Eastern Europe and the Soviet Union, where cities are provided with appropriate adjacent garrisons. The abundance of uniforms on the streets of almost any Soviet city strikes visitors. The military forces also carry on extensive military-patriotic indoctrination, ranging from the collection of battle trophies to lessons in nuclear defense for schoolchildren, who spend much time playing war. Paramilitary training is given through DOSAAF, a voluntary organization for cooperation with the armed forces, which is said to enlist about 65 million citizens. The flood of books and movies about war, particularly the Great Patriotic War, is unceasing; and these do not emphasize the sordid aspects of war, but its heroics as seen from the right side. The fixation with things military has grown sharply since the latter 1960s.

The army has rarely been needed to keep order in the Soviet Union and seldom in Eastern Europe; it is mostly a presence. But the semimilitary secret police, the KGB, is always active. Abroad, the KGB not only gathers data but carries on a multitude of activities, including the surveillance of Soviet citizens abroad. Any Soviet group traveling

[26]Andrew Cockburn, *The Threat: Inside the Soviet Military Machine* (New York: Random House, 1983), passim.

outside Russia is accompanied by an agent or guard. But most of the operations of the KGB are domestic, directed not against capitalists but nonconformists. It has a force of at least 300,000, including the guards at the virtually impenetrable borders, perhaps a million if collaborators are counted. Its recruits are picked for intelligence and reliability, which often means family connections; its officers have true elite status, with access to foreign goods and housing far above the standards of the masses. Under Khrushchev there was a reaction against the great power of the secret police of Stalin's day, and it was pushed a little into the background. Since Khrushchev, however, the KGB has been exalted as a glorious institution for the protection of socialism. Its stature reached a peak in the general secretaryship of its long-time chief.

The KGB does not arrest by any means so freely as in Stalin's time, but its presence is felt. According to CIA information, the numbers of forced labor camps and prisoners (including nonpoliticals) have been slowly growing to about 1,100 camps in 1982 holding 2.5 million inhabitants.[27] It is estimated that nine to ten thousand dissidents are detained as psychiatric patients, most of them in ordinary mental hospitals, the remainder in "psychiatric prisons."[28] The primary task of the KGB is to nip dissent. For this role it has varied and generally adequate means, including persuasion, threats, beatings, discharge from employment, reprisals against friends and relatives, exile to remote and intemperate regions, and psychiatric hospitalization, as well as possible sentence to a labor camp. The authorities can do in practice almost as they please; they observe the law only as far as they wish.

[27]*New York Times*, November 8, 1982, p. 3.
[28]*Science News*, May 28, 1983, p. 350.

Control of Opinion

In principle, compulsion should be necessary only against survivals of the past, agents or dupes of foreign capitalism, and a few eccentrics. The party seeks to govern primarily by convincing everyone of its legitimate authority, based on the accepted creed of Marxism-Leninism and the approval of the people.

To secure voluntary consent, contradictory messages are excluded as far as possible. To use Western journals and papers, Soviet scholars must demonstrate an approved need. Even scientists have difficulty securing access to scientific journals. All organized means of information—the press, broadcasting, art and literature, schools, public gatherings (except church services), theater, and so forth—are to be used for education and enlightenment, with concessions to entertainment as necessary. In addition to state-managed agencies, there is a vast apparatus of party indoctrination, from lectures and discussion groups to a network of party schools with many millions of students.

The inescapable, permanent bath of propaganda is undoubtedly effective, at least in largely excluding unwanted ideas. Soviet newpapers often seem unbearably dull, and always uninformative. In 1978 Soviet authorities asserted that the price of gasoline was doubled because Soviet citizens complained they were paying too little in comparison with prices elsewhere.[29] Repetition, however, makes mental habits, and propaganda is often skillful and effective. It seems especially so when it touches emotions without direct reference to the interests of the party. Soviet citizens are engrossed by spy stories with KGB heroes and capitalist hireling villains. The appeal to patriotism outweighs many complaints. For example, the

[29]*New York Times*, March 2, 1978, p. 3.

writer Lev Kopelev, having emerged from nine years of imprisonment, expressed pride in Soviet satellites.[30]

Mind control has psychological benefits. The Soviet picture of the world is simple and comforting, a picture of triumphs in the forward march of socialism and Soviet power, with only temporary setbacks. The struggle against the forces of evil goes well, as it must; and life is steadily getting better. People are not alarmed by news of natural calamities, sensational crimes, industrial accidents or disasters; as far as the Soviet press is concerned, such mishaps mar life only in capitalist countries. Discontent is not aroused by reports of prosperity outside their sphere or by information regarding the luxuries or indulgences of their betters. There are no scandals, except when the party attacks abuses from time to time. There is no gossip or society news, no sensationalism, no pornography, and only minor nonpolitical controversy. An accident killing about a thousand people in the mainline city of Sverdlovsk remained unknown to the outside world for more than a year.[31] The exalted chief of state may be for months unseen without a word of explanation, except that foreign reporters are told that he has a cold.

Decades of propaganda do away with the ability, perhaps the desire, to think critically about slogans; and the Soviet people enjoy "the happiness of simplification,"[32] along with the assurance that their society, whatever its temporary or superficial shortcomings, is the most just and progressive on earth. The Soviet citizen lives in a reassuring universe of clear answers and no problems of values, harmonious voices, and little burden of choice. The Soviet order is by definition socialism, and socialism is incontestably superior, even though there may still be something to learn from Western technology. Capitalism means greed, jealousy, selfishness, perversions, insecurity, and unemployment. Western society is disorderly and decadent. The West retains an enormous fascination for educated Soviet citizens, however; travel to the West and the acquisition of stylish Western goods is the dream of many and the privilege of few.

The party calls on people to serve their own interests by cooperating with the powers above them and with the system no one can hope to change. Nearly everyone does so. People become adept at cultural bilingualism, using different tongues according to the occasion. The dissidents who say in public what many say in private are eccentrics in the Soviet context. In Soviet psychiatric theory, nonconformity is ipso facto abnormal, and apparent sanity is only temporary remission.[33]

The upper hierarchy of the Russian Orthodox Church, of the Georgian and Armenian churches, the Baptists, and others, know well enough that the Soviet government despises their faiths and works for their undoing. Yet they mostly praise it, serve its purposes abroad, deny the existence of the discrimination they suffer, and urge the faithful to be submissive.

There is, withal, a counterculture; and time seems to be on its side. Soviet young people commonly say, "Nobody believes in anything any more" or "There are no more heroes."[34] People look for hidden meanings, and writers use Aesopian language. With hard facts scarce, rumor proliferates; Moscow is a city

[30]Ibid., October 1977, p. 15.
[31]Ibid., July 16, 1980, p. 7
[32]Solzhenitsyn, *The Gulag Archipelago*, vol. 1, p. 162.

[33]Walter Reich, "Soviet Psychiatry on Trial," *Commentary* 65 (January 1978), pp. 44–46. See also Sidney O. Block and Peter Reddaway, *Psychiatric Terror: How Soviet Psychiatry Is Used to Suppress Dissent* (New York: Basic Books, 1977).
[34]*New York Times*, March 6, 1978, p. A-10.

of hearsay and gossip.[35] Rumors of price rises, disasters, bombings, or the leader's illness compete with hopeful tales of goods to be sold or freer emigration. Many people speak frankly and critically in private, as they can do with relatively little fear nowadays. A crowd of ten to thirty thousand youths jeered police at the funeral of a singer of protest songs.[36] A few feminists have been expelled.[37]

The revival of traditional national feelings implies skepticism for a party that inevitably carries an antinational flavor. Russianism merges into love for the past, fondness for old churches, and a revival of Orthodoxy. Although the church hierarchy has been thoroughly corrupted by the state, there are from 25 to 40 million members, and Easter seems to be more popular each year. In order to compete, there have been instituted "socialist rites" modeled after those of the church for events from consecration of a newborn Soviet citizen to the receipt of a passport, marriage, and death, all laden with Lenin and the duty to socialism.[38] Priestly garb is highly respected after sixty-five years of official atheism.

Artists and writers, who want to be part of the modern world, press against the limits set by censorship. Occasionally slightly critical theater is permitted, mostly for the elite; cinema for the masses is more constricted. Avant garde painters get to exhibit some of their works in return for refraining from outdoor showings. Since 1974 they have been permitted their own union, membership in which protects them from the charge of parasitism. One means of pressure is the threat to cause a ruckus; nowadays Soviet authorities want tranquillity.

To cause a scandal means particularly to

furnish material for the foreign press, which is the chief support for dissidents. There are perhaps 45 million shortwave receivers in the Soviet Union, and jamming is only partially effective. Foreign radio is the principal means for protesters to communicate with like-minded persons and potential supporters, and hearing their thoughts broadcast enormously reinforces their morale. Soviet leaders are usually mindful of foreign opinion, although they often disregard it; as an émigré artist said, "People who are more or less accepted in the West are more or less protected in the East."[39] Trade and other contacts, apparently regarded as necessary for the economy, have their political costs, as thousands of Soviet officials are exposed to Western ideas and ways of life. However, contacts are minimized so far as feasible; foreigners are nearly as much set apart in Russia as in China.

Dissidents

Since the time of Khrushchev, who raised more expectations than he satisfied, there has been a tiny minority of outright protesters who have written and published illegally in what came to be called *samizdat*, "self-publisher." There are or have been numerous overlapping sectors of critical opinion. One is that of the Russian traditionalists, of whom Alexander Solzhenitsyn is an impassioned and forceful spokesman. They see Leninism as an assault on cherished Russian values, of which the visible custodian is the Orthodox Church. Another form of dissent is the Jewish demand for self-expression and the right to emigrate. Numerous groups, from Lithuanian Catholics to Russian Adventists, hope for freedom of religion. Although the Orthodox hierarchy is more or less domesticated, there is pressure among the faithful

---

[35]Ibid., April 10, 1978, p. 1.
[36]Ibid., July 29, 1980, p. 1.
[37]*Time,* August 4, 1980, p. 40.
[38]*New York Times,* March 15, 1983, p. 6.

[39]Ibid., December 21, 1977, p. A-2.

for freedom to do more than meet in the few remaining churches. Ethnic minorities push for more rights. Finally, there are those with a more strictly political program for liberalization, civil rights, and representative government. These may be divided into those who believe the party can be democratized, returning to an idealized pre-Stalinist tradition, and those who have given up hope of the party rectifying itself. The first are represented by historian Roy Medvedev. Symbol of the second tendency, the human rights advocates, is Andrei Sakharov, whose convictions cost him his career as a physicist and eventually his freedom. Another category of dissident, possibly most worrisome of all to Soviet authorities, is the aggrieved worker. There have been occasional strikes, mostly over shortages, reports of which filter through the mantle of secrecy; and there have been some small attempts to organize the workers to protect their rights against capricious bosses.[40] The dislike of the workers for the privileged intelligentsia, popular anti-Semitism, and the hauteur of the educated toward the laborers have generally kept the two sectors apart. It is a major weakness of the dissident movements that they go in different and partly conflicting directions.

The threat to the Soviet system from dissidents, especially the few intellectual outsiders, would seem very feeble; it may be that the authorities magnify the movement by the attention given to it. It is hence understandable that tolerance for vocal dissent has diminished. The movement probably reached its zenith in the atmosphere of détente in 1976; pressure became heavier as international tension increased in 1979 and after.[41]

[40]Ibid., September 15, 1977, p. A-9.
[41]See Peter Reddaway, "Policy toward Dissent since Khrushchev," in *Authority, Power, and Policy*, chap. 9; also, Leonid Plyushch, *History's Carnival: A Dissident's Autobiography.* (New York: Harcourt Brace Jovanovich, 1977).

By late 1982, one of the late groups, that formed to monitor Soviet compliance with the Helsinki convention on human rights, gave up the fight. The number of agents employed in surveillance and harassment of a handful of usually passive nonconformists is very large, and the worldwide damage to Soviet prestige has been disproportionate to the harm that a few advocates of freedom could do if they were merely isolated and ignored. Yet the dissidents represent a potential for infection, not so much of the mass of the people as of the privileged strata of Soviet society. Children of the nobility in tsarist Russia became populists and sometimes terrorists, and the weakening of the convictions of the elite may make it again vulnerable. Soviet officials cannot easily dismiss the ideas of people of the new Soviet generation educated like themselves, some of them from families of old Bolsheviks.

Economic Performance

The party proclaims it can manage the economy for the benefit of the masses far better than the anarchic and rapacious system of capitalism. For this purpose, the party works out directives, five-year and annual plans, administered by the ministries in cooperation with the State Planning Commission and other agencies. All should theoretially be coordinated, especially heavy industry, which receives close to nine-tenths of investment and attention. The results have been well publicized as successes of socialism: a high rate of growth of industrial production over a long period, and the urbanization and education of the people. At the same time, the party, in control of all important organizations and means of influencing thinking, is theoretically improving Soviet society in a coordinated fashion no Western leadership can approach.

The growth rate, however, has tended to

decline virtually continually since the frantic times of the First Five-Year Plan (1928–1932) and the high rates of the reconstruction period after World War II. The goals of the Eleventh Five-Year Plan (1981–1985) were modest by world standards, contemplating a growth of per capita income that may be no greater than inflation. Production of basic materials, such as steel, has tended to level off, in some cases decline, since the late 1970s. The Soviet industrial structure is, on balance, evidently aging and decaying, as the productivity of capital investments has declined sharply.

Until 1971, the Soviet Union was a net grain exporter; since then it has become a heavy importer. Supplies of meat, fruit, and vegetables have deteriorated markedly since 1975. Meat is commonly not to be found, or to be found, like fresh fruits and vegetables, only in peasant free markets at several times the prices in state stores. Brezhnev called food "the central problem of the economy,"[42] and the standard of nourishment has clearly declined in the last decade. Supplies of all kinds are so erratic that citizens spend the equivalent of about a day per week standing in line.[43] There has been little if any overall improvement since 1975; possibly the standard of living by 1983 had slipped back to the 1965 level.[44]

The country is not rushing into the automotive age; passenger car production is static at about one-tenth the American. Gas stations and repair garages are almost nonexistent. Solid roads are few, and the countryside is isolated by a sea of mud each spring. The number of telephones per 100 persons is like that of a less developed country, not a leading economic power. There are no "bullet trains" in the Japanese or French style; railroads have slowed down rather than speeded up in recent years. The computer industry and applications lag badly, and the state seems to rely heavily on espionage to reduce the gap. Not only is there difficulty in innovation, but also the party seems to fear that the use of computers would take away its decision-making function. The Soviet Union has made a few innovations in production technology, but it has developed virtually nothing for use—no new drugs, new fibers, or new gadgets of any kind.

The command economy has clearly become less effective, by some reports incredibly so. It appears that only one-fifth of the capital allocated to new projects in 1977 was usefully employed,[45] and a defecting Soviet official claimed that only 15 percent of the orders placed by the State Committee on Material-Technical Supply were filled.[46] Construction workers were five times as productive on their own as on a state project.[47] As much as one-third of Soviet produce and grains is lost, pilfered, or spoiled before it gets to market.[48] Prices in the free markets are inflated by the requirement that peasants must themselves bring their goods, from perhaps thousands of miles away. Factories have positive incentives to make machines as heavy as possible.[49] The planning apparatus has never found a way to motivate managers adequately to make the best economic decisions without giving them freedom to make a profit—that is, surrendering party control. A State Prices Committee tries to fix and monitor over 10 million prices; the result is a bureaucratic shambles. A Soviet commen-

[42]*New York Times,* January 15, 1982, p. 5.
[43]Ibid., June 26, 1980, p. 12.
[44]Walter Laqueur, "What We Know about the Soviet Union," *Commentary* 75 (February 1983), p. 16.

[45]*Christian Science Monitor,* January 16, 1978.
[46]Rabbot, "A Letter to Brezhnev," p. 60.
[47]*New York Times,* January 4, 1983, p. 4.
[48]*Time,* November 30, 1981, p. 23; *Wall Street Journal,* August 23, 1982, p. 11
[49]George Feiwel, "Economic Performance and Reform," in *Soviet Politics in the Brezhnev Era,* pp. 89–90.

tator asserted that the state generated an incredible 800 billion documents per year.[50]

The system can work tolerably well only because the rules are often disregarded. Uncontrolled markets of various degrees of illegality flourish and supply an apparently growing part of the needs of the population. For example, in 1978 to get a New Year's tree in Moscow it was virtually necessary to go to the black market.[51] Afghans made a regular business of smuggling chewing gum from Iran; Soviet authorities were indifferent.[52] According to *Pravda*,[53] many railway conductors take money in lieu of tickets, and tickets may be unavailable at stations because "there is no room on the train." There are many other distortions, such as placing nonworkers on the payroll in return for a kickback.[54] A Moscow Research Institute had to employ twenty persons to occupy three desks.[55] Not only do officials require tips, but store clerks save desirable merchandise for friends or sell it on the side, and hospital orderlies expect monetary incentives to provide a bedpan.

How well the Soviet economy functions we do not really know, and it may well be that the Soviet leadership does not know either. The system of rewards is a set of incentives to misinform higher authorities. For example, enterprises make up high production totals by counting goods moved from one plant to another. The value of production is calculated on the basis of materials and labor used; in other words, the more waste, the higher the registered productivity.[56] Similarly, it appears that Soviet officials do not know, and do not want to know, the

real extent of crime because high figures are undesirable. A police precinct commander was quoted as saying, "If I were to send in to police headquarters the genuine figures about juvenile crime in my precinct, I would not last a day in my job."[57]

From time to time there are minor reforms, but they have been insufficient to reverse negative trends, such as the decline of productivity of capital through several decades.[58] Innovation by Soviet scientists and engineers, which was already very low, declined by more than half from 1965 to 1978.[59] There have been some efforts to improve responsibility by setting expectations for small groups or brigades, of perhaps fifteen or thirty members, in both industry and agriculture,[60] but it seems impossible to change economic management substantially without political change. The Soviet managers have largely lost the concept of market economies and take for granted that they should have instructions on how much to produce; they believe the United States must have a hidden planning mechanism.[61] The party seems to prefer stagnation to the costs and risks of change.

Social Performance

In many ways, the guidance of the Party is less competent than might be expected.

The system has been effective in providing basic education and health care (despite the growing problem of corruption), and most people seem to feel it is a big improvement over the past. But education, especially higher, has been increasingly politicized and

---

[50]*Christian Science Monitor,* May 19, 1983, p. 10.
[51]*New York Times,* January 1, 1978, p. 6.
[52]Ibid., March 10, 1978, p. A–10.
[53]*Pravda,* December 18, 1977.
[54]*Washington Post,* January 27, 1978, p. A–25.
[55]*Business Week,* February 7, 1983, p. 56.
[56]*New York Times,* December 4, 1977, p. 3.

[57]Ibid., March 5, 1978, p. 16.
[58]Feiwel, "Economic Performance and Reform," p. 77.
[59]Zaslavsky, *The Neo-Stalinist State,* p. 150.
[60]*Business Week,* August 1, 1983, p. 44.
[61]Joseph Berliner, "Managing the USSR Economy: Alternative Models," *Problems of Communism* 32 (January-February 1983), p. 49.

stresses conformity at the expense of knowledge. The Soviet school is not in the computer age. Health care suffers prevalent corruption and lack of investment. Preventive medicine is weak, and there are practically no wheelchairs, pacemakers, or kidney machines; and the pharmacopeia is rudimentary.[62] Male life expectancy is less than in many Third World countries; more surprisingly, life expectancy for men dropped, 1964 to 1980, from 67 to 62 years; for women, from 75.6 to 73.5[63]—whereas in all Western and the big majority of Third World countries life expectancy rose substantially. Infant mortality fell for many years but began to rise in 1971, and in 1974 statistics were discontinued.

A major cause for the lowered life expectancy, especially for males, is alcoholism, a very major problem. Alcohol is not glamorized, there are many regulations to discourage its use, and prices are high. Yet its use is encouraged because stores can more easily fulfill sales quotas by liquor sales than other common merchandise, and the government makes large revenues from alcohol, whatever the social and economic cost. Raising prices increases the incentive to sell it and also encourages the competition of moonshine, made by peasants from sugar or potatoes stolen from collective farms. Vodka is the only commodity always freely available. Per capita consumption has increased four or five times in the past forty years.[64] Soviet consumers spend as large a percentage of their budgets (17 percent) on alcohol as Americans do on food. About 40,000 Soviet men die yearly of alcoholism, forty times the U.S. figure.[65] In spite of theoretically strict regulations, the highway death rate is about ten times as high per vehicle as in the United States.[66]

MINORITY NATIONALISM

Beneath the surface, Soviet society is permeated by ethnic antagonisms and competition between Russians and other nationalities, and there is much evidence that the self-assertion of major ethnic groups outgrows the rate of assimilation to the Russian-dominated Soviet system[67] The largely sham federal structure designed to facilitate central control with ostensible concessions furnishes a territorial and organizational basis for ethnic demands, and the local party-state apparatus has in most places become more of a preserve for persons of the local nationality. Economic development has not brought the poor nationalities to the level of the Russians but has made them more aware of the undiminished gap.

The root of the nationality problem is the waning of the common goal that united Balts, Russians, Asiatics, and Caucasians in Lenin's time. The Bolshevik party began as an internationalist movement in which diverse peoples could join in opposition to the tsarist state, which for Russians represented a backward and arbitrary government, and for the minorities of the empire, foreign domination as well. In their hatred of the old order, they could cooperate in making the revolution, crushing the overwhelmingly Russian ruling class, setting up a new egalitarian state, and seeking to spread the revolutionary conflagration everywhere. But

---

[62]*New York Times*, October 11, 1981, p. E-11.
[63]Muray Feshbach, "The Soviet Population, Trends and Dilemmas," *Population Bulletin* 37, August 1983.
[64]Zaslavsky, *The Neo-Stalinist State*, pp. 53–54.
[65]*New York Times*, January 4, 1983, p. 4.

[66]Smith, *The Russians*, p. 57.
[67]Teresa Rakowska-Harmstone, "Ethnicity and Change in the Soviet Union," in *Perspectives for Change in Communist Societies*, Rakowska-Harmstone, ed. (Boulder, Colo.: Westview Press, 1978), p. 169.

when the state settled down under Stalin as a fixed system of rule, the common purpose was lost and the predominance of the Russians inevitably returned. They were by far the largest single group, they dominated the center, and theirs was the common language and the prevalent culture. They were also the most reliable people, or became so as the state became essentially theirs. The core of the party apparatus and power structure became increasingly Russian, until now it is almost entirely so; the Politburo, Secretariat, high officer corps, and so forth have a few Ukrainians but only a sprinkling of non-Slavs. The revolution has turned full circle.

As Russian domination at the center grows, the reaction of minorities in the republics stiffens. They cannot openly contradict the system, but they can dilute or bypass policies imposed by outsiders. They can use the sacred works of Lenin subtly to argue for more latitude for themselves—citing, for example, his policy of promoting local cadres. There have been many complaints of political preference for the locals. They battle in the planning commissions for a larger share of resources and for keeping more of their produce at home. There have been de-Russification campaigns in several minority languages, including Ukrainian, the most important.

It is virtually a necessity to speak Russian if one hopes for a career, and vigorous promotion of that language has left only about a third of the population without it. But the policy has rather promoted bilingualism than led people to give up the native language or be assimilated into the Russian community. Indeed, this is made difficult by the passport system, whereby everyone is branded as of a certain nationality, which cannot be changed; children take their parents' nationality no matter where they were born

and educated—a practice that seems to be valued as a means of control.[68]

There are problems with many minorities. The Baltic peoples feel themselves superior and resent subjection to the Russians; Catholic Lithuania especially has seen anti-Soviet disorders. The former Volga Germans resist Russianization and seek permission to emigrate to West Germany. The Jews, who have come into new self-awareness, are subject to discrimination and anti-Semitic propaganda. In the official ideology, Zionism is akin to nazism and Jews are capitalist exploiters; in 1983 there were more anti-Semitic books and articles than any other year since Stalin. Even tsarist pogroms, unlike Lenin's close aides, have been rehabilitated. Emigration of Jews, which came to 51,000 in 1979, was almost completely halted by 1983.

Central Asia probably represents the most serious problem for the Soviet regime. The high birthrate of the Muslims indicates that by 2000 AD about 30 percent of the Soviet population and a third of the armed forces recruits will be Central Asians. The Central Asians push for local autonomy; the Islamic faith is strong, although 99 percent of the mosques have been closed,[69] and their relative poverty gives them a grievance. There is a tendency for Russian settlers to move away from Muslim areas.[70]

The ability of the ethnic minorities to press for real change remains limited, however. This is clearly demonstrated by the ability of the Soviet Union to dominate East Europeans with their nationalistic and anti-Russian traditions. Minority sentiments could acquire greater importance if they coalesced with Russian dissidence.

It remains the weakness of the minorities

[68]Zaslavsky, *The Neo-Stalinist State*, p. 96.
[69]*New York Times*, January 13, 1980, p. 14.
[70]*Christian Science Monitor*, June 12, 1981, p. 13.

that their cause is particularistic and divisive; Central Asians resent Ukrainians much as they do Russians. Old enmities helped the Bolsheviks incorporate the Caucasus area in the 1920s. When Armenia and Azerbaidzhan quarrel over a border territory, the Russians act as arbiters. The party presents itself as the necessary arch of unity, and unity is precious. In short, if agitation seems to threaten the dominance of the elites, Russians may feel all the more compelled to uphold the Marxist-Leninist ideology and the party position on which their status rests. The party holds the instruments of force and is prepared to employ whatever means are necessary to sustain itself. And ethnic division makes it difficult to loosen party rule, just as it makes economic decentralization dangerous.

THE OUTLOOK

Russia was the originator of the Marxist-Leninist state by virtue of its ambivalence toward the West, its mixture of autocratic temper and radical thinking, its multinational society, its messianism, its pride, and its determination to catch up with and surpass the West. It has been the center from which communism has flowed outward in a great historical movement, the most striking political tide of this century. The vitality of the Communist movement still depends, despite the apostasy of China, on its strength and inspiration in Russia.

Yet the most striking aspect of the contemporary Soviet polity is its general resemblance to the tsarist state. It has become again Russian-dominated and bureaucratic-military-authoritarian. There has rearisen a certain antithesis between the official state and the intelligentsia, or a sector of it. Censorship has become a little leaky. Corruption

and lawbreaking are probably as widespread as in the old days. A proverb runs, "the Russians always find an antidote for the poison of the law." Cynicism is rampant; typical is the Moscow racetrack, where thousands of nonproletarians gamble legally and illegally on the sport of kings.[71] The state is arbitrary but hardly terroristic. It may be that the general secretary and president, like a latter-day tsar, receives more adulation than he exercises actual power.

The revolution gave Russia a mighty renewal. Clearing away encumbrances and irrationalities, it set the stage for an economic upsurge and the appropriation of technology on a grand scale. It represented, on the one hand, a powerful drive to economic and social modernization, and on the other, traditional Russian authoritarianism, the rule of a small oligarchy through a bureaucratic elite, supported by political police, propaganda, and an official creed or ideology. In smashing the old state, it also demolished the slight restraints on political power that had grown up during the last decades of the empire. Economic and social progressiveness was joined to political primitivism. The fundamental problems of the old political order were not solved but plastered over. The ways of today are reminiscent of the old regime not because of memories and traditions but because of the continuation of the old problems of government of a multinational empire technologically dependent on the West.

Now, nearing its eighth decade, the revolution's youthful progressiveness seems increasingly submerged by its political backwardness. The economic controls that an inspired elite once employed to build in-

[71] *New York Times*, August 24, 1983, p. 4. For impressions of Soviet society, see David K. Shipler, *Russia: Broken Idols and Solemn Dreams* (New York: Times Books, 1983).

dustry more rapidly than industry had ever been built have come to suffocate the economy. The political structure has become rigid and immobile. The faith that once energized millions has turned into an exercise in official hypocrisy, irrelevant to the needs of the people and the conservative state. The party, once dedicated to remaking the world, is devoted above all to the preservation of its privileges. For a generation after the revolution, the Soviet leadership was the youngest in the world; now it is among the oldest.

The ills compound themselves. The insecure gerontocrats are fearful of dynamic and talented younger leaders. The rising generation of the "new class" lacks community with the people from whom its parents rose, sees less need to justify by work and dedication the position that comes by birth, and becomes more defensive of its privileges as they are less earned. The weakening of economic growth undermines the ideology essential for the proper functioning of the planned economy. To prevent education from subverting communism, it is made chauvinistic, narrow, and politicized; but the more politicized it is, the less educational. Fearful of dissent, the leaders deprive themselves by censorship and by the din of incessant indoctrination of the feedback and criticism that should help them understand and deal with problems.

It is clear that the Soviet Union cannot remain static. Outwardly, unlike Poland, Yugoslavia, and China, it has changed little in the past twenty years. But it must continue to evolve, and probably rather rapidly. One clear possibility is increased influence by the strongest organization other than the party, the armed forces. In most countries of the non-Western world, the holders of instruments of force have elbowed civilian authority aside when they believed that the government could not adequately maintain order, stand for the national interest, or provide for their needs. In the Soviet Union, it doubtless represents a failure of old-style party rule that the top place was given to the chief of the semimilitary KGB; and under his rule military influence in the government seemed to become more pervasive. A full-dress military coup could come with the breakdown of party controls, in case of grave disorders, economic collapse, or the excessively obvious incompetence of the civilian leadership. But the Soviet military forces would have, like the party, the problem of managing a multinational dominion, and would probably need the ideology and organization of the party. A coup might represent not a rejection of Marxism-Leninism but its renewal. Military domination was perfectly consistent with communism while the party was fighting its way to power in China and for a few years after victory, and again in the breakdown of the Cultural Revolution. In each case, the generals handed administration back to the civilians in due course.

Reversion to strong dictatorship is also conceivable. Many persons in the Soviet Union seem nostalgic for the steel hand of Stalin, who kept people in line and slapped down the petty bosses. Members of the party apparatus remember Stalin as the man who made the masses respect the powers. Yet a new leadership capable of restoring discipline seems distant. It would require abolition of the security the high cadres have achieved and prize, it seems, above all else. It is difficult to envision their sacrificing it or permitting anyone to snatch it from them unless a crisis seemed to threaten the entire system. Moreover, a new despotism, unless it could find a new inspiration, would be simple tyranny, without the spirit that gave meaning to Stalinism.

An opposite current would be toward relaxation or liberalization. Some loosening is implicit in the slackening of the party grip, contrary to the desires of the leadership. Workers loaf more, people talk more freely, some uncensored writings circulate, and the extralegal market flourishes. It seems obvious, apparently even to high Soviet authorities, that the economy could perform much better if it were unshackled. For better productivity, most prices should be freed, the rationing of producer goods should be ended, and enterprises should be allowed to determine their production according to the market—that is, for profit. But such measures would cause inflation and unemployment, at least at first. A more serious obstacle is that they would be injurious to a horde of officials, controllers, and party and state bosses. How could they justify their authority and status if the party-state were to give up detailed supervision of the economy? Political hacks could only watch with envy as nonpoliticians became richer than they. A similar situation prevails in agriculture. It is well known that production could be raised sharply by decentralizing the oversized collective or state farms and linking rewards more closely to effort. But to do so would be to cut across the vested interests of an army of loyal party members.

Khrushchev made a serious attempt at economic decentralization; in 1965 his successors introduced a limited reform to give managers more latitude, but nothing came of this and similar initiatives. It seems too difficult even to legalize the private repairmen. The party seems to fear that any one concession might lead to others, and that economic backsliding would have political effects and ideological costs and so potentially lead to disaster. Similarly, it is impossible to end censorship not only because the present regime is vulnerable to criticism but also because too many ugly skeletons are waiting to be exposed. The party apparently does not

dare make any concessions to democracy, such as permitting voters to choose between party-approved candidates, for fear that a crack in the system might become a fissure.

The determination to keep intact the heritage of Lenin is obviously very strong. There is a sense of responsibility; Poles or Hungarians may waver and experiment without danger as long as the rulership remains solid in Moscow. But if Moscow should waver, the entire edifice might fall. Probably also, uncertainty as to what people might do if set free breeds fear; it may be guessed that a breakdown of party controls would release tremendous bitterness, as people began telling themselves that the frustrations and sufferings of past decades were for no noble revolutionary purposes but for the satisfaction of a self-appointed clique.

There may be some relaxation of bonds as the idea of general purpose fades, the picture of external threat fades, the leadership ages, and Western influences continue to infiltrate the educated classes. But the fear of disorder and loss is compulsive. Few Russians have any real idea of political freedom, which is commonly equated with license and disorder. Police surveillance is taken for granted, like the omnipresent slogans. Quite probably, a movement of renewal would be based on Marxism-Leninism and reliance on a reformed party, in the conviction that trouble came from bad leadership straying from the true faith.

Real change must probably wait for the departure of those who rose during the Stalin era and whose careers were associated with Stalin's crimes. The new generation will certainly have a different mentality, but we can only guess how they will behave in power. The sense of legitimacy of the ruling class is subject to erosion both from their desire somehow to measure themselves by the general standards of civilized humanity and from their sense of the inadequacies of their state and its possible future inferiority. A deep shame arising from the comparison of Russia and the West was the greatest moving force for change prior to the revolution. If current trends continue, it may be so in the future. Yet Marxism-Leninism is strongest in the land of its birth. Russia can be proud of it; for all other countries, it is a more or less alien importation or imposition. Lenin is fairly sure to be revered in his homeland longer than anywhere else.

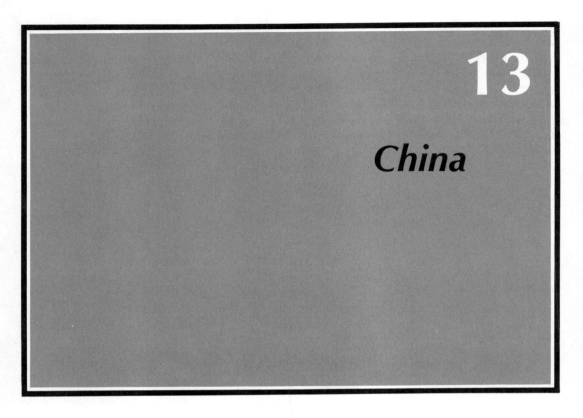

China

In the historical view, it is incredible that China, the most populous nation on earth, the Middle Kingdom disdainful of the barbarian outer world, should have adopted Russian political institutions and remodeled its national life on the Russian pattern. This amazing victory of communism, sealed by the proclamation of the People's Republic of China in October 1949, after twenty years of combat, was the high point of the world Communist movement and the greatest hope of victory. If communism could conquer China, it might well overrun all Asia and perhaps the world. Yet the apparent congruity of Russian-Soviet and Chinese communism was deceptive. They had to part company, if not become enemies, as we can see in hindsight. The two great autocratic empires, Russia and China, reacted similarly to the intrusion of Western power; and in

carrying out their anti-Western revolution, the Chinese Communists leaned on the moral support and example of the Russians, who had faced similar problems. When the Chinese learned to stand on their own feet, however, the bonds of ideology were broken by divergent interests and outlooks, and Chinese Communists became fiercely hostile to their Russian teachers.

There were marked differences of background. When the respective imperial regimes were faltering in the first part of this century, China was far poorer than Russia, its masses hungrier and more ignorant. In China, unlike Russia, there were hardly any industrial workers; and the intelligentsia was much smaller and less Westernized. Chinese culture and mentality were much more alien to the West. In the nineteenth century the Russians, who lived on the edge of the West, wanted to be accepted as Europeans, although they were suspected of being Asiatic at heart; the Chinese regarded the West as barbaric.

Chinese imperial civilization was relatively self-sufficient and geographically isolated. It was almost entirely endogenous, in contrast to the Russian tradition of eager and often indiscriminate borrowing. The impact of the West became important for China only toward the middle of the nineteenth century, and China tried only halfheartedly to learn what seemed necessary for survival. Present-day China has much less consistently than Russia striven to catch up materially. Instead, it has usually emphasized self-sufficiency and Chinese answers to the problems of modernization, although since the departure of Mao it has turned avidly to learning technology from abroad. The Chinese were less concerned than the Russians about what the West thought of them and less infatuated than the Russians with Western clothes, popular music, and other badges of foreign culture. An attack on Western classical music as "bourgeois poison," such as the Maoists conducted in 1974, would hardly be thinkable in the Soviet Union even in the worst times of Stalinism. Moreover, the impact of the West was far more humiliating to China, which could not defend itself, than to Russia, which usually could. The Chinese were both prouder and worse treated.

BUILDING THE NEW CHINA

Soviet Model

The breakdown of order following the fall of the dynasty in 1911 was deeper than in Russia, and the period of disorder was long and painful. In this situation, the most ef-

fective leaders of the masses were men who (except Zhou Enlai and Deng Xiaoping) had no direct experience of the West and even less knowledge of it than most Chinese intellectuals of their generation.[1] To make a radical, mobilizing revolution, rejecting both the injurious Western and the bankrupt native tradition, they needed a doctrine and a model. They found both in Soviet Russia. For this reason, they remained ostensibly obedient to the Comintern, even when it proved its incapacity to guide them, and to the Soviet state, which served itself by helping the anti-Communist Nationalists. They continued to be loyal when Mao achieved victory much sooner than Stalin (and probably Mao) had expected. The Soviet Union was adopted wholeheartedly as China's model, and it was accepted that the Chinese revolution was an integral and subordinate part of the Russian-led movement.

Chinese pragmatism and the virtual absence of a proletarian class in traditional terms led to the state's being organized formally not as a "dictatorship of the proletariat" but as a "people's democratic dictatorship" under Communist leadership, with the participation of a half-dozen subservient "parties" to represent various "classes" faithful to the revolution.[2] However, the Soviet framework of the governing party, secretaries, committees, Central Committee, and Politburo was adopted with slight modifications. Bodies corresponding to the Soviets were set up at all levels, with a written constitution on the Soviet pattern. In 1953–1954 Soviet-style general elections were held.[3] The former guerrilla army was reshaped to the Soviet

---

[1]Robert A. Scalapino, *Elites in the People's Republic of China* (Seattle: University of Washington Press, 1972), p. 74.

[2]Lucian W. Pye, *China: An Introduction* (Boston: Little, Brown, 1972), p. 186.

[3]L. La Dany, "Shrinking Political Life," *Problems of Communism* 23 (September–October 1974), pp. 25–26.

UNION OF SOVI

M O N

Lake
Balkhash

Urumchi •

SINKIANG — UIGHUR
AUTONOMOUS REGION

K

A

AFGHANISTAN

TSINGHAI

Indus River

PAKISTAN

TIBET AUTONOMOUS
REGION

New Delhi •

Lhasa •

I N D I A

NEPAL

Yangtze

BHUTAN

Brahmaputra River

BANGLADESH

Chindwin River

CHINA

·····——··· International Boundaries

——— —— Indefinite Boundaries

············ Boundaries Defined by
Communist China

BURMA

Irrawaddy River

Salween River

Scale of Miles

0   100   200   300   400   500

THAIL

CIALIST REPUBLICS

Lake Baikal

• Ulan Bater

HEILUNGKIANG

• Harbin

• Chang-chun

KIRIN

Vladivostok •

Sea of Japan

JAPAN

• Mukden •

LIAONING

NORTH KOREA

A HUI OMOUS ION

Hua-ho-hao-t'e •

★ Peking

Port Arthur • Dairen

KOREA

SOUTH KOREA

Osaka •

• Tientsin

Gulf of Chihli

T'ai-yuan •

HOPEH

River

SHANSI

• Tsinan

SHANTUNG

Yellow Sea

Yellow

River

Sian •

• Cheng-chu

KIANGSU

ou

SHENSI

HONAN

Huai

Ho-fei •

Nanking •

Shanghai •

WAN

HUPEH

Hankow •

ANHWEI

Hangchow •

East China Sea

heng-tu

River

CHEKIANG

Yangtze

Nam-ch'ang •

Ch'ang-sha •

HUNAN

KIANGSI

Foochow •

RYUKYU ISLANDS

Kuei-yang •

FUKIEN

Amoy •

Formosa Strait

KWEICHOW

g

KWANGSI CHUANG AUTONOMOUS REGION

KWANGTUNG

• Canton

PACIFIC OCEAN

• Nahning

Macao • (Port.)

Hong Kong (Brit.)

NAM

HAINAN

LUZON

PHILIPPINES

LIA

INNER MONGOLIAN AUTONOMOUS REGION

mold. The chief thrust of ideology was to learn from the Soviet big brother, with loyal adherence to the Soviet line in world affairs and gratitude for Soviet assistance at home. Thousands of Soviet engineers planned and modernized Chinese factories, and Chinese schoolchildren learned Russian and used translated Russian books.

Perhaps in imitation of Soviet policies of the mid-1920s, small-scale private industry and commerce were treated leniently; this was easier for China because the Chinese party enjoyed popular support such as the Soviet did not obtain until World War II. Otherwise, the Chinese took the Soviet economic model for granted. Land reform, begun soon after Communist occupation of a given area, was carried to completion by 1952. It was accompanied by the killing of several million landowners, a much smaller percentage of the population than the 5 million "kulaks" whom Stalin destroyed. Land reform was followed by collectivization, but this was more judiciously managed than Stalin's. First, mutual aid teams were formed, then small and incomplete collectives. The goal, however, was the same, and by 1957 the Chinese masses had been brought into collective farms much like the Soviet. For industrial reconstruction, rudimentary economic planning was begun immediately. A five-year plan was officially inaugurated in 1953, with disproportionate stress, in the Soviet style, on heavy and urban industry. Only 8 percent of investment was budgeted for agriculture, which occupied nine-tenths of the population.[4] The idea of economic incentives was also taken over, and wage differentials were wide. The Soviet educational system was copied, with emphasis on professional and technical training. Such policies, tried and certified by Soviet experience, brought rapid industrial growth—during the first decade, 14 to 19 percent yearly, according to various reports.

Emancipation

The event that set the Chinese on the way to divorce was the death of Stalin in March 1953. Although he had been no benefactor of the Chinese—he always treated Mao shabbily—Stalin was the old Comintern leader, Lenin's comrade whom the Chinese leaders had respected for three decades. But Mao was not prepared to defer to the secondary figures who followed. A serious revolutionary and leader of a much larger party, he doubtless expected Khrushchev's deference; but Khrushchev regarded him as a simpleminded bumpkin.[5]

A turning point was the February 1956 Twentieth Congress of the Soviet party, at which Khrushchev enunciated officially his line of Peaceful Coexistence and also denounced Stalin as a bungler, egomaniac, and murderer. Peaceful coexistence was unacceptable to the Chinese because they saw their revolution as still incomplete, with Taiwan in the hands of the Nationalists. And in the eyes of the Chinese, the denunciation of Stalin deprived the Khrushchev regime of legitimacy as his successor. It also implied condemnation of the Maoist cult of personality. Soviet prestige was further shaken a few months later by disorders in Eastern Europe. Soviet economic aid to China, never generous, dwindled as Khrushchev courted Third World nations, especially China's rival, India. The termination of the Soviet nuclear assistance program in 1959 was a manifestation of distrust. In 1960, Soviet economic

---

[4]Edgar Snow, *The Other Side of the River* (New York: Random House, 1971), p. 179.

[5]N. Khrushchev, *Khrushchev Remembers: The Last Testament* (Boston: Little, Brown, 1970), pp. 240, 257, 260.

experts were withdrawn to coerce China economically.

But leaving the Soviet road meant uncertainty and instability. The first independent experiment was the Hundred Flowers period of 1956–1957. Mao invited a "blooming and contending" of intellectuals, offering a freedom of criticism the Soviets have never dared. He seems to have believed that the writers would support him and his policies while criticizing the party apparatus he disliked. But criticism soon became deep and bitter,[6] and the flowers were branded poisonous weeds and cut down in an Anti-Rightist campaign. Bad feelings remained on both sides; Mao was disappointed in the ungrateful, conceited intellectuals and resolved to turn to the masses. The intellectuals felt they had been deceived and continued sniping covertly during subsequent years.

Mao was secure as chief ideologue and heroic leader of the revolution, but his power as head of the party was diminished by his distaste for the administrative drudgery and intrigues on which Stalin's supremacy rested.[7] In 1957, Mao's opponents high in the party sought to shunt him away from practical affairs while keeping him as the symbol of the revolution. Mao counterattacked by a new program, "placing politics in command," and leading China into a new "revolution from above." This program of people's communes and the Great Leap Forward was strikingly parallel to Stalin's violent collectivization and the First Five-Year Plan of twenty years earlier, likewise launched as soon as the country had recovered from the pre-

vious war. It led China toward a break with the Soviet Union, however, although the two powers continued to pretend to be revolutionary allies for several more years.

The people's communes could be established rapidly and with little resistance because peasants had already lost individual holdings. Announced as the social form of the future in August 1958, they were imposed generally by the end of the year. About 740,000 collective farms were amalgamated into 26,000 communes with 20,000 to 30,000 members each. The communes were production units, combining agriculture with local industry for self-sufficiency, and also local governments. They represented a leap into the propertyless utopian society, since it was proposed that tens of thousands of persons should live like a giant family, enjoying socialized meals, clothing, housing, entertainment, haircuts, and burials. Children were placed in nurseries. Members worked together in the fields, on irrigation projects, and in small-scale manufacturing without specific economic reward. Some city communes were also formed, partly to make full use of housewives and others not fully employed, partly to produce as much of the cities' food as possible on adjacent farmlands.[8] Mao was not only trying to fulfill the old dream of Marxism under quite un-Marxist conditions but was taking a leaf from the book of a nineteenth-century Chinese reformer, Kang Yuwei, who sought to save China from the West by introducing a communal society.[9]

Mao also sought to demonstrate Chinese superiority by a Great Leap Forward in production thanks to leadership, indoctrination, and inspiration. While peasants were ad-

---

[6]For the extent of the criticisms, see René Goldman, "The Rectification Campaign at Peking University, May–June 1957," in Roderick MacFarquhar, ed., *China Under Mao: Politics Takes Command* (Cambridge, Mass.: MIT Press, 1966), pp. 255–270.

[7]For a biography of Mao, see Ross Terrill, *Mao* (New York: Harper & Row, 1980).

[8]E. F. Vogel, *Canton under Communism* (New York: Harper & Row, 1971), p. 267.

[9]Immanuel C. Y. Hsu, *The Rise of Modern China* (New York: Oxford University Press, 1970), p. 753.

justing to life in the communes, they were also to double or triple grain production. They and city workers were to raise production of basic commodities at incredible rates. The most celebrated campaign was for immediate multiplication of steel output in the Stalinist passion for that metal. The already overburdened peasants were to build steel furnaces in every commune and somehow find raw materials. It was "walking on two legs," with rural industry, based on mass mobilization, supplementing modern industry, based on an unprecedented rate of capital investment, to quickly make China a great industrial power. With the party joining hands with the masses and putting politics in command, China should far outdo the Soviet Union.

The Maoists also attempted to enroll all able-bodied adults in militias, more for political than military purposes. Ideology became dedication to the communal task. Cadres went out and shared the peasants' work and life. Army officers were to serve one month a year as ordinary soldiers; colonels swept floors, and generals took orders from corporals.[10] Art, too, was made egalitarian. Writers went into the ricefields, and illiterate peasants composed poems exalting the revolution.[11]

The red banners of the people's communes and the Great Leap Forward raised China to a fever, and statistics poured out indicating incredible successes. Probably the leaders believed at first, as many abroad believed, that they had found an answer to China's troubles and a quick way to prosperity by putting hundreds of millions of

peasants to building a new life. But the capacity for mobilization far outstripped the capacity for rational direction. The statistics reflected wishes—the peasants pulled up good railroad tracks to make worthless steel to fill quotas—and production sank in confusion and disorder. In retreat, the fabulous targets were forgotten, priority was shifted back to agriculture, and industry languished. The management of production was devolved from the commune to brigades, almost equivalent to the previous collective farms; the commune became mostly a local government. Peasants were permitted household garden plots, the produce of which was theirs to sell. The household again became the basic economic unit. Urban communes disappeared. Ideological mobilization was largely replaced by economic incentives; and utopian goals, by a program for getting the country back on its feet.

The ideological deviation of the communes and the Leap completed the divorce of Chinese from Soviet communism, to which the Soviets contributed most effectively by withdrawing technical assistance in 1960. Thereafter, relations between the two giants worsened year by year, until they were frank enemies by the mid-1960s, and after President Nixon's 1972 visit to China, the Chinese, although denouncing both superpowers, usually seemed to find stronger language for the Soviet "revisionists."

The Cultural Revolution

The debacle of the Great Leap was never officially admitted, but it was a severe blow to its chief architect, Chairman Mao. Liu Shaoqi, who took Mao's place as head of state (Mao remained party chairman) in April 1959, and Deng Xiaoping, leader of the party secretariat, seemed to be in charge of the

---

[10]Ellis Joffe, "The Conflict Between the Old and the New in the Chinese Army," in *China under Mao*, p. 52.

[11]On Maoist campaigns, see Charles P. Cell, *Revolution at Work: Mobilization Campaigns in China* (New York: Academic Press, 1977).

retreat.[12] Mao, still the symbolic leader and ideologist of the revolution, went into semiretirement away from the capital, making pronouncements from time to time to which the apparatus paid little attention. Marshal Peng Dehuai ventured a far-reaching attack on Mao, perhaps intending his removal from leadership. But Mao demanded that the party support him, and it did so. Peng was replaced as military chief by the most fervent of Maoists, Lin Biao. Lin proceeded to politicize the army and indoctrinate it in Maoism.

Thereafter there was a covert split in the party, a division between the increasingly settled and practical-minded governing apparatus on the one side, and Mao, some discontented young revolutionaries, and part of the military on the other. The growing bureaucracy was increasingly unsympathetic to Mao's revolutionary romanticism, while Mao saw "revisionist" and "bourgeois" tendencies in the bureaucracy's reversion toward traditional Chinese ways as a new educated elite above the masses. There was a running battle, concealed by phrases of respect for the Great Helmsman, between Mao, who was not prepared to manage the administration but was increasingly impatient with the party majority, and the administrators, who wanted to be allowed to run the country but felt they needed Mao as a symbol.

The showdown came in 1966, perhaps brought on partly by tensions arising out of the escalation of the Vietnam war, of which the Chinese saw themselves as targets. The supporters of Liu Shaoqi wanted to restore the Soviet alliance; Mao, fearful of the Russians, wanted to mobilize the people for guerrilla war if necessary.[13] Mao was also vexed by criticism. In one instance a play appeared dealing with the unjust discharge of a faithful servant by a capricious emperor. In view of the custom of making political points by historical examples, knowing Chinese understood that it condemned Mao's dismissal of Marshal Peng.[14]

This sparked an amazing episode, the Great Proletarian Cultural Revolution, in which an autocrat called on the popular masses, especially the students, to put down and remake the apparatus of government over which he presided. It seems to have been motivated by a mixture of egotism and idealism. On the one hand, Mao was angry that anyone should question his judgment; on the other, he considered criticism of himself to be degradation of the revolution; by striking at his enemies, he was seeking renewal of his life's purpose and revitalizing his revolution.

Mao launched his campaign in Shanghai, stronghold of the radicals. In the spring of 1966, with army support, the Maoists gained control of the *People's Daily* and other important papers; a flood of articles descended upon Mao's critics. In July, Mao vindicated himself by swimming the Yangtse with a speed worthy of Superman. Attacks on party leaders multiplied, aiming ever higher, ultimately at the top managers, Liu and Deng.

What Mao proposed is unclear; the Cultural Revolution, like Stalin's big purges, was apparently not planned in advance. Mao moved forward and called on forces as he

[12]Lowell Dittmer, *Liu Shao-ch'i and the Chinese Cultural Revolution* (Berkeley: University of California Press, 1974), pp. 49–50.

[13]William F. Dorrill, "Power, Policy, and Ideology in the Making of the Chinese Cultural Revolution," in Thomas W. Robinson, ed., *The Cultural Revolution in China* (Berkeley: University of California Press, 1971), p. 73.

[14]Peter R. Mordy, *Opposition and Dissent in Contemporary China* (Stanford, Calif.: Hoover Institution Press, 1977).

needed to. Presumably aware of student revolts about this time in the United States, Western Europe, and Japan, he took up the students as a revolutionary force. "It is right to rebel," he pronounced; and they responded enthusiastically when he urged, "Bombard the headquarters."[15] In August 1966 Mao put on a red armband and ceremonially joined the Red Guards springing up among students and other youths everywhere. Schools closed (elementary schools for some months, universities for several years), and millions of young people were encouraged to parade, shout, maraud, and make pseudorevolution. Railroads were devoted to transporting them; about 10 million traveled to Peking to pay homage to the supreme figure. They could be sent anywhere to humiliate or drive anyone from office, and the apparatus could resist them only with difficulty because they were acting in the name of the semisacred leader with, for a time, the support of the army.

Liu Shaoqi and his principal aides were accused of promoting the restoration of capitalism, of treason, and of favoring the Soviet Union. About half of the top elite were forced from office.[16] The politburo and Central Committee ceased to function, replaced by the Central Cultural Revolution Committee, headed by Mao's wife, the former actress Jiang Qing. Many ministries were largely or entirely dissolved. In the provinces, party and most state structures gave way to something near chaos. It was speculated that the party might be abolished entirely.[17] Trade unions and other party-led mass organiza-

tions also became inoperative, and economic planning ceased. Mao seems to have thought that by direct contact with the people, incorporated in the Red Guards, he could rule better than through the "revisionist" party apparatus. It was proposed and briefly attempted to make cities into giant communes in imitation of the Paris Commune celebrated by Marx.[18] Conflicts surfaced between workers and students and between or among local and central organizations. Xenophobia reached a pitch reminiscent of the Boxer uprising of 1900. Foreign embassies were assaulted, and almost all Chinese ambassadors were recalled from abroad.

Maoists claimed to uncover many "representatives of the bourgeoisie" and "capitalist roaders" high in the party and government Mao had set up and presided over for more than thirty years. The revolution makers stressed humiliation and ridicule, such as parading sinners in dunce caps; but many persons were beaten, driven to suicide, put to hard labor, or murdered.[19]

Yet the Cultural Revolution had the purpose, like the people's communes and the Great Leap Forward, of raising China to a higher social level. It was cultural in seeking to make a new people without pride and greed, spartan creatures without interest in personal pleasures or vanity. Not only did everyone dress austerely alike, even the keeping of goldfish was forbidden as self-indulgence.[20] All thoughts were to be of the revolution, correct doctrine, and service to the cause incorporated in Mao. Mao was venerated like a deity and his words were scripture; it was ritual to open meetings with a

[15]William Hinton, *Hundred Day War: The Cultural Revolution at Tsinghua University* (New York: Monthly Review Press, 1972), p. 20.

[16]James T. Townsend, *Politics in China* (Boston: Little, Brown, 1974), p. 135.

[17]For a general treatment, see C. L. Chiou, *Maoism in Action: The Cultural Revolution* (New York: Crane and Russak, 1974).

[18]Stanley Karnow, *Mao and China: From Revolution to Revolution* (New York: Viking, 1972), p. 286.

[19]For a personal account, see Liang Heng and Judith Shapiro, *Son of the Revolution* (New York: Knopf, 1983).

[20]Simon Leys (Pierre Ryckmans), *Chinese Shadows* (New York: Viking, 1971), p. 26.

Mao reading and prayer for long life for the Chairman. Nonpolitical journals were closed, for a time no books but Mao's works were printed, and no others were to be had except for a few textbooks.[21] Chinese theater was reduced to six similar Maoist-revolutionary operas, which were made into the only six movies.

The Cultural Revolution was an attempt to revive the heroic and inspiring times of pure Communist spirit and Mao's glory, when the young leader and his comrades were conducting a holy war from the caves of Yenan. By determination and the ingenuity of the people, China would achieve self-sufficiency and strength as the Red Army did in those days of happy spartanism. Everyone would be wholeheartedly dedicated to the cause as the brave soldiers had been. Even Mao's model for education reverted to the university set up by the guerrillas.

The enormous adulation must have been gratifying, and Mao's critics were driven out, not a few to suicide. The organization was torn down. Even though many radical bands contended, sometimes bloodily, all claimed to be faithful adherents of Mao, and everyone talked in moral terms. Yet the attempt of the old man to recapture past success and halt the aging of a genuine revolution by making a synthetic one could not succeed. Mao and his close aides, including his wife, could not govern the country without a political apparatus; and in the chaos, anti-Communist feelings surfaced. It was necessary to bring in the army to restore order, to form revolutionary committees, and through them, to govern the land.

Late Maoism

In the fall of 1968, after the Soviet Union had invaded another dissident Communist country, Czechoslovakia, and after the United States had begun to turn away from its involvement in Vietnam, the Cultural Revolution was wound down. Anti-Americanism ceased to be the main theme of foreign policy. The Red Guards were finally suppressed as a political force—Mao seemed to have decided that they too were really "bourgeois."[22] In late 1970 universities began to reopen with simplified work-and-learning courses for youths of certified political rectitude with work or military experience. Rebuilding of the party began, and in a few years a large majority of those found unworthy during the Cultural Revolution were reinstated. The party was again recognized as a "vanguard," necessary to lead the country. The rule of the military gradually receded, although the army continued to supply a large share of the Central Committee and politburo.

During Mao's last years he continued to enjoy adulation extraordinary by any standards; but the days when everyone had to have the Little Red Book of Mao quotations in one's pocket and a Mao saying on the tip of one's tongue, were over. A running battle went on beneath the surface between radicals around Mao, who wanted to stress revolutionary egalitarianism and self-reliance, and the leadership of the revived apparatus. One of the first episodes of this contest was the fall of Marshal Lin Biao. Having Maoized the army, he made the Cultural Revolution possible; and in 1966 he was consecrated as Mao's second in command and successor. But with the recovery of the party apparatus, he lost stature. He was killed, apparently in attempted flight to the Soviet Union, in September 1971, and a number of his associates were purged. Subsequently, he was accused of having tried to murder Mao and seize power.

[21]Edgar Snow, *The Long Revolution* (New York: Vintage Books, 1971), p. 25.

[22]Hinton, *Hundred Day War*, p. 68.

The state increasingly reverted to old forms. It was said that there must be a whole series of "revolutions" on the way to communism, but this echo of the turbulence slowly receded. Zhou Enlai, a gifted and practical man who had been at Mao's side since 1933 and premier since the founding of the People's Republic, and whom the radicals never managed to topple, emerged as manager of the state. In January 1975 a new People's Congress adopted a new constitution reaffirming the supremacy of the party and consecrating such non-Maoist principles as payment according to work. Zhou outlined a program of long-term industrialization by conventional methods. Deng Xiaoping, the second-highest victim of the Cultural Revolution, who had resurfaced in 1973 (Liu Shaoqi was dead), was given status in the administration immediately behind Zhou. His famous antiradical aphorism was "It doesn't matter whether a cat is black or white as long as it catches mice."

Thereafter the ailing Mao had little influence on current policies, although his instructions or supposed instructions were announced from time to time by the radicals, led or supported by his fourth wife, Jiang Qing. As long as Zhou lived, he and his protégé, Deng, were able to manage the state in fairly pragmatic fashion while praising Mao and revolution. But the old conflicts remained unresolved: ideology versus expertise in the economy and education, moral versus material incentives, self-reliance versus modernization, revolutionism versus stability.

Relative stability ended with the illness and death of Zhou in January 1976. Without his patron, Deng was attacked in the press as the "capitalist roader in the party." A mass meeting in Peking in honor of Zhou turned into a demonstration in favor of Deng and precipitated his removal from office; prob-

ably the radicals persuaded Mao that a man with a popular following of his own was dangerous. Deng was replaced by a virtual unknown entirely without revolutionary glory, the chief of the security forces, Hua Guofeng. Hua, who became vice chairman of the party, appears not to have been a forceful leader, and after April the radicals seem to have been effectively in control. Disorders had been increasing for some time; in the summer of 1976 there were many strikes and riots, and the peasants in some areas divided up collective fields.[23]

Away from Maoism

Mao's death on September 9, 1976, deprived the radicals of their chief strength. The office of chairman of the party might have been left vacant for a decent interval—many positions have gone unfilled for years—but the unexceptional Hua was elevated to the post within a month, although his base in the party was slight and his claim to legitimacy was only an alleged statement of the dying Mao, "With you in charge, I rest assured." Immediately thereafter, the army arrested the Shanghai-based radicals, Jiang Qing and three associates, and charged them with planning an armed coup.

This set off a torrent of changes that amounted, within two years of Mao's death, to a virtual reversal of all major Maoist policies except hostility to the Soviet Union—a betrayal of Maoism in the eyes of many foreign adherents to Mao's ideals.[24] The Gang of Four were vilified as capitalist-roaders and criminals although they had been Mao's closest associates in his last decade. The sins and follies of the radical clique became the prin-

[23]Jürgen Domes, "The 'Gang of Four' and Hua Kuofeng: Analysis of Political Events 1975–76," *China Quarterly* 71 (September 1977), p. 491.

[24]See Bill Brugger, ed., *China since the "Gang of Four"* (New York: St. Martin's Press, 1980).

cipal theme of the Chinese press for more than a year. Everywhere peasants and workers denounced the Gang of Four as the source of their troubles, and kindergarten children recited their crimes. The Four were placed on show trial in 1980, but apparently they were not sent to their deaths.

"Smashing" the Gang of Four, removing thousands of their adherents, and throwing their ideological demands to the winds was almost a revolution. The nearest parallel in another Communist country to such a long and ferocious denunciation of previous rulers was the Stalinist blackening of Lenin's associates; that, however, came about a decade after Lenin's death. De-Stalinization by comparison was trivial; there was never a rooting out of Stalinists. To deprive the radicals of their last stronghold, in March 1978 the committees set up during the Cultural Revolution to give workers, peasants, and students a share in the administration of factories, farms, and schools were dissolved.[25] At the same time, thousands of old-line bureaucrats who had suffered during the Cultural Revolution were rehabilitated. In June 1978 over a hundred thousand persons who had been imprisoned since the Hundred Flowers fiasco of 1957 were released, and hundreds of thousands who had been degraded as "rightists" were restored to respectability. It was as though the inmates of Stalin's concentration camps had been brought back after his death to replace the dictator's henchmen.

For many months Mao was still exalted as spiritual guide, and his corpse remained on view in a magnificent mausoleum. Mao's quotations continued to be used both against the Gang of Four and to justify current policies. However, the Cultural Revolution, the talk of a decade, was forgotten. The works

[25]*New York Times,* March 7, 1978, p. 1.

of Mao brought out for the guidance of the masses were writings of the 1950s and before. Deng, while praising Mao as maker of the revolution, urged that his words be applied pragmatically. In the constitution adopted in March 1978, Mao Zedong Thought was retained as a general principle of the state. However, in January 1978 the leading paper, *The People's Daily,* for the first time in memory began placing in the corner citations from other than Mao, and Mao's words were no longer in boldface type.

DENGISM

Chairman Hua was given the routine title of "our wise leader," and his portraits were displayed with Mao's. He seemed, however, more of a ceremonial leader than the driver of state and party. He did not appear to promote any particular policies. He would greet diplomats but say nothing of consequence.

Hua was soon overshadowed by the indomitable Deng Xiaoping, who celebrated his second rehabilitation in July 1977. Born in 1904 of a landlord family, Deng spent several years in France in the 1920s with Zhou Enlai, his senior by six years. Returning to China, he entered Mao's guerrilla struggle; he is a survivor of the Long March. He rose rapidly under Zhou in the 1950s, becoming vice premier and secretary general of the Central Committee. He often clashed with Mao until in 1966, as the second highest victim of the Cultural Revolution, he was retired to menial labor. Brought back by Zhou in 1973, he reasserted himself, thanks to his close association with the leadership of the People's Liberation Army, as a major power in the government; he was de facto chief of the government from the death of

Zhou in January 1976 until the celebrated riots and his removal in April.

Deng, although nominally third in the hierarchy (after Hua and ailing Deputy Chairman Marshal Ye Jianying), acted as the man in charge and was so recognized. Hua appeared to be troubled by no particular ideas, although he talked of "political consciousness" and the masses when Deng was speaking of production and skills. Hua was apparently a symbolic head and link with the past, another Chinese deviation from ordinary Communist ways, in which the nominal chief has always been the real chief. It accords with Chinese tradition, however, that the monarch should leave the government to his servants.

By late 1978 there were cautious attacks against the policies of Mao's later years, and posters denounced him for his role in the suppression of the demonstrations of April 1976 that led to the ouster of Deng. There was no such shock as Khrushchev's attack on Stalin, but Mao was gradually lowered from demigod to fallible mortal, even while party pronouncements denied there was any de-Maoization.[26] He was cited as mere mouthpiece of the Central Committee, his giant portraits were taken down, and he was displaced as a hero by the better-liked Zhou Enlai. Early in 1981 Liu Shaoqi was completely rehabilitated. By March 1981, Mao was only one of a dozen outstanding leaders. In September 1982, the Twelfth Party Congress declared the Maoist cult a heresy. General Secretary Hu Yaobang then spoke of the "Marxist ideologial line of seeking truth from facts."[27] Mao Thought was retained formally as party doctrine, but was regarded as party, not personal, wisdom.[28]

It was Mao's merit, however, that he left most of his enemies alive, and from 1977 Deng placed or replaced more and more of his supporters, mostly victims of the Cultural Revolution, in high positions. A long-term Deng associate, Hu Yaobang, born 1916, was made head of the department of party organization, and in 1979 he took the office of general secretary, which had been vacant since the purge of Deng in 1966. Hua modestly asked to be referred to no longer as "the wise leader." Deng resigned as army chief of staff but occupied the chairmanship of the Military Commission of the state, which commanded the armed forces, and of the party Military Commission. By 1980, the Politburo was solid with Deng supporters. In September, an eminently practical administrator, Zhao Ziyang, born in 1924, replaced Hua as premier. The supremacy of Deng was sealed by the September 1982 Party Congress. He then was made chairman of the party's Central Advisory Commission, and Hua was left only with membership on the Central Committee. Subsequently, as many as 200 new senior officials were brought into the government of provinces and cities, many in their forties and with higher education, to carry out Deng's policies.[29]

Deng thus proceeded patiently and gradually to change party leadership, against stiff resistance of both Maoist loyalists and remaining adherents of the Cultural Revolution. As late as September 1982, the People's Liberation Army daily in Shanghai accused Deng of "bourgeois liberalism," but it was compelled to retract. A few months later it was officially declared that the elimination of Maoist ideology should have top priority in the revamping of the armed forces.[30] In 1983, the selected works of Deng Xiaoping went on sale.

[26]Bill Brugger, *China: Radicalism and Revisionism, 1962–1979* (London: Croom Helm, 1981), p. 230.

[27]*New York Times*, September 12, 1982, p. 1.

[28]Richard T. Thornton, *China, A Political History* (Boulder, Colo.: Westview Press, 1982), p. 426.

[29]*Los Angeles Times*, April 14, 1983, p. I–B 1.

[30]*Los Angeles Times*, April 14, 1983, p. 2.

New Policies

Deng and his practical-minded followers turned Maoist policies on their head in almost every department. Banned plays returned to the stage. It was discovered that the newspapers had been excessively dull, and editors were urged to enliven them. Many artists and writers banished to rural communes returned to their profession.[31] Deng allowed diversified literature and art, although excluding "decadent" works and warning that there could be "no absolute liberty."[32] Love stories, nonpolitical folk music, and so on, all banished by the radicals, were welcome. Many Chinese classics and foreign books were published; Mark Twain, Shakespeare, Beethoven, and other Western artists were again acceptable. After the bleak austerity of the Maoist years, Chinese crowds were wildly enthusiastic over Chaplin movies. Universities resumed the study of history, law, religion, philosophy, and economics, all stopped since 1966. Colorful and individual clothing was no longer forbidden; skirts reappeared. In 1978 beauty parlors were opening in major cities, and cosmetics appeared in stores. The puritanism of the Cultural Revolution retreated enough to permit sex education, and love was found to be in good form. Television, at first very restricted, became a passion. Billboards in major cities told of the virtues not of labor but of Japanese televisions and tape players. Rock music came, along with blue jeans. By 1983 the leadership was partly converted to the standard Western business suit, and fashion shows displayed modes acceptable to New York. For the first time since 1966, Chinese were allowed to attend the Protestant and Catholic churches for foreigners in Peking,[33] although party cadres were prohibited from practicing religion openly.

Deng's modernism meant a reversal of attitudes toward science and education. Scientists, especially the most qualified and above all the many trained in the United States, were persecuted during the Cultural Revolution. Deng brought them back from the ricefields, proclaimed them heroes, and promised them support and freedom. The party acknowledged that Chinese science lagged fifteen to twenty years behind world levels and proposed to close the gap in the next twenty-five by stepping energetically into all branches of modern research.

The release of science was accompanied by the depoliticization and strengthening of education. During and for years after the Cultural Revolution, there were no entrance examinations to the universities and no grades. Reliable peasants were admitted to medical school on the basis of party and ideological qualifications, and secondary school graduates could hope for higher education only after years of proving their worth by growing rice. Looking back at the loss of a generation of technical intelligentsia, especially in mathematics, physics, chemistry, and biology, the new regime instituted stiff written examinations and relaxed the rustication program for promising youths. Political qualifications were deemphasized, but the recommendation of the Communist Youth League was still helpful.[34] Students were expected to study and learn useful knowledge, which became a recognized "production factor." Academic degrees were revived. Perhaps even more politically significant, special primary and secondary schools for the gifted were established. A tracking system was introduced, separating superior, average, and slow pupils, in gross contradiction to Maoist

[31]Harrison Salisbury, "Now It's China's Cultural Thaw," *New York Times Magazine*, December 4, 1977, p. 49.

[32]*Christian Science Monitor*, October 25, 1977, p. 13.

[33]*New York Times*, March 10, 1978, p. 7.

[34]Ibid., July 13, 1980, p. 3.

tenets. A large number of scientific exchange programs were inaugurated, and thousands of students were sent to study abroad, especially in the United States.

China turned from modernization by revolutionism to modernization by technology and production, reverting to many of the policies of the 1950s and the program of reconstruction set forth by Zhou Enlai in January 1975 but blocked by the radicals. There was good reason for the change. The average industrial wage in 1977 was only about $30 a month (although the prices of necessities were very low) and had hardly increased for thirty years. As the Chinese pointed out with new frankness, Japan and China in 1957 both produced 10 million tons of steel; but in 1977 Japan produced 100 million tons, China only 20 million. The countryside was much poorer than the cities, as became evident when Western observers were given new freedom to travel. From 1952 through 1976, grain production increased at an average rate of only 2 percent per year, no more than population growth.

The great goal became the "Four Modernizations" (agriculture, industry, defense, and science and technology), and the Chinese people were spurred to a "New Long March" to make China a leading industrial country by the year 2000 with a per capita income of $1,000. After the "ten lost years," the course was changed from ideology to material advancement with remarkable thoroughness. In the leftist view, the dictatorship of the proletariat required the removal of experienced but less than totally enthusiastic managers regardless of the cost in production, and a program of industrial expansion was inherently undesirable because it would strengthen the managerial and technical elites.[35] In the view of their opponents, the

leftists preferred socialist weeds to capitalist grain. In the new era, managers and technicians were to be asked not what they believed but what they could do. Family background was no longer to be considered.

There were no more attacks on "money-seeking." Political meetings were reduced or ended, and workers were pressed to produce. Wages were raised and bonuses were offered for good performance. It was not at first admitted that these were "material incentives," because this was an exploitative device of capitalists and Soviet revisionists, but the Chinese offered socialist "material encouragement." For the peasant majority, work on private plots was encouraged, rural free markets were sanctioned, and more investment was put into irrigation and mechanization of agriculture. By the end of 1978 there were moves toward a limited market economy. In January 1979 the capital and salaries of the former possessing class, confiscated during the Cultural Revolution, were returned, apparently in order to stimulate economic confidence. Such measures may have been successful, because the government claimed large advances in production after several years' stagnation.

Rapid modernization meant securing technology from the advanced industrialized countries, and China undertook this task more eagerly and enthusiastically than any other Communist country has ever done. Foreign trade was increased rapidly; in 1978 it was nearly double in volume over 1977. Trade agreements were made with Japan, France, and other countries on a scale that the leftists would have deemed incompatible with independence. The country went on a buying spree, making commitments by the end of 1978 for about $60 billion of capital goods, although many of the contracts had to be cancelled because the Chinese overspent their resources. Cooperative ventures with foreign corporations were promoted,

---

[35]Tang Tsou, "Mao Tse-tung Thought, the Last Struggle for Succession, and the Post-Mao Era," *China Quarterly* 71 (September 1977), p. 513.

concessions were offered, and Western interests scrambled to participate in the development of Chinese oil. Hong Kong firms set up plants in China. The Chinese, who under Mao declined even long-term commercial credits as detrimental to self-sufficiency, went shopping for dollar loans. Previously a trip to China was a political event; now swarms of tourists grew more rapidly than the capacity to accommodate them, about a million in 1982.

The Chinese suddenly found much to admire in the United States, the imperialist monster of a decade earlier. Millions of Chinese took up the study of English. Japan was taken as an example of successful modernization, and relations between the two countries became quite intense. Tens of thousands of Japanese, mostly businesspersons, traveled to China, and many Chinese went to Japan, especially after a treaty of friendship sealed the reconciliation of the long-time rivals and enemies. In even more heretical fashion, wall posters were permitted pointing to the economic progress of Nationalist China on Taiwan and asking why socialist China had not been able to do so well. American visitors arriving in China found people eager to talk and friendly in a way Russians seldom are. In 1979 and 1980 new regulations severely restricted informal contacts with foreigners, but relations continued to be much easier than in Maoist times.

In November 1978, a Beijing crowd of some 10,000 cheered a speaker calling for democracy and applauded Deng's advocacy of the right to criticize. A Beijing crowd about this time was reported to have beaten up a youth who ventured to shout praise for Mao. Previously banned writings appeared, and a small uncensored press also sprang up, like Soviet samizdat but openly for sale.

In the spirit of release from Maoism, the state allowed almost full freedom of criticism, in a sort of replay of the Hundred Flowers period twenty years earlier. "Freedom of posters" was enshrined in the constitution, and for several months it was permitted to attack Maoism or even party rule. However, authorities warned from time to time that socialism was not to be challenged, insisted on the primacy of Marxism-Leninism and the evils of capitalism, and chided the "excesses of democracy." In March and April 1979, "antisocialist" writing was banned, and the popular posters in Beijing were first limited to a single Democracy Wall, then put under strict control. Democracy Wall was given to commercial billboards. Subsequently some human rights leaders were arrested, but there were no mass repressions or rectification campaigns like those Mao conducted after the Hundred Flowers experiment.

The party clearly had no intention of relaxing its grip on the country. Hu Yaobang assailed "bourgeois liberalism" and "pernicious writing" and called on authors to be "good troops with good weapons" in the fight for socialism.[36] Deng defined democracy as "the right to make suggestions" and to advance modernization.[37] The spate of freedom may have been partly an experiment, a hope to achieve the benefits of relaxation (and a good image abroad) without excessive cost. It also seems to have been a tactic in Deng's battle, as the critics directed their shafts chiefly against Maoism, and thus by association, against Hua. When this end had been attained, it rather served Deng's purpose to placate the apparatchiks and conservatives by closing the little opening to free expression.

Reconstructed Political Institutions

Part of Deng's liberalization was the regularization of state and party structures, many

---

[36]*New York Times,* September 3, 1981, p. 6.
[37]*Los Angeles Times,* April 14, 1982, p. 14.

of which had fallen into desuetude during and after the Cultural Revolution. A new constitution was adopted in 1978 and another in 1982, the fourth of the People's Republic. The constitution provides the customary freedoms, subject, however, to the leadership of the party. Local elections (with elements of choice at times) were held fairly regularly from 1978 on, mostly at workplaces, after over a decade without. Elections (Soviet style) for the National People's Congress had been held in 1953 and 1958, new elections were promised for 1984. The National People's Congress, somewhat obscurely chosen, met yearly after 1977, usually for about two weeks. In 1978 it included representatives of intellectuals, non-Communist parties, and other groups, and many delegates were non-Communists.[38] In 1983, a seventy-four-year-old moderate was chosen head of state (for a five-year term), filling an office vacant for years after the downfall of Liu Shaoqi in 1966. Probably the most important governmental organ was the military commission headed by Deng Xiaoping.

Below the central authority were the 21 provinces and 2,138 counties,[39] the latter divided into some 50,000 communes or (as they became) townships. These in turn were composed of production brigades, made up of production teams of a hundred or more. From the point of view of the people, government was exercised mostly through the block, workplace, or school organization, called *danwei*. To this body a Chinese had to go for permission to travel, change jobs, go to a higher school, have a child, or virtually anything out of the routine. Permission was likely to be denied.

The party charged with directing the immense apparatus also needed reconstruction. Formal party structures at the top were operative only during five of the years between 1949 and 1979,[40] as Mao's ideas of organization were somewhat romantic. The congress convened in September 1982 was the first ever to meet on schedule. The party chairmanship, an institution made for Mao, was abolished, and the general secretaryship was restored, in the conventional Communist pattern. The Central Committee, in 1977 still composed mostly (two-thirds) of veterans of the Long March of the 1930s,[41] was enlarged to 384 and was renewed (60 percent new) and rejuvenated, bringing in many technocrats. The Advisory Commission was made a resting place for senile leaders, but the politburo of September 1982 still had an average age of over seventy. The Politburo was large by Communist standards, with twenty-five members plus three alternates, but six formed its Standing Committee. Three octogenarian marshals remained in top spots.

Despite the purge of many associated with the Gang of Four, party membership was stated to have grown from 28 million in 1973 to 40 million in 1983, making it the world's largest organization. New members came mostly from the youth organization. Party schools were reestablished, and criteria for admission were stiffened.[42] The complete authority of the party was frankly stated in the constitution, and from the viewpoint of the people, party and state were hardly distinguishable. Some steps were taken, however, to separate the party from administration at the provincial level and below.

The Communist party was supplemented

[38]*Christian Science Monitor,* June 6, 1983, p. 9.

[39]For setup, see Derek A. Waller, *The Government and Politics of the People's Republic of China* (London: Hutchinson, 1981).

[40]Jürgen Domes, *Politische Soziologie der Volksrepublik China* (Wiesbaden, Ger.: Akademische Verlagsgesellschaft, 1980), p. 92.

[41]James R. Townsend, *Politics in China,* 2nd ed. (Boston: Little, Brown, 1980), p. 268.

[42]Brugger, *China: Radicalism and Revisionism,* p. 204.

by eight "democratic" parties. These practically lapsed during the Cultural Revolution but were reorganized in 1979, with a total membership of around 80,000, mostly intellectuals, teachers, and journalists. They were privileged to make suggestions to the People's Consultative Congress.[43]

Politically, China was an enormous pyramid, with a base of over a billion people. Perhaps 20 to 30 percent of the adults were enrolled in "mass organizations," such as the unions. Four percent of the population were party members, about a fifth of them, or 8 million, belonging to the inner party. About a million were regular party cadres, over whom stood an elite leadership of less than a thousand, headed by about thirty of the wielders of supreme authority.[44]

THE CHINESE DEVIATION

Chinese communism began under Soviet patronage, paid total verbal respect to the Soviet movement while fighting for power, and faithfully copied the elder Communist state for nearly ten years. Then it deviated sharply toward mobilization and ideology in the Great Leap Forward, the Cultural Revolution, and the commune movement. The Great Leap fell flat, but after a few years the revolutionary drive was fired up again in the Cultural Revolution. After it ended and especially since the death of Mao and the overthrow of the group closest to his outlook, China has tended to revert to institutions and modes basically similar to those of the despised Soviet model. Many of the new policies, which strike the outside world as marked liberalizations by comparison with Maoist practice—such as welcoming tourists, importing industrial

[43]*Los Angeles Times*, March 16, 1980, p. 2.
[44]Domes, *Politische Soziologie*, pp. 210–211.

equipment and processes, economic incentives for productive work, stress on science and technology, education for learning, and stress on modern weaponry—are accepted Soviet practices. China remains a strongly centralized state, characterized, like the Soviet Union, by decision making in the party framework; party supervision throughout society; military influence and participation in decision making; democratic formal institutions; popular participation in the execution of party policies; nominal egalitarianism; and a controlled economy, ideology, and public opinion.

The Chinese derided the Soviets for inequality, but the new policies cannot but produce a similar division of Chinese society, a reversion toward the old mandarinate, whose long fingernails and baggy sleeves signified detachment from manual labor. Stress on production leads to inequality, as some push above others and expect to be rewarded for it. Education is antiegalitarian at higher levels, because it gives to a few special qualifications and a claim to superiority. Moreover, it builds a nonideological and nonpolitical basis for authority. Consequently, the radicals were distrustful of education in general; insofar as it was indispensable, they wanted it to be mixed with physical work and to consist in large part of the sayings of Mao. But the new educational policies produce a highly qualified elite. City youths have an enormous advantage over peasants, and those of upper-class educated families over ordinary workers. Chinese society is about as unequal as Soviet.

Everything in the Chinese background and tradition was conducive to a more extreme authoritarianism than the Soviet. Western influence on the Chinese educated classes was slight before the revolution; to be educated in the old days meant not, as in nineteenth-century Russia, to be imbued with

Western culture and philosophy but to be formed in the philosophy of the secular Chinese autocracy. Russia always felt the need to prove itself in the eyes of the Western world; in the self-sufficiency of China, there was no concern for Western standards. China, in contrast to Russia, had no tradition of intellectual dissidence but of docility to authority. Russian Marxism and Lenin's party began as a movement of talkers and writers, arguing mostly among themselves. The Chinese party began in a time of near breakdown of government and struggle against foreign encroachment. Lenin spent the years prior to 1917 as an exile in European cafés, and his party became a military movement only in the civil war. The Chinese party was engaged in combat almost from the start, and for twenty years it was nearly equivalent to the People's Liberation Army. The epics of Chinese communism are military, from the fabulous Long March to countless battles against the Nationalists and Japanese.

In the first years after the 1949 victory, army and state were inseparable. By 1954, civilian rule was fairly effective, but the army had a large role in propaganda. In the Cultural Revolution the army was Mao's only reliable and disciplined support. Called on to end the chaos, it became again the chief organ of government. Military leaders came to head most of the tripartite Revolutionary Committees, became governors of most provinces, and dominated the Central Committee. The army managed or shared in many construction projects, and companies worked regularly with commune brigades. The faithful soldier was the model most used in propaganda. As Zhou Enlai remarked, "We are all connected with the army."[45]

After the Cultural Revolution, the army mostly stood on the side of the moderates,

[45]Snow, *The Long Revolution*, p. 99.

but it could not directly oppose Chairman Mao. Army figures remained prominent in the highest circles; high officers made up about half the Politburo and a third of the Central Committee. But the radicals tried to build up popular militias and hindered the army's acquisition of modern armaments. For twenty years the soldiers had to make do with armaments of Soviet design from the 1950s. It was perhaps mostly for this reason that the military was ready to act against the Gang of Four after Mao's death. The generals and marshals seem from the first to have been behind the government headed by Hua, and Deng was chief of staff and close to the high command.[46] Deng's strong position with the military seems to have been his chief instrument in building his supremacy over the head of the party hierarchy.

While the role of the army has been relatively greater than in the Soviet Union, that of the party has been less. The vanguard role of the party has never been emphasized as in the Soviet case. Mao's authority was that of military leader and maker of the revolution, somewhat apart from his position as party leader. He was able to act outside or even against the party hierarchy as Stalin never did, and in the Cultural Revolution the party was set aside. The Chinese have been less impressed than the Soviets with the logic of party control over and separate from government administration; the party instead has been part of the administration. The party secretariat plays no such role as it has in the Soviet Union. Its central secretariat was dissolved in the Cultural Revolution and reconstituted only after the death of Mao.

The Chinese, moreover, do not seem to

[46]Concerning the army, see Harvey Nelson, *The Chinese Military System: An Organizational Study of the Chinese People's Liberation Army* (Boulder, Colo.: Westview Press, 1977).

have been so obsessed with the necessity for unity as the Russians, perhaps because of the absence of important ethnic divisions. There has been a certain un-Soviet and un-Communist looseness and factionalism, like that which occurred in the Soviet party after Lenin's death, from 1924 to 1927. Divisions have centered on Kao Kang, Marshal Peng, President Liu, Marshal Lin, and others. Mao's call to arms against the party was the highest support for freedom of factions. Mao himself was indirectly criticized with the acquiescence of high party figures in the years before the Cultural Revolution. Zhou Enlai was apparently the target of a propaganda campaign in 1974, and Deng Xiaoping, while vice premier and chief administrator in 1976, was the butt of many insults from the radicals who controlled the press.

The fact that the Chinese party has never been subject to blood purges has doubtless made discipline less stern. From time to time people have been ousted, especially in the Cultural Revolution and after Mao's death, but tenure has been the usual rule. Not many of the upper circles have lost their lives; Kao Kang, Liu Shaoqi, and Lin Biao died in various ways, although none is known to have been executed. There were never Stalinesque purge trials. The return to power of thousands of persons denounced and removed during the Cultural Revolution was without parallel in Soviet history.

In the governmental sphere, China has also shown more instability than the Soviet Union. Many high offices have been left unfilled for long periods. The Soviets ritually hold nominal elections; the Chinese have had general elections only once. The Supreme Soviet duly meets to rubberstamp policies twice yearly; the Chinese National People's Congress, several thousand delegates supposedly indirectly elected by the corresponding bodies of provinces and munici-

palities directly under the central government, has not convened for long periods, although it should be the equivalent of a parliament approving the ministry or state council. For ten years up to 1975, nothing was heard of it. Provinces and communes seem to have had a good deal more de facto autonomy, managing their own resources to a considerable extent, sometimes in contradiction to central policies. Provinces have protected their own markets and applied directives in their own way.[47] Many enterprises are said to cheat the state of taxes.[48] Law is quite informal; only in 1979 were civil, criminal, and commercial codes adopted.

Although the Chinese system is quite as compelling as the Soviet, the former has relied more on informal controls. Instead of the police, the danwei controls daily lives, and almost totally; but it operates mostly by social pressure. A women pregnant without authorization is probably not dragged to the abortionist but subjected to endless visits until she agrees. Mao, who once prepared to be a teacher and always regarded himself as such,[49] wished to rule by moral suasion, in the manner traditionally deemed appropriate for Chinese emperors. No country has ever been more propagandized; the inescapable public loudspeakers in the villages and urban compounds saturated the air, and countless meetings filled afterwork hours. A merciful implication is that violence is unnecessary, that deviants are not to be punished (except as a last resort) but persuaded and spiritually remolded. A further implication is that "thought reform" or "brainwashing" is or was a Chinese specialty. The methods were originally developed in the guerrilla war to convert captured soldiers to the Communist cause. They relied on iso-

[47]*Business Week*, October 18, 1982, p. 67.
[48]*New York Times*, March 23, 1983, p. 41.
[49]Snow, *The Long Revolution*, p. 71.

lation, endless repetition, and social pressure, preferably from friends and associates. The errant individual must be brought to see his errors until he is overwhelmed by guilt and shame and led to thorough and presumably enthusiastic repentance.[50] China has never known the labor camps of Soviet Russia, and the percentage of the population in forced labor, never over 2 million,[51] has been small by Soviet standards. Since the early antilandlord campaigns, designed to cement the peasant masses to the party, no large group has been liquidated. The old propertied classes were allowed to live as long as they cooperated with the new order, although generally not to aspire to influence.

But Marxism was drained of its logical content. In the Marxist view, class depends on economic factors, and economic class determines the superstructure of ideas, philosophy, and government. In fact, both Marx and Lenin saw attitudes as much more important than class origins, but the Chinese Communists further loosened the relationship of politics to economics. They made "bourgeois" and "proletarian" equivalent simply to "rich" and "poor," divesting these terms of the classical Marxist relation to the means of production,[52] and "class" standing was made a matter of mentality. It seemed that a "proletarian" was a person of popular consciousness, loyal to the party and devoted to the people; a "capitalist" was a selfish person attached to past or elitist ways or in practice one whose policies were disapproved. In this view, the victory of socialism and the end of private capital did not mean the end of class conflict, since backward or "bourgeois" tendencies of character persisted indefinitely.

Maoism remained poorly integrated, lacking the fairly coherent scholasticism of Marxism-Leninism. Chinese "reeducation" has been more character training, moral remolding, and improvement of attitudes,[53] more like religious conversion than the learning of any particular truths. In practice, its words often lack operative meaning. The necessity to "make class struggle the key link" was much repeated in the years following the fall of the Gang of Four, but it seemed to call merely for uniting behind the party leadership. "Dictatorship of the proletariat" was exalted at great length; it could be taken to mean the building up of the economy under party leadership.

Hatred for the Western powers, especially the United States, was a dominant theme for many years. The Soviet Union took the place of the United States as principal threat about 1969, when there was a bloody border clash, and Chinese foreign policy was increasingly directed against the Russians. But the ideological picture was changed only gradually, and for years schoolchildren were throwing darts at caricatures of Uncle Sam. In 1975, three years after President Nixon was welcomed rather warmly in China, the constitution stated that China's main enemies were "imperialism" (the United States) and "social imperialism" (the Soviet Union). Only in the 1978 constitution was priority given to "social imperialism."

Mao made frequent use of historical examples and precedents, including the wisdom of Confucius.[54] He linked his revolu-

[50]For an account of "thought reform" in action, see Bao Ruo-wong (Jean Pasqualini), *Prisoner of Mao* (New York: Coward, McCann, and Geohagen, 1973).

[51]Harold C. Hinton, *An Introduction to Chinese Politics* (New York: Praeger, 1973), p. 212.

[52]James C. Hsuing, *Ideology and Practice: The Evolution of Chinese Communism* (New York: Praeger, 1970), p. 58.

[53]See Jack Gray, "Communism and Confucianism in China," in A. Brown and J. Gray, eds., *Political Culture and Political Change in Communist States* (New York: Holmes and Meier, 1977).

[54]Stuart R. Schram, "Mao Tse-tung: A Self-Portrait," *China Quarterly* 57 (January–March 1974), p. 164.

tion to previous Chinese revolutions, and he saw himself as successor on a higher plane to the emperor who unified China in the third century B.C. But Chinese history had to be mangled to squeeze the revolution, made by peasants in a precapitalist society, into the Marxist framework of feudalism generating capitalism, which generates socialism via the proletarian revolution. The Chinese simply asserted that they skipped the capitalist stage.

The key focus of the vague and fluctuating set of ideas called ideology was the people. At one time, the "people" included all those who opposed the Japanese; subsequently, they were all who stood with the Communists, while others were "enemies of the people." During the Cultural Revolution the "people" comprised only those who supported the coterie around Mao; after Mao, the "people" were those engaged in crushing the Gang of Four. Anything disapproved by the party was "restoration of capitalism"; such opposite and mutually opposed characters of Liu Shaoqi and Lin Biao were guilty of this sin, as were the Gang of Four, which assailed both of them. Nonetheless, proletarianism, class struggle, the superiority of socialism, and the evils of capitalism, mixed with elements of Confucianism and much nationalism, remain indispensable doctrines, the rationalization of party authority.

PROBLEMS

The task of the rulers of China is formidable, if not impossible, as they try to steer their unwieldy country into modernity. Perhaps the insolubility of the basic problems accounts for China's erratic course since 1949. The Chinese feel strongly that they should be far more successful, but no direction seems to carry them far.

Before the People's Republic, China was,

like India, extremely poor and backward in terms of modern culture. Like India, China has seen improvement, but much of it has been consumed by population increase and much has been lost because of political turmoil. Food production per capita decreased slightly from 1952 to 1977,[55] and available land also decreased. China feeds nearly a quarter of the world's population on one-fourteenth of the world's farmland. Peasants have been paid about fifteen cents per day. Some question whether many Chinese peasants were not materially better off before the Revolution. For better or worse, they are more controlled by the cadres than they were by the landlords. Wages in China are only about a tenth of those across the border in Hong Kong. Per capita income, variously reported, is among the world's lowest. Seventy percent of the labor force is agricultural, and only 6.4 percent is in the tertiary sector.[56] Unemployment is high for a centrally controlled economy; graduates may wait a year before receiving their job assignment. Poverty impedes improvement; massive tree-planting campaigns have been negated because peasants cut down anything burnable and so increase soil erosion. China uses three times as much energy per unit of production as do industrial states.[57] A modern infrastructure is rudimentary. Telephones are for officials only; Taiwan, with one-sixtieth of the population, has more telephones.

Illiteracy, despite mass campaigns, was recently reported between 30 and 60 percent by different Chinese sources,[58] having in-

[55]*Business Week*, June 15, 1981, p. 60.
[56]Alan P. L. Liu, *Social Change on Mainland China and Taiwan*, Occasional Papers/Reprint Series in Contemporary Asian Studies (Baltimore: University of Maryland School of Law, 1982), p. 11; Steven W. Mosher, *The Broken Earth: The Rural Chinese* (New York: Free Press, 1983).
[57]*Wall Street Journal*, October 26, 1981, p. 27.
[58]Domes, *Politische Soziologie*, p. 13.

creased during the Cultural Revolution. Only 30 percent of the school children achieve the fifth-grade level,[59] and the quality of education fell markedly after 1958. Only 1 percent of youths of college age are in school, compared to nearly 50 percent in the United States. China was 113th of 140 states of the world in that regard. In per capita expenditures on education, it was ranked 131.[60] The party has been and perhaps still is fearful of a large educated class, but without it modernization is doubtful.

China is overpopulated, perhaps more so than India. Mao regarded people as an asset to be mobilized, but after his departure, China's leaders saw the difficulty of providing food, education, and jobs and inaugurated the world's sternest population policy. The rule was established that each couple should have only one child, and severe penalties were placed on those who transgressed. Quotas were set down to the block level; the danwei planned allowed births, checked menstrual cycles and the contraceptives used, and in case of unauthorized pregnancy, virtually compelled abortion. If a woman, authorized to have a baby, delivered twins, one was subject to infanticide. Some provinces required sterilization of the parents after the birth of a child, a policy that led to female infanticide. Because of the desirability of having a son (girls leave their parents' household; sons stay), many girl babies were killed to permit the couple to try for a son. This was perhaps encouraged by cadres, who were rewarded for fewness of births, but it raised the prospect of a highly unbalanced population of pampered only sons, with unforeseeable consequences. It is unclear how long this policy is likely to be continued, how effective it is in the more backward areas, and how thoroughly it is applied to the ruling classes. But the imposition of such measures, sure to be passionately disliked by very many, potential grandparents as well as parents, is testimony to an extraordinary degree of control, much beyond that of the Soviet Union. Perhaps only North Korea could subject its people to such discipline. The compulsory sterilization campaign in India in 1976 was superficial and almost trivial by comparison.

The party apparently hopes to solve or reduce the economic problem by limiting the number of mouths to feed and hands to occupy. In the shorter run, however, it has to decide how to manage the economy. Policy has several times changed radically, and the economic curve has gone up and down—up from 1949 to 1957, down from 1958 to 1962, up from 1962 to 1965, down from 1966 to 1977, and since 1977 generally up.[61] The recent tendency, with some hesitations and reversals, has been toward more freedom of production and sale for the peasants. Communes were to set aside 5 to 7 percent of their land for private plots; peasants farming them had to deliver quotas at fixed prices but could sell the surplus, plus handicrafts, as they pleased.[62] Street vendors were permitted, and small shops, employing not more than five hands, could manufacture as they pleased. Communes were relieved of most of their economic functions and called "townships." State enterprises were partly freed from planning and allowed to keep much of their profits.[63]

[59]*Christian Science Monitor*, November 3, 1980, p. B 5.

[60]*New York Times*, July 13, 1980, p. 3.

[61]Immanuel C. Y. Hsu, *China Without Mao: The Search for a New Order* (New York: Oxford University Press, 1982), p. 161.

[62]*Time*, November 23, 1981, p. 51.

[63]*New York Times*, March 23, 1983, p. 41.

Wages were paid for work done—communism was defined as state ownership plus payment by work. Some small enterprises were set practically free to produce for their own account.[64]

Results were good. Peasant incomes increased sharply, and the goals of the people rose from radio and wristwatch to television and tape player. But when some peasants began earning forty to fifty times the average by entrepreneurship, by raising ducks, for example, cadres were angered, and they saw peasant markets as dens of dirty money-making. There were moves to try out workers' control, but the leadership saw what happened in Poland and drew back. Basic prices, fixed in 1949 with little change since, remained under state control because of fears of enrichment. The prosperity of private dealers—small-scale capitalists—was a challenge to the bases of party rule.

If China were to accept individualism, admit foreign ideas, and encourage people to enrich the country by enriching themselves, there would not be much place for socialism or a reason for party supremacy. China seemed to drift in a sort of morality crisis, having broken with the Soviet Union, cast Maoism aside, and found the radical leftists criminal. The Chinese leaders found themselves in the old dilemma of wanting the support of the intellectuals for modernization but not wanting any questioning of the system. The educated, especially the youth, turned away from Maoism, some taking up religion. Former Red Guards felt they had been used and cheated; former victims of the Cultural Revolution wanted material enjoyments in compensation. Youths illegally returned from the countryside were bitter. Ideology had been too changeable for cred-

ibility; hardly any college students pretended to believe in socialism; most were fatalist or cynical.[65] Impressed with the glitter of the West, they were hard to persuade of the superiority of socialism.[66]

Many poorly educated party cadres find this cynicism and boredom with ideology threatening. The motto "Seek truth from facts" is conditioned by unquestioned party superiority. Even against the teachings of Deng, cadres seek to assert themselves over scientists and intellectuals by refusing them admittance to the party.[67] On the contrary, they demand more study of Marxism and Mao Thought and insist that "literature and art must serve the people." They distrust all outside the inner circle; most trusted are those who were members before 1949 and are of uneducated peasant background. Many of the cadres would like to go back to the Soviet Union as a model of order, planning, and unequivocal party authority.[68]

The Chinese leaders are virtually compelled to combat admiration for the United States and the undercurrent of democratic thought and to treat that nation as basically hostile. The press inveighs against "spiritual pollution." They remained tied to Marxism as an explanation of poverty (exploitation by the United States and other capitalist-imperialist powers), and to compensate present poverty with the virtues and bright future of socialism. The defense of the party is not limited to exhortation, however. Critics who only lose their jobs are fortunate; there were reportedly hundreds of thousands of political prisoners at the zenith of Dengism, and

---

[64]*Los Angeles Times*, April 25, 1983, p. IV-1.

[65]Susan L. Shirk, *Competitive Comrades: Career Incentives and Student Strategies in China* (Berkeley: University of California Press, 1982), p. 2.

[66]For the atmosphere, see Richard Bernstein, *From the Center of the Earth* (Boston: Little, Brown, 1982).

[67]*Christian Science Monitor*, July 21, 1983, p. 13.

[68]*Business Week*, January 31, 1983, p. 48.

it was admitted that police torture is frequent.[69]

It may be, thirty-five years after the proclamation of the new China, that the country has settled down and left the traumatic changes and mass movements behind; in 1978 it was formally declared that they were no longer necessary. But it does not seem to be a healthy polity. There is the corruption common to such systems; grease of some kind is used to get meat, theater tickets, or repairs; to enter a hospital; or for a factory to secure timely delivery of supplies.[70] Much is done, as in the Soviet Union, by barter of privileges, and personal friendship is the chief political asset. There is still dense secrecy, even beyond the Soviet style. Cadres have virtual life tenure. The 1982 Party Congress rejected the idea of limits on office-holding, and the upper levels are still clogged with veterans. The bureaucracy is stiff and immobile; dealing with it tests the patience of foreign businessmen. There is great and widening inequality, between city and country, between provinces (Shanghai having seven times the per capita income of Honan)[71] and between levels of status. There are twenty-four grades of bureaucrats, with a differential of ten to one in effective income plus perquisites, as in the Soviet Union, of access to special shops and use of automobiles (chauffered for officials, denied to ordinary people entirely). Officers have personal servants,[72] and in 1984 they regained insignia. It is held honorable to make money, and millions of persons strive to do so on their own, even employing a few hands.[73]

[69]*New York Times*, August 30, 1980, p. 21; *Los Angeles Times*, May 5, 1983, p. 3.

[70]*Newsweek*, May 24, 1982, p. 46.

[71]Liu, *Social Change*, p. 24.

[72]*New York Times*, January 2, 1981, p. 6.

[73]Orville Scheel, "The Wind of Wanting to Go it Alone," *New Yorker*, January 23, 1984, pp. 43–85.

OUTLOOK

Mao led one of the greatest political movements of history, an effort to use doctrine and new organizational forms to reshape, mobilize, and modernize the immense Chinese nation. Where there had been chaos, his movement brought order and unity. It restored the national image, making China respected militarily and politically. It energetically attacked the hunger, disease, and ignorance that had been the lot of the Chinese masses for centuries and proclaimed equality and renewal.

Many people who saw or learned about the new China were profoundly inspired. Many American intellectuals found Maoist China a new and more promising model for the industrialization, without capitalism, of the Third World. Revolutionaries repelled by the staidness and bureaucratism of the Soviet Union made China their model for total social change. But since the death of Mao there has been general disillusionment. The change of policies has been so complete that the radicals who looked to China for leadership could only conclude that the Maoist revolution had been betrayed. Some turned their gaze elsewhere, a few to Albania; others remained loyal to the memory of Mao, although unable to understand why his people had permitted traitors to take charge. For the intellectuals who wanted to see in China the way to the future of the less developed world, there came a painful recognition—thanks mostly to the greater frankness of the new Chinese regime—that the achievements of Maoism were much fewer than had been touted. Hunger and disease had not been eliminated, only reduced; illiteracy had not been abolished. Economic growth had not been spectacular but, over the whole period, less than the world average. If China had clear accomplishments, such as avoiding the urban hypertrophy of most Third World countries or reducing the birthrate, they were achieved at an enormous cost in coercion. And the price in terms of intellectual compression has been fearful.

China remains a poor country, with its share of crime and corruption, while the inspiration of renewal has evaporated. This does not mean that the Communist state has been a failure or that another order could have done better. It is difficult to approve both the policies of Maoism and those of Dengism, however; if the one was good, the other can only be the opposite. And neither could solve the riddle of how to sustain the total rule of the party while modernizing the nation. Dengism has brought a remarkable increase of production, but there is no surety that political disorder may not again undo economic progress.

China is obviously unpredictable. However, it is possible that China may leave behind much of the specialness of communism more rapidly than most other states dedicated to Marxism-Leninism. The dominant preoccupation of the leadership was not much different from the chief preoccupation of the intelligentsia in 1910 or 1920—the modernization and strengthening of China by the direct means of borrowing from the modernized and stronger powers of the Western world. If this means a pragmatic, nonideological openness to Western influences as well as technology, and ultimately the acceptance of more pluralism in politics and society, China may evolve away from the Leninist model.

China may do so more easily than the Soviet Union, because the creed and convictions of Leninism are much less important for China. Lenin, after all, was a Russian, not only alien but a member of the nation the Chinese like least. For Russians, Leninism is almost equivalent to destiny in the world; for the Chinese, it is slightly humiliating. Marxism-Leninism is the rationalization of the unity of the Soviet Union through its consecration of class over nationality and of the Soviet dominion in Eastern Europe; China is a solid national unit (95 percent Han Chinese) with no need for such symbolic cement. Marxism-Leninism, moreover, affirms the Soviet position as a superpower and leader of the expected world transformation. For China it is antinational, the chief antagonist and only real danger being Marxist-Leninist. China has powerful reasons for accommodating to the West, with which it shares a security interest. At the same time, Marxism-Leninism somewhat impedes the acquisition and assimilation of the Western technology that mean modernization. Chinese doctrines have been in a continual flux: to change further and redefine "socialism" in strictly Chinese terms would be no shock.

It is to be hoped that China may find its way to its own means of dealing with the need for openness, freedom of information, and external inputs to the political system, along with the need for central direction and the realities of oligarchy for a people who cannot realistically expect self-rule. China remains an authoritarian power with the full panoply of instruments of control and rule by a small group that characterizes Communist states. It is a difficult country to govern, and there is no reason to expect it to move away from approximately its present condition in any foreseeable future. It remains to be seen whether the ailments of authoritarianism will grow to choke its progress, or whether the time of turmoil and confusion has been successfully surmounted and now the country can hope to harvest material and social progress. In either case, Chinese communism has probably played the dramatic part of its historical role.

Maoism was not thought but passion; and its passions derived from the humiliations of China's time of weakness and the long battle that led to reunification and the formation of a strong government. The wounds and emotions are now remembered only by those past midlife, and the governing apparatus is more interested in possession than in change. If change is to come, it is not to be social, the dispossession of the elite, but economic, the building of a more productive and stronger country.

China like Russia, is losing distinctiveness.

In the modern world of easy and instantaneous communication, mass travel, and economic interdependence, cities everywhere look more and more alike. China is no exception; it too seems drawn into the floodtide of modernity. As the new regime stresses modernization over revolution, the specialness of the Chinese way is diluted, and China looks much less different from India than a decade ago. Partly surrendering the dreams of socialism, China increasingly encounters the disorders of capitalism. As often in the past, it seems uncertain of its true direction. But it is a big chunk of humanity, and how its problems may be solved is one of the great questions of the future.

Conclusion

A tour of world governments is not a very cheerful journey, unless the gargantuan problems of some make our own troubles seem less forbidding. But some knowledge of the kinds of governments in the world and the way major foreign powers are organized should be a vital part of a liberal education. Political institutions are an essential cap of civilized society and human culture. Without a political order, there is no literature, science, sport, or large-scale production; and the nature and prosperity of such endeavors depend on the environment created for them by the state. Well-crafted political forms are necessary for the resolution of differences, the expression of shared purposes, and the avoidance of abuses of power. Defective political systems bring overwhelming waste, oppression, and massive cruelty.

A survey of major governments should serve various purposes of understanding. Our nation is engaged in cooperative and competitive relations—economic, political, and military—with many others; and these relations are greatly influenced by the politics of the nations involved. For example, relations between the United States and the Soviet Union have been poor to bad for almost all of the many decades they have coexisted, except when Hitler forced Stalin into semi-alliance with the West. There has been no economic cause of antagonism; the economies of the two countries are more complementary than competitive. Political philosophy and institutions set them at odds. Their relationship may be influenced by negotiations, but it depends fundamentally on the evolution of the two political systems, which is unfortunately not negotiable.

On the other hand, the fact that the advanced non-Communist industrial countries are definitely democratic has much to do with the fact that their quarrels are nonthreatening. There has been no war between democratic states for over a century. Differences among the industrial democracies are rather like differences among political parties within them—generally not about the character of the system or threats to one another's existence but contention for material advantages, conducted within a legal framework, such as questions of tariffs or airline routes. If Germany or Japan were to become dictatorships, they would be much more likely to seek to enlarge their power by force or threat of force, and world politics would be quite turned around.

Another reason for seeking understanding of foreign governments is to improve understanding of our own. By comparison with others, we gain a clearer idea of the qualities and defects of American government. It would be comforting to believe that the American system is generally superior to others, and it is certainly true that Americans have some reason to congratulate themselves. Their federal structure has functioned satisfactorily for 200 years (except for the troubles of 1861–1865), and under it this country progressed to the world's highest level of prosperity. The United States has produced more than its share of science and invention, and it has led the world into the postindustrial age; modernization has become for much of the world almost equivalent to Americanization.

Less familiar is the fact that among democratic countries the United States is in some ways exceptionally democratic. No other large country so frequently submits proposals for the direct decision of the voters. In France this device has been used occasionally on the initiative of the government; to use it, as in the United States, on the initiative of the voters, is a considerable concession to the principle of popular sovereignty. More important, the United States is unique in shifting the choice of candidates for elective office from party organizations to voters in primary elections. In other democracies, a more or less oligarchic party organization decides who gets on the ballot with the party label. Giving the choice to the voters increases not only responsibility but also flexibility and mobility; if Britain had such a device its party system would not be mired in the present morass. The use of primaries is closely related to the fact that the American Congress is the most independent legislative body in major countries by a large margin. Not only does the administration lack the power of dissolution held by prime ministers of parliamentary nations; it lacks a party whip, because the party organization cannot exclude a maverick and prevent his running as a party candidate in the next election. Americans also invented judicial review, the power of an independent judicial organ to judge the constitutionality of laws. This has been copied, of course, by Germany and Japan and partially by France; and it is an important contribution to the engineering of constitutionalism.

On the other hand, the United States may have much to learn from other countries; Americans should use foreign experiences as a guide for the improvement of their own institutions. The fact that an institution, such as the question hour or the use of civil servants at all but the top level of administration, seems to work well in various lands does not necessarily mean that it would work the same way in the United States, but it suggests a possibility. From time to time, the suggestion is made that the United States would be better off with a parliamentary system, thus guaranteeing control of the executive and legislative organs by the same party.

The fact that in the last two decades American success has been less impressive, as economic growth has lagged and social problems have multiplied, underlines the desirability of taking lessons from countries whose performance in the postwar period has been more dynamic. Somewhat belatedly, American business has undertaken to study Japanese management; but there is an equally good case for considering the political methods of the Japanese. For example, more systematic elite recruitment has advantages, although narrowing the choice to a few universities is hardly admirable; and the customary early retirement of senior Japanese bureaucrats certainly contributes to mobility and increases the effectiveness of the civil service and the quality of leadership.

Political institutions everywhere are imperfect, and it is not clear that any of the industrial democracies are able to ensure strong economic growth along with stability and social justice, or know how to check antisocial deviance without infringing freedoms, or how to harmonize the rights and demands of minorities with those of the majority. For Third World states in general, the quality of government is still more clearly a problem. States feel called on to press for modernization without the organizational capacity to manage the economy or impose priorities; and the less developed the society, the more difficult it is to prevent the abuse of power and the maldirection of resources. The Communist political systems, with their lack of external checks on centralized authority, seem to have evolved to a condition where once-dynamic regimes have become ossified, incapable of reform, and less and less effective.

The evaluation of a political system depends on what it is expected to accomplish. This is by no means clear. In the eighteenth and early nineteenth centuries, it was widely assumed that the chief purpose of the state was to conduct foreign relations, defend the country, get the better of rivals, and raise its prestige and standing in the international community. Interference with the economy was justified mostly for reasons of national strength; otherwise it could be argued that the best government was the one that governed least. The fostering of industry became a major concern in subsequent generations, especially as the United States, Russia, Germany, and Japan promoted manufacturing to catch up with Britain.

The state gradually assumed more responsibility for the welfare of the citizenry. Since the economic depression of the 1930s, it has been taken for granted that it is a major duty of the state to soften or overcome the hardships of the business cycle. Since World War II the welfare state has undertaken increasingly to protect its people from adversity, to redistribute wealth to the needier sectors of the population, and to counter undesirable side effects of modernization. It is still indispensable that a state have the capacity to conduct foreign policy, protect the national interest as far as possible, and do whatever it can for the preservation of peace in a nuclear age. However, the modern state is called on to promote the well-being of its citizens in a thousand ways—prohibiting, regulating, offering incentives and benefits, influencing if not guiding the economy, administering legal justice and advancing social equity, while maintaining as much freedom as is compatible with other needs.

How these goals are to be accomplished and at what cost, and who is to have the privilege of commanding and controlling the apparatus needed to accomplish them, is the subject of politics. Satisfactory management of a modern economy is perhaps beyond the ability of humans and computers, and there is likely to be some contradiction between production of wealth and its distribution. For example, taxes may be designed to promote equality or to encourage enterprise and investment; they can hardly do both at the same time, and they commonly do something else again, favor politically powerful interests. Justice and equality cannot be defined to everyone's satisfaction. Traditionally, equality has been understood as equality under the law, equal treatment of persons often very unequal in resources. It has been extended to equality of opportunity: the state should try to assure all citizens an equal opportunity to use their abilities. Many would go beyond this to make it the goal of the community to equalize rewards—equality of results in a sense compensating for unequal talents and efforts.

All this raises questions for which there are no answers: how personal interests are to be weighed against collective interests, how freedom can be squared with order, how people are to be rewarded for independence or obedience, how the desires of today are to be weighed against the supposed needs of the next decade or the next century. The more government gives to people, the more it must take, and the balance always leaves many dissatisfied. There is also an unsolvable question how far the state should try to follow the wishes of the people and how far to employ its own supposedly superior knowledge and understanding for their benefit. It is often impossible to find a satisfactory balance between the demands of activist minorities and passive majorities.

The government should be the organization best able to plan for the distant tomorrow and provide for the ultimate survival of the community, but there is little incentive for leaders to incur costs for the benefit of their successors. It may well be that accommodation to a new age requires more social orientation with more controls over the economy, restriction of freedom of expression, and the setting of priorities by the state.[1] It may be, on the contrary, that political action is too cumbersome and that the modern state must rely primarily on the enlightenment, idealism, and involvement of its citizens, pursuing their own ideas of right and self-interest, to find the way to the future.

Political institutions are to some extent shaped by goals; the welfare state, for example, implies a corresponding apparatus. However, the state that is effective for one purpose is likely to be effective for others. This is true even of military strength. Although a dictatorship may be more mobilized at the outset, it would seem from the record of recent wars that democratic states have at least as much endurance. The same qualities that have enabled the Israelis to build a more productive economy than their Arab neighbors have given them superior fighting capacity. A well-organized state is capable of selecting goals and realizing them, regardless of their character, whereas a poorly organized state is as incapable of warring on poverty as it is of warring on its neighbors.

The chief thing we might hope to learn, then, from the study of political institutions is what constitutes the well-ordered state. Concerning this there can be no complete agreement, because values and perceptions differ too widely. But there are obvious requirements if the state is to come near to

---

[1]As argued by Alexander Solzhenitsyn and his associates. See Mikhail Agursky, "Contemporary Socioeconomic Systems and their Future Prospects," in *From under the Rubble*, ed. Solzhenitsyn et al., (Boston: Little, Brown, 1975), pp. 81–87.

meeting the demands on it. These include legitimacy, adequate feedback, and means of renewal. For effectiveness and stability, the state should be accepted by the citizenry and properly ordained and entitled to tax, regulate, and if necessary apply coercion in the public interest. For sound direction, it is indispensable that persons outside the leadership are able to make their needs and wants known. It is unlikely that, over the long term, decision making will be in the interests of the people as a whole unless there is a broad input into that decision making. Finally, it is essential for effective government that capable persons be placed in high positions and that there be means of change and renewal of leadership.

Various governments seek these ends, or fail to seek them, in different ways. The Communist states rest their legitimacy on the historical role of the Leninist party, making more or less use of electoral forms as an auxiliary mode. In this they have had some success, although securing input conflicts with a major axiom of the system, the monopoly of information. They have not been entirely unaware of the problems of regularizing access to leadership and its tenure, but again the problem may be insoluble within the nature of the Communist system and its concentration of power. In Nigeria, the weakness of legitimacy of the military government was the principal force propelling the country toward electoral politics; and the need for a more open society to permit progress has led many military regimes, like that of Brazil, to relax their grip. Mexico has a unique hybrid system in which semifree elections and a degree of openness and toleration provide some legitimacy and feedback, and deficiencies in these respects are more or less compensated by the thoroughgoing renewal of the sexenio. For the democratic states, elections at regular intervals, coupled with civil rights, fairly well provide legitimacy, feedback, and renewal. Renewal of leadership, it may be noted, does not require heads of government to be voted out of office in an election, only that they be subject to this threat. If a British leader, for example, becomes unpopular, a party fearful of losing an election will depose him; and the Japanese Liberal-Democratic party has managed to retain power for a generation by virtue of frequent changes of its leadership.

A different quality, one that seems more necessary in the face of modern demands on government, is the ability to take action. This requires an effective bureaucracy or civil service, and the way in which the civil service, especially its leading cadres, is recruited, is a major characteristic of the political system. Much depends on the caliber, integrity, and motivation of the civil servants. It may at times almost seem, especially in France, Germany, and Japan, that the function of the democratic apparatus is to give legitimacy to government by the permanent officials.

The ability of the government to act may also entail the capacity to take strong but necessary action despite disagreement—that is, to override minority or vested interests or to carry out measures that the people might not sanction but that may be in their long-term interests. This is a basic claim of authoritarian states, especially in the Third World; they can push policies unpopular in their immediate effects but ultimately beneficial, such as postponement of consumption in favor of investment. It is also the claim, usually rather implied than explicit, of the Communist states; and it is apparent that a social revolution endows a state with such capacity.

In times of tranquillity, however, it seems too difficult to sustain authoritarian effectiveness without adequate legitimacy, feedback, and renewal. People learn to cheat a state that is not seen as legitimate and to obey its laws only insofar as they can be enforced by coercion; corruption vitiates all endeavors. Without ample feedback, it is much more difficult to determine for what purpose the state should exert its capacities, and they are more likely to be ineffectively applied. For example, Soviet control of agriculture should make it possible to raise yields to high levels; misapplied controls result in fact in low yields. Without a means of renewal of leadership, moreover, the capacities of the state are eventually frustrated. The most general fault of governments is the self-perpetuation in office of the rulers and their dedication to their own power and privilege, to the detriment of their responsibilities to the governed. Especially as an elite wears out the mission with which it came into the possession of power, it may be expected increasingly to devote its energies to self-maintenance. This seems to be the most acute problem of the otherwise fairly successful Soviet system. The regular and orderly change of top leadership is consequently a prime principle for keeping government competent and reasonably dedicated. It is more basic that elections provide a means of orderly change of leadership than that they reflect a popular choice.

For these reasons, it seems that the way of the future lies in the general direction of what we commonly understand by democracy—a legal order with some form of responsibility of the governors to the governed. Perhaps unfortunately, there is a lack of serious rivals. The Communist states have enjoyed advantages of freshness, dedication, and purposefulness; but these advantages wear out, and they appear gradually to become less distinctively Communist and more plainly authoritarian in the old sense of self-appointed and irresponsible government. The Soviet Union has ceased to be an im-

portant model except for a few developing countries. It is no longer possible to see Maoism as a promise of a better way.

It does not follow, of course, that American democracy should be imitated around the world. But to reject democracy as a general standard because Americans like to apply that qualification to their own institutions is ethnocentric. Modern representative government is largely a British creation, and republican and democratic institutions are ancient. Switzerland has never had a monarchy, and the Netherlands has had constitutional government since gaining independence in the seventeenth century. In ancient times, there were democracies or republics in Greece and India. Nowadays, people around the world approve of the rule of law, freedom of expression, responsibility of the rulers to the people, guarantees against arbitrary official violence, and so forth. Much of what one might include under the rubric of "democratic" is little more than human decency and fair play. The fundamental premise is simple and philosophically very strong, the equality of rights. This is a legal and political principle; but on the one hand, economic and social equality makes political equality achievable, and on the other, economic and social equality must be based on political equality.

The democratic system has not only ethical appeal. Historically there has been a rather close association between representative or constitutional government and material prosperity,[2] as there is today. This fact certainly suggests that less developed countries, if they desire a higher level of productivity (as they generally seem to do), would be well advised to study and borrow from the institutions of the most successful West-

---

[2]Robert Wesson, *State Systems: International Pluralism, Politics, and Culture* (New York: Macmillan, 1978).

ern countries, not uncritically but in conformity with their own conditions. No set of institutions is perfect, and government will always require reshaping with changing needs and circumstances. Political, like other institutions, may be expected to lag behind the technologically induced evolution of society. Government represents not only habits resistant to alteration but also positions of influence that people desire to retain. Moreover, we all live by and with collective myths, which help to hold society together. It is difficult to rethink basic propositions without a shock to force the mind to reorient itself; and war, which has chiefly served that function in the past, is no longer available. The problem of political reform is not only what should be done but what can be done in the real world, when change has to be accepted by the powers to be changed. But if political institutions fail to adapt to the difficult requirements of the new age, civilization will go down with them.

Political science has often skirted crucial questions or permitted itself to be used for partisan causes; and there has been lamentably little effort to think out better means of control and direction of the central authority of society. Only through better understanding of political affairs is it possible to improve essential political institutions in a world that is equally promising and threatening.

Index

DATE DUE
DATE DE RETOUR

FEB 1 5 1989			
APR 2 4 1989			

LOWE MARTIN No. 1137